W9-AZD-845

THE WILLIAM STALLINGS BOOKS ON COMPUTER AND DATA COMMUNICATIONS TECHNOLOGY

OPERATING SYSTEMS

A state-of-the art survey of operating system principles. Covers fundamental technology as well as contemporary design issues, such as threads, real-time systems, multiprocessor scheduling, distributed systems, and security.

HANDBOOK OF COMPUTER-COMMUNICATIONS STANDARDS VOLUME 1
THE OPEN SYSTEMS INTERCONNECTION (OSI) MODEL AND OSI-RELATED STANDARDS, SECOND EDITION

A description of the master plan for all computer-communications standards: the OSI model. The book also provides a detailed presentation of OSI-related standards at all 7 layers, including HDLC, X.25, ISO internet, ISO transport, ISO session, ISO presentation, Abstract Syntax ONE (ASN.1), and common application service elements (CASE).

HANDBOOK OF COMPUTER-COMMUNICATIONS STANDARDS VOLUME 2
LOCAL AREA NETWORK STANDARDS, SECOND EDITION

A detailed examination of all current local network standards, including logical link control (LLC, IEEE 802.2), CSMA/CD (IEEE 802.3), token bus (IEEE 802.4), token ring (IEEE 802.5), and fiber distributed data interface (FDDI, ANS X3T9.5).

HANDBOOK OF COMPUTER-COMMUNICATIONS STANDARDS VOLUME 3
THE TCP/IP PROTOCOL SUITE, SECOND EDITION

A description of the protocol standards that are mandated on all DOD computer procurements and are becoming increasingly popular on commercial local network products, including TCP, IP, FTP, SMTP, and TELNET. The network management standards, SNMP and CMOT, are also presented.

Local and
Metropolitan
Area Networks

Local and Metropolitan Area Networks

FOURTH EDITION

William Stallings

MACMILLAN PUBLISHING COMPANY
New York

MAXWELL MACMILLAN CANADA
Toronto

MAXWELL MACMILLAN INTERNATIONAL
New York   Oxford   Singapore   Sydney

Editor: John Griffin
Production Supervisor: John Travis
Production Manager: Roger Vergnes
Text Designer: Natasha Sylvester
Cover Designer: Robert Vega

This book was set in Palatino by Compset, Inc., and printed and bound by
Book Press. The cover was printed by Lehigh Press.

Macmillan Publishing Company is part
of the Maxwell Communication Group of Companies.

Macmillan Publishing Company
866 Third Avenue, New York, New York 10022

Maxwell Macmillan Canada, Inc.
1200 Eglinton Avenue East
Suite 200
Don Mills, Ontario M3C 3N1

Library of Congress Cataloging-in-Publication Data
Stallings, William.
    Local and metropolitan area networks / William Stallings. — 4th
ed.
        p.   cm.
    Rev. ed. of: Local networks. 3rd ed. © 1990.
    Includes bibliographical references and index.
    ISBN 0-02-415465-2
    1. Local area networks (Computer networks)   2. Metropolitan area
networks (Computer networks)   I. Stallings, William.   Local
networks.   II. Title.
TK5105.7.S77   1993
004.6—dc20   92-16096
                                                                        CIP

Printing: 2 3 4 5 6 7 8   Year: 3 4 5 6 7 8 9 0 1

To my wife, Tricia

Preface

The local area network (LAN) has come to play a central role in information distribution and office functioning within businesses and other organizations. The major factor driving the widespread introduction of the LAN has been the proliferation of small computer systems, especially personal computers, but also including workstations and mini-computers.

With the dropping price of LAN hardware and software, LANs have become more numerous and larger, and they have taken on more and more functions within the organization. The upshot is that the LAN, once installed, quickly becomes almost as essential as the telephone system. At the same time, there is a proliferation of LAN types and options and a need to interconnect a number of LANs at the same site and with LANs at other sites. This has led to the development of LANs of higher and higher data rates and the relatively recent introduction of the metropolitan area network (MAN).

Objectives

This book focuses on the broad and evolving field of local and metropolitan area networks. The aim of the text is to provide a reasoned balance among breadth, depth, and timeliness. The book emphasizes topics of fundamental importance concerning the technology and architecture of these networks. Certain key related areas, such as performance, internetworking, and network management are also treated in some detail.

The book explores the key topics in the field in the following general categories:

- *Technology and architecture:* There is a small collection of ingredients that serves to characterize and differentiate local and metropolitan area networks, including transmission medium, topology, communication protocols, switching technique, and hardware/software interface.
- *Network type:* It is convenient to classify the networks covered in this book into three types, based partly on technology and partly on application: These are local area network (LAN), metropolitan area network (MAN), and digital switch/digital private branch exchange (PBX).
- *Design approaches:* The book examines alternative design choices and assesses their relative merits.

Intended Audience

This book is intended for a broad range of readers interested in local networks:

- *Students and professionals in computer science and data communications:* The book is intended as both a textbook for study and a basic reference volume for this exciting area within the broader fields of computer science and data communications.
- *Local network designers and implementors:* The book discusses the critical design issues and illustrates alternative approaches to meeting user requirements.
- *Local network customers and system managers:* The book alerts the reader to some of the key issues and tradeoffs, and what to look for in the way of network services and performance.

The book is intended for both an academic and a professional audience. As a textbook, it is intended as a one-semester course. It covers much of the material in the Computer Communication Networks course of The joint ACM/IEEE Computing Curricula 1991.

The book also serves as a basic reference volume and is suitable for self-study. For the reader with little or no background in data communications, a brief primer is included.

Plan of the Text

The book is organized to clarify both the unifying and the differentiating concepts that underlie this field. The organization of the chapters is as follows:

1. *Introduction:* The chapter defines the term *local network* and looks at some of the applications and benefits.
2. *Topics in Data Communications and Computer Networking:* This necessarily brief survey explains the relevant concepts used throughout the book.
3. *Overview of LAN/MAN Technology:* Introduces the key elements of transmission medium and topology. A classification of networks into LANs, MANs, and WANs is developed.
4. *Topologies and Transmission Media for LANs and MANs:* Examines the design issues relating to the implementation of LANs and MANs, with emphasis on the topology and transmission medium alternatives.
5. *Local Area Network Architecture:* Describes the logical link control and medium access control architecture of LANs. LAN standards are also described.
6. *Metropolitan Area Network Architecture:* Treats the two most important MANs: FDDI and IEEE 802.6.
7. *Circuit-Switched Local Networks:* Networks in this category constitute the major alternative to LANs for meeting general local interconnection needs. The category includes the data-only digital switch and the voice/data digital private branch exchange (PBX).
8. *The Network Interface:* The nature of the interface between an attached device and a LAN or MAN is an important design issue. This chapter explores some alternatives.
9. *LAN/MAN Performance:* This chapter gives some insight into the performance problems and the differences in performance of various LANs and MANs.
10. *Internetworking:* In the majority of cases, LANs will be connected in some fashion to other networks, either by means of other LANs, by way of MANs, or using wide-area networks. The key alternatives of bridge and router are explored.
11. *Network Management:* Network management tools and systems are indispensable for LANs and MANs. This chapter explores the types of systems that are available and examines the standards developed for general network management and LAN/MAN management.

In addition, the book includes an extensive glossary, a list of frequently-used acronyms, and a bibliography. Each chapter includes problems and suggestions for further reading.

Throughout, there is a heavy emphasis on standards, including standards based on the Open Systems Interconnection (OSI) model and specific LAN and MAN standards, such as IEEE 802 and FDDI. This emphasis reflects the growing importance of such standards in defining the available products and future research directions in this field.

Related Materials

The author has produced other material that may be of interest to students and professionals. *Advances in Local and Metropolitan Area Network Technology* (1993, IEEE Computer Society Press, 10662 Los Vaqueros Circle, P.O. Box 3014, Los Alamitos, CA 90720, telephone 714-821-8380) is a companion to this text, and follows the same topical organization. It contains reprints of many of the key references used herein.

A set of videotape courses specifically designed for use with this book is available from The Media Group, Boston University, 565 Commonwealth Avenue, Boston, MA 02215; telephone (617) 353-3227.

Data and Computer Communications, Third Edition (Macmillan, 1991) covers fundamental concepts in the areas of data transmission, communication networks, and computer-communications protocols. *ISDN and Broadband ISDN, Second Edition* (Macmillan, 1992) covers the concepts and technology of integrated services digital networks (ISDN) and broadband ISDN, which are all-digital networks gradually being introduced to replace existing wide-area networks. *Networking Standards* (Addison-Wesley, 1993) covers the leading-edge standards that are defining the networks and distributed applications recently introduced or currently under development.

The Fourth Edition

I began work on the first edition of this book in 1982. At the time of its publication, it was the only book-length technical treatment of LANs (and remains the only textbook on the subject). Little did I anticipate that it would still be going strong over a decade later. To paraphrase a recent Oscar-winner, you like this book! You really like it! Any author is bound to feel a sense of pride and satisfaction on being asked to produce a fourth edition of a book that covers such a fast-moving field as this one. The book has withstood the test of time, and its success confirms that the basic organization and emphasis of the book is sound. However, because the field is fast-moving, each new edition requires a major revision to keep up.

This edition is no exception. The revision in this case even extends to the title, which now includes the phrase Metropolitan Area Networks. The inclusion of MANs is dictated by three developments:

1. The fiber distributed data interface (FDDI), which is generally referred to as a local area network (LAN), is finding increasing application as a backbone MAN, thanks to the increased demand for this service and the maturing of bridge and router technologies.
2. FDDI-II has been adopted. This revision of FDDI addresses some of the integrated-voice data requirements of a MAN.

3. After an almost uncountable number of false starts, the IEEE 802.6 committee has finally settled on a MAN standard, and that standard has received broad industry and customer support.

So the inclusion of MANs is a major new addition to the book. Another significant change in this edition is the revision of the chapter on internetworking. The material on bridge routing standards has been expanded. The spanning tree and source routing approaches, introduced in the third edition, receive expanded coverage. In addition, a new bridge standard, SRT, is introduced. In the area of routing, the new routing protocol standards, ES-IS and IS-IS are examined.

A final major change in this edition is the expansion of the coverage on network management to an entire chapter. The chapter covers the basis technology of network management systems and local network management. In addition, the ISO network management standards and the IEEE 802 LAN/MAN management standards are covered.

In addition to these major changes, there have been expansions and updates in every chapter. To give some feel for the overall scope of this revision, approximately 33% of the tables, 30% of the figures, and 24% of the references in this edition are new. All in all, this fourth edition constitutes a major revision. I have tried in a balanced manner to provide a comprehensive survey of the technology and architecture of local and metropolitan area networks.

Acknowledgment

My association with Macmillan's college division now stretches back over more than a decade. I have always had the strong and enthusiastic support of the division's staff and am grateful for all the support and encouragement I have received over the years. Two people in particular I would like to thank.

In a changing world, it is remarkable that the production editor for every one of my dozen books, going back to the first edition of this book, has been the same man: John Travis. Over the years, John has caught many errors, both editorial and—more important—technical, and he has managed to bring every single one of these books out on time. Quite an achievement.

My current, and I hope permanent, editor is John Griffin. His feel for both the technical and marketing side of the business has helped direct my writing into the most fruitful channels.

Of course, I have dealt with many other people in the College Division over the years. The names have changed from time to time, but the supportive atmosphere and the professionalism have not.

W. S.

Contents

CHAPTER 11

Network Management   477

Local and Metropolitan Area Networks

CHAPTER 1

Introduction

1.1

LANs, MANs, AND WANs

For businesses, government agencies, universities, and other organizations, data communications networks have become indispensable. Of most importance are networks that interconnect equipment within a single building or a group of buildings. For want of a better term, we will refer to such networks as *local networks*. In fact, this book is concerned with three types of local networks: local area networks (LANs), metropolitan area networks (MANs), and circuit-switching local networks. Before defining these terms, we need to understand the trends responsible for the importance of local networks.

Of most importance is the dramatic and continuing decrease in computer hardware costs, accompanied by an increase in computer hardware capability. Today's microprocessors have speeds, instruction sets, and memory capacities comparable to the most powerful minicomputers of a few years ago. This trend has spawned a number of changes in the way information is collected, processed, and used in organizations. There is increasing use of small, single-function systems, such as word processors and small business computers, and of general-purpose microcomputers, such as personal computers and Unix-based multiuser workstations. These small, dispersed systems are more accessible to the user, more responsive, and easier to use than large central time-sharing systems.

All of these factors lead to an increased number of systems at a single site: office building, factory, operations center, and so on. At the same time there is likely to be a desire to interconnect these systems for a variety of reasons, including:

- To share and exchange data between systems
- To share expensive resources

The ability to exchange data is a compelling reason for interconnection. Individual users of computer systems do not work in isolation and will want to retain some of the benefits provided by a central system. These include the ability to exchange messages with other users, the ability to access data from several sources in the preparation of a document or for an analysis, and the opportunity for multiple users to share information in a common file.

To appreciate the second reason, consider that although the cost of data processing hardware has dropped, the cost of essential electromechanical equipment, such as bulk storage and line printers, remains high. In the past, with a centralized data processing facility, these devices could be attached directly to the central host computer. With the dispersal of computer power, these devices must somehow be shared.

A Definition of Local Networks

We will elaborate on these and other reasons later in this chapter. For now, the discussion above should be enough to motivate the following definition of a *local network:*

> A local network is a communications network that provides interconnection of a variety of data communicating devices within a small area.

There are three elements of significance in this definition. First, a local network is a communications network. That is, it is a facility for moving bits of data from one attached device to another. The application-level software and protocols that are required for attached devices to function cooperatively are beyond the scope of this book. As a corollary to this definition, note that a collection of devices interconnected by individual point-to-point links is not included in the definition or in this book.

Second, we interpret the phrase *data communicating devices* broadly, to include any device that communicates over a transmission medium. Examples:

- Computers
- Terminals

- Peripheral devices
- Sensors (temperature, humidity, security alarm sensors)
- Telephones
- Television transmitters and receivers
- Facsimile

Of course, not all types of local networks are capable of handling all of these devices.

Third, the geographic scope of a local network is small. The most common occurrence is a network that is confined to a single building. Networks that span several buildings, such as on a college campus or military base, are also common. A borderline case is a network with a radius of a few tens of kilometers. With appropriate technology, such a system will behave like a local network.

Another element that could be added to the definition is that a local network is generally privately owned rather than a public or commercially available utility. Indeed, typically, a single organization will own both the network and the attached devices.

Some of the typical characteristics of local networks are:

- High data rates (0.1 to 100 Mbps)
- Short distances (0.1 to 25 km)
- Low error rate (10^{-8} to 10^{-11})

The first two parameters serve to differentiate local networks from two cousins: multiprocessor systems and wide-area networks.

Other distinctions can be drawn between local networks and their two cousins, and these have a significant impact on design and operation. Local networks generally experience significantly fewer data transmission errors and significantly lower communications costs than those of long-haul networks. Cost-performance trade-offs are thus significantly different. Also, because local networks are generally owned by the same organization as the attached devices, it is possible to achieve greater integration between the network and the devices; this topic is explored in Chapter 8.

A distinction between local networks and multiprocessor systems is the degree of coupling. Multiprocessor systems are tightly coupled, usually have some central control, and completely integrate the communications function. Local networks tend to exhibit the opposite characteristics.

Types of Local Networks

There are two basic types of local networks: those based on circuit switching and those based on a technology referred to as packet broadcasting (Figure 1.1). We will define the terms *circuit switching* and *packet*

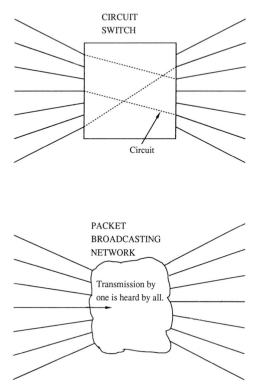

FIGURE 1.1 Transmission Methods for Local Networks

broadcasting in more detail in Chapter 2. For now, a brief definition of each should suffice:

- *Packet broadcasting:* Devices share a communications network in which a transmission from any one device is heard by all other devices. Data to be transmitted are broken up into small blocks, called *packets*. Packets include both user data and control information that indicate the destination of the data. Each packet is sent onto a network and may be received by all other devices on the network.
- *Circuit switching.* The network consists of a central switch to which all devices attach. Two devices communicate by setting up a circuit through the switch. The circuit consists of a path and dedicated resources for transferring data between the two devices through the switch.

The key to packet broadcasting is the use of a transmission medium shared by a number of devices. An early example of the use of a shared transmission medium is the multidrop line. The multidrop line, however, is used to permit communication between one primary station (usually a host computer) and a number of secondary stations (usually terminals). Communication on the multidrop line is controlled by the primary, and secondary-to-secondary exchange is generally not allowed. For a local network, peer communication among a number of cooperating devices is required. This type of local network is generally referred to as a **local area network (LAN)** and has the following key characteristics:

- A transmission medium is shared among the attached devices.
- Transmission is in the form of packets.
- A transmission from any one station is received by all other stations (hence the term *packet broadcasting*).
- There is no master station; rather, all of the stations cooperate to assure orderly use of the transmission medium.

In recent years, a new type of network, referred to as a **metropolitan area network (MAN),** has been developed. A metropolitan area network shares the characteristics listed above with the LAN; the difference is that the MAN covers larger distances and, generally, operates at higher data rates.

The most familiar example of a circuit-switching local network is the **private branch exchange (PBX).** The PBX was originally developed to provide an on-premise telephone exchange system. The voice PBX provides a point of interconnection for extension telephones within the office and a trunk connection to the nearest central office telephone exchange. Calls within the office are made through the PBX; calls outside the office are directed by the PBX to the public telephone network or a leased line.

With the advent of digital technology, the **digital PBX** has appeared on the scene and now dominates the PBX market. The digital PBX handles all signals internally as digital signals but still uses circuit-switching technology. The digital PBX is suited to handle both voice and data connections.

A final example of a local network that employs circuit switching is the **digital data switch.** The digital data switch is designed specifically to deal with data rather than voice. The main difference between the digital data switch and the digital PBX is that the former does not contain many of the call processing features normally found in the digital PBX, such as call forwarding and camp-on.

All the above networks can be distinguished from **wide-area networks (WANs).** As the name implies, WANs are networks that cover substantial distances. Public telephone networks and packet-switching networks are examples of WANs.

The focus of this book is on LANs and MANs, with a chapter devoted to circuit-switching local networks.

1.2

BENEFITS AND PITFALLS

Table 1.1 lists some of the major benefits of a local network. Whether these are realized or not, of course, depends on the skill and wisdom of those involved in selecting and managing the local network.

One of the most important potential benefits of a local network relates to system evolution. In a nonnetworked installation such as a time-sharing system, all data processing power is in one or a few systems. In order to upgrade hardware, existing applications software must be either converted to new hardware or reprogrammed, with the risk of error in either case. Even adding new applications on the same hardware, or enhancing those that exist, involves the risk of introducing errors and reducing the performance of the entire system. With a local network it is possible to gradually replace applications or systems, avoiding the "all-or-nothing" approach. Another facet of this capability is that old equipment can be left in the system to run a single application if the cost of moving that application to a new machine is not justified.

A local network tends to improve the reliability, availability, and survivability of a data processing facility (see Section 12.2). With multiple interconnected systems, the loss of any one system should have minimal impact. Further, key systems can be made redundant so that other systems can quickly take up the load after a failure.

We have already mentioned resource sharing. This includes not only expensive peripheral devices, but data. Data may be housed and con-

TABLE 1.1   Benefits and Pitfalls of Local Networks

Potential Benefits

System evolution: incremental changes with contained impact
Reliability/availability/survivability: multiple interconnected systems disperse
  functions and provide backup capability
Resource sharing: expensive peripherals, hosts, data
Multivendor support: customer not locked in to a single vendor
Improved response/performance
User needs single terminal to access multiple systems
Flexibility of equipment location
Integration of data processing and office automation

Potential Pitfalls

Interoperability is not guaranteed: software, data
A distributed database raises problems of integrity, security/privacy
Creeping escalation: more equipment will be procured than is actually needed
Loss of control: more difficult to manage and enforce standards

trolled from a specific facility but, via the network, may be available to many users.

A local network provides at least the potential of connecting devices from multiple vendors, thus giving the customer greater flexibility and bargaining power. However, a local network will provide only a rather low or primitive level of interconnection. For the network to function properly, higher levels of networking software must be supplied within the attached devices (see Section 2.3 and Chapter 8).

These are, in most cases, the most significant benefits of a local network. Several others are also listed in Table 1.1.

Alas, there are also some pitfalls, or at least potential pitfalls. As we mentioned, a local network does not guarantee that two devices can be used cooperatively, a concept known as *interoperability*. For example, two word processors from different vendors can be attached to a local network and can perhaps exchange data. But they probably will use different file formats and different control characters, so that it is not possible, directly, to take a file from one and begin editing it on the other. Some sort of format-conversion software is needed.

With a local network, it is likely that data will be distributed or, at least, that access to data may come from multiple sources. This raises questions of integrity (e.g., two users trying to update the database simultaneously) and security and privacy.

Another pitfall might be referred to as "creeping escalation." With the dispersal of computer equipment and the ease of incrementally adding equipment, it becomes easier for managers of suborganizations to justify equipment procurement for their department. Although each procurement may be individually justifiable, the totality of procurements throughout an organization may well exceed the total requirements.

There is also a loss of control problem. The prime virtue of networking—distributed systems—is also its prime danger. It is difficult to manage this resource, to enforce standards for software and data, and to control the information available through a network.

1.3

APPLICATIONS

The range of applications for local networks is wide, as indicated by the broad definition given above. Table 1.2 lists some of the potential applications. Again, we emphasize that not all local networks are capable of supporting all applications. To give some feeling for the use of local networks, we discuss in this section five rather different types of applications.

TABLE 1.2   Local Network Applications

Data Processing	Energy management
Data entry	Heating
Transaction processing	Ventilation
File transfer	Air conditioning
Inquiry/response	Process control
Batch/RJE	Fire and security
Office automation	Sensors/alarms
Document/word processing	Cameras and monitors
Electronic mail	Telephones
Intelligent copying/facsimile	Teleconferencing
Factory automation	Television
CAD/CAM	Off-the-air
Inventory control/order entry/shipping	Video presentations
Monitor and control of factory floor	
equipment	

Personal Computer Networks

We start at one extreme, a system designed to support microcomputers, such as personal computers. With the relatively low cost of such systems, individual managers within organizations are independently procuring personal computers for stand-alone applications, such as spreadsheet and project management tools. Today's personal computers put processor, file storage, high-level languages, and problem-solving tools in an inexpensive, "user-friendly" package. The reasons for acquiring such systems are compelling.

But a collection of stand-alone processors will not meet all of an organization's needs; central processing facilities are still required. Some programs, such as econometric forecasting models, are too big to run on a small computer. Corporate-wide data files, such as accounting and payroll, require a centralized facility but should be accessible to a number of users. In addition, there are other kinds of files that, although specialized, must be shared by a number of users. Further, there are sound reasons for connecting individual intelligent workstations not only to a central facility but to each other as well. Members of a project or organizational team need to share work and information. By far the most efficient way to do so is electronically.

Figure 1.2 is an example of a local network of personal computers for a hypothetical engineering group or department. The figure shows four types of users who have personal computers, each equipped with particular applications.

Each type of user is provided with electronic mail and word processing to improve the efficiency of creating and distributing messages, memos, and reports. Managers are also given a set of program and bud-

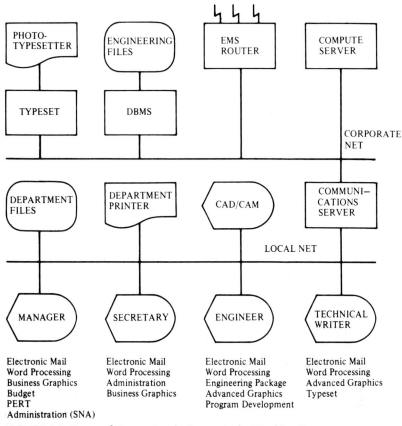

FIGURE 1.2 Personal Computers in Support of a Working Team

get management tools. With the amount of automation that personal computers supply, the role of secretaries becomes less that of a typist and more that of an administrative assistant. Tools such as electronic calendar and graphics support become valuable for these workers. In the same fashion, engineers and technical writers can be supplied with tailored systems.

Certain expensive resources, such as a disk and printer, can be shared by all users of the departmental local network. In addition, the network can tie into larger corporate network facilities. For example, the corporation may have a building-wide local network (see Office Automation below) and a long-haul corporate-wide network using, for example, IBM's SNA. A communications server can provide controlled access to these resources.

A key requirement for the success of such a network is low cost. The cost of attachment to the network for each device should be on the order of one to a few hundred dollars; otherwise, the attachment cost will approach the cost of the attached device. However, the capacity and data rate need not be high, so this is a realizable goal. For example, see [THUR85].

Computer Room Networks

At the other extreme from a personal computer local network is one designed for use in a computer room containing large, expensive mainframe computers. This type of network is likely to find application at very large data processing sites. Typically, these sites will be large companies or research installations with large data processing budgets. Because of the size involved, a small difference in productivity can mean millions of dollars. Further, although such networks are few in number, the collective cost of the equipment they support is very high. Consequently, this type of application deserves a close look.

Consider a site that uses a dedicated mainframe computer. This implies a fairly large application or set of applications. As the load at the site grows, the existing model may be replaced by a more powerful one, perhaps a multiprocessor system. At some sites, a single-system replacement will not be able to keep up; equipment growth rates will be exceeded by demand growth rates. The facility will eventually require multiple independent computers. Again, there are compelling reasons for interconnecting these systems. The cost of system interrupt is high, so it should be possible, easily and quickly, to shift applications to backup systems. It must be possible to test new procedures and applications without degrading the production system. Large bulk storage files must be accessible from more than one computer. Load leveling should be possible to maximize utilization.

An example of this type of installation is the one at the National Center for Atmospheric Research (NCAR), shown in Figure 1.3. This entails storage of massive amounts of data and the use of huge number-crunching simulation and analysis programs. There is also an extensive on-site graphics facility.

Initially, the NCAR facility consisted of a single mainframe run in batch mode. When it became clear that additional batch machines were needed, NCAR investigated the requirements for a new configuration to meet their needs. The result was four objectives:

1. Provide front-end processors to remove job and file preparation tasks from the batch computers
2. Provide an efficient method for interactive processing
3. Design a system architecture that would allow different services for special needs and purposes

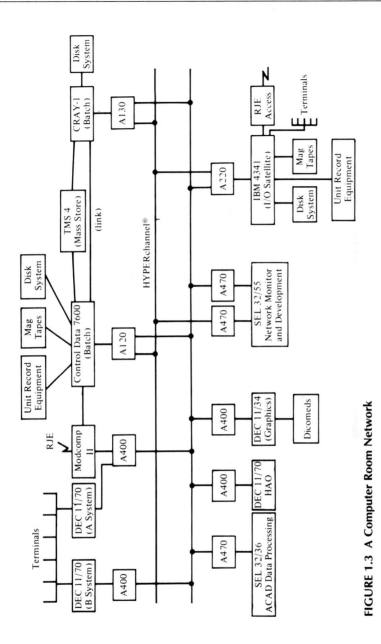

FIGURE 1.3 A Computer Room Network

4. Provide a system that would allow configuration flexibility without excessive modification to existing resources

The result of this study was a plan that called for the procurement of front-end processors, special-purpose computers, and bulk storage systems. A network was needed that met two requirements:

- Easy addition and subtraction of equipment
- High sustained data transfer speeds

It can be seen that some key requirements for computer-room networks are the opposite of those for personal computer local networks. High data rates are required to keep up with the work, which typically involves the transfer of large blocks of data. The electronics for achieving high speeds are expensive, on the order of tens of thousands of dollars per attachment. Fortunately, given the much higher cost of attached devices, such costs are reasonable.

Office Automation

Most local network applications will fall between these two extremes. Moderate data rates and moderate attachment costs are requirements. In some cases, the local network will support one or a few types of devices and rather homogeneous traffic. Others will support a wide variety of device and traffic types.

A good generic example of the latter is an office automation system, which can be defined as the incorporation of appropriate technology to help people manage information.

The key motivation for the move to office automation is productivity. As the percentage of white-collar workers has increased, the information and paper-work volume has grown. In most installations, secretarial and other support functions are heavily labor intensive. Increased labor costs combined with low productivity and increasing work load have caused employers to seek effective ways of increasing their rather low capital investment in this type of work.

At the same time, principals (managers, skilled "information workers") are faced with their own productivity bind. Work needs to be done faster with less wait time and waste time between segments of a job. This requires better access to information and better communication and coordination with others.

Table 1.3 lists elements of a hypothetical integrated office automation system. A study of this list gives some idea of the range of devices and information types that are part of the system. For this system to work and be truly effective, a local network is needed that can support the

TABLE 1.3 Elements of an Integrated Office Automation System

Basic IOAS Components

Action elements
  Word management (keying and
    editing)
  Terminal-oriented computer-based
    message system
  Automated file indexing
  Electronic filing and retrieval
  Off-line connection to computer-
    operated micrographics (for system
    purging)
Control elements
  Electronic calendar
  Electronic tickler file
Inquiry elements
  Automated file searching and retrieval
  Directory of users (names, addresses,
    telephone numbers, etc.)
  Capability for open-loop computer-
    aided retrieval (CAR) of
    micrographics
  Capability for input/output control of
    physical files

**Extended-Application IOAS
  Components**

Action elements
  Automated departmental billing for
    IOAS usage
  Individual applications
  Personal computing (permits
    individual to program)
  Unit applications
  Departmental applications
  Divisional applications
  Regional applications
  Line-of-business applications
  Functional applications
    (mathematical formulas)
Control elements
  System usage monitoring
    (departmental level)
  Specialized applications (as above)
Inquiry elements: specialized
  applications (as above)

Optional IOAS Components

Action elements
  Interconnection to other
    terminal-oriented, computer-
    based message systems
  Interconnection to public
    teletypewriter systems
  OCR (optical character
    recognition) input
  Digitized, hard-copy input
    (temporary; for incoming mail)
  Store-and-forward fax
  Soft-copy fax
  Interconnection to external fax
    devices and networks
  Audio output electronic mail
    (digital-to-audio conversion)
  Business graphics
    (black-and-white)
  Electronic calculator
  Sorting capabilities
  Photocomposer output
  On-line output of computer-
    operated micrographics (COM)
  Computer teleconferencing
Control elements
  COM format previewing
  Project management and control
  Management of multiauthored
    document preparation
Inquiry elements
  Soft-copy CAR
  Electronic publishing (manuals,
    price lists, news, etc.)
  Interconnection to other internal
    systems and data bases
  Interconnection to external
    research data base services

Source: [BARC81].

various devices and transmit the various types of information. A discussion of the use of local networks to tie together office automation equipment such as this can be found in [STAL90c].

Factory Local Networks

The factory environment is increasingly being dominated by automated equipment: programmable controllers, automated materials handling devices, time and attendance stations, machine vision devices, and various forms of robots. To manage the production or manufacturing process, it is essential to tie this equipment together. And, indeed, the very nature of the equipment facilitates this. Microprocessor devices have the potential to collect information from the shop floor and accept commands. With the proper use of the information and commands, it is possible to improve the manufacturing process and to provide detailed machine control.

The more that a factory is automated, the greater is the need for communications. Only by interconnecting all of the devices and by providing mechanisms for their cooperation can the automated factory be made to work. The means of interconnection is the factory local area network [SCHO84, MCGA85, HALL85].

To get some feeling for the requirements for a factory local network, consider the requirements developed by General Motors [STAL90a]. GM's specification of a communications network is driven by the sophisticated communications strategy it has evolved to meet its requirements. These requirements reflect those that obtain in other factory and robotics environments. Among the key areas are the following:

- Work force involvement has proven to be a valuable tool for GM's quality and cost-improvement effort. In an attempt to provide facts about the state of the business, employees are told GM's competitive position in relation to quality and costs. This information is communicated by video setups at numerous locations in the plant complex.
- An indirect effect on manufacturing costs has been the escalating cost of utilities. To try to control this area, GM measures usage of water, gas, pressurized air, steam, electricity, and other resources—often by means of computers and programmable controllers.
- GM is investigating and, in some cases, implementing asynchronous machining and assembly systems that are much more flexible than the traditional systems of the past. To facilitate flexibility, the communication requirements increase an order of magnitude.

- To protect its large investment in facilities, GM uses closed-circuit TV surveillance and computerized monitoring systems to warn of fires or other dangers.
- Accounting systems, personnel systems, material and inventory control systems, warranty systems, and others use large mainframe computers with remote terminals located throughout the manufacturing facility.
- The nature of process-control and factory environments dictates that communications be extremely reliable and that the maximum time required to transmit critical control signals and alarms be bounded and known.

To innerconnect all of the equipment in a facility, a local network is needed. The requirements listed above dictate the following characteristics of the local network:

- High capacity
- Ability to handle a variety of data traffic
- Large geographic extent
- High reliability
- Ability to specify and control transmission delays

Integrated Voice and Data Local Networks

In virtually all offices today, the telephone system is separate from any local network that might be used to interconnect data processing devices. With the advent of digital voice technology, the capability now exists to integrate the telephone switching system of a building with the data processing equipment, providing a single local network for both.

Such integrated voice/data networks might simplify network management and control. It will also provide the required networking for the kinds of integrated voice and data devices to be expected in the future. An example is an executive voice/data workstation that provides verbal message storage, voice annotation of text, and automated dialing.

Summary

This section has only scratched the surface of possible applications of local networks. This book focuses on the common principles underlying the design and implementation of all local networks, and so will not pursue the topic of specific applications. Nevertheless, in the course of the book, the reader will gain an appreciation of the variety of uses of local networks.

1.4

INFORMATION DISTRIBUTION

In determining the requirements for local networking, it is important to examine the traffic patterns that are reasonable to expect. Figure 1.4 illustrates the distribution of nonvoice information that has been consistently reported in a number of studies. About half of the information generated within a small unit of an organization (e.g., a department) remains within that unit. Typically only summary-type information or consolidated data are disseminated beyond the basic unit of an organization. Another 25% is normally shared with peer departments within a somewhat larger grouping (e.g., a division) and the immediate superior of the department. In a typical office layout, this would translate to a radius of about 600 feet. Another 15% goes elsewhere within the organization, such as to other departments within other divisions, central staff organizations, and top management. Finally, only about 10% of the total generated information is distributed beyond the confines of a single building or cluster of buildings. Example destinations include remote corporate headquarters, customers, suppliers, and government agencies.

Another way of looking at local network requirements is to consider the kinds of data processing equipment to be supported. In rough terms, we can group this equipment into three categories:

1. *Personal computers and terminals:* the workhorse in most office environments is the microcomputer, including personal computers and workstations. Additionally, when shared systems are present

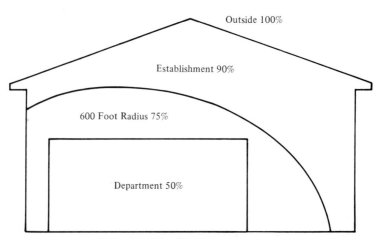

FIGURE 1.4 Information Distribution

in an organization, terminals are also to be found. Most of this equipment is found at the departmental level, used by individual professionals and secretarial personnel. When used for network applications, the load generated tends to be rather modest.

2. *Minicomputers:* minicomputers may function as servers within a department or be shared by users in a number of departments. In many organizations, a number of commonly used applications will be provided on time-shared minicomputers. Because of this shared use, these machines may generate more substantial traffic than microcomputers.

3. *Mainframes:* for large database and scientific applications, the mainframe is still the machine of choice. When the machines are networked, bulk data transfers dictate that a high-capacity network be used.

Figure 1.5 illustrates the performance spectrum involved. Larger, more expensive machines tend to require a higher data rate on the local network to support them. The higher the data rate, the greater the cost of the network.

The requirements indicated by Figures 1.4 and 1.5 suggest that a single local network will not, in many cases, be the most cost-effective solution. A single network would have to be rather high speed to support the aggregate demand. However, the cost of attachment to a local net-

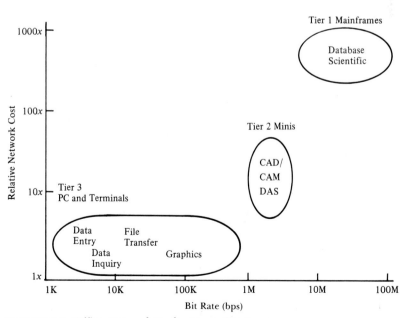

FIGURE 1.5 Office Network Performance Spectrum

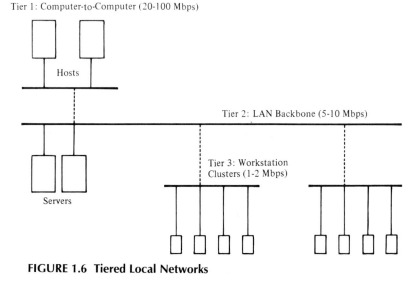

FIGURE 1.6 Tiered Local Networks

work tends to increase as a function of the network data rate. Accordingly, a high-speed local network would be very expensive for attachment of low-cost personal computers.

An alternative approach, which is becoming increasingly common, is to employ two or three tiers of local networks (Figure 1.6). Within a department, a low-cost, low-speed local network supports a cluster of microcomputers and terminals. These departmental local networks are then lashed together with a backbone local network of higher capacity. In addition, shared systems are also supported off of this backbone. If mainframes are also part of the office equipment suite, then a separate high-speed local network supports these devices and may be linked, as a whole, to the backbone local network to support a modest amount of traffic between the mainframes and other office equipment. We will see that local network standards and products address the need for all three types of local networks.

1.5

OUTLINE OF THE BOOK

This chapter, of course, serves as an introduction to the entire book. A brief synopsis of the remaining chapters follows.

Topics in Data Communications and Computer Networking

This book focuses on a specific aspect of data communications and computer networking. In order to provide context, and to make the book as self-contained as possible, Chapter 2 provides a basic overview of the entire field. The chapter begins with a look at some data communications concepts, including techniques for encoding analog and digital data for both analog and digital signaling, and the concept of multiplexing; the concepts of asynchronous and synchronous transmission are also discussed. The chapter then examines the properties of circuit switching and packet switching. Finally, communications architecture is discussed, using the Open Systems Interconnection (OSI) model as a basis for discussion.

LAN/MAN Technology

The essential technology underlying all forms of local networks comprises topology, transmission medium, and medium access control technique. Chapter 3 provides an overview of the first two of these elements. Four topologies are in common use: star, ring, bus, tree. The most common transmission media for local networking are twisted pair (unshielded and shielded), coaxial cable (baseband and broadband), and optical fiber. These topologies and transmission media are discussed, and the most promising combinations are described. The chapter closes with a discussion of various types of local networks.

Topologies and Transmission Media for LANs and MANs

Chapter 4 is concerned with the topologies and transmission media used in LANs and MANs. The use of twisted pair and coaxial cable in bus/tree LANs is examined first, followed by a discussion of twisted pair for star and ring LANs. The remainder of the chapter examines the increasingly important use of optical fiber in LANs and MANs; star, ring, and bus topologies are covered.

Local Area Network Architecture

Chapter 5 focuses on the protocols needed for stations attached to a LAN to cooperate with each other in the exchange of packets. Specifically, the chapter deals with link control and medium access control protocols. The latter include token-passing and contention-based protocols, such as token ring, token bus, and CSMA/CD. An appendix to Chapter 5 summarizes the standards for LANs that have been issued by the IEEE 802 committee.

Metropolitan Area Network Architecture

Chapter 6 is devoted to a study of the medium access control and physical layer specifications for MANs. The chapter concentrates on the two standards that have been developed: the fiber-distributed data interface (FDDI) and the IEEE 802.6 MAN standard.

Circuit-Switched Local Networks

There is a class of local networks based on the use of circuit switching, including the digital data switch and digital private branch exchange (PBX). Circuit switching is achieved by the use of time-division switching techniques. Chapter 7 begins with an overview of time-division switching techniques, and then examines their application in digital data switches and digital PBXs.

The Network Interface

A local network is a communications facility that supports a number of attached devices. Each device attaches to the network via a *network interface*. Chapter 8 examines the logic required at this interface. A number of issues, including the use of host-to-front-end protocols, is discussed. The differences in handling terminals and computers are also described.

Network Performance

In a LAN or MAN, the data rate, length, and medium access control technique of the network are the key factors in determining the effective capacity of the network. Chapter 9 examines performance of LANs and MANs, and introduces a key parameter, a, that provides a concise but powerful means of characterizing network performance. The issue of end-to-end performance is also considered. Chapter 10 looks at the rather different issues involved in assessing performance on circuit-switched local networks.

Internetworking

The increasing deployment of local networks has led to an increased need to interconnect local networks with each other and with wide-area networks. Chapter 10 focuses on the two most important devices used in internetworking involving local networks: bridges and routers. In both cases, there are two types of protocols involved: protocols for forwarding packets and protocols for exchanging routing information.

Network Management

The final chapter looks at the important issue of network management. Following a general discussion of network management requirements and systems, the OSI-based standards for network management are introduced. The remainder of the chapter looks at network management functions and services that are specific to LANs and MANs, including a discussion of standards in this area.

1.6

RECOMMENDED READING

[SLON91], [MART89], and [NAUG91] are book-length treatments of LANs. [KESS92] covers MANs. [STAL93a] is a collection of reprints of key articles on LANs and MANs. [STAL90b] and [STAL90c] provide a more detailed discussion of applications of local networks.

1.7

PROBLEMS

1.1 A computer network is an interconnected set of computers and other devices (terminals, printers, etc.) that can communicate and cooperate with each other to perform certain applications. A subset of a computer network is a communications network (sometimes called a subnetwork) that provides the necessary functions for transferring data between network devices. List functions and capabilities that should be part of the subnetwork and those that should be part of the computer network outside the subnetwork.

1.2 On what grounds should a collection of devices connected by point-to-point links be excluded from the definition of local network?

1.3 An alternative to a local network for meeting local requirements for data processing and computer applications is a centralized time-sharing system plus a large number of terminals dispersed throughout the local area. What are the major benefits and pitfalls of this approach compared to a local network?

1.4 What are the key factors that determine the response time and throughput performance of a local network? Of a centralized system?

1.5 In what ways is the human-machine interface of a local network likely to differ from that of a centralized system for:
   • Application users?
   • System operator/managers?

CHAPTER 2

Topics in Data Communications and Computer Networking

The purpose of this chapter is to make this book self-contained for the reader with little or no background in data communications. For the reader with greater interest, references for further study are supplied at the end of the chapter.

2.1

DATA COMMUNICATIONS CONCEPTS

Analog and Digital Data Communications

The terms *analog* and *digital* correspond, roughly, to continuous and discrete, respectively. These two terms are used frequently in data communications in at least three contexts:

- Data
- Signaling
- Transmission

Very briefly, we define *data* as entities that convey meaning. A useful distinction is that data have to do with the form of something; *information* has to do with the content or interpretation of those data. *Signals* are electric or electromagnetic encoding of data. *Signaling* is the act of propagating the signal along some suitable medium. Finally, *transmission* is the communication of data by the propagation and processing of signals. In what follows, we try to make these abstract concepts clear by discussing the terms *analog* and *digital* in these three contexts.

The concepts of analog and digital data are simple enough. *Analog data* take on continuous values on some interval. For example, voice and video are continuously varying patterns of intensity. Most data collected by sensors, such as temperature and pressure, are continuous-valued. *Digital data* take on discrete values; examples are text and integers.

In a communications system, data are propagated from one point to another by means of electric signals. An *analog signal* is a continuously varying electromagnetic wave that may be transmitted over a variety of media, depending on frequency; examples are wire media, such as twisted pair and coaxial cable, fiber optic cable, and atmosphere or space propagation. A *digital signal* is a sequence of voltage pulses that may be transmitted over a wire medium; for example, a constant positive voltage level may represent binary 1 and a constant negative voltage level may represent binary 0.

The principal advantages of digital signaling are that it is generally cheaper than analog signaling and is less susceptible to noise interference. The principal disadvantage is that digital signals suffer more from attenuation than do analog signals. Figure 2.1 shows a sequence of voltage pulses, generated by a source using two voltage levels, and the received voltage some distance down a conducting medium. Because of the attenuation or reduction of signal strength at higher frequencies, the pulses become rounded and smaller. It should be clear that this attenuation can rather quickly lead to the loss of the information contained in the propagated signal.

Both analog and digital data can be represented, and hence propagated, by either analog or digital signals. This is illustrated in Figure 2.2. Generally, analog data are a function of time and occupy a limited frequency spectrum. Such data can be directly represented by an electromagnetic signal occupying the same spectrum. The best example of this is voice data. As sound waves, voice data have frequency components in the range 20 Hz to 20 kHz. However, most of the speech energy is in a much narrower range. The standard spectrum of voice signals is 300 to 3400 Hz, and this is quite adequate to propagate speech intelligibly and clearly. The telephone instrument does just that. For all sound input

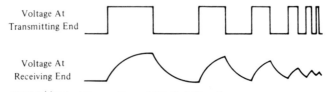

Voltage At Transmitting End

Voltage At Receiving End

FIGURE 2.1 Attenuation of Digital Signals

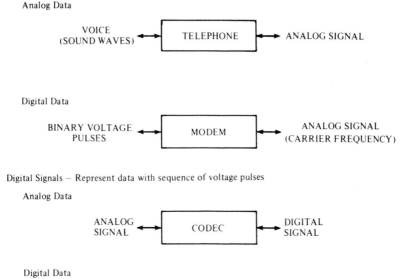

FIGURE 2.2 Analog and Digital Signaling for Analog and Digital Data

in the range of 300 to 3400 Hz, an electromagnetic signal with the same frequency-amplitude pattern is produced. The process is performed in reverse to convert the electromagnetic energy back into sound.

Digital data can also be represented by analog signals by use of a *modem* (modulator/demodulator). The modem converts a series of binary (two-valued) voltage pulses into an analog signal by modulating a *carrier frequency*. The resulting signal occupies a certain spectrum of frequency centered about the carrier and may be propagated across a medium suitable for that carrier. The most common modems represent digital data in the voice spectrum and hence allow those data to be propagated over ordinary voice-grade telephone lines. At the other end of the line, a modem demodulates the signal to recover the original data. Various modulation techniques are discussed below.

In an operation very similar to that performed by a modem, analog data can be represented by digital signals. The device that performs this function for voice data is a *codec* (coder-decoder). In essence, the codec takes an analog signal that directly represents the voice data and approximates that signal by a bit stream. At the other end of a line, the bit stream is used to reconstruct the analog data.

Finally, digital data can be represented directly, in binary form, by two voltage levels. To improve propagation characteristics, however, the binary data are often encoded, as explained below.

TABLE 2.1   Analog and Digital Transmission

(a) Treatment of Signals

	Analog Transmission	**Digital Transmission**
Analog Signal	Is propagated through amplifiers; same treatment for both analog and digital data	Assumes digital data; at propagation points, data in signal are recovered and new analog signal is generated
Digital Signal	Not used	Repeaters retransmit new signal; same treatment for both analog and digital data

(b) Possible Combinations

	Analog Transmission	**Digital Transmission**
Analog Signal	Analog signal	Digital signal
Digital Signal	Analog signal	Digital signal Analog signal

A final distinction remains to be made. Both analog and digital signals may be transmitted on suitable transmission media. The way these signals are treated is a function of the transmission system. Table 2.1 summarizes the methods of data transmission. Analog transmission is a means of transmitting analog signals without regard to their content; the signals may represent analog data (e.g., voice) or digital data (e.g., data that pass through a modem). In either case, the analog signal will attenuate after a certain distance. To achieve longer distances, the analog transmission system includes amplifiers that boost the energy in the signal. Unfortunately, the amplifier also boosts the noise components. With amplifiers cascaded to achieve long distances, the signal becomes more and more distorted. For analog data, such as voice, quite a bit of distortion can be tolerated and the data remain intelligible. However, for digital data, cascaded amplifiers will introduce errors.

Digital transmission, in contrast, is concerned with the content of the signal. We have mentioned that a digital signal can be transmitted only a limited distance before attenuation endangers the integrity of the data. To achieve greater distances, repeaters are used. A repeater receives the digital signal, recovers the pattern of 1's and 0's, and retransmits a new signal. Thus the attenuation is overcome.

The same technique may be used with an analog signal if it is assumed that the signal carries digital data. At appropriately spaced points, the transmission system has retransmission devices rather than amplifiers. The retransmission device recovers the digital data from the analog signal and generates a new, clean analog signal. Thus noise is not cumulative.

For long-haul communications, digital signaling is not as versatile and practical as analog signaling. For example, digital signaling is impossible for satellite and microwave systems. However, digital transmission is superior to analog, both in terms of cost and quality, and wide-area communications systems are gradually converting to digital transmission for both voice and digital data.

We will see that in local networks the trade-offs do not always lead to the same solutions as for wide-area communications. It is still true, within the local context, that digital techniques tend to be cheaper because of the declining cost of digital circuitry. However, the limited distances of local networks limit the severity of the noise and attenuation problems, and the cost and quality of analog techniques approach those of digital. Consequently, there is a secure place for analog signaling and analog transmission in local networks.

Data Encoding Techniques

As we have pointed out, data, either analog or digital, must be converted into a signal for purposes of transmission.

In the case of **digital data,** different signal elements are used to represent binary 1 and binary 0. The mapping from binary digits to signal elements is the *encoding scheme* used for transmission. To understand the significance of the encoding scheme, consider that there are two important tasks in interpreting signals (analog or digital) that carry digital data at the receiver. First, the receiver must know when a bit begins and ends, so that the receiver may sample the incoming signal once per bit time. Second, the receiver must recognize the value of each bit. A number of factors determine how successful the receiver will be in interpreting the incoming signal. For example, the greater the strength of the signal, the more it will withstand attenuation and the more it will stand out from any noise that is present. Also, the higher the data rate, the more difficult the receiver's task is, since each bit occupies a smaller amount of time: the receiver must be more careful about sampling properly and will have less time to make decisions. Finally, the encoding scheme will affect receiver performance. We will describe a number of different encoding techniques for converting digital data to both analog and digital signals.

In the case of **analog data,** the encoding scheme will also affect transmission performance. In this case, we are concerned about the quality, or fidelity, of the transmission. That is, we would like the received data to be as close as possible to the transmitted data. For the purposes of this text, we are concerned about the encoding of analog data in digital form, and techniques for this encoding are presented below.

Digital Data, Analog Signals. The basis for analog signaling is a continuous constant-frequency signal known as the *carrier signal*. Digital data are encoded by modulating one of the three characteristics of the

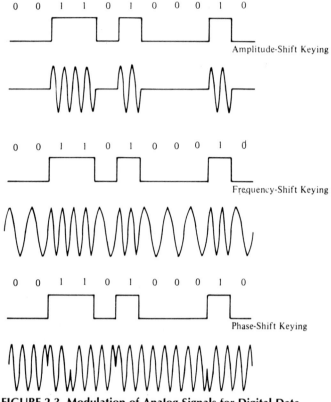

FIGURE 2.3 Modulation of Analog Signals for Digital Data

carrier: amplitude, frequency, or phrase, or some combination of these. Figure 2.3 illustrates the three basic forms of modulation of analog signals for digital data:

- Amplitude-shift keying (ASK)
- Frequency-shift keying (FSK)
- Phase-shift keying (PSK)

In all these cases, the resulting signal contains a range of frequencies on both sides of the carrier frequency. That range is referred to as the *bandwidth* of the signal.

In ASK, the two binary values are represented by two different amplitudes of the carrier frequency. In some cases, one of the amplitudes is zero; that is, one binary digit is represented by the presence, at constant amplitude, of the carrier, and the other is represented by the absence of the carrier. ASK is susceptible to sudden gain changes and is a rather inefficient modulation technique. On voice-grade lines, it is typically used up to only 1200 bps.

In FSK, the two binary values are represented by two different frequencies near the carrier frequency. This scheme is less susceptible to error than ASK. On voice-grade lines, it is typically used up to 1200 bps. It is also commonly used for high-frequency (3 to 30 MHz) radio transmission. It can also be used at even higher frequencies on local networks that use coaxial cable.

Figure 2.4 shows an example of the use of FSK for full-duplex operation over a voice-grade line. *Full duplex* means that data can be transmitted in both directions at the same time. To accomplish this, one bandwidth is used for sending, another for receiving. The figure is a specification for the Bell System 108 series modems. In one direction (transmit or receive), the modem passes frequencies in the range 300 to 1700 Hz. The two frequencies used to represent 1 and 0 are centered on 1170 Hz, with a shift of 100 Hz on either side. Similarly, for the other direction (receive or transmit) the modem passes 1700 to 3000 Hz and uses a center frequency of 2125 Hz. The shaded area around each pair of frequencies indicates the actual bandwidth of each signal. Note that there is little overlap and thus little interference.

In PSK, the phase of the carrier signal is shifted to represent data. Figure 2.3 shows an example of a two-phase system. In this system, a 0 is represented by sending a signal burst of the same phase as the previous signal burst sent. A 1 is represented by sending a signal burst of opposite phase to the previous one. PSK can use more than two phase shifts. A four-phase system would encode 2 bits with each signal burst. The PSK technique is more noise resistant and efficient than FSK; on a voice-grade line, rates up to 9600 bps are achieved.

Finally, the techniques discussed above may be combined. A common combination in PSK and ASK, where some or all of the phase shifts may occur at one of two amplitudes.

Digital Data, Digital Signals.   Although a common means of transmitting digital data is to pass them through a modem and transmit them as an analog signal, we will see that the transmission of digital data as

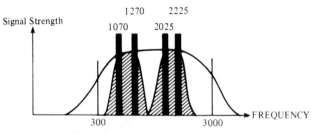

FIGURE 2.4 Full-Duplex FSK Transmission on a Voice-Grade Line

digital signals is the technique used in a number of local networks. The use of digital signals may be less expensive and, under some circumstances, provide better performance than analog signaling. In this subsection, we consider two families of coding techniques: NRZ codes and biphase codes.

With **Nonreturn-to-Zero (NRZ) codes,** two different voltage levels, one positive and one negative, are used as the signal elements for the two binary digits. The name refers to the fact that the voltage level never returns to zero, but is always positive or negative. NRZ is the most common and easiest way to transmit digital signals. However, we shall see that its use is not appropriate for local networks.

Figure 2.5a shows the use of a constant negative voltage to represent binary 1 and a constant positive voltage to represent binary 0. This code is known as **NRZ-L** (NRZ-level). This code is often used for very short connections, such as between a terminal and a modem or a terminal and a nearby computer.

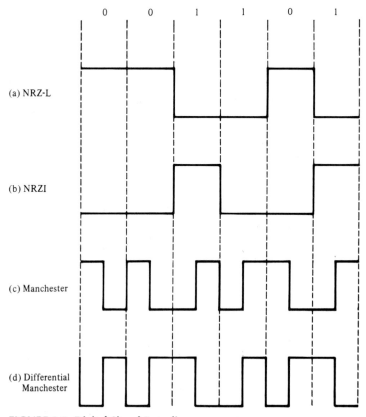

FIGURE 2.5 Digital Signal Encoding

A variation on NRZ is **NRZI** (NRZ, invert on ones). As with NRZ-L, NRZI maintains a constant voltage pulse for the duration of a bit time. The data themselves are encoded as the presence or absence of a signal transition at the beginning of the bit time. A transition (low-to-high or high-to-low) at the beginning of a bit time denotes a binary 1 for that bit time; no transition indicates a binary 0 (Figure 2-5b).

NRZI is an example of differential encoding. In differential encoding, the signal is decoded by comparing the polarity of adjacent signal elements rather than determining the absolute value of a signal element. One benefit of this scheme is that it may be more reliable to detect a transition in the presence of noise than to compare a value to a threshold. Another benefit is that with a complex transmission layout, it is easy to lose the sense of the polarity of the signal. For example, on a twisted-pair medium, if the leads from an attached device to the twisted pair are accidentally inverted, all 1's and 0's will be inverted. This cannot happen with differential encoding.

There are several disadvantages to NRZ transmission. It is difficult to determine where one bit ends and another begins. To picture the problem, consider that with a long string of 1's or 0's for NRZ-L, the output is a constant voltage over a long period of time. Under these circumstances, any drift between the timing of transmitter and receiver will result in the loss of synchronization between the two. Also, there is a direct-current (dc) component during each bit time that may accumulate if positive or negative pulses predominate. Thus, alternating-current (ac) coupling, which uses a transformer and provides excellent electrical isolation between data communicating devices and their environment, is not possible. Furthermore, the dc component can cause plating or other deterioration at attachment contacts.

There is a set of alternative coding techniques, grouped under the term **biphase codes,** which overcomes these problems. Two of these techniques, Manchester and Differential Manchester, are in common use for local networks. All of the biphase techniques require at least one transition per bit time and may have as many as two transitions. Thus, the maximum modulation rate is twice that for NRZ; this means that the bandwidth or transmission capacity required is correspondingly greater. To compensate for this, the biphase schemes have several advantages:

- *Synchronization:* Because there is a predictable transition during each bit time, the receiver can synchronize on that transition. For this reason, the biphase codes are known as self-clocking codes.
- *No dc component:* Because of the transition in each bit time, biphase codes have no dc component, yielding the benefits just described.
- *Error detection:* The absence of an expected transition can be used to detect errors. Noise on the line would have to invert both the

signal before and after the expected transition to cause an unde-tected error.

In the **Manchester** code (Figure 2.5c), there is a transition at the mid-dle of each bit period. The mid-bit transition serves as a clock and also as data: a low-to-high transition represents a 1, and a high-to-low tran-sition represents a 0. In **Differential Manchester** (Figure 2.5d), the mid-bit transition is used only to provide clocking. The encoding of a 0 is represented by the presence of a transition at the beginning of a bit pe-riod, and a 1 is represented by the absence of a transition at the begin-ning of a bit period. Differential Manchester exhibits the further advantage of being a differential encoding technique.

Analog Data, Digital Signals.   The most common example of the use of digital signals to encode analog data is *pulse code modulation* (PCM), which is used to encode voice signals. This section describes PCM and then looks briefly at a similar, less used scheme, *delta modulation* (DM).

PCM is based on the sampling theorem, which states [JORD85]:

> If a signal *f(t)* is sampled at regular intervals of time and at a rate higher than twice the highest significant signal frequency, then the samples con-tain all the information of the original signal. The function *f(t)* may be reconstructed from these samples by the use of a low-pass filter.

If voice data are limited to frequencies below 4000 Hz, a conservative procedure for intelligibility, then 8000 samples per second would be suf-ficient to completely characterize the voice signal. Note, however, that these are analog samples. To convert to digital, each of these analog samples must be assigned a binary code. Figure 2.6 shows an example in which each sample is approximated by being "quantized" into one of 16 different levels. Each sample can then be represented by 4 bits. Of course, it is now impossible to recover the original signal exactly. By using a 7-bit sample, which allows 128 quantizing levels, the quality of the recovered voice signal is comparable to that achieved via analog transmission. Note that this implies that a data rate of 8000 samples per second $\times$ 7 bits per sample = 56 kbps is needed for a single voice signal.

Typically, the PCM scheme is refined using a technique known as *nonlinear encoding*, which means, in effect, that the 128 quantization lev-els are not equally spaced. The problem with equal spacing is that the mean absolute error for each sample is the same, regardless of signal level. Consequently, lower-amplitude values are relatively more dis-torted. By using a greater number of quantizing steps for signals of low amplitude, and a small number of quantizing steps for signals of large amplitude, a marked reduction in overall signal distortion is achieved.

PCM can, of course, be used for other than voice signals. For exam-ple, a color TV signal has a useful bandwidth of 4.6 MHz, and reason-

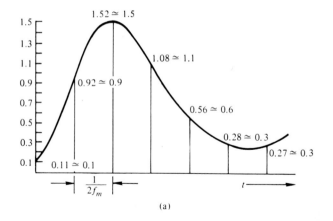

(a)

Digit	Binary equivalent	Pulse-code waveform
0	0000	
1	0001	
2	0010	
3	0011	
4	0100	
5	0101	
6	0110	
7	0111	
8	1000	
9	1001	
10	1010	
11	1011	
12	1100	
13	1101	
14	1110	
15	1111	

(b)

FIGURE 2.6 Pulse Code Modulation

able quality can be achieved with 10-bit samples, for a data rate of 92 Mbps.

With DM, a bit stream is produced by approximating the derivative of an analog signal rather than its amplitude. A 1 is generated if the current sample is greater in amplitude than the immediately preceding sample; a 0 is generated otherwise. For equal data rates, DM is comparable to PCM in terms of signal quality. Note that for equal data rates, DM requires a higher sampling rate: a 56-kbps voice signal is generated from 8000 PCM samples per second but 56,000 DM samples per second. In general, DM systems are less complex and less expensive than comparable PCM systems. A discussion of these and other encoding schemes can be found in [CROC83] and [JAYA84].

Multiplexing

In both local and long-haul communications, it is almost always the case that the capacity of the transmission medium exceeds that required for the transmission of a single signal. To make cost-effective use of the transmission system, it is desirable to use the medium efficiently by having it carry multiple signals simultaneously. This is referred to as *multiplexing*, and two techniques are in common use: frequency-division multiplexing (FDM) and time-division multiplexing (TDM).

FDM takes advantage of the fact that the useful bandwidth of the medium exceeds the required bandwidth of a given signal. A number of signals can be carried simultaneously if each signal is modulated onto a different carrier frequency, and the carrier frequencies are sufficiently separated so that the bandwidths of the signals do not overlap. A simple example of FDM is full-duplex FSK transmission (Figure 2.4). A general case of FDM is shown in Figure 2.7a. Six signal sources are fed into a multiplexer that modulates each signal onto a different frequency $(f_1, \ldots, f_6)$. Each signal requires a certain bandwidth centered around its carrier frequency, referred to as a *channel*. To prevent interference, the channels are separated by guard bands, which are unused portions of the spectrum.

An example is the multiplexing of voice signals. We mentioned that the useful spectrum for voice is 300 to 3400 Hz. Thus a bandwidth of 4 kHz is adequate to carry the voice signal and provide a guard band. For both North America (Bell System standard) and internationally [Consultative Committee on International Telegraphy and Telephony (CCITT) standard], a standard voice multiplexing scheme is twelve 4-kHz voice channels from 60 to 108 kHz. For higher-capacity links, both Bell and CCITT define larger groupings of 4-kHz channels.

TDM takes advantage of the fact that the achievable bit rate (sometimes, unfortunately, called bandwidth) of the medium exceeds the required data rate of a digital signal. Multiple digital signals can be carried on a single transmission path by interleaving portions of each signal in time. The interleaving can be at the bit level or in blocks of bytes or larger quantities. For example, the multiplexer in Figure 2.7b has six inputs that might each be, say, 9.6 kbps. A single line with a capacity of 57.6 kbps could accommodate all six sources. Analogously to FDM, the sequence of time slots dedicated to a particular source is called a *channel*. One cycle of time slots (one per source) is called a *frame*.

The TDM scheme depicted in Figure 2.7 is also known as *synchronous TDM*, referring to the fact that time slots are preassigned and fixed. Hence the timing of transmission from the various sources is synchro-

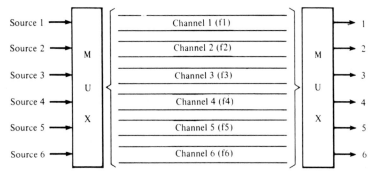

(a) Frequency-Division Multiplexing

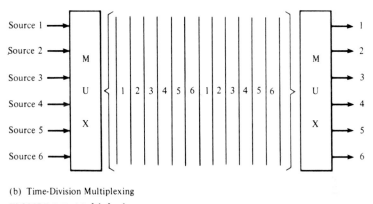

(b) Time-Division Multiplexing

FIGURE 2.7 Multiplexing

nized. In contrast, asynchronous TDM allows time on the medium to be allocated dynamically. Examples of this will be discussed later. Unless otherwise noted, the term TDM will be used to mean synchronous TDM only.

One example of TDM is the standard scheme used for transmitting PCM voice data, known in Bell parlance as *T1 carrier*. Data are taken from each source, one sample (7 bits) at a time. An eighth bit is added for signaling and supervisory functions. For T1, 24 sources are multiplexed, so there are $8 \times 24 = 192$ bits of data and control signals per frame. One final bit is added for establishing and maintaining synchronization. Thus a frame consists of 193 bits and contains one 7-bit sample per source. Since sources must be sampled 8000 times per second, the required data rate is $8000 \times 193 = 1.544$ Mbps. As with voice FDM, higher data rates are defined for larger groupings.

TDM is not limited to digital signals. Analog signals can also be interleaved in time. Also, with analog signals, a combination of TDM and

FDM is possible. A transmission system can be frequency-divided into a number of channels, each of which is further divided via TDM. This technique is possible with broadband local networks, discussed in Chapter 4.

Asynchronous and Synchronous Transmission

A fundamental requirement of digital data communication (analog or digital signal) is that the receiver know the starting time and duration of each bit that it receives.

The earliest and simplest scheme for meeting this requirement is asynchronous transmission. In this scheme, data are transmitted one character (of 5 to 8 bits) at a time. Each character is preceded by a start code and followed by a stop code (Figure 2.8a). The *start code* has the encoding for 0 and a duration of 1 bit time; in other words, the start code is 1 bit with a value of 0. The *stop code* has a value of 1, and a minimum duration, depending on the system, of from 1 to 2 bit times. When there are no data to send, the transmitter sends a continuous stop code. The receiver identifies the beginning of a new character by the transition from 1 to 0. The receiver must have a fairly accurate idea of the duration of each bit in order to recover all the bits of the character. However, a small amount of drift (e.g., 1% per bit) will not matter since the receiver resynchronizes with each stop code. This means of communication is simple and cheap but requires an overhead of 2 to 3 bits per character. This technique is referred to as *asynchronous* because characters are sent independently from each other. Thus characters may be sent at a nonuniform rate.

A more efficient means of communication is synchronous transmission. In this mode, blocks of characters or bits are transmitted without start and stop codes, and the exact departure or arrival time of each bit is predictable. To prevent timing drift between transmitter and receiver,

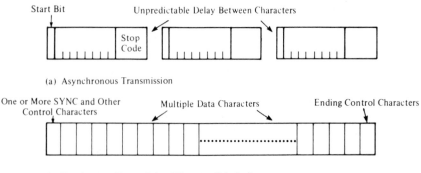

(a) Asynchronous Transmission

(b) Synchronous Transmission (Character-Oriented)

FIGURE 2.8 Asynchronous and Synchronous Transmission

their clocks must somehow be synchronized. One possibility is to provide a separate clock line between transmitter and receiver. Otherwise, the clocking information must be embedded in the data signal. For digital signals, this can be achieved with biphase encoding. For analog signals, a number of techniques can be used; the carrier frequency itself can be used to synchronize the receiver based on the phase of the carrier.

With synchronous transmission, there is another level of synchronization required, to allow the receiver to determine the beginning and end of a block of data. To achieve this, each block begins with a *preamble* bit pattern and ends with a *postamble* bit pattern. The data plus preamble and postamble are called a *frame*. The nature of the preamble and postamble depends on whether the block of data is character-oriented or bit-oriented.

With *character-oriented* schemes, each block is preceded by one or more synchronization characters (Figure 2.8b). The synchronization character, usually called *SYNC*, is chosen such that its bit pattern is significantly different from any of the regular characters being transmitted. The postamble is another unique character. The receiver thus is alerted to an incoming block of data by the SYNC characters and accepts data until the postamble character is seen. The receiver can then look for the next SYNC pattern.

Character-oriented schemes, such as IBM's BISYNC, are gradually being replaced by more efficient and flexible *bit-oriented schemes*, which treat the block of data as a bit stream rather than a character stream. The preamble-postamble principle is the same, with one difference. Since the data are assumed to be an arbitrary bit pattern, there is no assurance that the preamble or postamble pattern will not appear in the data. This event would destroy the higher-level synchronization.

For example, two common bit-oriented schemes, HDLC and SDLC, use the pattern 01111110 (called a *flag*) as both preamble and postamble. To avoid the appearance of this pattern in the data stream, the transmitter will always insert an extra 0 bit after each occurrence of five 1's in the data to be transmitted. When the receiver detects a sequence of five 1's, it examines the next bit. If the bit is 0, the receiver deletes it. This procedure is known as *bit stuffing*. HDLC is examined in more detail in Section 2.3.

2.2

COMMUNICATION SWITCHING TECHNIQUES

So far we have discussed how data can be encoded and transmitted over a communication link. In its simplest form, data communication takes place between two devices that are directly connected by some form of transmission medium (many of these media are described in Chapter 3). Often, however, it is impractical for two devices to be directly connected. This is so for one (or both) of the following contingencies:

- The devices are very far apart. It would be inordinately expensive, for example, to string a dedicated link between two devices thousands of miles apart.
- There is a set of devices, each of which may require a link to many of the others at various times. Examples are all of the telephones in the world and all of the terminals and computers owned by a single organization. Except for the case of a very few devices, it is impractical to provide a dedicated wire between each pair of devices.

The solution to this problem is to attach each device to a communication network. Communication is achieved by transmitting data from source to destination through a network of intermediate nodes. These nodes are not concerned with the content of the data; rather, their purpose is to provide a switching facility that will move the data from node to node until they reach their destination. Figure 2.9 illustrates the situation. We have a collection of devices that wish to communicate; we will refer to them generically as *stations*. The stations may be computers, terminals, telephones, or other communicating devices. We also have a collection of devices whose purpose is to provide communications, which we will refer to as *nodes*. The nodes are connected to each other in some fashion by transmission links. Each station attaches to a node. The collection of nodes is referred to as a *communications network*. If the

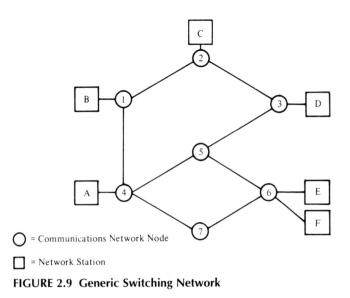

FIGURE 2.9 Generic Switching Network

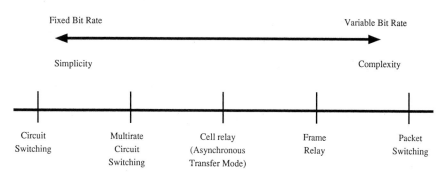

FIGURE 2.10 Spectrum of Switching Techniques [PRYC91]

attached devices are computers and terminals, then the collection of nodes plus stations is referred to as a *computer network.*

Figure 2.10 describes a spectrum of switching techniques available to transport information across a network. The two extreme ends of the spectrum represent the two traditional switching techniques: circuit switching and packet switching; the remaining techniques are of more recent vintage. In general, the techniques toward the left end of the line provide transmission with little or no variability and with minimal processing demands on attached stations, while techniques toward the right end provide increased flexibility to handle varying bit rates and unpredictable traffic at the expense of increasing processing complexity.

We begin with a detailed look at the two most common switching techniques, and then examine briefly the more advanced techniques.

Circuit Switching

Communication via circuit switching implies that there is a dedicated communication path between two stations. That path is a connected sequence of links between nodes. On each physical link, a channel is dedicated to the connection. The most common example of circuit switching is the telephone network.

Communication via circuit switching involves three phases, which can be explained with reference to Figure 2.9.

1. *Circuit establishment:* Before any data can be transmitted, an end-to-end (station-to-station) circuit must be established. For example, station A sends a request to node 4 requesting a connection to station E. Typically, the circuit from A to 4 is a dedicated line, so that part of the connection already exists. Node 4 must find the next leg in a route leading to node 6. Based on routing information and measures of availability and perhaps cost, node 4 selects the circuit to node 5, allocates a free channel (using TDM or FDM) on

that circuit, and sends a message requesting connection to E. So far, a dedicated path has been established from A through 4 to 5. Since a number of stations may attach to 4, it must be able to establish internal paths from multiple stations to multiple nodes. How this is done is explained in Chapter 7. The remainder of the process proceeds similarly. Node 5 dedicates a channel to node 6 and internally ties that channel to the channel from node 4. Node 6 completes the connection to E. In completing the connection, a test is made to determine if E is busy or is prepared to accept the connection.

2. *Data transfer:* Signals can now be transmitted from A through the network to E. The data may be digital (e.g., terminal to host) or analog (e.g., voice). The signaling and transmission may each be either digital or analog. In any case, the path is: A-4 circuit, internal switching through 4, 4-5 channel, internal switching through 5, 5-6 channel, internal switching through 6, 6-E circuit. Generally, the connection is full duplex, and data may be transmitted in both directions.

3. *Circuit disconnect:* After some period of data transfer, the connection is terminated, usually by the action of one of the two stations. Signals must be propagated to 4, 5, and 6 to deallocate the dedicated resources.

Note that the connection path is established before data transmission begins. Thus channel capacity must be available and reserved between each pair of nodes in the path, and each node must have internal switching capacity to handle the connection. The switches must have the intelligence to make these allocations and to devise a route through the network.

Circuit switching can be rather inefficient. Channel capacity is dedicated for the duration of a connection, even if no data are being transferred. For a voice connection, utilization may be rather high, but it still does not approach 100%. For a terminal-to-computer connection, the capacity may be idle during most of the time of the connection. In terms of performance, there is a delay prior to data transfer for call establishment. However, once the circuit is established, the network is effectively transparent to the users. Data are transmitted at a fixed data rate with no delay other than the propagation delay through the transmission links. The delay at each node is negligible.

Packet Switching

Long-haul circuit-switching telecommunications networks were originally designed to handle voice traffic, and the majority of traffic on these networks continues to be voice. A key characteristic of circuit-switching networks is that resources within the network are dedicated to a particular call. For voice connections, the resulting circuit will enjoy a high percentage of utilization since, most of the time, one party or the other is talking. However, as the circuit-switching network began to be used increasingly for data connections, two shortcomings became apparent:

1. In a typical terminal-to-host data connection, much of the time the line is idle. Thus, with data connections, a circuit-switching approach is inefficient.
2. In a circuit-switching network, the connection provides for transmission at constant data rate. Thus each of the two devices that are connected must transmit and receive at the same data rate as the other, which limits the utility of the network in interconnecting a variety of host computers and terminals.

To understand how packet switching addresses these problems, let us briefly summarize packet-switching operation. Data are transmitted in blocks, called *packets*. A typical upper bound on packet length is 1000 octets (bytes). If a source has a longer message to send, the message is broken up into a series of packets (Figure 2.11). Each packet consists of a portion of the data (or all of the data for a short message) that a station wants to transmit, plus a packet header that contains control information. The control information, at a minimum, includes the information that the network requires in order to be able to route the packet through the network and deliver it to the intended destination. At each node en route, the packet is received, stored briefly, and passed on to the next node.

Figure 2.12 illustrates the basic operation. A transmitting computer or other device sends a message as a sequence of packets (a). Each

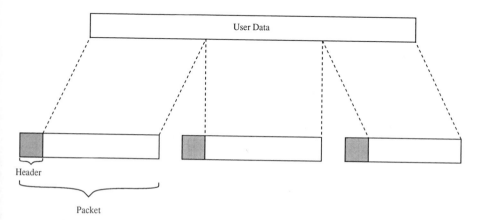

FIGURE 2.11 The Use of Packets

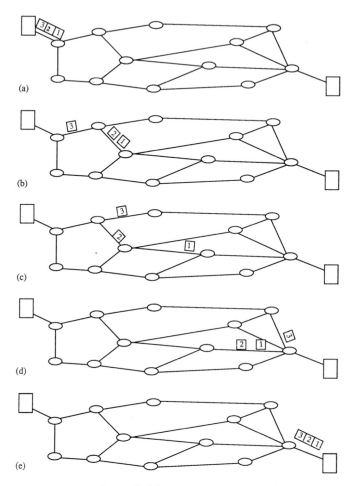

FIGURE 2.12 Packet Switching (Datagram Approach)

packet includes control information indicating the destination station (computer, terminal, etc.). The packets are initially sent to the node to which the sending station attaches. As each packet arrives at this node, it stores the packet briefly, determines the next leg of the route, and queues the packet to go out on that link. Each packet is transmitted to the next node (b) when the link is available. All of the packets eventually work their way through the network and are delivered to the intended destination.

The packet-switching approach has a number of advantages over circuit switching:

1. Line efficiency is greater, since a single node-to-node link can be dynamically shared by many packets over time. The packets are

queued up and transmitted as rapidly as possible over the link. By contrast, with circuit switching, time on a node-to-node link is preallocated using synchronous time-division multiplexing. Much of the time, such a link may be idle because a portion of its time is dedicated to a connection that is idle.

2. A packet-switching network can carry out data-rate conversion. Two stations of different data rates can exchange packets, since each connects to its node at its proper data rate.

3. When traffic becomes heavy on a circuit-switching network, some calls are blocked; that is, the network refuses to accept additional connection requests until the load on the network decreases. On a packet-switching network, packets are still accepted, but delivery delay increases.

4. Priorities can be used. Thus, if a node has a number of packets queued for transmission, it can transmit the higher-priority packets first. These packets will therefore experience less delay than lower-priority packets.

Let us now consider the operation of a packet-switching network. Consider that a station has a message to send through a packet-switching network that is of greater length than the maximum packet size. It therefore breaks up the message into packets and sends these packets, one at a time, to the network. A question arises as to how the network will handle this stream of packets as it attempts to route them through the network and deliver them to the intended destination. There are two approaches that are used in contemporary networks: datagram and virtual circuit.

In the **datagram** approach, each packet is treated independently, with no reference to packets that have gone before. This approach is illustrated in Figure 2.12. Each node chooses the next node on a packet's path, taking into account information received from neighboring nodes on traffic, line failures, and so on. So the packets, each with the same destination address, may not all follow the same route (c), and they may arrive out of sequence at the exit point. In this example, the exit node restores the packets to their original order before delivering them to the destination. In some datagram networks, it is up to the destination rather than the exit node to do the reordering. Also, it is possible for a packet to be destroyed in the network. For example, if a packet-switching node crashes momentarily, all of its queued packets may be lost. Again, it is up to either the exit node or the destination to detect the loss of a packet and to decide how to recover it. In this technique, each packet, treated independently, is referred to as a *datagram.*

In the **virtual circuit** approach, a preplanned route is established before any packets are sent; this route serves to support a logical connection between the end systems. Once the route is established, all of the

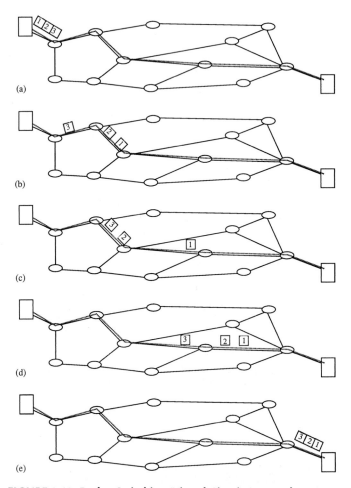

(a)

(b)

(c)

(d)

(e)

FIGURE 2.13 Packet Switching (Virtual Circuit Approach)

packets between a pair of communicating parties follow this same route through the network, as illustrated in Figure 2.13. Because the route is fixed for the duration of the logical connection, it is somewhat similar to a circuit in a circuit-switching network and is referred to as a *virtual circuit*. Each packet now contains a virtual circuit identifier as well as data. Each node on the preestablished route knows where to direct such packets; no routing decisions are required. At any time, each station can have more than one virtual circuit to any other station and can have virtual circuits to more than one station.

So the main characteristic of the virtual circuit technique is that a route between stations is set up prior to data transfer. Note that this setup does not mean that the route is a dedicated path, as in circuit switching. A packet is still buffered at each node and queued for output over a line. The difference from the datagram approach is that, with virtual circuits, the node need not make a routing decision for each packet. It is made only once for all packets using that virtual circuit.

If two stations wish to exchange data over an extended period of time, there are certain advantages to virtual circuits. First, the network may provide services related to the virtual circuit, including sequencing, error control, and flow control. *Sequencing* is provided since all packets follow the same route; and therefore they arrive in the original order. *Error control* is a service assuring not only that packets arrive in proper sequence, but that all packets arrive correctly. For example, if a packet in a sequence from node 4 to node 6 fails to arrive at node 6, or arrives with an error, node 6 can request a retransmission of that packet from node 4. *Flow control* is a technique for assuring that a sender does not overwhelm a receiver with data. For example, if station E is buffering data from station A and perceives that it is about to run out of buffer space, it can request, via the virtual circuit facility, that station A suspend transmission until further notice. Another advantage is that packets should transit the network more rapidly with a virtual circuit; it is not necessary to make a routing decision for each packet at each node.

One advantage of the datagram approach is that the call setup phase is avoided. Thus, if a station wishes to send only one or a few packets, datagram delivery will be quicker. Another advantage of the datagram service is that because it is more primitive it is more flexible. For example, if congestion develops in one part of the network, incoming datagrams can be routed away from the congestion. With the use of virtual circuits, packets follow a predefined route, and thus it is more difficult for the network to adapt to congestion. A third advantage is that datagram delivery is inherently more reliable. With the use of virtual circuits, if a node fails, all virtual circuits that pass through that node are lost. With datagram delivery, if a node fails, subsequent packets may find an alternate route that bypasses that node.

Table 2.2 summarizes the main features of circuit switching and the two forms of packet switching that we have discussed.

Multirate Circuit Switching

One of the drawbacks of circuit switching is its inflexibility with respect to data rate. If a station attaches to an ordinary circuit-switching network, it is committed to operating at a particular data rate. This data rate must be used regardless of the application, whether it is digitized voice or some data application. Thus, an application with a low data rate requirement would make inefficient use of the network link.

To overcome this inflexibility, an enhanced service, known as multirate circuit switching, was developed. This technique combines circuit switching with multiplexing. The station attaches to the network by

TABLE 2.2   Comparison of Communication Switching Techniques

Circuit Switching	Datagram Packet Switching	Virtual Circuit Packet Switching
Dedicated transmission path	No dedicated path	No dedicated path
Continuous transmission of data	Transmission of packets	Transmission of packets
Fast enough for interactive	Fast enough for interactive	Fast enough for interactive
Messages are not stored	Packets may be stored until delivered	Packets stored until delivered
Path is established for entire conversation	Route established for each packet	Route established for entire conversation
Call setup delay; negligible transmission delay	Packet transmission delay	Call setup delay; packet transmission delay
Busy signal if called party busy	Sender may be notified if packet not delivered	Sender notified of connection denial
Overload may block call setup; no delay for established calls	Overload increases packed delay	Overload may block call setup; increases packet delay
Electromechanical or computerized switching nodes	Small switching nodes	Small switching nodes
User responsible for message-loss protection	Network may be responsible for individual packets	Network may be responsible for packet sequences
Usually no speed or code conversion	Speed and code conversion	Speed and code conversion

TABLE 2.2   (Cont.)

Circuit Switching	Datagram Packet Switching	Virtual Circuit Packet Switching
Fixed bandwidth transmission	Dynamic use of bandwidth	Dynamic use of bandwidth
No overhead bits after call setup	Overhead bits in each packet	Overhead bits in each packet

means of a single physical link. That link is used to carry multiple fixed-data-rate channels between the station and a network node. The traffic on each channel can be switched independently through the network to various destinations.

For this technique, it is possible to develop a scheme in which all of the available channels operate at the same data rate, or a scheme that uses various data rates. For example, integrated services digital network (ISDN) is a standardized digital telecommunications specification. It defines a variety of station-network interfaces, all of which employ multirate circuit switching. The simplest ISDN interface consists of two 64-kbps channels and one 16-kbps channel.

Although this technique is more flexible than simple circuit switching, the same fundamental limitation exists. The user now has the choice of a number of data rates, but each rate remains fixed and the likelihood of inefficient use of a particular channel remains.

Frame Relay

Packet switching was developed at a time when digital long-distance transmission facilities exhibited a relatively high error rate compared to today's facilities. As a result, there is a considerable amount of overhead built into packet-switching schemes to compensate for errors. The overhead includes additional bits added to each packet to enhance redundancy, and additional processing at the end stations and the intermediate network nodes to detect and recover from errors.

With modern, high-speed telecommunications systems, this overhead is unnecessary and counterproductive. It is unnecessary because the rate of errors has been dramatically lowered and any remaining errors can easily be caught by logic in the end systems that operates above the level of the packet-switching logic. It is counterproductive because the overhead involved soaks up a significant fraction of the high capacity provided by the network.

To take advantage of the high data rates and low error rates of contemporary networking facilities, frame relay was developed. Whereas the original packet-switching networks were designed with a data rate to the end user of about 64 kbps, frame relay networks are designed to operate at user data rates of up to 2 Mbps. The key to achieving these high data rates is to strip out most of the overhead involved with error control.

Cell Relay

Cell relay, also known as asynchronous transfer mode, is in a sense a culmination of all of the developments in circuit switching and packet switching over the past 20 years. One useful way to view cell relay is as an evolution from frame relay. The most obvious difference between cell relay and frame relay is that frame relay uses variable-length packets and cell relay uses fixed-length packets, called cells. As with frame relay, cell relay provides minimum overhead for error control, depending on the inherent reliability of the transmission system and on higher layers of logic to catch and correct remaining errors. By using a fixed packet length, the processing overhead is reduced even further for cell relay compared to frame relay. The result is that cell relay is designed to work in the range of 10's and 100's of Mbps, compared to the 2 Mbps of frame relay.

Another way to view cell relay is as an evolution from multirate circuit switching. With multirate circuit switching, only fixed-data-rate channels are available to the end system. Cell relay allows the definition of virtual channels with data rates that are dynamically defined at the time that the virtual channel is created. By using small, fixed-size cells, cell relay is so efficient that it can offer a constant-data-rate channel even though it is using a packet-switching technique. Thus cell relay extends multirate circuit switching to allow multiple channels with the data rate of each channel dynamically set on demand.

2.3

COMPUTER NETWORKING

Communications Architecture

In Chapter 1 we discussed some of the motivations for and benefits of local networking. Many of these factors apply equally well to computer networks in general, whether local or long-haul. Indeed, the move to distributed nonlocal computer networks predates the coming of local networks.

When work is done that involves more than one computer, additional elements are needed: the hardware and software to support the communication between or among the systems. Communications hardware is reasonably standard and generally presents few problems. However, when communication is desired among heterogeneous (different vendors, different models of the same vendor) machines, the software development effort can be a nightmare. Different vendors use different data formats and data exchange conventions. Even within one vendor's product line, different model computers may communicate in unique ways.

As the use of computer communications and computer networking proliferates, a one-at-a-time special-purpose approach to communications software development is too costly to be acceptable. The only alternative is for computer vendors to adopt and implement a common set of conventions. For this to happen, a set of international or at least national standards must be promulgated by appropriate organizations. Such standards would have two effects:

1. Vendors feel encouraged to implement the standards because of an expectation that, because of wide usage of the standards, their products would be less marketable without them.
2. Customers are in a position to require that the standards be implemented by any vendor wishing to propose equipment to them.

It should become clear from the ensuing discussion that no single standard will suffice. The task of communication in a truly cooperative way between applications on different computers is too complex to be handled as a unit. The problem must be decomposed into manageable parts. Hence before one can develop standards, there should be a structure or *architecture* that defines the communications tasks.

This line of reasoning led the International Organization for Standardization (ISO) in 1977 to establish a subcommittee to develop such an architecture. The result was the *Open Systems Interconnection* (OSI) model, which is a framework for defining standards for linking heterogeneous computers. OSI provides the basis for connecting open systems for distributed applications processing. The term *open* denotes the ability of any two systems conforming to the reference model and the associated standards to connect.

Before introducing the OSI model, we consider a simpler architecture that clarifies some of the key concepts involved.

A Three-Layer Model

In very general terms, communications can be said to involve three agents: applications, computers, and networks. The applications that we are concerned with here are distributed applications that involve the exchange of data between two computer systems. These applications and others execute on computers that can often support multiple simultaneous applications. Computers are connected to networks and the data to be exchanged are transferred by the network from one computer to another. Thus the transfer of data from one application to another involves first getting the data to the computer in which the application resides and then getting them to the intended application within the computer.

With these concepts in mind, it appears natural to organize the communication task into three relatively independent layers:

- Network access layer
- Transport layer
- Application layer

The *network access layer* is concerned with the exchange of data between a computer and the network to which it is attached. The sending computer must provide the network with the address of the destination computer, so that the network may route the data to the appropriate destination. The sending computer may wish to invoke certain services, such as priority, that might be provided by the network. The specific software used at this layer depends on the type of network to be used; different standards have been developed for circuit switching, packet switching, local area networks, and others. Thus it makes sense to separate those functions having to do with network access into a separate layer. By doing this, the remainder of the communications software, above the network access layer, need not be concerned about the specifics of the network to be used. The same higher-layer software should function properly regardless of the particular network to which the computer is attached.

Regardless of the nature of the applications that are exchanging data, there is usually a requirement that data be exchanged reliably. That is, we would like to be assured that all of the data arrive at the destination application and that the data arrive in the same order in which they were sent. The mechanisms for providing reliability are essentially independent of the nature of the applications. Thus it makes sense to collect those mechanisms in a common layer shared by all applications, referred to as the *transport layer.*

Finally, the *application layer* contains the logic needed to support the various user applications. For each different type of application, such as file transfer, a separate module is needed that is particular to that application.

Figures 2.14 and 2.15 illustrate this simple architecture. Figure 2.14 shows three computers connected to a network. Each computer contains software at the network access and transport layers, and software at the

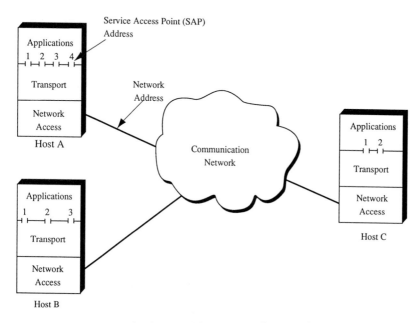

FIGURE 2.14 Communications Architectures and Networks

application layer for one or more applications. For successful communication, every entity in the overall system must have a unique address. Actually, two levels of addressing are needed. Each computer on the network must have a unique network address to allow the network to deliver data to the proper computer. Each application on a computer must have an address that is unique within that computer to allow the transport layer to deliver data to the proper application. These latter addresses are known as *service access points* (SAPs), connoting the fact

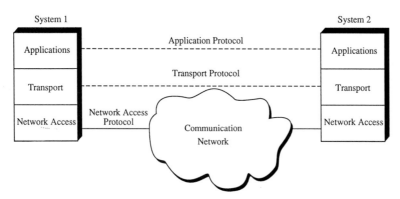

FIGURE 2.15 Protocols in a Simplified Architecture

that each application is individually accessing the services of the transport layer.

Figure 2.15 indicates the way in which modules at the same level on different computers communicate with each other: by means of a protocol. A *protocol* is the set of rules or conventions governing the way in which two entities cooperate to exchange data. A *protocol specification* details the control functions that may be performed, the formats and control codes used to communicate those functions, and the procedures that the two entities must follow.

Let us trace a simple operation. Suppose that an application, associated with SAP 1 at computer A, wishes to send a message to another application, associated with SAP 2 at computer B. The application at computer A hands the message over to its transport layer with instructions to send it to SAP 2 on computer B. The transport layer hands the message over to the network access layer, which instructs the network to send the message to computer B. Note that the network need not be told the identity of the destination service access point. All that it needs to know is that the data are intended for computer B.

To control this operation, control information, as well as user data, must be transmitted, as suggested in Figure 2.16. Let us say that the sending application generates a block of data and passes this to the transport layer. The transport layer may break this block into two smaller pieces to make it more manageable. To each of these pieces the transport layer appends a transport header, containing protocol control information. The combination of data from the next higher layer and control information is known as a *protocol data unit* (PDU); in this case, it is referred to as a transport protocol data unit. The header in each

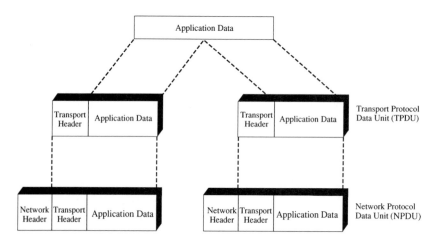

FIGURE 2.16 Protocol Data Units

transport PDU contains control information to be used by the peer transport protocol at computer B. Examples of items that may be stored in this header include:

- *Destination SAP:* When the destination transport layer receives the transport protocol data unit, it must know to whom the data are to be delivered.
- *Sequence number:* Since the transport protocol is sending a sequence of protocol data units, it numbers them sequentially, so that if they arrive out of order, the destination transport entity may reorder them.
- *Error-detection code:* The sending transport entity may calculate and insert an error-detecting code, so that the receiver can determine if an error has occurred and discard the protocol data unit.

The next step is for the transport layer to hand each protocol data unit over to the network layer, with instructions to transmit it to the destination computer. To satisfy this request, the network access protocol must present the data to the network with a request for transmission. As before, this operation requires the use of control information. In this case, the network access protocol appends a network access header to the data it receives from the transport layer, creating a network access PDU. Examples of the items that may be stored in the header include:

- *Destination computer address:* The network must know to whom (which computer on the network) the data are to be delivered.
- *Facilities requests:* The network access protocol might want the network to make use of certain facilities, such as priority.

Figure 2.17 puts all of these concepts together, showing the interaction between modules to transfer one block of data. Let us say that the file transfer module in computer X is transferring a file one record at a time to computer Y. Each record is handed over to the transport layer module. We can picture this action as being in the form of a command or procedure call, A-SEND (application-send). The arguments of this procedure call include the destination computer address, the destination service access point, and the record. The transport layer appends the destination service access point and other control information to the record to create a transport PDU, which is then handed down to the network access layer in a T-SEND command. In this case, the arguments for the command are the destination computer address and the transport protocol data unit. The network access layer uses this information to construct a network PDU. Suppose the network is an X.25 packet-switching network. In this case, the network protocol data unit is an X.25 data packet. The transport protocol data unit is the data field of the

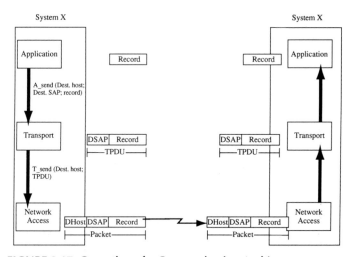

FIGURE 2.17 Operation of a Communication Architecture

packet, and the packet header includes the virtual circuit number for a virtual circuit connecting X and Y.

The network accepts the data packet from X and delivers it to Y. The network access module in Y receives the packet, strips off the packet header, and transfers the enclosed transport protocol data unit to X's transport layer module. The transport layer examines the transport protocol data unit header and, on the basis of the SAP field in the header, delivers the enclosed record to the appropriate application, in this case the file transfer module in Y.

The Concept of Open Systems

Open Systems Interconnection is based on the concept of cooperating distributed applications. In the OSI model, a system consists of a computer, all of its software, and any peripheral devices attached to it, including terminals. A distributed application is an activity that involves the exchange of information between two open systems. Examples of such activities include:

- A user at a terminal on one computer is logged onto an application such as transaction processing on another computer.
- A file management program on one computer transfers a file to a file management program on another computer.
- A user sends an electronic mail message to a user on another computer.
- A process control program sends a control signal to a robot.

OSI is concerned with the exchange of information between open systems and not with the internal functioning of each individual system. Specifically, it is concerned with the capability of systems to cooperate in the exchange of information and in the accomplishment of tasks.

The objective of the OSI effort is to define a set of standards that will enable open systems located anywhere in the world to cooperate by being interconnected through some standardized communications facility and by executing standardized OSI protocols.

An open system may be implemented in any way provided that it conforms to a minimal set of standards allowing communication to be achieved with other open systems. An open system consists of a number of applications, an operating system, and system software such as a data base management system and a terminal handling package. It also includes the communications software that turns a closed system into an open system. Different manufacturers will implement open systems in different ways, in order to achieve a product identity, which will increase their market share or create a new market. However, virtually all manufacturers are now committed to providing communications software that behaves in conformance with OSI in order to provide their customers with the ability to communicate with other open systems.

The OSI Model

A widely accepted structuring technique, and the one chosen by ISO, is layering. The communications functions are partitioned into a hierarchical set of layers. Each layer performs a related subset of the functions required to communicate with another system. It relies on the next lower layer to perform more primitive functions and to conceal the details of those functions. It provides services to the next higher layer. Ideally, the layers should be defined so that changes in one layer do not require changes in the other layers. Thus we have decomposed one problem into a number of more manageable subproblems.

The task of ISO was to define a set of layers and the services performed by each layer. The partitioning should group functions logically, and should have enough layers to make each layer manageably small, but should not have so many layers that the processing overhead imposed by the collection of layers is burdensome. The resulting OSI architecture has seven layers, which are listed with a brief definition in Table 2.3.

Table 2.3 defines, in general terms, the functions that must be performed in a system for it to communicate. Of course, it takes two to communicate, so the same set of layered functions must exist in two systems. Communication is achieved by having the corresponding (peer) layers in two systems communicate. The peer layers communicate

TABLE 2.3 The OSI Layers

Layer	Definition
1. Physical	Concerned with transmission of unstructured bit stream over physical link; involves such parameters as signal voltage swing and bit duration; deals with the mechanical, electrical, and procedural characteristics to establish, maintain, and deactivate the physical link (RS-232-C, RS-449, X.21)
2. Data link	Provides for the reliable transfer of data across the physical link; sends blocks of data (frames) with the necessary synchronization, error control, and flow control (HDLC, SDLC, BiSync)
3. Network	Provides upper layers with independence from the data transmission and switching technologies used to connect systems; responsible for establishing, maintaining, and terminating connections (X.25, layer 3)
4. Transport	Provides reliable, transparent transfer of data between end points; provides end-to-end error recovery and flow control
5. Session	Provides the control structure for communication between applications; establishes, manages, and terminates connections (sessions) between cooperating applications
6. Presentation	Performs generally useful transformations on data to provide a standardized application interface and to provide common communications services; examples: encryption, text compression, reformatting
7. Application	Provides services to the users of the OSI environment; examples: transaction server, file transfer protocol, network management

by means of a set of rules, or conventions, known as a protocol. The key elements of a protocol are:

- *Syntax:* The form in which information is exchanged (format, coding)
- *Semantics:* The interpretation of control information for coordination and error handling
- *Timing:* The sequence in which control events occur

Figure 2.18 illustrates the OSI architecture. Each computer contains the seven layers. Communication is between applications in the two computers, labeled application X and application Y in the figure. If application X wishes to send a message to application Y, it invokes the application layer (layer 7). Layer 7 establishes a peer relationship with layer 7 of the target computer, using a layer 7 protocol (application pro-

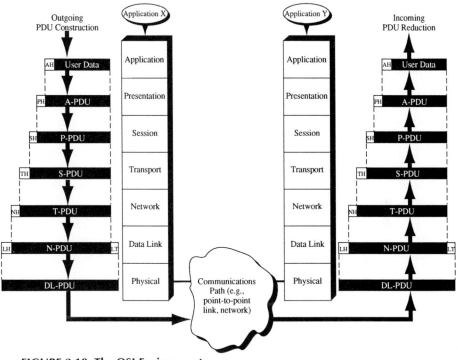

FIGURE 2.18 The OSI Environment

tocol). This protocol requires services from layer 6, so the two layer 6 entities use a protocol of their own, and so on down to the physical layer, which actually transmits bits over a transmission medium.

The figure also illustrates the way in which the protocols at each layer are realized. When application X has a message to send to application Y, it transfers those data to an application layer module. That module appends an application header to the data; the header contains the control information needed by the peer layer on the other side. The original data plus the header, referred to as an application protocol data unit (PDU), is passed as a unit to layer 6. The presentation module treats the whole unit as data and appends its own header. This process continues down through layer 2, which generally adds both a header and a trailer. This layer-2 protocol data unit, usually called a *frame*, is then transmitted by the physical layer onto the transmission medium. When the fame is received by the target computer, the reverse process occurs. As we ascend the layers, each layer strips off the outermost header, acts on the protocol information contained therein, and passes the remainder up to the next layer.

We have already seen several examples of the use of control information in headers and trailers. With synchronous communication, a preamble and postamble are added to each block of data. For packet-switching networks, each packet includes not only data but also (at least) an address.

Note that there is no direct communication between peer layers except at the physical layer. Even at that layer, the OSI model does not stipulate that two systems be directly connected. For example, a packet-switching or circuit-switching network may be used to provide the communications link. This point should become clearer below, when we discuss the network layer.

The attractiveness of the OSI approach is that it promises to solve the heterogeneous computer communications problem. Two systems, no matter how different, can communicate effectively if they have the following in common:

- They implement the same set of communications functions.
- These functions are organized into the same set of layers. Peer layers must provide the same functions, but note that it is not necessary that they provide them in the same way.
- Peer layers must share a common protocol.

To assure the above, standards are needed. Standards must define the functions and services to be provided by a layer (but not how it is to be done—that may differ from system to system). Standards must also define the protocols between peer layers (each protocol must be identical for the two peer layers). The OSI model, by defining a seven-layer architecture, provides a framework for defining these standards.

Protocols

In this section we discuss briefly each of the layers and, where appropriate, give examples of standards for protocols at those layers. Table 2.4 shows the relationship to the OSI model of some of the most important standards. Remember that the OSI layers are not standards; they merely provide a framework for standards.

The Consultative Committee on International Telegraphy and Telephony (CCITT) has developed standards for connecting *data terminal equipment* (DTE) to a packet-switching network that provides *data circuit-terminating equipment* (DCE). These terms correspond to the stations and nodes of Figure 2.9. The standard, X.25, specifically addresses layer 3 and subsumes standards for layers 2 and 1. (Observers are fond of saying that X.25 is an interface, not a protocol. This point is discussed under Network Layer below.) Layer 2 is referred to as LAP-B (Link Access Protocol—Balanced) and is almost identical with ISO's HDLC (High-Level Data Link Control) and ANSI's ADCCP (Advanced Data Communication Control Procedures).

TABLE 2.4   Some Well-Known Layers

OSI	CCITT	ISO	DOD	IEEE 802	ANS X3T9.5
7. Application		Various	Various		
6. Presentation					
5. Session		Session	TCP		
4. Transport		Transport (TP)			
3. Network	X.25	Internet	IP		
		Sublayer			
2. Link	LAP-B			Logical link	
				control	Data link
				Medium	
				access	Physical
				control	
1. Physical	X.21			Physical	

ISO has issued standards for layers 4 and 5 and is in the process of issuing a variety of standards that cover layers 6 and 7. ISO has also developed a sublayer of layer 3 that deals with internetworking, which involves communication across multiple networks.

An internetworking protocol, called IP, has been developed by the Department of Defense (DOD) for its own needs, plus a Transmission Control Protocol (TCP). TCP subsumes all the functions of layer 4 plus some of layer 5. DOD intends to mandate these standards for its procurements. In addition, DOD has issued various standards at the upper layers [STAL86b]. The mismatch with the ISO protocols is, unfortunately, unresolved.

For the type of local network that we refer to as a *local area network* (LAN), the Institute of Electrical and Electronics Engineers (IEEE), through its 802 committee, has developed a three-layer architecture that corresponds to layers 1 and 2 of the OSI model. A number of standards have been developed by the committee for these layers. Similarly, a subcommittee responsible to the American National Standards Institute (ANSI), known as ANS X3T9.5, has developed standards for the type of local network we refer to as a *high-speed local network* (HSLN). These standards, one per layer, correspond nicely to layers 1 and 2 of the OSI model.

This variety may be disheartening, given the alleged benefit of standards, which is to put everyone on the same road. There is certainly room for pessimism. The DOD-ISO disparity makes a uniform federal government position unlikely. For LANs, the 802 committee has produced a number of options and alternatives at each layer.

However, the picture is not as bleak as Table 2.4 makes it seem. With the exception of local networks, which must be treated separately, standards have settled out quite well for layers 1 through 3. Above that, there is considerable cooperation among the various groups, so that uniform or nearly uniform standards are possible in many cases.

Physical Layer.   The *physical layer* covers the physical interface between devices and the rules by which bits are passed from one to another. The physical layer has four important characteristics [BERT80, MCCL83]:

- Mechanical
- Electrical
- Functional
- Procedural

The most common standard in use today is RS-232-C. A typical use of RS-232-C is to connect a digital device to a modem, which in turn connects to a voice-grade telephone line. We will refer to this standard in describing these four characteristics.

The *mechanical characteristics* pertain to the point of demarcation. Typically, this is a pluggable connector. RS-232-C specifies a 25-pin connector, so that up to 25 separate wires are used to connect the two devices.

The *electrical characteristics* have to do with the voltage levels and timing of voltage changes. These characteristics determine the data rates and distances that can be achieved.

Functional characteristics specify the functions that are performed by assigning meaning to various signals. For RS-232-C, and for most other physical layer standards, this is done by specifying the function of each of the pins in the connector. For example, pin CA (Request to Send) is used for the device to signal the modem that it has data to send and that a carrier should be established for modulation. Pin CF (Received Line Signal Detector or Carrier Detect) is used for the modem to alert the device that a carrier is present on the line.

Procedural characteristics specify the sequence of events for transmitting data, based on the functional characteristics. For RS-232-C, the use of the various pins is defined. For example, when a device asserts Request to Send, the modem will assert Clear to Send if it is ready to transmit data. The device can then send data from pin BA (Transmitted Data) over that line to the corresponding pin on the modem.

The physical layer differs from the other OSI layers in that it cannot rely on a lower layer to transmit its PDUs. Rather, it must make use of a transmission medium whose characteristics are not part of the OSI model. There is no physical layer PDU structure as such; no header of protocol control information is used. The PDU simply consists of a block or stream of bits.

Data Link Layer.   The data link layer must deal with both the requirements of the communications facility and the requirements of the user.

Whereas the physical layer provides only a raw-bit-stream service, the data link layer attempts to make the physical link reliable and provides the means to activate, maintain, and deactivate the link. The principal service provided by the data link layer to higher layers is that of error detection and control. Thus, with a fully functional data link layer protocol, the next higher layer may assume error-free transmission over the link.

In this subsection we will spend some time defining HDLC, which is a synchronous bit-oriented protocol. We do so for two reasons:

1. HDLC is the ancestor of the link layer protocol standard for LANs (IEEE 802).
2. Many of the concepts concerning protocols are illustrated.

HDLC, and bit-oriented protocols in general, are intended to provide the following capabilities [CARL80]:

- *Code-independent operation (transparency):* The protocol and the data it carries are independent.
- *Adaptability to various applications, configurations, and uses in a consistent manner:* For example, point-to-point, multidrop, and loop configurations should be supported.
- *Both two-way alternate and two-way simultaneous (full-duplex) data transfer.*
- *High efficiency:* The protocol should have a minimum of overhead bits. Also, it should work efficiently over links with long propagation delays and links with high data rates.
- *High reliability:* Data should not be lost, duplicated, or garbled.

With these requirements in mind, we turn to a description of HDLC.

Three modes of operation are defined: The *normal response mode* (NRM), *asynchronous response mode* (ARM), and *asynchronous balanced mode* (ABM). Both NRM and ARM can be used in point-to-point or multipoint configurations. For each there is one *primary station* and one or more *secondary stations.* The primary station is responsible for initializing the link, controlling the flow of data to and from secondary stations, recovering from errors, and logically disconnecting secondary stations. In NRM, a secondary station may transmit only in response to a poll from the primary; in ARM, the secondary may initiate a transmission without a poll. NRM is ideally suited for a multidrop line consisting of a host computer and a number of terminals. ARM may be needed for certain kinds of loop configurations.

ABM is used on point-to-point links only, and each station assumes the role of both primary and secondary. ABM is more efficient for point-to-point lines since there is no polling overhead and both stations may initiate transmissions.

Data are transmitted in frames that consist of six fields (Figure 2.19).

Frame Structure:

8 bits	8	8	$\geqslant 0$	16	8
FLAG	ADDRESS	CONTROL	DATA	CRC	FLAG

Control Field Structure

	1	2	3	4	5	6	7	8
Information	0		N(S)		P/F		N(R)	
Supervisory	1	0	TYPE		P/F		N(R)	
Unnumbered	1	1	TYPE		P/F		MODIFIER	

FIGURE 2.19 The HDLC Frame Structure

- FLAG: Used for synchronization, this field indicates the start and end of a frame. The flag pattern, 01111110, is avoided in the data by bit stuffing.
- ADDRESS: This field identifies the secondary station for this transmission.
- CONTROL: This field identifies the function and purpose of the frame. It is described below.
- DATA: This field contains the data to be transmitted.
- CRC: This is a frame check sequence field. It uses a 16-bit *cyclic redundancy check* (CRC). The CRC field is a function of the contents of the address, control, and data fields. It is generated by the sender and again by the receiver. If the receiver's result differs from the CRC field, a transmission error has occurred (see Appendix 2A).

Three types of frames are used, each with a different control-field format. Information frames carry the data. Supervisory frames provide basic link control functions, and unnumbered frames provide supplemental link control functions.

The P/F (poll/final) bit is used by a primary station to solicit a response. More than one frame may be sent in response, with the P/F bit set to indicate the last frame. The P/F may be used with supervisory and unnumbered frames to force a response.

The N(S) and N(R) fields in the information frame provide an efficient technique for both flow control and error control. A station numbers the frames that it sends sequentially modulo 8, using the N(S) field. When a station receives a valid information frame, it acknowledges that frame with its own information frame by setting the N(R) field to the number of the next frame it expects to receive. This is known as a *piggybacked acknowledgment,* since the acknowledgment rides back on an information frame. Acknowledgments can also be sent on a supervisory frame. This scheme accomplishes three important functions.

1. *Flow control:* Once a station has sent seven frames, it can send no more until the first frame is acknowledged.
2. *Error control:* If a frame is received in error, a station can send a NAK (negative acknowledgment) via a supervisory frame to specify which frame was received in error. This is done in one of two ways. In the *go-back-n protocol,* the sending station retransmits the NAK'ed frame and all subsequent frames that have already been sent. In the *selective repeat technique,* the sending station retransmits only the frame in error.
3. *Pipelining:* More than one frame may be in transit at a time; this allows more efficient use of links with high propagation delay, such as satellite links.

The N(S)/N(R) technique is known as a *sliding-window protocol* because the sending station maintains a window of messages to be sent that gradually moves forward with transmission and acknowledgment. The process is depicted in Figure 2.20.

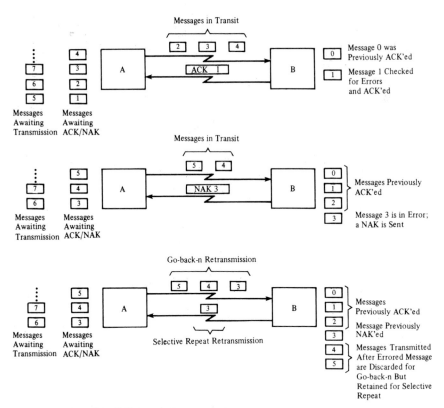

FIGURE 2.20 The Sliding-Window Technique

There are four types of supervisory frames:

1. *Receive Ready (RR):* used to acknowledge correct receipt of frames up through N(R)—1. Alternatively, this is a poll command instructing secondary to begin transmission with sequence number N(R).
2. *Receive Not Ready (RNR):* used to indicate a temporary busy condition. N(R) is used for a possibly redundant acknowledgment.
3. *Reject (REJ):* used to indicate an error in frame N(R) and to request retransmission of that and all subsequent frames.
4. *Selective Reject (SREJ):* used to request retransmission of a single frame.

The unnumbered frames have no sequence number and are used for a number of special purposes, such as to initialize a station, set the mode, disconnect a station, and reject a command.

Network Layer.   The network layer provides for the transfer of information between end systems across some sort of communications network. It relieves higher layers of the need to know anything about the underlying data transmission and switching technologies used to connect systems. At this layer, the computer system engages in a dialogue with the network to specify the destination address and to request certain network facilities, such as priority.

There is a spectrum of possibilities for intervening communications facilities to be managed by the network layer. At one extreme, there is a direct point-to-point link between stations. In this case, there may be no need for a network layer because the data link layer can perform the necessary function of managing the link.

Next, the systems could be connected across a single network, such as a circuit-switching or packet-switching network. Figure 2.21 shows how the presence of a network is accommodated by the OSI architecture. The lower three layers are concerned with attaching to and communicating with the network. The packets that are created by the end system pass through one or more network nodes that act as relays between the two end systems. The network nodes implement layers, 1, 2, and 3 of the architecture. In the figure, two end systems are connected through a single network node. Layer 3 in the node performs a switching and routing function. Within the node, there are two data link layers and two physical layers, corresponding to the links to the two end systems. Each data link (and physical) layer operates independently to provide service to the network layer over its respective link.

Note that the layer 1 and 2 protocols are local and they support the exchange of information between an end system and a network node. The upper four layers are end-to-end protocols between the attached end systems. Layer 3 has characteristics of both. The layer 3 protocol is

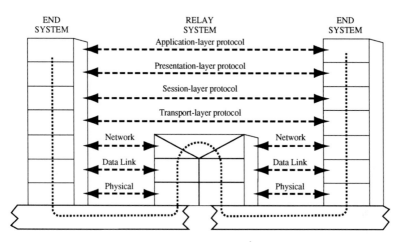

FIGURE 2.21 Communication Across a Network

local in the sense of interfacing to the network and requesting network services. It is end-to-end in the sense that it provides an address for transferring data to the other end system. The X.25 standard is a specification of the lowest three layers of OSI for interfacing an end system to a packet-switching network. A brief description is given in Chapter 8.

At the other extreme, two end systems might wish to communicate but are not even connected to the same network. Rather, they are connected to networks that, directly or indirectly, are connected to each other. This case requires the use of some sort of internetworking technique; we explore this approach in Chapter 10.

Transport Layer.   The transport layer provides a reliable mechanism for the exchange of data between computers. It ensures that data are delivered error-free, in sequence, with no losses or duplications. The transport layer may also be concerned with optimizing the use of network services and providing a requested quality of service. For example, the session layer may specify acceptable error rates, maximum delay, priority, and security features.

The mechanisms used by the transport protocol to provide reliability are very similar to those used by data link control protocols such as HDLC: the use of sequence numbers, error-detecting codes, and retransmission after timeout. The reason for this apparent duplication of effort is that the data link layer deals with only a single, direct link, whereas the transport layer deals with a chain of network nodes and links. Although each link in that chain is reliable because of the use of HDLC, a node along that chain may fail at a critical time. Such a failure will affect data delivery, and it is the transport protocol that addresses this problem.

The size and complexity of a transport protocol depends on the type of service it can get from layer 3. For a reliable layer 3 with a virtual circuit capability, a minimal layer 4 is required. If layer 3 is unreliable and/or supports only datagrams, then the layer 4 protocol should include extensive error detection and recovery. Accordingly, ISO has defined five classes of transport protocol, each oriented toward a different underlying network layer service.

Session Layer.   The session layer provides the mechanism for controlling the dialogue between the two end systems. In many cases, there will be little or no need for session-layer services, but for some applications, such services are used. The key services provided by the session layer include:

- *Dialogue discipline:* this can be two-way simultaneous (full-duplex) or two-way alternate (half-duplex).
- *Grouping:* the flow of data can be marked to define groups of data. For example, if a retail store is transmitting sales data to a regional office, the data can be marked to indicate the end of the sales data for each department. This would signal the host computer to finalize running totals for that department and start new running counts for the next department.
- *Recovery:* the session layer can provide a checkpointing mechanism, so that if a failure of some sort occurs between checkpoints, the session entity can retransmit all data since the last checkpoint.

ISO has issued a standard for the session layer that includes as options services such as those described above.

Presentation Layer.   The presentation layer defines the format of the data to be exchanged between applications, and offers application programs a set of data transformation services. For example, data compression or data encryption could occur at this level.

Application Layer.   The application layer provides a means for application programs to access the OSI environment. This layer contains management functions and generally useful mechanisms to support distributed applications. In addition, general-purpose applications such as file transfer, electronic mail, and terminal access to remote computers are considered to reside at this layer.

Perspective on the OSI Model

Figure 2.22 provides a useful perspective on the OSI architecture. The annotation suggests viewing the seven layers in three parts. The lower three layers contain the logic for a computer to interact with a network.

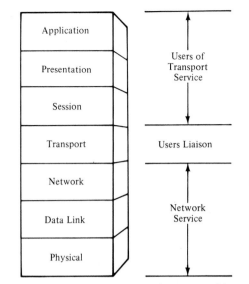

FIGURE 2.22 A Perspective on the OSI Architecture

The host is attached physically to the network, uses a data link protocol to reliably communicate with the network, and uses a network protocol to request data exchange with another device on the network and to request network services. The X.25 standard for packet-switching networks encompasses these three layers. Continuing from this perspective, the transport layer provides a reliable end-to-end service regardless of the intervening network facility; in effect, it is the user's liaison to the communications facility. Finally, the upper three layers, taken together, are involved in the exchange of data between end users, making use of a transport service for reliable data transfer.

2.4

RECOMMENDED READING

[STAL91] covers all of the topics in this chapter. [MART88] also provides a readable but less technical treatment of these topics. A thorough treatment of both analog and digital communications can be found in [COUC90]. Two books by Freeman also provide excellent coverage: [FREE91] concentrates on issues involved with the transmission of data; [FREE89] looks at design issues for communication systems, particularly circuit-switching systems. Another in-depth treatment is offered in the three-volume [BELL90]. [MCNA88] is a popular and well-respected treatment of the topics in Section 2.1, focusing on digital data communications.

A thorough discussion of the OSI model can be found in [TANE88], which averages about one chapter per layer. [STAL93] covers the standards at each layer of the OSI model, emphasizing the more recent, leading-edge standards. [STAL92] contains reprints of key articles covering OSI and the standards at each layer.

2.5

PROBLEMS

2.1 Write a program to do bit stuffing.

2.2 A user may wish to use a character-oriented synchronous transmission protocol to send arbitrary bit streams. How can the protocol ensure that none of its control characters (e.g., SYNC) appear in the character stream? Write a program to do this.

2.3 Write a program that implements the sliding window technique for (1) selective repeat and (2) go-back-n.

2.4 Consider a transmission link between stations A and B with a probability of error in a frame of p.

    a. Assume a selective repeat protocol and assume that station A is sending data and station B is sending acknowledgments only (RR, SREJ) and that it individually acknowledges each frame. Assume that acknowledgments are never lost. What is the mean number of transmissions required per frame?

    b. Now assume a go-back-n protocol and that the link is such that A will transmit three additional frames before receiving RR or REJ for each frame. Also assume that acknowledgments are never lost. What is the mean number of transmissions required per frame?

2.5 Are the modem and the codec functional inverses (i.e., could an inverted modem function as a codec, and vice versa)?

2.6 List the major disadvantages with the layered approach to protocols.

2.7 Compare bit-oriented and character-oriented data link protocols in terms of advantages and disadvantages.

2.8 Among the principles used by ISO to define the OSI layers were:

- The number of layers should be small enough to avoid unwieldly design and implementation, but large enough so that separate layers handle functions that are different in process or technology.
- Layer boundaries should be chosen to minimize the number and size of interactions across boundaries.

Based on these principles, design an architecture with eight layers and make a case for it. Design one with six layers and make a case for that.

2.9 Another form of digital encoding of digital data is known as delay modulation or *Miller coding*. In this scheme, a logic 1 is represented by a midbit transition (in either direction). A logic 0 is represented by a transition at the end of the bit period if the next bit is 0, and is represented by the absence of a transition if the next bit is a 1. Draw a Miller code waveform for the bit stream of Figure 2.5. Why might this technique be preferable to NRZ? To Manchester?

2.10 What is the percentage of overhead in a T1 carrier (percentage of bits that are not user data)?

2.11 Define the following parameters for a switching network:
N = number of hops between two given stations
L = message length, in bits
B = data rate, in bps, on all links
P = packet size, in bits
H = overhead (header) bits per packet
S = call setup time (circuit switching or virtual circuit) in seconds
D = propagation delay per hop in seconds
   a. For $N = 4$, $L = 3200$, $B = 9600$, $P = 1024$, $H = 16$, $S = 0.2$, $D = 0.001$, compute the end-to-end delay for circuit switching, message switching, virtual circuit packet switching, and datagram packet switching. Assume that there are no acknowledgments.
   b. Derive general expressions for the four techniques, taken two at a time (six expressions in all), showing the conditions under which the delays are equal.

2.12 What value of P, as a function of N, B, and H, results in minimum end-to-end delay on a datagram network? Assume that L is much larger than P, and D is zero.

2.13 Two stations communicate via a 1-Mbps satellite link. The satellite serves merely to retransmit data received from one station to the other, with negligible delay. The up-and-down propagation delay for a synchronous orbit is 270 ms. Using HDLC frames of length 1024 bits, what is the maximum possible data throughput (not counting overhead bits)?

APPENDIX 2A: THE CYCLIC REDUNDANCY CHECK

In HDLC and other data link control protocols, an error-detection technique is required so that the receiver can detect any bit errors in received frames and request that the sender retransmit those frames. This technique requires the addition of a **frame check sequence (FCS),** or **error-detecting code,** to each frame. On transmission, a calculation is performed on the bits of the frame to be transmitted; the result is inserted as an additional field in the frame. On reception, the same calculation is performed on the received bits and the calculated result is compared to the value stored in the incoming frame. If there is a discrepancy, the receiver assumes that an error has occurred.

One of the most common, and one of the most powerful, of the error-detecting codes is the cyclic redundancy check (CRC). For this technique, the message to be transmitted is treated as one long binary number. This number is divided by a unique prime binary number (a number divisible only by itself and 1), and the remainder is attached to the frame to be transmitted. When the frame is received, the receiver performs the same division, using the same divisor, and compares the calculated remainder with the remainder received in the frame. The most commonly used divisors are a 17-bit divisor, which produces a 16-bit remainder, and a 33-bit divisor, which produces a 32-bit remainder.

The measure of effectiveness of any error-detecting code is the percentage of errors it detects. It can be shown that all the following errors are indivisible by a prime divisor and hence are detectable [STAL88a]:

- All single-bit errors
- All double-bit errors, as long as the divisor has at least three 1's
- Any odd number of errors, as long as the divisor contains a factor of 11

TABLE 2.5 Effectiveness of the Cyclic Redundancy Check (CRC)

Type of Error	16-bit CRC Probability of Detection	32-bit CRC Probability of Detection
Single bit errors	1.0	1.0
Two bits in error (separate or not)	1.0	1.0
Odd number of bits in error	1.0	1.0
Error burst of length less than the length of the CRC (16 or 32 bits, respectively)	1.0	1.0
Error burst of length equal to the length of the CRC	$1-\dfrac{1}{2^{15}}$	$1-\dfrac{1}{2^{31}}$
Error burst of length greater than the length of the CRC	$1-\dfrac{1}{2^{16}}$	$1-\dfrac{1}{2^{32}}$

- Any burst error for which the length of the burst is less than the length of the divisor polynomial; that is, less than or equal to the length of the FCS
- Most larger burst errors

These results are summarized in Table 2.5. As you can see, this is a very powerful means of error detection and requires very little overhead. As an example, if a 16-bit FCS is used with frames of 1000 bits, then the overhead is only 1.6%. With a 32-bit FCS, the overhead is 3.2%.

CHAPTER 3

Overview of LAN/MAN Technology

The principal technology ingredients that determine the nature of a LAN or MAN are:

- Topology
- Transmission medium
- Medium access control technique

Together, they in large measure determine the type of data that may be transmitted, the speed and efficiency of communications, and even the kinds of applications that a network may support.

This chapter surveys the topologies and transmission media that, within the state of the art, are appropriate for LANs and MANs. The issue of access control is also briefly raised. With this survey as background, three classes of local networks are defined. The discussion is brief, with the objective of providing a context for the material in Chapters 4 through 7.

3.1

TOPOLOGIES

The term *topology*, in the context of a communications network, refers to the way in which the end points or stations of the network are interconnected. A topology is defined by the layout of communications links and switching elements, and it determines the data paths that may be used between any pair of stations.

To begin the discussion of topology, consider the question of why a communications network is needed at all. According to our definition in Chapter 1, the local network provides a means for interconnecting devices in a small area. Why not provide a direct connection between any pair of devices that need to communicate? Then no intermediate network of communications devices is required.

The problem with this approach is illustrated in Figure 3.1. Each device has a direct, dedicated link, called a *point-to-point link,* with each other device. If there are N devices, then N(N − 1) links are required, and each device requires (N − 1) input/output (I/O) ports. Thus, the cost of the system, in terms of cable installation and I/O hardware, grows with the square of the number of devices.

The infeasibility of this approach, sometimes known as the *mesh topology,* was recognized early for wide-area communications. The solution, as shown in Figure 2.9, was to introduce a network of switching nodes with the ability to route messages, creating logical links and eliminating the need for so many direct physical connections. In this approach, each device or station connects directly to a communication network node and communicates to other stations via the network.

This approach—the use of a collection of switching nodes—is not generally used for local networks. Because the distances involved are small, the expense of the switching nodes can be avoided. Topologies have been developed that require no or only one intermediate switching node and yet avoid the problems of the mesh topology.

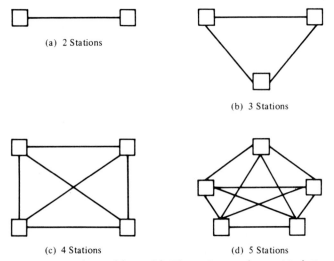

(a) 2 Stations

(b) 3 Stations

(c) 4 Stations   (d) 5 Stations

FIGURE 3.1 The Problem with Direct Connection or Mesh Topology

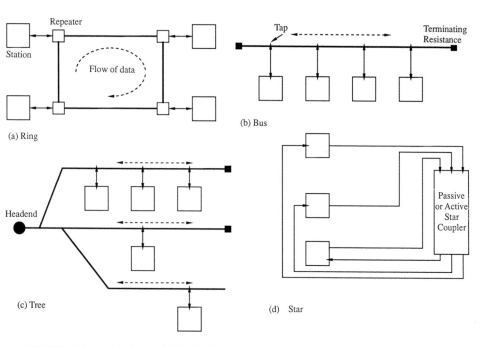

FIGURE 3.2 Local Network Topologies

Four simple topologies are described below: bus, tree, ring, and star
(Figure 3.2). These are commonly used, as is, to construct LANs and
MANs. They can also be used as building blocks for networks with more
complex topologies. These refinements are discussed in later chapters.

Ring Topology

In the *ring topology*, the network consists of a set of *repeaters* joined by
point-to-point links in a closed loop. Hence each repeater participates in
two links. The repeater is a comparatively simple device, capable of receiving data on one link and transmitting it, bit by bit, on the other link
as fast as it is received, with no buffering at the repeater. The links are
unidirectional; that is, data are transmitted in one direction only and all
are oriented in the same way. Thus data circulate around the ring in one
direction (clockwise or counterclockwise).

Each station attaches to the network at a repeater. Data are transmitted in packets. So, for example, if station X wishes to transmit a message
to station Y, it breaks the message up into packets. Each packet contains
a portion of the data plus some control information, including Y's address. The packets are inserted into the ring one at a time and circulate
through the other repeaters. Station Y recognizes its address and copies
the packets as they go by.

Since multiple devices share the ring, control is needed to determine at what time each station may insert packets. This is almost always done with some form of distributed control. Each station contains access logic that controls transmission and reception; various techniques are explored in Chapter 5.

Bus and Tree Topologies

With the *bus topology,* the communications network is simply the transmission medium—no switches and no repeaters. All stations attach, through appropriate hardware interfacing, directly to a linear transmission medium, or *bus.* A transmission from any station propagates the length of the medium and can be received by all other stations.

The tree topology is a generalization of the bus topology. The transmission medium is a branching cable with no closed loops. The tree layout begins at a point known as the *headend.* One or more cables start at the headend, and each of these may have branches. The branches in turn may have additional branches to allow quite complex layouts. Again, a transmission from any station propagates throughout the medium and can be received by all other stations. For both bus and tree topologies, the medium is referred to as *multipoint.*

Because all nodes on a bus or tree share a common transmission link, only one station can transmit at a time. Some form of access control is required to determine which station may transmit next. Again, we examine this topic in Chapter 5.

As with the ring, packet transmission is typically used for communication. A station wishing to transmit breaks its message into packets and sends these one at a time. For each packet that a station wishes to transmit, it waits for its next turn and then transmits the packet. The intended destination station will recognize its address as the packets go by and copy them. There are no intermediate nodes and no switching or repeating is involved.

Star Topology

In the star topology, each station is directly connected to a common central switch. One example of the use of this topology is the case in which the central switch uses circuit-switching technology. The digital data switch and digital private branch exchange are examples of this approach.

The star topology is also employed for implementing a packet broadcasting local area network. In this case, each station attaches to a central node, referred to as the *star coupler,* via two point-to-point links, one for transmission in each direction. A transmission from any one station enters the central node and is retransmitted on all of the outgoing links. Thus, although the arrangement is physically a star, it is logically a bus: a transmission from any station is received by all other stations, and only one station at a time may successfully transmit. Thus, the medium access control techniques used for the packet star topology are the same as for bus and tree.

There are two ways of implementing the star coupler. In the case of the **passive star coupler,** there is an electromagnetic linkage in the coupler, so that any incoming transmission is physically passed to all of the outgoing links. In the case of optical fiber, this coupling is achieved by fusing together a number of fibers, so that incoming light is automatically split among all of the outgoing fibers. In the case of coaxial cable or twisted pair, transformer coupling is used to split the incoming signal.

The other type of star coupler is the **active star coupler.** In this case, there is digital logic in the central node that acts as a repeater. As bits arrive on any input line, they are automatically regenerated and repeated on all outgoing lines. If multiple input signals arrive simultaneously, a collision signal is transmitted on all outgoing lines.

Choice of Topology

The choice of topology depends on a variety of factors, including reliability, expandability, and performance. This choice is part of the overall task of designing a local network. As the text proceeds, the trade-offs between the various approaches should become clear. A few general observations follow.

The bus/tree topology appears to be the most flexible one. It is able to handle a wide range of devices, in terms of number of devices, data rates, and data types. High bandwidth is achievable. Because the medium is passive, it would appear at first blush to be highly reliable. As we shall see, this is not necessarily the case. In particular, a break in the cable can disable a large part or all of the network.

Very high-speed links (e.g., optical fiber) can be used between the repeaters of a ring. Hence, the ring has the potential of providing the best throughput of any topology. There are practical limitations, in terms of numbers of devices and variety of data types. Finally, the reliability problem is obvious: a single link or repeater failure could disable the entire network.

The star topology, using circuit switching, readily integrates voice with data traffic. It lends itself well to low-data-rate ($\leq$64 kbps) devices. The star topology is good for terminal-intensive requirements because of the minimal processing burden that it imposes on the attached devices.

3.2

TRANSMISSION MEDIA

The *transmission medium* is the physical path between transmitter and receiver in a communications network. Figure 3.3 shows the basic elements of a transmission system. The most common configuration is a point-to-point link between two transmitting/receiving devices, which, through appropriate interfaces, insert analog or digital signals onto the medium. One or more intermediate devices may be used to compensate for attenuation or other transmission impairments. Point-to-point links are used in the ring topology to connect adjacent repeaters, and in the star topology to connect devices to the central switch. Point-to-point links may also be used to connect two local networks in different buildings: we elaborate on this point below. Multipoint links are used to connect multiple devices, as in the bus and tree topologies. Devices attach to the medium at various points; again, repeaters (digital signals) or amplifiers (analog signals) may be used to extend the length of the medium.

Transmission media may be classified as guided or unguided. In both cases, communication is in the form of electromagnetic waves. With *guided media*, the waves are guided along a physical path. Examples of guided media are twisted pair, coaxial cable, and optical fiber, all of

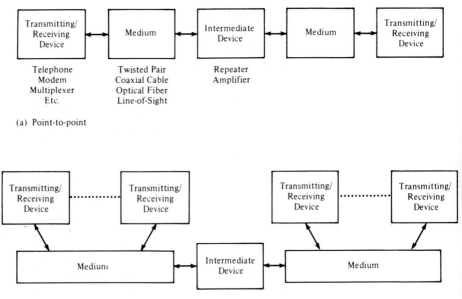

(a) Point-to-point

(b) Multipoint

FIGURE 3.3 Simplified Transmission System Block Diagram

which are used in local networks. The atmosphere and outer space are examples of *unguided media*, which provide a means for transmitting electromagnetic waves but do not guide them. Various forms of transmission through the atmosphere are employed for building-to-building connections.

In this section, we describe these media using the following characteristics:

- *Physical description:* the nature of the transmission medium
- *Transmission characteristics:* include whether analog or digital signaling is used, modulation technique, capacity, and the frequency range over which transmission occurs
- *Connectivity:* point-to-point or multipoint
- *Geographic scope:* the maximum distance between points on the network; whether suitable for intrabuilding, interbuilding, and/or intracity use
- *Noise immunity:* resistance of medium to contamination of the transmitted data
- *Relative cost:* based on cost of components, installation, and maintenance

Twisted Pair

By far the most common transmission medium, for both analog and digital data, is *twisted pair*. The wiring within a building to connect the telephones is twisted pair, as are the local loops that connect all of the phones in a limited geographic area to a central exchange.

Physical Description. A twisted pair consists of two insulated wires arranged in a regular spiral pattern. The wires are copper or steel coated with copper. The copper provides conductivity; steel may be used for strength. A wire pair acts as a single communication link. Typically, a number of these pairs are bundled together into a cable by wrapping them in a tough protective sheath. Over longer distances, cables may contain hundreds of pairs. The twisting of the individual pairs minimizes electromagnetic interference between the pairs. The wires in a pair have thicknesses of from 0.016 to 0.036 inch.

Transmission Characteristics. Wire pairs may be used to transmit both analog and digital signals. For analog signals, amplifiers are required about every 5 to 6 km. For digital signals, repeaters are used every 2 or 3 km.

The most common use of wire pair is for analog transmission of voice. Although frequency components of speech may be found between 20 Hz and 20 kHz, a much narrower bandwidth is required for intelligible speech reproduction [FREE91]. The standard bandwidth of a full-duplex voice channel is 300 to 3400 Hz. Multiple voice channels can be multiplexed, using FDM, on a single wire pair. A bandwidth of 4 kHz per channel provides adequate separation between channels. Twisted pair has a capacity of up to 24 voice channels using a bandwidth of up to 268 kHz.

Digital data may be transmitted over an analog voice channel using a modem. With a current modem design, speeds of up to 19.2 kbps using phase-shift keying (PSK) are practical. On a 24-channel wire pair, the aggregate data rate is 230 kbps.

It is also possible to use digital or baseband signaling on a wire pair. Bell offers a T1 circuit using twisted pair that handles 24 PCM voice channels, for an aggregate data rate of 1.544 Mbps. Higher data rates, depending on distance, are possible. A data rate of 4 Mbps represents a reasonable upper limit.

Connectivity.   Twisted pair can be used for point-to-point and multipoint applications. As a multipoint medium, twisted pair is a less expensive, lower-performance alternative to coax cable but supports fewer stations. Point-to-point usage is far more common.

Geographic Scope.   Twisted pair can easily provide point-to-point data transmission to a range of 15 km or more. Twisted pair for local networks is typically used within a single building or just a few buildings.

Noise Immunity.   Compared to other guided media, twisted pair is limited in distance, bandwidth, and data rate. The medium is quite susceptible to interference and noise because of its easy coupling with electromagnetic fields. For example, a wire run parallel to an ac power line will pick up 60-Hz energy. Signals on adjacent pairs of cables may interfere with each other, a phenomenon known as *cross-talk*.

Several measures can be taken to reduce impairments. Shielding the wire with metallic braid or sheathing reduces interference. The twisting of the wire reduces low-frequency interference, and the use of different twist lengths in adjacent pairs reduces cross-talk. These measures are effective for wavelengths much greater than the twist length of the cable. Noise immunity can be as high or higher than for coaxial cable for low-frequency transmission. However, above 10 to 100 kHz, coaxial cable is typically superior.

Cost.   Twisted pair is less expensive than either coaxial cable or fiber in terms of cost per foot. However, because of its connectivity limitations, installation costs may approach that of other media.

Coaxial Cable

The most versatile transmission medium is *coaxial cable*. In this section we discuss two types of coaxial cable currently in use for LAN applications: 75-ohm cable, which is the standard used in *community antenna television* (CATV) systems, and 50-ohm cable. As Table 3.1 illustrates, 50-ohm cable is used only for digital signaling, called *baseband*; 75-ohm cable is used for analog signaling with FDM, called *broadband*, and for high-speed digital signaling and analog signaling in which no FDM is possible. The latter is sometimes referred to as *single-channel broadband*.

Physical Description. Coaxial cable, like twisted pair, consists of two conductors, but it is constructed differently to permit it to operate over a wider range of frequencies. It consists of a hollow outer cylindrical conductor that surrounds a single inner wire conductor. The inner conductor can be either solid or stranded; the outer conductor can be either solid or braided. The inner conductor is held in place by either regularly spaced insulating rings or a solid dialectric material. The outer conductor is covered with a jacket or shield. A single coaxial cable has a diameter of from 0.4 to about 1 inch.

Transmission Characteristics. The 50-ohm cable is used exclusively for digital transmission. Manchester encoding is typically used. Data rates of up to 10 Mbps can be achieved.

CATV cable is used for both analog and digital signaling. For analog signaling, frequencies up to 300 to 400 MHz are possible. Analog data, such as video and audio, can be handled on CATV cable in much the same way as free-space radio and TV broadcasting. TV channels are each allocated 6 MHz of bandwidth; each radio channel requires much less. Hence a large number of channels can be carried on the cable using FDM.

When FDM is used, the CATV cable is referred to as broadband. The frequency spectrum of the cable is divided into channels, each of which carries analog signals. In addition to the analog data referred to above, digital data may also be carried in a channel. Various modulation schemes have been used for digital data, including ASK, FSK, and PSK. The efficiency of the modem will determine the bandwidth needed to support a given data rate. A good rule of thumb [STAH82] is to assume 1 Hz per bps for rates of 5 Mbps and above and 2 Hz per bps for lower rates. For example, a 5-Mbps data rate can be achieved in a 6-MHz TV channel, whereas a 4.8-kbps modem might use about 10 kHz. With current technology, a data rate of about 20 Mbps is achievable; at this rate, the bandwidth efficiency may exceed 1 bps/Hz.

To achieve data rates above 20 Mbps, two approaches have been taken. Both require that the entire bandwidth of the 75-ohm cable be dedicated to this data transfer; no FDM is employed. One approach is to use digital signaling on the cable, as is done for the 50-ohm cable. A data rate of 50 Mbps has been achieved with this scheme. An alternative is to use a simple PSK system; using a 150-MHz carrier, a data rate of 50 Mbps has also been achieved. Much lower data rates are achieved using FSK.

Connectivity. Coaxial cable is applicable to point-to-point and to multipoint configurations. Baseband 50-ohm cable can support on the order of 100 devices per segment, with larger systems possible by linking segments with repeaters. Broadband 75-ohm cable can support thousands of devices. The use of 75-ohm cable at high data rates (50 Mbps) introduces technical problems that limit the number of devices to 20 to 30.

Geographic Scope. Maximum distances in a typical baseband cable are limited to a few kilometers. Broadband networks can span ranges of tens of kilometers. The difference has to do with the relative signal integrity of analog and digital signals. The types of electromagnetic noise usually encountered in industrial and urban areas are of relatively low frequencies, where most of the energy in digital signals resides. Analog signals may be placed on a carrier of sufficiently high frequency to avoid the main components of noise.

High-speed transmission (50 Mbps), digital or analog, is limited to about 1 km. Because of the high data rate, the physical distance between signals on the bus is very small. Hence very little attenuation or noise can be tolerated before the data are lost.

Noise Immunity. Noise immunity for coaxial cable depends on the application and implementation. In general, it is superior to that of twisted pair for higher frequencies.

Cost. The cost of installed coaxial cable falls between that of twisted pair and optical fiber.

Optical Fiber Cable

One of the most significant technological breakthroughs in information transmission has been the development of practical fiber optic communications systems. Optical fiber already enjoys considerable use in long-distance telecommunications, and its use in military applications is growing. The continuing improvements in performance and decline in prices, together with the inherent advantages of optical fiber, have made it increasingly attractive for local area networking. The following characteristics distinguish optical fiber from twisted pair or coaxial cable:

- *Greater capacity:* The potential bandwidth, and hence data rate, of optical fiber is immense; data rates of 2 Gbps over tens of kilometers have been demonstrated. Compare this to the practical maximum of hundreds of Mbps over about 1 km for coaxial cable and just a few Mbps over 1 km for twisted pair.
- *Smaller size and lighter weight:* Optical fibers are considerably thinner than coaxial cable or bundled twisted-pair cable—at least an order of magnitude thinner for comparable information transmission capacity. For cramped conduits in buildings and underground along public rights of way, the advantage of small size is considerable. The corresponding reduction in weight reduces structural support requirements.
- *Lower attenuation:* Attenuation is significantly lower for optical fiber than for coaxial cable or twisted pair and is constant over a wide range.
- *Electromagnetic isolation:* Optical fiber systems are not affected by external electromagnetic fields. Thus the system is not vulnerable to interference, impulse noise, or cross-talk. By the same token, fibers do not radiate energy, causing little interference with other equipment and providing a high degree of security from eavesdropping. In addition, fiber is inherently difficult to tap.

Physical Description.   An optical fiber is a thin (2 to 125 μm), flexible medium capable of conducting an optical ray. Various glasses and plastics can be used to make optical fibers [JORD85]. The lowest losses have been obtained using fibers of ultrapure fused silica. Ultrapure fiber is difficult to manufacture; higher-loss multicomponent glass fibers are more economical and still provide good performance. Plastic fiber is even less costly and can be used for short-haul links, for which moderately high losses are acceptable.

An optical fiber cable has a cylindrical shape and consists of three concentric sections: the core, the cladding, and the jacket. The *core* is the innermost section, and consists of one or more very thin strands, or fibers, made of glass or plastic. Each fiber is surrounded by its own *cladding,* a glass or plastic coating that has optical properties different from those of the core. The outermost layer, surrounding one or a bundle of cladded fibers, is the *jacket.* The jacket is composed of plastic and other materials layered to protect against moisture, abrasion, crushing, and other environmental dangers.

Transmission Characteristics.   Optical fiber transmits a signal-encoded beam of light by means of total internal reflection. Total internal reflection can occur in any transparent medium that has a higher index of refraction than the surrounding medium. In effect, the optical fiber acts as a waveguide for frequencies in the range 10^{14} to 10^{15} Hz, which covers the visible spectrum and part of the infrared spectrum.

Figure 3.4 shows the principle of optical fiber transmission. Light from a source enters the cylindrical glass or plastic core. Rays at shallow angles are reflected and propagated along the fiber; other rays are absorbed by the surrounding material. This form of propagation is called multimode, referring to the variety of angles that will reflect. When the fiber core radius is reduced, fewer angles will reflect. By reducing the radius of the core to the order of a wavelength, only a single angle or mode can pass: the axial ray. This provides superior performance to multimode for the following reason. With multimode transmission, multiple propagation paths exist, each with a different path length and hence time to traverse the fiber. This causes signal elements to spread out in time and limits the rate at which data can be accurately received. Since there is a single transmission path with single-mode transmission, such distortion cannot occur. Finally, by varying the index of refraction of the core, a third type of transmission, known as multimode graded index, is possible. This type is intermediate between the other two in characteristics. The variable refraction has the effect of focusing the rays more efficiently than ordinary multimode, also known as multimode step index. Table 3.1 compares the three fiber transmission modes. As can be seen, tremendous capacities can be achieved, far exceeding those of coaxial cable or twisted pair.

Two different types of light source are used in fiber optic systems: the *light-emitting diode* (LED) and the *injection laser diode* (ILD). The LED is a solid-state device that emits light when a current is applied. The ILD is

TABLE 3.1   Comparison of Three Types of Optical Fibers

	Step-index Multimode	Graded-index Multimode	Single-mode
Light Source	LED or laser	LED or laser	laser
Bandwidth	wide (up to 200 MHz/ km)	very wide (200 MHz to 3 GHz/km)	extremely wide (3 GHZ to 50 GHZ/km)
Splicing	difficult	difficult	difficult
Typical Application	computer data links	moderate-length telephone lines	telecommunication long lines
Cost	least expensive	more expensive	most expensive
Core Diameter (μm)	50 to 125	50 to 125	2 to 8
Cladding Diameter (μm)	125 to 440	125 to 440	15 to 60

Source: [SHUF84]

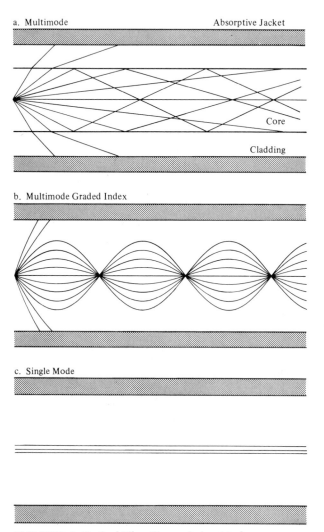

a. Multimode   Absorptive Jacket

Core

Cladding

b. Multimode Graded Index

c. Single Mode

FIGURE 3.4   Optical Fiber Transmission Modes

a solid-state device that works on the laser principle in which quantum electronic effects are stimulated to produce a superradiant beam of narrow bandwidth. The LED is less costly, operates over a greater temperature range, and has a longer operational life. The ILD is more efficient and can sustain greater data rates.

The detector used at the receiving end to convert the light into electrical energy is a *photodiode*. Two solid-state devices have been used: the PIN detector and the APD detector. The PIN photodiode has a segment of intrinsic (I) silicon between the P and N layers of a diode. The APD, avalanche photodiode, is similar in appearance but uses a stronger electric field. Both devices are basically photon counters. The PIN is less expensive and less sensitive than the APD.

The amplitude-shift keying technique is commonly used to transmit digital data over optical fiber; in this context, it is known as *intensity modulation*. For LED transmitters, binary one is represented by a short pulse of light and binary zero by the absence of light. Laser transmitters normally have a fixed bias current that causes the device to emit a low light level. This low level represents binary zero, while a higher-amplitude lightwave represents another signal element.

Data rates as high as a few gigabits per second have been demonstrated in the laboratory. Current practical applications are in the range of a few hundreds of megabits per second over a few kilometers.

There is a relationship among the wavelength employed, the type of transmission, and the achievable data rate. Both single mode and multimode can support several different wavelengths of light and can employ laser or LED light sources. In glass-composition fiber, light propagates best in three distinct wavelength "windows," centered on 850, 1300, and 1500 nanometers (nm). The loss is lower at higher wavelengths, allowing greater data rates over longer distances (Table 3.2). Most local applications today use 850-nm LED light sources. Although this is relatively inexpensive, this combination is generally limited to data rates under 100 Mbps and distances of a few kilometers. To achieve higher data rates and longer distances, a 1300-nm LED or laser source is needed. Thus, although the 850-nm source is attractive for LANs, the 1300-nm source is more appropriate for HSLNs. The highest transmission capacities and longest distances achievable today require 1500-nm light sources. These require lasers and are used in some long-distance applications, but are currently too expensive for local networks.

TABLE 3.2   Transmission Losses of Various Types of Optical Fiber [FREE85]

Mode	Material Core/Cladding	Transmission Loss, dB/km		
		850 nm	**1300 nm**	**1500 nm**
Single mode	Silica glass/silica glass	2	0.5	0.2
Step-index multimode	Silica glass/silica glass	2	0.5	0.2
	Silica glass/plastic	2.5	High	High
	Multicomponent glass/ multicomponent glass	3.4	High	High
Graded-index multimode	Silica glass/silica glass	2	0.5	0.2
	Multicomponent glass/ multicomponent glass	3.5	High	High

Currently, a single carrier frequency is used for optical fiber transmission. Future advances will permit practical FDM systems, also referred to as wavelength division multiplexing or color division multiplexing.

Connectivity. The most common use of optical fiber is for point-to-point links. Experimental multipoint systems using a bus topology have been built, but are too expensive to be practical today. In principle, however, a single segment of optical fiber could support many more drops than either twisted pair or coaxial cable, due to lower power loss, lower attenuation characteristics, and greater bandwidth potential.

Geographic Scope. Present technology supports transmission over distances of 6 to 8 km without repeaters. Hence optical fiber is suitable for linking local networks in several buildings via point-to-point links.

Noise Immunity. Optical fiber is not affected by electromagnetic interference or noise. This characteristic permits high data rates over long distance and provides excellent security.

Cost. Fiber optic systems are more expensive than twisted pair and coaxial cable in terms of cost per foot and required components (transmitters, receivers, connectors). While costs of twisted pair and coaxial cable are unlikely to drop, engineering advances should reduce the cost of fiber optics to be competitive with these other media.

Line-of-Sight Media

In this section we look at three techniques for transmitting electromagnetic waves through the atmosphere: microwave, infrared, and laser. All three require a *line-of-sight path* between transmitter and receiver.

Because of the high-frequency ranges at which these devices operate (microwave, 10^9 to 10^{10} Hz; infrared, 10^{11} to 10^{14} Hz; laser, 10^{14} to 10^{15} Hz), there is the potential for very high data rates. Practical systems for short links have been built with data rates of several megabits per second.

These transmission techniques are primarily useful for connecting local networks that are in separate buildings. It is difficult to string cable between buildings, either underground or overhead on poles, especially if the intervening space is public property. The line-of-sight techniques require equipment only at each building.

The *infrared* link consists of a pair of transmitter/receivers (transceivers) that modulate noncoherent infrared light. Transceivers must be within the line of sight, installed on either a rooftop or within a building with data transmitted through adjacent exterior windows. The system is highly directional; it is extremely difficult to intercept, inject data, or to jam such systems. No licensing is required and the system can be installed in just a few days. Data rates of a few megabits per second over a few kilometers are practical [SEAM82].

A similar system can be installed with *laser* transceivers using coherent light modulation. The major difference is that the Food and Drug Administration (FDA) requires that laser hardware, which emits low-level radiation, be properly shielded. The licensing process takes from 2 to 6 months [CELA82].

Both infrared and laser are susceptible to environmental interference, such as rain and fog. A system with less sensitivity is *microwave.* As with laser and infrared, installation is relatively easy; the major difference is that microwave transceivers can be mounted only externally to a building. Microwave is less directional than either laser or infrared; hence there is a security problem of data eavesdropping, insertion, or jamming. As with all radio-frequency systems, microwave requires Federal Communications Commission (FCC) licensing, which takes about 2 to 3 months. Comparable data rates and distances to laser and infrared can be achieved [RUSH82].

Table 3.3 summarizes the key characteristics of these techniques and includes, for comparison, the use of cable for building-to-building links.

Choice of Transmission Medium

The choice of transmission medium is determined by a number of factors. It is, we shall see, constrained by the topology of the network. Other factors come into play, such as:

- *Capacity:* to support the expected local network traffic
- *Reliability:* to meet availability requirements
- *Types of data supported:* tailored to the application
- *Environmental scope:* to provide service over the range of environments required

And so on. The choice is part of the overall task of designing a network, which is addressed in later chapters. Here we can make a few general observations.

Twisted pair is an inexpensive, well-understood medium. Typically, office buildings are wired to meet the anticipated telephone system demand plus a healthy margin. Compared to coax, the bandwidth is limited. Twisted pair is likely to be the most cost effective for a single-building, low-traffic, local network installation. An office automation system, with a preponderance of dumb terminals and/or intelligent workstations plus a few minis, is a good example.

Coaxial cable is more expensive than twisted pair, but has greater capacity. For a broad range of LAN/MAN requirements, and with the

TABLE 3.3 Transmission Media for Local Networks: Point-to-Point Across Public Property

Medium	Ease of Installation	Regulatory Licensing (months)	Data Rate (Mbps)	Ease of Maintenance	Cost
Infrared	1–2 days, easy	None	1–3	Excellent	Low
Laser	1–2 days, easy	2–6	1–3	Excellent	Low
Microwave	1 week, easy	2–3	1–3	Excellent	Low
Underground coax/ optical fiber	1–18 months, moderate to hard	6–18	10+	Fair to good	Moderate to high
Aerial coax/optical fiber	1–6 months, moderate	6–18	10+	Good	Moderate to high

Source: [CELA82].

exception of terminal-intensive systems, it is the medium of choice. For most requirements, a coaxial-based local network can be designed to meet current demand with plenty of room for expansion, at reasonable cost. Coaxial systems excel when there are a lot of devices and a considerable amount of traffic. Examples include large data processing installations and sophisticated office automation systems, which may include facsimile machines, intelligent copiers, and color graphics devices.

At the current state of the art, fiber optic links are suited for point-to-point communications. Hence they do not compete with coaxial cable. The exception is for ring topology networks. However, when the cost of multidrop fiber cable becomes competitive with that of coaxial cable, its advantages—low noise susceptibility, low loss, small size, light weight—will make it a serious contender for many network applications.

The line-of-sight media are not well suited to local network requirements. They are, however, good choices for point-to-point links between buildings, each of which has a twisted-pair or coaxial-based LAN.

3.3

RELATIONSHIP BETWEEN MEDIUM AND TOPOLOGY

Combinations

The choices of transmission medium and topology are not independent. Table 3.4 shows the preferred combinations. The ring topology requires point-to-point links between repeaters. Twisted-pair wire, baseband coaxial cable, and optical fiber can all be used to provide the links. However, broadband coaxial cable would not work well in this topology. Each repeater would have to be capable of receiving and transmitting data simultaneously on multiple channels. It is doubtful that the expense of such devices could be justified. Table 3.5 summarizes representative parameters for transmission media for commercially available ring LANs and MANs. Remember, however, that tables such as this one and Table 3.6 will always be overtaken by new developments in technology.

TABLE 3.4   Relationship Between Medium and Topology

Medium	Topology			
	Bus	Tree	Ring	Star
Twisted pair	X		X	X
Baseband coaxial cable	X		X	
Broadband coaxial cable	X	X		
Optical fiber	X		X	X

TABLE 3.5   Characteristics of Transmission Media for LAN/MAN Ring

Transmission Medium	Data Rate (Mbps)	Repeater Spacing (km)	Number of Repeaters
Twisted Pair	16	0.3	250
Baseband Coaxial Cable	16	1.0	250
Optical Fiber	100	2.0	500

For example, the possibility of standardizing a twisted-pair ring LAN at 100 Mbps is now under study, and a number of manufacturers have developed designs and expressed an interest in introducing such a product [VERE91].

For the bus topology, twisted-pair and both baseband and broadband coaxial cable are appropriate, and numerous products exist for each of these media. Until recently, optical fiber cable has not been considered feasible; the multipoint configuration was not considered cost effective, due to the difficulty in constructing low-loss optical taps. However, recent advances have made the optical fiber bus practical, even at quite high data rates.

The tree topology can be employed with broadband coaxial cable. The unidirectional nature of broadband signaling allows the construction of a tree architecture. On the other hand, the bidirectional nature of baseband signaling on either twisted pair or coaxial cable is not suited to the tree topology. Table 3.6 summarizes representative parameters for transmission media for commercially available bus and tree LANs and MANs.

The reader will note that the performance for a given medium is considerably better for the ring topology compared with the bus/tree topology. In the bus/tree topology, each station is attached to the medium by a tap, and each tap introduces some attenuation and distortion to the

TABLE 3.6   Characteristics of Transmission Media for LAN/MAN: Bus/Tree

Transmission Medium	Data Rate (Mbps)	Range (km)	Number of Taps
Unshielded Twisted Pair	1–2	<2	10's
Baseband Coaxial Cable	10/70	<3/<1	100's/10's
Broadband Coaxial Cable	20 per channel	<30	100's–1,000's
Optical Fiber	45	<150	500

signal as it passes by. In the ring, each station is attached to the medium by a repeater, and each repeater generates a new signal to compensate for effects of attenuation and distortion.

The star topology requires a point-to-point link between each device and the central node. For circuit switching, where the central node performs the circuit-switching task, twisted pair has traditionally been used. The higher data rates of coaxial or fiber would overwhelm the typical circuit-switching node. For packet switching, the performance of the star topology will depend on whether an active or pass star configuration is used.

Layout

One very practical issue is related to the selection of both medium and topology, and that is the actual layout of the transmission medium in the building. To address this issue, we need to make a distinction between topology and geometry. The net illustrations in Figure 3.2 depict the various topologies of local networks; this defines the way in which the devices are interconnected. But, as a practical matter, the actual path that the cable follows is constrained by physical characteristics of the building. The cable must follow routes that accommodate the walls and floors of the building. Typically, predefined cable paths are used, sometimes defined by the existence of conduits. Thus the geometry, or actual layout, of the cable will be distorted to some extent relative to the intended topology.

Let us consider some of the requirements that dictate the layout of the installed cable. Of prime importance is the need to minimize cost while providing the required capacity. One determinant of cost, of course, is the medium itself. As was mentioned, twisted pair is cheaper than coaxial cable, which is in turn cheaper than optical fiber. It is often the case, however, that the installation costs, which are primarily labor costs, far exceed the cost of the materials. This is particularly true in existing buildings, which may present difficulties in finding pathways for new cable. In new buildings, the problems and costs can be minimized if the cable layout for a local network can be designed ahead of time. Then the cable can be installed during construction.

A second important requirement is that the layout be suitable for accommodating equipment relocation and network growth. It is not unusual for 50% of the installed data terminals in an office building to be moved each year [IBM84]. And, with the continued proliferation of personal and other microcomputers, virtually any local network can be expected to grow. The safest way to plan for both relocation and growth is to install a network that reaches every office, or at least to install a smaller network that can easily be expanded to include additional offices with little or no disruption of the existing network. Finally, the layout

TABLE 3.7   The Use of Alternative Wiring Strategies

Medium	Topology		
	Star	Ring	Bus
Twisted pair	S	L, S	L, S
Coaxial cable		L	L
Optical fiber		L	L

L = linear wiring strategy
S = star wiring strategy

should be such as to facilitate servicing and maintenance. When a fault occurs somewhere in the network, we would like to be able to locate the fault, isolate it from the rest of the network, and fix it as soon as possible.

With the above considerations in mind, we can identify two general strategies for laying out the local network transmission medium: linear and star. Table 3.7 summarizes the relationship of the layout strategy to the transmission media and topologies of local networks.

The linear strategy attempts to provide the desired topology with the minimum cable, subject to the physical constraints of the building. The medium is propagated to the subscriber locations, which may be some or all of the offices in the building. Any of the guided media that have been described can be used, and either a bus or ring topology can be provided.

The star layout strategy uses an individual cable from a concentration point to each subscriber location. This is clearly the proper approach for the star topology local network. It can also be used for bus and ring topologies, as depicted in Figure 3.5. In the case of the bus topology, the bus is very short and resides at the concentration point; the drop cables to the attached devices are relatively long. In the case of the ring topology, the ring is distorted so that each link of the ring loops through the concentration point. Typically, this layout is used separately on each floor of a building. The concentration point is referred to as a wiring closet; some or all of the offices on the floor are connected to the closet. Connections between floors are provided by linking the closets. This type of layout is invariably used to support telephones in an office building and is becoming increasingly popular for local networks.

Although the star strategy is logical for the star topology, it may seem inappropriate for the ring and bus topologies. Its main disadvantage is that, for the ring and bus, the star strategy will require more cable than the linear strategy, increasing cost and cable congestion. For this reason, the star strategy is rarely used for coaxial cable or optical fiber local networks. However, the star approach is well suited for twisted-pair local

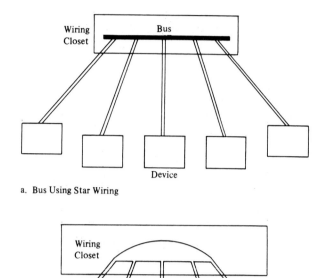

a. Bus Using Star Wiring

b. Ring Using Star Wiring

FIGURE 3.5 Bus and Ring Topologies Using Star Wiring

networks, where the cost penalty is lower. Some of the advantages of the star strategy are:

1. It lends itself to prewiring of the building. The layout is a regular one and conforms to normal installation practice in office buildings. Furthermore, most existing buildings are prewired with excess unshielded twisted pair. Thus, for local networks that employ unshielded twisted pair, it may be possible to use existing wiring. Even in the case of shielded twisted pair, installation will be easier since the paths for the new cable are well defined.
2. The system can be easily expanded, simply by patching additional cables into the network at the wiring closet.
3. Servicing and maintenance are easier. Diagnosis of problems can be performed from centralized points. Faults can easily be isolated by patching cables out of the network.

Further discussion of the star strategy will be provided as we look at some specific uses in the next two chapters.

3.4

CLASSES OF NETWORKS

There are a number of ways of classifying communications networks. We touched on this topic briefly in Chapter 1 and are now in a position to examine it in more depth.

One way to classify networks is in terms of the technology used: specifically, in terms of topology and transmission medium. This chapter has introduced these basic elements. As we shall see, the same topologies and transmission media are repeated in a wide variety of networks.

Perhaps the most commonly used means of classification is on the basis of geographical scope. Traditionally, networks have been classified as either local area networks (LANs) or wide-area networks (WANs). A category that has recently begun to receive much attention is the metropolitan area network (MAN).

Figure 3.6 illustrates these categories, plus some special cases. Table 3.8 summarizes key performance parameters. We examine each of these in turn.

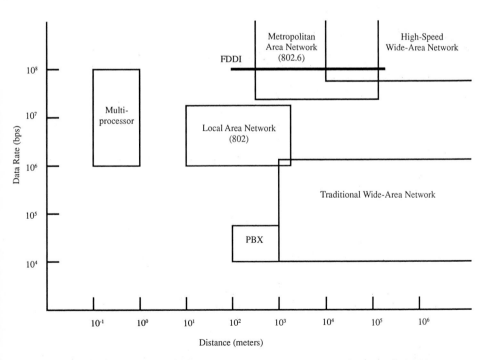

FIGURE 3.6 Comparison of Multiprocessor Systems, LANs, MANs, and WANs

TABLE 3.8   Characteristics of LANs, MANs, and WANs

Network	Data Rate	Distance Covered
Local Area Network (IEEE 802)	1–20 Mbps	< 25 km
Fiber Distributed Data Interface	100 Mbps	< 200 km
Metropolitan Area Network (IEEE 802.6)	30 Mbps–1$^+$Gps	<160 km
Traditional Wide-Area Network	10 kbps–1.5 Mbps	unlimited
High-Speed Wide-Area Network	50 Mbps–1$^+$Gbps	unlimited

Wide-Area Network

Wide-area networks have traditionally been considered to be those that cover a large geographical area, require the crossing of public right-of-ways, and rely at least in part on circuits provided by a common carrier. Such WANs are typically switched communications networks, consisting of an interconnected set of switching nodes (see Figure 2.9); each station attaches to one of the nodes. As was discussed in Chapter 2, a WAN may be either circuit-switched or packet-switched.

Until recently, WANs have provided only relatively modest capacity to subscribers. For data attachment, either to a packet-switching network or to a circuit-switching network by means of a modem, data rates of 9600 bps or even less have been common. Business subscribers have been able to obtain higher rates, with a service known as T-1, which operates at 1.544 Mbps. The most important recent development in WANs in this range of performance has been the development of the integrated services digital network (ISDN), which provides circuit-switching and packet-switching services at rates up to 1.544 Mbps (2.048 Mbps in Europe). The basic user interface to ISDN is multirate circuit switching using twisted pair.

The continuing development of practical optical fiber facilities has led to the standardization of much higher data rates for WANs, and we can expect these services to become widely available over the next few years, certainly by the end of the 1990s. These high-speed WANs provide user connections in the 10's and 100's of Mbps. The most important effort in this regard is the standardization of a broadband integrated services digital network (B-ISDN) that uses cell relay rather than circuit switching.

WANs are beyond the scope (no pun intended) of this book.

Local Area Network

As with wide-area networks, a local area network is a communications network that interconnects a variety of devices and provides a means for information exchange among those devices. There are several key distinctions between LANs and WANs:

1. The scope of the LAN is small, typically a single building or a cluster of buildings. This difference in geographic scope leads to different technical solutions. In particular, LANs almost invariably employ a shared medium topology (bus, tree, ring, passive, or active star) as opposed to a switching network architecture, and they use a packet broadcasting technique.
2. It is usually the case that the LAN is owned by the same organization that owns the attached devices. For WANs, this is less often the case, or at least a significant fraction of the network assets are not owned. This has two implications. First, care must be taken in the choice of LAN, since there may be a substantial capital investment (compared to dial-up or leased charges for wide-area networks) for both purchase and maintenance. Second, the network management responsibility for a local network falls solely on the user.
3. The internal data rates of LANs are much greater than those of wide-area networks.

LANs have been the focus of a standardization effort by the IEEE 802 committee, and it is perhaps useful to quote their definition of a LAN [IEEE90]:

> The LANs described herein are distinguished from other types of data networks in that they are optimized for a moderate size geographic area such as a single office building, a warehouse, or a campus. The IEEE 802 LAN is a shared medium peer-to-peer communications network that broadcasts information for all stations to receive. As a consequence, it does not inherently provide privacy. The LAN enables stations to communicate directly using a common physical medium on a point-to-point basis without any intermediate switching node being required. There is always need for an access sublayer in order to arbitrate the access to the shared medium. The network is generally owned, used, and operated by a single organization. This is in contrast to Wide Area Networks (WANs) that interconnect communication facilities in different parts of a country or are used as a public utility. These LANs are also different from networks, such as backplane buses, that are optimized for the interconnection of devices on a desk top or components within a single piece of equipment.

The committee was given a charter to develop standards for networks in the range of 1 to 20 Mbps.

Metropolitan Area Networks

As the name suggests, a MAN occupies a middle ground between LANs and WANs. Interest in MANs has come about as a result of a recognition that the traditional point-to-point and switched network techniques used in WANs may be inadequate for the growing needs of organizations. While broadband ISDN, with cell relay, holds out promise for meeting a wide range of high-speed needs, there is a requirement now for both private and public networks that provide high capacity at low costs over a large area. The high-speed shared-medium approach of the LAN standards provides a number of benefits that can be realized on a metropolitan scale.

Over many years of research on MANs, a number of alternatives have been explored and rejected. One approach has emerged that has received widespread support from providers and users, and has been standardized by the IEEE 802 committee as IEEE 802.6. Again, it is useful to look at their definition:

> A MAN is optimized for a larger geographical area than a LAN, ranging from several blocks of buildings to entire cities. As with local networks, MANs can also depend on communications channels of moderate-to-high data rates. Error rates and delay may be slightly higher than might be obtained on a LAN. A MAN might be owned and operated by a single organization, but usually will be used by many individuals and organizations. MANs might also be owned and operated as public utilities. They will often provide means for internetworking of local networks. Although not a requirement for all LANs, the capability to perform local networking of integrated voice and data (IVD) devices is considered an optional function for a LAN. Likewise, such capabilities in a network covering a metropolitan area are optional functions of a MAN.

Whereas the LANs defined by IEEE 802 are typically used only to support data traffic, the 802.6 MAN is intended for the support of both data and voice traffic. As Figure 3.6 indicates, MANs cover greater distances at higher data rates than LANs, although there is some overlap in geographical coverage.

The primary market for MANs is the customer that has high-capacity needs in a metropolitan area. A MAN is intended to provide the required capacity at lower cost and greater efficiency than obtaining an equivalent service from the local telephone company.

The MAN, as defined in IEEE 802.6, shares many characteristics with LANs. As with LANs, the MAN uses packet broadcasting over a shared transmission medium. As we will see, the MAN defined by 802.6 uses a bus topology.

Fiber Distributed Data Interface

The fiber distributed data interface (FDDI) is a network standard developed by the American National Standards Institute (ANSI) that specifies a 100-Mbps optical fiber ring network. In the literature, FDDI is generally considered to be a LAN and, indeed, most of the existing installations are within a single building or small cluster of buildings. FDDI is designed to provide high end-to-end throughput between expensive, high-speed devices such as mainframes and mass storage devices. It is also used as a backbone network to connect a number of lower-speed LANs.

As with the typical LAN, FDDI was originally defined to use packet broadcasting and to support data traffic. A recent enhancement to the standard, known as FDDI-II, provides support for voice traffic and other applications that normally use circuit switching.

As Table 3.8 and Figure 3.6 indicate, FDDI can be considered either to be a high-speed LAN or a MAN. The classification is somewhat arbitrary. However, for purposes of this book, it is more convenient to present the technical details of FDDI in the chapter on MANs, and that is the course that is followed.

Circuit-Switched Local Networks

In contrast to LANs and MANs, which use packet broadcasting, there is another approach to local networking using circuit switching. Typically, circuit-switching local networks have a star or hierarchical star topology using twisted-pair wire to connect end points to the switch. In the hierarchical star, high-speed trunks of coaxial cable or optical fiber may be used to connect satellite switching units to the central switching unit. Data rates to individual stations are typically low (≤64 kbps), but bandwidth is guaranteed and there is essentially no network delay once a connection is made.

One form of circuit-switched local network is the digital private branch exchange (PBX). This is an on-premise switch designed to handle both voice and data connections. Although the strength of these systems is their support from telephones, they are also well suited to terminal-to-host data traffic. Another form of circuit-switched local network is the digital data switch. Devices in this category are designed to handle data only, not voice, and are typically lower in cost than a digital PBX of comparable size.

Traditionally, the term *LAN* has been reserved for the packet-broadcasting, shared-medium networks of relatively high data rates indicated in Figure 3.6. Although a circuit-switched local network certainly provides local area coverage, the differences in architecture and data rate compared to LANs is such that these networks need to be treated separately.

3.5

RECOMMENDED READING

Detailed descriptions of the transmission characteristics of the transmission media discussed in this chapter can be found in [FREE91] and [BELL90]. A number of books provide detailed coverage of optical fiber transmission. Two that can be recommended are [DIAM90] and [ZANG91]; the former concentrates on the principles of optical transmission, while the latter is concerned with optical communications systems. [STAL93a] contains reprints of many key articles on LAN/MAN technology.

3.6

PROBLEMS

3.1 What functions should be performed by the network layer (layer 3) in a bus topology local network? Ring topology? Star topology?

3.2 Could HDLC be used as a link layer for a bus topology local network? If not, what is missing? Answer for ring and star.

3.3 An asynchronous device, such as a teletype, transmits characters one at a time with unpredictable delays between characters. What problems, if any, do you foresee if such a device is connected to a local network and allowed to transmit at will (subject to gaining access to the medium)? How might such problems be resolved? Answer for ring, bus, and star.

3.4 Which combination or combinations of medium and topology would be appropriate for the following applications, and why?

a. Terminal intensive: many terminals throughout an office: one or a few shared central computers

b. Small network: fewer than 50 devices, all low speed (<56 kbps)

c. Office automation: a few hundred devices, mostly terminals and minicomputers

3.5 Consider the transfer of a file containing one million characters from one section to another. What is the total elapsed time and effective throughput for the following cases:

a. A circuit-switched, star topology local network. Call setup time is negligible, and the data rate on the medium is 64 kbps.

b. A bus topology local network with two stations a distance D

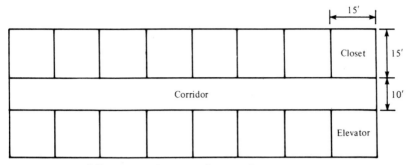

FIGURE 3.7 Building Layout for a Local Network

apart, a data rate of B bps, and a packet size P with 80 bits of overhead. Each packet is acknowledged with an 88-bit packet before the text is sent. The propagation speed on the bus is 200 m/μsec. Solve for:

(1): $D = 1$ km, $B = 1$ Mbps, $P = 256$ bits
(2): $D = 1$ km, $B = 10$ Mbps, $P = 256$ bits
(3): $D = 10$ km, $B = 1$ Mbps, $P = 256$ bits
(4): $D = 1$ km, $B = 50$ Mbps, $P = 10,000$ bits

c. A ring topology with a total circular length of $2D$, with the two stations a distance D apart. Acknowledgment is achieved by allowing a packet to circulate past the destination station, back to the source station. There are N repeaters on the ring, each of which introduces a delay of 1 bit time. Repeat the calculation for each of b1 through b4 for $N = 10; 100; 1000$.

3.6 A 10-story office building has the floor plan of Figure 3.7 for each floor. A local network is to be installed that will allow attachment of a device from each office on each floor. Attachment is to take place along the outside wall at the baseboard. Cable or wire can be run vertically through the indicated closet and horizontally along the baseboards. The height of each story is 10 ft. What is the minimum total length of cable or wire required for bus, tree, ring, and star topologies?

3.7 A tree-topology local network is to be provided that spans two buildings. If permission can be obtained to string cable between the two buildings, then one continuous tree layout will be used. Otherwise, each building will have an independent tree topology network and a point-to-point link will connect a special communications station on one network with a communications station on the other network. What functions must the communications stations perform? Repeat for ring and star.

CHAPTER 4

Topologies and Transmission Media for LANs and MANs

Recall that the three principal characteristics of a LAN or MAN are transmission medium, topology, and medium access control. In this chapter, we examine the first two of these in some detail. The complex subject of medium access control is dealt with for LANs and MANs separately in the following two chapters. The first two sections examine metallic media (twisted pair, coaxial cable) and the various topologies that are employed. The next two sections concentrate on optical fiber. Throughout, reference is made to the IEEE 802 standards, developed by a committee of the Institute of Electrical and Electronic Engineers, and the FDDI standard, developed by a committee of the American National Standards Institute. These committees and their work are discussed in the appendices to Chapters 5 and 6.

4.1

METALLIC MEDIA: BUS/TREE TOPOLOGY

Characteristics of Bus/Tree LANs

Of the topologies discussed in the preceding chapter, only the bus/tree topology is a multipoint medium. That is, there are more than two devices connected to and capable of transmitting on the medium.

The operation of this type of LAN can be summarized briefly. Because multiple devices share a single data path, only one may transmit at a time. A station usually transmits data in the form of a packet containing the address of the destination. The packet propagates throughout the medium and is received by all other stations. The addressed station copies the packet as it goes by.

Two transmission techniques are in use for bus/tree LANs on metallic media: baseband and broadband. *Baseband,* using digital signaling, can be employed on twisted-pair or coaxial cable. *Broadband,* using analog signaling in the radio-frequency (RF) range, employs coaxial cable. Some of the differences are highlighted in Table 4.1, and this section explores the two methods in some detail. There is also a variant, known as *single-channel broadband,* that has the signaling characteristics of broadband but some of the restrictions of baseband. This is also covered below.

The multipoint nature of the bus/tree topology gives rise to several rather stiff problems. First is the problem of determining which station on the medium may transmit at any point in time. With point-to-point links (only two stations on the medium), this is a fairly simple task. If the line is full-duplex, both stations may transmit at the same time; if the line is half-duplex, a rather simple mechanism is needed to ensure that the two stations take turns. Historically, the most common shared access scheme has been the multidrop line, in which access is determined by polling from a controlling station. The controlling station may send data to any other station, or it may issue a poll to a specific station, asking for an immediate response. This method, however, negates some of the advantages of a distributed system and is awkward for communication between two noncontroller stations. A variety of distributed strategies, referred to as *medium access control protocols,* have now been developed for bus and tree topologies. These are discussed in Chapter 5.

A second problem has to do with signal balancing. When two devices exchange data over a link, the signal strength of the transmitter must be adjusted to be within certain limits. The signal must be strong enough so that after attenuation across the medium it meets the receiver's minimum signal strength requirements. It must also be strong enough to

TABLE 4.1   Bus/Tree Transmission Techniques

Baseband	**Broadband**
Digital signaling	Analog signaling (requires RF modem)
Entire bandwidth consumed by signal—no FDM	FDM possible—multiple data channels, video, audio
Bidirectional	Unidirectional
Bus topology	Bus or tree topology
Distance: up to a few kilometers	Distance: up to 10's of kilometers

maintain an adequate signal-to-noise ratio. On the other hand, the signal must not be so strong that it overloads the circuitry of the transmitter, which creates harmonics and other spurious signals. Although easily done for a point-to-point link, signal balancing is no easy task for a multipoint line. If any device can transmit to any other device, then the signal balancing must be performed for all permutations of stations taken two at a time. For n stations that works out to $n \times (n - 1)$ permutations. So for a 200-station network (not a particularly large system), 39,800 signal strength constraints must be satisfied simultaneously. With interdevice distances ranging from tens to thousands of meters, this is an impossible task for any but small networks. In systems that use radio-frequency (RF) signals, the problem is compounded because of the possibility of RF signal interference across frequencies. The solution is to divide the medium into segments within which pairwise balancing is possible, using amplifiers or repeaters between segments.

Baseband Systems

The principal characteristics of a baseband system are listed in Table 4.1. As mentioned earlier, a baseband LAN is defined as one that uses digital signaling. (This is a restricted use of the word *baseband*, which has become accepted in local network circles. More generally, *baseband* refers to the transmission of an analog or digital signal in its original form, without modulation.) Digital signals are inserted on the line as voltage pulses, usually using either Manchester or Differential Manchester encoding. The entire frequency spectrum of the medium is used to form the signal; hence frequency-division multiplexing (FDM) cannot be used. Transmission is bidirectional. That is, a signal inserted at any point on the medium propagates in both directions to the ends, where it is absorbed (Figure 4.1a). The digital signaling requires a bus topology. Unlike analog signals, digital signals cannot easily be propagated through the splitters and joiners required for a tree topology. Baseband systems can extend only a limited distance, about 1 km at most. This is because the attenuation of the signal, which is most pronounced at higher frequencies, causes a blurring of the pulses and a weakening of the signal to the extent that communication over larger distances is impractical.

Baseband Coax. The most well-known form of baseband bus LAN uses coaxial cable. We concentrate on those systems in this section. Unless otherwise indicated, the discussion is based on the Ethernet system [METC76. SHOC82, DIGI80] and the almost-identical IEEE standard [IEEE90b].

Most baseband coaxial cable systems use a special 50-ohm cable rather than the standard CATV 75-ohm cable. These values refer to the

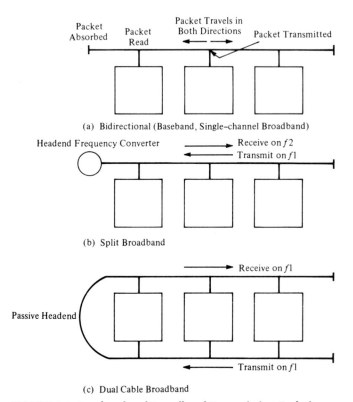

(a) Bidirectional (Baseband, Single–channel Broadband)

(b) Split Broadband

(c) Dual Cable Broadband

FIGURE 4.1 Baseband and Broadband Transmission Techniques

impedance of the cable. Roughly speaking, impedance is a measure of how much voltage must be applied to the cable to achieve a given signal strength (see Appendix 4A). For digital signals, the 50-ohm cable suffers less intense reflections from the insertion capacitance of the taps and provides better immunity against low-frequency electromagnetic noise. The simplest baseband coaxial bus LAN consists of an unbranched length of coaxial cable with a terminating resistance at each end. The value of the resistance is set equal to the impedance of the cable; this prevents reflection by absorbing any signal on the cable.

As with any transmission system, there are engineering trade-offs involving data rate, cable length, number of taps, and the electrical characteristics of the transmit and receive components for a baseband coaxial system. For example, the lower the data rate, the longer the cable can be. That latter statement is true for the following reason: when a signal is propagated along a transmission medium, the integrity of the signal suffers due to attenuation, noise, and other impairments. The longer the length of propagation, the greater the effect, increasing the probability of error. However, at a lower data rate, the individual pulses of a digital signal last longer and can be recovered in the presence of impairments more easily than higher-rate, shorter pulses.

With the above in mind, we give one example that illustrates some of the trade-offs. The Ethernet specification and the original IEEE standard specified the use of 50-ohm cable with a 0.4-inch diameter and a data rate of 10 Mbps. With these parameters, the maximum length of the cable is set at 500 meters. Stations attach to the cable by means of a tap, with the distance between any two taps being a multiple of 2.5 m; this is to ensure that reflections from adjacent taps do not add in phase [YEN83]. A maximum of 100 taps is allowed. In IEEE jargon, this system is referred to as "10base5." The first two digits give the data rate in megabits per second; the four letters are an abbreviation for the medium (baseband); and the final digit is the maximum cable length in hundreds of meters.

To provide a lower-cost system for personal computer local networks, IEEE later added a 10base2 specification [METC83, FLAT84, JONE85]. Table 4.2 compares this system, dubbed Cheapernet, with the 10base5 specification. The key difference is the thinner (0.25 in) cable used in products like public address systems. The thinner cable is more flexible; thus it is easier to bend around corners and bring to a workstation cabinet rather than installing cable in the wall and having to provide a drop cable to the station. The cable is easier to install and requires cheaper electronics than the thicker cable. On the other hand, the thinner cable suffers greater attenuation and lower noise resistance than the thicker cable. Thus it supports fewer taps over a shorter distance.

Figure 4.2, from the Ethernet specification, illustrates typical components and their functions. The main components are:

- Transceiver
- Transceiver cable
- Controller
- 50-ohm coaxial cable
- 50-ohm terminators

TABLE 4.2   IEEE Specifications for 10-Mbps Baseband Coaxial Bus Local Networks

Parameter	10base5	10base2
Data Rate	10 Mbps	10 Mbps
Maximum Segment Length	500 m	200 m
Network Span	2500 m	1000 m
Nodes per Segment	100	30
Node Spacing	2.5 m	0.5 m
Cable Diameter	0.4 in	0.25 in

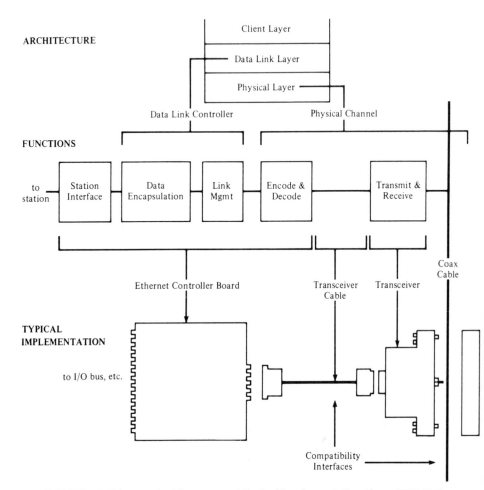

FIGURE 4.2 Ethernet Architecture and Typical Implementation (from [DIGI80])

The transceiver taps into the coaxial cable. It transmits signals from the station to the cable, and vice versa. It also contains the electronics necessary to recognize the presence of a signal on the coaxial cable and to recognize a collision of two signals. This last function is needed for Ethernet and 802 because of the CSMA/CD protocol that they use (discussed in Chapter 5). A baseband bus LAN using some other protocol would not require this complexity. The transceiver also provides ground isolation between the signals from the station and the signals on the cable. Since two local grounds may differ by several volts, connection of local grounds to the cable could cause a large current to flow through the cable's shield, introducing noise and creating a safety hazard.

The transceiver cable comprises two twisted pair (referred to as twin pair) and connects the transceiver to the controller, which contains the bulk of the intelligence required to communicate over the LAN. This split is arbitrary: all of the electronics could be included at the transceiver end. The split is motivated by the assumption that the station will be located some distance from the cable and that the cable tap may be in a relatively inaccessible location. Hence the electronics at the tap should be as simple as possible to reduce maintenance costs. The cable supplies power to the transceiver and passes data signals between the transceiver and the controller as well as control signals. The latter includes a collision presence signal from transceiver to controller. Other signals are possible. For example, the 802 standard has isolate and cease-to-isolate signals that allow the controller to enable and disable the transceiver.

The controller is an implementation of all the functions (other than those performed by the transceiver) needed to manage access to the coax cable for the purpose of exchanging packets between the coax cable and the attached station. More will be said about the particular functions in Chapter 5.

Finally, the transmission system consists of 50-ohm coaxial cable and terminators. The terminators absorb signals, preventing reflection from the ends of the bus.

These five types of components are sufficient for building a baseband bus LAN of up to about 1 km with up to about 100 stations. In many cases, this will be enough, but for greater requirements, an additional component is needed: the repeater.

The repeater is used to extend the length of the network. It consists, in essence, of two transceivers joined together and connected to two different segments of coaxial cable. The repeater passes digital signals in both directions between the two segments, amplifying and regenerating the signals as they pass through. A repeater is transparent to the rest of the system; since it does no buffering, it in no sense isolates one segment from another. So, for example, if two stations on different segments attempt to transmit at the same time, their packets will interfere with each other (collide). To avoid multipath interference, only one path of segments and repeaters is allowed between any two stations. The 802 standard allows a maximum of four repeaters in the path between any two stations, extending the effective cable length of 2.5 km. Figure 4.3 is an example of a baseband system with three segments and two repeaters.

Broadband Systems

Like the term *baseband*, the term *broadband* is co-opted into the local network vocabulary from the telecommunications world, with a change in meaning. In general, broadband refers to any channel having a bandwidth greater than a voice-grade channel (4 kHz). In the local network

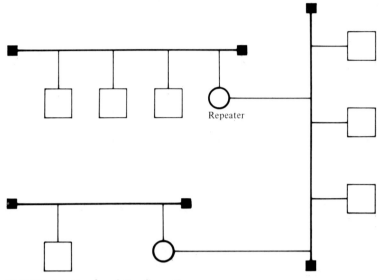

FIGURE 4.3 Baseband Configuration

context, the term refers to coaxial cable on which analog signaling is used. A further restriction to transmission techniques that allow frequency-division multiplexing (FDM) on the cable is usually applied. We will mean systems capable of FDM when using the term *broadband*. Systems intended to carry only a single analog signal will be referred to as *carrierband*.

Table 4.1 summarizes the key characteristics of broadband systems. As mentioned, broadband implies the use of analog signaling. FDM is possible: the frequency spectrum of the cable can be divided into channels or sections of bandwidth. Separate channels can support data traffic, television, and radio signals. Broadband components allow splitting and joining operations; hence both bus and tree topologies are possible. Much greater distance—tens of kilometers—are possible with broadband compared to baseband. This is because the analog signals that carry the digital data can propagate greater distances before the noise and attenuation damage the data.

Dual and Split Configurations.   As with baseband, stations on a broadband LAN attach to the cable by means of a tap. Unlike baseband, however, broadband is inherently a unidirectional medium; the taps that are used allow signals inserted onto the medium to propagate in only one direction. The primary reason for this is that it is infeasible to build amplifiers that will pass signals of one frequency in both directions. This unidimensional property means that only those stations "downstream" from a transmitting station can receive its signals. How, then, can full connectivity be achieved?

Clearly, two data paths are needed. These paths are joined at a point on the network known as the **headend.** For a bus topology, the headend is simply one end of the bus. For a tree topology, the headend is the root of the branching tree. All stations transmit on one path toward the headend (inbound). Signals arriving at the headend are then propagated along a second data path away from the headend (outbound). All stations receive on the outbound path.

Physically, two different configurations are used to implement the inbound and outbound paths. (Figure 4.1 b and c). On a **dual-cable** configuration, the inbound and outbound paths are separate cables, with the headend simply a passive connector between the two. Stations send and receive on the same frequency.

By contrast, on a **split** configuration, the inbound and outbound paths are different frequency bands on the same cable. Bidirectional amplifiers[1] pass lower frequencies inbound and pass higher frequencies outbound. Between the inbound and outbound frequency bands is a guardband that carries no signals and serves merely as a separator. The headend contains a device for converting inbound frequencies to outbound frequencies.

The frequency-conversion device at the headend can be either an analog or a digital device. An analog device, known as a **frequency translator,** converts a block of frequencies from one range to another. A digital device, known as a **remodulator,** recovers the digital data from the inbound analog signal and then retransmits the data on the outbound frequency. Thus, a remodulator provides better signal quality by removing all of the accumulated noise and attenuation and transmitting a cleaned-up signal.

Split systems are categorized by the frequency allocation of the two paths, as shown in Table 4.3. Subsplit, commonly used by the cable television industry, was designed for metropolitan area television distribution, with limited subscriber-to-central office communication. It provides the easiest way to upgrade existing one-way cable systems to two-way operation. Subsplit has limited usefulness for local area networking because a bandwidth of only 25 MHz is available for two-way communication. Midsplit is more suitable for LANs, since it provides a more equitable distribution of bandwidth. However, midsplit was developed at a time when the practical spectrum of a cable-TV cable was 300 MHz, whereas a spectrum of 400 to 450 MHz is now available. Ac-

[1]Unfortunately, this terminology is confusing, since we have said that broadband is inherently a unidirectional medium. At a given frequency, broadband is unidirectional. However, there is no difficulty in having signals in nonoverlapping frequency bands traveling in opposite directions on the cable, and in amplifying those signals.

TABLE 4.3   Common Cable Frequency Splits

Format	Inbound Frequency Band	Outbound Frequency Band	Maximum Two-way Bandwidth
Subsplit	5 to 30 MHz	54 to 400 MHz	25 MHz
Midsplit	5 to 116 MHz	168 to 400 MHz	111 MHz
High-split	5 to 174 MHz	232 to 400 MHz	168 MHz
Dual Cable	40 to 400 MHz	40 to 400 MHz	360 MHz

cordingly, a high-split specification has been developed to provide greater two-way bandwidth for a split-cable system.

The differences between split and dual configurations are minor. The split system is useful when a single-cable plant is already installed in a building. If a large amount of bandwidth is needed, or the need is anticipated, then a dual-cable system is indicated. Beyond these considerations, it is a matter of a trade-off between cost and size. The single-cable system has the fixed cost of the headend remodulator or frequency translator. The dual-cable system makes use of more cable, taps, splitters, and amplifiers. Thus, dual cable is cheaper for smaller systems, where the fixed cost of the headend is noticeable, and single cable is cheaper for larger systems, where incremental costs dominate.

Broadband Components.   Broadband systems use standard, off-the-shelf cable television components, including 75-ohm coaxial cable. All endpoints are terminated with a 75-ohm terminator to absorb signals (see Appendix 4A). Broadband is suitable for tens of kilometers radius from the headend and hundreds or even thousands of devices. The main components of the system are:

- Cable
- Terminators
- Amplifiers
- Directional couplers
- Modems
- Controllers

Cables used in broadband networks are of three types. **Trunk cable** forms the spine of a large LAN system. Trunk cables use a semirigid construction. As the name implies, semirigid cable is not flexible. The outer portion of the cable is made of solid aluminum. The cable can be bent, but not too many times and not very easily. Trunk lines come in six sizes, ranging from 0.412 to 1 inch in diameter. The greater the diameter of the cable, the lower the attenuation. Semirigid cable has excellent noise rejection characteristics and can be used indoors and outdoors. Typically, a trunk cable will extend from a few kilometers to tens of kilometers.

Distribution cables, or **feeder cables,** are used for shorter distances and for branch cables. They may be semirigid or flexible, and are typically 0.4 to 0.5 inch in diameter. Whereas trunk cables may be used indoors or outdoors, feeder cables are generally limited to indoor use. The choice of cable depends on a number of criteria [COOP84]:

- The physical constraints of the route: smaller-diameter cables are easier to install.
- The required signal level for the distribution network: larger-diameter cables have less signal loss.
- Local and national building codes.

The flexible cable most commonly used for feeder cable has the designation RG-11. With a diameter of 0.405 inches, and with poorer noise resistance than semirigid cable, distance is limited to about 800 meters.

Drop cables are used to connect outlets and stations to distribution cables. These are short (10 to 50 feet) and therefore need not be very large in diameter; although attenuation per unit length is greater for narrower cable, the short distance means that the total attenuation will be small even with a narrow cable. The cables used are flexible and include RG-59 (0.242 in diameter), RG-6 (0.332 inch), and RG-11 (0.405 inch) cables.

Amplifiers may be used on trunk and distribution cables to compensate for cable attenuation. As Figure 4.4 indicates, attenuation on a cable is an increasing function of frequency. Therefore, amplifiers must have a slope to account for the variability of attenuation. For split systems, amplifiers must be bidirectional, passing and amplifying lower frequencies in one direction and higher frequencies in the other.

Directional couplers provide a means for dividing one input into two outputs and combining two inputs into one output. **Splitters,** used to branch the cable, provide roughly equal attenuation along the split branches. **Taps,** used to connect drop cables and hence stations to the LAN, provide more attenuation to the drop cable. Figure 4-5 illustrates these concepts.

Modems are needed to convert between the digital data on the attached stations and the analog signal on the medium. A variety of modulation techniques are in use. The two most common, which are endorsed for use on IEEE-802-standard LANs (see Appendix 5A), are differential phase-shift keying (DPSK), used with IEEE 802.3 and duobinary AM/PSK, used with IEEE 802.4.

In ordinary PSK, a binary zero is represented by a carrier with a particular phase, and a binary one is represented by a carrier with the opposite phase (180-degree difference). DPSK makes use of differential

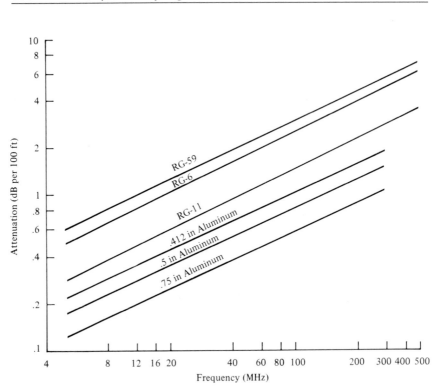

FIGURE 4.4 Cable Attenuation versus Frequency for Various Sizes of Coaxial Cable

encoding, in which a change of phase occurs when a zero occurs, and there is no change of phase when a one occurs. The advantage of differential encoding is that it is easier for the receiver to detect the presence or absence of a change of phase than it is to determine the phase itself.

In duobinary AM/PSK, a special narrow-bandwidth pulse is created that is used to amplitude-modulate an RF carrier. Such pulse is illustrated in Figure 4.6 for a 10-Mbps data rate; the pulse of opposite polarity is also used. Note that the pulse spreads over a number of bit time. Thus, pulses that are generated in nearby bit slots will overlap. However, the overlap is highly predictable: at each sample point, a pulse has a value of 0 or 1. Thus, at any sample point, a 0, 1, or 2 can be detected. To encode digital data, two pulses, one bit time apart, are used. A binary one is represented by two consecutive pulses of the same polarity, which will produce a sample of +2 or −2, and a binary zero is represented by two consecutive pulses of opposite polarity, which produces a sample of 0. Each pulse participates in 2 bits; that is, each pulse is both the second pulse of one bit and the first pulse of the next bit.

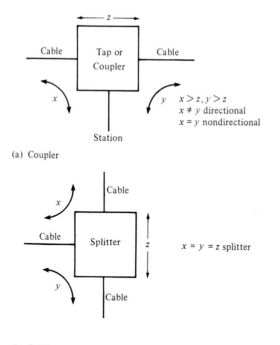

(a) Coupler

(b) Splitter

x, y, z = attenuation

FIGURE 4.5 Directional Couplers and Splitters

A characteristic common to virtually all broadband LAN modems is the use of scrambling. This gives the data a pseudorandom nature that helps the receiver extract bit-timing information. It also improves the spectral characteristics of the signal, giving it a more uniform power distribution, as opposed to the potentially strong discrete spectral lines

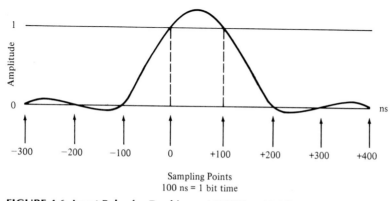

Sampling Points
100 ns = 1 bit time

FIGURE 4.6 Input Pulse for Duobinary AM/PSK at 10 Mbps

in nonscrambled data. This gives the signal better noise resistance. The scrambling process is explained in Appendix 4C.

Finally, **controllers** are needed, as in baseband, to provide the basic LAN service.

Data Transmission Services.   As mentioned earlier, the broadband LAN can be used to carry multiple channels, some used for analog signals, such as video and voice, and some for digital. Digital channels can generally carry a data rate of somewhere between 0.5 and 2 bps/Hz. Figure 4.7 shows a possible allocation of a 350-MHz cable.

Three kinds of digital data transfer service are possible on a broadband cable: dedicated, switched, and multiple access (Figure 4.8). For dedicated service, a small portion of the cable's bandwidth is reserved for exclusive use by two devices. No special protocol is needed. Each of the two devices attaches to the cable through a modem; both modems are tuned to the same frequency. This technique is analogous to securing a dedicated leased line from the telephone company. The dedicated service could be used to connect two devices when a heavy traffic pattern is expected; for example, one computer may act as a standby for another and may need to get frequent updates of state information and file and database changes. Transfer rates of up to 20 Mbps are achievable.

The switched technique requires the use of a number of frequency bands. Devices are attached through *frequency-agile modems,* capable of changing their frequency by electronic command. Initially, all attached devices, together with a controller, are tuned to the same frequency. A station wishing to establish a connection sends a request to the controller, which assigns an available frequency to the two devices and signals their modems to tune to that frequency. This technique is analogous to a dial-up line. Because the cost of frequency-agile modems rises dramatically with data rate, rates of 56 kbps or less are typical. The switched technique is used in Wang's local network for terminal-to-host connections [STAH82] and could also be used for voice service.

Finally, the multiple-access service allows a number of attached devices to be supported at the same frequency. This provides for distributed peer communications among many devices, which is the primary motivation for a local network. As with baseband, some form of medium access control protocol is needed to control transmission. These protocols are discussed in Chapter 5.

Baseband versus Broadband

Table 4.4 summarizes the pros and cons of the two technologies. Baseband has the advantage of simplicity, and, in principle, lower cost. The layout of a baseband cable plant is simple; there are just five rules for

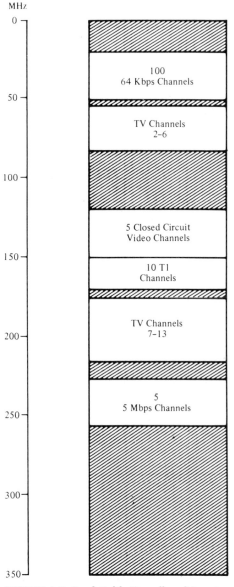

FIGURE 4.7 Dual-Cable Broadband Spectrum Allocation

trunk layout in the Ethernet specification. An office-building electrician should be able to do the job.

The potential disadvantages of baseband include the limitations in capacity and distance—disadvantages only if your requirements exceed those limitations. Another concern has to do with grounding. Because dc components are on the cable, it can be grounded in only one place.

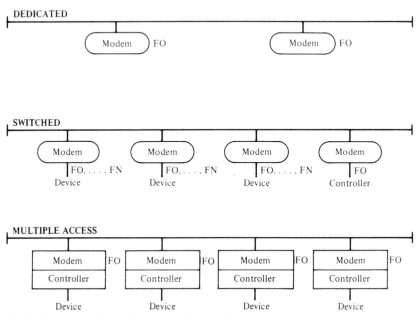

FIGURE 4.8 Broadband Data Transfer Services

Care must be taken to avoid potential shock hazards and antenna effects.

Broadband's strength is its tremendous capacity; it can carry a wide variety of traffic on a number of channels. With the use of amplifiers, broadband can achieve very wide area coverage. Also, the system is based on a mature CATV technology. Components are reliable and readily available.

TABLE 4.4   Baseband versus Broadband

Advantages	Disadvantages
Baseband	
Cheaper—no modem	Single channel
Simpler technology	Limited capacity
Easy to install	Limited distance
	Grounding concerns
Broadband	
High capacity	Modem cost
Multiple traffic types	Installation and maintenance complexity
More flexible configurations	Doubled propagation delay
Large area coverage	
Mature CATV technology	

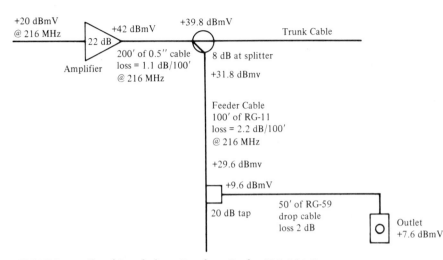

FIGURE 4.9 Signal Levels from Trunk to Outlet [COOP84]

Broadband systems are more complex than baseband to install and maintain. The layout design must include cable type selection, and placement and setting of all amplifiers and taps. To get some feeling for the complexity of broadband cable layout design, consider Figure 4.9, which shows a small portion of a cable plant.[2] In order to assure that the signal level at each station or outlet is within prescribed tolerances, the engineer must consider the attenuation loss along each cable segment, the loss at each splitter and tap, and the gain at each amplifier. These losses and gains must be balanced to provide proper signal levels throughout the LAN. Maintenance involves periodic testing and alignment of all network parameters. These are jobs for experienced radio-frequency engineers.

Finally, the average propagation delay between stations on broadband is twice that for a comparable baseband system. This reduces the efficiency and performance of the broadband system, as discussed in Chapter 9.

As with all other network design choices, the selection of baseband or broadband must be based on relative costs and benefits. It is likely that some installations will have both types. Neither is likely to win the LAN war.

Carrierband Systems

There is another application of analog signaling on a LAN, known as carrierband, or single-channel broadband. In this case, the entire spec-

___
[2]The figure uses dB and dBmV units: these are explained in Appendix 4B.

trum of the cable is devoted to a single transmission path for the analog signals; no frequency-division multiplexing is possible.

Typically, a carrierband LAN has the following characteristics. Bidirectional transmission, using a bus topology, is employed. Hence there can be no amplifiers, and there is no need for a headend. Although the entire spectrum is used, most of the signal energy is concentrated at relatively low frequencies. This is an advantage, because attenuation is less at lower frequencies.

Because the cable is dedicated to a single task, it is not necessary to take care that the modem output be confined to a narrow bandwidth. Energy can spread over the entire spectrum. As a result, the electronics are simple and relatively inexpensive. Typically, some form of frequency-shift keying (FSK) is used.

Carrierband would appear to give comparable performance, at a comparable price, to baseband.

4.2

METALLIC MEDIA: STAR TOPOLOGY

In recent years, there has been increasing interest in the use of twisted pair as a transmission medium for LANs. From the earliest days of commercial LAN availability, twisted-pair bus LANs have been popular. However, such LANs suffer in comparison with a coaxial cable LAN. First of all, the apparent cost advantage of twisted pair is not as great as it might seem when a linear bus layout is used. True, twisted-pair cable is less expensive than coaxial cable. On the other hand, much of the cost of LAN wiring is the labor cost of installing the cable, which is no greater for coaxial cable than for twisted pair. Second, coaxial cable provides superior signal quality, and therefore it can support more devices over longer distances at higher data rates than twisted pair.

The renewed interest in twisted pair, at least in the context of bus/tree–type LANs, is in the use of unshielded twisted pair in a star wiring arrangement (see discussion in Section 3.3). The reason for the interest is that unshielded twisted pair is simply telephone wire, and virtually all office buildings are equipped with spare twisted pairs running from wiring closets to each office. This yields two benefits when deploying a LAN:

1. There is essentially no installation cost with unshielded twisted pair, since the wire is already there. Coaxial cable has to be pulled. In older buildings, this may be difficult since existing conduits may be crowded.
2. In most office buildings, it is impossible to anticipate all the locations where network access will be needed. Since it is extrava-

gantly expensive to run coaxial cable to every office, a coaxial cable–based LAN will typically cover only a portion of a building. If equipment subsequently has to be moved to an office not covered by the LAN, a significant expense is involved in extending the LAN coverage. With telephone wire, this problem does not arise, since all offices are covered.

The most popular approach to the use of unshielded twisted pair for a LAN is therefore a star-wiring approach. In Figure 3.5a we indicated how a star-wiring approach was compatible with a bus topology. In general, however, the products on the market use a scheme suggested by Figure 4.10, in which the central element of the star is an active element, referred to as the **hub.** Each station is connected to the hub by two twisted pairs (transmit and receive). The hub acts as a repeater: when a single station transmits, the hub repeats the signal on the outgoing line to each station.

Note that although this scheme is physically a star, it is logically a bus: a transmission from any one station is received by all other stations, and if two stations transmit at the same time, there will be a collision.

Multiple levels of hubs can be cascaded in a hierarchical configuration. Figure 4.11 illustrates a two-level configuration. There is one **header hub** (HHUB) and one or more **intermediate hubs** (IHUB). Each hub may have a mixture of stations and other hubs attached to it from below. This layout fits well with building wiring practices. Typically, there is a wiring closet on each floor of an office building and a hub can be placed in each one. Each hub could service the stations on its floor.

Figure 4.12 shows an abstract representation of the intermediate and header hubs. The header hub performs all the functions described previously for a single-hub configuration. In the case of an intermediate

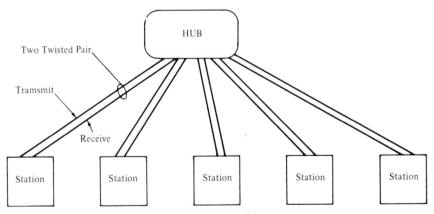

FIGURE 4.10 Twisted-Pair, Star-Wiring, Logical-Bus Arrangement

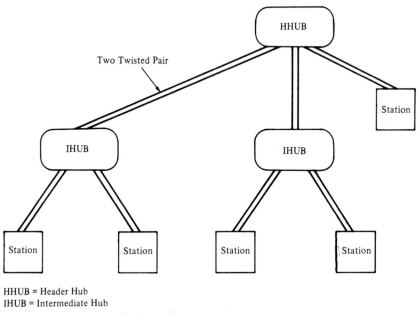

HHUB = Header Hub
IHUB = Intermediate Hub
FIGURE 4.11 Two-Level Hierarchy

hub, any incoming signal from below is repeated upward to the next higher level. Any signal from above is repeated on all lower-level outgoing lines. Thus, the logical bus characteristic is retained: a transmission from any one station is received by all other stations, and if two stations transmit at the same time, there will be a collision.

The initial version of the above scheme employed a data rate of 1 Mbps and was dubbed StarLAN [PARL85]. More recently, products op-

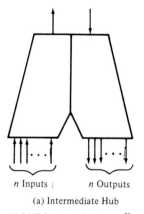

(a) Intermediate Hub

(b) Header Hub

FIGURE 4.12 Intermediate and Header Hubs

erating at 10 Mbps have begun to appear [SCHM88, MULQ88b]. These are intended to be compatible with the 10-Mbps baseband coaxial cable bus systems, requiring only a change of transceiver. Although there is now a fair amount of practical experience with these higher-speed systems, there remains a controversy about their practicality [CLAI88, ORLO88]. Two reasons for this controversy can be stated:

1. Existing telephone wire in buildings can be inadequate for data transmission. Problems include twisted pair that is not twisted, splicing and other connections, and other faults that are not noticeable for voice transmission but that would produce very high error rates at 10 Mbps.
2. Twisted-pair cables are rather tightly packed together in conduits. The mutual capacitance from adjacent pairs adversely affects attenuation, cross-talk, and velocity of propagation. The effects on data transmission may not be noticeable at 1 Mbps, but become a problem at 10 Mbps.

These problems can to some extent be overcome by the use of signal processing techniques and by careful design of the transceiver. However, just as we saw with the 10-Mbps coaxial cable bus, there are trade-offs to be made. In this case, IEEE recommends a maximum distance between station and hub of 250 meters at 1 Mbps and 100 meters at 10 Mbps.

4.3

METALLIC MEDIA: RING TOPOLOGY

Description

The ring consists of a number of repeaters, each connected to two others by unidirectional transmission links to form a single closed path (Figure 4.13). Data are transferred sequentially, bit by bit, around the ring from one repeater to the next. Each repeater regenerates and retransmits each bit.

For a ring to operate as a communications network, three functions are required: data insertion, data reception, and data removal. These functions are provided by the repeaters. Each repeater, in addition to serving as an active element on the ring, serves as a device attachment point for data insertion. Data are transmitted in packets, each of which contains a destination address field. As a packet circulates past a repeater, the address field is copied to the attached station. If the station recognizes the address, then the remainder of the packet is copied.

A variety of strategies can be used for determining how and when packets are added to and removed from the ring. The strategy can be

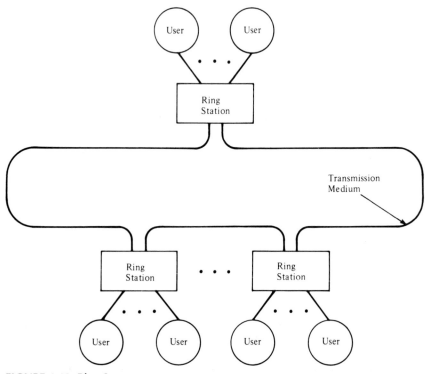

FIGURE 4.13 Ring System

viewed, at least conceptually, as residing in a medium access control layer, discussed in Chapter 5.

Repeaters perform the data insertion and reception functions in a manner not unlike that of taps, which serve as device attachment points on a bus or tree. Data removal, however, is more difficult on a ring. For a bus or tree, signals inserted onto the line propagate to the end points and are absorbed by terminators. Hence, shortly after transmission ceases, the bus or tree is clear of data. However, because the ring is a closed loop, data will circulate indefinitely unless removed. A packet may be removed by the addressed repeater. Alternatively, each packet could be removed by the transmitting repeater after it has made one trip around the loop. The latter approach is more desirable because (1) it permits automatic acknowledgement, and (2) it permits multicast addressing: one packet sent simultaneously to multiple stations.

The repeater, then, can be seen to have two main purposes: (1) to contribute to the proper functioning of the ring by passing on all the data that come its way, and (2) to provide an access point for attached stations to send and receive data. Corresponding to these two purposes are two states (Figure 4.14): the listen state and the transmit state.

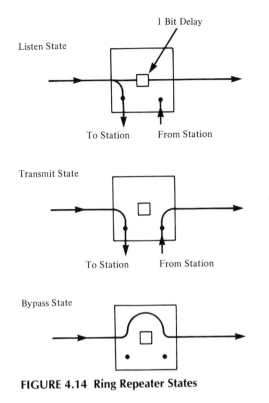

FIGURE 4.14 Ring Repeater States

In the *listen state*, each bit that is received is retransmitted with a small delay, required to allow the repeater to perform necessary functions. Ideally, the delay should be on the order of 1 bit time (the time it takes for a repeater to transmit 1 complete bit onto the outgoing line). These functions are:

- Scan passing bit stream for pertinent patterns. Chief among these is the address or addresses of attached devices. Another pattern, used in the token control strategy explained later, indicates permission to transmit. Note that to perform the scanning function, the repeater must have some knowledge of packet format.
- Copy each incoming bit and send it to the attached station, while continuing to retransmit each bit. This will be done for each bit of each packet addressed to this station.
- Modify a bit as it passes by. In certain control strategies, bits may be modified to, for example, indicate that the packet has been copied. This would serve as an acknowledgment.

When a repeater's station has data to send and when the repeater, based on the control strategy, has permission to send, the repeater enters the *transmit state*. In this state, the repeater receives bits from the station and retransmits them on its outgoing link. During the period of transmission, bits may appear on the incoming ring link. There are two possibilities, and they are treated differently:

1. The bits could be from the same packet that the repeater is still sending. This will occur if the bit length of the ring is shorter than the packet. In this case, the repeater passes the bits back to the station, which can check them as a form of acknowledgment.
2. For some control strategies, more than one packet could be on the ring at the same time. If the repeater, while transmitting, receives bits from a packet it did not originate, it must buffer them to be transmitted later.

These two states, listen and transmit, are sufficient for proper ring operation. A third state, the *bypass state*, is also useful. In this state, a bypass relay is activated, so that signals propagate past the repeater with no delay other than medium propagation. The bypass relay affords two benefits: (1) it provides a partial solution to the reliability problem, discussed later, and (2) it improves performance by eliminating repeater delay for those stations that are not active on the network.

Ring Benefits

A good deal of research into overcoming some of the weaknesses of the ring has been done at Massachusetts Institute of Technology [SALT79, SALT83] and at IBM [BUX83, STRO83, DIXO83]. The result has been a proliferation of ring-based LAN products, most notably the appearance of the IBM product in 1985, followed by a number of compatible products from other vendors [DERF86, STRO86].

Like the bus and tree, the ring is a shared-access or multiaccess network (although the medium itself is a collection of point-to-point links). Hence the ring shares the same benefits as the bus/tree, including ability to broadcast and incremental cost growth. There are other benefits provided by the ring that are not shared by the bus/tree topology.

The most important benefit or strength of the ring is that it uses point-to-point communication links. There are a number of implications of this fact. First, because the transmitted signal is regenerated at each node, greater distances can be covered than with baseband bus. Broadband bus/tree can cover a similar range, but cascaded amplifiers can result in loss of data integrity at high data rates. Second, the ring can accommodate optical fiber links that provide very high data rates and excellent electromagnetic interference (EMI) characteristics. Finally, the electronics and maintenance of point-to-point lines are simpler than for multipoint lines.

Another benefit of the ring is that fault isolation and recovery are simpler than for bus/tree. This is discussed in more detail later in this section.

With the ring, the duplicate address problem is easily solved. If, on a bus or tree, two stations are by accident assigned the same address, there is no easy way to sort this out. A relatively complex algorithm must be incorporated into the LAN protocol. On a ring, the first station with an address match that is encountered by a packet can modify a bit in the packet to acknowledge reception. Subsequent stations with the same address will easily recognize the problem.

Finally, there is the potential throughput of the ring. Under certain conditions, the ring has greater throughput than a comparable bus or tree LAN. This topic is explored in Chapter 9.

Potential Ring Problems

The potential problems of a ring are, at first blush, more obvious than the benefits:

1. *Cable vulnerability:* A break on any of the links between repeaters disables the entire network until the problem can be isolated and a new cable installed. The ring may range widely throughout a building and is vulnerable at every point to accidents.
2. *Repeater failure:* As with the links, a failure of a single repeater disables the entire network. In many networks, it will be common for many of the stations not to be in operation at any time; yet all repeaters must always operate properly.
3. *Perambulation:* When either a repeater or a link fails, locating the failure requires perambulation of the ring, and thus access to all rooms containing repeaters and cable. This is known as the "pocket full of keys" problem.
4. *Installation headaches:* Installation of a new repeater to support new devices requires the identification of two nearby, topologically adjacent repeaters. It must be verified that they are in fact adjacent (documentation could be faulty or out of date), and cable must be run from the new repeater to both of the old repeaters. There are several unfortunate consequences. The length of cable driven by the source repeater may change, possibly requiring retuning. Old cable, if not removed, accumulates. In addition, the geometry of the ring may become highly irregular, exacerbating the perambulation problem.
5. *Size limitations:* There is a practical limit to the number of repeaters on a ring. This limit is suggested by the reliability and maintenance problems cited earlier, the timing jitter discussed below, and

the accumulating delay of large numbers of repeaters. A limit of a few hundred repeaters seems reasonable.

6. *Initialization and recovery:* To avoid designating one ring node as a controller (negating the benefit of distributed control), a strategy is required to assure that all stations can cooperate smoothly when initialization and recovery are required. This need arises, for example, when a packet is garbled by a transient line error; in that case, no repeater may wish to assume the responsibility of removing the circulating packet.

7. *Timing jitter:* This is a subtle problem having to do with the clocking or timing of a signal in a distributed network. It is discussed below.

Problems 1 and 2 are reliability problems. However, these two problems, together with problems 3, 4, and 5 can be ameliorated by a refinement in the ring architecture, explained in the next section. Problem 6 is a software problem, to be dealt with by the various LAN protocols discussed in Chapter 5. Problem 7 is discussed next.

Timing Jitter.   On a twisted-pair or coaxial-cable ring LAN, digital signaling is generally used with biphase encoding, typically Differential Manchester. As data circulate around the ring, each receiver must recover the binary data from the received signal. To do this, the receiver must know the starting and ending times of each bit, so that it can sample the received signal properly. This requires that all the repeaters on the ring be synchronized, or clocked, together. Recall from Chapter 2 that biphase codes are self-clocking; the signal includes a transition in the middle of each bit time. Thus each repeater recovers clocking as well as data from the received signal. This clock recovery will deviate in a random fashion from the mid-bit transitions of the received signal for several reasons, including noise during transmission and imperfections in the receiver circuitry. The predominant reason, however, is delay distortion. Delay distortion is caused by the fact that the velocity of propagation of a signal through a guided medium varies with frequency. The effect is that some of the signal components of one pulse will spill over into other pulse positions; this is known as *intersymbol interference.* The deviation of clock recovery is known as *timing jitter.*

As each repeater receives data, it recovers the clocking for two purposes: first to know when to sample the incoming signal to recover the data, and second, to use the clocking for transmitting the Differential Manchester signal to the next repeater. The repeater issues a clean signal with no distortion. However, since the clocking is recovered from the incoming signal, the timing error is not eliminated. Thus the digital pulse width will expand and contract in a random fashion as the signal travels around the ring and the timing jitter accumulates. The cumulative effect of the jitter is to cause the bit latency, or bit length, of the ring to vary. However, unless the latency of the ring remains constant, bits will be dropped (not retransmitted) as the latency of the ring decreases or added as the latency increases.

Thus timing jitter places a limitation on the number of repeaters in a ring. Although this limitation cannot be entirely overcome, several measures can be taken to improve matters [KELL83, HONG86]; these are illustrated in Figure 4.15. First, each repeater can include a phase-locked loop (PLL). This is a device that uses feedback to minimize the deviation from one bit time to the next. Although the use of phase-locked loops reduces the jitter, there is still an accumulation around the ring. A supplementary measure is to include a buffer in one of the repeaters, usually designated as the monitor repeater or station. Bits are written in using the recovered clock and are read out using a crystal master clock. The buffer is initialized to hold a certain number of bits and expands and contracts as needed. For example, the IEEE standard specifies a 6-bit buffer, which is initialized to hold 3 bits. That is, as bits come in, they are placed in the buffer for 3 bit times before being retransmitted. If the received signal at the monitor station is slightly faster than the master clock, the buffer will expand, as required, to 4, 5, or 6 bits to avoid dropping bits. If the received signal is slow, the buffer will contract to 2, 1, or 0 bits to avoid adding bits to the repeated bit stream. Thus the cleaned-up signals that are retransmitted are purged of the timing jitter. This combination of PLLs and a buffer significantly increases maximum feasible ring size. The actual limit will depend on the characteristics of the transmission medium, which determine the amount of delay distortion and therefore the amount of accumulated jitter. For example, the IBM ring product specifies a maximum of 72 repeaters in a ring using

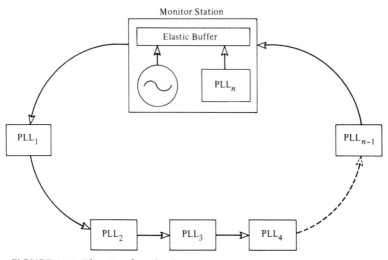

FIGURE 4.15 Ring Synchronization

unshielded twisted pair, and a maximum of 260 repeaters in a ring using shielded twisted pair.

The Star-Ring Architecture

Two observations can be made about the basic ring architecture described above. First, there is a practical limit to the number of repeaters on a ring. As was mentioned above, a number of factors combine to limit the practical size of a ring LAN to a few hundred repeaters. Second, the cited benefits of the ring do not depend on the actual routing of the cables that link the repeaters.

These observations have led to the development of a refined ring architecture, the star ring, which overcomes some of the problems of the ring and allows the construction of large local networks [SALW83]. This architecture uses the star wiring strategy discussed in the previous chapter. It is the basis of IBM's ring product and similar products.

As a first step, consider the rearrangement of a ring into a star. This is achieved by having the interrepeater link all threads through a single site (Figure 4.16). This ring wiring concentrator has a number of advantages. Because there is access to the signal on every link, it is a simple matter to isolate a fault. A message can be launched into the ring and tracked to see how far it gets without mishap. A faulty segment can be disconnected—no pocket full of keys needed—and repaired at a later time. New repeaters can easily be added to the ring: simply run two cables from the new repeater to the site of ring wiring concentration and splice into the ring.

The bypass relay associated with each repeater can be moved into the ring wiring concentrator. The relay can automatically bypass its repeater and two links for any malfunction. A nice effect of this feature is that the transmission path from one working repeater to the next is approximately constant; thus the range of signal levels to which the transmission system must automatically adapt is much smaller.

The ring wiring concentrator greatly alleviates the perambulation and installation problems mentioned earlier. It also permits rapid recovery from a cable or repeater failure. Nevertheless, a single failure could, at least temporarily, disable the entire network. Furthermore, throughput and jitter considerations still place a practical upper limit on the number of repeaters in a ring. Finally, in a spread-out network, a single wire concentration site dictates a lot of cable.

To attack these remaining problems, consider a local network consisting of multiple rings. Each ring consists of a connected sequence of wiring concentrators, and the set of rings is connected by a bridge (Figure 4.17). The bridge routes data packets from one ring subnetwork to another, based on addressing information in the packet so routed. From a physical point of view, each ring operates independently of the other

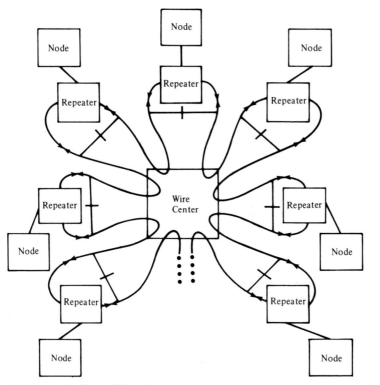

FIGURE 4.16 Ring Wiring Concentrator

rings attached to the bridge. From a logical point of view, the bridge provides transparent routing among the rings.

The bridge must perform five functions:

1. *Input filtering:* For each ring, the bridge monitors the traffic on the ring and copies all packets addressed to other rings on the bridge. This function can be performed by a repeater programmed to recognize a family of addresses rather than a single address.
2. *Input buffering:* Received packets may need to be buffered, either because the inter-ring traffic is peaking, or because the target output buffer is temporarily full.
3. *Switching:* Each packet must be routed through the bridge to its appropriate destination ring.
4. *Output buffering:* A packet may need to be buffered at the threshold of the destination ring, waiting for an opportunity to be inserted.
5. *Output transmission:* This function can be performed by an ordinary repeater.

For a small number of rings, a bridge can be a reasonably simple device. As the number of rings on a bridge grows, the switching com-

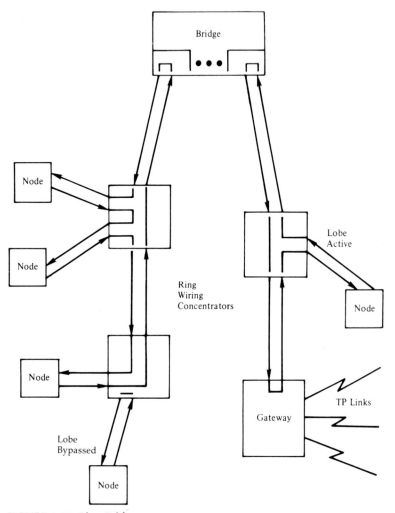

FIGURE 4.17 Ring Bridge

plexity and load on the bridge also grow. For very large installations, multiple bridges, interconnected by high-speed trunks, may be needed (Figure 4.18).

Three principal advantages accrue from the use of a bridge. First, the timing jitter problem, which becomes more difficult as the number of repeaters on a ring grows, is bounded by restricting the size of the ring. Second, the failure of a ring, for whatever reason, will disable only a portion of the network; failure of the bridge does not prevent intraring traffic. Finally, multiple rings may be employed to obtain a satisfactory level of performance when the throughput capability of a single ring is exceeded.

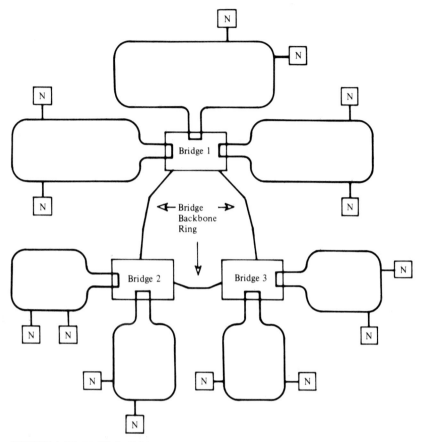

FIGURE 4.18 Multiple Bridges

There are several pitfalls to be noted. First, the automatic acknowl-edgment feature of the ring is lost; higher-level protocols must provide acknowledgment. Second, performance may not significantly improve if there is a high percentage of inter-ring traffic. If it is possible to do so, network devices should be judiciously allocated to rings to minimize inter-ring traffic.

4.4

OPTICAL FIBER STAR

The earliest work on optical fiber LANs focused on the star topology. Two general approaches have been investigated: the passive star and the active star. We examine each of these in turn.

Passive Star

One of the first commercially available approaches for fiber LANs was the passive star coupler [RAWS78, SCHO88]. The passive star coupler is fabricated by fusing together a number of optical fibers. Any light input to one of the fibers on one side of the coupler will be equally divided among and output through all the fibers on the other side. To form a network, each device is connected to the coupler with two fibers, one for transmit and one for receive (Figure 4.19). All of the transmit fibers enter the coupler on one side, and all of the receive fibers exit on the other side. Thus, although the arrangement is physically a star, it acts like a bus: a transmission from any one device is received by all other devices, and if two devices transmit at the same time, there will be a collision.

Two methods of fabrication of the star coupler have been pursued: the biconic fused coupler, and the mixing rod coupler. In the biconic fused coupler [STRA87], the fibers are bundled together. The bundled fibers are heated with an oxyhydrogen flame and pulled into a biconical tapered shape. That is, the rods come together into a fused mass that tapers into a conical shape and then expands back out again. The mixing rod approach [OHSH86] begins in the same fashion. Then, the biconical taper is cut at the waist and a cylindrical rod is inserted between the tapers and fused to the two cut ends. This latter technique allows the use of a less narrow waist and is easier to fabricate.

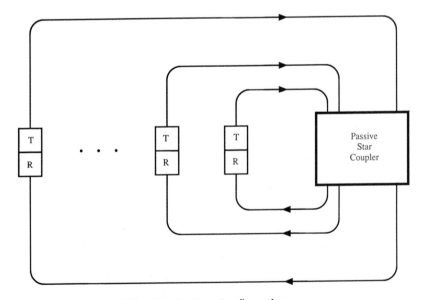

FIGURE 4.19 Optical Fiber Passive Star Configuration

Commercially available passive star couplers can support a few tens of stations at a radial distance of up to a kilometer or more. Figure 4.20 shows the operating range of the two types of couplers. The limitations on number of stations and distances are imposed by the losses in the network. With today's equipment, the optical power loss between transmitter and receiver that can be tolerated is on the order of 25 to 30 dB. In the figure, the outer edge of each region is defined by a maximum end-to-end attenuation of 30 dB. The attenuation that will occur in the network consists of the following components:

- *Optical connector losses:* Connectors are used to splice together cable segments for increased length. Typical connector losses are 1.0 to 1.5 dB per connector. A typical passive star network will have from 0 to 4 connectors in a path from transmitter to receiver, for a total maximum attenuation of 4 to 6 dB.
- *Optical cable attenuation:* Typical cable attenuation for the cable that has been used in these systems ranges from 3 to 6 dB per kilometer.
- *Optical power division in the coupler:* The coupler divides the optical power from one transmission path equally among all reception paths. Expressed in decibels, the loss seen by any node is 10 log N, where N is the number of nodes. For example, the effective loss in a 16-port coupler is about 12 dB.

As Figure 4.20 indicates, the passive star coupler is quite limited. One promising approach to improving performance is to use an optical amplifier. In 1989, it was demonstrated that an optical signal can be directly

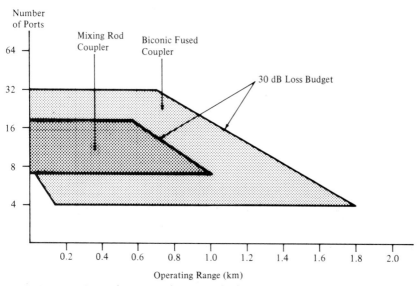

FIGURE 4.20 Operating Range for Optical Fiber Passive Star LAN [SCHO88]

amplified with low noise by an amplifier known as the erbium-doped fiber amplifier (EDFA). The EDFA is applicable as a high-power post-amplifier at the sending port, as a low-noise preamplifier at the receiving port, and as an intermediate repeating in-line optical amplifier [NAKA90, PARK92]. In the context of the passive star topology, the EDFA can be used to amplify signals as they pass through the star coupler.

The basic technique of the EDFA is as follows (Figure 4.21). A short segment of optical fiber is doped with erbium atoms. A constant laser input at a given wavelength, known as a laser pump, is applied to that portion of the fiber. When a laser signal at a different wavelength encounters erbium atoms that are excited to higher energy levels by a pumping light, the power of the signal light gradually increases along the optical fiber.

The use of the EDFA at the star coupler allows the implementation of networks with a greater number of stations operating over longer distances at higher data rates than can be achieved with an ordinary passive star coupler [IRSH92]. As yet, these devices are not commercially practical, but we can expect to see products in a few years.

Active Star

For a number of years, work has been underway at the Xerox Palo Alto Research Center to develop an improved version of the star topology fiber LAN. The result is Fibernet II [SCHM83], which differs from the passive star only in that the central coupler is an active repeater rather than a passive device. However, like the passive star, the active star appears as a bus to the attached devices: a transmission from any one device is received by all other devices, and only one device at a time can successfully transmit.

Figure 4.22 is a schematic diagram of Fibernet II. As before, each device attaches to the central node through two optical fiber cables, one for transmit and one for receive. Figure 4.16 reveals the internal organization of the node. When a station transmits, the receiver module de-

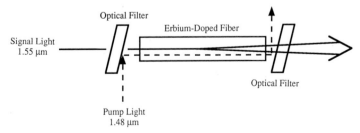

FIGURE 4.21 Erbium-Doped Fiber Amplifier [NAKA90]

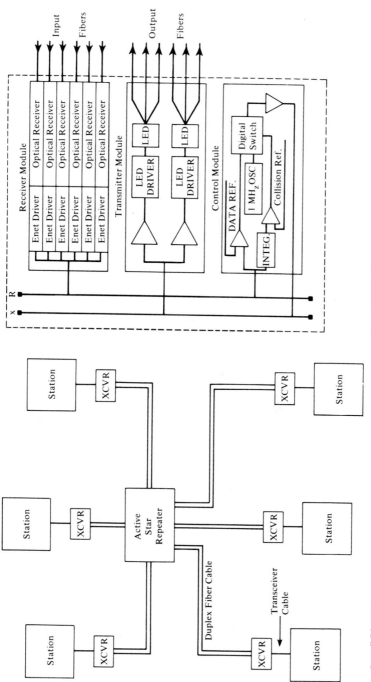

b. Active Star Organization

a. Overall Diagram

FIGURE 4.22 Fibernet II Active Star Configuration

tects the optical signal on the inbound optical fiber and retransmits it on a backplane bus designated R. The bus is in fact a miniature 50-ohm coaxial cable. The signal on the R bus is received by the control module, which retransmits it on another 50-ohm coaxial bus designated X. The purpose of this intermediate module is to perform collision detection, a function discussed in the next chapter. Finally, the transmitter module picks up the signal from bus X and retransmits it in optical form on all output fibers. The delay for this entire process is on the order of a few bit times. It can be seen that this arrangement is in fact simply a bus topology using star wiring, as depicted in Figure 3.5a.

The active star has several advantages over the passive star. In the passive star, the incoming signal is split equally among all outgoing fibers, so that the greater the number of fibers, the greater the loss on any one path. With the active star, this loss does not occur. Thus the active star can support more devices over a greater distance. Fibernet II is designed to support up to over a hundred devices at a maximum radius of 2.5 km. The disadvantage of the active star is that it is more expensive due to the active components in the central node.

4.5

OPTICAL FIBER RING

Even with the use of EDFAs, the optical fiber star configuration, at least for the near future, will be limited to relatively low speeds (for optical fiber) and modest distances. The optical fiber ring, on the other hand, is well suited to providing high data rates over long distances, better exploiting the potential of optical fiber. The ring consists of a series of point-to-point links, and the technology for point-to-point fiber transmission is well understood and widely available. In addition to the other advantages of fiber cited earlier, it exhibits significantly less delay distortion than coaxial cable or twisted pair and hence suffers less from timing jitter, which means that larger ring networks can be constructed.

Because of the high data rates attainable with optical fiber, the fiber ring is a natural choice for a very high-speed LAN or for a MAN. The fiber-distributed data interface (FDDI) is such a network, and we look at the details of its physical-layer specification in Chapter 6. In this section, we briefly look at some considerations for a fiber ring LAN of lower speed and smaller geographic extent than FDDI. The trade-off, clearly, is one of cost. By limiting the design to a relatively low speed and to a relatively short distance, a relatively inexpensive fiber LAN can be developed.

As an example, we will use the specifications developed by IBM for its fiber ring product [SEE86]; these are representative of what is com-

**TABLE 4.5   IBM Optical Fiber Ring
Specification (SEE86)**

Core Diameter	100 μm
Cladding Diameter	143 μm
Wavelength	850 nm
Attenuation	<6 dB/km
Bandwidth	>150 MHz
Data Rate	up to 20 Mbps
Distance	1.5 to 2.0 km

mercially available and commercially feasible. IBM's fiber ring specification was written to satisfy current transmission requirements using a light wavelength of 840 nm. The fiber specification also supports upward migration to higher-performance networks operating at a wavelength of 1300 nm. Although the latter could support a higher data rate, the transmitters and receivers operating at that wavelength are considerably more expensive than 850-nm devices.

Table 4.5 lists the key parameters of the specification. At an 850-nm wavelength, relatively low-cost LED transmitters and PIN detectors are used. Transmission is in the graded-index mode. A data rate of up to 20 Mbps is achievable with a maximum single-link distance of up to 1.5 to 2 km. The system should be able to support at least as many repeaters on a single ring as shielded twisted pair, on the order of 250.

4.6

OPTICAL FIBER BUS

Several approaches can be taken in the design of a fiber bus topology LAN or MAN [MUKH91]. The differences have to do with the nature of the taps into the bus and the detailed topology.

Optical Fiber Taps

With an optical fiber bus, either an active or passive tap can be used; both are permissible with the 802.6 standard. In the case of an active tap (Figure 4.23a), the following steps occur:

1. Optical signal energy enters the tap from the bus.
2. Clocking information is recovered from the signal and the signal is converted to an electrical signal.

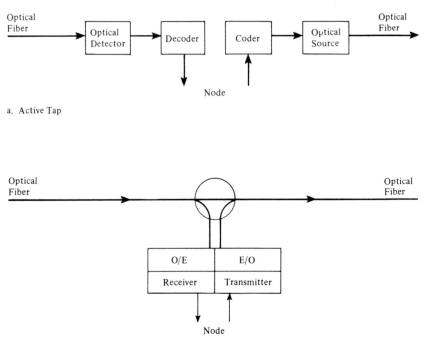

a. Active Tap

b. Passive Tap

FIGURE 4.23 Optical Fiber Bus Taps

3. The converted signal is presented to the node and perhaps modified by the latter.
4. The optical output (a light beam) is modulated according to the electrical signal and launched into the bus.

In effect, the bus consists of a chain of point-to-point links, and each node acts as a repeater. Each tap actually consists of two of these active couplers and requires two fibers. This is because of the inherently unidirectional nature of the device in Figure 4.23a.

In the case of a passive tap (Figure 4.23b), the tap extracts a portion of the optical energy from the bus for reception and it injects optical energy directly into the medium for transmission. Thus, there is a single run of cable rather than a chain of point-to-point links. This passive approach is equivalent to the type of taps typically used for twisted pair and coaxial cable. Each tap must connect to the bus twice, once for transmit and once for receive.

The electronic complexity and interface cost are drawbacks for the implementation of the active tap. Also, each tap will add some increment of delay, just as in the case of a ring. For passive taps, the lossy nature of pure optical taps limits the number of devices and the length of the medium. However, the performance of such taps has improved sufficiently in recent years to make fiber bus networks practical [ZANG91].

Optical Fiber Bus Configurations

A variety of configurations for the optical fiber bus have been proposed. All of these fall into two categories: those that use a single bus and those that use two buses.

Figure 4.24a shows a typical single-bus configuration, referred to as a loop bus. The operation of this bus is essentially the same as for the dual-bus broadband coaxial system described earlier. Each station transmits on the bus in the direction toward the headend and receives on the bus in the direction away from the headend. In addition to the two connections shown, some medium access control (MAC) protocols require that each station have an additional *sense tap* on the inbound (toward the headend) portion of the bus. The sense tap is able to sense the presence or absence of light on the fiber, but is not able to recover data.

Figure 4.24b shows the two-bus configuration. Each station attaches to both buses and has both transmit and receive taps on both buses. On each bus, a station may transmit only to those stations downstream from it. By using both buses, a station may transmit to and receive from

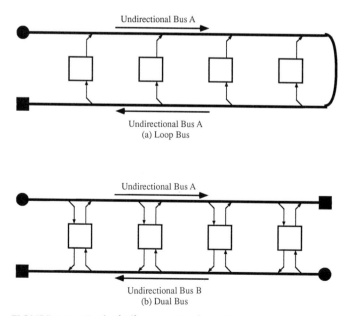

FIGURE 4.24 Optical Fiber Bus Configurations

all other stations. A given node, however, must know which bus to use to transmit to another node; if not, all data would have to be sent out on both buses. This is the configuration used in the IEEE 802.6 MAN, and it is described in Chapter 6.

4.7

RECOMMENDED READING

[MART89] covers many of the topics in this chapter and discusses commercial implementations. [NAUG91] does the same at a less technical level. [SLON91] contains a number of useful papers on these topics.

For a detailed look at baseband systems, the original Ethernet article [METC76] and a later follow-up article [SHOC82] remain informative, Detailed discussions of broadband LANs can be found in [COOP84] and [KIM88]. [MUKH91] and [HENR89] are good surveys of fiber LAN/MAN technology.

4.8

PROBLEMS

4.1 Consider a baseband bus with a number of equally spaced stations. As a fraction of the end-to-end propagation delay, what is the mean delay between stations? What is it for broadband bus? Now, rearrange the broadband bus into a tree with N equal-length branches emanating from the headend; what is the mean delay?

4.2 Give examples of appropriate applications of the broadband dedicated service and the switched service.

4.3 Consider a baseband bus with a number of equally spaced stations with a data rate of 10 Mbps and a bus length of 1 km. What is the average time to send a packet of 1000 bits to another station, measured from the beginning of transmission to the end of reception? Assume a propagation speed of 200 m/μs. If two stations begin to transmit at exactly the same time, their packets will interfere with each other. If each transmitting station monitors the bus during transmission, how long before it notices an interference, in seconds? In bit times?

4.4 Repeat Problem 4.3 for a data rate of 1 Mbps.

4.5 Repeat Problems 4.3 and 4.4 for broadband bus.

4.6 Repeat Problems 4.3 and 4.4 for a broadband tree consisting of 10 cables of length 100 m emanating from a headend.

4.7 Reconsider Problem 3.6. Can a baseband bus following the IEEE 802 rules (500-m segments, maximum of four repeaters in a path) span the building? If so, what is the total cable length?

4.8 Reconsider Problem 3.6 for a broadband tree. Can the total length be reduced compared to the broadband bus?

4.9 Reconsider Problem 3.6, but now assume that there are two rings, with a bridge on floor 5 and a ring wiring concentrator on each floor. The bridge and concentrators are located in closets along the vertical shaft.

4.10 At a propagation speed of 200 m/μs, what is the effective length added to a ring by a bit delay at each repeater:
   a. At 1 Mbps?
   b. At 40 Mbps?

4.11 System A consists of a single ring with 300 stations, one per repeater. System B consists of three 100-station rings linked by a bridge. If the probability of a link failure is P_l, a repeater failure is P_r, and a bridge failure is P_b, derive an expression for parts (a) through (d):
   a. Probability of failure of system A.
   b. Probability of complete failure of system B.
   c. Probability that a particular station will find the network unavailable, for systems A and B.
   d. Probability that any two stations, selected at random, will be unable to communicate, for systems A and B.
   e. Compare values of 4a through 4d for $P_l = P_b = P_r = 10^{-2}$.

4.12 Consider two rings of 100 stations each joined by a bridge. The data rate on each link is 10 Mbps. Each station generates data at a rate of 10 packets of 2000 bits each per second. Let F be the fraction of packets on each ring destined for the other. What is the minimum throughput of the bridge required to keep up?

APPENDIX 4A: CHARACTERISTIC IMPEDANCE

An important parameter associated with any transmission line is its characteristic impedance. To understand its significance, we need to consider the electrical properties of a transmission line. Any transmission line has both inductance and capacitance, which are distributed along the entire length of the line. These quantities can be expressed in terms of inductance and capacitance per unit length.

An infinite transmission line has similar electrical properties to the circuit depicted in Figure 4.24a and b. Of course, the actual inductance and capacitance are distributed uniformly along the line and not lumped as shown in the figure, but the equivalent circuit is good enough to explain the behavior of an actual line.

Figure 4.25a shows a section of an infinite line connected to a voltage source. Closing the switch (Figure 4.25b) will cause current to flow. Now, in a finite line, at steady state, the inductors will behave as short circuits (zero resistance) and the capacitors as open circuits (infinite resistance). However, at the instance that the switch is closed, current will flow and be resisted by the inductance and capacitance. The process will continue indefinitely because there is an infinite number of capacitors to be charged. There will be a definite relationship between the applied voltage and the amount of current that will flow. The relationship will depend only on the value of inductance and capacitance, which in turn depend on the physical dimensions of the line. In our example, an applied voltage of 100 volts causes a current of 2 amperes to flow into the

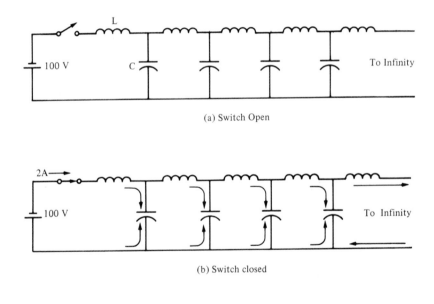

(a) Switch Open

(b) Switch closed

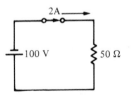

FIGURE 4.25 Characteristic Impedance

line when the switch is closed. As far as the source is concerned, it has no way of knowing whether it is connected to a transmission line that is infinitely long or to a 50-ohm resistor, as shown in Figure 4.25. In both cases, a current of 2 amperes would flow. For this reason, we say that this particular line has a characteristic impedance, or surge impedance, of 50 ohms.

The characteristic impedance is given by the equation:

$$Z_0 = \sqrt{\frac{L}{C}}$$

where

Z = characteristic impedance of the line, in ohms
L = inductance, in henrys per unit length
C = capacitance, in farads per unit length

Since the inductance and capacitance depend on the construction of the line, the characteristic impedance can also be determined from the physical dimensions of the line. In particular, for coaxial cable,

$$Z_0 = \frac{138}{\sqrt{\varepsilon}} \log \frac{D}{d}$$

where

$\log$ = logarithm to the base 10
D = diameter of outside conductor
d = diameter of inside conductor
ε = dielectric constant of the insulating
    material between the two conductors;
    for air, the value is 1

For a dielectric of 1 and an impedance of 50 ohms, the ratio D/d is 2.3, and for an impedance of 75 ohms, the ratio is 3.5.

It is important to realize that the characteristic impedance of a transmission line is a function of the construction of the line itself; it does not depend on the signal carried or on what is connected to the line.

The significance of characteristic impedance is this: When a line is terminated in its characteristic impedance, any signal on the line is absorbed when it reaches the terminating resistance. There are no reflections. Obviously, such reflections are to be avoided since they would interfere with the signal being transmitted.

More detail on these matters can be found in any text on transmission line theory, for example, [LIBO85].

APPENDIX 4B: DECIBELS

An important parameter in any transmission system is the strength of the signal being transmitted. As a signal propagates along a transmission medium, there will be a loss, or attenuation, of signal strength. Additional losses occur at taps and splitters. To compensate, amplifiers may be inserted at various points to impart a gain in signal strength. It is customary to express gains, losses, and relative levels in decibels, because:

- Signal strength often falls off logarithmically, so loss is easily expressed in terms of the decibel, which is a logarithmic unit.
- The net gain or loss in cascaded transmission path can be calculated with simple addition and subtraction.

The decibel is a measure of the difference in two signal levels:

$$N_{dB} = 10 \log \frac{P_1}{P_2}$$

where

$$N_{dB} = \text{number of decibels}$$
$$P_{1,2} = \text{voltage values}$$

For example, if a signal with a power level of 10 mw is inserted onto a transmission line and the measured power some distance away is 5 mw, the loss can be expressed as

$$\text{LOSS} = 10 \log(5/10) = 10(-.03) = -3 \text{ dB}$$

Note that the decibel is a measure of relative, not absolute, difference. A loss from 1000 mw to 500 mw is also a -3 dB loss. Thus, a loss of 3 dB halves the voltage level; a gain of 3 dB doubles the magnitude.

The decibel is also used to measure the difference in voltage, taking into account that power is proportional to the square of the voltage:

$$P = \frac{V^2}{R}$$

where

$$P = \text{power dissipated across resistance } R$$
$$V = \text{voltage across resistance } R$$

Thus

$$N_{dB} = 10 \log \frac{P_1}{P_2} = 10 \log \frac{V_1^2/R}{V_2^2/R} = 20 \log \frac{V_1}{V_2}$$

Decibel values refer to relative magnitudes or changes in magnitude, not to an absolute level. It is convenient to be able to refer to an absolute level of voltage in decibels so that gains and losses with reference to an initial signal level may easily be calculated. One unit in common use in cable television and broadband LAN applications is the dBMV (decibel-millivolt). This is an absolute unit with 0 dBMV equivalent to 1 mV. Thus

$$\text{Voltage(dBmV)} = 20 \log \frac{\text{Voltage(mV)}}{1\text{mV}}$$

The voltage levels are assumed to be across a 75-ohm resistance.

The decibel is convenient for determining overall gain or loss in a signal path. For example, Figure 4.9 shows a path from a point on a broadband trunk cable at which the signal level is 20 dBmV to an outlet. The amplifier gain and the losses due to the cables, tap, and splitter are expressed in decibels. By using simple addition and subtraction, the signal level at the outlet is easily calculated to be 7.6 dBmV.

APPENDIX 4C: SCRAMBLING AND DESCRAMBLING

For some digital data encoding techniques, a long string of binary zeros or ones in a transmission can degrade system performance. For example, in the differential phase-shift keying (DPSK) scheme used in some broadband LAN modems, a phase shift occurs only when the input is a zero bit. If there is a long strong of ones, it is difficult for the receiver to maintain synchronization with the transmitter. A similar problem arises with the other common broadband LAN modulation scheme, duobinary AM/PSK. Also, other transmission properties are enhanced if the data are more nearly of a random nature rather than constant or repetitive [BELL82a]. A technique commonly used with modems to improve signal quality is scrambling and descrambling. The scrambling process tends to make the data appear more random.

The scrambling process consists of a feedback shift register, and the matching descrambler consists of a feedforward shift register. An example is shown in Figure 4.26. In this example, the scrambled data sequence may be expressed as follows:

$$B_m = A_m \oplus B_{m-3} \oplus B_{m-5}$$

where $\oplus$ indicates the *exclusive or* operation. The descrambled sequence is

$$
\begin{aligned}
C_m &= B_m + B_{m-3} \oplus B_{m-5} \\
&= (A_m \oplus B_{m-3} \oplus B_{m-5}) \oplus B_{m-3} \oplus B_{m-5} \\
&= A_m
\end{aligned}
$$

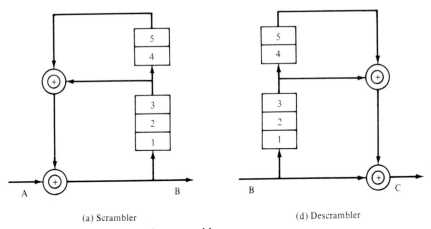

(a) Scrambler   (d) Descrambler

FIGURE 4.26 Scrambler and Descrambler

As can be seen, the descrambled output is the original sequence.

We can represent this process with the use of polynomials. Thus, for this example, the polynomial is $P = 1 + X^{-3} + X^{-5}$. The input is divided by this polynomial to produce the scrambled sequence. At the receiver the received scrambled signal is multiplied by the same polynomial to reproduce the original input. Figure 4.27 is an example using the polynomial P and an input of 101010100000111. The scrambled transmission, produced by dividing by $P(100101)$, is 101110001101001. When this number is multiplied by P, we get the original input. Note that the input sequence contains the periodic sequence 10101010 as well as a long string of zeros. The scrambler effectively removes both patterns.

```
                        1 0 1 1 1 0 0 0 1 1 0 1 0 0 1  ← B
                      _____
P  → 1 0 0 1 0 1 ) 1 0 1 0 1 0 0 0 0 0 1 1 1 – – – – – ← A
                   1 0 0 1 0 1
                   _____
                       1 1 1 1 1 0
                       1 0 0 1 0 1
                       _____
                         1 1 0 1 1 0
                         1 0 0 1 0 1
                         _____
                           1 0 0 1 1 0
                           1 0 0 1 0 1
                           _____
                               1 1 0 0 1 1
                               1 0 0 1 0 1
                               _____
                                 1 0 1 1 0 1
                                 1 0 0 1 0 1
                                 _____
                                   1 0 0 0 0 0
                                   1 0 0 1 0 1
                                   _____
                                     1 0 1 0 0 0
```

(a) Scrambling

```
                        1 0 1 1 1 0 0 0 1 1 0 1 0 0 1 ← A
                                    1 0 0 1 0 1 ← P
                        _____
                        1 0 1 1 1 0 0 0 1 1 0 1 0 0 1
                      1 0 1 1 1 0 0 0 1 1 0 1 0 0 1
                    1 0 1 1 1 0 0 0 1 1 0 1 0 0 1
                    _____
        C = A ⟶ 1 0 1 0 1 0 1 0 0 0 0 0 1 1 1 – – – – –
```

(b) Descrambling

FIGURE 4.27   Example of Scrambling with $p(x) = 1 + x^{-3} + x^{-5}$

CHAPTER 5

Local Area Network Architecture

The preceding chapter examined some key issues relating to the architecture and physical properties of LANs. Because of its scope and importance, the subject of communications architecture or protocols was deferred and is presented here in its own chapter.

This chapter begins with an overall discussion of LAN protocols and seeks to determine what layers of functionality are required. Then the specific areas of link control and medium access control are explored. Throughout, reference is made to the IEEE 802 standard. This is for two reasons:

1. The standard is well thought out, providing a framework for exposing and clarifying LAN communication architectural issues.
2. The standard has had a major influence on LAN products.

A brief rationale and summary of the IEEE 802 standard is contained in an appendix to this chapter.

5.1

LAN PROTOCOLS

A LAN Reference Model

Chapter 2 summarized an architecture for communications, the OSI reference model, based on seven layers of protocols. We saw in that discussion (see Figure 2.14) that layers 1, 2, and 3 were required for the functioning of a packet-switching network. To recall, these layers were described as follows:

1. *Physical layer:* concerned with transmission of unstructured bit stream over physical link. Involves such parameters as signal voltage swing and bit duration. Deals with the mechanical, electrical, and procedural characteristics to establish, maintain, and deactivate the physical link.
2. *Data link layer:* provides for the reliable transfer of data across the physical link; sends blocks of data (frames) with the necessary synchronization, error control, and flow control.
3. *Network layer:* provides upper layers with independence from the data transmission and switching technologies used to connect systems; responsible for establishing, maintaining, and terminating connections.

We now turn to the question of what layers are required for the proper operation of the LAN. For the sake of clarity, we examine the question in the context of the OSI reference model. Two characteristics of LANs are important in this context. First, data are transmitted in addressed frames. Second, there is no intermediate switching, hence no routing required (repeaters are used in rings and may be used in baseband bus LANs, but do not involve switching or routing). One exception to the second characteristic is the ring bridge. A discussion of that and other exceptions is deferred until Chapter 10.

These two characteristics essentially determine the answer to the question: What OSI layers are needed? Layer 1, certainly. Physical connection is required. Layer 2 is also needed. Data transmitted across the LAN must be organized into frames and control must be exercised. But what about layer 3? The answer is yes and no. If we look at the functions performed by layer 3, the answer would seem to be no. First, there is routing. With a direct link available between any two points, this is not needed. The other functions—addressing, sequencing, flow control, error control, and so on—are, we learned, also performed by layer 2. The difference is that layer 2 performs these functions across a single link, whereas layer 3 may perform them across the sequence of links required to traverse the network. But since only one link is required to traverse the LAN, these layer 3 functions are redundant and superfluous!

From the point of view of an attached device, the answer would seem to be yes, the LAN must provide layer 3. The device sees itself attached to an access point into a network supporting communication with multiple devices. The layer for assuring that a message sent across that access point is delivered to one of a number of each points would seem to be a layer 3 function. So we can say that although the network provides services up through layer 3, the characteristics of the network allow these services to be implemented on two OSI layers. We shall explore this topic more fully in Chapter 8. For the purpose of this chapter it is sufficient to understand that the minimum essential communications functions that must be performed by the LAN correspond to layers 1 and 2 of the OSI model.

With the points above in mind, let us now think about the functional requirements for controlling a local network and examine these from the top down. We follow the reasoning, illustrated in Figure 5.1, used by the IEEE 802 committee.

At the highest level are the functions associated with accepting transmissions from and delivering receptions to attached stations. These functions include:

- Provide one or more service access points. A service access point (SAP), recall, is a logical interface between two adjacent layers.
- On transmission, assemble data into a frame with address and CRC fields.
- On reception, disassemble frame, perform address recognition and CRC validation.
- Govern access to the link.

These are the functions typically associated with layer 2, the data link layer. The first function and related functions are grouped into a logical link control (LLC) layer by IEEE 802. The last three functions are treated as a separate layer, called *medium access control* (MAC). This is done for the following reasons:

- The logic required to manage access to a multiple-source, multiple-destination link is not found in traditional layer 2 link control.

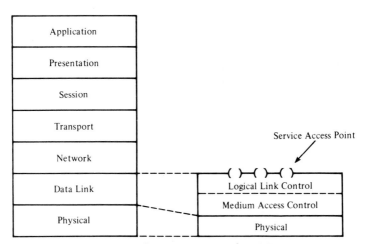

FIGURE 5.1 LAN Protocol Layers Compared to OSI

- For the same LLC, several MAC options may be provided, as we shall see.

Finally, at the lowest layer, are the functions generally associated with the physical layer. These include:

- Encoding/decoding of signals
- Preamble generation/removal (for synchronization)
- Bit transmission/reception

As with the OSI model, these functions are assigned to a physical layer in the IEEE 802 standard.

In the remainder of this section, we touch briefly on two aspects of LAN protocols. First, since the MAC layer is not found in the traditional OSI model, and to provide a context for later discussions, the characteristics and types of medium access control techniques are discussed. Then the structure for LAN frames is discussed briefly, using the IEEE 802 standard as an example.

We are then prepared to get more specific about LAN protocols. Section 5.2 discusses link control. Sections 5.3 and 5.4 provide details for various LAN medium access control techniques. Physical layer functions were discussed in Chapter 4.

Medium Access Control for Local Networks

All local networks (LAN, MAN, circuit-switched local network) consist of collections of devices that must share the network's transmission capacity. Some means of controlling access to the transmission medium is needed so that two particular devices can exchange data when required.

The key parameters in any medium access control technique are where and how. *Where* refers to whether control is exercised in a centralized or distributed fashion. In a centralized scheme, a controller is designated that has the authority to grant access to the network. A station wishing to transmit must wait until it receives permission from the controller. In a decentralized network, the stations collectively perform a medium access control function to dynamically determine the order in which stations transmit. A centralized scheme has certain advantages, such as:

- It may afford greater control over access for providing such things as priorities, overrides, and guaranteed bandwidth.
- It allows the logic at each station to be as simple as possible.
- It avoids problems of coordination.

Its principal disadvantages include:

- It results in a single point of failure.
- It may act as a bottleneck, reducing efficiency.

The pros and cons for distributed control are mirror images of the points made above.

The second parameter, *how*, is constrained by the topology and is a trade-off among competing factors: cost, performance, and complexity. In general, we can categorize access control techniques as being either synchronous or asynchronous. With synchronous techniques, a specific capacity is dedicated to a connection. We will see this in the circuit-switched local networks. Such techniques are not optimal in LANs and MANs because the needs of the stations are generally unpredictable. It is preferable to be able to allocate capacity in an asynchronous (dynamic) fashion, more or less in response to immediate needs. The asynchronous approach can be further subdivided into three categories: round robin, reservation, and contention.

Round Robin. Round robin techniques are conceptually simple, being based on the philosophy of "give everybody a turn." Each station in turn is given an opportunity to transmit. During that opportunity, the station may decline to transmit or may transmit subject to a certain upper bound, usually expressed as a maximum amount of data or time for this opportunity. In any case, the station, when it is finished, must relinquish its turn, and the right to transmit passes to the next station in logical sequence. Control of turns may be centralized or distributed. Polling on a multidrop line is an example of a centralized technique.

When many stations have data to transmit over an extended period of time, round robin techniques can be very efficient. If only a few stations have data to transmit at any given time, other techniques may be preferable, largely depending on whether the data traffic is stream or bursty. *Stream traffic* is characterized by lengthy and fairly continuous transmissions. Examples are voice communication, telemetry, and bulk file transfer. *Bursty traffic* is characterized by short, sporadic transmissions. Interactive terminal-host traffic fits this description.

Reservation. For stream traffic, reservation techniques are well suited. In general, for these techniques, time on the medium is divided into slots, much as with synchronous TDM. A station wishing to transmit reserves future slots for an extended or indefinite period. Again, reservations may be made in either a centralized or distributed fashion.

Contention. For bursty traffic, contention techniques are usually appropriate. With these techniques, no control is exercised to determine whose turn it is; all stations contend for time in a way that can be, as we shall see, rather rough and tumble. These techniques are of necessity distributed in nature. Their principal advantage is that they are simple to implement and, under light to to moderate load, efficient. For some

TABLE 5.1   Medium Access Control Techniques

	Centralized	Distributed
Round robin	Polling	Token bus Token ring Delay scheduling Implicit token

Reservation	Centralized
	  reservation
		Distributed
		  reservation

Contention		CSMA/CD Slotted ring Register insertion

of these techniques, however, performance tends to collapse under heavy load.

Although both centralized and distributed reservation techniques have been implemented in some LAN products, round robin and contention techniques are the most common.

The discussion above has been somewhat abstract and should become clearer as specific techniques are discussed in this chapter and the next. For future reference, Table 5.1 places the techniques that will be discussed into the classification just outlined. Table 5.2 lists the MAC protocols that are defined in the LAN and MAN standards.

IEEE 802 Frame Format

This section presents the formats used for frames in the IEEE 802 standard. These formats are similar to those used by most proprietary networks. They are the basis for the LLC, MAC, and physical layer functionality.

At this point it is worth reviewing the HDLC format presented in Chapter 2. The requirements for a local network frame are very similar.

TABLE 5.2   Standardized Medium Access Control Techniques

	Bus Topology	Ring Topology
Round Robin	Token Bus (IEEE 802.4)	Token Ring (IEEE 802.5, FDDI)
Reservation	DQDB (IEEE 802.6)	FDDI-II
Contention	CSMA/CD (IEEE 802.3)	

Note: The DQDB and FDDI-II protocols for circuit-switched traffic are not fully specified in the standards and may be either distributed or centralized. All other standardized MAC protocols are distributed.

There must, of course, be a data or information field. A control field is needed to pass control bits and identify frame type. Starting and ending patterns are usually required to serve as delimiters. Addressing is required. Here is the main difference. Because LAN links are multiple-source, multiple-destination, both source and destination addresses are required. Further, unlike HDLC and virtually all other layer 2 protocols, the IEEE 802 LAN protocols support a form of multiplexing common in layer 3 protocols. As we shall see, this is accomplished in IEEE 802 by identifying service access points at each station.

Figure 5.2 shows the IEEE 802 formats. As can be seen, a separate format is used at the LLC level, and this is then embedded in the appropriate MAC frame. IEEE 802 supports three MAC alternatives: CSMA/CD, token bus, and token ring.

5.2

LINK LAYER PROTOCOL FOR LANS

In this section we look first at the general link level requirements for a local area network, then examine the IEEE 802 specification.

Principles

The link layers for LANs should bear some resemblance to the more common link layers extant. Like all link layers, the LAN link layer is concerned with the transmission of a frame of data between two stations, with no intermediate switching nodes.

It differs from traditional link layers in three ways:

1. It must support the multiaccess nature of the link (this differs from multidrop in that there is no primary node).
2. It is relieved of some details of link access by the MAC layer.
3. It must provide some layer 3 functions.

Figure 5.3 will help clarify the requirements for the link layer. We consider two stations or systems that communicate via a LAN (bus or ring). Higher layers (the equivalent of transport and above) provide end-to-end services between the stations. Below the link layer, a medium MAC layer provides the necessary logic for gaining access to the network for frame transmission and reception.

At a minimum, the link layer should perform those functions normally associated with that layer:

- *Error control:* End-to-end error control and acknowledgment. The link layer should guarantee error-free transmission across the LAN.
- *Flow control:* End-to-end flow control.

Logical Link Control (LLC)

1	1	1–2	N	bytes or octets
DSAP	SSAP	Control	DATA	

CSMA/CD

7	1	2, 6	2, 6	2	0–1500		4
Preamble	SFD	DA	SA	Length	LLC	PAD	FCS

Token Bus

≥ 1	1	1	2, 6	2, 6	≥ 0	4	1
Preamble	SD	FC	DA	SA	LLC	FCS	ED

Token Ring

1	1	1
SD	AC	ED

1	1	1	2,6	2,6	≥ 0	4	1	1
SD	AC	FC	DA	SA	LLC	FCS	ED	FS

```
AC   = Access Control
DA   = Destination Address
DSAP = Destination Service Access Point
ED   = Ending Delimiter
FC   = Frame Control
FCS  = Frame Check Sequence
FS   = Frame Status
SA   = Source Address
SD   = Starting Delimiter
SFD  = Start Frame Delimiter
SSAP = Source Service Access Point
```

FIGURE 5.2 IEEE 802 Frame Formats

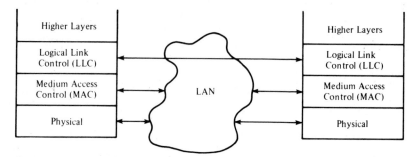

FIGURE 5.3 LAN Communication Architecture

These functions can be provided in much the same way as for HDLC and other point-to-point link protocols—by the use of sequence numbers (N(S), N(R)).

It has already been mentioned that because of the lack of intermediate switching nodes, a LAN does not require a separate layer 3; rather, the essential layer 3 functions can be incorporated into layer 2:

- *Connectionless:* A service that does not require the overhead of establishing a logical connection is needed for efficient support of highly interactive traffic.
- *Connection-oriented;* A connection-oriented service is also usually needed.
- *Multiplexing:* Generally, a single physical link attaches a station to a LAN; it should be possible to provide data transfer with multiple end points over that link.

Because there is no need for routing, the above functions are easily provided. The connectionless service simply requires the use of source and destination address fields, as discussed previously. The station sending the frame must designate the destination address, so that the frame is delivered properly. The source address must also be indicated so that the recipient knows where the frame came from.

Both the connection-oriented and multiplexing capabilities can be supported with the concept of the service access point (SAP), introduced in Chapter 2. An example may make this clear. Figure 5.4 shows three stations attached to a LAN. Each station has an address. Further, the link layer supports multiple SAPs, each with its own address. The link layer provides communication between SAPs. Assume that a process or application X in station A wishes to send a message to a process in station C. X may be a report generator program in minicomputer A. C may be a printer and a simple printer driver. X attaches itself to SAP 1 and requests a connection to station C, SAP 1 (station C may have only one SAP if it is a single printer). Station A's link layer then sends to the LAN a connection-request frame that includes the source address (A, 1), the destination address (C, 1), and some control bits indicating that this is a connection request. The LAN delivers this frame to C, which, if it is free, returns a connection-accepted frame. Henceforth, all data from X will be assembled into a frame by A's LLC, which includes source (A,1) and destination (C,1) addresses. Incoming frames addressed to (A,1) will be rejected unless they are from (C, 1); these might be acknowledgment frames, for example. Similarly, station C's printer is declared busy and C will accept frames only from (A,1).

Thus a connection-oriented service is provided. At the same time, process Y could attach to (A,2) and exchange data with (B,1). This is an example of multiplexing. In addition, various other processes in A could use (A,3) to send datagrams to various destinations.

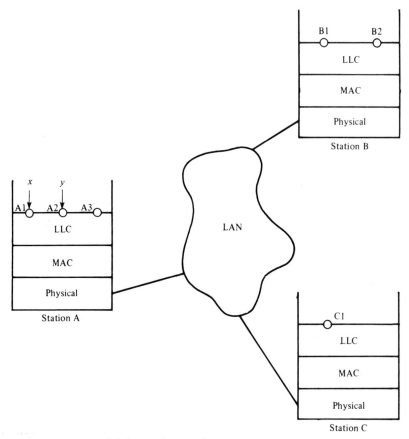

FIGURE 5.4 LAN Link Control Scenario

One final function of the link layer should be included, to take advantage of the multiple access nature of the LAN:

- *Multicast, broadcast:* The link layer should provide a service of sending a message to multiple stations or all stations.

Addressing

The preceding discussion referred to both station and LLC addresses. A further elaboration of this point is warranted. To understand the function of addressing, we need to consider the requirements for exchanging data.

In very general terms, communication can be said to involve three agents: processes, stations, and networks. *Processes* are the fundamental entities that communicate. One example is a file transfer operation. In this case, a file transfer process in one station exchanges data with a file transfer process in another station. Another example is remote terminal access. In this case, a user terminal is attached to one station and controlled by a terminal-handling process in that station. The user, through the terminal-handling process, is remotely connected to a time-sharing system; data are exchanged between the terminal-handling process and the time-sharing process. Processes execute on *stations,* which can often support multiple simultaneous processes. Stations are connected by a *network,* and the data to be exchanged are transmitted by the network from one station to another. From this point of view, the transfer of data from one process to another involves first getting the data to the station in which the process resides and then getting the data to the process within the station.

These concepts suggest the need for two levels of addressing. To see this, consider Figure 5.5, which shows the overall format of data transmitted using the LLC and MAC protocols (compare Figure 2.18). User data to be sent are passed down to LLC, which appends a header. This header contains control information that is used to manage the protocol between the local LLC entity and the remote LLC entity. The combination of user data and LLC header is referred to as an LLC *protocol data unit* (PDU). After the sending LLC has prepared a PDU, the PDU is then passed as a block of data down to the MAC entity. The MAC entity appends both a header and a trailer, to manage the MAC protocol. The result is a MAC-level PDU. To avoid confusion with an LLC-level PDU, the MAC-level PDU is typically referred to as a *frame.*

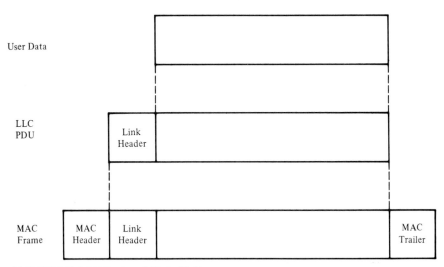

FIGURE 5.5 LAN Protocol Data Units

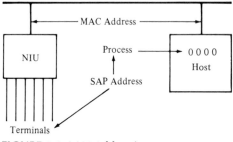

FIGURE 5.6 LAN Addressing

Now, the MAC header must contain a destination address that uniquely identifies a station on the local network. This is needed since each station on the local network will read the destination address field to determine if it should capture the MAC frame. When a MAC frame is captured, the MAC entity strips off the MAC header and trailer and passes the resulting LLC PDU up to the LLC entity. The LLC header must contain a destination SAP address so the LLC can determine to whom the data are to be delivered. Hence, two levels of addressing are needed:

1. *MAC address:* identifies a station on the local network
2. *LLC address:* identifies an LLC user

Figure 5.6 illustrates the two levels of addresses. The MAC address is associated with a physical attachment point on the network. The LLC SAP is associated with a particular user within a station. In some cases, the SAP corresponds to a host process. Another case relates to a common type of attached equipment, referred to as a network interface unit (NIU).[1] Often, an NIU is used as a terminal concentration device. In this case, each terminal port on the NIU has a unique SAP.

So far, we have discussed the use of addresses that identify unique entities. In addition to these **individual addresses,** group addresses are also employed. A **group address** specifies a collection of one or more entities. For example, one might wish to send a message to all terminal users attached to a particular NIU, or all terminal users on the entire LAN. Two types of group addresses are used. A **broadcast address** refers to all entities within some context; this is also referred to as an all-stations address. A **multicast address** refers to some subset of entities within some context.

Table 5.3 depicts the possible combinations. The first five combinations are straightforward. A specific user can be addressed. A group of

[1]NIUs are examined in detail in Chapter 8.

TABLE 5.3   LAN Addressing

MAC Address	LLC User Address (Service Access Point)
Individual	Individual
Individual	Multicast
Individual	Broadcast
Multicast	Broadcast
Broadcast	Broadcast
Multicast	Individual
Multicast	Multicast
Broadcast	Individual
Broadcast	Multicast

users or all users at a specific station can be addressed. And all users on some stations or all users on all stations can be addressed.

The last four combinations in the table are less obvious. It should be clear that LLC addresses are unique only within a single station. It is only the LLC entity within a station that examines the LLC header and determines the user. However, it is possible to assign LLC addresses uniquely across all stations; this is undesirable for the following reasons:

- The total number of users on all stations would be limited by the SAP field length in the LLC header.
- Central management of SAP assignment would be required, no matter how large and heterogeneous the user population.

On the other hand, it may be desirable to assign the same SAP value to entities in different stations. For example, a station management entity in a station may always be given an SAP value of 1, to facilitate network management. Or a group of management and control entities within a station may always be given the same multicast SAP address. When such a convention is followed, then it becomes possible to address data to one SAP address or a multicast SAP address in a group of stations or all stations.

IEEE 802 Logical Link Control

The IEEE 802 LLC standard [IEEE89a] is a good example of a LAN link control layer. It is well thought out and offers a variety of services. This section summarizes the features of LLC.

Figure 5.2 depicts the LLC frame. As can be seen, it specifies the source and destination service access points (thus allowing link multiplexing), a 1- or 2-byte control field, and a data field. The source and destination address fields are needed by the LLC, but are also used by MAC, and are included in the outer MAC frame. The LLC can be specified in three parts:

1. The interface with the station, specifying the services that LLC (and hence the LAN) provides to the network subscriber
2. The LLC protocol, specifying the LLC functions
3. The interface with MAC, specifying the services that LLC requires to perform its function

A variety of functions were mentioned in the previous section. Not all of these functions are needed in all environments. Accordingly, the 802 standard defines two general categories of data link control operation. The first is a connectionless operation that provides minimum service with minimum protocol complexity. This is useful and efficient when higher layers (e.g., network, transport) provide error control, flow control, and sequencing functions. It is also useful when the guaranteed delivery of data is not required. The second category is connection-oriented operation that provides the functions referred to above using a protocol similar to HDLC. These two types of operations are reflected in the specifications of both the LLC services and the LLC protocol.

LLC Services.   LLC provides three services:

1. *Unacknowledged connectionless service:* This is a datagram service that simply allows for sending and receiving frames. It supports point-to-point, multipoint, and broadcast.
2. *Connection-oriented service:* This provides a logical connection between service access points. It provides flow control, sequencing, and error recovery.
3. *Acknowledged connectionless service:* This is also a connectionless service, but provides for acknowledgment, relieving higher layers of this burden. It supports point-to-point transfers.

These services are specified in terms of primitives that can be viewed as commands or procedure calls with parameters.[2] Table 5.4 summarizes the LLC primitives.

The **Unacknowledged Connectionless Service** is a datagram style of service that simply allows for sending and receiving LLC frames, with no form of acknowledgment to assure delivery. It supports point-to-point, multipoint, and broadcast addressing.

---

[2]These primitives always include one of four standard modifiers: request, indication, response, confirm. The interpretation of these primitives is discussed in Appendix 5B at the end of this chapter.

TABLE 5.4   Logical Link Control Primitives

UNACKNOWLEDGED CONNECTIONLESS SERVICE
DL-UNITDATA.request (source-address, destination-address, data, priority)
DL-UNITDATA.indication (source-address, destination-address, data, priority)

CONNECTION-MODE SERVICE
DL-CONNECT.request (source-address, destination-address, priority)
DL-CONNECT.indication (source-address, destination-address, priority)
DL-CONNECT.response (source-address, destination-address, priority)
DL-CONNECT.confirm (source-address, destination-address, priority)

DL-DATA.request (source-address, destination-address, data)
DL-DATA.indication (source-address, destination-address, data)

DL-DISCONNECT.request (source-address, destination-address)
DL-DISCONNECT.indication (source-address, destination-address, reason)

DL-RESET.request (source-address, destination-address)
DL-RESET.indication (source-address, destination-address, reason)
DL-RESET.response (source-address, destination-address)
DL-RESET.confirm (source-address, destination-address)

DL-CONNECTION-FLOWCONTROL.request (source-address,
  destination-address, amount)
DL-CONNECTION-FLOWCONTROL.indication (source-address,
  destination-address, amount)

ACKNOWLEDGED CONNECTIONLESS SERVICE
DL-DATA-ACK.request (source-address, destination-address, data, priority,
  service-class)
DL-DATA-ACK.indication (source-address, destination-address, data, priority,
  service-class)
DL-DATA-ACK-STATUS.indication (source-address, destination-address, priority,
  service-class, status)
DL-REPLY.request (source-address, destination-address, data, priority, service-class)
DL-REPLY.indication (source-address, destination address, data, priority,
  service-class)
DL-REPLY-STATUS.indication (source-address, destination-address, data, priority,
  service-class, status)

DL-REPLY-UPDATE.request (source-address, data)
DL-REPLY-UPDATE-STATUS.indication (source-address, status)

This service provides for only two primitives across the interface between the next higher layer and LLC. DL-UNITDATA.request is used to pass a block of data down to LLC for transmission. DL-UNITDATA.indication is used to pass that block of data up to the destination user from LLC upon reception. The source-address and destination-address parameters specify the local and remote LLC users, respectively. Each of these parameters actually is a combination of LLC service access point and the MAC address. The data parameter is the block of data transmitted from one LLC user to another. The priority parameter specifies the desired priority. This (together with the MAC portion of the address) is passed down through the LLC entity to the MAC entity, which has the responsibility of implementing a priority mechanism. As we shall see, token bus and token ring are capable of this, but the 802.3 CSMA/CD system is not.

The **Connection-Oriented Service** provides a virtual-circuit style connection between service access points (between users). It provides a means by which a user can request or be notified of the establishment or termination of a logical connection. It also provides flow control, sequencing, and error recovery. It supports point-to-point addressing.

This service includes the DL-CONNECT set of primitives (request, indication, response, confirm) to establish a logical connection between SAPs. Once the connection is established, blocks of data are exchanged using DL-DATA.request and DL-DATA.indication. Because the existence of a logical connection guarantees that all blocks of data will be delivered reliably, there is no need for an acknowledgment (via indication and confirm primitives) of individual blocks of data. At any point, either side may terminate the connection with a DL-DISCONNECT.request; the other side is informed with a DL-DISCONNECT.indication.

The DL-RESET primitives are used to reset a logical connection to an initial state. Sequence numbers are reset and the connection is reinitialized. Finally, the two flow control primitives regulate the flow of data across the SAP. The flow can be controlled in either direction. This is a local flow control mechanism that specifies the amount of data that may be passed across the SAP.

The **Acknowledged Connectionless Service** provides a mechanism by which a user can send a unit of data and receive an acknowledgment that the data were delivered, without the necessity of setting up a connection.

This service includes DL-DATA-ACK.request and DL-DATA-ACK.indication with meanings analogous to those for the Unacknowledged Connectionless Service, plus DL-DATA-ACK-STATUS.indication to provide acknowledgment to the sending user. The DL-REPLY primitives provide a data exchange service. It allows a user to request that data be returned from a remote station or that data units be exchanged with a remote station. Associated with these primitives are the DL-REPLY-UPDATE primitives. These primitives allow a user to pass data to LLC to be held and sent out at a later time when requested to do so (by a DL-REPLY primitive) by some other station.

The specification of three types of service is intended to allow LLC to be used to support a variety of user requirements and to enable implementors to implement subsets of LLC to meet their specific needs and to optimize the implementation to those needs. The Unacknowledged Connectionless Service is the simplest and requires the minimum implementation. In cases where higher layer protocols (usually transport) provide end-to-end error control and flow control, this minimum service is all that is needed. On the other hand, when the supported devices are very simple (e.g., terminals), it might make sense to forgo elaborate upper layers and rely on LLC to provide end-to-end control. Finally, the Acknowledged Connectionless Service may be useful in some real-time environments, such as factory LANs. For example, certain alarm or control signals may be very important and time-critical. Because of their importance, an acknowledgment is needed so that the sender can be assured that the signal got through. Because of the urgency of a signal, the user might not want to take the time to first establish a logical connection and then send the data.

LLC Protocol

The basic LLC protocol is modeled after the HDLC balanced mode, and it has similar formats and functions. These are summarized briefly in this section. The reader should be able to see how this protocol supports the LLC services defined above.

The format of an LLC protocol data unit is shown in Figure 5.2. First are the address fields. Both the DSAP and SSAP fields actually contain 7-bit addresses. The least significant bit of DSAP indicates whether this is an individual or group address. The least significant bit of SSAP indicates whether this is a command or response frame.

Figure 5.7 shows the format for the LLC control field (compare Figure 2.19). It is identical to that of HDLC and the functioning is the same, with four exceptions:

1. LLC makes use of only the asynchronous balanced mode of operation and does not employ HDLC's normal response mode or asynchronous response mode. This mode is used to support connection-oriented service. The set asynchronous balanced mode (SABME) command is used to establish a connection, and disconnect (DISC) is used to terminate the connection.
2. LLC supports a connectionless (datagram) service by using the unnumbered information (UI) frame.
3. LLC permits multiplexing by the use of SAPs.
4. LLC supports an acknowledged connectionless service by using two new unnumbered frames.

A brief summary follows.

As with HDLC, three frame formats are defined for LLC: information transfer, supervisory, and unnumbered. Their use depends on the type of operation employed. The types are Type 1 (connectionless), Type 2 (connection-oriented), and Type 3 (acknowledged connectionless).

	1	2	3	4	5	6	7	8	9	10-16
Information Transfer Command/Response (I–Format PDU)	0				N(S)				P/F	N(R)
Supervisory Commands/Responses (S–Format PDUs)	1	0	S	S	X	X	X	X	P/F	N(R)
Unnumbered Commands/Response (U–Format PDUs)	1	1	M	M	P/F	M	M	M		

Where

N(S)–Transmitter Send Sequence Number (Bit 2–Low–order Bit)
N(R)–Transmitter Receive Sequence Number (Bit 10–Low–order Bit)
S–Supervisory Function Bit
M–Modifier Function Bit
X–Reserved and Set to Zero
P/F–Poll Bit–Command LLC PDU Transmissions
    Final Bit–Response LLC PDU Transmissions
    (1–Poll/Final)

FIGURE 5.7 IEEE 802 LLC Control Field Format

With Type 1 Operation, protocol data units (PDUs) are exchanged between LLC entities without the need to establish a logical connection. There is no acknowledgment, flow control, or error control. This type of operation supports the Unacknowledged Connectionless Service.

Three unnumbered frame formats are used. The UI (unnumbered information) frame is used to send a connectionless data frame, containing data from an LLC user. The XID (exchange identification) frame is used to convey station class (which operation types are supported). The TEST (test) frame is used to a request a TEST frame in response, to test the LLC-to-LLC path.

With Type 2 Operation, a data link connection is established between two LLC entities prior to data exchange. This type of operation supports Connection-Oriented Service and uses all three frame formats. The information transfer frames are used to send data (as opposed to control information). N(S) and N(R) are frame sequence numbers that support error control and flow control. A station sending a sequence of frames will number them, modulo 128, and place the number in N(S). N(R) is a piggybacked acknowledgment. It enables the sending station to indicate which number frame it expects to receive next. These numbers support flow control since, after sending seven frames without an acknowledgment, a station can send no more. The numbers support error control, as explained below. The P/F field is set to 1 only on the last frame in a series, to indicate that the transmission is over.

The supervisory frame is used for acknowledgment and flow control. The 2-bit SS field is used to indicate one of three commands: Receive

Ready (RR), Receive Not Ready (RNR), and Reject (REJ). RR is used to acknowledge the last frame received by indicating in N(R) the next frame expected. The frame is used when there is no reverse traffic to carry to piggybacked acknowledgment. RNR acknowledges a frame, as with RR, but also asks the transmitting station to suspend transmission. When the receiving station is again ready it sends an RR frame. REJ is used to indicate that the frame with number N(R) is rejected and that it and any subsequently transmitted frames must be sent again.

Unnumbered frames are used for control purposes in Type 2 operation. The 5-bit MMMMM field specifies a particular command or response. The commands are:

- SABME (set asynchronous balanced mode extended): used by an LLC entity to request logical connection with another LLC entity.
- DISC (disconnect): used to terminate a logical connection; the sending station is announcing that it is suspending operations.

The foregoing frames are commands, initiated by a station at will. The following frames are responses:

- UA (unnumbered acknowledgment): used to acknowledge SABME and DISC commands
- DM (disconnected mode): used to respond to a frame in order to indicate that the station's LLC is logically disconnected
- FRMR (frame reject): used to indicate that an improper frame has arrived—one that somehow violates the protocol

The P/F bit is used to indicate that a response is requested to a command frame.

With Type 3 Operation, each transmitted frame is acknowledged. A new unnumbered frame, the Acknowledged Connectionless (AC) Information frame, is defined. Unlike the other frames used in LLC, this frame is not defined in HDLC. User data are sent in an AC command frame and must be acknowledged using an AC response frame. To guard against lost frames, a 1-bit sequence number is used. The sender alternates the use of 0 and 1 in its AC command frames, and the receiver responds with an AC frame with the corresponding number.

LLC-MAC Interface. The IEEE 802 LLC is intended to operate with any of the three MAC protocols (CSMA/CD, token bus, token ring). A single logical interface to any of the MAC layers is defined. The 802 standard does not define an explicit interface, but provides a model. The basic primitives are:

- MA-UNITDATA.request: to request transfer of an LLC frame from local LLC to destination LLC. This includes information transfer, supervisory, and unnumbered frames.

- MA-UNITDATA.indicate: to transfer incoming LLC frame from local MAC to local LLC.

5.3
MEDIUM ACCESS CONTROL—BUS/TREE

Of all the local network topologies, the bus/tree topologies present the greatest challenges and the most options for medium access control. This section will not attempt to survey the many techniques that have been proposed; good discussions can be found in [LUCZ78] and [FRAN81]. Rather, emphasis is placed on the two techniques that seem likely to dominate the marketplace: CSMA/CD and token bus. Standards for these techniques have been developed by the IEEE 802 committee.

A third technique, centralized reservation, is reviewed briefly. This is for the sake of completeness; virtually all access techniques for bus/tree are related to one of these three techniques.

Table 5.5 compares the three techniques on a number of characteristics. The ensuing discussion should clarify their significance.

CSMA/CD

The most commonly used medium access control technique for bus-tree topologies is carrier sense multiple access with collision detection (CSMA/CD). The original baseband version of this technique was developed and patented by Xerox [METC77] as part of its Ethernet local network [METC76]. The original broadband version was developed and patented by MITRE [HOPK80] as part of its MITREnet local network [HOPK79, HOPK77]. A baseband version inspired by Ethernet has been issued as an IEEE 802 standard [IEEE90b].

TABLE 5.5   Bus/Tree Access Methods

	CSMA/CD	Token Bus	Centralized Reservation
Access determination	Contention	Token	Reservation
Packet length restriction	Greater than twofold propagation delay	None	No greater than slot size
Principal advantage	Simplicity	Regulated/fair access	Regulated/fair access
Principal disadvantage	Performance under heavy load	Complexity	Required central controller

Before examining this technique, we look at some earlier schemes from which CSMA/CD evolved.

Precursors.   All of the techniques discussed in this section, including CSMA/CD, can be termed *random access* or *contention* techniques. They are designed to address the problem of how to share a common broadcast transmission medium—the "Who goes next?" problem. The techniques are random access in the sense that there is no predictable or scheduled time for any station to transmit; station transmissions occur randomly. They are contention in the sense that no control is exercised to determine whose turn it is—all stations must contend for time on the network.

The earliest of these techniques, known as *ALOHA,* was developed for ground-based packet radio broadcasting networks [ABRA70]. However, it is applicable to any transmission medium shared by uncoordinated users. ALOHA, or *pure ALOHA* as it is sometimes called, is a true free-for-all. Whenever a station has a frame to send, it does so. The station then listens for an amount of time equal to the maximum possible round-trip propagation time on the network (twice the time it takes to send a frame between the two most widely separated stations). If the station hears an acknowledgment during that time, fine; otherwise, it resends the frame. After repeated failures, it gives up. A receiving station determines the correctness of an incoming frame by examining the check sum. If the frame is valid, the station acknowledges immediately. The frame may be invalid, due to noise on the channel or because another station transmitted a frame at about the same time. In the latter case, the two frames may interfere with each other so that neither gets through; this is known as a *collision.* In that case, the receiving station simply ignores the frame. ALOHA is as simple as can be, and pays a penalty for it. Because the number of collisions rises so rapidly with increased load, the maximum utilization of the channel is only about 18%.

To improve efficiency, a modification of ALOHA [ROBE75] was developed in which time on the channel is organized into uniform slots whose size equals the frame transmission time. Some central clock or other technique is needed to synchronize all stations. Transmission is permitted to begin only at a slot boundary. Thus frames that do overlap will do so totally. This increases the maximum utilization of the system to about 37%. The scheme is known as *slotted ALOHA.*

Both ALOHA and slotted ALOHA exhibit poor utilization. Both fail to take advantage of one of the key properties of both packet radio and local networks, which is that the propagation delay between stations is usually very small compared to frame transmission time. Consider the following observations. If the station-to-station propagation time is large compared to the frame transmission time, then, after a station launches a frame, it will be a long time before other stations know about it. During that time, one of the other stations may transmit a frame; the two frames may interfere with each other and neither gets through. Indeed, if the distances are great enough, many stations may begin transmitting, one after the other, and none of their frames get through unscathed. Suppose, however, that the propagation time is extremely small compared to frame transmission time. In that case, when a station launches a frame, all the other stations know it almost immediately. So, if they had any sense, they would not try transmitting until the first station was done. Collisions would be rare since they would occur only when two stations began to transmit almost simultaneously. Another way to look at it is that the short delay time provides the stations with better feedback about the state of the system; this information can be used to improve efficiency.

The foregoing observations led to the development of a technique known as carrier sense multiple access (CSMA) or listen before talk (LBT). A station wishing to transmit first listens to the medium to determine if another transmission is in progress. If the medium is in use, the station backs off some period of time and tries again, using one of the algorithms explained below. If the medium is idle, the station may transmit. Now, it may happen that two or more stations attempt to transmit at about the same time. If this happens, there will be a collision. To account for this, a station waits a reasonable amount of time after transmitting for an acknowledgment, taking into account the maximum round-trip propagation delay, and the fact that the acknowledging station must also contend for the channel in order to respond. If there is no acknowledgment, the station assumes that a collision has occurred and retransmits.

One can see how this strategy would be effective for systems in which the frame transmission time is much longer than the propagation time. Collisions can occur only when more than one user begins transmitting within a short time (within the period of propagation delay). If a station begins to transmit, and there are no collisions during the time it takes for the leading edge of the frame to propagate to the farthest station, then the station has seized the channel and the remainder of the frame will be transmitted without collision.

The maximum utilization achievable using CSMA can far exceed that of ALOHA or slotted ALOHA. The maximum utilization depends on the length of the frame and on the propagation time; the longer the frames or the shorter the propagation time, the higher the utilization. This subject will be explored in Chapter 9.

With CSMA, an algorithm is needed to specify what a station should do if the medium is found to be busy. Three approaches are depicted in

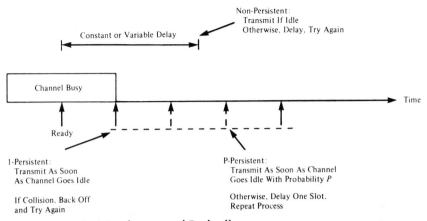

FIGURE 5.8 CSMA Persistence and Back-off

Figure 5.8. One algorithm is *nonpersistent* CSMA. A station wishing to transmit listens to the medium and obeys the following rules:

1. If the medium is idle, transmit.
2. If the medium is busy, wait an amount of time drawn from a probability distribution (the retransmission delay) and repeat step 1.

The use of random retransmission times reduces the probability of collisions. The drawback is that even if several stations have a frame to send, there is likely to be some wasted idle time following a prior transmission.

To avoid channel idle time, the *1-persistent protocol* can be used. A station wishing to transmit listens to the medium and obeys the following rules:

1. If the medium is idle, transmit.
2. If the medium is busy, continue to listen until the channel is sensed idle; then transmit immediately.
3. If there is a collision (determined by a lack of acnowledgment), wait a random amount of time and repeat step 1.

Whereas nonpersistent stations are deferential, 1-persistent stations are selfish. If two or more stations are waiting to transmit, a collision is guaranteed. Things get sorted out only after the collision.

A compromise that attempts to reduce collisions, like nonpersistent, and reduce idle time, like 1-persistent, is *p-persistent*. The rules are:

1. If the medium is idle, transmit what probability p, and delay one time unit with probability $(1 - p)$. The time unit is typically equal to the maximum propagation delay.

2. If the medium is busy, continue to listen until the channel is idle and repeat step 1.

3. If transmission is delayed one time unit, repeat step 1.

The question arises as to what is an effective value of p. The main problem to avoid is one of instability under heavy load. Consider the case in which n stations have frames to send while a transmission is taking place. At the end of that transmission, the expected number of stations that will attempt to transmit is np. If np is greater than 1, multiple stations will attempt to transmit and there will be a collision. What is more, as soon as all these stations realize that they did not get through, they will be back again, almost guaranteeing more collisions. Worse yet, these retries will compete with new transmissions from other stations, further increasing the probability of collision. Eventually, all stations will be trying to send, causing continuous collisions, with throughput dropping to zero. To avoid this catastrophe np must be less than one for the expected peaks of n. As p is made smaller, stations must wait longer to attempt transmission but collisions are reduced. At low loads, however, stations have unnecessarily long delays.

Description of CSMA/CD.   All of the techniques described above could be used in a bus/tree topology with an electrical conductor medium or in a packet radio scheme. We now introduce *carrier sense multiple access with collision detection* (CSMA/CD), which, because of the CD part, is appropriate only for a bus/tree topology [it is also referred to as *listen while talk* (LWT)]. CSMA/CD can be used with either baseband or broadband systems. Where details differ between baseband and broadband, we will use IEEE 802 and MITREnet as examples for comparison.

CSMA, although more efficient than ALOHA or slotted ALOHA, still has one glaring inefficiency. When two frames collide, the medium remains unusable for the duration of transmission of both damaged frames. For long frames, compared to propagation time, the amount of wasted bandwidth can be considerable. This waste can be reduced if a station continues to listen to the medium while it is transmitting. In that case, these rules can be added to the CSMA rules:

1. If a collision is detected during transmission, immediately cease transmitting the frame, and transmit a brief jamming signal to assure that all stations know that there has been a collision.

2. After transmitting the jamming signal, wait a random amount of time, then attempt to transmit again using CSMA.

Now the amount of wasted bandwidth is reduced to the time it takes to detect a collision. Question: How long does that take? Figure 5.9 illustrates the answer for a baseband system. Consider the worst case of two stations that are as far apart as possible. As can be seen, the amount

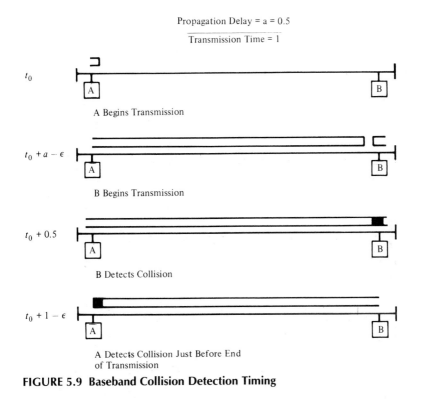

$$\text{Propagation Delay} = a = 0.5$$
$$\overline{\text{Transmission Time} = 1}$$

t_0

A Begins Transmission

$t_0 + a - \epsilon$

B Begins Transmission

$t_0 + 0.5$

B Detects Collision

$t_0 + 1 - \epsilon$

A Detects Collision Just Before End
of Transmission

FIGURE 5.9 Baseband Collision Detection Timing

of time it takes to detect a collision is twice the propagation delay. For broadband bus, the wait is even longer. Figure 5.10 shows a dual-cable system. This time, the worst case is two stations close together and as far as possible from the headend. In this case, the time required to detect a collision is four times the propagation delay from the station to the headend. The results would be the same for a midsplit system.

Both figures indicate the use of frames long enough to allow CD prior to the end of transmission. In most systems that use CSMA/CD, it is required that all frames be at least this long. Otherwise, the performance of the system is the same as the less efficient CSMA protocol, since collisions are detected only after transmission is complete.

Now let us look at a few details of CSMA/CD. First, which persistence algorithm should we use: non-, 1-, or p-? You may be surprised to learn that the most common choice is 1-persistent. It is used by both Ethernet and MITREnet, and in the IEEE 802 standard. Recall that both nonpersistent and p-persistent have performance problems. In the nonpersistent case, capacity is wasted because the medium will generally remain idle following the end of a transmission even if there are stations waiting to send. In the p-persistent case, p must be set low enough to avoid

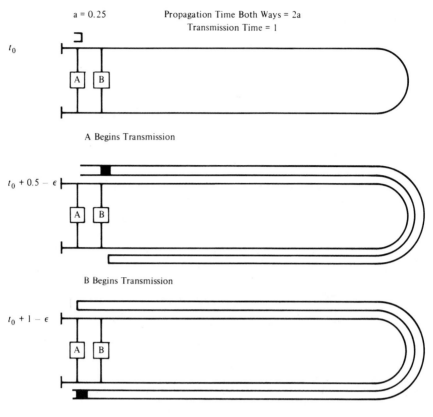

$a = 0.25$ Propagation Time Both Ways = 2a

Transmission Time = 1

t_0

A Begins Transmission

$t_0 + 0.5 - \epsilon$

B Begins Transmission

$t_0 + 1 - \epsilon$

A Detects Collision Just Before End
of Transmission

FIGURE 5.10 Broadband Collision Detection Timing

instability, with the result of sometimes atrocious delays under light load. The 1-persistent algorithm, which after all means $p = 1$, would seem to be even more unstable than p-persistent due to the greed of the stations. What saves the day is that the wasted time due to collisions is mercifully short (if the frames are long relative to propagation delay!), and with random back-off, the two stations involved in a collision are unlikely to collide on their next tries. To ensure that back-off maintains stability, IEEE 802 and Ethernet use a technique known as binary exponential back-off. A station will attempt to transmit repeatedly in the face of repeated collisions, but after each collision, the mean value of the random delay is doubled. After 16 unsuccessful attempts, the station gives up and reports an error.

The beauty of the 1-persistent algorithm with binary exponential back-off is that it is efficient over a wide range of loads. At low loads, 1-

persistence guarantees that a station can seize the channel as soon as it goes idle, in contrast to the non- and p-persistent schemes. At high loads, it is at least as stable as the other techniques. However, one unfortunate effect of the back-off algorithm is that it has a last-in, first-out effect; stations with no or few collisions will have a chance to transmit before stations that have waited longer.

Although the implementation of CSMA/CD is substantially the same for baseband and broadband, there are differences. One example is the means for performing carrier sense. For baseband systems using Manchester encoding, carrier is conveniently sensed by detecting the presence of transitions on the channel. Strictly speaking, there is no carrier to sense digital signaling; the term was borrowed from the radio lexicon. With broadband, carrier sense is indeed performed. The station's receiver listens for the presence of a carrier on the outbound channel.

Collision detection also differs for the two systems. In a baseband system, a collision should produce substantially higher voltage swings than those produced by a single transmitter. Accordingly, Ethernet and the IEEE standard dictate that a transmitting transceiver will detect a collision if the signal on the cable at the transceiver exceeds the maximum that could be produced by the transceiver alone. Because a transmitted signal attenuates as it propagates, there is a potential problem with collision detection. If two stations far apart are transmitting, each station will receive a greatly attenuated signal from the other. The signal strength could be so small that when it is added to the transmitted signal at the transceiver, the combined signal does not exceed the CD threshold. For this reason, among others, IEEE 802 restricts the maximum length of cable to 500 m. Because frames may cross repeater boundaries, collisions must cross as well. Hence if a repeater detects a collision on either cable, it must transmit a jamming signal on the other side. Since the collision may not involve a transmission from the repeater, the CD threshold is different for a nontransmitting transceiver: a collision is detected if the signal strength exceeds that which could be produced by two transceiver outputs in the worst case.

A much simpler collision detection scheme is possible with the twisted-pair star-wiring approach (Figure 4.10). In this case, collision detection is based on logic rather than sensing voltage magnitudes. For any hub, if there is activity (signal) on more than one input, a collision is assumed. A special signal called the *collision presence* signal is generated. This signal is generated and sent out as long as activity is sensed on any of the input lines. This signal is interpreted by every node as an occurrence of collision. Figure 5.11 gives examples of the operation of a star-wired system with and without collisions. In the first example, a frame transmitted from station A propagates up to HHUB and is eventually received by all stations in the network. In the second example, a

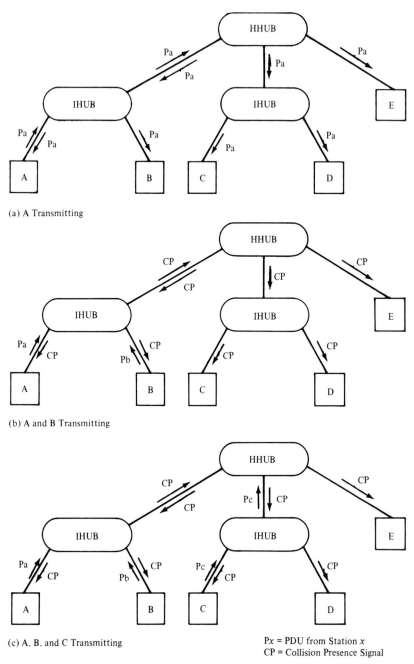

(a) A Transmitting

(b) A and B Transmitting

(c) A, B, and C Transmitting

Px = PDU from Station x
CP = Collision Presence Signal

FIGURE 5.11 Operation of a Two-Level Star-Wired CSMA/CD Configuration

collision is detected by A's IHUB. The collision presence signal propagates up to HHUB and is rebroadcast down to all hubs and stations. The third example shows the result of a three-way collision.

There are several possible approaches to collision detection in broadband systems. The most common of these is to perform a bit-by-bit comparison between transmitted and received data. When a station transmits on the inbound channel, it begins to receive its own transmission on the outbound channel after a propagation delay to the headend and back. In the IEEE 802.3 specification, the bits up through the last bit of the source address field of the transmitted and received signals are compared, and a collision is assumed if they differ. There are several problems with this approach. The most serious is the danger that differences in signal level between colliding signals will cause the receiver to treat the weaker signal as noise and fail to detect a collision. The cable system, with its taps, splitters, and amplifiers, must be carefully tuned so that attenuation effects and differences in transmitter signal strength do not cause this problem. Another problem for dual-cable systems is that a station must simultaneously transmit and receive on the same frequency. Its two RF modems must be carefully shielded to prevent cross-talk.

An alternative approach for broadband is to perform the CD function at the headend. This is most appropriate for the split system, which has an active component at the headend anyway. This reduces the tuning problem to one of making sure that all stations produce approximately the same signal level at the headend. The headend would detect collisions by looking for garbled data or higher-than-expected signal strength.

IEEE 802 CSMA/CD.   The IEEE 802 CSMA/CD standard [IEEE90b] is very close to that of Ethernet, and conforms to the preceding discussion. Figure 5.2 shows the MAC CSMA/CD frame structure. The individual fields are as follows:

- *Preamble:* a 7-byte pattern used by the receiver to establish bit synchronization and then locate the first bit of the frame.
- *Start frame delimiter (SFD):* indicates the start of a frame.
- *Destination address (DA):* specifies the station(s) for which the frame is intended. It must be a unique physical address (one destination transceiver), a multicast-group address (a group of stations), or a global address (all stations on the local network). The choice of a 16- or 48-bit address is an implementation decision and must be the same for all stations on a particular LAN.
- *Source address (SA):* specifies the station that sent the frame. The SA size must equal the DA size.
- *Length:* Specifies the number of LLC bytes that follow.

- *LLC:* field prepared at the LLC level.
- *Pad:* a sequence of bytes added to assure that the frame is long enough for proper CD operation.
- *Frame check sequence (FCS):* a 32-bit cyclic redundancy check value. Based on all fields, starting with destination address.

Token Bus

This is a relatively new technique for controlling access to a broadcast medium, inspired by the token ring technique discussed later. We will first provide a general description, then look at some of the IEEE 802 details.

Description. The token bus technique is more complex than CSMA/CD. For this technique, the stations on the bus or tree form a logical ring; that is, the stations are assigned logical positions in an ordered sequence, with the last member of the sequence followed by the first. Each station knows the identity of the stations preceding and following it. The physical ordering of the stations on the bus is irrelevant and independent of the logical ordering (Figure 5.12).

A control frame known as the *token* regulates the right of access. The token frame contains a destination address. The station receiving the token is granted control of the medium for a specified time. The station may transmit one or more frames and may poll stations and receive responses. When the station is done, or time has expired, it passes the token on to the next station in logical sequence. This station now has permission to transmit. Hence steady-state operation consists of alternating data transfer and token transfer phases. Nontoken-using stations are allowed on the bus. These stations can respond only to polls or requests for acknowledgment.

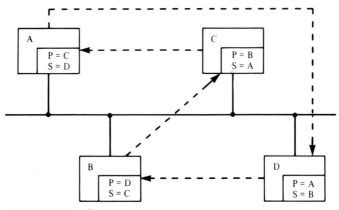

FIGURE 5.12 Token Bus

This scheme requires considerable maintenance. The following functions, at a minimum, must be performed by one or more stations on the bus:

- *Ring initialization:* When the network is started up, or after the logical ring has broken down, it must be initialized. Some cooperative, decentralized algorithm is needed to sort out who goes first, who goes second, and so on.
- *Addition to ring:* Periodically, nonparticipating stations must be granted the opportunity to insert themselves in the ring.
- *Deletion from ring:* A station must be able to remove itself from the ring by splicing together its predecessor and successor.
- *Recovery:* A number of errors can occur. These include duplicate address (two stations think it is their turn) and broken ring (no station thinks that it is its turn).

IEEE 802 Token Bus. The IEEE 802 token bus protocol follows the general principles outlined above [IEEE90c]. Figure 5.2 shows the MAC frame structure for token bus. The individual fields are as follows:

- *Preamble:* a one or more byte pattern used by receivers to establish bit synchronization and locate the first bit of the frame.
- *Start delimiter (SD):* indicates start of frame.
- *Frame control (FC):* indicates whether this is an LLC data frame. If not, bits in this field control operation of the token bus MAC protocol. An example is a token frame.
- *Destination address (DA):* as with CSMA/CD.
- *Source address (SA):* as with CSMA/CD.
- *LLC:* field prepared by LLC.
- *Frame check sequence (FCS):* as with CSMA/CD.
- *End delimiter (ED):* indicates end of frame.

The details of the protocol can be grouped into the following categories, which will be considered in turn:

- Addition of a node
- Deletion of a node
- Fault management by token holder
- Ring initialization
- Classes of service

First, let us consider how *addition of a node* is accomplished, using a controlled contention process called *response windows.* Each node in the ring has the responsibility of periodically granting an opportunity for new nodes to enter the ring. While holding the token, the node issues a *solicit-successor* frame, inviting nodes with an address between itself and the next node in logical sequence to demand entrance. The transmitting node then waits for one response window or slot time (equal to twice the end-to-end propagation delay of the medium). One of four events can occur.

1. *No response:* Nobody wants in. The token holder transfers the token to its successor as usual.
2. *One response:* One node issues a *set-successor* frame. The token holder sets its successor node to be the requesting node and transmits the token to it. The requestor sets its linkages accordingly and proceeds.
3. *Multiple responses:* The token holder will detect a garbled response if more than one node demands entrance. The conflict is resolved by an address-based contention scheme. The token holder transmits a *resolve-contention* frame and waits four response windows. Each demander can respond in one of these windows based on the first 2 bits of its address. If a demander hears anything before its window comes up, it refrains from demanding. If the token-holder receives a valid set-successor frame, it is in business. Otherwise, it tries again, and only those nodes that responded the first time are allowed to respond this time, based on the second pair of bits in their address. This process continues until a valid set-successor frame is received, no response is received, or a maximum retry count is reached. In the latter two cases, the token holder gives up and passes the token.
4. *Invalid response:* If the token holder hears a frame other than set-successor, it assumes that some other station thinks it holds the token. To avoid conflict, the station reverts to an idle or listen state.

Deletion of a node is much simpler. If a node wishes to drop out of the logical ring, it waits until it receives the token, and then sends a set-successor frame to its predecessor (the station that transmitted the token to it) containing the address of its successor. The existing station then sends the token as usual to its successor. On the next go-round, the former predecessor of the exited node will send the token to the former successor of the exited node. Each time that a station receives a token, it automatically sets its predecessor address to equal the source address of the token frame. Thus, the exited station is spliced out of the logical ring. If a node fails, it will not pick up the token when the token is passed to it, and this will be detected by the token sender, as explained below.

Fault management by the token holder covers a number of contingencies, listed in Table 5.6. First, while holding the token, a node may hear a frame indicating that another node has the token. If so, it immediately drops the token by reverting to listener mode. In this way, the number of token holders drops immediately to 1 or 0, thus overcoming the mul-

TABLE 5.6   Token Bus Error Handling

Condition	Action
Multiple token	Defer/drop to 1 or 0
Unaccepted token	Retry
Failed station	"Who follows" process
Failed receiver	Drop out of ring
No token	Initialize after time-out

tiple-token problem (which could be caused by two nodes having the same address). The next three conditions listed in the table are manifested during token passing. Upon completion of its turn, the token holder will issue a token frame to its successor. The successor should immediately issue a data or token frame. Therefore, after sending a token, the token issuer will listen for one slot time, to make sure that its successor is active. This precipitates a sequence of events:

1. If the successor node is active, the token issuer will hear a valid frame and revert to listener mode.
2. If the token issuer hears a garbled transmission, it waits four time slots. If it hears a valid frame, it assumes that its token got through. If it hears nothing, it assumes the token was garbled and reissues the token.
3. If the issuer does not hear a valid frame, it reissues the token to the same successor one more time.
4. After two failures, the issuer assumes that its successor has failed and issues a *who-follows* frame, asking for the identity of the node that follows the failed node. The issuer should get back a set-successor frame from the second node down the line. If so, the issuer adjusts its linkage and issues a token (back to step 1).
5. If the issuing node gets no response to its who-follows frame, it tries again.
6. If the who-follows tactic fails, the node issues a solicit-successor frame with the full address range (i.e., every node is invited to respond). If this process works, a two-node ring is established and life goes on.
7. If the solicit-successor tactic fails, it assumes that some major fault has occurred; either all other stations have failed, all stations have left the logical ring, the medium has broken, or the station's own receiver has failed. At this point, if the station has any more data to send, it sends that data and tries passing the token again. It then ceases transmission and listens to the bus.

Logical *ring initialization* occurs when one or more stations detect a lack of bus activity of duration longer than a time-out value: the token has been lost. This can be due to a number of causes, such as the network has just been powered up, or a token-holding station fails. Once its time-out expires, a node will issue a *claim-token* frame. Contending claimants are resolved in a manner similar to the response-window process. Each claimaint issues a claim-token frame padded by 0, 2, 4, or 6 slots based on the first 2 bits of its address. After transmission, a claimant listens to the medium and if it hears anything, drops its claim. Otherwise, it tries again, using the second pair of its address bits. The process repeats. With each iteration, only those stations who transmitted the longest on the previous iteration try again, using successive pairs of address bits. When all address bits have been used, a node that succeeds on the last iteration considers itself the token holder. The ring can now be rebuilt by the response window process described previously.

As an option, a token bus system can include *classes of access* that provide a mechanism of prioritizing access to the bus. Four access classes are defined, in descending order: class 6, 4, 2, and 0.

Any station may have data to send in one or more of these classes. The object is to allocate network capacity to the higher-priority frames and send only lower-priority frames when there is sufficient capacity. To explain, let us define the following variables:

- THT = token holding time: the maximum time that a station can hold the token to transmit class 6 data
- TRT4 = token rotation time for class 4; maximum time that a token can take to circulate and still permit class 4 transmission
- TRT2 = token rotation time for class 2: as above
- TRT0 = token rotation time for class 0: as above

When a station receives the token, it can transmit classes of data according to the following rules (Figure 5.13):

1. It may transmit class 6 data for a time THT. Hence for an *n*-station ring, during one circulation of the token, the maximum amount of time available for class 6 transmission is $n \times$ THT.
2. After transmitting class 6 data, or if there were no class 6 data to transmit, it may transmit class 4 data only if the amount of time for the last circulation of the token (including any class 6 data just sent) is less than TRT4.
3. The station may next send class 2 data only if the amount of time for the last circulation of the token (including any class 6 and 4 data just sent) is less than TRT2.
4. The station may next send class 0 data only if the amount of time for the last circulation of the token (including any class 6, 4, and 2 data just sent) is less than TRT0.

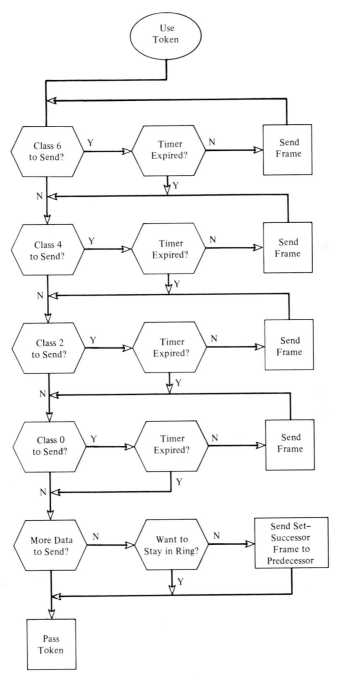

FIGURE 5.13 Token Bus Priority Scheme

This scheme, within limits, gives preference to frames of higher priority. More definitively, it guarantees that class 6 data may have a certain portion of the capacity. Two cases are possible. If $n \times$ THT is greater than MAX[TRT4, TRT2, TRT0], the maximum possible token circulation time is $n \times$ THT, and class 6 data may occupy the entire cycle to the exclusion of other classes. If $n \times$ THT is less than MAX[TRT4, TRT2, TRT0], the maximum circulation time is MAX[TRT4, TRT2, TRT0], and class 6 data are guaranteed $n \times$ THT amount of that time. This analysis ignores the time it takes to transmit the token and any other overhead, such as the reaction time at a station upon receipt of a token. However, these overhead quantities will generally be small compared to data transmission time.

Figure 5.14, which is adapted from one in [JAYA87], illustrates the average behavior of the 802.4 capacity-allocation scheme. That is, the plots ignore temporary load fluctuations, instead depicting the steady-state performance. For convenience, we assume that TRT4 > TRT2 > TRT0 and that the load generated in each class of data is the same.

Figure 5.14a depicts the first case ($n \times$ THT > TRT4). At very low loads, the token circulation time is very short, and all of the data offered in all four classes are transmitted. As the load increases, the average token circulation time reaches TRT0. There is then a range, as indicated in the figure, in which the load continues to increase but the token circulation time remains at TRT0. In this range, the other classes of data increase their throughput at the expense of class 0 data, whose throughput declines. At some point, the load is such that the token circulation time equals TRT0, but the amount of transmission in classes 2, 4, and 6

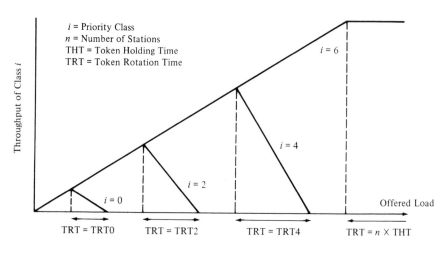

(a) Case I: $n \times$ THT > TRT4

FIGURE 5.14 Throughput of Token Bus Priority Classes

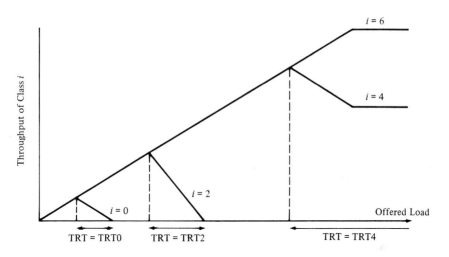

(b) Case IIa: $(TRT4/2) < n \times THT < TRT4$

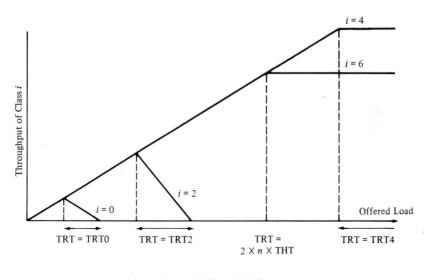

(c) Case IIb: $n \times THT < (TRT4/2)$

FIGURE 5.14 (Cont.)

uses up all of that time and no class 0 data can be transmitted. Further increase in offered load results in renewed increase in the token circulation time. The same pattern repeats for class 2 and class 4 data. There is a period when the load increases at a constant token circulation time of TRT2, and during that period, class 2 data are gradually crowded out. Class 4 data are similarly crowded out at a higher level of load. Finally, a situation is reached in which only class 6 data are being transmitted, and the token circulation time stabilizes at $n \times$ THT.

For the second case just mentioned ($n \times$ THT $<$ TRT4), we need to examine two subcases. Figure 5.14b shows the case in which $\frac{TRT4}{2} <$ ($n \times$ THT) $<$ TRT4. As before, with increasing load, class 0 and class 2 traffic are eliminated and the token circulation time increases. At some point, the increasing load drives the token circulation time to TRT4. Using our simple example, when this point is reached, approximately half of the load is class 4 data and the other half is class 6. But, since $n \times$ THT $> \frac{TRT4}{2}$, if the load on the network continues to increase, the portion of the load that is class 6 traffic will also increase. This will cause a corresponding decrease in class 4 traffic. Eventually, a point is reached at which all of the allowable class 6 traffic is being handled during each token circulation. This will take an amount of time $n \times$ THT and still leave some time left over for class 4 data. Thereafter, the total token circulation time remains stable at TRT4.

Finally, Figure 5.14c shows the case in which $n \times$ THT $< \frac{TRT4}{2}$. As before, increasing load eliminates class 0 and class 2 traffic. A point is reached at which the token circulation time is $2 \times n \times$ THT, with half of the traffic being class 4 and half being class 6. This is a maximum throughput-per-token-circulation for class 6. However, the amount of class 4 data can continue to increase until the token circulation time is TRT4.

Figure 5.15 is a simplified example of a 4-station logical ring with THT = 610 and TRT4 = TRT2 = TRT0 = 1600. Time is measured in *octet times*. Station 9 always transmits three class 6 frames of 128 octets each. Stations 7 and 5 send as many lower-priority frames as possible, of lengths 400 and 356 octets, respectively. Station 1 transmits class 6 frames of 305 octets each. Initially, Station 1 has two frames to transmit each time it gets the token, and later has only one frame to send per token possession. We assume that the time to pass the token is 19 octet times. In the figure, there are two columns of numbers under each station. The value in the left-hand column is the token circulation time observed at that station for the previous rotation of the token. The right-hand value is the number of frames that station transmits. Each row represents one rotation of the token.

The example begins after a period during which no data frames have been sent, so that the token has been rotating as rapidly as possible; thus each station measures a token circulation time of 76. In the first rotation, Station 9 transmits all of its class 6 frames. When Station 7 receives the token, it measures a rotation time of 460 since it last received

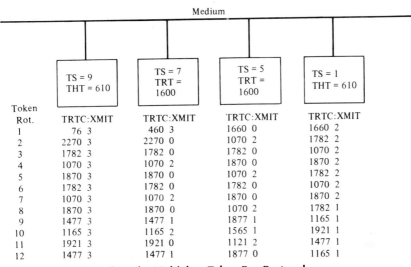

Token Rot.	TRTC:XMIT	TRTC:XMIT	TRTC:XMIT	TRTC:XMIT
1	76 3	460 3	1660 0	1660 2
2	2270 3	2270 0	1070 2	1782 2
3	1782 3	1782 0	1782 0	1070 2
4	1070 3	1070 2	1870 0	1870 2
5	1870 3	1870 0	1070 2	1782 2
6	1782 3	1782 0	1782 0	1070 2
7	1070 3	1070 2	1870 0	1870 2
8	1870 3	1870 0	1070 2	1782 1
9	1477 3	1477 1	1877 1	1165 1
10	1165 3	1165 2	1565 1	1921 1
11	1921 3	1921 0	1121 2	1477 1
12	1477 3	1477 1	1877 0	1165 1

FIGURE 5.15 Operation of a Multiclass Token Bus Protocol

the token (3*128 + 4*19). Thus it is able to send three of its frames before its TRT is exhausted. Station 5 measures a rotation time of 1660 (3*400 + 3*128 + 4*19) and thus is prevented from sending any data. Finally, Station 1 sends two class 6 frames.

Note that rotations 5 through 7 repeat rotations 2 through 4, showing a stable bandwidth allocation: Stations 1 and 9 use 69% of the bandwidth for class 6 data and Stations 5 and 7 share equally the remaining bandwidth for lower-priority data. Starting on the eighth rotation, Station 1 reduces it use of the LAN. This reduces the bandwidth used for class 6 data to 52%, and lower-priority data are allowed to fill in the unused bandwidth.

CSMA/CD versus Token Bus

At present, CSMA/CD and token bus are the two principal contenders for medium access control technique on bus/tree topologies. Table 5.7 attempts to summarize the pros and cons of the two techniques. A brief discussion follows.

Let us look at CSMA/CD first. On the positive side, the algorithm is simple; good news for the VLSI folks, and also good news for the user, in terms of cost and reliability. The protocol has been widely used for a long time, which also leads to favorable cost and reliability. The protocol provides fair access—all stations have an equal chance at the bandwidth; good if you require only fair access. As we shall see in Chapter 9, CSMA/CD exhibits quite good delay and throughput performance, at least up to a certain load, around 5 Mbps under some typical conditions.

TABLE 5.7   CSMA/CD versus Token Bus

Advantages	Disadvantages
CSMA/CD	
Simple algorithm	Colision detection requirement
Widely used	Fault diagnosis problems
Fair access	Minimum packet size
Good performance at low to medium load	Poor performance under very heavy load
	Biased to long transmissions
Token Bus	
Excellent throughput performance	Complex algorithm
Tolerates large dynamic range	Unproven technology
Regulated access	

There are, unfortunately, quite a few "cons" for CSMA/CD. From an engineering perspective, the most critical problem is the collision detection requirement. In order to detect collisions, the differences in signal strength from any pair of stations at any point on the cable must be small; this is no easy task to achieve. Other undesirable implications flow from the CD requirement. Since collisions are allowed, it is difficult for diagnostic equipment to distinguish expected errors from those induced by noise or faults. Also, CD imposes a minimum frame size, which is wasteful of bandwidth in situations where there are a lot of short messages, such as may be produced in highly interactive environments.

There are some performance problems as well. For certain data rates and frame sizes, CSMA/CD performs poorly as load increases. Also, the protocol is biased toward long transmissions.

For token bus, perhaps its greatest positive feature is its excellent throughput performance. Throughput increases as the data rate increases and levels off but does not decline as the medium saturates. Further, this performance does not degrade as the cable length increases. A second "pro" for token bus is that, because stations need not detect collisions, a rather large dynamic range is possible. All that is required is that each station's signal be strong enough to be heard at all points on the cable; there are no special requirements related to relative signal strength.

Another strength of token bus is that access to the medium can be regulated. If fair access is desired, token bus can provide this as well as CSMA/CD. Indeed, at high loads, token bus may be fairer; it avoids the last-in, first-out phenomenon mentioned earlier. If priorities are required, as they may be in an operational or real-time environment, these can be accommodated. Token bus can also guarantee a certain bandwidth; this may be necessary for certain types of data, such as voice, digital video, and telemetry.

An advertised advantage of token bus is that it is deterministic; that is, there is a known upper bound to the amount of time any station must wait before transmitting. This upper bound is known because each station in the logical ring can hold the token only for a specified time. In contrast, with CSMA/CD, the delay time can be expressed only statistically. Furthermore, since every attempt to transmit under CSMA/CD can in principle produce a collision, there is a possibility that a station could be shut out indefinitely. For process control and other real-time applications, this nondeterministic behavior is undesirable. Alas, in the real world, there is always a finite possibility of transmission error, which can cause a lost token. This adds a statistical component to token bus.

The main disadvantage of token bus is its complexity. The reader who made it through the description above can have no doubt that this is a complex algorithm. A second disadvantage is the overhead involved. Under lightly loaded conditions, a station may have to wait through many fruitless token passes for a turn.

Which to choose? That is left as an exercise to the reader, based on requirements and the relative costs prevailing at the time. The decision is also influenced by the baseband versus broadband debate. Both must be considered together when comparing vendors.

Centralized Reservation

The CSMA/CD technique was developed to deal with bursty traffic, such as is typically produced in interactive applications (query response, data entry, transactions). In this environment, stations are not transmitting most of the time; hence, a station with data to transmit can generally seize the channel quickly and with a minimum of fuss. Token bus, on the other hand, incurs the overhead of passing the token from one idle station to another.

For applications that have a stream rather then bursty nature (file transfer, audio, facsimile), token bus can perform quite well, especially if some priority scheme is used. If the collective load is great enough, CSMA/CD has difficulty keeping up with this kind of demand.

A number of schemes have been proposed, based on the use of reservations, that appear to offer the strengths of both CSMA/CD and token bus. In this section we look at a technique that requires centralized control. This is a likely candidate for a broadband system, with the control function performed at the headend. In Chapter 6 we will examine a decentralized control technique specifically designed for the high data rates of HSLNs.

The centralized scheme described in this section was developed by AMDAX for its broadband LAN [KARP82]. (Other centralized reservation schemes for bus systems have been described in [WILL73] and [MARK78].) Fixed-size frames of 512 bits are used, of which 72 are overhead bits. Time is organized into cycles, each cycle consisting of a set of equal-size time slots, and each time slot is sufficient for transmitting one frame. At the conclusion of one cycle, another cycle begins. The central controller at the headend may allocate slot or frame positions, within one or more future cycles, to particular stations. Frame positions not assigned to any station are referred to as *unallocated frames.* All stations must remain informed as to which frames are allocated to them and which are unallocated.

From the point of view of the station, communication is as follows. If a station has a small message to send, one that will fit in a single frame, it sends it in the next available unallocated frame on the inbound channel. The frame contains the message, source and destination addresses, and control information indicating that this is a data frame. Because the frame position used by the station is unallocated, it may also be used by another station, causing a collision. Hence the transmitting station must listen to the outbound channel for its transmission. If the station does not see its frame within a short defined time, it continues to send the frame at random times until it gets through.

To send messages too big to fit into a single frame, a station may reserve time on the bus. It does this by sending a reservation request to the central controller on the inbound channel. The request uses an unallocated frame and contains an indication that this is a request frame, the source address, and the number of frames to be sent. The station then listens to the outbound channel a short defined time, expecting to get a reservation confirmation frame containing its address and the number and order of frames in future cycles it has been allocated (if the line is too heavily loaded, it may not get all the bandwidth requested). When confirmation is received, the station may transmit its data in the frames allocated to it. If confirmation is not received, the station assumes that its reservation suffered a collision and tries again.

From the point of view of the central controller, communication is as follows. Frames are received one at a time on the inbound channel. Allocated frames are repeated on the outbound channel with no further processing. Unallocated frames must be examined. If the frame is garbled or contains an error, it is ignored. If it is a valid data frame, it is repeated on the outbound channel. If it is a valid reservation frame, the controller fills the reservation within the limits of its available frames in future cycles and sends a confirmation.

It should be clear that this technique exhibits the strengths of both CSMA/CD and token bus. Its principal disadvantage is that it requires a rather complex central controller, with the attendant reliability problems.

5.4

MEDIUM ACCESS CONTROL—RING

Over the years, a number of different algorithms have been proposed for controlling access to the ring. The three most common access techniques are discussed in this section: register insertion, slotted ring, and token ring. The first two will be briefly described; the token ring is discussed in some detail, as this is now an IEEE 802 standard.

Table 5.8 compares these three methods on a number of characteristics:

- *Transmit opportunity:* When may a repeater insert a packet onto the ring?
- *Packet purge responsibility:* Who removes a packet from a ring to avoid its circulating indefinitely?
- *Number of packets on ring:* This depends not only on the bit length of the ring relative to the relative packet length, but on the access method.
- *Principle advantage.*
- *Principal disadvantage.*

The significance of the table entries will become clear as the discussion proceeds.

TABLE 5.8   Ring Access Methods

Characteristic	Register Insertion	Slotted Ring	Token Ring
Transmit opportunity	Idle state plus empty buffer	Empty slot	Token
Packet purge responsibility	Receiver or transmitter	Transmitter	Transmitter
Number of packets on ring	Multiple	Multiple	One
Principal advantage	Maximum ring utilization	Simplicity	Regulated/fair access
Principal disadvantage	Purge mechanism	Bandwidth waste	Token maintenance

Token Ring

Token ring is probably the oldest ring control technique, originally proposed in 1969 [FARM69] and referred to as the *Newhall ring*. It has become the most popular ring access technique in the United States. This technique is the one ring access method selected for standardization by the IEEE 802 Local Network Standards Committee [IEEE89b].

Description.   The token ring technique is based on the use of a small frame, called a *token*, that circulates around the ring when all stations are idle. A station wishing to transmit must wait until it detects a token passing by. It then seizes the token by changing one bit in the token, which transforms it from a token to a start-of-frame sequence for a frame. The station then appends and transmits the remainder of the fields needed to construct a frame (Figure 5.16).

There is now no token on the ring, so other stations wishing to transmit must wait. The frame on the ring will make a round trip and be purged by the transmitting station. The transmitting station inserts a new token on the ring when both of the following conditions have been met:

- The station has completed transmission of its frame.
- The leading edge of its transmitted frame has returned (after a complete circulation of the ring) to the station.

If the bit length of the ring is less than the frame length, the first condition implies the second. If not, a station could release a free token after it has finished transmitting but before it begins to receive its own transmission; the second condition is not strictly necessary. However, use of the first condition alone might complicate error recovery, since several frames may be on the ring at the same time. In any case, the use of a token guarantees that only one station at a time may transmit.

When a transmitting station releases a new free token, the next station downstream with data to send will be able to seize the token and transmit.

Several implications of the token ring technique can be mentioned. Note that under lightly loaded conditions, there is some inefficiency since a station must wait for the token to come around before transmitting. However, under heavy loads, which is where it matters, the ring functions in a round-robin fashion, which is both efficient and fair. To see this, refer to Figure 5.16. Note that after station A transmits, it releases a token. The first station with an opportunity to transmit is D. If D transmits, it then releases a token and C has the next opportunity, and so on. Finally, the ring must be long enough to hold the token. If

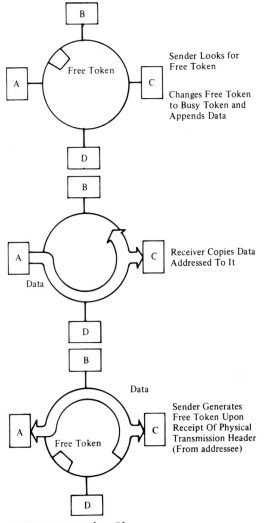

Sender Looks for
Free Token

Changes Free Token
to Busy Token and
Appends Data

Receiver Copies Data
Addressed To It

Sender Generates
Free Token Upon
Receipt Of Physical
Transmission Header
(From addressee)

FIGURE 5.16   Token Ring

stations are temporarily bypassed, their delay may need to be supplied artificially.

The principal advantage of token ring is the control over access that it provides. In the simple scheme described above, the access is fair. As we shall see, schemes can be used to regulate access to provide for priority and guaranteed bandwidth services.

The principal disadvantage of token ring is the requirement for token maintenance. Loss of the free token prevents further utilization of the ring. Duplication of the token can also disrupt ring operation. One station must be elected monitor to assure that exactly one token is on the ring and to reinsert a free token if necessary.

IEEE 802 Token Ring.   The IEEE 802 token ring specification is a refinement of the scheme just outlined. The key elements are as follows:

1. *Single-token protocol:* A station that has completed transmission will not issue a new token until the busy token returns. This is not as efficient for small frames as a multiple-token strategy of issuing a free token at the end of a frame. However, the single-token system simplifies priority and error-recovery functions.
2. *Priority bits:* These indicate the priority of a token and therefore which stations are allowed to use the token. In a multiple-priority scheme, priorities may be set by station or by message.
3. *Monitor bit:* Used by the ring monitor, as explained below.
4. *Reservation indicators:* They may be used to allow stations with high-priority messages to request in a frame that the next token be issued at the requested priority.
5. *Token-holding timer:* Started at the beginning of data transfer, it controls the length of time a station may occupy the medium before transmitting a token.
6. *Acknowledgment bits:* There are three: error detected (E), address recognized (A), and frame copied (C). These are set to 0 by the transmitting station. Any station may set the E bit. Addressed stations may set the A and C bits.

Figure 5.2 shows the two frame formats for token ring. The individual fields are as follows:

- *Starting delimiter (SD):* a unique 8-bit pattern used to start each frame.
- *Access control (AC):* has the format PPPTMRRR, where PPP and RRR are 3-bit priority and reservation variables, M is the monitor bit, and T indicates whether this is a token or data frame. In the case of a token frame, the only additional field is ED.
- *Frame control (FC):* indicates whether this is an LLC data frame. If not, bits in this field control operation of the token ring MAC protocol.
- *Destination address (DA):* as in CSMA/CD and token bus.
- *Source address (SA):* as in CSMA/CD and token bus.
- *LLC:* as in CSMA/CD and token bus.
- *FCS:* as in CSMA/CD and token bus.
- *Ending delimiter (ED):* contains the error detection (E) bit and the intermediate frame (I) bit. The I bit is used to indicate that this is a frame other than the final one of a multiple-frame transmission.

• *Frame status (FS):* contains the address recognized (A) and frame copied (C) bits.

Let us first consider the operation of the ring when only a single priority is used. In this case, the priority and reservation bits are not used. A station wishing to transmit waits until a free token goes by, as indicated by a token bit of 0 in the AC field. The station seizes the token by setting the token bit to 1. The SD and AC fields of the received token now function as the first two fields of a data frame. It then transmits one or more frames, continuing until either its output is exhausted or its token-holding timer expires. When the AC field of the last transmitted frame returns, the station transmits a free token by setting the token bit to 0 and appending an ED field.

Stations in the receive mode listen to the ring. Each station can check passing frames for errors and set the E bit if an error is detected. If a station detects its own address, it sets the A bit to 1; it may also copy the frame, setting the C bit to 1. This allows the originating station to differentiate three conditions:

• Station nonexistent/nonactive
• Station exists but frame not copied
• Frame copied

Token Ring Priority.   The 802.5 standard includes a specification for an optional priority mechanism. Eight levels of priority are supported by providing two 3-bit fields in each data frame and token: a priority field and a reservation field. To explain the algorithm, let us define the following variables:

$$P_f = \text{priority of frame to be transmitted by station}$$
$$P_s = \text{service priority: priority of current token}$$
$$P_r = \text{value of } P_s \text{ as contained in the last}$$
$$\text{token received by this station}$$
$$R_s = \text{reservation value in current token}$$
$$R_r = \text{highest reservation in the frames received by}$$
$$\text{this station during the last token rotation}$$

The scheme works as follows:

1. A station wishing to transmit must wait for a token with $P_s \leq P_f$.
2. While waiting, a station may reserve a future token at its priority level (P_f). If a data frame goes by, and if the reservation field is less than its priority $(R_s < P_f)$, then the station may set the reservation field of the frame to its priority $(R_s \leftarrow P_f)$. If a token frame goes by, and if $(R_s < P_f \text{ AND } P_f < P_s)$, then the station sets the reservation

field of the frame to its priority ($R_s \leftarrow P_f$). This has the effect of preempting any lower-priority reservation.

3. When a station seizes a token, it sets the token bit to 1 to start a data frame, sets the reservation field of the data frame to 0, and leaves the priority field unchanged (the same as that of the incoming token frame).

4. Following transmission of one or more data frames, a station issues a new token with the priority and reservation fields set as indicated in Table 5.9.

The effect of the above steps is to sort the competing claims and allow the waiting transmission of highest priority to seize the token as soon as possible. A moment's reflection reveals that, as stated, the algorithm has a ratchet effect on priority, driving it to the highest used level and keeping it there. To avoid this, a station that raises the priority (issues a

TABLE 5.9   Actions Performed by the Token Holder to Implement the Priority Scheme [VALE92]

Conditions	Actions
Frame available AND $P_s \leq P_f$	Send frame
(Frame not available OR THT expired) AND $P_r \geq$ MAX $[R_r, P_f]$	Send token with: $P_s \leftarrow P_f$ $Rs \leftarrow$ MAX $[R_r, P_f]$
(Frame not available OR THT expired) AND $P_r <$ MAX $[R_r, P_f]$ AND $P_r > S_x$	Send token with: $P_s \leftarrow$ MAX $[R_r, P_f]$ $Rs \leftarrow 0$ Push $S_r \leftarrow P_r$ Push $S_x \leftarrow P_s$
(Frame not available OR THT expired) AND $P_r <$ MAX $[R_r, P_f]$ AND $P_r = S_x$	Send token with: $P_s \leftarrow$ MAX $[R_r, P_f]$ $Rs \leftarrow 0$ Pop S_x Push $S_x \leftarrow P_s$
(Frame not available OR (Frame available and $P_f < S_x$)) AND $P_s = S_x$ AND $R_r > S_r$	Send token with: $P_s \leftarrow R_r$ $Rs \leftarrow 0$ Pop S_x Push $S_x \leftarrow P_s$
(Frame not available OR (Frame available and $P_f < S_x$)) AND $P_s = S_x$ AND $R_r \leq S_r$	Send token with: $P_s \leftarrow R_r$ $Rs \leftarrow 0$ Pop S_r Pop S_x

token that has a higher priority than the token that it received) has the responsibility of later lowering the priority to its previous level. Therefore, a station that raises priority must remember both the old and the new priorities and downgrade the priority of the token at the appropriate time. In essence, each station is responsible for assuring that no token circulates indefinitely because its priority is too high. By remembering the priority of earlier transmissions, a station can detect this condition and downgrade the priority to a previous, lower priority or reservation.

To implement the downgrading mechanism, two stacks are maintained by each station, one for reservations and one for priorities:

S_x = stack used to store new values of token priority

S_r = stack used to store old values of token priority

The reason that stacks rather than scalar variables are required is that the priority can be raised a number of times by one or more stations. The successive raises must be unwound in the reverse order.

To summarize, a station having a higher-priority frame to transmit than the current frame can reserve the next token for its priority level as the frame passes by. When the next token is issued, it will be at the reserved priority level. Stations of lower priority cannot seize the token, so it passes to the reserving station or an intermediate station with data to send of equal or higher priority than the reserved priority level. The station that upgraded the priority level is responsible for downgrading it to its former level when all higher-priority stations are finished. When that station sees a token at the higher priority, it can assume that there is no more higher-priority traffic waiting, and it downgrades the token before passing it on. Figure 5.17 is an example of the operation of the priority mechanism.

Token Maintenance.   To overcome various error conditions, one station is designated as the active monitor. The active monitor periodically issues an active-monitor-present control frame to assure other stations that there is an active monitor on the ring. To detect a lost token condition, the monitor uses a valid frame timer that is greater than the time required to completely traverse the ring. The timer is reset after every valid token or data frame. If the timer expires, the monitor issues a token. To detect a persistently circulating data frame, the monitor sets a monitor bit to 1 on any passing data frame the first time it goes by. If it sees a data frame with the monitor bit already set, it knows that the transmitting station failed to absorb the frame. The monitor absorbs the frame and transmits a token. The same strategy is used to detect a failure in the priority mechanism: no token should circulate completely around the ring at a constant nonzero priority level. Finally, if the active

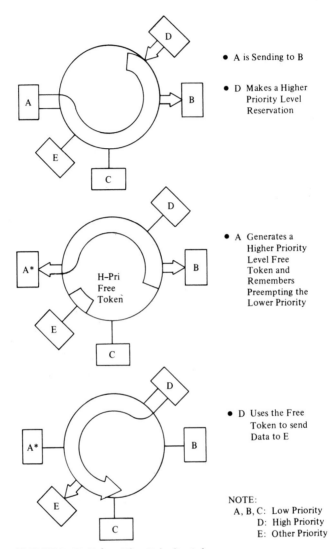

FIGURE 5.17 Token Ring Priority Scheme

monitor detects evidence of another active monitor, it immediately goes into standby monitor status.

In addition, all of the active stations on the ring cooperate to provide each station with a continuous update on the identity of its upstream neighbor. Each station periodically issues a standby-monitor-present (SMP) frame. Its downstream neighbor absorbs this frame, notes its ending address, and after a pause, sends its own SMP frame. The absence of SMP frames can be used in fault isolation.

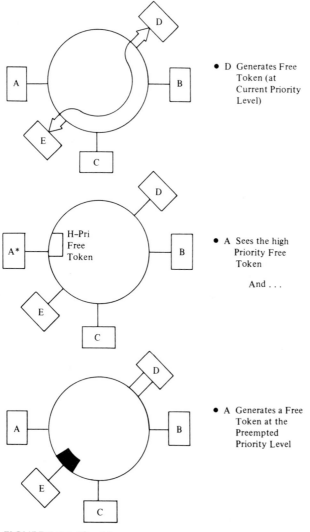

- D Generates Free Token (at Current Priority Level)

- A Sees the high Priority Free Token

  And . . .

- A Generates a Free Token at the Preempted Priority Level

FIGURE 5.17 (Cont.)

Register Insertion

This strategy was originally proposed in [HAFN74] and has been developed by researchers at Ohio State University [REAM75, LIU78]. It is also the technique used in the IBM Series 1 product [IBM82] and a Swiss product called SILK [HUBE83]. It derives its name from the shift register associated with each node on the ring. The shift register, equal in size to the maximum frame length, is used for temporarily holding frames that circulate past the node. In addition, the node has a buffer for storing locally produced frames.

The register insertion ring can be explained with reference to Figure 5.18, which shows the shift register and buffer at one node. First consider the case in which the station has no data to send, but is merely handling frames of data that circulate by its position. When the ring is idle, the input pointer points to the rightmost position of the shift register, indicating that it is empty. When data arrive from the ring, they are inserted bit by bit in the shift register, with the input pointer shifting left for each bit. The frame begins with an address field. As soon as the entire address field is in the register, the station can determine if it is the addressee. If not, the frame is forwarded by shifting one bit out on the right as each new bit arrives from the left, with the input pointer stationary. After the last bit of the frame has arrived, the station continues to shift bits out to the right until the frame is gone. If, during this time, no additional frames arrive, the input pointer will return to its initial position. Otherwise, a second frame will begin to accumulate in the register as the first is shifted out.

Two observations are in order. First, the last few sentences imply that more than one frame may be on the ring at a time. How this can be is described below. Second, picture a series of frames, with gaps in between, passing a station. The effect of the actions described in the preceding paragraph is to compress the gaps between the earlier arrivers and stretch them out for later arrivers. As we shall see, the widening gaps provide an opportunity for new frames to be inserted into the ring.

Returning to the main line of our discussion: If an arriving frame is addressed to the station in question, the station has two choices. First, it can divert the remainder of the frame to itself and erase the address bits from the register, thus purging the frame from the ring. This is the

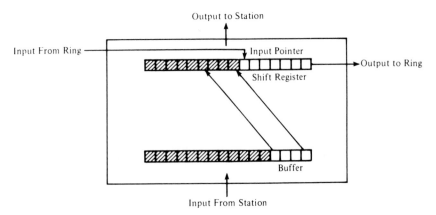

FIGURE 5.18 Register Insertion Ring

approach taken by IBM. A moment's thought will reveal that such a strategy can result in a total bandwidth utilization that at times exceeds actual bit transmission rate. However, this may be false economy since, if the receiver rather than the transmitter purges the ring, some other means of acknowledgment must be employed, thus wasting bandwidth. The second alternative is to retransmit the frame as before, while copying it to the local station.

Now consider the case in which the station has data to transmit. A frame to be transmitted is placed in the output buffer. If the line is idle and the shift register is empty, the frame can be transferred immediately to the shift register. If the frame consists of some length n bits, less than the maximum frame size, and if at least n bits are empty in the shift register, the n bits are parallel-transferred to the empty portion of the shift register immediately adjacent to the full portion; the input pointer is adjusted accordingly.

We can see that there is a delay at each station, whose minimum value is the length of the address field and whose maximum value is the length of the shift register. This is in contrast to slotted ring and token ring, where the delay at each station is just the repeater delay—typically one or two bit times. To get a feeling for the effect, consider a station transmitting a 1000-bit frame on a 10-Mbps register insertion ring. The time it takes the station to transmit the frame is $1000/10^7 = 0.10$ ms. If the frame must pass 50 stations to reach its destination and if the address field is 16 bits, then the minimum delay, exclusive of propagation time, is $(16 \times 50)/10^7 = 0.08$ ms. This is a substantial delay compared to transmission time. Worse, if each station has a 1000-bit shift register, the maximum delay the frame could experience is $(1000 \times 50)/10^7 = 5$ ms.

The register insertion technique enforces an efficient form of fairness. As long as the ring is idle, a station with a lot of data to be sent can send frame after frame, utilizing the entire bandwidth of the ring. If the ring is busy, however, a station will find that, after sending a frame, the shift register will not accommodate another frame right away. The station will have to wait until enough intermessage gaps have accumulated before sending again. As a refinement, certain high-priority nodes can be given shift registers whose length is greater than the minimum shift register length (which is equal to the maximum frame length).

The principal advantage of the register insertion technique is that it achieves the maximum ring utilization of any of the methods. There are several other favorable features. Like the token system, it allows variable-length frames, which is efficient from the point of view of both the stations and the ring. Like the slotted ring, it permits multiple frames to be on the ring—again, an efficient use of bandwidth.

The principal disadvantage is the purge mechanism. Allowing multiple frames on the ring requires the recognition of an address prior to removal of a frame, whether it be removed by sender or receiver. If a frame's address field is damaged, it could circulate indefinitely. One possible solution is the use of an error-detecting code on the address field; IBM's Series 1 employs a parity bit. The requirement for address field recognition also dictates that each frame be delayed at each node by the length of that field. No such requirement exists in the other two methods.

Slotted Ring

For the slotted ring (Figure 5.19), a number of fixed-length slots circulate continuously on the ring. This strategy was first developed by Pierce [PIER72] and is sometimes referred to as the *Pierce loop*. Most of the development work on this technique was done at the University of Cambridge in England [HOPP83], and a number of British firms market commercial versions of the *Cambridge ring* [HEYW81]. The Cambridge ring is the basis for an ISO standard for slotted ring (ISO 8802-7).

In the slotted ring, each slot contains a leading bit to designate the slot as empty or full. All slots are initially marked empty. A station with data to transmit must break the data up into fixed-length frames. It then waits until an empty slot arrives, marks the slot full, and inserts a frame of data as the slot goes by. The station cannot transmit another frame until this slot returns. The full slot makes a complete round-trip, to be marked empty again by the source. Each station knows the total number of slots on the ring and can thus clear the appropriate full/empty bit as it goes by. Once the now-empty slot goes by, the station is free to transmit again.

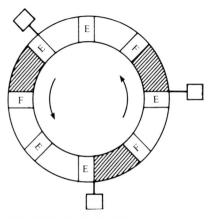

FIGURE 5.19 Slotted Ring

In the Cambridge ring, each slot contains room for one source address byte, one destination address byte, two, four, six, or eight data bytes, and five control bits, for a total length of 40, 56, 72, or 88 bits.

The Cambridge ring contains several interesting features. A station may decide that it wishes to receive data from only one other station. To accomplish this, each station includes a source select register. When this register contains all ones, the station will receive a packet addressed to it from any source; when it contains all zeros, the station will not accept packets from any source. Otherwise the station is open to receive packets from only the source whose address is specified by the register.

The Cambridge ring specifies two response bits in each packet to differentiate four conditions:

- Destination nonexistent/nonactive
- Packet accepted
- Destination exists but packet not accepted
- Destination busy

Finally, the Cambridge ring includes a monitor, whose task it is to empty a slot that is persistently full.

Typically, there will be very few slots on a ring. Consider, for example, a 100-station ring with an average spacing of 10 m between stations and a data rate of 10 Mbps. A typical propagation velocity for signals is 2×10^8 m/s. A moment's thought should reveal that the bit length of the link between two stations is $(10^7$ bps $\times$ 10 m$)(2 \times 10^8$ m/s$) = 0.5$ bit. Say that the delay at each repeater is one bit time. Then the total bit length of the ring is just 1.5×150 bits. This is enough for four slots.

The principal disadvantage of the slotted ring is that it is wasteful of bandwidth. First, each frame contains only 16 bits, resulting in a tremendous amount of overhead. Second, a station may send only one frame per round-trip time. If only one of a few stations have frames to transmit, many of the slots will circulate empty.

The principal advantage of the slotted ring appears to be its simplicity. The interaction with the ring at each node is minimized, improving reliability.

5.5

RECOMMENDED READING

[KURO84] is a good overall survey of MAC protocols. [BERT92] and [SPRA91] provide detailed, performance-oriented analyses of many bus and ring MAC protocols. A description of the IEEE 802 standards is provided in [MART89]; more technical treatments are to be found in [VALE92] and [STAL90a].

5.6

PROBLEMS

5.1 What arguments or parameters are essential for each of the LLC primitives in Table 5.4?

5.2 Why is there not an LLC primitive L-CONNECTION-FLOWCON-TROL confirm?

5.3 Show, with an example, how the LLC protocol provides the LLC services as defined by the LLC primitives.

5.4 A simple medium access control protocol would be to use a fixed assignment time-division multiplexing (TDM) scheme, as described in Section 2.1. Each station is assigned one time slot per cycle for transmission. For the bus and tree, the length of each time slot is the time to transmit 100 bits plus the end-to-end propagation delay. For the ring, assume a delay of one bit time per station, and assume that a round-robin assignment is used. Stations monitor all time slots for reception. What are the limitations, in terms of number of stations, and throughput per station for:

   a. A 1-km, 10-Mbps baseband bus?

   b. A 1-km (headend to farthest point), 10-Mbps broadband bus?

   c. A 10-Mbps broadband tree consisting of a 0.5-km trunk emanating from the headend and five 0.1-km branches from the trunk at the following points: 0.05 km, 0.15 km, 0.25 km, 0.35 km, 0.45 km?

   d. A 10-Mbps ring with a total length of 1 km?

   e. A 10-Mbps ring with a length of 0.1 km between repeaters?

   f. Compute throughput per station for all of the above for 10 and 100 stations.

5.5 The binary exponential back-off algorithm is defined by IEEE 802 thus: "The delay is an integral multiple of slot time. The number of slot times to delay before the nth retransmission attempt is chosen as a uniformly distributed random integer r in the range $0 < r < 2^{**}K$, where $K = \min(n,10)$." Slot time is, roughly, twice the round-trip propagation delay. Assume that two stations always have a frame to send. After a collision, what is the mean number of retransmission attempts before one station successfully retransmits? What is the answer if three stations always have frames to send?

5.6 Consider two stations on a baseband bus at a distance of 1 km from each other. Let the data rate be 1 Mbps, the packet length be 100 bits, and the propagation velocity be 2×10^8 m/s. Assume that each station generates packets at an average rate of 1000 packets per second. For the ALOHA protocol, if one station begins to transmit a packet at time t, what is the probability of collision? Repeat for slotted-ALOHA. Repeat for ALOHA and slotted-ALOHA at 10 Mbps.

5.7   Repeat Problem 5.6 for a broadband bus. Assume that the two stations are 1 km apart and that one is very near the headend.

5.8   For a p-persistent CSMA, what is the probability that the next transmission after a successful transmission will be successful for $np = 0.1, 1.0,$ and 10?

5.9   In what sense are the slotted ring and token ring protocols the complement of each other?

5.10   A promising application of fiber optics for local networks is in the ring topology. Which, if any, of the three ring protocols is inappropriate for this medium?

5.11   For a token ring system, suppose that the destination station removes the data frame and immediately sends a short acknowledgment frame to the sender, rather than letting the original frame return to sender. How will this affect performance?

5.12   Consider a Cambridge ring of length 10 km with a data rate of 10 Mbps and 500 repeaters, each of which introduces a 1-bit delay. How many slots are on the ring?

5.13   For the ring in Problem 5.12, assume a constant user data load of 4 Mbps. What is the mean number of slots that a station must wait to insert a packet?

5.14   Write a program that implements the token ring priority mechanism.

5.15   If the token ring active monitor fails, it is possible that two stations will timeout and claim that status. Suggest an algorithm for overcoming this problem.

5.16   The IEEE 802 refers to the token bus service class scheme as a bandwidth allocation scheme rather than a priority scheme. A priority scheme would provide that all frames of higher priority would be transmitted before any lower-priority frames would be allowed on the bus. Show by counterexample that the 802 scheme is not a priority scheme.

5.17   Compare the token bus service class scheme with the token ring and priority scheme. What are the relative pros and cons? Is it possible, with appropriate parameter settings, to achieve the same behavior from both?

APPENDIX 5A: IEEE 802 STANDARDS

The key to the development of the LAN market is the availability of a low-cost interface. The cost to connect equipment to a LAN must be much less than the cost of the equipment alone. This requirement, plus the complexity of the LAN protocols, dictate a VLSI solution. However, chip manufacturers will be reluctant to commit the necessary resources unless there is a high-volume market. A LAN standard would assure that volume and also enable equipment of a variety of manufacturers to intercommunicate. This is the rationale of the IEEE Project 802 [CLAN82], a committee established by the IEEE Computer Society in February 1980 to prepare local area network standards. In 1985, the 802 committee issued a set of four standards, which were subsequently adopted in 1985 by the American National Standards Institute (ANSI) as American National Standards [IEEE85a-d]. These standards were subsequently revised and reissued as international standards by the International Organization for Standardization (ISO) in 1987, with the designation ISO 8802.

Two conclusions were quickly reached by the committee. First, the task of communication across the local network is sufficiently complex that it needs to be broken up into more manageable subtasks. Second, no single technical approach will satisfy all requirements.

The second conclusion was reluctantly reached when it became apparent that no single standard would satisfy all committee participants. There was support for both ring and bus topologies. With the bus topology, there was support for two access methods (CSMA/CD and token bus) and two media (baseband and broadband). The response of the committee was to standardize all serious proposals rather than to attempt to settle on just one. Figure 5.20 illustrates the results.

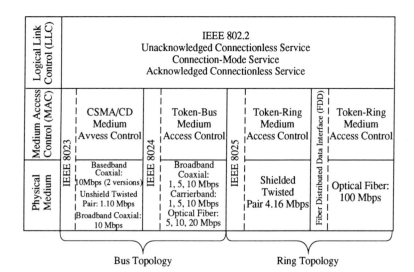

FIGURE 5.20 Local Area Network Standards

This chapter has described in some detail the LLC and MAC standards. It remains to briefly summarize the physical layer standards.

CSMA/CD (IEEE 802.3)

The IEEE 802.3 committee has been the most active in defining alternative physical configurations. This is both good and bad. On the good side, the standard has been responsive to evolving technology. On the bad side, the customer, not to mention the potential vendor, is faced with a bewildering array of options. However, the committee has been at pains to ensure that the various options can be easily integrated into a configuration that satisfies a variety of needs. Thus, the user that has a complex set of requirements may find the flexibility and variety of the 802.3 standard to be an asset.

To distinguish the various implementations that are available, the committee has developed a concise notation:

<data rate in Mbps> <signaling method><maximum segment length in hundreds of meters>

The defined alternatives are:

- 10BASE5
- 10BASE2
- 1BASE5
- 10BASET (this does not quite follow the notation; "T" stands for twisted pair)
- 10BROAD36

Table 5.10 summarizes these options.

The 10BASE5 specification is the **original 802.3 standard;** it specifies a 10-Mbps baseband coaxial cable LAN using standard baseband coaxial cable. The maximum length of a segment of cable is 500 meters, with a maximum of 100 taps per segment allowed. The length of the network can be extended using repeaters (see Figure 4.3). The standard allows a maximum of four repeaters in the path between any two stations, extending the effective length of the network to 2.5 km.

This original version, issued in 1985, was soon followed by a new option, 10BASE2, sometimes called **Cheapernet.** This provides for the use of a thinner coaxial cable at the same data rate. The thinner cable results in significantly cheaper electronics, at the penalty of fewer stations and shorter length. Segment length is reduced to 185 meters with a maximum of 30 taps per segment. It is targeted to lower-cost devices, such as UNIX workstations and personal computers.

Another option, known as **StarLAN,** specifies an unshielded twisted-pair version operating at 1 Mbps. As the name suggests, the layout of StarLAN makes use of star wiring. In particular, the hub arrangement

TABLE 5.10 IEEE 802.3 Physical Layer Medium Alternatives

Parameter	10BASE5	10BASE2	1BASE5	10BASET	10BROAD36
Transmission medium	Coaxial Cable (50 ohm)	Coaxial Cable (50 ohm)	Unshielded twisted pair	Unshielded twisted pair	Coaxial Cable (75 ohm)
Signaling technique	Baseband (Manchester)	Baseband (Manchester)	Baseband (Manchester)	Baseband (Manchester)	Broadband (DPSK)
Data rate (Mbps)	10	10	1	10	10
Maximum sement length (m)	500	185	500	100	1800
Network span (m)	2500	925	2500	500	3600
Nodes per segment	100	30	—	—	—
Cable diameter (mm)	10	5	0.4–0.6	0.4–0.6	0.4–1.0

described in Chapter 2 is employed (Figures 4.10, 4.11, and 4.12). This option is substantially lower in cost than either of the coaxial cable options and is targeted specifically at personal computer installations that do not require high capacity. This option could be appropriate for a departmental-level LAN.

The attraction of the 1BASE5 specification is that it allows the use of inexpensive unshielded twisted-pair wire, which is ordinary telephone wire. Such wire is often found prewired in office buildings as excess telephone cable and can be used for LANs. Of course, the disadvantage of this specification is the rather low data rate of 1 Mbps. By sacrificing some distance, it is possible to develop a 10-Mbps LAN using the unshielded twisted-pair medium. Such an approach is specified in the latest physical medium addition to the 802.3 family, the 10BASET specification.

As with the 1BASE5 specification, the **10BASET** specification defines a star-shaped topology. The details of this topology differ sightly from those of 1BASE5. In both cases, a simple system consists of a number of stations connected to a central point. In both cases, stations are connected to the central point via two twisted pairs. The central point accepts input on any one line and repeats it on all of the other lines. In the case of the 10BASET specification, the central point is referred to as a multiport repeater.

Stations attach to the multiport repeater via a point-to-point link. Ordinarily, the link consists of two unshielded twisted pairs. The data rate is 10 Mbps using Manchester encoding. Because of the high data rate and the poor transmission qualities of of unshielded twisted pair, the length of a link is limited to 100 meters. As an alternative, an optical fiber link may be used. In this case, the maximum length is 500 m.

The distinction between a 1BASE5 hub and a 10BASET multiport repeater becomes clear when we consider a multistar arrangement. Figure 5.21 shows a sample configuration for 10BASET. The medium access unit (MAU) denotes the logic required for interfacing a device to the LAN. Note that the connection between one repeater and the next is a link that appears the same as an ordinary station link. In fact, the repeater makes no distinction between a station and another repeater. Recall that in the 1BASE5 system, there is a distinction between intermediate hubs and header hubs. In the 10BASET system, all multiport repeaters function in the same manner as an ordinary repeater on a 10BASE5 or 10BASE2 system:

- A valid signal appearing on any input is repeated on all other links.
- If two inputs occur, causing a collision, a collision enforcement signal is transmitted on all links.
- If a collision enforcement signal is detected on any input, it is repeated on all other links.

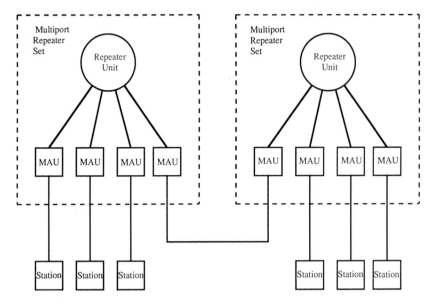

FIGURE 5.21 A Simple 10BASET Configuration

One advantage of the use of repeaters and the use of a data rate of 10 Mbps is that the 10BASET system can be mixed with 10BASE2 and 10BASE5 systems. All that is required is that the MAU conform to the appropriate specification. Figure 5.22 shows a configuration containing four 10BASET systems and one 10BASE5 system.

Table 5.11 summarizes the allowable connections. The maximum transmission path permitted between any two stations is five segments and four repeater sets. A segment is either a point-to-point link segment or a coaxial 10BASE5 or 10BASE2 segment. The maximum number of coaxial cable segments in a path is three.

Finally, a 10-Mbps **broadband** option has been added, 10BROAD36. This provides for the support of more stations over greater distances than the baseband versions, at greater cost.

TABLE 5.11   Allowable Connections to a 10BASET Multiport Repeater

Transmission Medium	Number of Attached Devices	Maximum Length (m)
Two unshielded twisted pairs	2	100
Two optical fiber cables	2	500
Coaxial cable (10BASE5)	30	185
Coaxial cable (10BASE2)	100	500

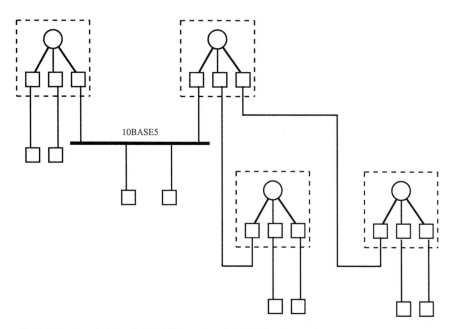

FIGURE 5.22 A Mixed 10BASET and 10BASE5 Configuration

Token Bus (IEEE 802.4)

The token bus standard specifies three physical layer options (Table 5.12). One is a **broadband** system, which supports data channels at 1, 5, and 10 Mbps with bandwidths of 1.5, 6, and 12 MHz, respectively. The standard recommends the use of a single-cable split system with a headend frequency translator. The dual-cable configuration is also allowed.

The second is a scheme known as **carrierband,** or single-channel broadband. Recall that carrierband signaling means that the entire spectrum of the cable is devoted to a single transmission path for analog signals. Because carrierband is dedicated to a single data channel, it is not necessary to take care that the modem output be confined to a narrow bandwidth. Energy can spread over the cable's spectrum. As a result, the electronics are simple and inexpensive compared with those for broadband. Carrierband data rates of 1, 5, and 10 Mbps are specified.

The most recent addition to the IEEE 802.4 physical layer standard is an **optical fiber** specification. Three data rates are specified: 5, 10, and 20 Mbps. In keeping with standard practice for optical fiber systems, the bandwidth and carrier are specified in terms of wavelength instead of frequency. For all three data rates, the bandwidth is 270 nm and the center wavelength is between 800 and 910 nm.

TABLE 5.12 IEEE 802.4 Physical Layer Medium Alternatives

Parameter	Phase-Continuous Carrierband	Phase Coherent Carrierband	Broadband			Optical Fiber
Data rate (Mbps)	1	5	10	1	5	5, 10, 20
Bandwidth	N.A.	N.A.	N.A.	1.5 MHz	6 MHz	270 nm
Center frequency	5 MHz	7.5 MHz	15 MHz	*	*	800–910 nm
Modulation	Manchester/phase continuous FSK	Phase coherent FSK	Multilevel duobinary AM/PSK			On-off
Topology	Omnidirectional bus	Omnidirectional bus	Directional bus (tree)			Active or passive star
Transmission medium	Coaxial cable (75 ohm)	Coaxial cable (75 ohm)	Coaxial cable (75 ohm)			Optical fiber
Scrambling	No	No	Yes			No

TABLE 5.13   IEEE 802.5 Physical Layer Medium Specification

Transmission Medium	Shielded Twisted Pair
Data rate (Mbps)	4 or 16
Maximum number of repeaters	250
Maximum length between repeaters	Not specified

The 802.4 optical fiber specification can be used with any topology that is logically a bus. That is, a transmission from any one station is received by all other stations, and if two stations transmit at the same time, a collision occurs. The standard recommends the use of active or passive stars.

Token Ring (IEEE 802.5)

Only a single medium option is specified in 802.5: **shielded twisted pair** at 4 and 16 Mbps (Table 5.13) using Differential Manchester encoding. An earlier specification of a 1-Mbps system has been dropped from the most recent edition of the standard.

APPENDIX 5B: SERVICE PRIMITIVES AND PARAMETERS

In a communications architecture, such as the OSI model or the LAN architecture (Figure 5.1), each layer is defined in two parts: the protocol between peer (at the same layer) entities in different systems, and the services provided by one layer to the next higher layer in the same system.

We have seen a number of examples of protocols, which are defined in terms of the formats of the protocol data units that are exchanged, and the rules governing the use of those protocol data units. The services between adjacent layers are expressed in terms of primitives and parameters. A primitive specifies the function to be performed, and the parameters are used to pass data and control information. The actual form of a primitive is implementation dependent. An example is a procedure call.

Four types of primitives are used in standards to define the interaction between adjacent layers in the architecture. These are defined in Table 5.14. The layout of Figure 5.23b suggests the time ordering of these events. For example, consider the transfer of a connection request

TABLE 5.14   Primitive Types

REQUEST	A primitive issued by a service user to invoke some service and to pass the parameters needed to fully specify the requested service.
INDICATION	A primitive issued by a service provided to either: 1. indicate that a procedure has been invoked by the peer service user on the connection and to provide the associated parameters, or 2. notify the service user of a provider-initiated action.
RESPONSE	A primitive issued by a service user to acknowledge or complete some procedure previously invoked by an indication to that user.
CONFIRM	A primitive issued by a service provider to acknowledge or complete some procedure previously invoked by a request by the service user.

from LLC user *A* to a peer entity *B* in another system. The following steps occur:

1. *A* invokes the services of LLC with a DL-CONNECT.request primitive. Associated wtih the primitive are the parameters needed, such as the destination address.
2. The LLC entity in *A*'s system prepares an LLC protocol data unit (PDU) to be sent to its peer LLC entity in *B*.

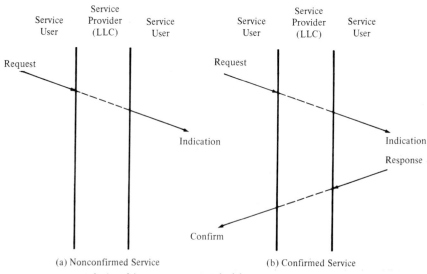

(a) Nonconfirmed Service   (b) Confirmed Service

FIGURE 5.23 Relationship Among LLC Primitives

3. The destination LLC entity delivers the data to *B* via a DL-CON-NECT.indication, which includes the source address and other parameters.
4. *B* issues a DL-CONNECT.response to its LLC entity.
5. *B*'s LLC entity conveys the acknowledgment to *A*'s LLC entity in a PDU.
6. The acknowledgment is delivered to *A* via a DL-CONNECT.confirm.

This sequence of events is referred to as a **confirmed service,** because the initiator receives confirmation that the requested service has had the desired effect at the other end. If only request and indication primitives are involved (corresponding to steps 1, 2, and 3), then the service dialogue is a **nonconfirmed service;** the initiator receives no confirmation that the requested action has taken place.

CHAPTER 6

Metropolitan Area Network Architecture

The newest area of interest in communications networking is that of metropolitan area networks (MANs). As the name suggests, a MAN occupies a middle ground between local area networks (LANs) and wide-area networks (WANs). Interest in MANs has come about as a result of a recognition that the traditional point-to-point and switched network techniques used in WANs may be inadequate for the growing needs of organizations. While broadband ISDN, with ATM, holds out promise for meeting a wide range of high-speed needs, there is a requirement now for both private and public networks that provide high capacity at low costs over a large area. The high-speed shared-medium approach of the LAN standards provides a number of benefits that can be realized on a metropolitan scale.

Some of the key characteristics of MANs are:

- *High speed:* A MAN is intended to support a relatively large number of devices, including a number of LANs. Therefore, high capacity is required.
- *Geographic scope:* As the name suggests, a MAN is intended to cover an area extending from a few blocks of buildings to a good-size metropolitan area.
- *Integrated voice/data support:* In many cases, a MAN will be used not only to support the interconnection of LANs and stand-alone computers, but also as an alternative to or supplement to the local telephone service. Thus, the MAN must support traffic generally

carried by circuit-switched networks as well as packet-switched traffic.

The focus of this chapter is on standardized approaches to MAN design. We begin with a look at the fiber distributed data interface (FDDI). This standard can be viewed as either a high-speed LAN standard or as a MAN standard; the architecture supports both applications. It is convenient to treat FDDI with other MANs in this chapter.

The original specification for FDDI supports only packet-switched traffic. An enhancement, known as FDDI-II, extends FDDI to provide circuit-switching traffic; this system is examined next.

Both FDDI and FDDI-II operate over a fiber optic ring. The remainder of the chapter is devoted to the fiber bus approach. The standard configuration is the IEEE 802.6 DQDB standard, which supports both packet-switched and circuit-switched traffic.

6.1

FDDI

As with the IEEE 802.3, 802.4, and 802.5 standards, the FDDI standard encompasses both the MAC and physical layers, and supports the use of IEEE 802.3 logical link control (LLC). Figure 6.1 depicts the overall FDDI protocol architecture, which below the LLC level consists of four parts:

1. *Medium access control (MAC):* As with the 802 standards, the FDDI MAC layer is the portion of the data link layer that regulates access to the LAN medium.

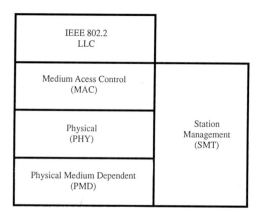

FIGURE 6.1 FDDI Protocol Architecture

2. *Physical (PHY):* This is the medium-independent portion of the physical layer, which includes the encoding of digital data.
3. *Physical medium dependent (PMD):* Characterizes the medium-dependent aspects of the physical layer.
4. *Station management (SMT):* Provides the control necessary at the station level to manage the processes underway in the various FDDI layers.

Both the FDDI and FDDI-II standards make use of a ring LAN topology with optical fiber medium, operating at 100 Mbps. We turn first to FDDI.

FDDI MAC Protocol

The FDDI MAC protocol is a token-ring protocol, similar to the IEEE 802.5 specification. There are several differences that reflect the requirements of the higher data rate (100 Mbps) of FDDI. Table 6.1 summarizes the key differences. Some of these are at the MAC layer and are discussed in this subsection; the remainder are at the physical layer and are examined in a subsequent subsection.

FDDI Frame Format. Figure 6.2 depicts the frame formats for the FDDI protocol. Compare these to those of 802.5 (Figure 5.2). The standard defines the contents of this format in terms of symbols, with each symbol corresponding to 4 bits. Symbols are used because at the physical layer data are encoded and transmitted in 4-bit chunks. However, MAC entities in fact must deal with individual bits, so the discussion that follows sometimes refers to 4-bit symbols and sometime to bits. A frame other than a token frame consists of the following fields:

- *Preamble:* Synchronizes the frame with each station's clock. The originator of the frame uses a field of 16 idle symbols (64 bits); subse-

TABLE 6.1 Differences Between FDDI and 802.5

FDDI	802.5
Optical fiber	Shielded twisted pair
100 Mbps	4, 16 Mbps
Reliability specification	No reliability specification
4B/5B code	Differential Manchester
Distributed clocking	Centralized clocking
Timed token rotation	Priority and reservation bits
New token after transmit	New token after receive

Bits	64	8	8	16 or 48	16 or 48	0	32	4	1
	Preamble	SD	FC	DA	SA	Info	FCS	ED	FS

SD = Starting delimiter
FC = Frame control
DA = Destination address
SA = Source address
FCS = Frame check sequence
ED = Ending delimiter
FS = Frame staus

(a) General Frame Format

Preamble	SD	FC	ED

(b) Token Frame Format

FIGURE 6.2 FDDI Frame Formats

quent repeating stations may change the length of the field consistent with clocking requirements. The idle symbol is a nondata fill pattern. The actual form of a nondata symbol depends on the signal encoding on the medium.

- *Starting delimiter (SD):* Indicates start of frame. It is coded as JK, where J and K are nondata symbols.
- *Frame control (FC):* Has the bit format CLFFZZZZ, where C indicates whether this is a synchronous or asynchronous frame (explained below); L indicates the use of 16- or 48-bit addresses; FF indicates whether this is an LLC, MAC control, or reserved frame. For a control frame, the remaining 4 bits indicate the type of control frame.
- *Destination address (DA):* Specifies the station(s) for which the frame is intended. It may be a unique physical address, a multicast-group address, or a broadcast address. The ring may contain a mixture of 16- and 48-bit address lengths.
- *Source address (SA):* Specifies the station that sent the frame.
- *Information:* Contains LLC data unit or information related to a control operation.
- *Frame check sequence (FCS):* A 32-bit cyclic redundancy check, based on the FC, DA, SA, and information fields.
- *Ending delimiter (ED):* Contains one or two nondata symbols (T) and marks the end of the frame, except for the FS field. The ED is 8 bits long for a token and 4 bits long for all other frames.
- *Frame status (FS):* Contains the error detected (E), address recognized (A), and frame copied (F) indicators. Each indicator is represented by a symbol, which is R for "off" or "false" and S for "on" or "true."

A comparison with the 802.5 frame shows that the two are very similar. The FDDI frame includes a preamble to aid in clocking, which is more demanding at the higher data rate. Both 16- and 48-bit addresses are allowed on the same network with FDDI; this is more flexible than the scheme used on all the 802 standards. Finally, there are some differences in the control bits. For example, FDDI does not include priority and reservation bits; capacity allocation is handled in a different way, as described below.

MAC Protocol. The basic (without capacity allocation) FDDI MAC protocol is fundamentally the same as IEEE 802.5. There are two key differences:

1. In FDDI, a station waiting for a token seizes the token by absorbing (failing to repeat) the token transmission as soon as the token frame is recognized. After the captured token is completely received, the station begins transmitting one or more data frames. The 802..5 technique of flipping a bit to convert a token to the start of a data frame was considered impractical because of the high data rate of FDDI.
2. In FDDI, a station that has been transmitting data frames releases a new token as soon as it completes data frame transmission, even if it has not begun to receive its own transmission. Again, because of the high data rate, it would be too inefficient to require the station to wait, as in 802.5.

Figure 6.3 gives an example of ring operation. After Station A has seized the token, it transmits frame F1, and immediately transmits a new token. F1 is addressed to Station C, which copies it as it circulates past. The frame eventually returns to A, which absorbs it. Meanwhile, B seizes the token issued by A and transmits F2 followed by a token. This action could be repeated any number of times, so that at any one time, there may be multiple frames circulating the ring. Each station is responsible for absorbing its own frames based on the source address field.

Capacity Allocation. The priority scheme used in 802.5 will not work in FDDI, as a station will often issue a token before its own transmitted frame returns. Hence, the use of a reservation field is not effective. Furthermore, the FDDI standard is intended to provide for greater control over the capacity of the network than 802.5 to meet the requirements for a high-speed LAN. Specifically, the FDDI capacity allocation scheme seeks to accommodate the following requirements:

- Support for a mixture of stream and bursty traffic
- Support for multiframe dialogue

With respect to the first requirement, a high-capacity LAN would be expected to support a large number of devices or to act as a backbone for a number of other LANs. In either case, the LAN would be expected

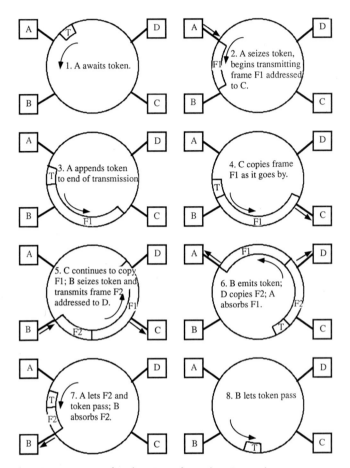

FIGURE 6.3 Example of FDDI Token Ring Operation

to support a wide variety of traffic types. For example, some of the stations may generate short, bursty traffic with modest throughput requirements but a need for a short delay time. Other stations may generate long streams of traffic that require high throughput, but they may be able to tolerate moderate delays prior to the start of transmission.

With respect to the second requirement, there may sometimes be a need to dedicate a fixed fraction or all of the capacity of the LAN to a single application. This permits a long sequence of data frames and acknowledgments to be interchanged. An example of the utility of this feature is a read or write to a high-performance disk. Without the ability to maintain a constant high-data rate flow over the LAN, only one sector of the disk could be accessed per revolution—an unacceptable performance.

To accommodate the requirement to support a mixture of stream and bursty traffic, FDDI defines two types of traffic: synchronous and asynchronous. Each station is allocated a portion of the total capacity (the portion may be zero); the frames that it transmits during this time are referred to as **synchronous frames.** Any capacity that is not allocated or that is allocated but not used is available for the transmission of additional frames, referred to as **asynchronous frames.**

The scheme works as follows. A target token rotation time (TTRT) is defined; each station stores the same value for TTRT. Some or all stations may be provided a synchronous allocation (SA_i), which may vary among stations. The allocations must be such that:

$$DMax + FMax + TokenTime + \Sigma SA_i \leq TTRT$$

where

$$
\begin{aligned}
SA_i &= \text{synchronous allocation for station } i \\
DMax &= \text{propagation time for one} \\
&\quad \text{complete circuit of the ring} \\
FMAX &= \text{time required to transmit a} \\
&\quad \text{maximum-length frame (4500 octets)} \\
TokenTime &= \text{time required to transmit a token}
\end{aligned}
$$

The assignment of values for SA_i is by means of a station management protocol involving the exchange of station management frames. The protocol assures that the above equation is satisfied. Initially, each station has a zero allocation and it must request a change in the allocation. Support for synchronous allocation is optional; a station that does not support synchronous allocation may transmit only asynchronous traffic.

All stations have the same value of TTRT and a separately assigned value of SA_i. In addition, several variables that are required for the operation of the capacity-allocation algorithm are maintained at each station:

- Token-rotation timer (TRT)
- Token-holding timer (THT)
- Late counter (LC)

Each station is initialized with TRT set equal to TTRT and LC set to zero.[1] When the timer is enabled, TRT begins to count down. If a token is received before TRT expires, TRT is reset to TTRT. If TRT counts down to 0 before a token is received, then LC is incremented to 1 and TRT is reset to TTRT and again begins to count down. If TRT expires a second

---

[1]All timer values in the standard are negative numbers with counters counting up to zero. For clarity, the discussion uses positive numbers.

time before receiving a token, LC is incremented to 2, the token is considered lost, and a claim process (described below) is initiated. Thus LC records the number of times, if any, that TRT has expired since the token was last received at that station. The token is considered to arrive early if TRT has not expired since the station received the token, that is, if LC = 0.

When a station receives the token, its actions will depend on whether the token is early or late. If the token is early, the station saves the remaining time from TRT in THT, resets TRT, and enables TRT:

$$\text{THT} \leftarrow \text{TRT}$$
$$\text{TRT} \leftarrow \text{TTRT}$$
$$\text{enable TRT}$$

The station can then transmit according to the following rules:

1. It may transmit synchronous frames for a time SA_i.
2. After transmitting synchronous frames, or if there were no synchronous frames to transmit, THT is enabled. The station may transmit asynchronous frames only as long as THT > 0.

If a station receives a token and the token is late, then LC is set to zero, and TRT continues to run. The station can then transmit synchronous frames for a time SA_i. The station may not transmit any asynchronous frames.

This scheme is designed to assure that the time between successive sightings of a token is on the order of TTRT or less. Of this time, a given amount is always available for synchronous traffic and any excess capacity is available for asynchronous traffic. Because of random fluctuations in traffic, the actual token circulation time may exceed TTRT [JOHN87, SEVC87], as demonstrated below.

The FDDI algorithm is similar to the 802.4 algorithm with only two classes of data: 6 and 4. Synchronous data corresponds to class 6 and the value of SA_i in FDDI corresponds to the token-holding time in 802.4. TTRT corresponds to TRT4. Since the sum of the SA_i (all the synchronous allocations) must be less than or equal to TTRT, the FDDI restrictions correspond to case IIa in Figure 5.14.

Figure 6.4 illustrates the use of the station variables in FDDI by displaying the values of TRT, THT, and LC for a particular station. In this example, taken from [MCCO88], the TTRT is 100 milliseconds (ms). The station's synchronous capacity allocation, SA_i, is 30 ms. The following events occur:

A. A token arrives early. The station has no frames to send. TRT is set to TTRT (100 ms) and begins to count down. The station allows the token to go by.
B. The token returns 60 ms later. Since TRT = 40 and LC = 0, the token is early. The station sets THT ← TRT and TRT ← TTRT, so

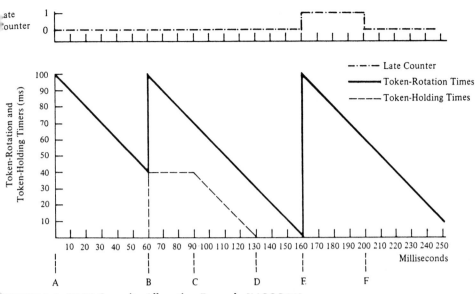

FIGURE 6.4 FDDI Capacity Allocation Example [MCCO88]

that THT = 40 and TRT = 100. TRT is immediately enabled. The station has synchronous data to transmit and begins to do so.

C. After 30 ms, the station has consumed its synchronous allocation. It has asynchronous data to transmit, so it enables THT and begins transmitting.

D. THT expires, and the station must cease transmission of asynchronous frames. The station issues a token.

E. TRT expires. The station increments LC to 1 and resets TRT to 100.

F. The token arrives. Since LC is 1, the token is late, and no asynchronous data may be transmitted. At this point, the station also has no synchronous data to transmit. LC is reset to 1 and the token is allowed to go by.

Figure 6.5 provides a simplified example of a 4-station ring. We assume that the traffic consists of fixed-length frames, and that TTRT = 100 frame times and SA_i = 20 frame times for all stations. We also assume that the total overhead during one complete token circulation is 4 frame times. One row of the table corresponds to one circulation of the token. For each station, the arrival time is shown, followed by the value of TRT at the time of arrival, followed by the number of synchronous and asynchronous frames transmitted while the station holds the token.

The example begins after a period during which no data frames have been sent, so that the token has been circulating as rapidly as possible (4 frame times). Thus, when Station 1 receives the token, it measures a

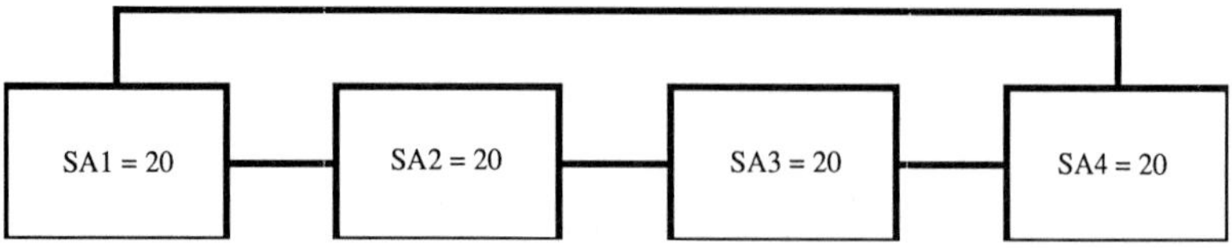

Arrival Time	TRT	Sync	Async	Arrival Time	TRT	Sync	Async	Arrival Time	TRT	Sync	Async	Arrival Time	TRT	Sync	Async
0	100	0	0	1	100	0	0	2	100	0	0	3	100	0	0
4	96	20	96	121	80*	20	0	142	60*	20	0	163	40*	20	0
184	20*	20	0	205	96	20	0	226	76*	20	0	247	56*	20	0
268	36*	20	0	289	16	20	16	326	76*	20	0	347	56*	20	0
368	36*	20	0	389	0	20	0	410	92*	20	0	431	72*	20	0
452	52*	20	0	473	16	20	16	510	92*	20	0	531	72*	20	0
552	52*	20	0	573	0	20	0	594	8	20	8	623	80*	20	0
644	60*	20	0	665	8	20	8	694	0	20	0	715	88*	20	0
736	68*	20	0	757	8	20	8	786	8	20	8	815	88*	20	0
836	68*	20	0	857	0	20	0	878	8	20	8	907	96*	20	0
928	76*	20	0	949	8	20	8	978	0	20	0	999	4	20	4
1024	80*	20	0	1045	4	20	4	1070	8	20	8	1099	0	20	0

FIGURE 6.5 Operation of FDDI Capacity Allocation Scheme

circulation time of 4 (its TRT = 96). It is therefore able to send not only its 20 synchronous frames but also 96 asynchronous frames; recall that THT is not enabled until after the station has sent its synchronous frames. Station 2 experiences a circulation time of 120 (20 frames + 96 frames + 4 overhead frames), but is nevertheless entitled to transmit its 20 synchronous frames. Note that if each station continues to transmit its maximum allowable synchronous frames, then the circulation time surges to 180 at time 184, but soon stabilizes at 100. With a total synchronous utilization of 80 and an overhead of 4 frame times, there is an average capacity of 16 frame times available for asynchronous transmission. Note that if all stations always have a full backlog of asynchronous traffic, the opportunity to transmit asynchronous frames is distributed among them.

This example demonstrates that the synchronous allocation does not always provide a guaranteed fraction of capacity $\dfrac{SA_i}{TTRT}$. Rather, the fraction of capacity available to a station for synchronous transmission during any token circulation is $\dfrac{SA_i}{\tau}$, where τ is the actual circulation time. As we have seen, τ can exceed TTRT. It can be shown that τ tends, in the steady state, to TTRT and has an upper bound of $2 \times$ TTRT [JOHN87].

Asynchronous traffic can be further subdivided into eight levels of priority. Each station has a set of eight threshold values, T_Pr(1), . . . , T_Pr(8), such that T_Pr(i) = maximum time that a token can take to circulate and still permit priority *i* frames to be transmitted. Rule 2 above is revised as follows:

2. After transmitting synchronous frames, or if there were no synchronous frames to transmit, THT is enabled and begins to run from its set value. The station may transmit asynchronous data of priority *i* only so long as THT > T_Pr(*i*). The maximum value of any of the T_Pr(*i*) must be no greater than TTRT.

This scheme is essentially the one used in the 802.4 token bus standard (Figure 5.13).

The above rules satisfy the requirement for support for both stream and bursty traffic and, with the use of priorities, provide a great deal of flexibility. In addition, FDDI provides a mechanism that satisfies the requirements for dedicated multiframe traffic mentioned earlier. When a station wishes to enter an extended dialog it may gain control of all the unallocated (asynchronous) capacity on the ring by using a restricted token. The station captures a nonrestricted token, transmits the first frame of the dialog to the destination station, and then issues a restricted token. Only the station that received the last frame may transmit asynchronous frames using the restricted token. The two stations may then exchange data frames and restricted tokens for an extended period, during which no other station may transmit asynchronous frames. The standard assumes that restricted transmission is predetermined not to violate the TTRT limitation, and it does not mandate the use of THT during this mode. Synchronous frames may be transmitted by any station upon capture of either type of token.

Figure 6.6 depicts the complete FDDI capacity allocation scheme.

FDDI Physical Layer Specification

The physical layer specification for FDDI includes a medium-independent part and a medium-specific part. In the medium-independent part, two key topics addressed are data encoding and jitter. We examine these first and then look at the physical medium specification.

Data Encoding. Recall from our discussion in Chapter 2 that digital data need to be encoded in some form for transmission as a signal. The type of encoding will depend on the nature of the transmission medium, the data rate, and other constraints, such as cost. Optical fiber is inherently an analog medium; signals can be transmitted only in the optical frequency range. Thus we might expect that one of the popular digital-to-analog encoding techniques (ASK, FSK, PDSK) would be used. Both FSK and PSK are difficult to do at high data rates and the optoelectronic equipment would be too expensive and unreliable

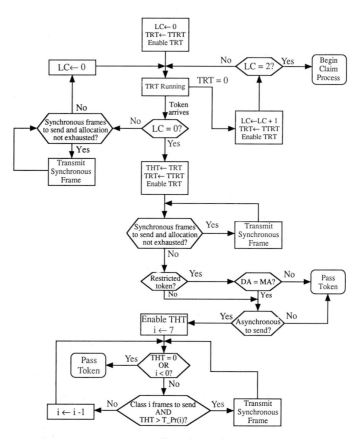

FIGURE 6.6 FDDI Capacity Allocation Scheme

[FREE91]. With amplitude-shift keying (ASK), recall, a constant-frequency signal is used, and two different signal levels are used to represent the two binary data values. In the simplest case, one value is represented by the absence of the carrier, and the other value by the presence, at constant amplitude, of the signal. This technique is often called *intensity modulation*.

Intensity modulation, then, provides a simple means for encoding digital data for transmission over optical fiber. A binary 1 can be represented by a burst or pulse of light, and a binary 0 by the absence of optical energy. The disadvantage of this approach is its lack of synchronization. Since transitions on the fiber are unpredictable, there is no way for the receiver to synchronize its clock to the transmitter. The solution to this problem is to first encode the binary data to guarantee the presence of transitions and then to present the encoded data to the optical source for transmission. For example, the data could first be encoded using Manchester encoding; the high and low codes depicted in Figure 2.5 could then be transmitted as light and nonlight, respectively. This is in fact a common signaling technique used for optical fiber transmission; it is used in the 802.4 optical fiber specification, for example. The disadvantage of this approach is that the efficiency is only 50%. That is, because there can be as many as two transitions per bit time, a signaling rate of 200 million signal elements per second (200 Mbaud) is needed to achieve a data rate of 100 Mbps. At the high data rate of FDDI, this represents an unnecessary cost and technical burden.

To achieve greater efficiency, the FDDI standard specifies the use of a code referred to as 4B/5B. In this scheme, encoding is done 4 bits at a time; each 4 bits of data are encoded into a symbol with five *cells*, such that each cell contains a single signal element (presence or absence of light). In effect, each set of 4 bits is encoded as 5 bits. The efficiency is thus raised to 80%: 100 Mbps is achieved with 125 Mbaud.

To understand how the 4B/5B code achieves synchronization, you need to know that there is actually a second stage of encoding: each cell of the 4B/5B stream is treated as a binary value and encoded using Nonreturn to Zero Inverted (NRZI) as shown in Figure 2.5. In this code, a binary 1 is represented with a transition at the beginning of the bit interval and a binary 0 is represented with no transition at the beginning of the bit interval; there are no other transitions. The advantage of NRZI is that it employs differential encoding. Recall from Chapter 2 that in differential encoding the signal is decoded by comparing the polarity of adjacent signal elements rather than the absolute value of a signal element. A benefit of this scheme is that it is generally more reliable to detect a transition in the presence of noise and distortion than to compare a value to a threshold. This aids the ultimate decoding of the signal after it has been converted back from the optical to the electrical realm.

Now we are in a position to describe the 4B/5B code and to understand the selections that were made. Table 6.2 shows the symbol encoding used in FDDI. Each possible 5-cell pattern is shown, together with its NRZI realization. Since we are encoding 4 bits with a 5-bit pattern, only 16 of the 32 possible patterns are needed for data encoding. The codes selected to represent the 16 4-bit data blocks are such that a transition is present at least twice for each 5-cell code. Given an NRZI format, no more than three zeros in a row are allowed.

The FDDI encoding scheme can be summarized as follows:

1. A simple intensity modulation encoding is rejected because it does not provide synchronization; a string of ones or zeros will have no transitions.
2. The data to be transmitted must first be encoded to assure transitions. The 4B/5B code is chosen over Manchester because it is more efficient.

TABLE 6.2   4B/5B Code

Code Group	NRZI Pattern	Symbol	Assignment
	Line State Symbols		
00000		Q	Quiet
11111		I	Idle
00100		H	Halt
	Starting Delimiter		
11000		J	1st of sequential SD Pair
10001		K	2nd of sequential SD Pair
	Data Symbols		
11110		0	0000
01001		1	0001
10100		2	0010
10101		3	0011
01010		4	0100
01011		5	0101
01110		6	0110
01111		7	0111
10010		8	1000
10011		9	1001
10110		A	1010
10111		B	1011
11010		C	1100
11011		D	1101

TABLE 6.2 (Cont.)

Code Group	NRZI Pattern	Symbol	Assignment
Data Symbols			
11100		E	1110
11101		F	1111
Ending Delimiter			
01101		T	Used to terminate the data stream
Control Indicators			
00111		R	Denoting logical ZERO (reset)
11001		S	Denoting logical ONE (set)
Invalid Code Assignments			
00001		V or H	Violation or Halt
00010		V or H	Violation or Halt
00011		V	Violation
00101		V	Violation
00110		V	Violation
01000		V or H	Violation or Halt
01100		V	Violation
10000		V or H	Violation or Halt

3. The 4B/5B code is further encoded using NRZI so that the resulting differential signal will improve reception reliability.
4. The specific 5-bit patterns chosen for the encoding of the 16 4-bit data patterns are chosen to guarantee no more than three zeros in a row to provide for adequate synchronization.

Only 16 of the 32 possible cell patterns are required to represent the input data. The remaining cell patterns are either declared invalid or assigned special meaning as control symbols. These assignments are listed in Table 6.2. The nondata symbols fall into the following categories:

- *Line state symbols:* Q indicates the absence of any transitions and loss of clock recovery ability. Halt indicates a forced logical break in activity while maintaining DC balance and clock recovery. I indicates normal condition between frame and token transmissions. The I symbol is used in frame absorption. When a frame returns to the originating station, it is stripped by that station by transmitting I's immediately following its recognition (following the source address field), instead of repeating the frame. Similarly, a token is absorbed by a station by transmitting I's after determining that the incoming frame is a token.
- *Starting delimiter:* The starting delimiter field consists of a J and K symbol pair used to designate the beginning of a frame.
- *Ending delimiter:* The ending delimiter field consists of one or two T symbols used to designate the end of the frame, except for the frame status field if present.
- *Control indicators:* The R and S symbols are used in the frame status field to indicate presence or absence of a condition, as explained earlier.
- *Invalid code assignments:* The remaining symbol codes are designated as violation (V) symbols, some of which may be recognized as off-alignment H symbols.

Timing Jitter. Recall that in Chapter 4 we defined timing jitter as the deviation of clock recovery that can occur when the receiver attempts to recover clocking as well as data from the received signal. The clock recovery will deviate in a random fashion from the timing of the transmitter due to signal impairments in transmission and imperfections in the receiver circuitry. If no countermeasures are taken, the jitter accumulates around the ring. We saw that the IEEE 802.5 standard specifies that only one clock will be used on the ring, and that the station with the clock is responsible for eliminating jitter by means of an elastic buffer. If the ring as a whole runs ahead of or behind the master clock, the elastic buffer expands or contracts accordingly. Even with this technique, the accumulation of jitter places a limitation on the size of the ring.

This centralized clocking approach is inappropriate for a 100-Mbps fiber ring. At 100 Mbps, the bit time is only 10 ns, compared to a bit time of 250 ns at 4 Mbps. Thus the effects of distortion are more severe, and a centralized clocking scheme would put very tough, and therefore expensive, demands on the phase-lock loop circuity at each node. Therefore, the FDDI standard specifies the use of a distributed clocking scheme. Each station uses its own autonomous clock to transmit bits from its MAC layer onto the ring. For repeating incoming data, a buffer is imposed between the receiver and the transmitter. Data are clocked into the buffer at the clock rate recovered from the incoming stream, but are clocked out of the buffer at the station's own clock rate. The buffer has a capacity of 10 bits and expands and contracts as needed. At any time, the buffer contains a certain number of bits. As bits come in, they are placed in the buffer and thus experience a delay equal to the time it takes to transmit the bits ahead of it in the buffer. If the received signal is slightly faster than the repeater's clock, the buffer will expand to avoid dropping bits. If the received signal is slow, the buffer will contract to avoid adding bits to the repeated bit stream.

The buffer in each repeater is initialized to its center position each time that it begins to receive a frame, during the preamble that begins the frame. This increases or decreases the length of the preamble, initially transmitted as 16 symbols, as it proceeds around the ring. Because the stability of the transmitter clock is specified as 0.005%, a buffer of 10 bits allows transmission of frames 4500 octets in length without overrunning or underrunning the limits of the buffer.

Physical Medium Specification.   The FDDI standard specifies an optical fiber ring with a data rate of 100 Mbps, using the NRZI-4B/5B encoding scheme described previously. The wavelength specified for data transmission is 1300 nm.

The specification indicates the use of multimode fiber transmission. Although today's long-distance networks rely primarily on single-mode fiber, that technology generally requires the use of lasers as light sources, rather than the cheaper and less powerful light-emitting diodes (LEDs), which are adequate for FDDI requirements. The dimensions of the fiber cable are specified in terms of the diameter of the core of the fiber and the outer diameter of the cladding layer that surrounds the core. The combination specified in the standard is 62.5/125 μm. The standard lists as alternatives 50/125, 82/125, and 100/140 μm. In general, smaller diameters offer higher potential bandwidths but also higher connector loss.

Station and FDDI Network Configurations

Each FDDI station is composed of logical entities that conform to the FDDI standards. The role of a given station depends on the number of entities it has. Networks with different physical topologies may be constructed, depending on the types of stations used.

Dual Ring.   To enhance the reliability of an FDDI ring, the standard provides for the construction of a dual ring, as illustrated in Figure 6.7. Stations participating in a dual ring are connected to their neighbors by two links that transmit in opposite directions. This creates two rings: a primary ring, and a secondary ring on which data may circulate in the opposite direction. Under normal conditions, the secondary ring is idle. When a link failure occurs, the stations on either side of the link reconfigure as shown in Figure 6.7b, isolating the link fault and restoring a

(a) Normal Operation

(b) Reconfigured After Link Failure

(c) Reconfigured After Station Failure

● = MAC Entity

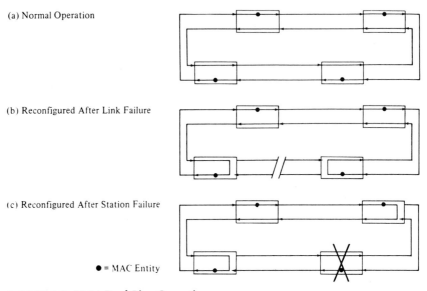

FIGURE 6.7 FDDI Dual-Ring Operation

closed ring. In this figure, a dark dot represents a MAC attachment within the station. Thus, in the counter direction, signals may be merely repeated, while the MAC protocol is involved in only the primary direction. As an option, a station may contain two MAC entities and therefore execute that MAC protocol in both directions.

Should a station fail, as shown in Figure 6.7c, then the stations on either side reconfigure to eliminate the failed station and both links to that station.

Station Types.   The type of station just described is only one of four station types defined in the FDDI standard (Table 6.3). The use of four different station types allows for the creation of complex topologies and for designs with high levels of reliability.

The dual attachment station (DAS), as just described, can be used to construct a dual ring. In some cases, this dual ring will constitute the entire FDDI LAN. In other cases, the dual ring can serve as the trunk ring for a more complex topology. In its most general form, the topology that can be achieved with FDDI is referred to as a *dual ring of trees.*

Figure 6.8 is an example that shows the use of all four station types. The main trunk is a dual ring consisting only of stations that are capable of supporting the two rings. Some of these stations are DASs, whose function is to provide an attachment point for end-user stations. Others are dual-attachment concentrators (DACs) that participate in the dual ring and may support an end-user station. In addition, each DAC may support stations that attach to a single ring. Each DAC therefore serves as the root of a tree. Single attachment stations (SASs) may attach to the

TABLE 6.3 FDDI Station Types

Station Type	Definition	Connects To
Dual Attachment (DAS)	Has two pairs of PHY and PMD entities and one or more MAC entities; participates in the trunk dual ring.	DAS, DAC
Dual Attachment Concentrator (DAC)	A DAS with additional PHY and PMD entities beyond those required for attachment to the dual ring. The additional entities permit attachment of additional stations that are logically part of the ring but are physically isolated from the trunk ring.	DAS, DAC, SAC, SAS
Single Attachment Station (SAS)	Has one each PHY, PMD, and MAC entities, and therefore cannot be attached into the trunk ring, but must be attached by a concentrator.	DAC, SAC
Single Attachment Concentrator (SAC)	A SAS with additional PHY and PMD entities beyond those required for attachment to a concentrator. The additional entities permit attachment of additional stations in a tree-structured fashion.	DAC, SAC, SAS

DAC by means of a single ring. The SAS connection does not provide the reliability of the dual-ring configuration available to the DAS. However, FDDI constrains the topology so that an SAS must attach to a concentrator. In the event of a failure of the SAS or its connection to the concentrator, the concentrator may isolate the SAS. Therefore, the reliability of the dual ring is maintained. To achieve a tree structure of depth greater than two, single-attachment concentrators (SACs) may be used. An SAC may attach to a DAC or another SAC and may support one or more SASs.

It is important to note that even with an elaborate tree structure, an FDDI configuration still maintains a ring topology. Figure 6.9 shows the circulation path for a simple configuration of a dual ring of two stations, one of which is a DAC. Note that the six stations form a single ring around which a single token will circulate. In addition, a secondary ring that encompasses the DASs and DACs is available for reliability.

FDDI Topologies. The definition of four station types allows for the creation of a wide variety of topologies. The following are of particular interest:

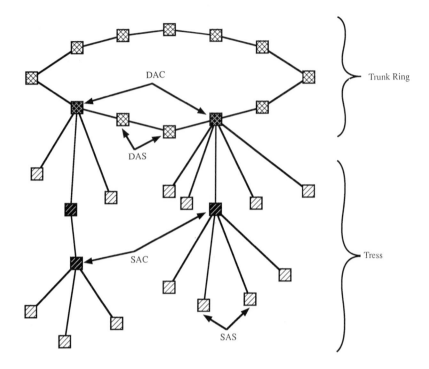

FIGURE 6.8 General FDDI Topology [WOLT90]

- *Stand-alone concentrator with attached stations:* a single concentrator and its attached stations. Such a configuration could be used to connect multiple high-performance devices in a work group or multiple LANs, with each FDDI station being a bridge.
- *Dual ring:* a set of DASs connected to form a single dual ring. This topology is useful when there are a limited number of users. It could also be used to interconnect departmental LANs, with each FDDI station being a bridge.
- *Tree of concentrators:* a good choice for interconnecting large groups of user devices. Concentrators are wired in a hierarchical star arrangement with one concentrator serving as the root of the tree. This topology provides great flexibility for adding and removing concentrators and stations or changing their location without disrupting the LAN.
- *Dual ring of trees:* the most elaborate and flexible topology. Key stations can be incorporated into the dual ring for maximum availability, and the tree structure provides the flexibility described in the preceding item.

Ring Monitoring

The responsibility for monitoring the functioning of the token ring algorithm is distributed among all stations on the ring. Each station mon-

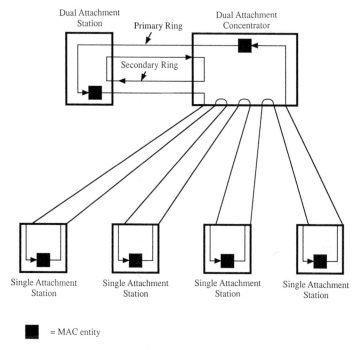

FIGURE 6.9 Star-Shaped Ring

itors the ring for invalid conditions requiring ring initialization. Invalid conditions include an extended period of inactivity or incorrect activity (e.g., persistent data frame). To detect the latter condition, each station keeps track of how long it has been since it last saw a valid token. If this time significantly exceeds TTRT, an error condition is assumed.

Three processes are involved in error detection and correction:

- Claim token process
- Initialization process
- Beacon process

Two MAC control frames are used: the Beacon frame and the Claim frame.

Claim Token Process. A station will detect the need for initialization of the ring by observing the lack of token; as explained above, this event occurs when the station sets LC to 2. Any station detecting a lost token initiates the claim-token process by issuing a sequence of Claim frames. The purpose of the claim-token process is to negotiate the value to be assigned to TTRT and to resolve contention among stations attempting to initialize the ring. Each claiming station sends a continuous stream of Claim frames. The information field of the Claim frame contains the station's bid for the value of TTRT. Each claiming station inspects incoming Claim frames and either defers (ceases to transmit its own Claim frames and just repeats incoming frames) or not (continues to transmit its own Claim frames and absorbs incoming frames), according to the following arbitration hierarchy:

- The frame with the lower TTRT has precedence.
- Given equal values of TTRT, a frame with a 48-bit address has precedence over a frame with a 16-bit address.
- Given equal values of TTRT and equal address lengths, the frame with the address of larger numerical value has precedence.

The process completes when one station receives its own Claim frame, which has made a complete circuit of the ring without being preempted. At this point, the ring is filled with that station's Claim frames and all other stations have yielded. All stations store the value of TTRT contained in the latest received Claim frame. The result is that the smallest requested value for TTRT is stored by all stations and will be used to allocate capacity.

The motivation for giving precedence to the lowest TTRT value is to make the LAN responsive to time-critical applications. If we define ring latency (RL) as the total overhead during one complete token circulation, then ring utilization can be expressed as:

$$\frac{TTRT - RL}{TTRT}$$

Low values of TTRT will provide a low guaranteed response time and thus support real-time applications. High values of TTRT allow very high ring use under heavy loads.

Initialization Process.   The station that has won the claim-token process is responsible for initializing the ring. All the stations on the ring recognize the initialization process as a result of having seen one or more Claim frames. The initializing station issues a nonrestricted token. On the first circulation of the token, it may not be captured. Rather, each station uses the appearance of the token for transition from an initialization state to an operational state, and to reset its TRT.

Beacon Process.   The Beacon frame is used to isolate a serious ring failure such as a break in the ring. For example, when a station is attempting the claim-token process, it will eventually time out if it does not come to a resolution (winning or losing), and it will enter the Beacon process.

Upon entering the Beacon process, a station continuously transmits Beacon frames. A station always yields to a Beacon frame received from an upstream station. Consequently, if the logical break persists, the Beacon frames of the station immediately downstream from the break will normally be propagated. If a station in the Beacon process receives its own Beacon frames, it assumes that the ring has been restored, and it initiates the claim-token process.

6.2

FDDI-II

FDDI-II is an upward-compatible extension to FDDI that adds the ability to support circuit-switched traffic in addition to the packet-mode traffic supported by the original FDDI.

With FDDI, all data are transmitted in frames of variable length. Each frame includes delimiters to mark its beginning and end, and address information indicating source and destination MAC stations. FDDI is not suitable to maintain a continuous, constant-data-rate connection between two stations. Even the so-called synchronous traffic class of FDDI guarantees only a minimum sustained data rate; it does not provide a uniform data stream with no variability. Such a continuous, constant data stream is typical of circuit-switched applications, such as digitized voice or video.

FDDI-II provides a circuit-switched service while maintaining the token-controlled packet-switched service of the original FDDI. With FDDI-II, it is possible to set up and maintain a constant-data-rate connection between two stations. Instead of using embedded addresses, the connection is established on the basis of a prior agreement, which may have been negotiated using packet messages or may have been established by some other suitable convention known to the stations involved.

The technique used in FDDI-II for providing circuit-switched services is to impose a 125-μsec frame structure on the ring. A circuit-switched connection consists of regularly repeating time slots in the frame. This mode of transmission is sometimes referred to as *isochronous*. The term is used in the FDDI documents with the generally accepted meaning. Note, however, that the terms *synchronous* and *asynchronous* are used in FDDI with special meanings that relate to ring transmission (Table 6.4).

FDDI-II Architecture

Figure 6.10 is a block diagram of an FDDI-II station. The physical layer and the presence of station management are the same as for the original FDDI. At the MAC level, two new components, referred to collectively as hybrid ring control (HRC), are added: the hybrid multiplexer (HMUX) and isochronous MAC (IMAC).

The IMAC module provides the interface between FDDI and the isochronous service, represented by the circuit-switched multiplexer

TABLE 6.4 Definitions of Data Transmission Modes

Term	FDDI Definition	CCITT Definition[1]	ISO Definition[2]
Asynchronous transmission	A class of data transmission service whereby all requests for service contend for a pool of dynamically allocated ring bandwidth and response time.	The essential characteristic of time-scales or signals such that their corresponding significant instants do not necessarily occur at the same average rate.	Data transmission in which the time of occurrence of the start of each character, or block of characters, is arbitrary; once started, the time of occurrence of each signal representing a bit within the character, or block, has the same relationship to significant instants of a fixed time frame.
Synchronous transmission	A class of data transmission service whereby each requester is preallocated a maximum bandwidth and guaranteed a maximum access time.	The essential characteristic of timescales or signals such that their corresponding significant instants occur at precisely the same average rate.	Data transmission in which the time of occurrence of each signal representing a bit is related to a fixed time base.
Isochronous transmission	The essential characteristic of a time-scale or a signal such that the time intervals between consecutive significant instants either have the same duration or durations that are integral multiples of the shortest duration.	The essential characteristic of a time-scale or a signal such that the time intervals between consecutive significant instants either have the same duration or durations that are integral multiples of the shortest duration.	A data transmission process in which there is always an integral number of unit intervals between any two significant instants.

[1]From CCITT G.701, Vocabulary of Digital Transmission and Multiplexing, and PCM Terms

[2]From the ISO 2382: Information Technology—Vocabulary.

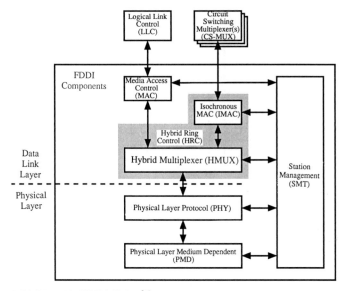

FIGURE 6.10 FDDI-II Architecture

(CS-MUX). The HMUX multiplexes the packet data from the MAC and the isochronous data from IMAC.

Hybrid Mode

An FDDI-II network can operate in either basic or hybrid mode. In **basic mode,** only the packet-switched service, controlled by a circulating to-ken, is available. In this mode, the network operates in the same fashion as the original FDDI. In **hybrid mode,** both packet and circuit services are available. An FDDI-II network typically starts out in basic mode to set up the timers and parameters necessary for the timed token protocol, then switches to hybrid mode.

When operating in hybrid mode, FDDI-II employs a continuously re-peating protocol data unit referred to as a *cycle.* The cycle is a framing structure similar in principle to that used in synchronous transmission systems. The contents of the cycle are visible to all stations as it circu-lates around the ring. A station called the cycle master generates a new cycle 8,000 times per second, or once every 125 μsec. At 100 Mbps, this works out to a cycle size of 12,500 bits. As each cycle completes its circuit of the ring, it is stripped by the cycle master.

Cycle Format and Channels.   Figure 6.11 illustrates the format of the cycle, which consists of the following components:

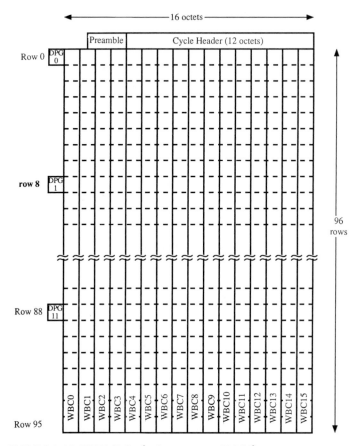

FIGURE 6.11 FDDI-II Cycle Structure at 100 Mbps

- *Preamble:* a 5-symbol (20-bit) nondata stream. The actual size of the preamble will vary from 4 to 6 symbols to maintain synchronization in the face of jitter.
- *Cycle header:* 12-octet header containing information that defines the usage of the remainder of the cycle, as described below.
- *Dedicated packet group:* 12 octets always available for token-controlled packet transfer.
- *Wideband channels:* each consisting of 96 octets per cycle.

Each of the wideband channels, at 96 octets, provides a capacity of 6.144 Mbps. Each channel may be set aside for circuit switching or packet switching. If the channel is used for packet switching, then it is merged with the dedicated packet group octets and any other WBCs set aside for packet switching, to form one large channel dedicated to packet switching. This channel, referred to as the **packet data channel,** is controlled by a circulating token; capacity is allocated on this channel as indicated in Figure 6.6. Thus the minimum capacity of the packet data channel is 768 Kbps, and it can grow in increments of 6.144 Mbps, to a maximum of 99.072 Mbps. The capacity allocation of FDDI-II can be summarized as follows:

	Number of bits per cycle	Data rate (Mbps)
Overhead (cycle header + preamble	116	0.928
N channels of circuit-switched data	$N \times 768$	$N \times 6.144$
Packet data channel	$96 + (16 - N) \times 768$	$0.768 + (16 - N) \times 6.144$
TOTAL	12,500	100

The IMAC sublayer within the HRC controls the WBCs that are used for circuit-switched traffic. Each 6.144-Mbps wideband channel can support a single isochronous channel. Alternatively, one WBC may be subdivided by IMAC into a number of subchannels. These separate subchannels permit simultaneous, independent, isochronous dialogues between different pairs of FDDI-II stations. Table 6.5 summarizes the possible subchannel sizes.

Cycle Header.   The FDDI-II cycle header consists of the following fields (Figure 6.12):

- *Starting delimiter:* indicates the beginning of a cycle; it is represented by the JK symbol pair.

TABLE 6.5   Possible WBC Subchannel Sizes

Bits/Cycle	Channel Rate (Kbps)	Possible Application and/or Current Channel Equivalents
1	8	Compressed voice, data
2	16	Compressed voice, data
4	32	Compressed voice, data
8	64	Voice, ISDN B channel
48	384	6 B channels, ISDN H0 channel
192	1536	24 B channels, ISDN H11 channel
192 + 1	1544	T1 carrier
240	1920	30 B channels, ISDN H12 channel
256	2048	E1 carrier
768	6144	FDDI-II WBC

2 Symbols	1	1	2	<———————————16———————————>				2
SD	C1	C2	CS	P0	P1		P15	IMC
Start Delimiter	Synch Control	Seq Control	Cycle Sequence					Isochronous Maint Chan

<———————— Programming Template ————————>

FIGURE 6.12 FDDI-II Cycle Header

- *Synchronization control:* used to establish the synchronization state of the ring. A value of R indicates that synchronization has not yet been established and that the cycle may be legally interrupted by another cycle. The C1 field is set to R during hybrid mode initialization or by any station that detects loss of cycle synchronization by not receiving a cycle with 125 μsec of the previous cycle. A value of S indicates that synchronization has been established; this value can be set only by the cycle master.
- *Sequence control:* indicates the status of cycle sequencing. A value of R indicates that either the cycle sequence has not yet been established or that a cycle sequence error has been detected; a value of S indicates that valid cycle sequence is established and stations can latch each CS value to compare to the CS value in the next cycle.
- *Cycle sequence:* takes the form NN where N is a data symbol. If the C1 and C2 fields both contain R, then the CS field is interpreted as containing a monitor rank. The monitor rank can take on a value from 0 to 63 and is used during the monitor contention process. During this process, monitor stations transmit their rank in the CS field and the station with the highest rank becomes the new cycle master. During normal operation, both C1 and C2 contain S, and CS contains a value between 64 and 255, representing the cycle sequence number. The cycle master increments this number by one for each new cycle, with 255 incremented to wrap around to 64.
- *Programming template:* Consists of 16 symbols, one for each WBC. An R value indicates that the corresponding WBC is part of the packet data channel, while an S indicates that the corresponding WBC is dedicated to isochronous traffic. The programming template is read by all stations, but may be modified only by the cycle master.
- *Isochronous maintenance channel:* dedicated to carry isochronous traffic for maintenance purposes. Its use is outside the scope of the present standard.

Operation

During normal operation, the activity on an FDDI-II network consists of a sequence of cycles generated by the cycle master. Stations communicate using circuit switching by sharing the use of a dedicated isochronous channel. Stations communicate using packet switching over the packet data channel, observing the rules imposed by the token ring protocol.

Initialization. Typically, the ring will be configured to initialize in basic mode. Once basic mode is established and operating, one or more stations may attempt to move the network to hybrid mode by issuing a cycle. One monitor station can be preassigned this task, or all monitor stations may compete. During the monitor contention process, each contending monitor station continually issues cycles with an R value in the C1 and C2 fields and its monitor value in the CS field. If a contender sees an incoming frame with a higher monitor value, it ceases to transmit its own cycles and simply repeats incoming cycles. Eventually, the monitor with the highest rank sees its own rank. It then issues cycles with an S value in the C1 and C2 fields and a cycle sequence number in the CS field.

Programming Template Maintenance. The cycle master maintains the programming template. The allocation of capacity between packet and circuit transmission may be modified dynamically by means of SMT requests to the cycle master. When a request for modification comes in, the cycle master waits until it receives the token on the packet data channel, to ensure that no other station's packet data are circulating on the ring. It then generates a new cycle with the new programming template and issues a new token on the packet data channel. Other FDDI-II stations will adjust to the new allocation as soon as they receive the new programming template.

6.3

IEEE 802.6

Although the IEEE 802.6 committee was chartered in 1982, it was only after a number of false starts that the committee has defined a technical approach to MANs that has achieved widespread support. The result is the IEEE 802.6 standard, which has been adopted by ANSI [IEEE90d].

The IEEE 802.6 standard is referred to as the Distributed Queue Dual Bus (DQDB) subnetwork standard. *DQDB* refers to the topology and access control technique employed, and *subnetwork* suggests that a single DQDB network will be a component in a collection of networks to provide a service.

Figure 6.13, based on one in IEEE 802.6, suggests the use of DQDB subnetworks. A subnetwork or set of subnetworks can be used as a public network controlled by a Bell operating company or other public pro-

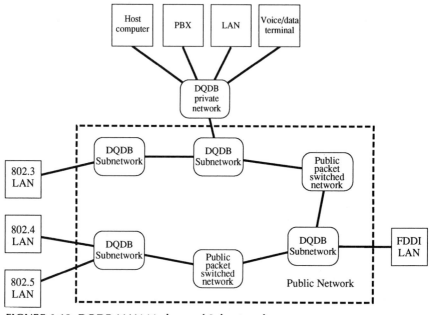

FIGURE 6.13 DQDB MAN Made up of Subnetworks

vider, or as a private backbone network covering a building or set of buildings for a given user. To support services across a metropolitan area, a single DQDB network may range from a few kilometers to more than 50 km in extent. Subnetworks can operate at a variety of data rates.

DQDB subnetworks can be connected by bridges or routers. The links between a pair of bridges or routers can be point-to-point, or they can be a network such as a packet-switched network, a circuit-switched network, or ISDN.

Topology

The DQDB topology is that of a dual bus using unidirectional taps. Figure 6.14 is a logical block diagram of the basic configuration. Transmissions on the two buses are independent; thus the effective data rate of a DQDB network is twice the data rate of the bus.

For clarity in our discussion, we use the following terminology (not part of the 802.6 standard): upstream(A) refers to upstream on bus A; downstream(A) refers to downstream on bus A. The node that is upstream(A) of all other nodes is designated head of bus A, or head(A). Upstream(B), downstream(B), and head(B) have the obvious corresponding meanings.

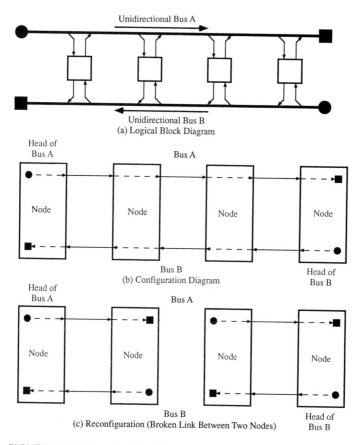

FIGURE 6.14 Open Bus Topology

Synchronization and Timing.   Transmission on each bus consists of a steady stream of fixed-size slots with a length of 53 octets. Nodes read and copy data from the slots; they also gain access to the subnetwork by writing to the slots. Head(A) is responsible for generating the slots on bus A, while head(B) is responsible for generating the slots on bus B. The slot-generation function is indicated by a solid circle in Figure 6.14b; the bus termination function is indicated by a solid square.

Operation of the subnetwork is controlled by a 125-μsec clock. The timing interval was chosen to provide support for isochronous services; it reflects the 8-kHz public networking frequency required by voice services. The slot generators in head(A) and head(B) transmit multiple slots to the shared medium every 125 μsec; the number of slots generated per clock cycle depend on the physical data rate.

Under normal conditions, the 125-μsec timing is provided by a single source. If the DQDB subnetwork is connected to a public telecommunications network, the timing may be provided by that network. Indeed, if the subnetwork is supporting certain isochronous services and is connected to a public network, it may be required that the timing be derived from the public network.

The alternative source of timing is a node within the DQDB subnetwork. One node would be designated for this purpose.

Looped Bus Topology.   The topology depicted in Figure 6.14a is, for self-evident reasons, referred to as an open-bus topology. There is an alternative topology, depicted in Figure 6.15a, known as the looped-bus

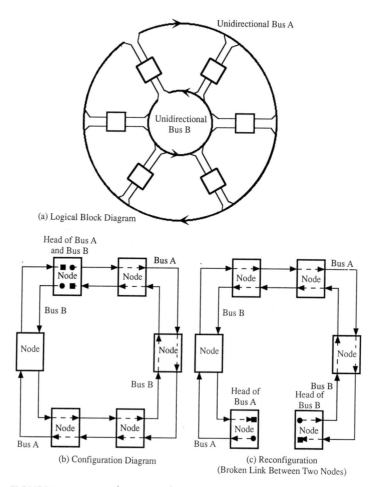

(a) Logical Block Diagram

(b) Configuration Diagram

(c) Reconfiguration
(Broken Link Between Two Nodes)

FIGURE 6.15 Looped Bus Topology

topology. In this topology, the nodes are attached to the two buses to form two closed loops. The head(A) and head(B) roles are both played by the same node.

Note that the looped-bus topology resembles a dual-ring topology. The two, however, are different since the head(A,B) node does not repeat incoming transmissions on the corresponding outgoing link.

Reconfiguration. The DQDB subnetwork includes a reconfiguration capability in the event of the failure of a link or node. This feature is particularly effective in the case of the looped-bus topology, since full connectivity can be maintained.

Figure 6.15c shows the effect of the loss of a link on the looped-bus topology. The head(A) and head(B) functions migrate from the original head(A,B) node to the two nodes adjacent to the fault. The result is a fully connected open-bus topology. If a node adjacent to a break is not capable of performing the head-of-bus functions, then the node on the side of the fault that is nearest to the fault and capable of performing the head-of-bus functions is designated as head of one of the buses. The nodes that are passed over thus become isolated from the subnetwork.

When a fault occurs on an open bus topology, the best that can be done is to reconfigure as two separate open-bus subnetworks, as shown in Figure 6.14c.

Protocol Architecture

Figure 6.16 depicts the protocol architecture of the IEEE 802.6 DQDB standard. As with the IEEE 802 LAN standards, the DQDB standard is divided into three layers. The upper layer corresponds to the upper portion of the OSI data link layer. In the case of the 802 LAN standards, this is the LLC layer. In the case of 802.6, a number of different protocols can be supported at this layer.

The middle layer of 802.6 is referred to as the DQDB layer. This corresponds roughly with the MAC layer of the 802 LAN standards and, as with the MAC layer, regulates access to the shared medium. It corresponds to the lower portion of the OSI data link layer.

The lowest layer of the 802.6 architecture is, of course, the physical layer. This layer is defined to support a variety of physical transmission schemes.

DQDB Services. The layer above the DQDB layer is not part of the 802.6 protocol architecture as such. Rather, it serves to define the services that an 802.6 subnetwork must support. Three types of services have so far been defined: connectionless service, connection-oriented data service, and isochronous services. Convergence functions within

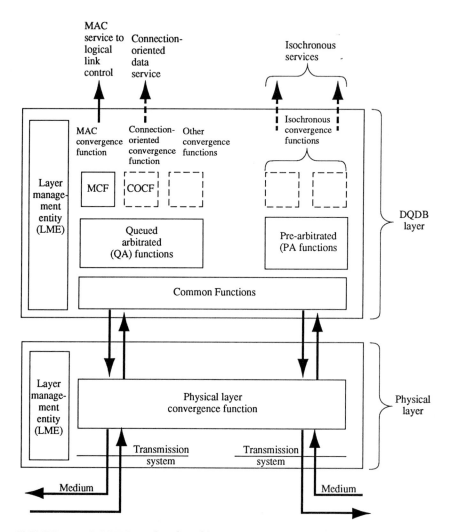

FIGURE 6.16 DQDB Functional Architecture

the DQDB layer adapt the underlying medium access service to provide a specific service to the user.

The **connectionless data service** provides support for connectionless communication via the LLC type 1 protocol (see Chapter 5). The connectionless media access service supports the transport of frames up to a length of 9188 octets. Transmission is in the form of fixed-length 52-octet segments. Accordingly, the service must include a segmentation and reassembly function.

The **connection-oriented service** supports the transport of 52-octet segments between nodes sharing a virtual channel connection. Thus, as with the connectionless service, segmentation and reassembly are required. The control signaling required to establish, maintain, and clear a connection is outside the scope of the current 802.6 standard.

The **isochronous service** provides support for users who require a constant interarrival time. The service is provided over a logical isochronous connection. The control signaling required to establish, maintain, and clear a connection is outside the scope of the current 802.6 standard.

DQDB Layer.   The DQDB layer can be viewed as being organized into three sublayers:

- Common functions
- Arbitrated functions
- Convergence functions

The **common functions** module deals with the relay of slots in the two directions and provides a common platform for asynchronous and isochronous services. In addition to the basic transmission and reception of slots, the common functions module is responsible for head-of-bus, configuration control, and MID page allocation functions.

The **head-of-bus function** is performed only by the one or two nodes designated as head of bus. It includes generating and transmitting slots. Each slot is a formatted data unit. Included in the header is a bit to indicate the type of slot; this is marked by the head-of-bus function to indicate whether this is a slot for isochronous data or asynchronous data. In the former case, the head also inserts the virtual channel identifier into the slot header.

The **configuration control function** is involved in the initialization of the subnetwork and its reconfiguration after a failure. An example of a configuration control function is the activation and deactivation of the head-of-bus functions at appropriate nodes during the process of reconfiguration.

The **MID page allocation function** participates in a distributed protocol with all nodes on the subnetwork to control the allocation of message ID values to nodes. The message ID is used in the segmentation and reassembly function, as described below.

The **arbitrated functions** are responsible for medium access control. There are two functions, corresponding to the two kinds of slots carried on the bus.

All slots on the bus are 53 octets in length, consisting of a 1-octet access control field and a 52-octet segment. The two types of slots generated on the network are queued arbitrated (QA) and prearbitrated (PA) slots.

PA slots are used to carry isochronous data. The **PA function** provides access control for the connection-oriented transfer over a guaranteed bandwidth channel of octets that form part of an isochronous octet stream. The PA function assumes the previous establishment of a connection. As a result of connection establishment, the PA function will be informed of the virtual channel ID (VCI) associated with this connection. The VCI is part of the access control field and is generated by the head-of-bus function. An isochronous connection may involve all of the segment octets in a slot; alternatively, a single segment may be shared by more than one isochronous connection. In the latter case, the PA will be informed of the VCI and the offset of the octets to be used for reading and writing within the multiple-user PA segment payload.

QA slots are used to carry asynchronous data. The **QA function** provides access control for asynchronous data transfer of 48-octet segment payloads. The QA function accepts the segment payloads from a convergence function and adds the appropriate segment header to form a segment. A distributed reservation scheme known as *distributed queuing* is used to provide medium access control. The MAC protocol is used to gain access to an available QA slot.

The DQDB layer is intended to provide a range of services. For each service, a **convergence function** is needed to map the data stream of the DQDB user into the 53-octet transmission scheme of the DQDB layer. The concept is the same as that of the ATM adaptation layer (AAL) used in BISDN. Three services have been identified so far:

- *Connectionless data transfer:* The standard fully specifies the convergence function to support the connectionless MAC data service to LLC.
- *Isochronous service:* The standard gives guidelines for the provision of an isochronous service.
- *Connection-oriented data service:* The convergence function for this service is under study.

The **MAC convergence function (MCF)** adapts the connectionless MAC service to the QA function. The key task here is one of segmentation and reassembly. MAC service units of a length up to 9188 octets must be transmitted in a sequence of slots. The MCF transmit process involves encapsulating the LLC PDU (MAC SDU) to form an initial MAC PDU (IMPDU). The IMPDU is segmented into segmentation units of 44 octets, each of which is carried in a QA slot. The segmentation and reassembly protocol is described below.

The **isochronous convergence function (ICF)** adapts an isochronous octet-based service to the guaranteed-bandwidth octet-based service of the PA function. The ICF is analogous to the isochronous MAC service of FDDI-II. The primary function of the ICF is buffering to allow for instantaneous rate differences between the PA service and the provided isochronous service. This is because the PA function guarantees the average arrival and transmission rate of isochronous services but cannot guarantee that octets will be supplied at regular fixed intervals. The buffering ensures that a fixed interarrival time can be maintained.

A **connection-oriented convergence function (COCF)** is mentioned in the standard but not defined. The COCF would use the QA slots and the same segmentation and reassembly procedures as the MCF.

Physical Layer. The DQDB layer is independent of the physical layer. Therefore, a variety of DQDB networks can be implemented using the same access layer but operating at different data rates over different transmission systems. Three transmission systems are referenced in the standard:

- ANSI DS3: transmits data at 44.736 Mbps over coaxial cable or optical fiber.
- ANSI SONET (CCITT SDH): transmits data at 155.52 Mbps and above over single-mode optical fiber.
- CCITT G.703: transmits data at 34.368 Mbps and 139.264 Mbps over a metallic medium.

For each transmission system, a physical-layer convergence protocol is used to provide a consistent physical-layer service to the DQDB layer. The only physical-layer convergence function defined in the current standard is for DS3.

Distributed Queue Access Protocol

Access to QA slots on the DQDB medium is provided by the distributed queue access protocol. Although the basic mechanism of this protocol at any one node is straightforward, the resulting distributed activity is complex. In addition, the basic protocol is augmented by two features designed to optimize the protocol: bandwidth balancing and priorities. We begin with a general description of the basic protocol. This is followed by a more detailed discussion of the protocol mechanism and a worked-out example. Bandwidth balancing and priorities are covered in the final two subsections.

In discussing the distributed queue protocol, we need to remember that there are actually two media: bus A and bus B. Since the access control mechanisms are exactly the same with respect to bus A and bus B, we will generally confine ourselves to a discussion of access control of bus A, unless otherwise noted.

Description of the Basic Protocol. The distributed queue access protocol is a distributed reservation scheme. The two words suggest the key characteristics of the protocol:

- *Reservation:* For most reservation schemes, including this one, time on the medium is divided into slots, much as with synchronous TDM. A node wishing to transmit reserves a future slot.
- *Distributed:* To accommodate changing requirements, the reservation scheme must be dynamic. That is, nodes make reservation requests when they have data to send. The function of granting requests in the IEEE 802.6 standard is distributed. That is, the network nodes collectively determine the order in which slots are granted.

The distributed reservation scheme for the DQDB subnetwork must take into account the nature of the topology. The essence of the protocol can be summarized as follows. Node X wishes to transmit a block of data to node Y. X must choose the bus on which Y is downstream from X. Let us assume that the bus is A; that is, Y is downstream(A) from X. For X to transmit a block of data in a slot to Y, it must use an available block coming from upstream(A). If the upstream(A) stations monopolize the medium, X is prevented from transmitting. Therefore, X's reservation request must be made to its upstream (A) peers. This requires the use of bus B, since those stations upstream(A) from X are also downstream(B) from X and capable of receiving a reservation request from X on bus B.

The protocol requires that each station defer its own need to transmit to the needs of its downstream peers. As long as one or more downstream peers have an outstanding reservation request, a station will refrain from transmitting, allowing unused slots to continue downstream. The key requirement for the protocol, then, is a mechanism by which each station can keep track of the requests of all of its downstream peers.

The actual behavior of a node will depend on its position on the bus. The four positions of significance (with respect to bus A) are illustrated in Figure 6.17, which shows a DQDB subnetwork with N nodes. Consider first **node (N-1)**, which is head(B). This node has no downstream(A) nodes, and therefore does not transmit data on bus A and does not need to make reservations on bus B. The only data transfer activity for node (N-1) on bus A is reception. The node reads all passing slots. Any QA slot with a destination address matching node (N-1) is copied.

Now consider the node closest to head(B), which in this case is labeled **node (N-2)**. Whenever this node needs to transmit a segment of data, it issues a request on bus B for an available slot on bus A. This is actually done by setting a request bit in a passing slot. Although node (N-2) makes reservations on bus B, it never receives any reservation requests on bus B: its only upstream(B) peer is node (N-1), which does not issue requests on bus B. On bus A, node (N-2) receives segments of

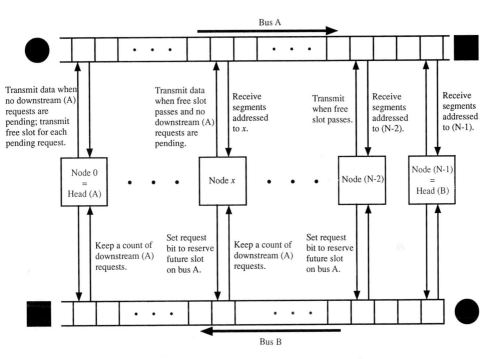

FIGURE 6.17 Basic Operation of the Distributed Queue Protocol (data transmission on bus A)

data addressed to it. In addition, when node (N-2) has data to send, and has issued a request, it may transmit its segment of data in the first free slot that passes. The first bit in each slot indicates whether the slot is free or busy.

A third node whose position is important is head(A), which is labeled **node 0** in the figure. As the head of bus A, this node is responsible for generating the stream of slots on bus A. Thus there will be no QA slots on bus A with data addressed to this node, and all QA slots originate as free slots. When this node has data to send to any other node, it can simply insert those data in the next QA slot that it generates. Because there are no upstream(B) peers of node 0, it has no need to issue requests.

However, head(A) is responsible for seeing that outstanding requests plus its own needs are satisfied in a round-robin, or first-come-first-served, basis. To do this, node 0 must keep a running count of how many requests have arrived on bus B that have not yet been satisfied. Table 6.6a summarizes the required behavior. Head(A) keeps track of the number of outstanding requests, which is simply the difference between incoming QA slots with a request and outgoing QA slots that are free. If head (A) has a segment of data to send at time T, it must wait

TABLE 6.6   Behavior of Nodes in Figure 6–17

(a) Behavior of Head(A)
At instant of time when it is ready to issue the next
QA slot on bus A

	No preceding requests outstanding	One or more preceding requests outstanding
Head(A) has no data to send	Issue a free QA slot (busy bit set to zero).	Issue a free QA slot and reduce by one the count of preceding requests.
Head(A) has a segment of QA data to send	Issue a QA slot containing the data (busy bit set to one; destination address and data inserted); following requests, if any, now become preceding requests.	Issue a free QA slot and reduce by one the count of preceding requests.

At instant of time when it is receives the next
QA slot on bus B

	Incoming slot contains a request	Incoming slot does not contain a request
Head(A) has no data to send	Add 1 to count of preceding requests	—
Head(A) has a segment of QA data to send	Add 1 to count of following requests	—

(b) Behavior of Node *x*
At instant of time when it observes a free
QA slot on bus A

	No preceding requests outstanding	One or more preceding requests outstanding
Node *x* has no data to send	Let free slot pass.	Let free slot pass and reduce by one the count of preceding requests.
Node has a segment of QA data to send and has previously issued a request on bus B	Set the busy bit to one on the passing slot and insert data; following requests, if any, now become preceding requests.	Let free slot pass and reduce by one the count of preceding requests.

At instant of time when it observes a
QA slot on bus B

	Incoming slot contains a request	Incoming slot does not contain a request
Node *x* does not have an outstanding request	Add 1 to count of preceding requests	—
Node *x* has a segment of QA data to send and has already issued a request for that segment	Add 1 to count of following requests	—
Node *x* has a segment of QA data to send and has not yet issued a request for that segment	Add 1 to count of preceding requests	Insert request into passing slot (set request bit to 1)

until it has satisfied all of the requests outstanding at that time by issuing free QA slots. Once it has satisfied all those requests, it may transmit its own segment. Meanwhile, head(A) must keep track of additional requests that arrive after time T. To distinguish between requests that arrive before and after time T, they are referred to as preceding and following requests respectively in Table 6.6.

One way to visualize this operation is to think of it in terms of tickets. Each time a request arrives, head(A) generates a ticket. Each time that head(A) issues a free QA slot, it discards the oldest ticket. When the node has its own data to send, it generates a ticket on its behalf and places it on the bottom of the stack. As additional tickets are generated by arriving requests, these are placed on the bottom of the stack. When head(A)'s ticket reaches the top of the stack, head(A) can issue a busy QA slot containing its data.

Finally, Figure 6.17 depicts the behavior of a node other than the three already discussed, labeled **node x.** Like node (N-2), whenever node x needs to transmit a segment of data, it issues a request on bus B for an available slot on bus A. In addition, like node 0, node x must keep a count of requests that pass by on bus B so that its own requests are handled fairly. On bus A, node x receives segments of data addressed to it. In order to enforce a round-robin discipline, node x must keep track of incoming requests that precede and follow its own request, in a manner similar to the behavior of node 0. When node x has data to send, and has issued a request, it may transmit its segment of data in a passing free slot only after all preceding requests have been satisfied. Table 6.6b, which is quite similar to Table 6.6a, summarizes the rules of behavior for node x.

Counter Mechanism.   This mechanism can be described in terms of a distributed collection of FIFO (first in, first out) queues. At each node, a queue is formed for each bus. For each request read in a passing slot, the node inserts one item in the queue. When the node itself issues a request, it adds an item to the queue for itself. When its own item is at the top of the queue, the node may transmit in the next free QA slot. A node may have only one item for itself in each queue (one for each bus) at any time.

This queueing mechanism can be simply implemented with a pair of counters for each queue, as illustrated in Figure 6.18, which shows the counters used for transmission on bus A; a corresponding pair of counters is used by the same node for transmission on bus B. When the node is not ready to send, it keeps track of requests on bus B from its downstream(A) neighbors in a request count. Each time a request is observed (request bit is set), the count is increased by 1; each time a free slot passes on bus A, the count is decremented by 1 to a minimum count of 0.

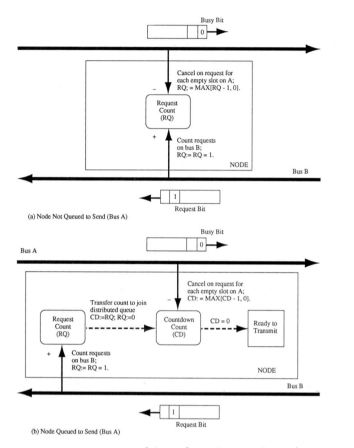

(a) Node Not Queued to Send (Bus A)

(b) Node Queued to Send (Bus A)

FIGURE 6.18 Request and Countdown Counter Operation

At any time, the value of RQ represents the unmet need for free QA slots by the node's downstream(A) peers. The node is obligated to let this number of free slots pass before itself using a QA slot to transmit. Therefore, when the node does have data to transmit on bus A, it issues a request on bus B as soon as possible. The earliest opportunity will be the first slot to pass in which the request bit has not yet been set. Of course, while waiting for the opportunity to set the request bit, the node must continue to count passing requests in RQ. When the node does set the request bit on a passing slot on bus B, it immediately transfers the current value of RQ to a countdown count (CD) and resets RQ to 0. The node then decrements CD until it reaches 0, at which time the node may transmit on bus A in the next free QA slot. Meanwhile, the node counts new requests on bus B in RQ. The effect of the above is to maintain a single FIFO queue into which the node may insert its own request.

Note that the queue formation is such that a slot is never wasted on the subnetwork if there is a segment queued for it, because the CD count in the queued nodes represents the number of segments queued ahead. Since at any point in time one segment must have queued first, then at least one node is guaranteed to have a CD count of zero. It is that node that will access the next passing free QA slot.

This is a remarkably effective protocol. Under conditions of light load, the value of CD will be small or 0 and free QA slots will be frequent. Thus, with a light load, delay is negligible, a property shared by CSMA/CD protocols. Under heavy loads, virtually every free QA slot will be utilized by one of the waiting nodes. Thus, with a heavy load, efficiency approaches 100%, a property shared by token bus and token ring protocols. This combination of quick access under light load and predictable queueing under heavy load makes the protocol suitable for a MAN of high data rate that will carry a mix of bursty traffic (e.g., interactive use) and more sustained stream-like traffic (e.g., file transfers).

A Simple Example.   Figure 6.19, adapted from an example in the 802.6 document, provides a simple example of the operation of the basic protocol. The example is limited to transmission of data on bus A; none of the nodes is a head-of-bus node.

The example starts at a point when there are no outstanding requests. At that point, all nodes have an RQ value of 0. Then, the following events occur:

a Node E issues a request on bus B by changing the busy bit in a passing slot from 0 to 1. Each downstream(B) node (nodes A–D) increments its RQ counter. At the same time, node E transfers its RQ count to its CD count. In this case, the count is 0, so node E can transmit on bus A as soon as it sees a free QA slot.
b Node B issues a request on bus B. The node transfers the value of RQ, which is 1, to CD and sets RQ to 0. This node will have to wait until a free QA slot passes on bus A before gaining access. Node A sees the request bit that has been set and increments its RQ value to 2.
c Node C issues a request on bus B. C sets its CD value to 1 and its RQ value to 0. Node B increments its RQ value to 1. Note that B's CD value is unchanged; the arrival of new requests after B has issued its own request does not affect the timing of B's access to bus A. Node A increments its RQ to 3.
d A free QA slot passes down bus A. Nodes A and D decrement their RQ counts. Nodes B and C decrement their CD counts. Node E has a CD of 0 and so can seize the free slot by changing the busy bit from 0 to 1 and inserting a QA segment.
e Another free QA slot passes down bus A. Node A decrements its RQ count. Both nodes B and C are eligible to seize the free slot. However,

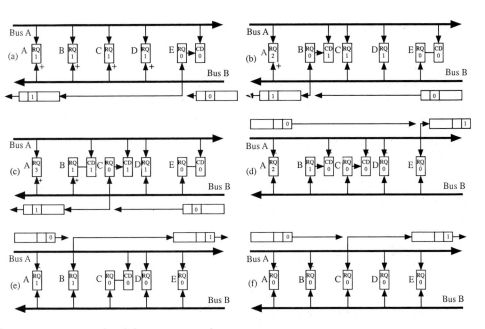

IGURE 6.19 Example of the QA Protocol

the free slot passes node B first, which uses it to transmit a QA segment.

f Node C uses the next passing free slot to transmit. The system returns to its original state, in which all nodes have an RQ value of 0.

Note that the three requests are satisfied in the order issued. Thus the behavior of the network as a whole is that of a FIFO queue.

Priority Distributed Queueing.   The distributed queueing protocol supports three levels of priority. Priority access control is absolute in that QA segments with a higher priority will always gain access ahead of segments at all lower levels. This is achieved by operating separate distributed queues for each level of priority.

Several refinements need to be made to the access method described so far to support priority. Each segment includes 3 request bits, one for each level of priority. A node wishing to transmit on bus A at a particular priority level sets the appropriate bit on the next slot on bus B for which that bit is 0. To keep track of these requests, each node must maintain 6 RQ counters, one for each priority level in each direction, and 6 CD counters.

The operation of the RQ and CD counters is specified in such a way as to achieve absolute priority. We need to consider the two cases of a request pending and no request pending by a node at a particular priority level for one of the buses.

First, let us consider the case of a node that has no requests pending at a given priority level for bus A; the same description will also apply to bus B. The RQ count operating at that priority level will count requests at the same and higher priority levels. Thus the RQ count records all queued segments at equal and higher priorities. As before, the RQ count is decremented for each passing QA slot on bus B.

Now suppose that the node has a QA segment queued at a particular priority level for bus A. In our original definition of the CD count, this variable is decremented with passing QA slots on one bus and unaffected by traffic on the other bus. To account for priorities, we continue to decrement CD with every passing free QA slot on one bus, but increment CD for every request on the other bus that is of higher priority. This allows the higher-priority segments to claim access ahead of already queued segments. To avoid double counting, the RQ count is incremented only for requests of the same priority level; the higher-priority requests are already being counted in the CD count.

At the present time, the use of the priority levels is unspecified in the standard. The standard dictates that connectionless data segments (carry LLC PDUs) must operate at the lowest priority level (level 0). It is possible that control signaling messages or connection-oriented data might be assigned to one of the two higher-priority levels; this is a matter for further study.

Bandwidth Balancing.   A problem can arise in the access control mechanism so far described under conditions of heavy load and a network of large extent. To understand the problem, which is one of bandwidth unfairness, we first need to clarify the relationship between data that a node needs to send, the use of requests, and the use of free slots. This relationship is illustrated in Figure 6.20, taken from the 802.6 document. The relationship concerns data generated at a node to be transmitted in QA segments. The DQDB user (i.e., LLC) provides service data units to the DQDB layer. Each block of arriving data is broken up into one or more segments and placed in a FIFO segment queue awaiting transmission. There are six such queues, one for each of three levels of priority on each of the two buses.

The figure shows the relationships for one of the six segment queues. A segment transmit queue is used to hold a segment that is awaiting a free slot on the bus. When a segment is transferred from the segment queue to the transmit queue, a request needs to be issued on the other bus. It may not be possible to issue the request immediately, since the node must wait for a passing slot in which the corresponding request bit has not yet been set. Therefore, a request queue is needed, which holds the requests until they can be issued. Each time that an empty

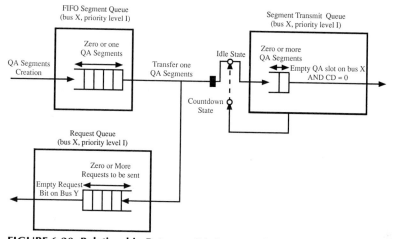

FIGURE 6.20 Relationship Between QA Segment Queue, Request Queue, and Segment Transmit Queue

request bit on a passing slot is set, one item is removed from the request queue.

The DQDB protocol dictates that once a node has issued a request for a free QA slot, it cannot issue another request until the first one is satisfied. To enforce this, the transmit queue can hold only one segment. If there is a segment in the transmit queue, it may be issued when the corresponding CD count is zero and an empty QA slot passes. If there is no segment in the transmit queue, one item from the segment queue may be transferred to the transmit queue, accompanied by the insertion of an entry in the request queue.

We are now in a position to explain the bandwidth unfairness problem, using an example in [HAHN90]. Consider two nodes that are transmitting very long messages on bus A: call the upstream(A) node 1 and the downstream (A) node 2; no other nodes require access to bus A. Define the following:

D = the number of slots in transit between nodes 1 and 2; this is obviously a direct function of the physical length of the medium between the two nodes. Assume an integer value.

Δ = the difference in the arrival times of the messages from DQDB users to the DQDB entities. That is, (time that the first segment is placed in the segment queue of node 2) − (time that the first segment is placed in the segment queue of node 1)

$c(\Delta) = $ a function that clips its argument to the range $[-D,D]$

$P = $ number of requests plus idle slots circulating between the two nodes

Once both nodes have received messages from their users (both nodes have begun filling their segment queues), node 1 leaves slots idle only in response to requests from node 2. Therefore, once node 2 begins to receive QA slots from node 1, the only idle slots node 2 receives are in response to its earlier requests. Each idle slot received by node 2 results in a segment being transmitted, a new segment being placed in the transmit queue, and a request being issued on bus B. Therefore the value of P is constant; let us refer to these conserved entities as *permits*. This quantity determines the throughput of the downstream node. We can express P as follows:

$$P = 1 + D - c(\Delta)$$

To verify this equation, consider two extreme cases. First, assume that a message arrives from node 1's user more than D time units before node 2 has a message to send ($\Delta \geqslant D$). In that case, node 1 will fill the bus with data and will allow a free slot to pass only when it receives a request from node 2. When node 2 is ready to transmit, it must issue a request and wait for that request to reach node 1 and for a free slot to return. In this instance, there is only one permit in the network: $P = 1$. At the other extreme is the case of $\Delta \leqslant -D$. Initially, only node 2 is active. It inserts its first segment in the transmit queue and sends its first reservation request. The first segment is transmitted immediately in a free slot. The node continues to transmit segments and issue requests in this fashion. By the time node 1 is ready to transmit, bus B is already carrying D requests. In the time that it takes for node 1's first segment to reach node 2, node 2 injects another D requests, so that $P \approx 2D$.

Now define the following quantities:

$\gamma_1 = $ steady-state throughput of node 1 (in segments per slot time)
$\gamma_2 = $ steady-state throughput of node 2 (in segments per slot time)
$Q = $ average value of CD at node 1

Note that, at any instant in time, permits can be stored in the request channel (bus B between nodes 1 and 2), in the data channel (bus A between nodes 1 and 2), and in the counter CD at node 1. Some thought should convince you that the following relationships hold:

$$\gamma_1 + \gamma_2 = 1$$
$$\gamma_1 = 1/Q$$
$$\gamma_2 = P/T$$
$$T = 2D + Q$$

Solving these equations, we have:

$$\gamma_1 = \frac{2}{2 - D - c(\Delta) + \sqrt{(D - c(\Delta) + 2)^2 + 4Dc(\Delta)}}$$

$$\gamma_2 = 1 - \gamma_1$$

Note that if the nodes are very close together ($D \approx 0$), or if they start transmitting at about the same time ($\Delta \approx 0$), then each node gets about half of the capacity. However, if D is very large (large network) and the downstream node starts later, its predicted throughput rate is only about $\frac{1}{2D}$. Node 1 also suffers a penalty if it starts later, though not as great; its worst case rate is approximately $\frac{1}{\sqrt{2D}}$.

As [HAHN90] points out, one way of explaining the bandwidth unfairness phenomenon of DQDB is that the protocol pushes the system too hard. In its attempt to use every single slot on the bus, the protocol causes request queues to build up in the nodes that never recede. The refinement proposed in the paper, and subsequently adopted by IEEE 802.6, "leaks" some bandwidth to prevent the hogging of bandwidth in overload situations. The technique is known as **bandwidth balancing.**

In ordinary DQDB, a node may transmit a segment when its CD count is zero and the current QA slot is free. Bandwidth balancing permits the node to transmit only a fraction α of that time. This is achieved by artificially incrementing RQ after every β segments are transmitted; thus $\alpha = \frac{\beta}{1 + \beta}$. This forces the node to send an extra free slot downstream after using β free slots. For example, if $\alpha = 0.9$ ($\beta = 9$), then after every 9 QA segments transmitted, the node lets an extra slot pass. To implement this scheme, one more counter, called the *trigger counter*, is needed for each direction at each node. The trigger counter is incremented by 1 every time a QA segment is transmitted. When the counter equals β, it is set to 0 and RQ is incremented by 1.

The parameter β, called *bandwidth balancing modulus*, or BWB_MOD, in the standard must be set in each node. The value may be set between 0 and 64, with a default value of 8. A value of 0 disables the bandwidth balancing function.

One BWB_MOD is associated with each bus, but no distinction is made on the basis of priority. When BWB_MOD resets to 0, the RQ counts for that bus are incremented for all priority levels for which no QA segment is queued, and the CD counts for that bus are incremented for all priority levels for which a QA segment is queued.

The standard recommends that bandwidth balancing be enabled for a bus that spans a distance that is greater than the effective length of one 53-octet slot, which is approximately the following:

2 km at 44.376 Mbps (DS3 rate)
546 m at 155.520 Mbps (STM-1 rate)
137 m at 622.080 Mbps (STM-4 rate)

DQDB Protocol Data Units

A rather complex set of protocol data unit formats is used to support the DQDB layer functions.

Slot. As we have already discussed, the basic unit of transfer on a DQDB subnetwork is the 53-octet slot. The slot consists of a 1-octet header and a 52-octet segment; its format is shown in Figure 6.21a.

The slot header, referred to as the *access control field*, contains the bits that control slot access. The fields are:

- *Busy:* indicates whether the slot contains information or is free.
- *Slot type:* indicates whether this is a QA slot or a PA slot. The combination of busy bit and slot-type bit is referred to as the slot access control field.
- *Previous slot reserved:* indicates whether the segment in the previous slot may be cleared or not. This bit is set by a node when the immediately preceding slot contains a QA segment destined only for that node. The use of this bit is for further study.
- *Reserved:* set to 00; reserved for future use.
- *Request:* three request bits for the three priority levels.

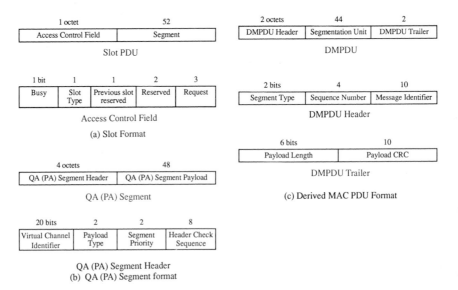

(a) Slot Format

(b) QA (PA) Segment format

(c) Derived MAC PDU Format

FIGURE 6.21 IEEE 802.6 PDU Formats

Segment.   Each slot contains a 52-octet segment that may be either a QA segment or a PA segment. Both types of segments consist of a 4-octet header followed by a 48-octet segment payload. The QA and PA segment headers have the identical format, with some differences in interpretation of the fields. The formats are shown in Figure 6.21b. The header fields are:

- *Virtual channel identifier:* identifies the virtual channel, or logical connection, to which the segment belongs. The VCI value of all ones corresponds to the connectionless MAC service. Other nonzero VCI values are available for use for the connection-oriented data service and isochronous services.
- *Payload type:* indicates the nature of the data to be transferred. The field could be used by DQDB subnetworks interconnected via bridges, where this value could differentiate between user data and network signaling and management data. The default value for both PA and QA segments is 00; all other values are for further study.
- *Segment priority:* reserved for future use with multiport bridges. A multiport bridge is one that connects three or more subnetworks.
- *Header check sequence:* covers the segment header, and is used for the detection of errors and the correction of single-bit errors.

Transfer of MAC Service Data Units.   The DQDB layer provides the MAC service by accepting MAC service data units (LLC PDUs) from a DQDB user and transmitting each to a destination DQDB user. Since the QA segment format limits the protocol to a segment payload of 48 octets, it is clear that a segmentation and reassembly function must be performed. The approach that is taken to this function is depicted in Figure 6.22. An arriving MAC SDU is encapsulated into an initial MAC PDU (IMPDU), which includes an IMPDU header and trailer plus the entire MAC SDU. This IMPDU is then segmented into 44-octet *segmentation units,* each of which can be fit into a derived MAC PDU (DMPDU). The DMPDU includes the 44-octet segmentation unit plus a header and trailer for a total length of 48 octets. Thus each 48-octet DMPDU fits into a single QA segment, which in turn fits into a single QA slot.

A MAC SDU is transferred within an **initial MAC Protocol Data Unit (IMPDU).** An IMPDU is transferred between peer MAC convergence function protocol entities. The format of an IMPDU is shown in Figure 6.23. The IMPDU is constructed by adding the following major elements to a variable-length MAC SDU, which is stored in the INFO field:

- *Common PDU header:* carried in all DQDB-layer PDUs supporting frame-based bursty data services.
- *MCP header:* specific to the MAC convergence protocol, and therefore specific to the transfer of a MAC SDU.

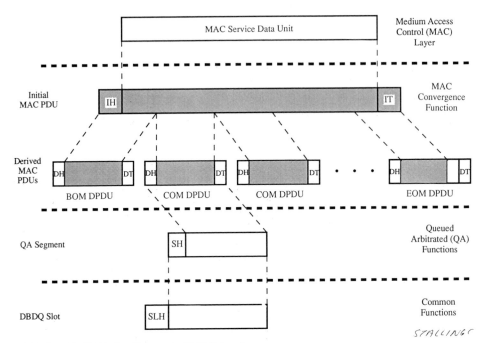

FIGURE 6.22 PDUs for Support of MAC Service

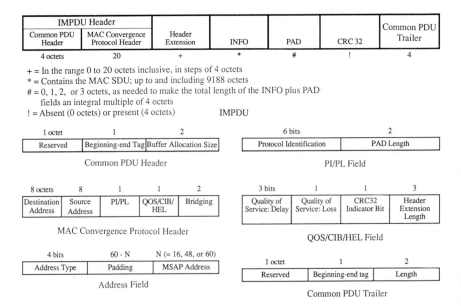

FIGURE 6.23 Initial MAC PDU Format

- *Header extension:* provides the optional capability to convey additional IMPDU protocol control information that may be standardized in the future. An example of its use would be to convey service-provider-specific information in cases where this protocol is used to access the services of a public network.
- *PAD:* contains the minimum number of octets so that the total length of the INFO field plus the PAD field is an integral multiple of four octets.
- *CRC 32:* provides the optional capability for including a 32-bit CRC, calculated over all the fields of the MCP header, the header extension field, the INFO field, and the PAD field.
- *Common PDU trailer:* carried in all DQDB-layer PDUs supporting frame-based bursty data services.

The **common PDU header** consists of three fields:

- *Reserved:* reserved for future use.
- *Beginning-end tag:* an 8-bit sequence number associated with an IMPDU and incremented by one (modulo 256) for successive IMPDUs sent by the node. This value is used in segmentation and reassembly, explained below.
- *Buffer allocation size:* the total length of the IMPDU, exclusive of the common PDU header and trailer. This alerts the receiver to buffer space requirements. Again, this value is used in segmentation and reassembly.

The **MCP header** consists of the following fields:

- *Destination address:* the MAC address of the destination node.
- *Source address:* the MAC address of the source node.
- *PI/PL:* the protocol identification subfield identifies the MAC service user to which the INFO field is to be sent. The pad-length subfield indicates the length of the PAD field in the IMPDU.
- *QOS/CIB/HEL:* the QOS delay subfield indicates the requested quality of service for an IMDPU with respect to delay in accessing the subnetwork. The value is based on the priority requested by the MAC user. The QOS loss bit is currently reserved. It may be used for congestion control at bridges by indicating which IMPDUs are eligible for discard. The CRC32 Indicator bit indicates the presence or absence of the CRC32 field in the IMPDU. The header-extension-length subfield gives the length of the header extension field in the IMPDU, in units of 4 octets.
- *Bridging:* Reserved for future use for MAC-level bridging. One use for this field would be a hop count: after an IMPDU has passed through a given number of bridges, it would be discarded.

The two address fields have the format shown in Figure 6.23. The first 4 bits indicate the address type. Support for 48-bit addresses is mandatory. Support for 16-bit addresses is optional. Both of these address types conform to the MAC address format for IEEE 802. Support is also optional for 60-bit addresses, which may be publicly administered (local MAN operator) or privately administered.

The **common PDU trailer** contains the same information in the same format as the common PDU header. The same value is inserted into the beginning-end tag field in both header and trailer, and the same value is inserted in the buffer allocation size and length fields.

As Figure 6.22 illustrates, an IMPDU is segmented into one or more **derived MAC protocol data units (DMPDUs).** Each DMPDU carries a 44-octet portion of the IMPDU, known as a **segmentation unit.** In addition, each DMPDU has a header and trailer.

The **DMPDU header** contains the following fields:

- *Segment type:* There are four types of DMPDUs. A single segment message (SSM) contains an entire IMPDU. If the IMPDU is segmented into two or more DMPDUs (Figure 6.22), the first DMPDU is the beginning of message (BOM), the last DMPDU is the end of message (EOM), and any intermediate DMPDUs are a continuation of message (COM).
- *Sequence number:* This is used in reassembling an IMPDU to verify that all of the DMPDU segmentation units have been received and concatenated properly. A value of the sequence number is set as a BOM and incremented for each successive COM and the EOM for a single IMPDU.
- *Message identifier:* This is a unique identifier associated with the set of DMPDUs that carry a single IMPDU. Again, this number is needed to ensure proper reassembly.

The **DMPDU trailer** contains the following fields:

- *Payload length:* indicates the number of octets from the IMPDU that occupy the segmentation unit of the DMPDU. The number has a value between 4 and 44 octets, in multiples of 4. The value will always be 44 for BOM and COM DMPDUs. It is a lesser number in an SSM if the IMPDU is less than 44 octets in length. It is a lesser number in an EOM if the length of the IMPDU is not an integer multiple of 44 octets in length, necessitating the use of a partially filled EOM.
- *Payload CRC:* a 10-bit CRC on the entire DMPDU.

6.4

RECOMMENDED READING

[KESS92] is a clear and technically detailed account of both FDDI and DQDB. [SLON91] contains good overviews of the two standards. Both

[ABEY91] and [RUBI90] compare FDDI and DQDB with many other high-speed LAN and MAN systems. [KARO90] summarizes the two standards and examines enhancements to each to improve performance. [SACH88] and [MAXE88] survey MAC techniques for fiber bus networks.

6.5

PROBLEMS

6.1 Compare the capacity allocation schemes of token bus, 803.5 token ring, and FDDI. What are the relative pros and cons?

6.2 Rework the example of Figure 6.5 using a TTRT of 12 frames and assuming that no station ever has more than 8 asynchronous frames to send.

6.3 Assess CSMA/CD, token bus, and the DQDB scheme as MAC algorithms for a MAN. Justify the assertion that DQDB is best suited to the requirements of a bus-based MAN.

6.4 How many slots are spread out on the DQDB bus in each direction for a 30-km bus running at 150 Mbps?

6.5 Suppose that two nodes are randomly placed on a bus; that is, each is placed independently and the position of each is chosen from a uniform distribution over the length of the bus. For a bus of length L, show that the expected distance between the two nodes is $1/3$.

6.6 The bandwidth balancing technique is one method of overcoming the unfairness of the DQDB protocol. Another proposed solution is referred to as reservation request control (RRC). The basic idea of RRC is to prevent unfair access to request bits. This is accomplished by providing downstream nodes with information about the number of upstream nodes, and allowing each node to have multiple outstanding requests for the same bus and priority level. If a node knows that there are N upstream(A) nodes that need access to bus A, it may send a request on the first available slot on bus B and then it must defer to the N upstream(A) nodes by allowing N slots available for sending requests to pass on bus B before it tries to send its next request. In this case, each upstream(A) node can use one of these slots to send a request.

a. Suggest a dynamic means of implementing RRC that allows the node to consider only the upstream nodes that may want to send rather than the physical total of all upstream nodes.

b. Compare RRC with bandwidth balancing, in terms of fairness and in terms of efficient use of the medium.

CHAPTER 7

Circuit-Switched Local Networks

Up until now, we have been looking at local networks that use packet switching. For many observers, this is the only kind of local network there is. But there is an alternative, based on the older circuit-switched approach. As we shall see, the differences in architecture and design issues are striking. We will also learn, perhaps to your surprise, that underneath, the similarities are equally striking.

The chapter begins by summarizing the characteristics of a star topology local network. Then we look at the digital switching concepts that underlie this type of network. Next we look at the devices most commonly used to build local networks (although these are rarely thought of as "true" local networks)—digital data switches. We are at last ready to look at the digital private branch exchange (PBX). Finally, the digital PBX and LAN are compared.

7.1

STAR TOPOLOGY NETWORKS

A star topology network, as described in Chapter 3, consists in essence of a collection of devices or stations attached to a central switching unit. Circuit switching is used; the central switch establishes a dedicated path between any two devices that wish to communicate.

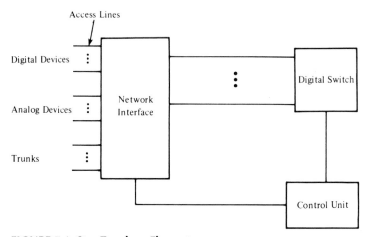

FIGURE 7.1 Star Topology Elements

Figure 7.1 depicts the major elements of a star topology network. The heart of a modern system is a digital switch. The advent of digital switching technology has dramatically improved the cost, performance, and capability of circuit-switched networks. Key to the operation of such systems are that (1) all signals are represented digitally, and (2) synchronous time-division multiplexing (TDM) techniques are used.

The network interface element represents the functions and hardware needed to connect digital devices, such as data processing devices and digital telephones, to the network. Analog telephones can also be attached if the network interface contains the logic for converting to digital signals. Trunks to external systems may also be attached. These may include analog voice trunks and digital TDM lines.

The control unit performs three general tasks. First, it establishes connections. This is generally done on demand, that is, at the request of an attached device. To establish the connection, the control unit must handle and acknowledge the request, determine if the intended destination is free, and construct a path through the switch. Second, the logic must maintain the connection. Since the digital switch uses time-division principles, this may require ongoing manipulation of the switching elements. However, the bits of the communication are transferred transparently. This is in contrast to the packet switching used on LANs and HSLNs, which are sensitive to the transmission protocol and can be considered content dependent. Third, the logic must tear down the connection, either in response to a request from one of the parties or for its own reasons.

Star networks may be either one-sided or two-sided. In a one-sided system, all attachment points are viewed the same: A connection can be established between any two devices. In a two-sided system, attachment points are grouped into two classes and a connection can be established only between two devices from different classes. A typical application of the latter is the connection of a set of terminals to a set of computer ports; in many cases, only terminal-to-port connections are allowed.

An important characteristic of a star topology network is whether it is blocking or nonblocking. Blocking occurs when the network is unable to connect two stations because all possible paths between them are already in use. A blocking network is one in which such blocking is possible. Hence a nonblocking network permits all stations to be connected at once and grants all possible connection requests as long as the called party is free. When a network is supporting only voice traffic, a blocking configuration is generally acceptable, since it is expected that most phone calls are of short duration and that, therefore, only a fraction of the telephones will be engaged at any time. However, when data processing devices are involved, these assumptions may be invalid. For example, for a data entry application, a terminal may be continuously connected to a computer for hours at a time. [BHUS85] reports that typical voice connections on a PBX have a duration of 120 to 180 seconds, whereas data calls can have a range of from 8 seconds to 15 hours. Hence, for data applications, there is a requirement for a nonblocking or "nearly nonblocking" (very low probability of blocking) configuration.

7.2

DIGITAL-SWITCHING CONCEPTS

The technology of switching has a long history, most of it covering an era when analog signal switching predominated. With the advent of PCM and related techniques, both voice and data can be transmitted via digital signals. This has led to a fundamental change in the design and technology of switching systems. Instead of dumb space-division systems, modern digital-switching systems rely on intelligent control of space- and time-division elements.

This section looks at the concepts underlying contemporary digital switching (good discussions can be found in [SKAP79], [JOEL77], [JOEL79a], [JOEL79b], and [FLEM79]). We begin with a look at space-division switching, which was originally developed for the analog environment and has been carried over into digital technology. Then the various forms of time-division switching, which were developed specifically to be used in digital switches, are examined. Later sections discuss how these concepts are implemented in digital data switches and digital PBXs.

Space-Division Switching

The *space-division switch* is, as its name implies, one in which paths between pairs of devices are divided in space. Each connection requires the establishment of a physical path through the switch that is dedicated solely to the transfer of signals between the two end points. The basic building block of the switch is an electronic crosspoint or semiconductor gate [ABBO84] that can be enabled and disabled by a control unit.

Figure 7.2a shows a simple crossbar matrix with n inputs and m outputs. Interconnection is possible between any input line and any output line by engaging the appropriate crosspoint. The crossbar depicts a bilateral arrangement: there is a distinction between input and output. For example, input lines may connect to terminals, while output lines connect to computer ports. The crossbar switch is said to perform concentration, distribution, or expansion according as $n > m$, $n = m$, or $n < m$.

The crossbar matrix makes a distinction between input and output: any input can connect to any output. It requires $n \times m$ crosspoints. However, if the inputs and outputs are the same, then $n = m$ and the requirement is that any end point can connect to any other end point. This requires only a triangular array of $n(n - 1)/2$ crosspoints (Figure 7.2b) and is referred to as a folded configuration.

The crossbar switch has a number of limitations or disadvantages:

- The number of crosspoints grows with n^2. This is costly for large n and results in high capacitive loading on any message path.

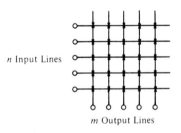

n Input Lines

m Output Lines

(a) Crossbar Matrix

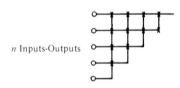

n Inputs-Outputs

(b) Triangular Switch

FIGURE 7.2 Single-Stage Space-Division Switch

- The loss of a crosspoint prevents connection between the two devices involved.
- The crosspoints are inefficiently utilized.

To overcome these limitations, multiple-stage switches are employed. The N input lines (inlets) are broken up into N/n groups of n lines. Each group of lines goes into a first-stage matrix. The outputs of the first-stage matrices become inputs to a group of second-stage matrices, and so on. Figure 7.3 depicts a three-stage network of switches that is symmetric; that is, the number of inlets to the first stage equals the number of outlets from the last stage. There are k second-stage matrices, each with N/n inlets and N/n outlets. Each first-stage matrix has k outlets so that it connects to all second-stage matrices. Each second-stage matrix has N/n outlets so that it connects to all third-stage matrices.

This type of arrangement has a couple of advantages over the simple crossbar switch:

- The number of crosspoints is reduced (see below), increasing crossbar utilization.
- There is more than one path through the network to connect two end points, increasing reliability.

Of course, a multistage network requires a more complex control scheme. To establish a path in a single-stage network, it is only neces-

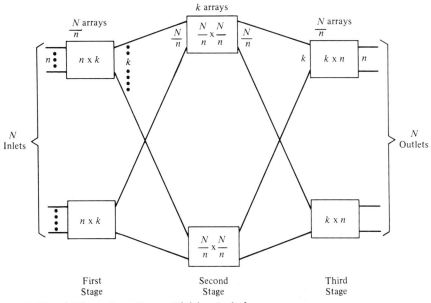

FIGURE 7.3 Three-Stage Space-Division Switch

sary to open a single gate. In a multistage network, a free path through the stages must be determined and the appropriate gates enabled.

A consideration with a multistage space-division switch is that it may be blocking. It should be clear from Figure 7.2 that a crossbar matrix is nonblocking; that is, a path is always available to connect an input to an output. That this is not always the case with a multiple-stage switch can be seen in Figure 7.4. The figure shows a three-stage switch with $N = 9$, $n = 3$, and $k = 3$. The heavier lines indicate lines that are already in use. In this stage, input line 9 cannot be connected to either output line 4 or 6, even though both of these output lines are available.

It should be clear that by increasing the value of k (the number of outlets from each first-stage switch and the number of second-stage switches), the probability of blocking is reduced. What value of K is required for a nonblocking three-stage switch? The answer is depicted in Figure 7.5. Consider that we wish to establish a path from input line a to output line b. The worst-case situation for blocking occurs if all of the remaining $n - 1$ input lines and $n - 1$ output lines are busy and are connected to different center-stage switches. Thus a total of $(n - 1) + (n - 1) = 2n - 2$ center switches are unavailable for creating a path from a to b. However, if one more center-stage switch exists, the appropriate links must be available for the connection. Thus, a three-stage network will be nonblocking if

$$k = 2n - 1 \qquad\qquad (7.1)$$

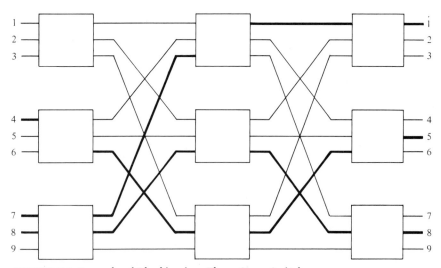

FIGURE 7.4 Example of Blocking in a Three-Stage Switch

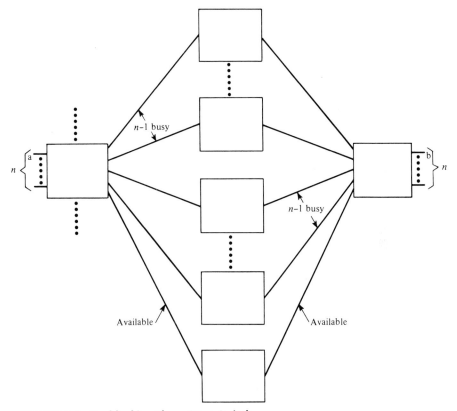

FIGURE 7.5 Nonblocking Three-Stage Switch

We now return to our claim that a multiple-stage switch requires fewer crosspoints than a single-stage switch. From Figure 7.3, the total number of crosspoints N_x in a three-stage switch is

$$N_x = 2Nk + k\left(\frac{N}{n}\right)^2 \tag{7.2}$$

Substituting Equation (7.1) into (7.2),

$$N_x = 2N(2n - 1) + (2n - 1)\left(\frac{N}{n}\right)^2 \tag{7.3}$$

for a nonblocking switch. The actual value as a function of N depends on the number of arrays (N/n) in the first and third stages. To optimize, differentiate N_x with respect to n and set the result to 0. For large N, the result converges to $n = (N/2)^{1/2}$. Substituting into (7.3),

$$N_x = 4N(\sqrt{2N} - 1) \tag{7.4}$$

**TABLE 7.1   Number of Crosspoints in a
Nonblocking Switch**

Number of Lines	Number of Crosspoints for Three-Stage Switch	Number of Crosspoints for Single-Stage Switch
128	7,680	16,384
512	63,488	262,144
3,048	516,096	4.2×10^6
8,192	4.2×10^6	6.7×10^7
32,768	3.3×10^7	1×10^9
131,072	2.6×10^8	1.7×10^{10}

Table 7.1 compares this value with the number of crosspoints in a single-stage switch. As can be seen, there is a savings, which grows with the number of lines.

A further discussion of this topic can be found in [JASJ83] and [JORD85].

Time-Division Switching

In contrast to space-division switching, in which dedicated paths are used, *time-division switching* involves the partitioning of a slower-speed data stream into pieces that share a higher-speed data stream with other data pieces. The individual pieces or slots are manipulated by the control logic to route data from input to output. Three concepts comprise the technique of time-division switching:

- TDM bus switching
- Time-slot interchange (TSI)
- Time-multiplex switching (TMS)

TDM Bus Switching

As discussed in Chapter 2, TDM is a technique that allows multiple signals to share a single transmission line by separating them in time. In this chapter we are concerned primarily with synchronous TDM, that is, a situation in which time slots are preassigned so that few or no overhead bits are required.

As shown in Figure 7.6a, synchronous TDM was designed to permit multiple low-speed streams to share a high-speed line. This permits multiple channels of data to be handled efficiently both within and outside switching systems. A set of inputs is sampled in turn. The samples are organized serially into slots (channels) to form a recurring frame of

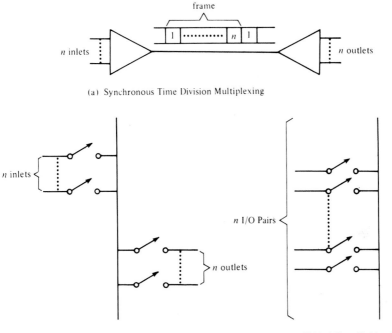

(a) Synchronous Time Division Multiplexing

(b) A Simple Time-Division Switch   (c) A Simple Folded Time-Division Switch

FIGURE 7.6 TDM Bus Switching

n slots. A slot may be a bit, a byte, or some longer block. An important point to note is that with synchronous TDM, the source and destination of the data in each time slot are known. Hence there is no need for address bits in each slot.

The mechanism for synchronous TDM may be quite simple. For example, each input line deposits data in a buffer; the multiplexer scans these buffers sequentially, taking fixed-size chunks of data from each buffer and sending them out on the line. One complete scan produces one frame of data. For output to the lines, the reverse operation is performed, with the multiplexer filling the output line buffers one by one.

The I/O lines attached to the multiplexer may be synchronous or asynchronous; the multiplexed line between the two multiplexers is synchronous and must have a data rate equal to the sum of the data rates of the attached lines. Actually, the multiplexed line must have a slightly higher data rate, since each frame will include some overhead bits—headers and trailers—for synchronization.

The time slots in a frame are assigned to the I/O lines on a fixed, predetermined basis. If a device has no data to send, the multiplexer must send empty slots. Thus the actual data transfer rate may be less than the capacity of the system.

Figure 7.6b shows a simple way in which TDM can be used to achieve switching. A set of buffered input and output lines is connected through controlled gates to a high-speed digital bus. Each input line is assigned a time slot. During that time, the line's gate is enabled, allowing a small burst of data onto the bus. For that same time slot, one of the output line gates is also enabled. Since the enabling and disabling of gates is controlled, the sequence of input and output line activations need not be in the same order. Hence a form of switching is possible. Curiously, this technique has no commonly used name; we shall refer to it as TDM bus switching.

Of course, such a scheme need not be two-sided. As shown in Figure 7.6c, a folded switch can be devised by attaching n I/O pairs to the bus. Any attached device achieves full-duplex operation by transmitting during one assigned time slot and receiving during another. The other end of the connection is an I/O pair for which these time slots have the opposite meanings.

The TDM bus switch has an advantage over a crossbar switch in terms of efficient use of gates. For n devices, the TDM bus switch requires $2n$ gates or switchpoints, whereas the most efficient multistage crossbar network requires on the order of $n\sqrt{n}$ switchpoints.

Let us look at the timing involved a bit more closely. First, consider a nonblocking implementation of Figure 7.6c. There must be n repetitively occurring time slots, each one assigned to an input and an output line. We will refer to one iteration for all time slots as a frame. The input assignment may be fixed; the output assignments vary to allow various connections. When a time slot begins, the designated input line may insert a burst of data onto the line, where it will propagate to both ends past all other lines. The designated output line will, during that time, copy the data if any as they go by. The time slot, then, must equal the transmission time of the input line plus the propagation delay between input and output lines. In order to keep the successive time slots uniform, time slot length should be defined as transmission time plus the end-to-end bus propagation delay. For efficiency, the propagation delay should be much less than the transmission time. Note that only one time slot or burst of data may be on the bus at a time.

To keep up with the input lines, the slots must recur sufficiently frequently. For example, consider a system connecting full-duplex lines at 19.2 kbps. Input data on each line are buffered at the gate. The buffer must be cleared, by enabling the gate, fast enough to avoid overrun. So if there are 100 lines, the capacity of the bus must be at least 1.92 Mbps. Actually, it must be higher than that to account for the wasted time due to propagation delay.

These considerations determine the traffic-carrying capacity of a blocking switch as well. For a blocking switch, there is no fixed assignment of input lines to time slots; they are allocated on demand. The data rate on the bus dictates how many connections can be made at a time. For a system with 200 devices at 19.2 kbps and a bus at 2 Mbps, about half of the devices can be connected at any one time.

The TDM bus-switching scheme can accommodate lines of varying data rates. For example, if a 9600-bps line gets one slot per frame, a 19.2-kbps line would get two slots per frame. Of course, only lines of the same data rate can be connected.

Figure 7.7 is an example that suggests how the control for a TDM bus switch could be implemented. Let us assume that propagation time on the bus is zero. Time on the bus is organized into 30-μs frames of six 5-μs slots each. A control memory indicates which gates are to be enabled during each time slot. In this example, six words of memory are needed. A controller cycles through the memory at a rate of one cycle every 30 μs. During the first time slot of each cycle, the input gate from device 1 and the output gate to device 3 are enabled, allowing data to pass from device 1 to device 3 over the bus. The remaining words are accessed in

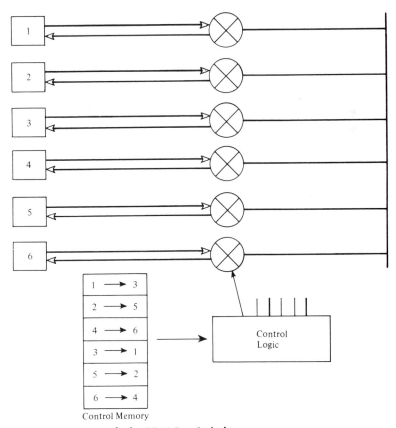

FIGURE 7.7 Control of a TDM Bus Switch

succeeding time slots and treated accordingly. As long as the control memory contains the contents depicted in Figure 7.7, connections are maintained between 1 and 3, 2 and 5, and 4 and 6.

Several questions may occur to you. For one, is this circuit switching? Circuit switching, recall, was defined as a technique in which a dedicated communications path is established between devices. This is indeed the case for Figure 7.6. To establish a connection between an input and output line, the controller dedicates a certain number of time slots per frame to that connection. The appropriate input and output gates are enabled during those time slots to allow data to pass. Although the bus is shared by other connections, it is nevertheless used to create a dedicated path between input and output. Another question: Is this synchronous TDM? Synchronous TDM is generally associated with creating permanent dedicated time slots for each input line. The scheme depicted in Figure 7.6 can assume a dynamic character, with the controller allocating available time slots among connections. Nevertheless, at steady state—a period when no connections are made or broken—a fixed number of slots is dedicated per channel and the system behaves as a synchronous time-division multiplexer.

The control logic for the system described above requires the enabling of two gates to achieve a connection. This logic can be simplified if the input burst into a time slot contains destination address information. All output devices can then always connect to the bus and copy the data from time slots with their address. This scheme blurs the distinction between circuit switching and packet switching.

This point bears further comment. In the bus reservation schemes described in Chapter 6, a device that has a quantity of data to send reserves sufficient future slots to handle that data. After the data are sent, the reservation goes away until the station again wants to send. In the TDM bus-switching scheme, a station reserves one or more time slots per frame for the indefinite future by requesting a connection. The reservation lasts until a disconnect is requested. The logic of the two schemes is very close.

Another point: The LAN/HSLN bus and the TDM bus switch differ only in geometry, not topology. The LAN or HSLN bus involves a relatively long bus with stations attached via relatively short lines. The star topology of the TDM bus switch actually involves a relatively short bus with stations attached via relatively long lines. This difference is crucial, of course: The timings on the shorter bus are amenable to greater control because of the much shorter propagation delay. Also, as we shall see, not all digital-switch architectures use a pure TDM bus switch. Nevertheless, the implication of the preceding discussion is valid: the differences between the technologies and architectures of the various types of networks discussed in this book are less than one might think.

Time-Slot Interchange.   The basic building block of many time-division switches is the *time-slot interchange* (TSI) mechanism. A TSI unit operates on a synchronous TDM stream of time slots, or channels, by interchanging pairs of slots to achieve full duplex operation. Figure 7.8a shows how the input line of device I is connected to the output line of device J, and vice versa.

We should note several points. The input lines of N devices are passed through a synchronous multiplexer to produce a TDM stream with N slots. To achieve interconnection, the slots corresponding to two inputs are interchanged. This results in a full-duplex connection between two lines. To allow the interchange of any two slots, the incoming data in a slot must be stored until they can be sent out on the right channel in the next frame cycle. Hence the TSI introduces a delay and produces output slots in the desired order. These are then demultiplexed and routed to the appropriate output line. Since each channel is provided a time slot in the frame, whether or not it transmits data, the

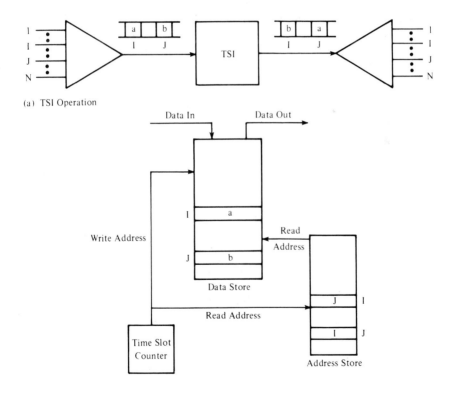

(a) TSI Operation

(b) TSI Mechanism

FIGURE 7.8 Time-Slot Interchange (TSI)

size of the TSI unit must be chosen for the capacity of the TDM line, not the actual data transfer rate.

Figure 7.8b depicts a mechanism for TSI. Individual lines are multiplexed and demultiplexed. These functions can be integrated as part of the switch itself, or they may be implemented remotely, as a device-clustering mechanism. A random-access data store whose width equals one time slot of data and whose length equals the number of slots in a frame is used. An incoming TDM frame is written sequentially, slot by slot, into the data store. An outgoing TDM frame is created by reading slots from the memory in an order dictated by an address store that reflects the existing connections. In the figure, the data in channels I and J are interchanged, creating a full-duplex connection between the corresponding stations.

TSI is a simple, effective way to switching TDM data. However, the size of such a switch, in terms of number of connections, is limited by the memory access speed. It is clear that, in order to keep pace with the input, data must be read into and out of memory as fast as they arrive. So, for example, if we have 24 sources operating at 64 kbps each, and a slot size of 8 bits, we would have an arrival rate of 192,000 slots per second (this is the structure of the PCM T1 carrier). Memory access time would need to be 1/192,000, or about 5 μs.

Let us look more closely at the operation of the data store; in particular, we need to view it as a function of time. As an example [DAV173], consider a system with eight input/output lines, in which the following connections exist: 1–2, 3–7, and 5–8. The other two stations are not in use. Figure 7.9 depicts the contents of the data store over the course of one frame (eight slots). During the first time slot, data are stored in location 1 and read from location 2. During the second time slot, data are stored in location 2 and read from location 1. And so on.

As can be seen, the write accesses to the data store are cyclic, that is, accessing successive locations in sequential order, whereas the read accesses are acyclic, requiring the use of an address store. The figure also depicts two frames of the input and output sequences and indicates the transfer of data between channels 1 and 2. Note that in half the cases, data slots move into the next frame.

As with the TDM bus switch, the TSI unit can handle inputs of varying data rates. Figure 7.10 suggests a way in which this may be done. Instead of presenting the input lines to a synchronous multiplexer, they are presented to a selector device. This device will select an input line based on a channel assignment provided from a store controlled by the time-slot counter. Hence, instead of sampling equally from each input, it may gather more slots from some channels than others.

Time-Multiplexed Switching.   As we have seen, a TSI unit can support only a limited number of connections. Further, as the size of the unit

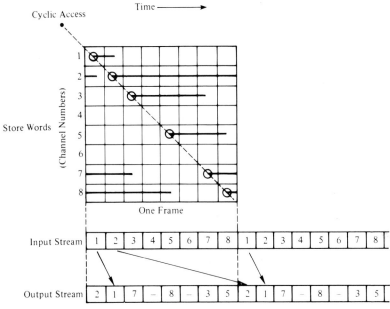

FIGURE 7.9 Operation of a TSI Store

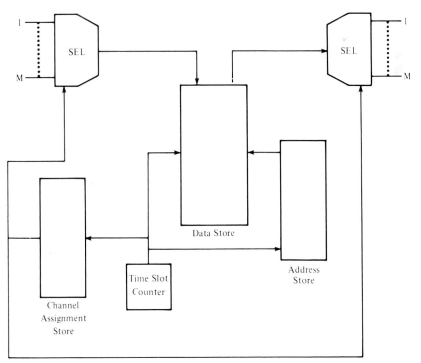

FIGURE 7.10 TSI Operation with Variable-Rate Input

grows, for a fixed-access speed, the delay at the TSI grows. To overcome both of these problems, multiple TSI units are used. Now, to connect two channels entering a single TSI unit, their time slots can be interchanged. However, to connect a channel on one TDM stream (going into one TSI) to a channel on another TDM stream (going into another TSI), some form of space-division multiplexing is needed. Naturally, we do not wish to switch all of the time slots from one stream to another; we would like to do it one slot at a time. The technique is known as *time-multiplexed switching* (TMS).

Multiple-stage networks can be built up by concatenating TMS and TSI stages: TMS stages, which move slots from one stream to another, are referred to as S, and TSI stages are referred to as T. Systems are generally described by an enumeration of their stages from input to output, using the symbols T and S. Figure 7.11 is an example of a two-stage TS network. Such a network is blocking. For example, if one channel in input stream 1 is to be switched to the third channel in output stream 1, and another channel in input stream 1 is to be switched to the third channel in output stream 2, one of the connections is blocked.

To avoid blocking, three or more stages are used. Some of the more common structures used in commercially available systems are [SKAP79]:

- TST
- TSSST
- STS

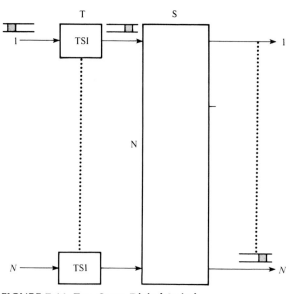

FIGURE 7.11 Two-Stage Digital Switch

- SSTSS
- TSTST

The requirements on the TMS unit are stringent. The unit must provide space-division connections between its input and output lines, and these connections must be reconfigured for each time slot. This requires, in effect, a control store whose width is sufficient to handle the number of ingoing and outgoing lines and whose length equals the number of time slots in a frame.

One means of implementing the TMS stage is the crossbar switch discussed earlier. This requires that the crosspoints be manipulated at each time slot. More commonly, the TMS stage is implemented by digital selectors (SEL) that select only one input at a time on a time-slot basis. These SEL devices are the same as those described in the preceding section, except that here each of their inputs is a TDM stream rather than a single line. Figure 7.12 shows STS and TST networks implemented with the SEL units.

In an STS network, the path between an incoming and outgoing channel has multiple possible physical routes equal to the number of TSI units. For a fully nonblocking network, the number of TSI units must be double the number of incoming and outgoing TDM streams. On the other hand, the multiple routes between two channels in a TST network are all in the time domain; there is only one physical path possible. Here, too, blocking is a possibility. One way to avoid blocking is by expanding the number of time slots in the space stage. In all multistage networks, a path-search algorithm is needed to determine the route from input to output.

It is interesting to compare the TDM bus switch with TSI and TMS. It does not exactly fit into either category. Compare it to a space switch. The TDM bus switch does connect any input with any output, as in a crossbar or SEI switch. The space switch operates simultaneously on all inputs, whereas the TDM bus switch operates on the inputs sequentially. However, because the frame time on the bus is less than the slot time of any input, the switching is effectively simultaneous. On the other hand, a comparison of Figures 7.8 and 7.6b reveals the similarity between TSI and TDM bus switching.

7.3

DIGITAL DATA-SWITCHING DEVICES

The techniques discussed in the preceding section have been used to build a variety of digital-switching products designed for data-only applications. These devices do not provide telephone service and are generally cheaper than a digital PBX of comparable capacity.

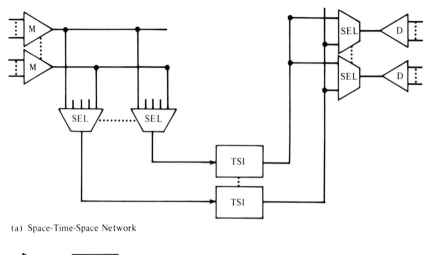

(a) Space-Time-Space Network

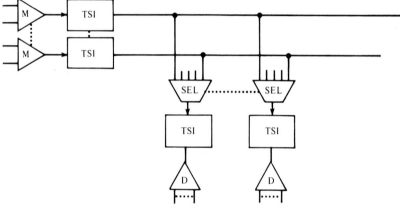

(b) Time-Space-Time Network

FIGURE 7.12 Three-Stage TDM Switches

The variety of devices is wide and the distinction between types is blurred. For convenience, we categorize them as follows:

• Terminal/port-oriented switch
• Data switch

In what follows we will look at the functions performed by each type of device and suggest an architecture that supports those functions. Keep in mind that usually any of the techniques in Section 7.2, or any combination, may be used to implement any of these switches. The discussion here is intended only to give examples.

Before turning to the specific device types, let us look at the requirements for data switching.

Data-Switching Requirements

For any circuit-switching system used to connect digital-data-transmitting devices, certain generic requirements can be defined. These requirements apply both to pure digital-data-switching devices and to digital PBX systems. We begin first by looking briefly at the data transmission techniques that must be supported by a data switch and then look at the functions to be performed.

The devices attached to a data switch will use either asynchronous or synchronous transmission. Asynchronous transmission, recall, is character-at-a-time. Each character consists of a start bit, 5 to 8 data bits, a parity bit, and a stop signal, which may be 1, 1.5, or 2 bit times in length. Logic is available that can automatically determine character length, parity, and even bit rate. Hence it is a relatively easy matter for a data switch to handle asynchronous transmission. On input, data are accumulated a character at a time and transmitted internally using synchronous transmission. At the other end of the connection, they are buffered and transmitted a character at a time to the output line. This applies to any switch using time-division switching techniques. Of course, a pure space-division switch need not concern itself with such matters; a dedicated physical path is set up and bits are transmitted transparently.

Synchronous transmission represents a greater challenge. Synchronous communication requires either a separate clock lead from the transmission point to the reception point or the use of a self-clocking encoding scheme, such as Manchester. The latter technique is typical. With synchronous communication, the data rate must be known ahead of time, as well as the synchronization pattern (bits or characters used to signal the beginning of a frame). Thus there can be no universal synchronous interface.

Of course, for either synchronous or asynchronous transmission, full duplex operation is required. Typically, this requires two twisted pairs (known as a *twin pair*) between a device and the switch, one for transmission in each direction. This is in contrast to the case with analog signaling where a single twisted-pair suffices (see Figure 2.4). Recently, however, some vendors have begun to offer full-duplex digital signaling on a single twisted pair, using a *ping-pong protocol*. In essence, data are buffered at each end and sent across the line at double the data rate, with the two ends taking turn. So, for example, two devices may communicate, full-duplex, at 56 kbps, if they are attached to a 112-kbps line and the line drivers at each end buffer the device data and transmit, alternately, at 112 kbps. In fact, a somewhat higher data rate is required to account for propagation delay and control signals.

We turn now to the functions to be provided by a data switch. The most basic, of course, is the making of a connection between two attached lines. These connections can be preconfigured by a system operator, but more dynamic operation is often desired. This leads to two additional functions: port contention and port selection. *Port contention* is a function that allows a certain number of designated ports to contend or access to a smaller number of ports. Typically, this is used for terminal-to-host connection to allow a smaller number of host ports to service a larger number of terminal ports. When a terminal user attempts to connect, the system will scan through all the host ports in the contention group. If any of the ports is available, a connection is made.

Port selection is an interactive capability. It allows a user (or an application program in a host) to select a port for connection. This is analogous to dialing a number in a phone system. Port selection and port contention can be combined by allowing the selection, by name or number, of a contention group. Port-selection devices are becoming increasingly common. A switch without this capability only allows connections that are preconfigured by a system operator. If one knows in advance what interconnections are required, fine. Otherwise, the flexibility of port selection is usually worth the additional cost.

An interactive capability carries with it an additional responsibility: the control unit of the switch must be able to talk to the requesting port. This can be done in two ways. In some cases, the manufacturer supplies a simple keypad device that attaches to and shares the terminal's line. The user first uses the keypad to dial a connection; once the connection is made, communication is via the terminal. As an alternative, the connection sequence can be effected through the terminal itself. A simple command language dialogue is used. However, this technique requires that the system understand the code and protocol being used by the terminal. Consequently, this feature is generally limited to asynchronous ASCII devices.

Terminal/Port-Oriented Switches

The devices discussed in this section were designed to address a specific problem: the connection of interactive terminals to computer ports. In many computer sites with one or more time-sharing systems and a population (usually growing) of terminals, means must be found for interconnection.

One means of connection is simply to assign each terminal to a specific computer port, even when not active. This is expensive in terms of computer ports, since generally only a fraction of the terminals are logged on. Further, the user cannot change to a different computer without making cable changes. Another approach is to use multiple dial-up telephone rotaries, for each computer and each transmission speed. The rotary allows a user to call a single number and gain access to one of several autoanswer modems; if all modems are busy, the rotary returns a busy signal. The approach ties up telephone lines for extended periods and requires the use of modems.

One early solution that avoided some of the expenses mentioned above was the patch panel. This device enabled manual connection of two lines and could also provide some system monitoring and diagnostics. The addition of intelligence to this type of device to eliminate the manual connection function has resulted in a variety of intelligent terminal/port-oriented switches. A variety of names are used, depending partly on function, including intelligent path panel, port selector, and port-contention device.

At a minimum, these devices permit a set of connections to be set up and periodically updated by a system operator. Port-selection and port-contention functions are also provided on many products.

Figure 7.13 is an example of a noninteractive (without port selection) system. The system allows connection of one I/O port to any other I/O port on the same or a different port card. Connections are set up at system initialization time and may be changed dynamically by the system operator (not the user). The means of establishing connections is simple. Each port has associated with it a destination address register. To connect two ports, the address of each is placed in the other. To transmit data, the sending device puts its data (8 bits) and the destination address (8 bits) on the bus. All devices continually monitor the bus for their own address. The switch is nonblocking, allowing the pre-assignment of time slots to transmitting devices. Receiving devices need not know the time slot for reception since they are looking for an address. Thus, at the cost of 100% overhead, the control logic is greatly simplified.

Figure 7.14 is an example of a port-selection system. A collection of line modules is scanned to produce a TDM stream that is passed over a bus to a switch module. The output of the switch module is a switched set of time slots that are directed to the proper port. Note the redundant architecture for reliability.

Data Switches

Not much else needs to be said about these devices. No distinction is made between terminal lines and ports. The switch simply has a set of I/O lines and is capable of establishing connections between lines. Any or a combination of the digital-switching techniques described in Section 7.2 may be used. Some or all of the functions described in this section may be provided.

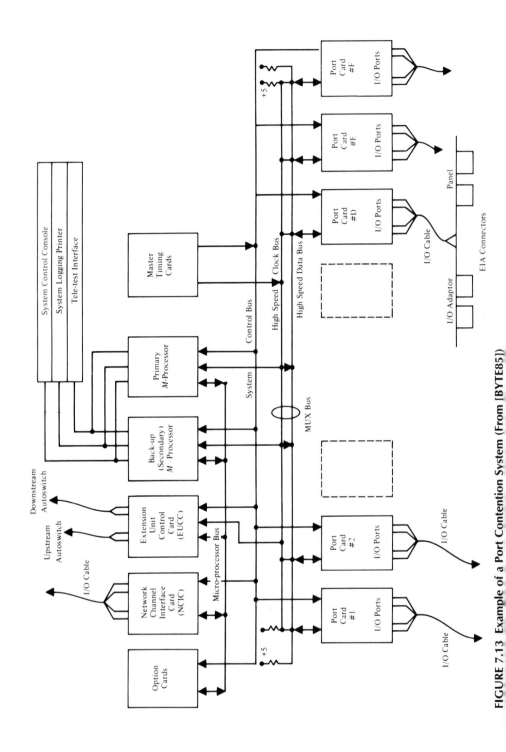

FIGURE 7.13 Example of a Port Contention System (From [BYTE85])

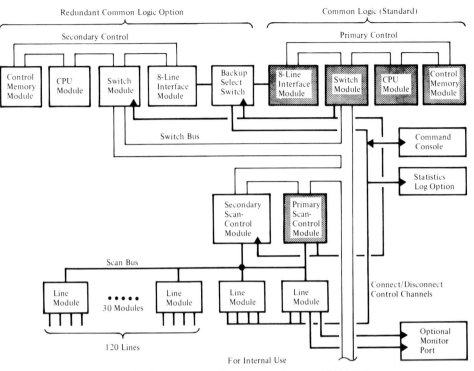

FIGURE 7.14 Example of a Port Selection System (From [VONA80])

7.4

THE DIGITAL PRIVATE BRANCH EXCHANGE

Evolution of the Digital PBX

The digital PBX is a marriage of two technologies: digital switching and telephone exchange systems. The forerunner of the digital PBX is the *private branch exchange* (PBX). A PBX is an on-premise facility, owned or leased by an organization, that interconnects the telephones within the facility and provides access to the public telephone system. Typically, a telephone user on the premises dials a three- or four-digit number to call another telephone on the premises, and dials one digit (usually 8 or 9) to get a dial tone for an outside line, which allows the caller to dial a number in the same fashion as a residential user.

The original private exchanges were manual, with one or more operators at a switchboard required to make all connections. Back in the 1920s, these began to be replaced by automatic systems, called *private automatic branch exchanges* (PABX), which did not require attendant intervention to place a call. These first-generation systems used electromechanical technology and analog signaling. Data connections could be made via modems. That is, a user with a terminal, a telephone, and a modem or acoustic coupler in the office could dial up an on-site or remote number that reached another modem and exchange data.

The second-generation PBXs were introduced in the mid-1970s. These systems use electronic rather than electromagnetic technology and the internal switching is digital. Such a system is referred to as a digital PBX, or *computerized branch exchange* (CBX). These systems were designed primarily to handle analog voice traffic, with the codec function built into the switch so that digital switching could be used internally. The systems were also capable of handling digital data connections without the need of a modem.

The third-generation systems are touted as "integrated voice/data" systems, although the differences between third generation and upgraded second generation are rather blurred. Perhaps a better term is "improved digital PBX." Some of the characteristics of these systems that differ from those of earlier systems include:

- *The use of digital phone:* This permits integrated voice/data workstations.
- *Distributed architecture:* Multiple switches in a hierarchical or meshed configuration with distributed intelligence provides enhanced reliability.
- *Nonblocking configuration:* Typically, dedicated port assignments are used for all attached phones and devices.

As new features and technologies are employed, incremental improvements make difficult the continuing classification of PBXs into generations. Nevertheless, it is worth noting recent advances in PBX products that, together, might be considered to constitute a fourth generation [JEWE85, COOV85]:

- *Integrated LAN link:* This capability provides a direct high-speed link to a LAN. This allows an optimum distribution of lower-speed devices (terminals) on the PBX and higher-speed devices (computers) on the LAN in a fashion that is fully transparent to the user.
- *Dynamic bandwidth allocation:* Typically, a PBX offers one or only a small number of different data rate services. The increased sophistication of capacity allocation within the PBX allows it to offer virtually any data rate to an attached device. This allows the system to grow as user requirements grow. For example, full-motion color video at 448 kbps or advanced voice codecs at 32 kbps could be accommodated.
- *Integrated packet channel:* This allows the PBX to provide access to an X.25 packet-switched network.

It is worthwhile to summarize the main reasons why the evolution described above has taken place. To the untrained eye, analog and digital PBXs would seem to offer about the same level of convenience. The analog PBX can handle telephone sets directly and it uses modems to accommodate digital data devices; the digital PBX can handle digital data devices directly and it uses codecs to accommodate telephone sets. Some of the advantages of the digital approach are

- *Digital technology:* By handling all internal signals digitally, the digital PBX can take advantage of low-cost LSI and VLSI components. Digital technology also lends itself more readily to software and firm-wave control.
- *Time-division multiplexing:* Digital signals lend themselves readily to TDM techniques, which provide efficient use of internal data paths, access to public TDM carriers, and TDM switching techniques that are more cost effective than older, cross-bar techniques.
- *Digital control signals:* Control signals are inherently digital and can easily be integrated into a digital transmission path via TDM. The signaling equipment is independent of the transmission medium.
- *Encryption:* This is more easily accommodated with digital signals.

Telephone Call Processing Requirements

The characteristic that distinguishes the digital PBX from a digital data switch is its ability to handle telephone connections. Freeman [FREE89] lists eight functions required for telephone call processing:

- Interconnection
- Control
- Attending
- Busy testing
- Alerting
- Information receiving
- Information transmitting
- Supervision

The interconnection function encompasses three contingencies. The first contingency is a call originated by a station bound for another station on the digital PBX. The switching technologies that we have discussed are used in this context. The second contingency is a call originated by a digital PBX station bound for an external recipient. For this, the PBX must not only have access to an external trunk, but must perform internal switching to route the call from the user station to the trunk interface. The PBX also performs a line-to-trunk concentration function to avoid the expense of one external line per station. The third contingency is a call originated externally bound for a PBX station. Referred to as *direct inward dialing,* this allows an external caller to use the unique phone number of a PBX station to establish a call without going through an operator. This requires trunk-to-line expansion plus internal switching.

The control function includes, of course, the logic for setting up and tearing down a connection path. In addition, the control function serves to activate and control all other functions and to provide various management and utility services, such as logging, accounting, and configuration control.

The PBX must recognize a request for a connection; this is the attending function. The PBX then determines if the called party is available (busy testing) and, if so, alerts that party (alerting). The process of setting up the connection involves an exchange of information between the PBX and the called and calling parties. Note how dramatically this differs from the distributed packet-switching approach of LANs and HSLNs.

Finally, a supervisory function is needed to determine when a call is completed and the connection may be released, freeing the switching capacity and the two parties for future connections.

Let us look more closely at the sequence of events required to successfully complete a call. First, consider an internal call from extension 226 to extension 280. The following steps occur:

1. 226 goes off-hook (picks up the receiver). The control unit recognizes this condition.
2. The control unit finds an available digit receiver and sets up a circuit from 226 to the digit receiver. The control unit also sets up a circuit from a dial-tone generator to 226.
3. When the first digit is dialed, the dial-tone connection is released. The digit receiver accumulates dialed digits.
4. After the last digit is dialed, the connection to the digit receiver is released. The control unit examines the number for legitimacy. If it is not valid, the caller is informed by some means, such as connection to a rapid busy signal generator. Otherwise, the control unit then determines if 280 is busy. If so, 226 is connected to a busy-signal generator.
5. If 280 is free, the control unit sets up a connection between 226 and a ring-back-tone generator and a connection between 280 and a ringer.
6. When 280 answers by going off-hook, the ringing and ring-back connections are dropped and a connection is set up between 226 and 280.
7. When either 280 or 226 goes on-hook, the connection between them is dropped.

For outgoing calls, the following steps are required:

1–3. As above. In this case the caller will be dialing an access code number (e.g., the single digit 9) to request access to an outgoing trunk.
  4. The control unit releases the connection to the digit receiver and finds a free trunk group and sends out an off-hook signal.
  5. When a dial tone is returned from the central office, the control unit repeats steps 2 and 3.
  6. The control unit releases the connection to the digit receiver and sends the number out to the trunk and makes a connection from the caller to the trunk.
  7. When either the caller or the trunk signals on-hook, the connection between them is dropped.

There are variations on the foregoing sequence. For example, if the PBX performs least-cost routing, it will wait until the number is dialed and then select the appropriate trunk.

Finally, incoming calls, when direct inward dialing is supported, proceed as follows.

  1. The control unit detects a trunk seizure signal from the central office and sends a start-dialing signal out on that trunk. It also sets up a path from the trunk to a digit receiver.
  2. After the last digit is received, the control unit releases the path, examines the dialed number, and checks the called station for busy, in which case a busy signal is returned.
  3. If the called number is free, the control unit sets up a ringing connection to the called number and a ring-back connection to the trunk. It monitors the called station for answer and the trunk for abandon.
  4. When the called station goes off-hook, the ringing and ring-back connections are dropped and a connection is set up between the trunk and the called station.
  5. When either the trunk or called station signals on-hook, the connection between them is dropped.

As you can see, the requirements for setting up a telephone connection are more complex than those for a data connection.

Advanced Services

The digital PBX is very application oriented. That is, a considerable portion of the design and development effort is spent fitting the product directly to the application.

In a digital PBX, a distinction is made between advanced services that are possible with digital control and the "plain old telephone services"

TABLE 7.2   Typical PBX Features

Automatic Call Distribution

A call to one number is spread among a group of telephones. When a call comes in, it is routed to the next available phone in rotary fashion.

Automatic Callback

When the caller rings a busy number the caller is alerted and may hang up. The system will monitor the called number until it is free; it may also alert the called party with a beep on the line. When the called number is free, the system rings the caller and re-places the call. The same service can be provided for gaining access to a special outside line, such as a WATS circuit.

Call Detail Recording

The details of telephone traffic are measured and recorded, including a history of numbers called and call duration from each phone. The record includes both internal calls and external calls plus the related charges.

Call Forwarding

Permits a station to be set so that incoming calls are automatically referred to another telephone: (1) when the station subscriber expects to be away and/or (2) when the subscriber is using the telephone line.

Call Intercept

When a busy number is called, the call is intercepted by a message center or operator.

Call Notification

Enables the PBX to notify a user already engaged in a call of an incoming call. The user than has the choice of accepting, rejecting, or ignoring the waiting call. Some systems permit "executive override," permitting a calling party literally to interrupt an ongoing conversation.

Call Pickup

This feature is useful in an office with many phones. If another phone in the room rings and there is no one to pick it up, a subscriber at a nearby phone can dial a code that transfers the call to that subscriber.

Call Transfer

When two subscribers are connected, one may transfer the call to a third party and leave the connection. This service is different from the call-forward service since, in this case, the call to be transferred must have an established end-to-end connection prior to the transfer.

Conference Call

Permits the addition of extensions to a two-party call.

Direct Inward Dialing

Enables an outside call to be placed directly to a PBX user without attendant intervention.

Direct Outward Dialing

A subscriber can dial a call on the public network without assistance from an operator.

Don't Disturb

Allows a station user to instruct the PBX not to ring through a call to the telephone.

TABLE 7.2   (Cont.)

External Number Repetition
  Similar to automatic callback but to an external number. The system will
  repeatedly call a busy external number until the number is free and begins
  ringing. At that point the system rings the caller.

Outgoing Call Restriction
  Certain extensions are prevented from making certain categories of calls (e.g.,
  any outgoing call, any outgoing long-distance call).

Route Optimization
  When more than one option exists for outside calls (e.g., more than one carrier,
  WATS, etc.) the system will pick the cheapest available route at each point in
  time.

Three-party Service
  The possibility for a busy subscriber to hold the existing call and make a call
  to a third party. The following arrangements may then be possible: the ability
  to switch between the two calls, the introduction of a common speech path
  between the three parties, and the connection of the other two parties.

(POTS) of an older PBX; the call processing functions just described are
examples of the latter. Table 7.2 lists advanced services that are typically
found in digital PBX products.

Data-Switching Requirements

The data-switching requirements for a digital PBX are the same as those
for a digital data switch. Typically, a terminal user will be requesting
connection to a computer port. The same issues of speed, asynchro-
nous/synchronous, and calling technique arise.

There are several new wrinkles. The PBX may support a voice/data
workstation with one twisted pair for the phone and two pairs for the
terminal. In such arrangements, the destination port may be selected
from the phone rather than the terminal or a keypad.

The PBX has the advantage of direct connection to outgoing telephone lines. The terminal user who wishes to access an external computer need not have a telephone and a modem; the PBX can provide the
link-up service. Typically, the connection is to an outgoing analog voice
line. To provide the proper service, the PBX maintains a pool of modems
that can be used by any data device to communicate over the external
lines.

The exact implementation of the modem pool depends on the architecture of the PBX, but some strange contortions may be required. Consider the case of a PBX whose switching capability consists of a TDM
bus switch. Figure 7.15 illustrates this. A device wishing to communicate outside will be connected to an available modem in the pool. The
modem produces analog signals that must be switched to an outgoing

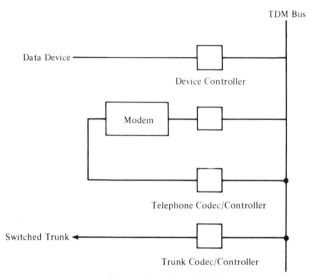

FIGURE 7.15 Use of a Modem in a Digital PBX

analog trunk. But the PBX switches only digital signals! Therefore, the modem output is routed to a codec that digitizes the data and puts them back onto the TDM bus. They are then routed to a trunk interface, where the signal is converted back to analog and sent on its way.

The most important characteristic is the internal integration of data and digitized voice. The same switching mechanism is used for both. Therefore, both must conform to common slot size and timing conventions. This is a requirement not faced by the digital switch designer.

Digital PBX Architecture

A variety of architectures have been developed by digital PBX manufacturers. Since these are proprietary, the details are not generally known in most cases. In this section, we attempt to present the general architecture features common to all PBX systems.

Digital PBX Components.   Figure 7.16 presents a generic PBX architecture. You should find it quite similar to the data-switching architecture we have discussed. Indeed, since the requirements for the PBX are a superset of those for the data switch, a similar architecture is not surprising.

As always, the heart of the system is some kind of digital-switching network. The switch is responsible for the manipulation and switching of time-multiplexed digital-signal streams, using the techniques described in Section 7.2. The digital-switching network consists of some

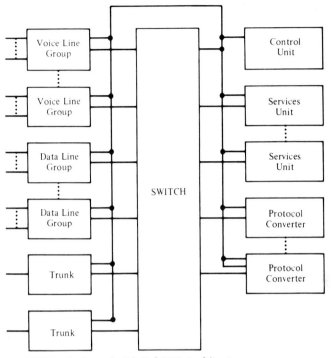

FIGURE 7.16 Generic Digital PBX Architecture

number of space- and time-switching stages. Many of the PBXs are not sufficiently large, in terms of lines or capacity, to require complex switching networks. Indeed, some have no network as such, but simply use a TDM bus switch.

Attached to the switch are a set of interface units that provide access to and from the outside world. Typically, an interface unit will perform a synchronous time-division multiplexing function in order to accommodate multiple incoming lines. On the other side, the unit requires two lines into the switch for full-duplex operation.

It is important to understand that the interface unit is performing synchronous and not asynchronous TDM, even though connections are dynamically changing. On the input side, the unit performs a multiplex operation. Each incoming line is sampled at a specified rate. For n incoming lines each of data rate x, the unit must achieve an input rate of nx. The incoming data are buffered and organized into chunks of time-slot size. Then, according to the timing dictated by the control unit, individual chunks are sent out into the switch at the internal PBX data rate, which may be in the range 50 to 500 Mbps. In a nonblocking switch, n time slots are dedicated to the interface unit for transmission, whether or not they are used. In a blocking switch, time slots are assigned for the duration of a connection. In either case, the time-slot assignment is fixed for the duration of the connection, and synchronous TDM techniques may be used.

On the output side, the interface unit accepts data from the switch during designated time slots. In a nonblocking switch these may be dedicated (requiring more than a simple TDM bus switch), but are in any case fixed for the duration of the connection. Incoming data are demultiplexed, buffered, and presented to the appropriate output port at its data rate.

Several types of interface units are used. A data line group unit handles data devices, providing the functions described in Section 7.3. An analog voice line group handles a number of twisted-pair phone lines. The interface unit must include codecs for digital-to-analog (input) and analog-to-digital (output) conversion. A separate type of unit may be used for integrated digital voice/data workstations, which present digitized voice at 64 kbps and data at the same or a lower rate. The range of lines accommodated by interface units is typically 8 to 24.

In addition to multiplexing interface units that accommodate multiple lines, trunk interface units are used to connect to off-site locations. These may be analog voice trunks or digital trunks, which may carry either data or PCM voice. Whereas a line interface unit must multiplex incoming lines to place on the switch, the demultiplex switch traffic to send to the lines, the trunk unit must demultiplex and multiplex in both directions (see Figure 7.17). Consider an incoming digital line with n channels of time-multiplexed data (the argument is the same for an analog trunk, which presents n channels of frequency-multiplexed voice). These data must be demultiplexed and stored in a buffer of length n units. Individual units of the buffer are then transmitted out to the switch at the designated time slots. Question: Why not pass the TDM stream directly from input to the bus, filling n contiguous time slots? Actually, in a nonblocking dedicated port system, this is possible. But for a system with dynamic time-slot assignment, the incoming data must be buffered and sent out on time slots that vary as connections are made and broken.

The other boxes in Figure 7.16 can be explained briefly. The control unit operates the digital switch and exchanges control signals with attached devices. For this purpose, a separate bus or other data path is used; control signals generally do not propagate through the switch itself. As part of this or a separate unit, network administration and control functions are implemented. Service units would include such things as tone and busy-signal generators and dialed-digit registers. Some PBX systems provide protocol converters for connecting dissimilar lines. A connection is made from each line to the protocol converter.

It should be noted that this generic architecture lends itself to a high degree of reliability. The failure of any interface unit means the loss of

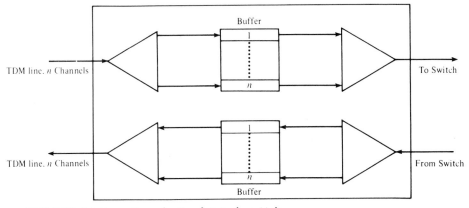

FIGURE 7.17 Operation of a Trunk Interface Unit

only a small number of lines. Key elements such as the control unit can be made redundant.

Distributed Architecture.   For reasons of efficiency and reliability, many PBX manufacturers offer distributed architectures for their larger systems. The PBX is organized into a central switch and one or more distributed modules, with coaxial or fiber optic cable between the central switch and the modules, in a two-level hierarchical star topology.

The distributed modules off-load at least some of the central-switch processor's real-time work load (such as off-hook detection). The degree to which control intelligence is off-loaded varies. At one extreme, the modules may be replicas of the central switch, in which case they function almost autonomously with the exception of certain overall management and accounting functions. At the other extreme, the modules are as limited as possible.

A distributed architecture means that it will often be necessary to concatenate several connections to achieve a connection between two devices. Consider Figure 7.18. A connection is desired between lines a and b. In module A, a connection is established between line a and one channel on a TDM trunk to the central switch. In the central switch, that channel is connected to a channel on a TDM trunk to module B. In module B, that channel is connected to line b.

There are several advantages to a distributed architecture:

- It permits growth beyond the practical size of a single digital switch.
- It provides better performance by off-loading of functions.
- It provides higher reliability: the loss of a single module need not disable the entire system.
- It reduces twisted-pair wiring distances.

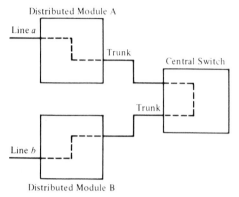

**FIGURE 7.18 Circuit Establishment in a
Distributed Digital PBX**

Modular Architecture.   The discussion so far has concerned what
might be termed "traditional" digital-switch architecture. More recently,
a modular-switch architecture has been developed based on the use of
one module type for all switching stages [KAJI83]. A single module contains both time and space switching.

A major motivation for going to a modular architecture is to overcome
some inherent disadvantages of the traditional multistage time-and-
space switch. With the traditional switch, the designer must decide in
advance the maximum exchange size in order to determine the number
of stages and the switch size at each stage. These decisions, in turn,
determine a lower size limit. In addition, central control is needed to set
up and tear down paths through the switch. As the size of the switch
grows, this task becomes increasingly complex. The modular architecture does not possess these disadvantages, as we shall see.

We can contrast the modular switch to the traditional digital switch
by listing some of the advantages of the former:

- *Flexible size:* The modules serve as building blocks, allowing a large
  number of different switch sizes, ranging from very small to very
  large.
- *Simplified control:* Path setup and tear-down is distributed. Each
  module is intelligent and control is provided via the data path.
- *Simplified manufacturing, testing, and maintenance:* There are fewer
  parts to build and install.

The principal disadvantage of the modular architecture is potentially
increased propagation delay. Each module performs a TSI function. In
a large switch, a circuit may pass through multiple modules, and the TSI
delays can become substantial.

In the remainder of this section, we briefly describe one example of a modular architecture, the ITT 1240 [COTT81, KEIS85]. For another example, the reader is referred to [ENOM85].

The basic building block of the ITT switch is depicted in Figure 7.19. This module is a plug-in printed circuit board that carries 16 identical LSI *switch ports* interconnected by a TDM bus switch. Each port has an incoming and an outgoing synchronous TDM line. Each line has a data rate of 4.096 Mbps and carries 32 channels. Each channel is used for either digital data or PCM voice. One TDM frame consists of 16 bits from each of the 32 channels. Eight of these bits are control or unused bits. A little arithmetic reveals that each channel is therefore 64 kbps.

There is no common mechanism or control processor to control the modules. Each module is controlled by the individual switch ports act-

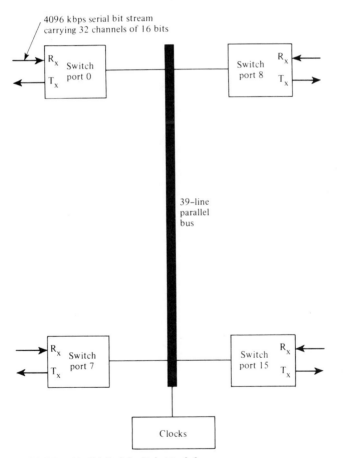

FIGURE 7.19 Digital Switch Module

ing together over the TDM bus to make and break connections. The receive (incoming) side of each switch port is in essence a synchronous demultiplexer. It sends the channel data, along with destination port number and channel number, out in 16-bit chunks onto the bus during assigned time slots. The transmit (outgoing) side recognizes its port number on the bus and places each slot of data in the appropriate frame slot of the outgoing line. Since the slots are then transmitted in a (possibly) different order than that in which they were received from the bus, the switch port performs, in effect, a TSI operation. With this architecture, any channel on any of the 16 incoming lines can be connected to any of the 512 (16 × 32) outgoing channels. Thus the module provides a combination of time and space switching.

To begin, let us consider the operation of the simplest switch, depicted in Figure 7.20. Individual terminals (digital data or PCM voice) attach to a *terminal control element* (TCE), which produces two 32-channel

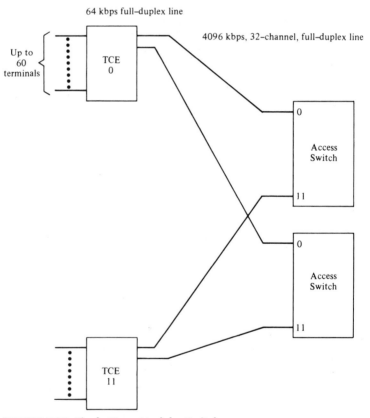

FIGURE 7.20 Single-Stage Modular Switch

TDM streams destined for the switch. Similarly, the TCE receives two 32-channel streams from the switch. Thus the TCE is nothing more than a synchronous TDM multiplexer/demultiplexer. Up to 60 terminals attach to the switch (the extra channels are used for control). The switch in this case consists of two modules that in this context are called *access switches,* with one full-duplex 32-channel link from each TCE going to each module. The use of two modules provides redundancy in the case of failure. Thus any two of the 60 devices on the TCE can be connected via the switch.

Note that one TCE uses up only one port on each of the access switches. The switches support up to 12 TCEs using 12 of the available 16 ports. The remaining ports are unused in this configuration. Thus the simplest one-stage switch consists of two modules and supports 720 terminals. Switching is accomplished as follows. When a terminal requests a connection, and if the destination terminal is attached to the same TCE, the TCE completely implements the connection without involving an access switch. Otherwise, the TCE selects an available outgoing channel (out of the 64) and transmits a path setup request over that channel, which includes the destination address. The access switch responds by selecting an available channel going to the appropriate TCE.

The way in which a switch may be expanded and the operation of a multistage switch can be explained with reference to Figure 7.21. The single-stage switch is enclosed in a box labeled A. For a first expansion, up to three more pairs of access switches may be added to the first stage, all interconnected by a second stage of switching. The four unused ports on each access switch (32 in all) connect to a second-stage switch called a *group switch.* This stage consists of up to four modules, with eight ports on each module utilized. The four ports on each access switch attach, one each, to the four modules of stage 2. Thus full connectivity is achieved. The full switch can now handle a total of 2880 terminals. Switching is accomplished as follows. If two terminals connect via TCEs to the same access switch, a path is set up that "reflects back" through the access switch without going to the second stage. Addresses have a hierarchical format, so it is easy for a module to determine if reflection is allowed. If not, an available channel to the stage 2 switch is selected and that switch in turn reflects back to a different access switch that connects to the TCE of the destination terminal.

The two-step configuration is labeled B in the diagram. Further expansion proceeds similarly. The eight unused ports on each second-stage module are used to connect to up to eight third-stage switches. Reflection can occur at stage 1, 2, or (boxes C and D). The maximum configuration consists of four stages and supports over 100,000 terminals.

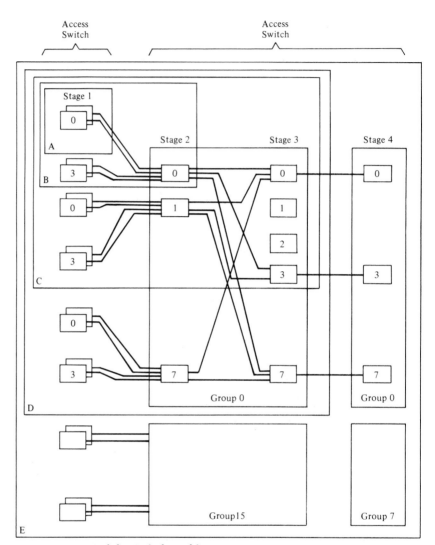

FIGURE 7.21 Modular Switch Architecture

Centrex

To conclude this section, we briefly describe another approach to supporting voice and data devices in an office environment. Known as Centrex, this approach provides the same service as a digital PBX and appears the same to the user [KLIN86, BRAY85]. In contrast to the digital PBX, however, Centrex performs switching functions in equipment located in the telephone company's central office as opposed to the customer's premises. Centrex utilizes public central-office switching technology enhanced to form a virtual private switch. All telephone and voice lines are routed from the customer site to the central switch. The user can still make local calls with an extension number, giving the appearance of a local switch.

There are several benefits associated with Centrex as opposed to PBXs:

- *Reliability and availability:* The central office equipment is engineered for reliability, with extensive use of redundancy. Maintenance and technical support personnel are available at the switch at all times.
- *Flexibility:* The user is not committed to a switch of a certain size. The customer can grow or shrink the service as required.
- *Avoidance of PBX-related expenses:* These include capital investment, space requirements, and insurance.
- *Continued updating of functionality:* New hardware and software features are regularly added to Centrex offerings.

Centrex is not a true local network because of the distances involved. However, from the user's point of view, this is irrelevant, and Centrex is a major competitor to the digital PBX.

7.5

DIGITAL PBX VERSUS LAN

There is a clear overlap between the capabilities provided by a digital PBX system and a LAN. Both can support a large number and wide variety of digital devices. In order to choose between the two technologies, the potential customer should lay out all the mandatory and desirable features, and then compare the two based on a match against requirements and cost (this process is described in [DERF83]). In this section we compare briefly the two approaches, based on a checklist suggested in [PFIS82]. PBX and LAN can be compared in the following categories:

- Installation
- Reliability
- Data types
- Distance
- Speed
- Capacity
- Cost

The *installation* of the cable for a LAN in an already finished building is without question a time-consuming and expensive task. It is not out of bounds to have the wire costs of a LAN installation be 50% of the total! Consider the requirements for a PBX. Phone connections require a two-wire (usually twisted-pair) connection. Data connections, using digital signaling, usually require two twisted pairs for a full-duplex line. Therefore, with many PBX systems, the user who wants both a phone and a terminal in the office requires three twisted-pair lines. The third-generation PBX systems often provide integrated digital voice/data workstations that require only two twisted pairs. Some vendors, using the ping-pong protocol, offer an integrated voice/data link consisting of a single 256-kbps twisted pair (128 kbps for full-duplex voice, 128 kbps for full-duplex data). In any case, just about all existing office sites are wired with twisted pairs for distribution of traditional phone services. Further, PBXs are almost always installed with two pairs of wiring per outlet—one for backup. So most PBXs have a number of available spare twisted-pair lines. This could represent a tremendous savings compared to a LAN.

With respect to *reliability*, there are problems with both PBX and LAN systems. The reliability problems of the LAN may be the more severe, contrary to the usual first impression. PBX systems can be made fully redundant, virtually eliminating network-wide failures. But it is easy to postulate situations that would disable all or a substantial part of a LAN.

Both the PBX and the LAN can adequately handle most *data type* requirements. The PBX is superior for handling voice. The centralized control nature of the PBX is ideal for the variety of voice processing requirements in an office environment. Another type of transmission—video—can at present only be practically handled by a broadband LAN.

The *distances* achievable by the PBX and the LAN are about equal. With a distributed architecture, a PBX can easily span a multibuilding complex by locating a switching center in each building, thus matching the range achievable with a broadband LAN.

In terms of *data rate*, the LAN has an edge. Third-generation PBX systems generally support data up to a maximum of 64 kbps (some vendors have plans for rates of up to 256 kbps). A LAN can, with proper interfaces, accommodate attachments in the Mbps range. To many users, 64 kbps may appear to be equivalent to infinity. However, some of the newer workstations, with high-resolution graphics, require much higher data rates. Furthermore, file transfer operations can get severely bogged down at those lower rates.

Closely related to this is the question of capacity and here the picture is murkier. On its face, it would appear that the PBX has the edge. The total digital transfer capacity of a PBX can go up to about 500 Mbps (the data rate on a TDM bus, for example). Baseband bus and ring systems are far less, and even a broadband tops out at about 300 Mbps over a number of channels. However, the nature of the traffic must be taken into account. Most digital data traffic in the office is bursty in nature (terminal to host traffic). On a LAN, the network is utilized by a node only for the duration of the burst. But on a PBX, a node will consume a dedicated portion of the capacity for the duration of a connection.

Last on our checklist is the question of *cost*. For this, there is no definitive answer, partly because component costs are changing rapidly and partly because they are installation dependent. There is a final point of comparison that was not included in the checklist because it relates to detailed design strategy rather than the pros and cons of the two approaches. This point has to do with the nature of the network interface. In a circuit-switched system, the network is usually "transparent"; that is, two connected devices communicate as if they had a direct connection. In a packet-switched system, the issue of the protocol between the network and the attached device arises. Of course, with the introduction of protocol-conversion services on the PBX, the distinctions blur. In any case, it is to this issue that we turn in the next chapter.

7.6

RECOMMENDED READING

[BELL91] provides a clear discussion of TSI and TMS. Other good treatments of digital switching include [FREE89], [RONA86], and [KEIS85]. An interesting analysis of the performance of TST switches is provided in [MANF91]

[HELD87], [MULL87], and [MEHT88] describe and discuss port selection and port-contention devices.

A very clear discussion of the PBX appears in [MART90], which also discusses the large list of features and services found in a modern PBX. This latter topic is also treated extensively in [DAV190]. [COOV89] contains reprints of a number of useful papers on the PBX.

7.7

PROBLEMS

7.1 Demonstrate that there is a high probability of blocking in a two-stage switch.

7.2 Explain the following statement in Section 7.2: "The timings on the shorter bus are amenable to greater control because of the much shorter propagation delay."

7.3 What is the magnitude of delay through a TSI stage?

7.4 For STS, give an example of blocking when the number of TSI units equals the number of incoming lines. What is the minimum number of TSI units for proper functioning (even in a blocking mode)?

7.5 In Figure 7.15, why is it not possible to route the digital data coming from the device directly to an outgoing trunk, where they will be converted to analog by the codec for transmission?

7.6 Assume that the velocity of propagation on a TDM bus is $0.7c$, its length is 10 m, and the data rate is 500 Mbps. How many bits should be transmitted in a time slot to achieve a bus efficiency of 99%?

7.7 Demonstrate that in a TSI data store at most only half of the memory is usefully occupied at any one time. Devise a means of reducing the TSI memory requirement while maintaining its nonblocking property.

7.8 Is it necessary to include address bits with each time slot in a statistical TDM stream? Is there a more efficient technique?

7.9 Justify the assertion in Section 7.2 that, for an STS network, the number of TSI units must be double the number of incoming and outgoing lines for nonblocking.

7.10 Reconsider Problem 3.6, but now assume that there is a central switching unit on floor 3 and a satellite switching unit on floor 6.

7.11 Consider the use of a 500-ns memory in a TSI device. How many full-duplex voice channels can be supported if the voice is encoded using PCM?

7.12 Determine the number of crosspoints and the total number of memory bits required for a TST switch defined as follows:

- Number of lines = 32
- Single-stage space switch
- Number of channels per frame = 30
- Time expansion = 2

7.13 How many bits of memory are needed in a TSI unit for a 60-channel signal with 9 bits per time slot?

7.14 Consider a three-stage crossbar switch system with 1000 input and 1000 output lines. It is nonblocking. For an optimum design, what is the total number of crosspoints required? How many arrays are needed for each stage and how many input and output lines are there per stage?

7.15 Repeat Problem 7.14 using 2048 as the number of input and output lines.

7.16 Consider the configuration of Figure 7.6b. Suppose that the maximum length of the bus is 1 meter. What is the maximum delay that could occur end-to-end on the bus? (Assume electricity travels in a copper wire at a rate of 0.8 times the speed of light.)

7.17 For the system of Problem 7.14, how many switch points would be needed if a TDM bus were used?

7.18 Consider a simple nonblocking implementation of Figure 7.6c. Suppose that the bus is 1500 meters long and that 2048 bits of data are to be input in each time slot. The data rate of the bus is 100 Mbps. The maximum number of stations attached to the bus is limited so that a station is guaranteed a slot every 10 milliseconds. Assume that electricity travels in copper wire at 0.8 times the speed of light.

a. What is the guaranteed data rate for a station?

b. What is the maximum sustained data rate of the system?

c. What is the maximum number of stations that can be serviced by this system?

7.19 Consider a simple time-slot interchange switching system. Assume a memory of 50-nsec cycle time. The memory is organized into 16-bit words. Frames are 1024 bits. What is the maximum data rate per channel? What is the data rate of the trunk lines to and from the switch?

CHAPTER 8

The Network Interface

Previous chapters have looked at the capabilities and features of the various types of local networks, but little has been said of the devices that connect to those networks. The purpose of a local network is to provide a means of communication for the various attached devices. To realize this purpose, the interface between the network and attached devices must be such as to permit cooperative interaction. This section addresses the complexities implicit in that seemingly simple notion.

We began with a statement of the problem: the networking requirements for cooperative interaction. Then we consider the connection of digital devices to packet-switched networks, the common case for LANs and HSLNs; this is the area in which most of the complexity arises. The simpler issues relating to circuit-switched networks and to analog devices are then considered.

8.1

THE REQUIREMENT

To understand the network interface requirement, let us first consider, from the computer vendor's point of view, how to provide a computer networking capability. Many vendors offer some sort of networking capability. Applications such as transaction processing, file transfer, and

electronic mail are available to run on a network of computers and intelligent terminals. The vendor supports these applications with a networking and communications software package. Examples are IBM's
SNA and DEC's DECNET. For clarity in the following discussion, we
will consider a generic package based on the OSI model; the principles
apply equally well to other proprietary architectures.

It is important to note that the OSI model does not provide an architecture for the *networking* of *multiple* computers; it is a model for the
communications between *two* computers, based on a set of protocols. Networking requires not only communications protocols but network management, a naming facility, network services, and so on. These issues
are addressed later. In this chapter we are concerned with the communications protocol implications of local networking.

Communications protocols, such as those compatible with the OSI
model, do provide a basis for computer networking. Traditionally, this
has been done in two ways, as depicted in Figure 8.1. A common vendor
offering is a private network (Figure 8.1a). Computers are connected by
point-to-point links that can be local direct connects (a special case of
"local network"!) or long-haul links, either dial-up or leased. Each node
in the network can act both as an end point for executing applications
and as a switch for passing along data. A layer 2 protocol, such as
HDLC, is sufficient to provide connectivity; the network can be viewed
as a set of computers hooked together by paired, point-to-point, layer 2
links. Any given computer supports more than one link by using more
than one physical port, as indicated in the diagram.

This figure is a bit misleading in that it shows a link at only one
protocol layer—layer 2. Of course, there is also a layer 1 link for each
layer 2 link. Furthermore, the figure suggests that there will be peer
communication at higher protocol layers. However, it would be possible with this configuration for a user to write a package for exchanging data between two machines that makes use of none of these
higher-layer services; the user still needs a physical connection and link-
control logic. Layer 2, then, is the highest *required* layer for this configuration to work.

For a long-haul network, the private network configuration can be
justified if there is either a very high volume of traffic or a very low
volume. With a high volume of traffic between nodes, the expense of
dedicated (leased) lines is reasonable. With a low volume of traffic, dial-
up lines are cost effective. Over some range between these two extremes
the public or value-added network (VAN) provides the most cost-effective communications support for computer networking (Figure 8.1b).
The VAN, discussed in Chapter 2, consists of switches and communication lines configured to provide connectivity among attached devices.
The VAN provides, among others, three services that are relevant here:

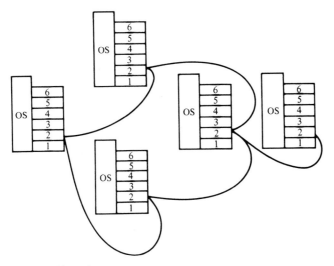

a. Private Network

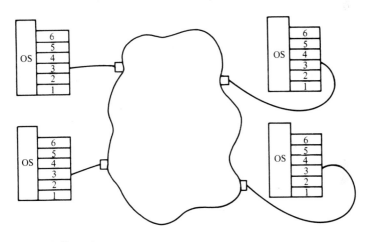

b. Public Network

FIGURE 8.1 Approaches to Computer Networking

1. *Routing:* To send data, an attached device specifies the address of the destination device; the VAN is responsible for routing those data through the network to their destination.
2. *Multiplexing:* An attached device does not need one physical port for each device with which it may communicate. Rather, the VAN supports multiple virtual circuits multiplexed on a single physical line.

3. *Standardized interface:* The use of a standardized interface allows the user to attach devices from a variety of vendors, since vendors readily support standards. If the VAN used a special-purpose proprietary interface, the user would be forced to develop or procure the needed hardware and software to attach to the VAN, and would have to do this for every different type of device to be attached to the VAN.

The reader will recognize that the first two items are functions requiring a layer 3 protocol. Typically, the X.25 standard is used. Most vendors who provide private networks can provide the same networking applications over a VAN. The discussion in Chapter 2 describes the mechanism by which this is accomplished.

Figure 8.1 thus serves to illustrate the network interface requirement. With a private network, the vendor's devices are directly connected to each other and the issue does not really arise. With a separate packet-switched communications network, the vendor must determine how to interface its devices to the network. The solution is to implement compatible layers 1, 2, and 3, as with X.25.

A multiaccess local network does not fit neatly into either of the categories noted above. Devices are not attached by point-to-point links as in a private network; instead, a multipoint link exists. Neither is a local network a VAN, with a network of intermediate switching nodes. The problem for the computer vendor is how to integrate the local network into its communications and networking software. The alternatives for this integration are discussed below.

From the customer's point of view, the local network interface is also an important issue. Typically, a customer will acquire some new data processing equipment in addition to the local network. The customer probably also has existing equipment to be hooked into the network. The customer would also like the flexibility of acquiring future equipment of various types, possibly from various vendors. The problem, then, for the customer is to procure a local network whose interface accommodates a variety of equipment with little or no special software required for that equipment. What approach should the customer take?

8.2

PACKET-SWITCHED INTERFACING

Approaches to LAN/MAN Attachment

Packet transmission is used on both LANs and MANs. As we have seen, packet switching implies that the data to be sent over the network by a device are organized into packets that are sent through the network one at a time. Protocols must be used to specify the construction and exchanges of these packets. At a minimum for a local network, protocols at layers 1 and 2 are needed to control the multiaccess network communication (e.g., these layers would comprise the LLC, MAC, and physical functions specified by IEEE 802).

Thus all attached devices must share these common local network protocols. From a customer's point of view, this fact structures the ways in which devices attach to a LAN or MAN into three alternatives, depicted in Figure 8.2:

- Homogeneous/single-vendor approach
- "Standards" approach
- Standard network interface approach

A homogeneous network is one in which all equipment—network plus attached devices—is provided by a single vendor. All equipment shares a common set of networking and communications software. The vendor has integrated a local network capability into its product line. Customers need not concern themselves with details of protocols and interfaces.

Undoubtedly, many customers will adopt this approach. The single-vendor system simplifies maintenance responsibility and provides an easy path for system evolution. On the other hand, the flexibility to obtain the best piece of equipment for a given task may be limited. Relying on a vendor, without consideration of its network architecture, to be able easily to accommodate foreign equipment is risky.

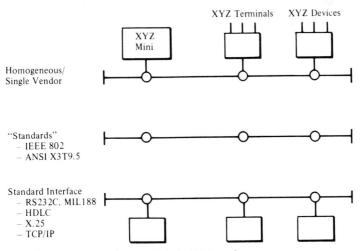

FIGURE 8.2 Approaches to LAN/MAN Attachment

Another approach that a customer may take is to procure a local network that conforms to a standard and dictate that all equipment be compatible with that standard. The local network would consist of a transmission medium plus an expandable set of "attachment points." This approach, although attractive, has some problems. The IEEE standard for LANs is loaded with options, so that two devices claiming to be IEEE compatible may not be able to coexist on the same network. Without a standard for network management, it is unlikely that local network equipment from different vendors can be mixed successfully in a single local network. The topic of network management is explored in Chapter 11.

The promise of local networks standards lies not in the solving of the interconnect problem. Standards offer the hope that the prospect of a mass market will lead to cheap silicon implementations of local network protocols. But the interconnect problem is an architectural issue, not a protocol issue.

Now consider a local network as consisting of not only a transmission medium, but also a set of intelligent devices that implement the local network protocols *and* provide an interface capability for device attachment. We will refer to this device as a *network interface unit* (NIU). The NIUs, collectively, control access to and communications across the local network. Subscriber devices attach to the NIU through some standard communications or I/O interface. The details of the local network operation are hidden from the device.

The NIU architecture is commonly used by independent local network vendors (those who sell only networks, not the data processing equipment that uses the network). Thus, in many cases, the NIUs in a local network configuration are supplied by a different vendor than the supplier of the terminal and computer equipment. This approach has several advantages. First, attached devices are relieved of the burden of the local network processing logic. Second, the user has more flexibility in selecting equipment to attach to the network. It is not necessary that the attached equipment support the particular type of local network that the user has implemented. It is necessary only that the NIU and the attached devices share a common, standardized interface.

Next, we look at the workings of an NIU. Following that, we consider the architectural implications for networking.

The Network Interface Unit

The NIU is a microprocessor-based device that acts as a communications controller to provide data transmission service to one or more attached devices. The NIU transforms the data rate and protocol of the subscriber device to that of the local network transmission medium and vice versa. Data on the medium are available to all attached devices, whose NIUs screen data for reception based on address. In general terms, the NIU performs the following functions:

- Accepts data from attached device
- Buffers the data until medium access is achieved
- Transmits data in addressed packets
- Scans each packet on medium for own address
- Reads packet into buffer
- Transmits data to attached device at the proper data rate

The hardware interface between the NIU and the attached device is typically a standard serial communications interface, such as RS-232-C. Almost all computers and terminals support this interface. For higher speed, a parallel interface, such as an I/O channel or direct memory access (DMA) interface can be provided. For example, a number of vendors offer an NIU interface directly into the UNIBUS of DEC's minicomputer line. Figure 8.3 gives a generic architecture for an NIU.

The NIU can either be an outboard or an inboard device. As an outboard device, the NIU is a stand-alone unit that may have one or more serial communications ports for device attachment. High-speed parallel ports are also used. As an inboard device, the NIU is integrated into the chassis of the data processing device, such as a minicomputer or terminal. An inboard NIU generally consists of one or more printed-circuit boards attached to the device's internal system bus.

From a customer's point of view, an NIU with standard interface options solves, at least at the electrical level, the interconnect problem. From a designer's point of view, the NIU is a useful architectural con-

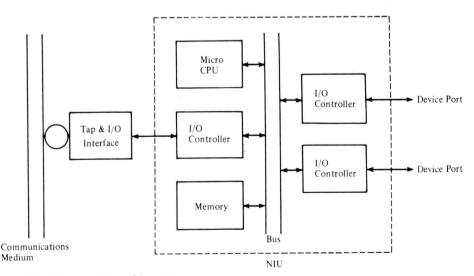

FIGURE 8.3 NIU Architecture

cept. Whether a network is homogeneous or not, and whether the interface provided to the local network is standard or not, there must be some distributed logic for controlling local network access. Conceptualizing this logic as an NIU clarifies some of the communications architectural issues associated with networking applications on a local network.

In what follows, we treat the NIU as a distinct device. Recognize that this device could be so integrated into the attached device as to be indistinguishable. This does not affect the reasoning involved.

8.3

THE DEVICE/NIU INTERFACE

Local Network Protocol Architecture

Having introduced the concept of the NIU, we can now turn to the problem of integrating local network protocols into the communications software of a system. Before beginning this discussion, it will be useful to examine the protocol architecture requirements for communication across a LAN.

Figure 5.3 suggests that a LAN communication architecture involves three layers: physical, medium access control (MAC), and logical link control (LLC). The physical layer provides for attachment to the medium. MAC enables multiple devices to share the medium's capacity in an orderly fashion. Finally, LLC provides for the management of a logical link across the network. The figure indicates that higher layers of software will make use of LLC. Put another way, LLC provides the service of transmitting frames of data across the LAN, and that service is invoked by a higher layer of software.

In pursuit of this line of reasoning, we need to consider what higher layers of software are appropriate in this context. In terms of the OSI model (Figure 2.11). the three IEEE 802 layers correspond to the lowest two layers (physical, data link) of the OSI model. The next layer, then, would be the network layer. But, from our discussion of Section 5.1, we have determined that a network layer is not really needed in the context of a local network. Thus, we can improve efficiency by eliminating the network layer and going directly to the transport layer.

Figure 8.4a reflects this line of reasoning. The LLC layer provides a service for moving frames of data from one station on the LAN to another. The transport layer provides end-to-end reliability. Thus, the user of transport is guaranteed that its data will be delivered with no losses and no misorderings. We can trace the operation of this architecture on a single unit of user data in Figure 8.4b, which is keyed to event times marked on Figure 8.4a. At some time t_o, the user of transport presents a block of data to transport. The transport entity encapsulates these data

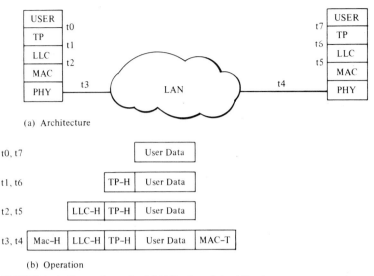

(a) Architecture

(b) Operation

FIGURE 8.4 Operation of a LAN Protocol Architecture

with a transport header and passes the resulting unit to LLC ($t+$). LLC adds to its own header (Figure 5.2) and passes the resulting unit to MAC (t_2). MAC produces a frame that includes both a MAC header and a MAC trailer and this frame is transmitted across the LAN (t_3). The MAC frame includes a destination station address, and the frame will be copied by the station with that address (t_4). The user's block of data then moves up through the layers, with the appropriate headers and trailers stripped off at each layer (t_5, t_6, t_7).

Modes of Attachment

The scenario of Figure 8.4 assumes that all of the protocol layers at each station are integrated and execute on a single processor. However, in most cases, some of the lower layers will execute on an NIU, with the upper layers executing on the main processor. The remainder of this section is devoted to an examination of various approaches to achieving this split.

All of the approaches fall into one of two general categories illustrated in Figure 8.5. For simplicity, the three LAN-related protocols (LLC, MAC, and physical) are represented by the two lowest layers of the OSI model in this figure.

To provide service to an attached device, the NIU can function as a gateway. A *gateway* is a device for connecting two systems that use different protocols: a protocol converter, if you like. In this case, the NIU contains logic for communicating with the attached device using some

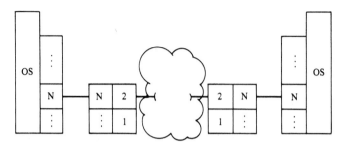

(a) THE NIU AS GATEWAY (PROTOCOL MODEL)

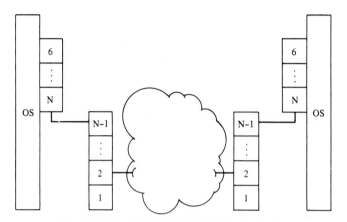

(b) THE NIU AS FRONT–END NETWORK PROCESSOR (INTERFACE MODE)

FIGURE 8.5 Protocol Layers for Local Networks

protocol native to that device; the level of communication is at some layer *n* (Figure 8.5a). The NIU converts between that protocol and that of the local network.

Compare this architecture with Figure 2.15 describing the VAN/PDN architecture. In that figure the level of communication between the DTE and DCE is at layer 3. The operation is as follows. The data that originate at the application layer, plus all the headers generated by layers 7 through 4, are treated as a unit of data by layer 3. Layer 3 has the responsibility of routing this data unit to the destination system. It does this by means of a protocol with the *local* DCE at layer 3. Of course, to transmit a layer 3 frame from DTE to DCE, a logical link (layer 2) over a physical link (layer 1) is needed. Hence the DTE-DCE conversation consists of protocols at layers 1, 2, and 3. Now, the DCE uses a different set of protocols to route the data unit through the network to the destination DCE, which in turn has a layer 1, 2, 3 protocol conversation with the destination DTE. The result is that a layer 4 packet has been routed from source to destination through gateways that convert the protocols up through layer 3.

In Figure 8.5b we see that the NIU can function instead as a front-end network processor (FNP). An FNP is a network processor that provides communications management services to an attached information processor. In contrast to a gateway, which *converts* from one set of protocols to another, the FNP *replaces* the protocols that might be found in the attached device. The attached device contains layers 7 down through n. There is an n/n-1 interface to the NIU that contains layers n-1 to 1, with layers 2 and 1 being the local network protocols.

The typical host–FNP situation is one in which the host is a mainframe and the front end is a minicomputer. In that case, a common interface boundary is between session (5) and transport (4). This is a reasonable break: layers 1 through 4 can be thought of as communications management, responsible for managing physical and logical links and providing a reliable end-to-end transport service. Layers 5 and 6 can be thought of as message management, responsible for maintaining a dialogue between end points and providing appropriate message formatting services. So the 5/4 break, although certainly not unique, is a logical one.

Within these two general categories, a number of specific approaches have been tried by various vendors and experimenters. The remainder of this section looks at those approaches that appear to be the most appropriate:

- Layer 1 Gateway (Transparent Mode)
- Layer 2 Gateway
- Layer 3 Gateway (X.25 Interface)
- Layer 4/2 FNP (LLC Interface)
- Layer 5/4 FNP (Transport Interface)

The NIU as Gateway

Layer 1 Gateway. This mode, which could be referred to as the transparent mode, permits protocol-compatible devices to communicate as if the NIUs and cable were not present. The NIU appears as a modem and provides signaling transparency. For example, for an RS-232C interface, when the originating device raises Request-to-Send to the originating NIU, the destination NIU raises Received-Line-Signal Detector (Carrier Detect) to the destination device. Data transfer is accomplished using buffering within the NIU. The transmitting NIU accumulates data from the transmitting device until either a buffer fills, a timer expires, or a control sequence is detected. The accumulated data are packaged in a frame and sent to the receiving NIU. The receiving NIU transmits the data to the receiving device.

Four parameters within each NIU control data transfer. These are: buffer size, time-out, control sequence(s), and destination address (NIU,

SAP). At least the address parameter is variable and must be set using a control mode. For intelligent attached devices, a small I/O program would be needed to set NIU parameters. For dumb terminals, the associated NIU would have to provide a user interface (terminal handler) for setting parameters.

There is a lot of appeal in this approach. If the local network is truly transparent to the attached devices, any networking or communications capability that operates over traditional communications lines will operate over the local network with no modification.

Of course, this mode is not quite "transparent." There are two phases (this is true of all the modes): a control phase, for requesting a connection, and a data transfer phase. But the logic needed for the control phase is minor.

There are some disadvantages to this approach, particularly for synchronous communications. Chief among these is flow control. Flow-control mechanisms for synchronous communication function at layer 2. If one device attached to the local network via its NIU is beginning to overrun the capacity of the destination device, the destination device can send, at layer 2, a message that will halt or reduce the flow of data. However, if the attached device sends data to the NIU faster than it can be accepted, there is no way for the NIU to exert flow control on the attached device. A similar problem exists with error control. If an attached device fails to receive an acknowledgment to a frame, it does not know whether the fault is in the NIU or the destination device.

These problems are not fatal, but they do present difficulties to the designer.

Layer 2 Gateway. In this mode, a layer 2 protocol is established between the attached device and the NIU. An example is HDLC.

As with a layer 1 gateway, there are two phases of communication: control and data transfer. For setting up a connection to some destination device, a dialogue is needed that is outside the layer 2 protocol. Again, this can be provided by a small I/O program. Once a connection is established, the layer 2 protocol would support data transfer.

This mode also presents a flow-control problem. In this case, the NIU can exercise flow control over the attached device. However, the remote device has no means, *at layer 2*, of exercising flow control on the source device. Higher-layer protocols must be relied on in the two devices.

Another problem, common to both layer 1 and 2 protocols, is that the NIU does not support multiplexing. That is, for each logical connection to another device on the network, the attached device must have one physical connection to the network. This situation most closely resembles that of a private network using dial-up lines.

Layer 3 Gateway.   In this mode, the local network presents the appearance of a VAN. Typically, the NIU provides the X.25 standard for attached intelligent devices. The advantage of this approach is that any networking capability that will work on X.25 VAN will work on the local network. The X.25 layer 3 protocol provides a multiplexing capability so that multiple virtual circuits are supported over a single physical link. In this mode, we at last get away from the necessity of a separate control dialogue. As the discussion will show, the network layer functionally includes a connection request capability.

X.25 is perhaps the best known and most widely used protocol standard. The standard specifies an interface between attached devices and a packet-switched network. The standard actually encompasses the three lowest layers of the OSI model (Figure 2.15). The physical layer makes use of a standard known as X.21, but in many cases, the RS-232-C standard is substituted. The data link layer is LAP-B, which is a subset of HDLC. The network layer is referred to in the standard as the packet level; it specifies a virtual-circuit service.

Figure 8.6 shows the layer 3 packet formats used in the X.25 standard. A 24-bit header is used for data packets. The header includes a 12-bit virtual-circuit number (expressed as a 4-bit group number and an 8-bit channel number). The N(S) and N(R) fields perform the same function

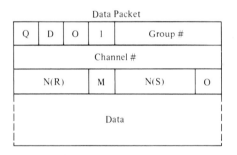

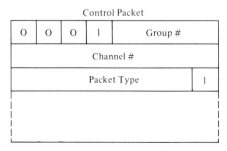

FIGURE 8.6 X.25 Layer 3 Packet Formats

on a virtual-circuit basis as they do on a link basis in HDLC. The control packet has a variable-length header, depending on the specific function; some of these functions are referred to in the following discussion.

Figure 8.7 shows a typical sequence of events in a virtual call. The left-hand part of the figure shows the packets exchanged between user machine A and its DCE (the NIU plays the role of the DCE in a local network); the right-hand part shows the packets exchanged between user machine B and its DCE. The routing of packets between the DCEs is the responsibility of the internal logic of the network.

The sequence of events is as follows:

1. A requests a virtual circuit to B by sending a Call Request packet to its DCE. The packet includes a virtual-circuit number (group, channel), as well as source and destination addresses. Future incoming and outgoing data transfers will be identified by the virtual circuit number.

2. B's DCE receives the call request and sends a Call Indication packet to B. This packet has the same format as the Call Request packet but a different virtual circuit number, selected by B's DCE from the set of locally unused numbers.

3. B indicates acceptance of the call by sending a Call Accepted packet specifying the same virtual-circuit number as that of the Call Indication packet.

4. A receives a Call Connected packet with the same virtual-circuit number as that of the Call Request packet.

5. A and B send Data and Control packets using their respective virtual circuit numbers.

6. A (or B) sends a Clear Request packet to terminate the virtual circuit and receives a local Clear Confirmation packet.

7. B (or A) receives a Clear Indication packet and transmits a Clear Confirmation packet.

Figure 8.8 depicts the operation of this architecture in transmitting one block of user data. In this case, the packet level of X.25 adds a network-layer header (t_2), and the link layer adds a link header and trailer (t_3). The resulting frame is then sent to the station's NIU, where the link header and trailer are peeled off and the packet is delivered to the network layer (t_4). Notice in the figure that there is no "user" of this layer. The NIU is an intermediate gateway whose job is to relay the data on. So the packet, or network, header is left in place to be examined at the other end. Relay logic within the NIU passes the packet to LLC, which appends its own header (t_5) and passes the result to MAC. The remainder of the figure should be self-explanatory.

The X.25 interface is already offered by a number of LAN vendors. Because this is such a common means of connecting to long-haul com-

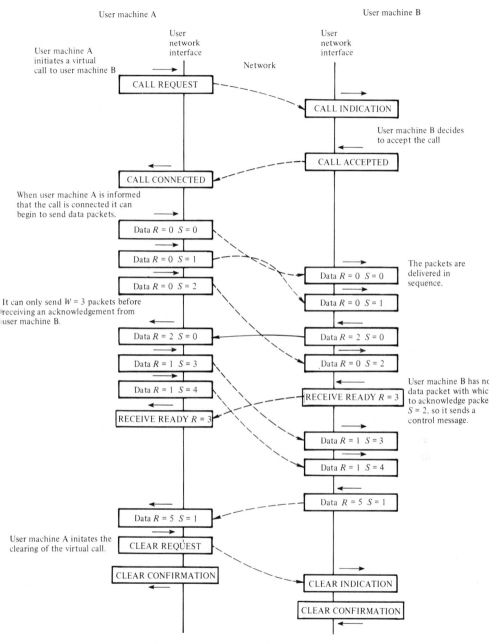

FIGURE 8.7 Sequence of Events: X.25 Protocol

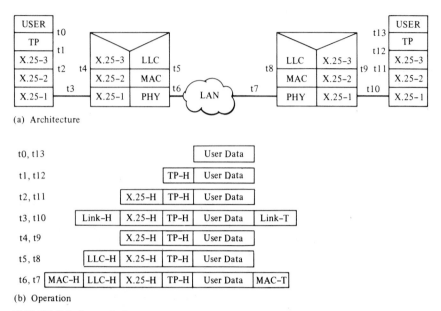

(a) Architecture

(b) Operation

FIGURE 8.8 Layer 3 Gateway

munications networks, its use for local networks is likely to become popular.

The NIU as Front-End Processor

Layer 4/2 FNP.   Figure 8.9 illustrates a layer 4/2 FNP mode. This is an attractive option that lends itself to a high-performance inboard NIU. The two layers needed to control the local network are in the NIU: all other layers are in the attached device. This configuration also provides high "visibility" for the local network. Software executing in the attached device can directly invoke layer 2 functions provided by the local network, such as broadcasting and priorities.

The architecture of this option is not as straightforward as you might have expected. First, there is no network layer, as has already been explained. However, there are additional layers needed to link an NIU and its attached station. In the figure, we assume a serial communication link between the NIU and the attached device. Thus, a physical-layer protocol and a link-layer protocol are needed to exchange data across that link. One more protocol is also needed. This protocol has no universally accepted name, but is often referred to as a *host-to-front-end protocol* (HFP). To identify this as referring to a front end whose highest layer is LLC, we shall identify it as LLC-HFP.

To understand the need for an HFP, consider again the case of an integrated architecture (Figure 8.4). At t_1, the transport entity passes a

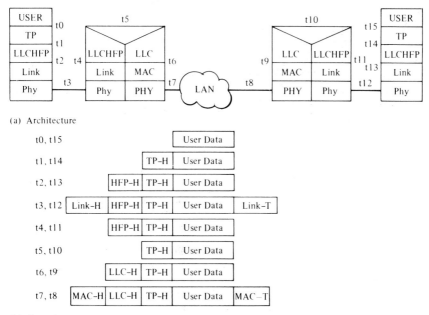

(a) Architecture

t0, t15				User Data		
t1, t14			TP–H	User Data		
t2, t13		HFP–H	TP–H	User Data		
t3, t12	Link–H	HFP–H	TP–H	User Data	Link–T	
t4, t11		HFP–H	TP–H	User Data		
t5, t10			TP–H	User Data		
t6, t9		LLC–H	TP–H	User Data		
t7, t8	MAC–H	LLC–H	TP–H	User Data	MAC–T	

(b) Operation

FIGURE 8.9 Layer 4/2 FNP

block of data to LLC for transmission. How does LLC know what to do with this data block? That information is contained in the link-control primitive used by the transport layer to invoke LLC. These primitives were listed in Table 5.2. For example, if the unacknowledged connectionless service is used, the transport entity would use the following primitive and associated parameters to invoke LLC:

DL-UNIDATA.request (source address, destination address, data, priority)

where

source address = local LLC user (service
access point plus MAC address)
destination address = remote LLC user (service
access point plus MAC address)
data = block of data to be transmitted
priority = desired priority for this data transfer

Exactly how this information is passed to an LLC entity from an LLC user will depend on the implementation. For example, if LLC is invoked by a subroutine call, then the DL-UNIDATA.request call is compiled into a machine-language subroutine branch, and the parameters of the call are placed somewhere in registers or memory to be picked up by the called routine. The details are not, and should not be, part of the LLC standard. The internal implementation of this interface depends on the machine language and operating system, and upon design choices made to optimize the implementation.

The subroutine-call approach works fine if the transport and LLC entities execute in the same processor. But in the case of Figure 8.9, they are in separate systems. We need a way for the transport and LLC entities to exchange commands (primitives) and parameters, and this is the function of the LLC-HFP. LLC-HFP provides a way for the transport and LLC entities to communicate. In the host, the LLC-HFP entity presents an interface to the transport entity that mimics LLC. This allows the transport entity to use calls such as L__DATA.request as if LLC were in the same system. In the NIU, LLC-HFP behaves like any other LLC user.

We can now trace the operation of the architecture of Figure 8.9. At t_1, the transport entity passes the user's data plus a transport header to LLC-HFP, using the L__DATA.request call. LLC-HFP appends a header and passes the result to the link layer (t_2). Table 8.1 suggests a format for the header. The remaining steps in Figure 8.9 should be clear.

Now, the above scenario assumes an outboard NIU and the use of a data link protocol such as HDLC across the host-NIU interface. If the NIU is a communications board, then there will be no link and physical-layer protocols as such between the NIU and the host. In most cases, the NIU and host processor will connect to the same backplane bus and exchange information through a common main memory; the NIU typically uses direct-memory access (DMA) to access the memory. In this case, a specific area of memory is shared and is used to construct a system control block for communication. As an example, Table 8.2 is the system control block format used in an Intel product [WEBB84].

One issue remains to be examined. Whether the host-NIU exchange is achieved by an LLC-HFP or by the exchange of system control blocks, a specification of that exchange is needed. If both the NIU and the host are provided by the same vendor, then that specification can be proprietary. If, however, the NIU and the host are from different vendors, then a standard specification would be preferable. As we have commented, it is likely that NIUs will be from a different vendor than the vendor for the attached devices. Indeed, there may be attached devices from a number of different vendors. Thus, the case for a standard for the host-NIU exchange is a strong one. Unfortunately, no such standard exists or is even contemplated by IEEE 802, ANSI X3T9.5, or ISO.

Layer 5/4 FNP.   In this mode, the NIU takes on the scope and characteristics of what is normally thought of as true FNP. All of the layers normally associated with communications management are implemented in the NIU; the higher message management layers are in the

TABLE 8.1 Example LLC-HFP PDU Header

a. Header Fields

Service Access Point	LLC User
Primitive code	LLC primitive being invoked. Codes are listed in (b)
Parameter count	Number of parameters
Parameter	This field occurs once for each parameter and consists of two subfields:
Length	Length in octets of value subfield
Value	Value of the parameter

b. Primitive codes

1	DL-UNITDATA.request
2	DL-UNITDATA.indication
3	DL-CONNECT.request
4	DL-CONNECT.indication
5	DL-CONNECT.response
6	DL-CONNECT.confirm
7	DL-DATA.request
8	DL-DATA.indication
9	DL-DISCONNECT.request
10	DL-DISCONNECT.indication
11	DL-RESET.request
12	DL-RESET.indication
13	DL-RESET.response
14	DL-RESET.confirm
15	DL-CONNECTION-FLOWCONTROL.request
16	DL-CONNECTION-FLOWCONTROL.indication
17	DL-DATA-ACK.request
18	DL-DATA-ACK.indication
19	DL-DATA-ACK-STATUS.indication
20	DL-REPLY.request
21	DL-REPLY.indication
22	DL-REPLY-STATUS.indication
23	DL-REPLY-UPDATE.request
24	DL-REPLY-UPDATE-STATUS.indication

attached device. For communication between two devices that implement these higher layers, this approach works well.

Figure 8.10 depicts this architecture. Note the similarity to Figure 8.9. The same reasoning applies. In this case, the user of transport executes on a different processor than the transport entity. A TP-HFP is needed to allow the transport user to exchange primitives and parameters with the transport entity. The same techniques discussed earlier can be used in this architecture. The TP-HFP header will contain a code specifying which primitive is being invoked, and the remainder of the header is a

TABLE 8.2   LLC-HFP System Control Block

Word	Name	Description
1	Status	NIU or host status information, such as whether or not ready to receive data.
2	Directive	Management-related commands and acknowledgements.
3	Command Pointer	Points to an area of memory that contains one or more commands. Each command consists of a command code and a list of parameters.
4	Frame Pointer	Points to a buffer containing a block of data being passed between LLC and the LLC user.
5–8	Error Counters	Error-related statistics.

list of parameter lengths and values. In the case of an inboard NIU, the primitives and parameters can be exchanged by means of a system control block.

Table 8.3 lists the primitives for the ISO transport protocol standard. The ISO transport protocol standard also has the concept of a service access point (SAP), so that there may be multiple users of a transport entity. The first six primitives listed in the table are used to establish and subsequently tear down a logical connection between transport SAPs. Most of the parameters are self-explanatory. The quality of service parameter allows the transport user to request specific transmission ser-

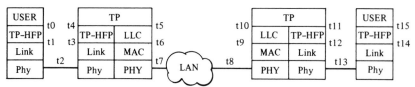

(a) Architecture

(b) Operation

FIGURE 8.10 Layer 5/4 FNP

TABLE 8.3   ISO Transport Service Primitives

T_CONNECT.request (Called Address, Calling Address, Expedited Data Option,
  Quality of Service, Data)
T_CONNECT.indication (Called Address, Calling Address, Expedited Data Option,
  Quality of Service, Data)
T_CONNECT.response (Quality of Service, Responding Address, Expedited Data
  Option, Data)
T_CONNECT.confirm (Quality of Service, Responding Address, Expedited Data
  Option, Data)
T_DISCONNECT.request (Data)
T_DISCONNECT.indication (Disconnect Reason, Data)

T_DATA.request (Data)
T_DATA.indication (Data)

T_EXPEDITED_DATA.request (Data)
T_EXPEDITED_DATA.indication (Data)

vices, such as priority and security levels. The remaining primitives are concerned with data transfer. The expedited version requests that the transport entity attempt to deliver the associated data as rapidly as possible. Note the similarity of these primitives to those for LLC.

Placement of transport layer and below in the NIU is becoming a popular option (e.g., sees [BAL85], [DAVI83], [WOOD79]). Again, a standard specification for TP-HFP and a transport-level system control block are desirable, but are not in sight.

Summary

The discussion in this section has dealt with the issue of which communications architecture layers should reside in the NIU and should therefore be considered part of the local network service, and which should reside in the attached device. The choice will depend on a variety of factors, including cost and performance. As yet, there is little operational experience with most of these alternatives to guide us. Consequently, we can close this section only with a few preliminary observations.

The principal advantage of placing as many layers as possible in the NIU is that this makes the task of intelligent device attachment as easy as possible. The customer or user must be assured that the various devices on the network are compatible. By placing more of the communications functionality in the network, the scope of this task is reduced. On the other hand, placing as little functionality as possible in the network may increase the network's flexibility. Functions in the attached device can be tailored to achieve certain objectives in such areas as performance, priorities, and security.

8.4

TERMINAL HANDLING FOR LANS

In the preceding section, the discussion focused on the requirements for attaching an intelligent device to a LAN or MAN. Such devices implement the necessary communication layers and can communicate across a network as described in Chapter 2. For simplicity, we will refer to all such devices as hosts. But there are other devices that do not have the processing power to implement the OSI layers, such as dumb terminals, printers, and even limited-function intelligent terminals. We will refer to these devices generically as terminals.

From a hardware point of view, terminals attach to a LAN in the same fashion as hosts: through NIUs. An NIU for terminals will provide a number of serial communication ports for terminal attachment; support for from 4 to 32 terminals on a single NIU is typical. From a software point of view, the approaches outlined in Section 8.3 are not directly applicable to terminal support. All of the approaches discussed assumed that some number of layers would be implemented in the attached device. How, then, are terminals attached?

Two general approaches are possible. The first is to treat terminal-host communication as fundamentally different from host-host communication. This approach can be explained using the concept of a secondary network, which is discussed next. The application of this concept in the local network context is then described. The second approach relies on the use of a virtual terminal protocol. This concept is defined and its use in the local network context is discussed.

The Secondary Network

Let us refer to the kind of computer network we have discussed in Section 2.3 and previously in this chapter as a primary network. A primary network consists of the hardware and software required to interconnect applications executing within the OSI architecture. These include mainframes, FNPs, minicomputers, and intelligent terminals (generically, hosts). Typically a mainframe will contain the higher-order layers (5, 6, 7), and all communications functions (layers 1 through 4) are off-loaded to an FNP. Minis and intelligent terminals typically contain all the OSI layers.

Within the OSI architecture, applications execute as modules sitting on top of the presentation layer (layer 6). Interconnection is logically achieved by means of a session established by session control (layer 5). To communicate with another application, an application requests that a session be established between a "logical port" attached to itself and a "logical port" attached to the other application. This service is provided by layer 5, which can establish both local and remote connections.

This mechanism works fine for devices containing all the software needed to implement the OSI layers. However, there are a number of devices, such as dumb terminals, printers, and so on (generically, terminals), that should be accessible over a network but that do not have the functionality of the various OSI layers. The secondary network consists of the hardware and software required to connect these devices to an OSI network. Whereas the primary network uses a 7-layer architecture, secondary connections use protocols tailored to the device in question.

Conceptually, we can think of these devices being serviced by application programs that act as gateways to the primary network. We will refer to these gateways as *secondary network servers* (SNSs). Since an SNS is an application, it can establish sessions with other applications over the primary network. A device such as a terminal local to a particular computer connects directly to a local SNS and, through it, participates on the primary network.

These concepts are illustrated in Figure 8.11. Applications are represented as bubbles resting on layer 6. Sessions are represented by dashed

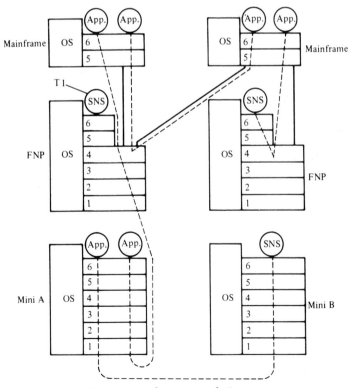

FIGURE 8.11 Primary/Secondary Network Concepts

lines. For example, consider the terminal T1 communicating with the SNS in minicomputer A. T1 could be directly connected to A or remotely via communications link or even by a network, as we will explain below. In any case, there is a connection between T1 and SNS that does not use the OSI layers; this we refer to as a secondary network connection. Now, suppose that T1 is logged on to A via the SNS and wishes to access an application on minicomputer B. The SNS, as an application, can invoke the communications functions of A to establish a session with the application on B; we refer to this as primary network connection.

With this brief background, we now look at the use of the secondary network approach for local networks. To provide a secondary network connection from terminal to host, the NIU must allow the terminal user to request a connection to an SNS in a host (alternatively, a host could set up the connection). Data transfer must occur as if the terminal were directly connected to the host. Note that the local network medium is being used to support both primary (host-host) and secondary (terminal-host) network connections.

As we shall see, in providing secondary network connections for terminals, the NIU functions in the gateway mode (Figure 8.5a). The specific approach taken depends on whether the terminals being supported are asynchronous or synchronous.

Asynchronous Terminals: Transparent Mode

Asynchronous terminals communicate by transmitting and receiving characters one at a time. Generally, no link-control protocol as such is used. Thus, there is usually no or only a primitive form of error and flow control provided.

The simplest, and most common, way of supporting asynchronous terminals on a LAN is to use a layer 1 gateway, which we referred to as a transparent mode. The architecture is illustrated in Figure 8.12a. Communication between the NIU and terminals is managed by an asynchronous handler, which simply transmits and receives using the asynchronous scheme described in Chapter 2 (Figure 2.8a). As characters come in from a terminal, they are placed in an input buffer by a buffer handler program; when a carriage return is received, or when a time-out occurs, the contents of the buffer are passed to LLC for transmission. The data are transmitted across the LAN to an NIU to which is attached the destination host. Data arriving from the host are delivered in a block by LLC to the buffer handler. These data are then transmitted to the terminal one character at a time. The host side of this architecture is identical to the terminal side. The NIU attaches to the host through one or more asynchronous communications lines. Thus, it appears to both the host and the terminal as though they were directly connected.

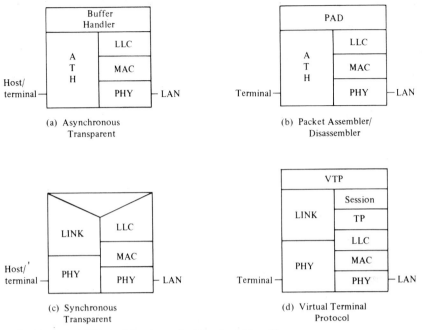

(a) Asynchronous
Transparent

(b) Packet Assembler/
Disassembler

(c) Synchronous
Transparent

(d) Virtual Terminal
Protocol

FIGURE 8.12 NTU Architectures for Terminal Handling

Asynchronous Terminals: PAD Approach

The approach just outlined is simple and effective. Its main drawback is evident in Figure 8.13. Because the connection is transparent, there must be one asynchronous port on the host for each terminal connection. This is referred to as the "milking machine" approach, and is clearly wasteful of host hardware. It would be preferable if the link to the host could be a multiplexed link that could carry traffic from a number of terminals at the same time. This approach has been standardized within the context of the X.25 standard.

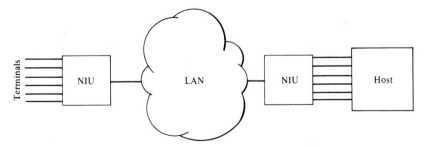

FIGURE 8.13 Asynchronous Terminal Support: Milking Machine Approach

As supplements to the X.25 standard, CCITT has developed a set of standards related to a facility known as a *packet assembler disassembler* (PAD). The PAD is designed to solve the two fundamental problems associated with the attachment of terminals to a network:

1. Many terminals are not capable of implementing the protocol layers for attaching in the same manner as a host. The PAD facility provides the intelligence for communicating with a host using the X.25 protocol.
2. There are differences among terminal types. The PAD facility provides a set of parameters to account for those differences. However, it deals with only asynchronous, start-stop terminals.

Three standards define the PAD facility:

- X.3: Describes the functions of the PAD and the parameters used to control its operation (Table 8.4)
- X.28: Describes the PAD–terminal protocol
- X.29: Describes the PAD–host protocol

TABLE 8.4   PAD Parameters (X.3)

Number	Description	Selectable Values
1	Whether terminal operator can escape from data transfer to PAD command state	0: not allowed 1: escape character 32–126: graphic characters
2	Whether PAD echoes back characters received from terminal	0: no echo 1: echo
3	Terminal characters that will trigger the sending of a partially full packet by the PAD	0: send full packets only 1: alphanumeric 2, 4, 8, 16, 32, 64: other control characters
4	Time-out value that will trigger the sending of a partially full packet by the PAD	0: no time-out 1–255: multiple of 50 ms
5	Whether PAD can exercise flow control over terminal output, using X-ON, X-OFF	0: not allowed 1: allowed
6	Whether PAD can send service signals (control information) to terminal	0: not allowed 1: allowed
7	Action(s) taken by PAD on receipt of break signal from terminal	0: nothing 1: send interrupt 2: reset 4: send break signal 8: escape 16: discard output

TABLE 8.4   (Cont.)

Number	Description	Selectable Values
8	Whether PAD will discard DTE data intended for terminal	0: normal delivery 1: discard
9	Number of padding characters inserted after carriage return (to terminal)	0: determined by data rate 1–255: number of characters
10	Whether PAD inserts control characters to prevent terminal line overflow	0: no 1–255: yes, line length
11	Terminal speed (bps)	0–18: 50 to 64,000
12	Whether terminal can exercise flow control over PAD, using X-ON, X-OFF	0: not allowed 1: allowed
13	Whether PAD inserts line feed after carriage return sent or echoed to terminal	0: no line feed 1, 2, 4: various conditions
14	Number of padding characters inserted after line feed (to terminal)	0: no padding 1–255: number of characters
15	Whether PAD supports editing during data transfer (defined in parameters 16–18)	0: no 1: yes
16	Character delete	0–127: selected character
17	Line delete	0–127: selected character
18	Line display	0–127: selected character
19	Terminal type for editing PAD service signals (e.g., character delete)	0: no editing signals 1: printing terminal 2: display terminal
20	Characters that are not echoed to terminal when echo is enabled	0: no echo mask Each bit represents certain characters
21	Parity treatment of characters to/from terminal	0: no parity treatment 1: parity checking 2: parity generation
22	Number of lines to be displayed at one time	0: page wait disabled 1–255: number of lines

Figure 8.14a indicates the architecture for use of the PAD. The terminal attached to the PAD sends characters one at a time. These are buffered in the PAD and then assembled into an X.25 packet and sent through the network to the host. Host packets are received at the PAD, disassembled by stripping off the X.25 header, and passed to the terminal one character at a time. Simple commands between terminal and PAD (X.28), used to set parameters and establish virtual circuits, consist of character strings. Similar host–PAD control information (X.29) is

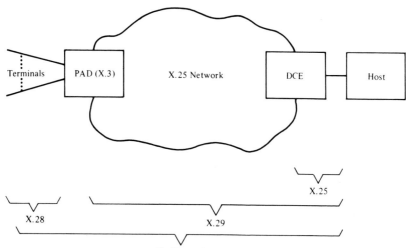

(a) Parameter-Defined Terminal

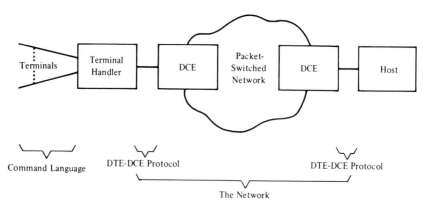

(b) Virtual Terminal Protocol

FIGURE 8.14 Two Views of Terminal-Network Architecture

transmitted in the data field of an X.25 packet, with a bit set in the X.25 header to indicate that this is control information.

Figure 8.12b shows the architecture of the NIU that provides the PAD function for terminals. The host NIU architecture is the same one shown in Figure 8.8.

Synchronous Terminals: Layer 2 Gateway

For synchronous terminals, a layer 2 gateway can be used (Figure 8.12c). This gateway accepts frames of data from the synchronous terminal and transmits them across the LAN; it also accepts frames from the LAN and delivers them to the terminal.

Support for synchronous terminals is complicated by the fact that most synchronous terminals employ a poll-and-select data link protocol. With this type of protocol, all communication is initiated by the host. When the host has data to send to a terminal, it issues a select command with the terminal's address. If the terminal is ready to receive data, it responds with a positive acknowledgment, and the host sends the data. When the host is prepared to receive data, it issues a poll command with the terminal's address. If the terminal has data to send, it can then send the data. This protocol was developed to allow multiple terminals to be connected to a host over a single multipoint line.

With terminals scattered around a LAN, some mechanism is needed for performing the polling and selecting. Two approaches have been used:

1. Poll and select commands are delivered across the LAN to the various terminals.
2. Poll and select commands terminate at the host NIU. Each terminal NIU does its own polling and selecting, and the data to be exchanged are buffered at the host and terminal NIUs. Thus, when a host issues a poll, data will be delivered to the host only if there is already data in the host NIU buffer for the polled terminal.

In both cases, the NIUs must know which terminals are logically connected to which hosts in order to exercise the poll-and-select protocol.

Virtual Terminal Protocols

We have surveyed various techniques for connecting terminals to packet-switched local networks so that they can effectively communicate with host devices. There is, however, a problem buried in this approach that relates to one of the advertised benefits of a local network. Specifically, the local network user typically would like not to be locked into a single vendor. The user would like to be able to procure hosts and terminals from a variety of vendors, but also to maintain complete connectivity.

What does this imply? Usually, in order to be able to use a terminal from one vendor with a host from another vendor, a special host software package must be built to accommodate the foreign terminal. Now consider a LAN with N types of terminals and M types of hosts. For complete connectivity, each host type must contain a package for handling each terminal type. In the worst case, MN I/O packages must be developed. Furthermore, if a new type of host is acquired, it must be equipped with N new I/O packages. If a new type of terminal is acquired, each host must be equipped with a new I/O package, for a total of M new packages. This is not the type of situation designed to encourage multivendor LANs.

To solve this problem, a universal terminal protocol is needed—one that can handle all types of terminals. Such a thing exists today in name only: *virtual terminal protocol* (VTP). However, rudimentary versions do already exist. One is the TELNET protocol of ARPANET [DAVI77]. The true VTP is a fundamentally different and more flexible approach than the PAD concept. In this section we present a brief overview of VTP principles; more detail may be found in [DAY80], [DAY81], [MAGN79], and [LOWE83].

As the name implies, the VTP is a protocol, a set of conventions for communication between peer entities. It includes the following functions:

- Providing the service of establishing and maintaining a connection between two application-level entities
- Controlling a dialogue for negotiating the allowable actions to be performed across the connection
- Creating and maintaining a data structure that represents the "state" of the terminal
- Translating between actual terminal characteristics and a standardized representation

The first two functions are in the nature of session control (layer 5); the latter two are presentation control (layer 6) functions. Figure 8.14 illustrates the difference in philosophy between this approach and that of the PAD. In the VTP approach, the terminal handler, which implements the terminal side of the protocol, is considered architecturally as a host attached to the network. Thus the protocol is end-to-end in terms of reliability, flow control, and so on. On the other hand, the X.29 standard is not a protocol as such. The PAD is considered part of the network, not a separate host. From the point of view of the host, the PAD facility is part of its local DCE's X.25 layer 3 functionality. Although the PAD concept affords an easily implemented capability, it does not provide the architectural base for a flexible terminal-handling facility.

The principal purpose of the VTP is to transform the characteristics of a real terminal into a standardized form or virtual terminal. Because of the wide differences in capabilities among terminals, it is unreasonable to attempt to develop a single virtual terminal type. Four classes of interest are:

1. *Scroll mode:* These are terminals with no local intelligence, including keyboard-printer and keyboard-display devices. Characters are transmitted as they are entered, and incoming characters are printed or displayed as they come in. On a display, as the screen fills, the top line is scrolled off.
2. *Page mode:* These are keyboard-display terminals with a cursor-addressable character matrix display. Either user or host can modify random-accessed portions of the display. I/O can be a page at a time.
3. *Form/data entry mode:* These are similar to page mode terminals, but allow definition of fixed and variable fields on the display. This permits a number of features, such as transmitting only the variable part and defining field attributes to be used as validity checks.
4. *Graphics mode:* These allow the creation of arbitrary two-dimensional patterns.

For any VTP, there are basically four phases of operation:

1. *Connection management:* includes session-layer-related functions, such as connection request and termination
2. *Negotiation:* used to determine a mutually agreeable set of characteristics between the two correspondents
3. *Control:* exchange of control information and commands (e.g., defining the attributes of a field)
4. *Data:* transfer of data between two correspondents

Figure 8.12d shows the terminal NIU architecture that supports a virtual terminal protocol. The VTP can be thought of as occupying layers 6 and 7 of the architecture. It interfaces to a session protocol entity at layer 5. On the host side, either of the FNP modes of attachment would work.

The ISO Virtual Terminal Service

The ISO virtual terminal service is an application-layer service defined within the framework of the open systems interconnection (OSI) model. The standard defines a model for a virtual terminal, which is an abstract representation of a real terminal. The standard defines operations that can be performed, such as reading text from the virtual keyboard, writing text on the virtual screen, and moving a cursor to a particular position on the virtual screen. The standard also defines a virtual terminal protocol for the exchange of data and control messages between a terminal and an application via the virtual terminal service. The protocol standard specifies the display data stream structure and the control messages by which the two sides can agree on the details of the terminal capabilities to be supported.

Rather than defining a single virtual terminal for all possible applications, the standard provides its users with the tools to define a virtual terminal suited to the application at hand and the physical limitations of the terminal. For example, if the physical terminal is monochrome, then the two sides agree not to use color information.

Table 8.5 lists some of the key aspects of the ISO standard. We examine each of these in turn.

Classes of Service. The ISO standard provides different classes of service. Each class meets the needs of a specific range of applications and terminal functions. So far, Basic, Forms, and Graphics classes have been identified. Of these, only the Basic class is fully defined and supported by vendors. We can expect to see the other classes available in the next few years.

The Basic class is a character-oriented service. In its simplest form, it meets the terminal access requirements of applications such as line editing and operating system command language interaction, which can be satisfied with simple scroll-mode terminals. The basic class also supports page-mode terminals and provides for the exchange of data in blocks instead of character-at-a-time. An extension to the basic class pro-

TABLE 8.5   Aspects of the ISO Virtual Terminal Service

Classes of Service
Basic
Forms
Graphics
Modes of Operation
Two-way alternate
Two-way simultaneous
Delivery Control
No delivery control
Simple delivery control
Quarantine delivery control
Echo Control
Local echo
Remote echo

vides a primitive set of forms-related services. It allows the definition and addressing of individual fields and the transmission of selected fields. With this capability, the service can transfer just the variable fields on a form. However, there is no facility for defining or using field attributes.

The Forms class is designed to handle all of the operations associated with forms-mode terminals, such as the 3270 terminals. This would allow any forms-mode terminals from any vendor to interact with forms-mode applications on any host from any vendor. Finally, the Graphics class will deal with graphics and image-processing terminals.

Modes of Operation.   The virtual terminal standard supports two modes of operation: two-way alternative (half-duplex) and two-way simultaneous (full-duplex). When a terminal sets up a connection to a host, the mode of operation is agreed on between the two virtual service modules.

Two-way alternate mode enforces the discipline that only one side at a time can transmit. This prevents the situation in which data from the computer begin to appear on the terminal display screen while the user is entering text from the keyboard. The two-way alternate mode is typical of synchronous forms-mode terminals such as the 3270. Most normal enquiry/response applications are naturally two-way alternate, for example.

The two-way simultaneous mode permits both sides to transmit at the same time. An example of the utility of this would be the control terminal for a complex real-time system such as a process control plant. For such an application, the terminal must be capable of being updated rapidly with status changes even if the operator is typing in a command.

Delivery Control.   Delivery control allows one side to control delivery of data to the other side to coordinate multiple actions. Normally, any data entered at a terminal are automatically delivered to the application on the other side as soon as possible, and any data transmitted by the application are delivered to the terminal as soon as possible. In some cases, however, one side may require explicit control over when certain data are delivered to its peer.

For example, suppose a user is logged on to a time-sharing system via the virtual terminal service. The time-sharing system may issue a single prompt character (e.g., ">") when it is ready for the next command. However, the terminal side of the virtual terminal service may choose to deliver data to the terminal for display only after several characters have been received, rather than one character at a time. Since this single prompt character must be displayed, and since the terminal side cannot reasonably be expected to know what the prompt character is, some mechanism is needed to force delivery. Another example is the use of special function keys that are often found on terminals and that can be set up to perform multiple actions, resulting in the transmission of multiple messages to the host. Sometimes it is desirable that all of the functions of the key be presented to the peer user simultaneously.

Three types of delivery control can be specified with any transmission:

1. *No delivery control:* This is the default type. In this case, data are made available to the peer at the convenience of the implementation of the virtual terminal service.
2. *Simple delivery control:* In this case, the service user (terminal or application) can issue a request that all undelivered data be delivered. The invoking side may also, optionally, request acknowledgment of the delivery to the other side.
3. *Quarantine delivery control:* This requires that the remote virtual terminal service module hold all incoming data until they are explicitly released for delivery by the other side. For example, an application could send a screenful of data in several small blocks but instruct the other side to defer delivery, so that the entire screen update is displayed at once. Another example is the function key action mentioned previously.

Echo Control.   Echo control is concerned with the control of how characters typed on a keyboard will cause updates to a display. In real terminals, characters typed on the keyboard may be displayed on the screen locally by the terminal as they are typed or may be "echoed back" to the display by the computer. The former option is less flexible but is often chosen when the communication link is half-duplex and echoing back would therefore not be practical. The latter option is used where the communication line is full-duplex and where greater control over the screen is required. For example, a time-sharing system may wish to suppress the display of the terminal user's password and identification code but display all other characters.

Virtual Terminal Parameters.   In addition to the aspects of the virtual terminal service listed in Table 8.5, a major feature of the service is the use of terminal parameters. These are similar to those used in X.3 in that they provide a way of defining various characteristics of the terminal. However, the parameters available in the ISO standard are much more complex and powerful than those of X.3. They allow the user to define various characteristics of displayable characters, such as font, size, intensity, and color. Control objects can be defined that are used to control formatting on the display, and to trigger various events such as ringing an alarm. Characteristics of other devices such as printers can also be specified.

8.5

CIRCUIT-SWITCHED NETWORKS

The interface issues relating to circuit-switched local networks are far simpler to deal with than those of packet-switched networks. With a circuit-switched local network, such as a digital PBX, the mode of attachment is essentially transparent, much like the layer 1 protocol mode discussed above.

As before, there are two phases of operation, a connection phase and a data transfer phase. The data transfer phase uses synchronous TDM; thus no protocols and no logic are required. As was mentioned, this is a truly transparent connection.

For the connection phase, the main issue is the means by which the attached device requests a connection. For this discussion, it is useful to refer back to Figure 7.16, which indicates that each digital data device attaches to the network via some form of data line group. At least three means of connection establishment have been used:

1. Data devices typically connect via a twisted pair; therefore, near the data device, there must be a line driver to which the device attaches. This driver can include a simple keypad for selecting a destination.
2. Either the line driver or the data line group (more likely the latter) can contain the logic for conducting a simple dialogue with a terminal. In this case, the terminal user enters the connection request via the terminal.
3. The attached device (host) could contain a simple I/O program that generates connection requests in a form understandable to the network.

Regardless of the means, the switch architecture can support the private network configuration shown in Figure 8.1a. The local network connection would appear as a dial-up line to the attached device.

Finally, we mention the protocol converter featured in Figure 7.16. This facility acts as a gateway between devices with dissimilar protocols. It is used, for example, to convert between asynchronous ASCII terminals and the synchronous IBM 3270 protocol. In the future, this might be used to implement a VTP.

8.6

ANALOG DEVICES

There are very few cases of analog device attachment to a local network to discuss. The most common is the telephone. Analog telephones are easily accommodated on a digital PBX that includes a codec in the line group (Figure 7.16). The other likely place to find analog devices is on a broadband network. As we have discussed, these networks easily accommodate video and audio attachments by dedicating channels for their use.

8.7

RECOMMENDED READING

As yet, there is not much literature on this subject. [STAC80] is perhaps the most systematic look at NIU interfaces for LANs; other articles of interest are [BAL85], [CERR87], [SPAN86], and [CZOT87]. [OLSE83] describes the layer 1 gateway approach for asynchronous terminals. A view of the issue for high-speed LANs is contained in [NESS81].

A readable description of X.3/X.28/X.29 is contained in [MART88]. [DAY80] contains a good discussion of virtual terminal protocols. [RICH90] discusses a host-to-front-end protocol, and [KANA88] details a proposal for one.

8.8

PROBLEMS

8.1 Consider Figure 8.8. Assume that the host–NIU protocol is X.25 and the NIU–NIU protocol is IEEE 802. Describe, with an example, how the layer 3 X.25 protocol is converted to the LLC protocol for transmission over the network.

8.2 Repeat Problem 8.1, but now assume the ANS LDDI link layer for NIU–NIU.

8.3 Consider Figure 8.9. Assume that the host–NIU interface is IEEE-802 LLC. Describe, with an example, how the host layer 4 software makes use of the layer 2 services to transmit data to a destination host.

8.4 Repeat Problem 8.3, but now assume the ANS LDDI interface.

8.5 Consider a layer 1 gateway being used by devices that communicate with a synchronous layer 2 protocol, such as HDLC or BISYNC. How is the NIU overflow problem handled?

8.6 Describe how a protocol convert in a digital switch architecture can be used to implement VTP.

8.7 In Figure 8.10, the transport layer is in the NIU rather than the host and therefore part of the communications subnetwork. Since the transport layer is supposed to provide end-to-end reliability, is there cause for concern? Describe any potential problems and ways of attacking them.

CHAPTER 9

LAN/MAN
Performance

This chapter has two objectives:

1. To give the reader some insight into the factors that affect performance and the relative performance of various local network schemes
2. To present analytic techniques that can be used for network sizing and to obtain first approximations of network performance

It is beyond the scope of this book to derive analytic expressions for all of the performance measures presented; that would require an entire book on local network performance. Further, this chapter can only sketch the techniques that would be useful to the analyst in approximating performance; for deeper study, references to appropriate literature are provided.

This chapter begins by presenting some of the key performance considerations for LANs and MANs; the section serves to put the techniques and results presented subsequently into perspective. Separate sections present results for LAN and MAN systems. Finally, the more difficult problem of end-to-end performance is broached.

9.1

LAN/MAN PERFORMANCE CONSIDERATIONS

The key characteristics of the LAN that structure the way its performance is analyzed are that there is a shared access medium, requiring a medium access control protocol, and that packet switching is used. MANs share these characteristics. It follows that the basic performance considerations, and the approaches to performance analysis, will be the same for both. With the above points in mind, this section explores these basic considerations. The section begins by defining the basic measures of performance, then looks at the key parameter for determining LAN/MAN performance, known affectionately to devotees as a. Having been introduced to a, the reader is in a position to appreciate the interrelationship of the various factors that affect LAN/MAN performance, which is the final topic.

The results that exist for the portion of performance within the local network boundary are summarized in subsequent sections. As we shall see, these results are best organized in terms of the medium access control protocol.

Measures of Performance

Three measures of LAN and MAN performance are commonly used:

- D: the delay that occurs between the time a packet or frame is ready for transmission from a node, and the completion of successful transmission.
- S: the throughput of the local network: the total rate of data being transmitted between nodes (carried load).
- U: the utilization of the local network medium; the fraction of total capacity being used.

These measures concern themselves with performance within the local network. How they relate to the overall performance of the network and attached devices is discussed later.

The parameter S is often normalized and expressed as a fraction of capacity. For example, if over a period of 1 s, the sum of the successful data transfers between nodes is 1 Mb on a 10-Mbps channel, then $S =$ 0.1. Thus S can also be interpreted as utilization. The analysis is commonly done in terms of the total number of bits transferred, including overhead (headers, trailers) bits; the calculations are a bit easier, and this approach isolates performance effects due to the local network alone. One must work backward from this to determine effective throughput.

Results for S and D are generally plotted as a function of the offered load G, which is the actual load or traffic demand presented to the local network. Note that S and G differ. S is the normalized rate of data packets successfully transmitted; G is the total number of packets offered to the network; it includes control packets, such as tokens, and collisions, which are destroyed packets that must be retransmitted. G, too, is often expressed as a fraction of capacity. Intuitively, we would expect D to increase with G: the more traffic competing for transmission time, the longer the delay for any individual transmission. S should also increase with G, up to some saturation point, beyond which the network cannot handle more load.

Figure 9.1 shows the ideal situation: channel utilization increases to accommodate load up to an offered load equal to the full capacity of the system; then utilization remains at 100%. Of course, any overhead or inefficiency will cause performance to fall short of the goal. The depiction of S versus G is a reasonable one from the point of view of the network itself. It shows the behavior of the system based on the actual load on it. But from the point of view of the user or the attached device, it may seem strange. Why? Because the offered load includes not only original transmissions but also acknowledgments and, in the case of errors or collisions, retransmissions. The user may want to know the throughput and the delay characteristics as a function of the device-generated data to be put through the system—the input load. Or if the network is the focus, the analyst may want to know what the offered load is given the input load. We will return to this discussion later.

The reader may also wonder about the importance of U. D and S are certainly of interest, but the efficiency or utilization of the channel may seem of minor importance. After all, local networks are advertised as having very high bandwidth and low cost compared to long-haul net-

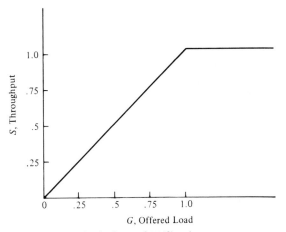

FIGURE 9.1 Ideal Channel Utilization

works. Although it is true that utilization is of less importance for local compared to long-haul links, it is still worth considering. Local network capacity is not free, and demand has a tendency to expand to fill available capacity.

In summary, we have introduced two additional parameters:

1. *G:* the offered load to the local network; the total rate of data presented to the network for transmission
2. *I:* the input load; the rate of data generated by the stations attached to the local network

Table 9.1 is a very simplified example to show the relationship among these parameters. Here we assume a network with a capacity of $C = 1000$ frames per second. For simplicity, I, S, and G are expressed in frames per second. It is assumed that 1% of all transmitted frames are lost and must be repeated. Thus at an input $I = 100$ frames per second, on the average 1 frame per second will be repeated. Thus $S = 100$ and $G = 101$. Assume that the input load arrives in batches, once per second. Hence, on average, with $I = 100$, $D = 0.0505$ s. The utilization is defined as $S/C = 0.1$.

The next two entries are easily seen to be correct. Note that for $I = 990$, the entire capacity of the system is being used ($G = 1000$). If I increases beyond this point, the system cannot keep up. Only 1000 frames per second will be transmitted. Thus S remains at 990 and U at 0.99. But G and D grow without bound as more and more backlog accumulates; there is no steady-state value. This pattern will become familiar as the chapter proceeds.

The Effect of Propagation Delay and Transmission Rate

Recall from Figure 3.6 that local networks are distinguished from long-haul networks on the one hand, and multiprocessor systems on the

TABLE 9.1   Example of Relationships Among LAN/MAN Measures of Performance[a,b]

I	*S*	*G*	*D*	*U*
100	100	101	0.0505	0.1
500	500	505	0.2525	0.5
990	990	1000	0.5	0.99
2000	990	—	—	0.99

[a]Capacity: 1000 frames/s.
[b]*I*, input load (frames per second); *S*, throughput (frames per second); *G*, offered load (frames per second;)*D*, delay (seconds); *U*, utilization (fraction of capacity).

other, by the data rate (R) employed and the distance (d) of the communications path. In fact, it is the product of these two terms, $R \times d$, that can be used to characterize local networks. Furthermore, as we shall see, this term, or cousins of it, is the single most important parameter for determining the performance of a local network. We shall see that a network's performance will be the same, for example, for both a 100-Mbps, 1 km-bus and a 10-Mbps, 10-km bus.

A good way to visualize the meaning of $R \times d$ is to divide it by the propagation velocity of the medium, which is nearly constant among most media of interest. A good approximation for propagation velocity is about two-thirds of the speed of light, or 2×10^8 m/s. A dimensional analysis of the formula

$$\frac{Rd}{V}$$

shows this to be equal to the length of the transmission medium in bits, that is, the number of bits that may be in transit between two nodes at any one time.

We can see that this does indeed distinguish local networks from multiprocessor and long-haul networks. Within a multiprocessor system, there are generally only a few bits in transit. For example, the latest IBM I/O channel offering operates at up to 24 Mbps over a distance of up to 120 m, which yields at most about 15 bits. Processor-to-processor communication within a single computer will typically involve fewer bits than that in transit. On the other hand, the bit length of a long-haul network can be hundreds of thousands of bits. In between, we have local networks. Several examples: a 500-m Ethernet system (10 Mbps) has a bit length of 25; both a 1-km HYPERchannel (50 Mbps) and a typical 5-km broadband LAN (5 Mbps) are about 250 bits long.

A useful way of looking at this is to consider the length of the medium as compared to the typical frame transmitted. Multiprocessor systems have very short bit lengths compared to frame length; long-haul nets have very long ones. Local networks generally are shorter than a frame up to about the same order of magnitude as a frame.

Intuitively, one can see that this will make a difference. Compare local networks to multiprocessor computers. Relatively speaking, things happen almost simultaneously in a multiprocessor system; when one component begins to transmit, the others know it almost immediately. For local networks, the relative time gap leads to all kinds of complications in the medium access control protocols, as we have seen. Compare long-haul networks to local networks. To have any hope of efficiency, the long-haul link must allow multiple frames to be in transit simultaneously. This places specific requirements on the link-layer protocol, which must deal with a sequence of outstanding frames waiting to be acknowledged. LAN and MAN protocol generally allow only one frame to be in transit at a time, or at the most a few for some ring protocols. Again, this affects the access protocol.

The length of the medium, expressed in bits, compared to the length of the typical frame is usually denoted by a:

$$a = \frac{\text{length of data path (in bits)}}{\text{length of frame}}$$

Some manipulation shows that

$$a = \frac{Rd}{VL}$$

where L is the length of the frame. But d/V is the propagation time on the medium (worst case), and L/B is the time it takes a transmitter to get an entire frame out onto the medium. So

$$a = \frac{\text{propagation time}}{\text{transmission time}}$$

Typical values of a range from about 0.01 to 0.1 for LANs and 0.01 to over 1 for MANs. Table 9.2 gives some sample values for a bus topology. In computing a, keep in mind that the maximum propagation time on a broadband network is double the length of the longest path from the headend, plus the delay, if any, at the headend. For baseband bus and ring networks, repeater delays must be included in propagation time.

The parameter a determines an upper bound on the utilization of a local network. Consider a perfectly efficient access mechanism that allows only one transmission at a time. As soon as one transmission is over, another node begins transmitting. Furthermore, the transmission is pure data—no overhead bits. (*Note:* These conditions are very close to

TABLE 9.2   Values of a

Data Rate (Mbps)	Packet Size (bits)	Cable Length (km)	a
1	100	1	0.05
1	1,000	10	0.05
1	100	10	0.5
10	100	1	0.5
10	1,000	1	0.05
10	1,000	10	0.5
10	10,000	10	0.05
50	10,000	1	0.025
50	100	1	2.5

being met in a digital switch but not, alas, in LANs and MANs.) What is the maximum possible utilization of the network? It can be expressed as the ratio of total throughput of the system to the capacity or bandwidth:

$$U = \frac{throughput}{R} = \frac{L/(propagation + transmission\ time)}{R} \quad (9.1)$$
$$= \frac{L/(d/V + L/R)}{R} = \frac{1}{1 + a}$$

So, utilization varies inversely with a. This can be grasped intuitively by studying Figure 9.2. This figure shows a baseband bus with two stations as far apart as possible (worst case) that take turns sending frames. If we normalize time such that the frame transmission time $= 1$, then $a =$ propagation time. The sequence of events can be expressed as follows:

1. A station begins transmission at t_0.
2. Reception begins at $t_0 + a$.
3. Transmission is completed at $t_0 + 1$.
4. Reception ends at $t_0 + 1 + a$.
5. The other station begins transmitting.

Event 2 occurs *after* event 3 if $a > 1.0$. In any case, the total time for one "turn" is $1 + a$, but the transmission time is only 1, for a utilization of $1/(1 + a)$.

The same effect can be seen to apply to a ring network in Figure 9.3. Here we assume that one station transmits and then waits to receive its own transmission before any other station transmits. The identical sequence of events outlined above applies.

Equation (9.1) is plotted in Figure 9.4. The implications for throughput are shown in Figure 9.5. As offered load increases, throughput remains equal to offered load up to the full capacity of the network (when $S = G = \frac{1}{1 + a}$), and then remains at $S = \frac{1}{1 + a}$ as load increases.

So we can say that an upper bound on the utilization or efficiency of a LAN or MAN is $1/(1 + a)$, regardless of the medium access protocol used. Two caveats: First, this assumes that the maximum propagation time is incurred on each transmission. Second, it assumes that only one transmission may occur at a time. These assumptions are not always true; nevertheless, the formula $1/(1 + a)$ is almost always a valid upper bound, because the overhead of the medium access protocol more than makes up for the lack of validity of these assumptions.

The overhead is unavoidable. Frames must include address and synchronization bits. There is administrative overhead for controlling the protocol. In addition, there are forms of overhead peculiar to one or

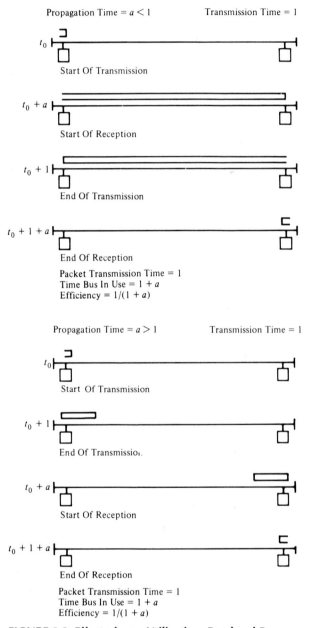

Propagation Time = $a < 1$ Transmission Time = 1

t_0 Start Of Transmission

$t_0 + a$ Start Of Reception

$t_0 + 1$ End Of Transmission

$t_0 + 1 + a$ End Of Reception

Packet Transmission Time = 1
Time Bus In Use = $1 + a$
Efficiency = $1/(1 + a)$

Propagation Time = $a > 1$ Transmission Time = 1

t_0 Start Of Transmission

$t_0 + 1$ End Of Transmission

$t_0 + a$ Start Of Reception

$t_0 + 1 + a$ End Of Reception

Packet Transmission Time = 1
Time Bus In Use = $1 + a$
Efficiency = $1/(1 + a)$

FIGURE 9.2 Effect of *a* on Utilization: Baseband Bus

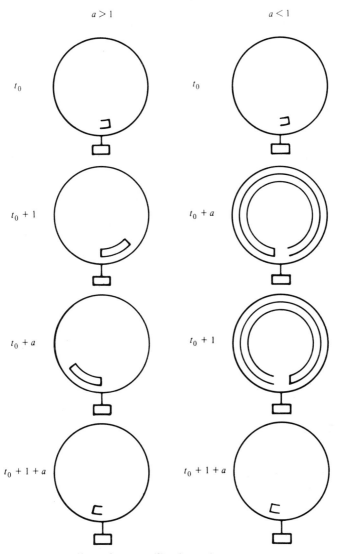

FIGURE 9.3 Effect of *a* on Utilization: Ring

more of the protocols. We highlight these briefly for the most important protocols:

- *Contention protocols (ALOHA, S-ALOHA, CSMA, CSMA/CD):* time wasted due to collisions; need for acknowledgment frames. S-ALOHA requires that slot size equal transmission plus maximum propagation time.

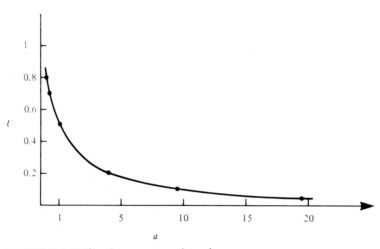

FIGURE 9.4 Utilization as a Function of *a*

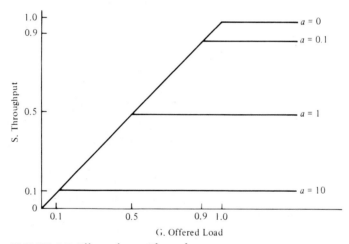

FIGURE 9.5 Effect of *a* on Throughput

- *Delay scheduling:* time spent waiting to see if other stations have data to send; acknowledgment frames.
- *Token bus:* time waiting for token if logically intervening stations have no data to send; token transmission; acknowledgment frames.
- *Token ring:* time waiting for token if intervening stations have no data to send.
- *Slotted ring:* time waiting for empty slot if intervening stations have no data to send.

- *Register insertion:* delay at each node of time equal to address length. From the point of view of a single station, the propagation time and hence *a* may increase due to insertion of registers on the ring.
- *Explicit reservation:* reservation transmission, acknowledgments.
- *Implicit reservation:* overhead of protocol used to establish reservation, acknowledgments.

There are two distinct effects here. One is that the efficiency or utilization of a channel decreases as *a* increases. This, of course, affects throughput. The other effect is that the overhead attributable to a protocol wastes bandwidth and hence reduces effective utilization and effective throughput. By and large, we can think of these two effects as independent and additive. However, we shall see that, for contention protocols, there is a strong interaction such that the overhead of these protocols increases as a function of *a*.

In any case, it would seem desirable to keep *a* as low as possible. Looking back to the defining formula, for a fixed network *a* can be reduced by increasing frame size. This will be useful only if the length of messages produced by a station is an integral multiple of the frame size (excluding overhead bits). Otherwise, the large frame size is itself a source of waste. Furthermore, a large frame size increases the delay for other stations. This leads us to the next topic: the various factors that affect LAN/MAN performance.

Factors That Affect Performance

We list here those factors that affect the performance of a LAN or a MAN. We are concerned here with that part which is independent of the attached devices—those factors that are exclusively under the control of the local network designer. The chief factors are:

- Capacity
- Propagation delay
- Number of bits per frame
- Local network protocols
- Offered load
- Number of stations

The first three terms have already been discussed; they determine the value of *a*.

Next are the local network protocols: physical, medium access, and link. The physical layer is not likely to be much of a factor; generally, it can keep up with transmissions and receptions with little delay. The link layer will add some overhead bits to each frame and some administrative overhead, such as virtual circuit management and acknowledgments. This area has not been studied much, and is best considered as part of the end-to-end performance problem discussed in Section 9.4. This leaves the medium access layer, which can have a significant effect on network performance. Sections 9.2 and 9.3 are devoted to this topic.

We can think of the first three factors listed above as characterizing the network; they are generally treated as constants or givens. The local network protocol is the focus of the design effort—the choice that must be made. The next two factors, offered load and the number of stations, are generally treated as the independent variables. The analyst is concerned with determining performance as a function of these two variables. Note that these two variables must be treated separately. Certainly, it is true that for a fixed offered load per station, the total offered load increases as the number of stations increases. The same increase could be achieved by keeping the number of stations fixed but increasing the offered load per station. However, as we shall see, the network performance will be different for these two cases.

One factor that was not listed above: the error rate of the channel. An error in a frame transmission necessitates a retransmission. Because the error rates on local networks are so low, this is not likely to be a significant factor.

9.2

LAN PERFORMANCE

A considerable amount of work has been done on the analysis of the performance of various LAN protocols for bus/tree and ring. This section is limited to summarizing the results for the protocols discussed in Chapter 5, those protocols that are most common for LANs.

We begin by presenting an easily used technique for quickly establishing bounds on performance. Often, this back-of-the-envelope approach is adequate for system sizing.

Next, a comparison of the three protocols standardized by IEEE 802 (CSMA/CD, token bus, token ring) is presented. These three protocols are likely to dominate the market and an insight into their comparative performance is needed.

We then look more closely at contention protocols and devote more time here to the derivation of results. This process should give the reader a feeling for the assumptions that must be made and the limitations of the results. More time is spent on the contention protocols because we wish to understand their inherent instability. As we shall see, the basis of this instability is a positive feedback mechanism that behaves poorly under heavy load.

Finally, we revisit token ring and view it in context with the other two common ring protocols: register insertion and slotted ring.

Bounds on Performance

The purpose of this section is to present a remarkably simple technique for determining bounds on the performance of a LAN. Although a considerable amount of work has been done on developing detailed analytic and simulation models of the performance of various LAN protocols, much of this work is suspect because of the restrictive assumptions made. Furthermore, even if the models were valid, they provide a level of resolution not needed by the local network designer.

A common-sense argument should clarify this point. In any LAN or MAN, there are three regions of operation, based on the magnitude of the offered load:

1. A region of low delay through the network, where the capacity is more than adequate to handle the load offered.
2. A region of high delay, where the network becomes a bottleneck. In this region, relatively more time is spent controlling access to the network and less in actual data transmission compared to the low-delay region.
3. A region of unbounded delay, where the offered load exceeds the total capacity of the system.

This last region is easily identified. For example, consider the following network:

- Capacity = 1 Mbps
- Number of stations = 1000
- Frame size = 1000 bits

If, on average, each station generates data at a rate exceeding 1 frame per second, then the total offered load exceeds 1 Mbps. The delay at each station will build up and up without bound.

The third region is clearly to be avoided. But almost always, the designer will wish to avoid the second region as well. The second region implies an inefficient use to the network. Further, a sudden surge of data while in the second region would cause corresponding increases in the already high delay. In the first region, the network is not a bottleneck and, as we will discuss in Section 9.4, will contribute typically only a small amount to the end-to-end delay.

Thus the crucial question is: What region will the network operate in, based on projected load and network characteristics? The third region is easily identified and avoided; it is the boundary between the first two regions that must be identified. If the network operates below that boundary, it should not cause a communications bottleneck. If it operates above the boundary, there is reason for concern and perhaps redesign. Now, the issue is: How precisely do we need to know the boundary? The load on the network will vary over time and can only be estimated. Because the load estimates are unlikely to be precise, it is not necessary to know exactly where that boundary is. If a good approximation for the boundary can be developed, then the network can be sized so that the estimated load is well below the boundary. In the example just described, the estimated load is 1 Mbps. If the capacity of the LAN is such that the boundary is approximately 4 Mbps, then the designer can be reasonably sure that the network will not be a bottleneck.

With the above points in mind, we present a technique for estimating performance bounds, based on the approach taken by the IEEE 802 committee [STUC85]. To begin, let us ignore the medium access control protocol and develop bounds for throughput and delay as a function of the number of active stations. Four quantities are needed:

1. T_{idle} = the mean time that a station is idle between transmission attempts: the station has no messages awaiting transmission.
2. T_{msg} = the time required to transmit a message once medium access is gained.
3. T_{delay} = the mean delay from the time a station has a packet to transmit until completion of transmission; includes queueing time and transmission time.
4. THRU = mean total throughput on the network of messages per unit time.

We assume that there are N active stations, each with the same load-generating requirements. To find an upper bound on total throughput, consider the ideal case in which there is no queueing delay: each station transmits when it is ready. Hence each station alternates between idle and transmission with a throughput of $1/(T_{idle} + T_{msg})$. The maximum possible throughput is just the summation of the throughputs of all N stations:

$$\text{THRU} \le \frac{N}{T_{idle} + T_{msg}} \tag{9.2}$$

This upper bound increases as N increases, but is reasonable only up to the point of raw capacity of the network, which can be expressed

$$\text{THRU} \le \frac{1}{T_{msg}} \tag{9.3}$$

The breakpoint between these two bounds occurs at

$$\frac{N}{T_{idle} + T_{msg}} = \frac{1}{T_{msg}} \tag{9.4}$$

$$N = \frac{T_{idle} + T_{msg}}{T_{msg}}$$

This breakpoint defines two regions of operation. With the number of stations below the breakpoint, the system is not generating enough load to utilize fully system capacity. However, above the breakpoint, the network is saturated: it is fully utilized and is not able to satisfy the demands of the attached stations.

To see the reasonableness of this breakpoint, consider that the capacity of the network is $1/T_{msg}$. For example, if it takes 1 μs to transmit a message, the data rate is 10^6 messages per second. The amount of traffic being generated by N stations is $N/(T_{idle} + T_{msg})$. If the traffic exceeds the network's capacity, messages get backlogged and delay increases. Note also that traffic increases either by increasing the number of stations (N) or increasing the rate at which stations transmit messages (reduce T_{idle}).

These same considerations allow us to place a lower bound on delay. Clearly,

$$T_{delay} \geq T_{msg} \qquad (9.5)$$

Now, consider that at any load the following relationship holds:

$$\text{THRU} = \frac{N}{T_{idle} + T_{delay}} \qquad (9.6)$$

since $1/(T_{idle} + T_{delay})$ is the throughput of each station. Combining (9.3) and (9.6) we have

$$T_{delay} \geq NT_{msg} - T_{idle}$$

The breakpoint calculation, combining (9.5) and the equation above, yields the same result as before (see Figure 9.6). Keep in mind that these bounds are asymptotes of the true delay and throughput curves. The breakpoint delimits two regions. Below the breakpoint, capacity is underutilized and delay is low. Above the breakpoint, capacity saturates and delay blows up. In actuality, the changes are gradual rather than abrupt.

Bounds on the other side are easily found. The delay would be maximized if all N stations had a message to transmit simultaneously:

$$T_{delay} \leq NT_{msg}$$

Combining with equation (9.6) gives us

$$\text{THRU} \geq \frac{N}{T_{idle} + NT_{msg}}$$

These bounds give one a rough idea of the behavior of a system. They allow one to do a simple back-of-the-envelope calculation to determine if a proposed system is within reasonable bounds. If the answer is no, much analysis and grief may be saved. If yes, the analyst must dig deeper.

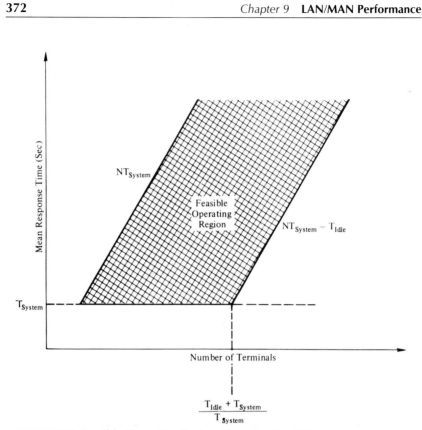

FIGURE 9.6 Feasible Operating Region, Zero-Overhead System

Two examples should clarify the use of these equations. First, consider a workstation attached to a 1-Mbps local network that generates, on average, three messages per minute, with messages averaging 500 bits. With message transmission time equal to 500 μs, the mean idle time is 20 s. The breakpoint number of stations is, roughly,

$$N = \frac{20}{500 \times 10^{-6}} = 40{,}000 \text{ stations}$$

If the number of stations is much less than this, say 1000, congestion should not be a problem. If it is much more, say 100,000, congestion may be a problem.

Second, consider a set of stations that generates PCM digitized voice packets on a 10-Mbps local network. Data are generated at the rate of 64 kbps. For 0.1-s packets, we have a transmission time per packet of 640 μs. Thus

$$N = \frac{0.1}{640 \times 10^{-6}} = 156 \text{ stations}$$

Generally, we would not expect all voice stations (telephones) to be active at one time; perhaps one-fourth is a reasonable estimate, so the breakpoint is around 600 stations.

Note that in both these examples, we have very quickly arrived at a first-order sizing of the system with no knowledge of the protocol. All that is needed is the load generated per station and the capacity of the network.

The calculations above are based on a system with no overhead. They provide bounds for a system with perfect scheduling. One way to account for overhead is to replace T_{msg} with T_{sys}, where the latter quantity includes an estimate of the overhead per packet. This is done in Figure 9.6.

A more accurate though still rough handle on performance can be had by considering the protocol involved. We develop the results for token passing. A similar analysis can be found in [HAYE81]. This protocol, for bus or ring, has the following characteristics:

- Stations are given the opportunity to transmit in a fixed cyclical sequence.
- At each opportunity, a station may transmit one message.
- Frames may be of fixed or variable length.
- Preemption is not allowed.

Some additional terms are needed:

- $R(K)$ = mean throughput rate (messages/second) of station K
- T_{over} = total overhead (seconds) in one cycle of the N stations
- C = duration (seconds) of a cycle
- $UTIL(K)$ = utilization of the network due to station K

Let us begin by assuming that each station always has messages to transmit; the system is never idle. The fraction of time that the network is busy handling requests from station K is just

$$UTIL(K) = R(K) \, T_{msg}(K)$$

To keep up with the work, the system must not be presented with a load greater than its capacity:

$$\sum_{K=1}^{N} UTIL(K) = \sum_{K=1}^{N} R(K)T_{msg}(K) \leq 1$$

Now consider the overhead in the system, which is the time during a cycle required to pass the token and perform other maintenance functions. Clearly,

$$C = T_{over} + \sum_{K=1}^{N} T_{msg}(K)$$

From this we can deduce that

$$R(K) = \frac{1}{C} = \frac{1}{T_{over} + \sum\limits_{K=1}^{N} T_{msg}(K)}$$

Now, let us assume that the medium is always busy but that some stations may be idle. This line of reasoning will lead us to the desired bounds on throughput and delay. Since we assume that the network is never idle, the fraction of time the system spends on overhead and transmission must sum to unity:

$$\frac{T_{over}}{C} + \sum\limits_{K=1}^{N} R(K)T_{msg}(K) = 1$$

Thus

$$C = \frac{T_{over}}{1 - \sum\limits_{K=1}^{N} R(K)T_{msg}(K)}$$

Note that the duration of a cycle is proportional to the overhead; doubling the mean overhead time should double the cycle time for a fixed load. This result may not be intuitively obvious; the reader is advised to work out a few examples.

With C known, we can place an upper bound on the throughput of any one source:

$$R(J) \leq \frac{1}{C} = \frac{1 - \sum\limits_{K=1}^{N} R(K)T_{msg}(K)}{T_{over}} \tag{9.7}$$

Now let us assume that all sources are identical: $R(K) = R$, $T_{msg}(K) = T_{msg}$. Then (9.7) reduces to

$$R \leq \frac{1 - NRT_{msg}}{T_{over}}$$

Solving for R:

$$R < \frac{1}{T_{over} + NT_{msg}}$$

But, by definition, $R = 1/(T_{delay} + T_{idle})$, so we can express:

$$T_{delay} = \frac{1}{R} - T_{idle}$$

$$T_{delay} \geq T_{over} + NT_{msg} - T_{idle}$$

In practice, T_{over} may consist of some fixed amount of time C_0 for each cycle plus an amount C_1 for each station that receives the token. These numbers will differ for token ring and token bus:

$$T_{delay} \geq C_0 + N(T_{msg} + C_1) - T_{idle}$$

We also have the inequality of (9.5) and can solve for the breakpoint:

$$N = \frac{T_{msg} + T_{idle} - C_0}{T_{msg} + C_1} \qquad (9.8)$$

Figure 9.7 depicts the delay-station plot, showing the two regions. Note that the slope of the line in the heavily loaded region is $T_{msg} + C_1$.

A similar analysis can be carried out for CSMA/CD. Figure 9.8 is a comparison developed in [STUC85]. The absolute positions of the various policies depend on specific assumptions about overhead and, in the case of CSMA/CD, the value of a. But the relative positions are generally true: under lightly loaded conditions CSMA/CD has a shorter delay time, but the protocol breaks down more rapidly under increasing load.

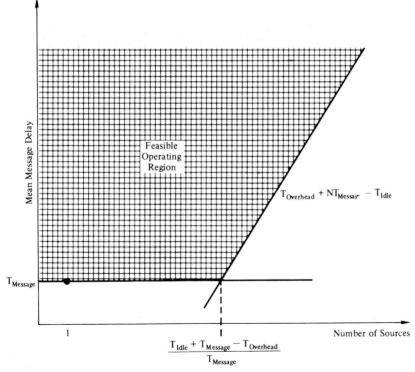

FIGURE 9.7 Bounds on Token-Passing Performance

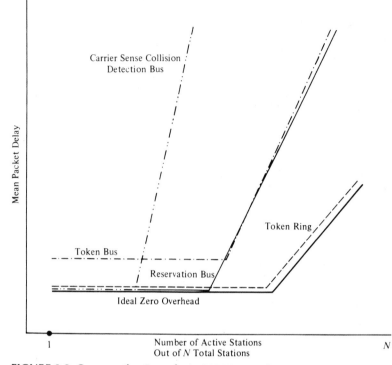

FIGURE 9.8 Comparative Bounds on LAN Protocols

Comparative Performance of Token Passing and CSMA/CD

The purpose of this section is to give the reader some insight into the relative performance of the most important LAN protocols: CSMA/CD, token bus, and token ring. We begin with simplified models that highlight the main points of comparison. Following this, a careful analysis performed by the IEEE 802 committee is reported.

For the models, we assume a local network with N active stations. Our purpose is to estimate the maximum throughput achievable on the LAN. For this purpose, we assume that each station is always prepared to send a frame.

First, let us consider token ring. Time on the ring will alternate between data frame transmission and token passing. Refer to a single instance of a data frame followed by a token as a cycle and define:

- C = average time for one cycle
- DF = average time to transmit a data frame
- TF = average time to pass a token

It should be clear that the average cycle rate is just $1/C = 1/(DF + TF)$. Intuitively,

$$S = \frac{DF}{DF + TF} \tag{9.9}$$

That is, the throughput, normalized to system capacity, is just the fraction of time that is spent transmitting data.

Refer now to Figure 9.3; time is normalized such that frame transmission time equals 1 and propagation time equals a. For the case of $a < 1$, a station transmits a frame at time t_0, receives the leading edge of its own frame at $t_0 + a$, and completes transmission at $t_0 + 1$. The station then emits a token, which takes time a/N to reach the next station (assuming equally spaced stations). Thus one cycle takes $1 + a/N$ and the transmission time is 1. So $S = 1/(1 + a/N)$.

For $a > 1$, the reasoning is slightly different. A station transmits at t_0, completes transmission at $t_0 + 1$, and receives the leading edge of its frame at $t_0 + a$. At that point, it is free to emit a token, which takes a time a/N to reach the next station. The cycle time is therefore $a + a/N$ and $S = 1/[a(1 + 1/N)]$. Summarizing,

$$Token:\ S = \begin{cases} \dfrac{1}{1 + a/N} & a < 1 \\[2mm] \dfrac{1}{a(1 + 1/N)} & a > 1 \end{cases} \tag{9.10}$$

The reasoning above applies equally well to token bus, where we assume that the logical ordering is the same as the physical ordering and that token-passing time is therefore a/N.

For CSMA/CD, we base our approach on a derivation in [METC76]. Consider time on the medium to be organized into slots whose length is twice the end-to-end propagation delay. This is a convenient way to view the activity on the medium; the slot time is the maximum time, from the start of transmission, required to detect a collision. Again, assume that there are N active stations, each generating the same load. Clearly, if each station always has a packet to transmit, it does, so there will be nothing but collisions on the line. Therefore, we assume that each station restrains itself to transmitting during an available slot with probability p.

Time on the medium consists of two types of intervals. First is a transmission interval, which lasts $1/2a$ slots. Second is a contention interval, which is a sequence of slots with either a collision or no transmission in each slot. The throughput is just the proportion of time spent in transmission intervals [similar to the reasoning for equation (9.1)].

To determine the average length of a contention interval, we begin by computing A, the probability that exactly one station attempts a transmission in a slot and therefore acquires the medium. This is just the binomial probability that any one station attempts to transmit and the others do not:

$$A = \binom{N}{1} p^1 (1 - p)^{N-1}$$
$$= Np(1 - p)^{N-1}$$

This function takes on a maximum over p when $p = 1/N$:

$$A = \left(1 - \frac{1}{N}\right)^{N-1}$$

Why are we interested in the maximum? Well, we want to calculate the maximum throughput of the medium. It should be clear that this will be achieved if we maximize the probability of successful seizure of the medium. During periods of heavy usage, a station should restrain its offered load to $1/N$. (This assumes that each station knows the value of N; in order to derive an expression for maximum possible throughput, we live with this assumption.) On the other hand, during periods of light usage, maximum utilization cannot be achieved because G is too low; this region is not of interest here.

Now we can estimate the mean length of a contention interval, w, in slots:

$$E[w] = \sum_{i=1}^{\infty} i \cdot \Pr\,[i \text{ slots in a row with a collision or no}$$

transmission followed by a slot with one transmission]

$$= \sum_{i=1}^{\infty} i(1 - A)^i A$$

The summation converges to

$$E[w] = \frac{1 - A}{A}$$

We can now determine the maximum utilization, which is just the length of a transmission interval as a proportion of a cycle consisting of a transmission and a contention interval.

$$CSMA/CD: S = \frac{1/2a}{1/2a + \dfrac{1 - A}{A}} = \frac{1}{1 + 2a\dfrac{1 - A}{A}} \qquad (9.11)$$

Figure 9.9 shows normalized throughput as a function of a for various values of N and for both token passing and CSMA/CD. For both protocols, throughput declines as a increases. This is to be expected. But the

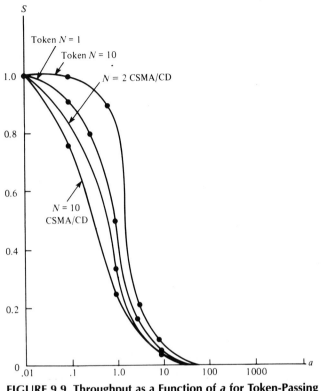

FIGURE 9.9 Throughput as a Function of *a* for Token-Passing and CSMA/CD

dramatic difference between the two protocols is seen in Figure 9.10, which shows throughput as a function of N. Token-passing performance actually improves as a function of N, because less time is spent in token passing. Conversely, the performance of CSMA/CD decreases because of the increased likelihood of collision.

It is interesting to note the asymptomatic value of S as N increases. For token:

$$\textit{Token: } \lim_{N\to\infty} S = \begin{cases} 1 & a < 1 \\ \dfrac{1}{a} & a > 1 \end{cases}$$

For CSMA/CD, we need to know that $\lim_{N\to\infty}(1 - 1/N)^{N-1} = 1/e$. Then

$$\textit{CSMA/CD: } \lim_{N\to\infty} S = \frac{1}{1 + 3.44a}$$

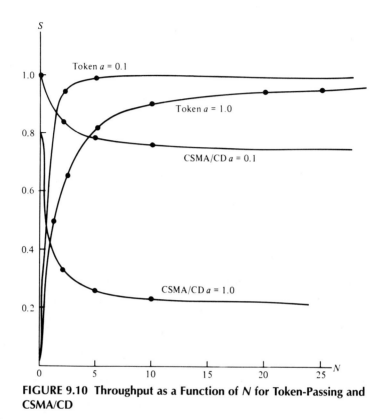

FIGURE 9.10 Throughput as a Function of *N* for Token-Passing and CSMA/CD

Continuing this example, it is relatively easy to derive an expression for delay for token passing. Once a station (station 1) transmits, it must wait for the following events to occur before it can transmit again:

- Station 1 transmits token to station 2.
- Station 2 transmits data frame.
- Station 2 transmits token to station 3.
- Station transmits data frame.

    •
    •
    •
        •

- Station *N* − 1 transmits token to station *N*.
- Station *N* transmits data frame.
- Station *N* transmits token to station 1.

Thus the delay consists of (*N* − 1) cycles plus *a/N*, the token passing time. We have

$$\text{Token: } D = \begin{cases} N + a - 1 & a < 1 \\ aN & a > 1 \end{cases} \tag{9.12}$$

Thus, delay increases linearly with load, and for a fixed number of stations delay is constant and finite even if all stations always have something to send. The delay for CSMA/CD is more difficult to express and depends on the exact nature of the protocol (persistence, retry policy). In general, we can say that the delay grows without bound as the system becomes saturated. As N increases, there are more collisions and longer contention intervals. Individual frames must make more attempts to achieve successful transmission. We explore this behavior further in the next station.

We now report the results of a deeper analysis done for the IEEE 802 committee [STUC85]. A similar analysis is also reported in [BUX81]. The analysis is based on considering not only mean values but second moments of delay and message length. Two cases of message arrival statistics are employed. In the first, only 1 station out of 100 has messages to transmit and is always ready to transmit. In such a case, one would hope that the network would not be the bottleneck, but could easily keep up with one station. In the second case, 100 stations out of 100 always have messages to transmit. This represents an extreme of congestion and one would expect that the network may be a bottleneck.

The results are shown in Figure 9.11. It shows the actual data transmission rate versus the transmission speed on a 2-km bus. Note that the abscissa is not offered load but the actual capacity of the medium. The 1 station or 100 stations provide enough input to utilize the network fully. Hence these plots are a measure of maximum potential utilization. Three systems are examined: token ring with a 1-bit latency per station, token bus, and CSMA/CD. The analysis yields the following conclusions:

- For the given parameters, the smaller the mean frame length, the greater the difference in maximum mean throughput rate between token passing and CSMA/CD. This reflects the strong dependence of CSMA/CD on a.
- Token ring is the least sensitive to work load.
- CSMA/CD offers the shortest delay under light load, while it is most sensitive under heavy load to the work load.

Note also that in the case of a single station transmitting, token bus is significantly less efficient than the other two protocols. This is so because the assumption is made that the propagation delay is longer than for token ring, and that the delay in token processing is greater than for token ring.

Another phenomenon of interest is seen most clearly in Figure 9.11b. For a CSMA/CD system under these conditions, the maximum effective throughput at 5 Mbps is only about 1.25 Mbps. If the expected load is, say, 0.75 Mbps, this configuration may be perfectly adequate. If, however, the load is expected to grow to 2 Mbps, raising the network data

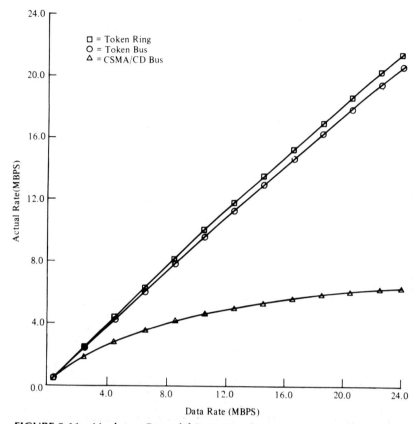

FIGURE 9.11a Maximum Potential Data Rate for LAN Protocols; 2000 bits per packet; 100 stations active out of 100 stations total

rate to 10 Mbps or even 20 Mbps will not accommodate the increase! The same conclusion, less precisely, can be drawn from the model presented at the beginning of this section.

As with all the other results presented in this chapter, these depend on the nature of the assumptions made and do not reflect accurately the nature of the real-world load. Nevertheless, they show in a striking manner the nature of the instability of CSMA/CD and the ability of token ring and token bus to continue to perform well in the face of overload conditions.

The Behavior of Contention Protocols

The preceding section revealed that CSMA/CD performs less well than token passing under increasing load or increasing *a*. This is characteristic of all contention protocols. In this section we explore this subject in

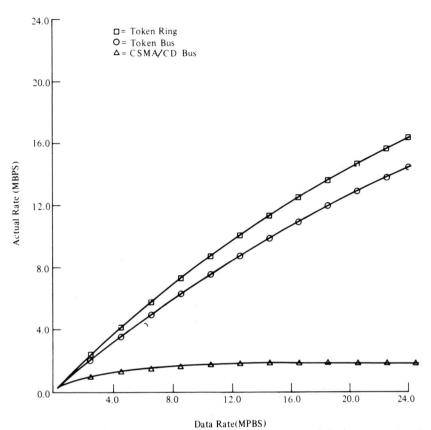

FIGURE 9.11b 500 bits per packet; 100 stations active out of 100 stations total

more detail for the interested reader. To do this, we present results based on the assumption that there is an infinite number of stations. This may strike the reader as an absurd tactic, but, in fact, it leads to analytically tractable equations that are, up to a point, very close to reality. We will define that point shortly. For now, we state the infinite-source assumption precisely: there is an infinite number of stations, each generating an infinitely small rate of frames such that the total number of frames generated per unit of time is finite.

The following additional assumptions are made:

1. All frames are of constant length. In general, such frames give better average throughput and delay performance than do variable-length frames. In some analyses, an exponential distribution of frame length is used.
2. The channel is noise-free.

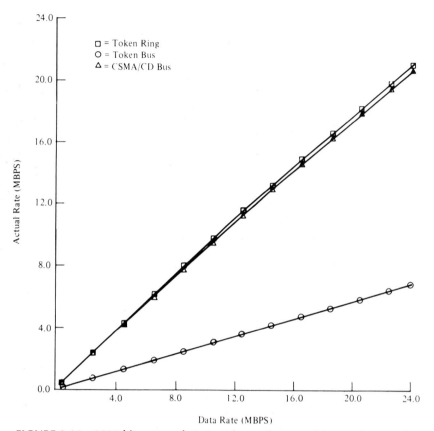

FIGURE 9.11c 2000 bits per packet; 1 station active out of 100 stations total

3. Frames do not collect at individual stations; that is, a station transmits each frame before the next arrives, hence $I = S$. This assumption weakens at higher loads, where stations are faced with increasing delays for each packet.
4. G, the offered load, is Poisson distributed.
5. For CSMA/CD, no time is lost for carrier sense and collision detection.

These assumptions do not accurately reflect any actual system. For example, higher-order moments or even the entire probability distribution of frame length or G may be needed for accurate results. These assumptions do provide analytic tractability, enabling the development of closed-form expressions for performance. Thus they provide a common basis for comparing a number of protocols and they allow the de-

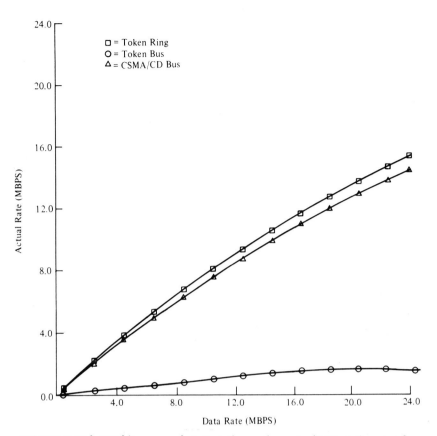

FIGURE 9.11d 500 bits per packet; 1 station active out of 100 stations total

velopment of results that give insight into the behavior of systems. In the following discussion, we shall cite simulation and measurement studies that indicate that these insights are valid.

Let us look first at the simplest contention protocol, pure ALOHA. Traffic, of course, is generated as so many frames per second. It is convenient to normalize this to the frame transmission time; then we can view S as the number of frames generated per frame time. Since the capacity of the channel is one frame per frame time, S also has the usual meaning of throughput as a fraction of capacity.

The total traffic on the channel will consist of new frames plus frames that must be retransmitted because of collision:

$$G = S$$
$$+ \text{(number of retransmitted frames per frame transmission time)}$$

Now, a frame must be retransmitted if it suffers a collision. Thus we can express the rate of retransmissions as $G•Pr$ [individual frame suffers a collision]. Note that we must use G rather than S in this expression. To determine the probability of collision, consider as a worst case, two stations, A and B, as far apart as possible on a bus (i.e., a normalized distance a, as in Figure 9.2). A frame transmitted by station A will suffer a collision if B begins transmission prior to A but within a time $1 + a$ of the beginning of A's transmission, or if B begins transmission after A within a time period $1 + a$ of the beginning of A's transmission. Thus the vulnerable period is of length $2(1 + a)$.

We have assumed that G is Poisson distributed. For a Poisson process with rate λ, the probability of an arrival in a period of time t is $1 - e^{-\lambda t}$. Thus the probability of an arrival during the vulnerable period is $1 - e^{-2(1 + a)G}$. Therefore, we have

$$G = S + G[1 - e^{-2(1 + a)G}]$$

So

$$ALOHA: \ S = Ge^{-2(1 + a)G} \tag{9.13}$$

This derivation assumes that G is Poisson, which is not the case even for I Poisson. However, studies indicate that this is a good approximation [SCHW77]. Also, deeper analysis indicates that the infinite population assumption results closely approximate finite population results at reasonably small numbers—say, 50 or more stations [KLEI76, PATE87]. This is also true for CSMA and CSMA/CD systems [TOBA80a, TOBA82].

Another way of deriving (9.13) is to note that S/G is the fraction of offered frames transmitted successfully, which is just the probability that for each frame, no additional frames arrive during the vulnerable period, which is $e^{-2(1 + a)G}$.

Throughput for slotted ALOHA is also easily calculated. All frames begin transmission on a slot boundary. Thus the number of frames transmitted during a slot time is equal to the number that was generated during the previous slot and await transmission. To avoid collisions between frames in adjacent slots, the slot length must equal frame transmission time plus propagation delay (i.e., $1 + a$). Thus the probability that an individual frame suffers collision is $1 - e^{-(1 + a)G}$. Thus we have:

$$S\text{-}ALOHA: \ S = Ge^{-(1 + a)G} \tag{9.14}$$

Differentiating (9.13) and (9.14) with respect to G, the maximum possible values for S are $1/[2e(1 + a)$ and $1/[e(1 + a)]$ respectively. These results differ from those reported in previous accounts of local network performance [TROP81, FRAN81], which ignore a and have $S = Ge^{-2G}$ for ALOHA and $S = Ge^{-G}$ for slotted ALOHA. The discrepancy arises because these formulas were originally derived for satellite channels, for which they are valid, but are often compared with CSMA-type protocols derived for local networks (e.g., [TOBA80b]). The results that correspond to $a = 0$ are plotted in Figure 9.12. For small values of $a(a \leq 0.01)$, these figures are adequate; but for comparison with CSMA protocols, equations (9.13) and (9.14) should be used.

Figure 9.12 provides insight into the nature of the instability problem with contention protocols. As offered load increases, so does throughput until, beyond its maximum value, throughput actually declines as G increases. This is because there is an increased frequency of collisions: more frames are offered, but fewer successfully escape collision. Worse, this situation may persist even if the input to the system drops to zero! Consider: For high G, virtually all offered frames are retransmissions and virtually none get through. So, even if no new frames are generated, the system will remain occupied in an unsuccessful attempt to clear the backlog; the effective capacity of the system is virtually zero. Thus, even in a moderately loaded system, a temporary burst of work could move the network into the high-collision region permanently. This type of instability is not possible with the noncontention protocols.

Delay is more difficult to calculate, but the following reasoning gives a good approximation. We define delay as the time interval from when a node is ready to transmit a frame until when it is successfully received. This delay is simply the sum of queueing delay, propagation delay, and transmission time. In ALOHA, the queueing delay is 0; that is, a node transmits immediately when it has a frame to transmit. However, because of collisions, we may consider the queueing delay time to be the total time consumed prior to successful transmission (i.e., the total time spent in unsuccessful transmissions). To get at this, we need to know the expected number of transmissions per frame. A little thought shows

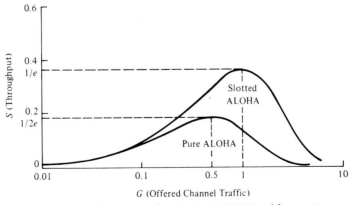

FIGURE 9.12   Performance of ALOHA, S-ALOHA with $a = 0$

that this is simply G/S. So the expected number of retransmissions per frame is just $G/S - 1 = e^{2(1 + a)G} - 1$. The delay D can then be expressed as

$$D = [e^{2(1 + a)G} - 1] \delta + a + 1$$

where δ is the average delay for one transmission. A common algorithm used for ALOHA is to retransmit after a time selected from a uniform distribution of from 1 to K frame-transmission times. This minimizes repeated collisions. The average delay is then $(K + 1)/2$. To this, we must add the amount of time a station must wait to determine that its frame was unsuccessful. This is just the time it would take to complete a transmission $(1 + a)$ plus the time it would take for the receiver to generate an acknowledgment (w) plus the propagation time for the acknowledgment to reach the station (a). For simplicity, we assume that acknowledgment packets do not suffer collisions. Thus:

$$ALOHA: D = [e^{2(1 + a)G} - 1] \left(1 + 2a + w + \frac{K + 1}{2} \right) + a + 1 \quad (9.15)$$

For S-ALOHA, a similar reasoning obtains. The main difference now is that there is a delay, averaging half a slot time between the time a node is ready to send a frame and the time the next slot begins:

$$S\text{-}ALOHA: D = [e^{(1 + a)G} - 1] \left(1 + 2a \right.$$

$$\left. + w + \frac{K + 1}{2} \right) + 1.5\, a + 1.5 \quad (9.16)$$

These formulas confirm the instability of contention-based protocols under heavy load. As the rate of new frames increases, so does the number of collisions. We can see that both the number of collisions and the average delay grow exponentially with G. Thus there is not only a trade-off between throughput (S) and delay (D), but a third factor enters the trade-off: stability. Figure 9.13 illustrates this point. Figure 9.13a shows that delay increases exponentially with offered load. But Figure 9.13b is perhaps more meaningful. It shows that delay increases with throughput up to the maximum possible throughput. Beyond that point, although throughput declines because of increased numbers of collisions, the delay continues to rise.

It is worth pondering Figures 9.12 and 9.13 to get a better feeling for the behavior of contention channels. Recall that we mentioned that both S and G are derived parameters, and what we would really like to estimate is the actual traffic generated by network devices, the input load I. As long as the input load is less than the maximum potential throughput, $Max_G(S)$, then $I = S$. That is, the throughput of the system equals the input load. Therefore, all frames get through. However, if $I >$

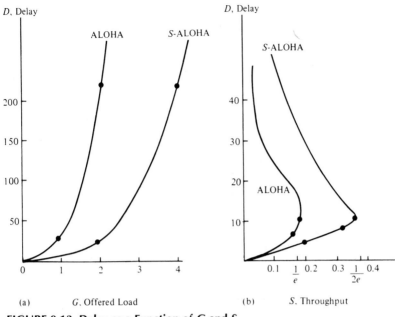

FIGURE 9.13 Delay as a Function of G and S

$Max_G(S)$, Figures 9.12 and 9.13 no longer apply. The system cannot transmit frames as fast as they arrive. The result: if I remains above the threshold indefinitely, then D goes to infinity, S goes to zero, and G grows without bound.

Figure 9.13b shows that, for a given value of S, there are two possible values of D. How can this be? In both cases, $I = S$, and the system is transmitting all input frames. The explanation is as follows: as the input, $I = S$, approaches the saturation point, the stochastic nature of the input will eventually lead to a period of a high rate of collisions, resulting in decreased throughput and higher frame delays.

Finally, we mention that these results depend critically on the assumptions made. For example, if there is only one station transmitting, then the achievable throughput is 1.0, not 0.18 or 0.37. Indeed, with a single user at a high data rate and a set of other users at very low data rates, utilization approaching 1 can be achieved. However, the delay encountered by the other users is significantly longer than in the homogeneous case. In general, the more unbalanced the source rates, the higher the throughput [KLEI76].

We now turn to the CSMA protocols. A similar line of reasoning can be used to derive closed-form analytic results as is done with ALOHA and S-ALOHA. Perhaps the clearest derivations can be found in

[LABA78]. The same or similar results can be found in [KLEI75], [KLEI76], [SCHW77], [HERR79], [TOBA80a], [TOBA82], and [HEYM82].

Figure 9.14 compares the various contention protocols for $a = 0.01$ and 0.05. Note the dramatic improvement in throughput of the various CSMA schemes over ALOHA. Also note the decline in performance for increased a. This is seen more clearly in Figure 9.15 [TAKA85]. As expected, the performance of all CSMA schemes declines with increasing a since the period of vulnerability grows. For high enough values of a, say 0.5 to 1.0, the slotted protocols approach S-ALOHA, and the unslotted protocols approach ALOHA. At these values, neither the carrier sense nor the collision detection are of much use. Thus the distributed reservation protocol for MANs in Chapter 6 does not suffer by using S-ALOHA rather than CSMA to contend for reservations.

Figure 9.16 shows delay as a function of throughput. As can be seen, CSMA/CD offers significant delay and throughput improvements over CSMA at $a = 0.05$. As a increases, these protocols converge with each other and with S-ALOHA.

One of the critical assumptions used in deriving all these results is that the number of sources is infinite. The validity of the assumption can be seen in Figure 9.10. Note that for small values of a, the efficiency of the system with a finite number of stations differs little from that achieved as the number of stations grows to infinity. For larger values of a, the differences are more marked. The figure shows that the infinite-population assumption underestimates efficiency but is still a good approximation.

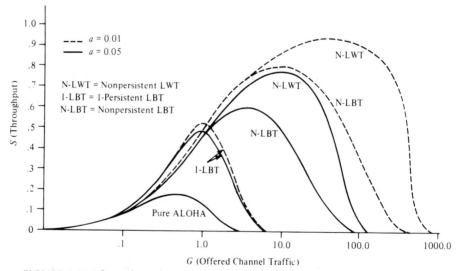

FIGURE 9.14 Throughput for Various Contention Protocols

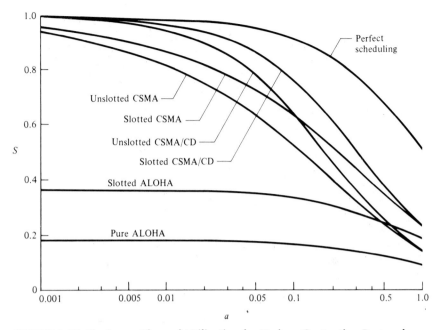

FIGURE 9.15 Maximum Channel Utilization for Various Contention Protocols

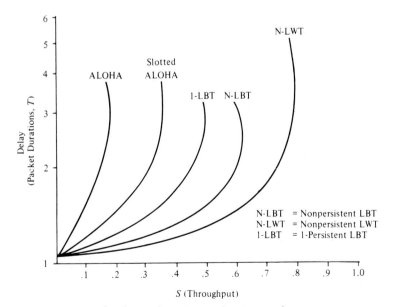

FIGURE 9.16 Delay for Various Contention Protocols

A second assumption that is unrealistic is that of fixed frame sizes. While a local network could enforce fixed frame sizes, this is clearly inefficient if the messages are of variable length. One common situation is to have one long frame size for file transfer and a shorter size for interactive traffic and acknowledgments. Now, as frame length decreases, *a* increases, so if all frames were short, then the utilization would be less than if all frames were long. Presumably, with a mixture of the two traffic types, the efficiency would be somewhere in between. This has been shown to be the case in [TOBA80a]. The analysis also showed that only a small percentage of longer frames is sufficient to achieve close to the higher throughput of the case of long frames only. However, this increased throughput is to the detriment of the throughput and delay characteristics of the shorter frames. In effect, they are crowded out.

A final point about the foregoing derivations: all represent analytic models of local network performance. Greater validity can be achieved through simulation, where some of the assumptions may be relaxed, and through actual performance measurement. In general, these efforts tend to confirm the validity of the analytic models. Although not entirely accurate, these models provide a good feel for the behavior of the network. Interested readers may consult [TASA86, LABA78, SHOC80a, MARA82, AIME79, OREI82, BEVE88, GONS88, MOLL87]. A general discussion of CSMA/CD modeling techniques is contained in [ROUN83].

Comparative Performance of Ring Protocols

It is far more difficult to do a comparative performance of the three major ring protocols than the comparison of bus and token ring protocols. The results depend critically on a number of parameters unique to each protocol. For example:

- *Token ring:* size of token, token processing time
- *Slotted ring:* slot size, overhead bits per slot
- *Register insertion:* register size

Thus it is difficult to do a comparison, and although there have been a number of studies on each one of the techniques [TROP81, PENN79], few have attempted pairwise comparisons, much less a three-way analysis. Given this unfortunate situation, this section will merely attempt to summarize the most significant comparative studies.

The most systematic work in this area has been done by two different groups: Hammond and O'Reilly [HAMM86], and Liu and his associates [LIU78, LIU82]. We report on the results of the former; those of the latter are virtually identical. The analysis compares token ring, slotted ring, and register insertion. The following parameters are varied:

- Number of stations: 10, 100
- Value of a: 1.0, 0.1
- Ratio of header size to data size for slotted ring: 1, 0

Figure 9.17 summarizes the results. They show that register insertion is best for a small number of stations or under low loads. Token ring seems to have the best performance under a variety of conditions. Note also that register insertion appears to be able to carry a load greater than 1.0; this is because the protocol permits multiple frames to circulate.

Bux performed an analysis comparing token ring, slotted ring, and CSMA/CD [BUX81]. This careful analysis produced several important conclusions. First, the delay-throughput performance of token ring versus CSMA/CD confirms our earlier discussion. That is, token ring suffers greater delay than CSMA/CD does at light load but less delay and stable throughput at heavy loads. Further, token ring has superior delay characteristics to slotted ring. The poorer performance of slotted ring seems to have two causes: (1) the relative overhead in the small slots of a slotted ring is very high, and (2) the time needed to pass empty slots around the ring to guarantee fair bandwidth is significant. Bux also reports several positive features of slotted ring: (1) the expected delay for a message is proportional to length (i.e., shorter packets get better service than long ones), and (2) overall mean delay is independent of packet length distribution. Bux extended his analysis to include register insertion [BUX83], achieving results comparable to Liu's.

Another study of token ring versus slotted ring is reported in [CHEN82]. Cheng's results confirm those of Bux; that is, the delay of slotted ring exceeds that of token ring. Interestingly, Cheng also showed that the performance of the ring improves as the number of slots increases at least to equal the number of nodes. However, for local area networks, which typically have $a < 1$, a multiple-slot ring is achieved only by having very small slots or artificial delays. With smaller slots, the overhead is proportionally greater.

Finally, we mention a study reported in [YU81], which also concluded that insertion ring had shorter delays than token ring. In this study, Yu looked at a ring with a data rate of 100 Mbps over a 5-km distance. The distribution of packet size was assumed to be bimodal, with half having a length of 4 Kbytes and half with a length of 100 bytes. Thus the value of a, using average packet size, was about 0.125.

It is difficult to draw conclusions from the efforts made so far. The slotted ring seems to be the least desirable over a broad range of parameter values, owing to the considerable overhead associated with each small packet. For example, the Cambridge ring, which is the ring most

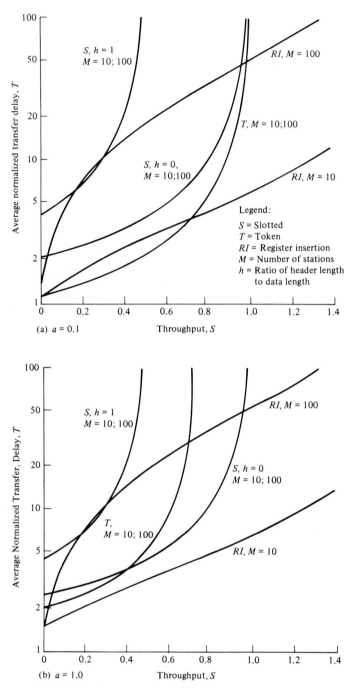

(a) $a = 0.1$

(b) $a = 1.0$

FIGURE 9.17 Delay for Various Ring Protocols

widely available commercially in Europe, uses a 37-bit slot with only 16 data bits! The designers of the Cambridge ring originally started out with register insertion but rejected it for slotted ring. The sole reason seems to have been reliability: a fault developing in a shift register can disrupt the entire ring [WILK79].

As between token ring and register insertion, the evidence suggests that at least for some sets of parameter values, register insertion gives superior delay performance. Interestingly, there are very few commercially available register insertion products. On the other hand, token ring in the United States, with a boost from IEEE 802 and IBM, and slotted ring in Europe, where many firms have licensed the Cambridge slotted ring, seem destined to dominate the marketplace.

The primary advantage of register insertion is the potentially high utilization it can achieve. In contrast with token ring, multiple stations can be transmitting at a time. Further, a station can transmit as soon as a gap opens up on the ring; it need not wait for a token. On the other hand, the propagation time around the ring is not constant, but depends on the amount of traffic.

A final point in comparing token ring and register insertion. Under light loads, register insertion operates more efficiently, resulting in slightly less delay. However, both systems perform adequately. Our real interest is under heavy load. A typical LAN will have $a < 1$, usually $a \ll 1$, so that a transmitting station on a token ring will append a token to the end of its packet. Under heavy load, a nearby station will be able to use the token. Thus about 100% utilization is achieved, and there is no particular advantage to register insertion.

9.3

MAN PERFORMANCE

There has been considerably less material published on MAN performance, compared to that on LAN performance. The principles, of course, remain the same. In this section, we look at some of the key performance aspects of FDDI and DQDB and at a comparative study of the two protocols.

FDDI Performance

One of the key performance factors for FDDI is TTRT, the target token rotation time. Recall from Chapter 6 that this parameter, negotiated among all participating stations, defines the expected time for successive sighting of a token by a station when the ring is busy. Since this parameter is set by user action, it is important to understand its effect on performance.

The FDDI standard specifies a number of rules for the selection of TTRT:

1. The token rotation time can be as twice the TTRT. Thus, a station with synchronous data to transmit may suffer a delay of up to 2 × TTRT. Therefore, a station requiring a guaranteed response time should request a TTRT value of one-half the required response time.

2. Each station has a parameter T_Min, which is the minimum value of TTRT that may be requested. T_Min may be set by station management (see Chapter 11) dynamically or it may be configured as a default value. The maximum default value of T_Min is 4 ms. That is, if stations are configured with a default value of T_Min, that value may not exceed 4 ms.

3. Each station has a parameter T_Max, which is the maximum value of TTRT that may be requested. T_Max may be set by station management (see Chapter 11) dynamically or it may be configured as a default value. The minimum default value of T_Min in basic mode is 165 ms, and the minimum default value in hybrid mode is 670 ms.

Within these constraints, TTRT should be chosen to optimize performance. We now consider some aspects of effect of TTRT on performance.

A simple analytic model for the effect of TTRT has been reported in [JAIN91]. In what follows, we summarize the derivation of this model and the key results.

Consider an FDDI ring with the following parameters:

$$D = \text{ring latency; total time}$$
$$\text{for a token to circulate the}$$
$$\text{ring in the absence of data traffic}$$
$$N = \text{number of stations on the ring}$$
$$T = \text{negotiated value of TTRT}$$

We will show that the following equations hold:

$$U = \frac{N \times (TTRT - D)}{(N \times TTRT) + D} \tag{9.17}$$

$$\text{Maximum access delay} = (N - 1) \times TTRT + 2D \tag{9.18}$$

Let us first demonstrate that this relationship holds for a ring with three stations. Figure 9.18 shows the ring and illustrates a sequence of events. Time proceeds vertically down the page. The token is shown as a thick horizontal line, and a frame transmission is indicated by a thick

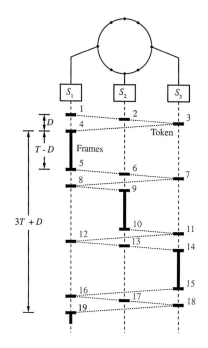

FIGURE 9.18 Sequence of Events for 3-Station FDDI Network

line along the time axis. We assume that, initially, all three stations are idle until $t + D$, when the three stations suddenly have a large number of asynchronous frames to send. The sequence of events is as follows:

1. $t = 0$. Station S_1 sees the token and resets its token rotation time (TRT). Since the station has no data to send, it does not capture the token, which proceeds around the ring.
2. $t = t_{12}$. Station S_2 resets its TRT and allows the token to pass.
3. $t = t_{13}$. Station S_3 resets its TRT and allows the token to pass.
4. $t = D$. Station S_1 captures the token. Its value of TRT is D, so it can hold the token and transmit data for a time $T - \text{TRT} = T - D$.
5. $t = T$. The token holding timer (THT) expires at S_1 and it issues a token.
6. $t = T + t_{12}$. Station S_2 observes the token. The elapsed time since its last sighting is T, so it is unable to transmit any asynchronous frames. The token is allowed to pass.
7. $t = T + t_{13}$. Station S_3 must also allow the token to pass.
8. $t = T + D$. Station S_1 must also allow the token to pass.
9. $t = T + D + t_{12}$. Station S_1 captures the token. Its value of TRT

is D, so it can hold the token and transmit data for a time $T - TRT = T - D$.

10. $t = T + D + t_{12} + (T - D) = 2T + t_{12}$. The token holding timer (THT) expires at S_1 and it issues a token.

The remainder of the steps are easily followed. The illustration ends at $t = 3T + D$. We can see that the system goes through a cycle in which each station can transmit for a total time of $T - D$, and the total elapsed time is $3T + D$. As long as each station has unlimited asynchronous frames to transmit, the cycle will repeat. During each cycle, the total time spent transmitting is $3(T - D)$. During each cycle, each station waits for an interval of $2T + 2D$ after releasing the token. This interval is the maximum access delay; it will be less at lower loads. Thus, for a ring with three active stations, the efficiency and maximum access delay under heavy load are:

$$U = \frac{3 \times (T - D)}{(3 \times T) + D}$$

$$\text{Maximum access delay} = (3 - 1) \times T + 2D$$

The above analysis can be generalized to N stations. Equations 9.17 and 9.18 can be used to compute the utilization and maximum access delay for any FDDI ring configuration. For example, consider a ring with 16 stations and a total fiber length of 20 km. Light travels along fiber at a speed of 5.085 μs/km, and a typical repeater delay is 1 μs. The ring latency can therefore be calculated as follows:

$$D = (20 \times 5.085) + (16 \times 1) = 0.12 \text{ ms}$$

Assuming a TTRT of 5 ms, and all 16 stations active, we have:

$$U = \frac{16 \times (5 - 0.12)}{(16 \times 5) + 0.12} = 0.975$$

$$\text{Maximum access delay} = (16 - 1) \times 5 + 2 \times 0.12 = 75.24 \text{ ms}$$

Figure 9.19 shows the effect of TTRT on utilization. Three configurations are considered:

1. *Typical:* Consists of 20 single-attachment stations (SASs) on a 4-km ring. This would be sufficient to interconnect a number of LANs and computers in a single office building. The ring latency for this configuration is about 0.04 ms.
2. *Big:* Consists of 100 SASs on a 100-km ring. The ring latency for this configuration is about 0.6 ms.
3. *Maximum:* Consists of 500 dual-attachment, dual-MAC stations (one MAC entity in each direction) on a 200-km ring. The ring latency for this configuration is about 2 ms.

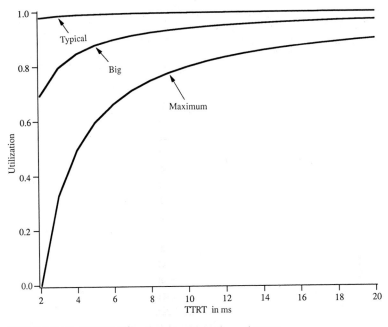

FIGURE 9.19 FDDI Utilization as a Function of TTRT

The figure shows that efficiency is low at values close to ring latency and increases as TTRT increases. This is intuitively reasonable: if TTRT is very small, then on many token circulations, many of the stations will have to let the token pass. Note also that beyond a certain point increases in TTRT bring very little increase in utilization. Of course, as might also be expected, as the utilization of the ring increases, there are increasing congestion and queueing delays for stations to transmit. This effect is shown in Figure 9.20. Thus, there is a trade-off in setting TTRT between efficient utilization of the ring and minimizing delay to active stations.

DQDB Performance

As with FDDI, there is a key user–settable parameter in DQDB that has a significant effect on performance: the bandwidth balancing modulus.

Recall from Chapter 6 that a node, without bandwidth balancing, may use an empty QA slot if it has placed a reservation and there are no downstream reservations in line ahead of it. With bandwidth balancing, after every BWB_MOD QA segments transmitted, a node must let an extra free QA slot pass, where BWB_MOD is the bandwidth balancing modulus.

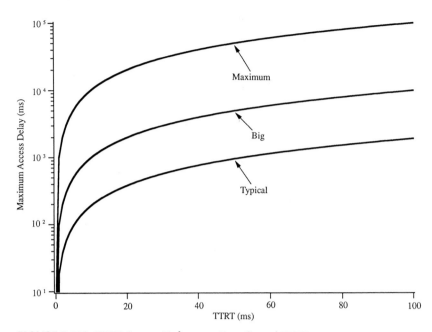

FIGURE 9.20* FDDI Access Delay as a Function of TTRT

To get a feel for the effect of BWB_MOD on performance, let us consider the following set of conditions, which yield maximum subnetwork throughput:

- No station has any PA traffic.
- Every station has QA traffic ready to transmit at all times.
- All QA segments have the same priority.
- All nodes have the same value for BWB_MOD.

Define

$$\gamma = \text{throughput of any one node}$$
$$N = \text{number of nodes}$$
$$\beta = \text{value of BWB\_MOD}$$

Recall that the maximum throughput of a node is limited by $\dfrac{\beta}{1 + \beta}$. We can express the throughput of a node as the amount of capacity not used by the other nodes, subject to the limitation. Therefore:

$$\gamma = \frac{\beta}{1 + \beta} \times [1 - (N - 1) \times \gamma]$$

Solving for γ:

$$\gamma = \frac{1}{N + (1/\beta)}$$

Thus the total normalized throughput, or utilization, for a bus with N stations is:

$$U = \frac{N}{N + (1/\beta)}$$

Figure 9.21 plots utilization as a function of the number of stations for various values of BWB_MOD. The smaller the value of BWB_MOD, the greater the number of slots that each station will let pass unused. Accordingly, the smaller the value of BWB_MOD, the lower the utilization. On the other hand, increasing the number of stations increases utilization, since there is an increased opportunity for passed slots to be used downstream.

Comparative Performance of FDDI and DQDB

As yet, little work has been reported on comparing the performance of FDDI and DQDB. As the figures of this section suggest, both schemes

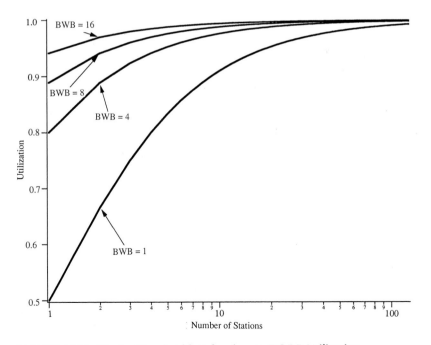

FIGURE 9.21* Effect of Bandwidth Balancing on DQDB Utilization

are capable of achieving very high levels of utilization. This is important because the high speed and large extent of these networks make efficient utilization difficult to achieve.

One of the few analyses that has been published is reported in [DRAV91]. Similar but less detailed results were reported in [NEWM88] and [RODR90].

Figure 9.22 shows the results reported in [DRAV91]. The figures assume a mixed application environment of interactive and bulk file transfer applications, with all stations uniformly loaded with 20% of the load from the file transfer application. A distinction is made between short packets generated by interactive applications and long packets generated by file transfer. In the case of FDDI, a short packet is transferred in a short frame; a long packet is transferred in one or a very few large frames. In the case of DQDB, a short packet is carried in a single QA slot; a long packet requires a number of QA slots. The figure yields several interesting results:

- DQDB provides much less delay for short packets for both network sizes. This is because, with multiple QA segments, a node must wait until one segment is transmitted before reserving for the next segment, and then must wait for a free slot after all intervening downstream reservations have been satisfied.
- Utilization above about 80% causes long queueing delays for all

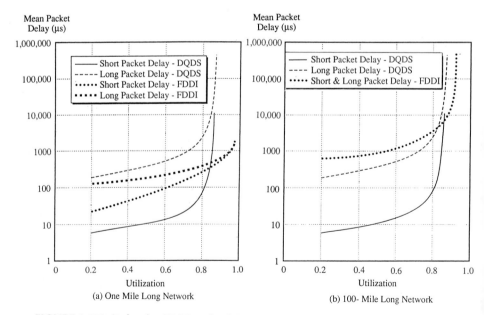

FIGURE 9.22* Delay for FDDI and DQDB

DQDB traffic, whereas a small FDDI network can sustain higher utilization.
- DQDB appears to be better suited to interactive traffic, whereas FDDI is better suited to bulk traffic.

9.4
END-TO-END PERFORMANCE

So far, we have been concerned with the throughput and delay performance for transmitting packets over a LAN or MAN. Some useful insights have been gained and techniques developed for estimating that performance. Alas, this is of no concern to the local network user. The user is concerned with *end-to-end* performance. Examples:

- Two hosts regularly exchange large files. What is the end-to-end throughput rate during file transfer?
- A user at a terminal is querying a data base on a host. What is the delay from the end of query entry to the beginning of response?

Consider the steps involved in sending data from one host to another. In general terms, we have:

1. Process in source host initiates transfer.
2. Host system software transfers data to NIU.
3. Source NIU transfers data to destination NIU.
4. Destination NIU transfers data to destination host.
5. Host system software accepts data, notifies destination process.
6. Destination process accepts data.

Each of these steps involves some processing and the use of a resource potentially shared by others. What we have discussed so far, and the focus of virtually all local network performance studies, is step 3.

To get a handle on end-to-end performance, the analyst must model the NIU, the host–NIU link, and the host, as well as the NIU–NIU link. This requires the development of computer system performance models. Although these techniques have been around for a while, one of the few attempts to apply these principles systematically to local network performance has been undertaken by a group at CONTEL Information Systems [LISS81, MAGL80, MAGL81, MAGL82, MITC81, MITC86]. We summarize their approach in this section.

The discussion will be with reference to Figure 9.23. As mentioned earlier, the total delay, say, from the time a message is generated at node A by some application until it reaches node B, is just the sum of the delays encountered at each step. Each such step can be modeled using queueing theory. A queueing situation arises when a "customer" arrives

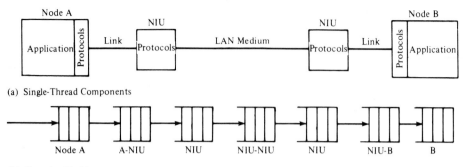

(a) Single-Thread Components

(b) Queueing Model

FIGURE 9.23 End-to-end Local Network Performance Model

at a service facility and, finding it busy, is forced to wait. The delay incurred by a customer is just the time spent waiting in the queue plus the time for service. The delay depends on the pattern of arriving traffic and the characteristics of the server. Table 9.3 summarizes some simple results. Results for more complex cases may be found in [MART72].

The system depicted in Figure 9.23 consists of a set of single-server queueing systems in tandem, that is, the output of one queue is the input to the next. In the general case, it is a complex task to characterize the behavior of this system, and closed-form analytic solutions do not exist. However, there is a theorem (Jackson's theorem) stating that under certain conditions each node in the network of queues can be treated independently. Thus the delay at each queue can be calculated separately and summed to give an overall figure. The assumptions [JACK63]:

- Work arrives from outside the system with a Poisson distribution.
- Exponential service time at each node is with a first-come, first-served policy.
- No saturated queues: queues are large enough to hold the maximum number of waiting customers.

There is some evidence that networks of the type we are discussing, which may violate these assumptions, are nevertheless closely approximated by the decomposition approach [MAGL81]. Furthermore, the assumption of exponential service time usually results in upper bounds to delays; thus the analysis will give conservative estimates.

Solving for total delay is thus computationally simple. Starting with the first queue, and given an arrival rate λ, the delay at that step is determined. As long as $\rho = \lambda S \leq 1$, the queue is stable and the output rate is equal to the input rate. This now becomes the input to the second stage, and so on. For a stable system, we must have

$$\lambda \leq \frac{1}{\text{Max}[S_i]}$$

TABLE 9.3   Isolated Queues

Parameters

w = mean number of items waiting for service (not including items being served)

q = mean number of items in system (waiting and being served)

t_w = mean time item spends waiting for service

t_q = mean time item spends in system, waiting and being served

ρ = utilization: fraction of time a server is busy

S = mean service time for an item

Assumption: Poisson arrivals with parameter λ, exponential service times

$$w = \frac{\rho^2}{1-\rho}$$

$$q = \frac{\rho}{1-\rho}$$

$$t_w = \frac{\rho S}{1-\rho}$$

$$t_q = \frac{S}{1-\rho}$$

$$\rho = \lambda S$$

This represents the maximum achievable throughput. As long as this condition is satisfied, the total delay for a message over N stages is simply

$$D = \sum_{i=1}^{N} D_i$$

Now, let us begin with the first stage, node A. Node A must perform a number of tasks related to the passing of a message, including applications processing and the processing for the various protocol layers. These tasks may have various priorities with preemptive interrupts allowed. For each class of task, the queueing equation is

$$t_{qj} = \frac{1}{1 - \sum_{i=1}^{j-1} \rho_i} \left\{ \frac{\sum_{i=1}^{j} \rho_i S_i}{1 - \sum_{i=1}^{j} \rho_i} + S_j \right\}$$

where $\rho_i = \lambda_1 S_i$.

To solve this equation, we need values for the λ_i and S_i. The λ_i depend on the rate at which messages are generated; this should become clear in the example below. The S_i can be approximated by estimating the execution path length of each service routine and dividing by the effective instruction per second rate of the processor. Since other activities, such as disk I/O, may be handled by the processor, its raw instruction execution rate needs to be modified by some overhead factor.

The next delay encountered is the communications link between node A and its NIU. This delay will depend on the nature of the interface. As an example, consider a half-duplex line with a given interface transfer rate. Here there are two classes of arrivals for a single server: node-to-NIU and NIU-to-node traffic. The λ_i ($i = 1, 2$) depend on the rate at which messages arrive for transmission across the link. The service time in either direction (S_1, S_2) is just the average message length divided by the data rate. It is easy to see that, assuming no priorities,

$$\rho = \lambda_1 S_1 + \lambda_2 S_2$$

$$S = \frac{\rho}{\lambda_1 + \lambda_2}$$

where S is the overall average service time. Then

$$t_{qj} = t_w + S_j$$

$$= \frac{\rho S}{1 - \rho} + S_j \qquad j = 1, 2$$

The NIU is the next source of delay and may be modeled in the same fashion as node A. Next comes the local network itself. The delay at this stage depends on the topology (ring, bus, or tree) and the medium access protocol. Sections 9.2 and 9.3 are devoted to developing results in this area. The remainder of the steps are symmetric with those already discussed and they need not be described.

Two refinements to the model above: First, an NIU often has multiple ports. Hence the arrival rate of work at an NIU consists of the rates from multiple hosts. This must be taken into account. Second, the node-NIU link may be multiplexed so that arrivals are from multiple remote nodes.

As an example, we consider an analysis reported in [MITC81]. In this example, node A is a host and node B is an intelligent workstation. Within node A, there is some application program exchanging messages with the workstation. There are five main classes of activities associated with the application. We assume that these are serviced by the host on a preemptive resume basis. The activities, in descending order of priority:

1. *Link-in:* link level functions for messages inbound from the NIU.
2. *Link-out:* link level functions for messages outbound to the NIU.
3. *Protocols-in:* higher-level protocol functions for inbound messages.
4. *Protocols-out:* higher-level protocol functions for outbound messages.
5. *Application:* application processing.

The host/NIU interface is assumed to have an effective transfer rate of 800 kbps, while the workstation/NIU interface is 9.6 kbps. This would be the case for an integrated host NIU and a stand-alone terminal NIU.

The NIU is assumed to implement up through the transport layer with the following priorities:

1. Network link-in
2. Node link-in
3. Network link-out
4. Node link-out
5. Higher-layer protocols

Finally, a nonpersistent CSMA/CD bus system operating at 1.544 Mbps is assumed.

The results are summarized in Table 9.4, which shows that, within the moderate utilization range of the bus, the bus contributes only 5% of the delay. The implication, confirmed by the other studies referenced earlier, is that the effect of the topology and medium access control on overall delay is negligible until the medium approaches saturation. In Section 9.2, we outlined a quick and simple means of estimating the saturation point. It is clearly desirable to operate below that point and, while operating below that point, only a rough approximation of the delay due to the medium will suffice.

Nevertheless, we have devoted considerable space to looking at the performance of various topology/MAC approaches. This is so because the saturation points for different approaches are different. But it needs to be pointed out that beyond the determination of a saturation point, the focus of activity should be the broader end-to-end delay issue.

This section has touched only briefly on the techniques for end-to-end delay analysis. The interested reader is referred to [MART67], [SAUE81], [KOBA78], and [IBM71].

9.5

RECOMMENDED READING

Books on the subject of LAN/MAN performance include [STUC85], [HAMM86], and [TASA86]. [LI87] is a special issue of the *IEEE Journal on Selected Areas in Communications* devoted to performance of broadcast networks, especially LANs. [KLEI86] presents a clever graphical technique for analyzing the effect of *a*. [GOOD88] is a careful study of CSMA/CD taking into account the use of binary exponential backoff. [TAKA88] is a rigorous analysis of polling schemes in general, with application to token bus and token ring. An interesting analysis of end-to-

TABLE 9.4   End-to-End Delay, CSMA/CD Network

Traffic Parameters
  Arrival rate: 0.017 message per second
  Aggregate load: 100,000 bps

CSMA/CD Parameters
  Propagation: 30 μs
  Retransmission interval: 5

MSG Lengths
  Input: 800 characters
  Output: 12,000 characters

I/F Transfer Rates
  Host: 800,000 bps
  Workstation: 9600 bps

Protocol Path-Length Parameters
  Node protocols
  Send: 12,000 instructions
  Receive: 12,000 instructions

  Node access link layer
  Send: 75 instructions
  Receive: 75 instructions

  Network access link layer
  Send: 75 instructiions
  Receive: 75 instructions

  TCP/IP: 12,000

  Multiprogram level: 32

Processor Capacities
  Host: 1.100 MIPS
  BIU: 0.615 MIPS
  Workstation: 0.115 MIPS

Host application program path length: 50,000 instructions
Cable utilization: 0.0565
Total normalized traffic, including retransmissions: 0.06

Delay Categories

Throughput	Response	Host	HI/F	WI/F	HBIU	WBIU	W/S	Cable
0.50	2.0066	0.04	0.01	0.84	0.01	0.02	0.02	0.05
1.00	2.0252	0.04	0.01	0.84	0.01	0.02	0.02	0.05
1.50	2.0444	0.04	0.01	0.84	0.01	0.02	0.02	0.05
2.00	2.0645	0.04	0.01	0.84	0.01	0.02	0.02	0.05
2.50	2.0853	0.04	0.01	0.83	0.02	0.02	0.02	0.05
3.00	2.1071	0.04	0.01	0.83	0.02	0.02	0.02	0.05
3.50	2.1298	0.04	0.01	0.83	0.02	0.02	0.02	0.05
4.00	2.1536	0.04	0.01	0.83	0.02	0.02	0.02	0.05
4.50	2.1785	0.05	0.01	0.83	0.02	0.02	0.02	0.05
5.00	2.2047	0.05	0.01	0.83	0.02	0.02	0.02	0.05
5.50	2.2324	0.05	0.01	0.83	0.02	0.02	0.02	0.05
6.00	2.2616	0.05	0.01	0.82	0.03	0.02	0.02	0.05
6.50	2.2927	0.05	0.01	0.82	0.03	0.02	0.02	0.05
7.00	2.3259	0.05	0.01	0.82	0.03	0.02	0.02	0.05
7.50	2.3615	0.06	0.01	0.82	0.03	0.01	0.02	0.05
8.00	2.4001	0.06	0.01	0.81	0.03	0.01	0.03	0.05
8.50	2.4424	0.06	0.01	0.81	0.03	0.01	0.03	0.05
9.00	2.4892	0.06	0.01	0.80	0.04	0.01	0.03	0.05
9.50	2.5423	0.07	0.01	0.79	0.04	0.01	0.03	0.05
10.00	2.6041	0.07	0.01	0.78	0.05	0.01	0.03	0.05

Source: [MITC81]

end performance is [MITC86]. Similar results are reported in [MURA88], [BUX84], and [WONG84].

[BERT92] and [SPRA91] cover network performance more generally, but have interesting and worthwhile sections on LAN/MAN performance.

As a balance to the many works on LAN/MAN performance, it is worthwhile to read [SMIT91], which compares some of the assumptions about LAN behavior underlying most analytic and simulation studies against empirical data on the actual behavior of some networks. The results indicate that there may be some cause for concern about the validity of many models when heavy loads are analyzed.

9.6

PROBLEMS

9.1 Equation (9.1) is valid for token ring and baseband bus. What is an equivalent expression for
  a. Broadband bus?
  b. Slotted ring?
  c. Register insertion ring?
  d. Broadband tree (use several different configurations)?

9.2 Develop a display similar to Figure 9.6 that shows throughput as a function of N.

9.3 Derive equations similar to (9.10) and (9.11) for the case where there are two types of frames, one 10 times as long as the other, that are transmitted with equal probability by each station.

9.4 Consider a 10-Mbps, 1-km bus, with N stations and frame size $= F$. Determine throughput and delay for token bus and throughput for CSMA/CD:
  a. $N = 10, F = 1000$
  b. $N = 100, F = 1000$
  c. $N = 10, F = 10{,}000$
  d. $N = 100, F = 10{,}000$.

9.5 Compare equations (9.1), (9.10), and (9.11). Under what circumstances does the throughput for the latter two equations exceed the theoretical maximum of (9.1)? Explain.

9.6 For the graphs in Figure 9.11, determine a and comment on the results.

9.7 Demonstrate that the number of stations and offered load affect performance independently for the following protocols:
  a. CSMA/CD
  b. Collision avoidance
  c. Token bus

     d. Token ring

     e. Slotted ring

     f. Register insertion

     g. Reservation

9.8 Consider an S-ALOHA system with a finite number of stations N and $a = 0$. The offered load from each station is G_1, the throughput S_i. Derive an equation for S as a function of G_i. Assume that the G_i are identical; what is the equation for S? Verify that this approaches Ge^{-G} as $N \to \infty$. Above what value of N is the difference negligible?

9.9 Demonstrate that CSMA/CD is biased toward long transmissions.

9.10 Show that, for $a = 0$, the following relationship holds for 1-persistent CSMA

$$S = \frac{G(1 + G)e^{-G}}{G + e^{-G}}$$

9.11 The performance of CSMA/CD depends on whether the collision detection is performed at the same site as the transmission (baseband) or at a time later whose average is a (broadband). What would you expect the relative performance to be?

9.12 Let $T_{msg}(K) = 0.1$ s and $T_{over} = 0.1$ s for a 50-station token system. Assume that all stations always have something to transmit. Compute C, $R(K)$, and $UTIL(K)$. What is the percentage of overhead? Now let $T_{over} = 0.2$. What is the percentage of overhead?

9.13 Consider the conditions extant at the end of Problem 9.12. Assume that individual stations may be busy or idle. What is the cycle time C? Now halve the overhead ($T_{over} = 0.1$). What is the cycle time C?

9.14 For equation (9.7), let the number of stations be two. Plot $R(2)$ versus $R(1)$ and show the admissible mean throughput rates. Interpret the result in terms of relative static priority policies.

9.15 Do an asymptotic breakpoint analysis for CSMA/CD.

9.16 Equations (9.10) and (9.12) are valid for token ring and for token baseband bus. What are equivalent equations for broadband bus?

9.17 For equations 9.17 and 9.18, consider the special cases of one active station ($N = 1$) and a large number of active stations (N approaches ∞). Discuss the resulting equations.

CHAPTER 10

Internetworking

In many, perhaps most, cases a local network will not be an isolated entity. An organization may have more than one type of local network at a given site to satisfy a spectrum of needs. An organization may have local networks at various sites and need them to be interconnected for central control of distributed information exchange. And an organization may need to provide a connection for one or more terminals and hosts on a local network to other computing resources.

Table 10.1 lists some commonly used terms relating to the interconnection of networks, or internetworking. An interconnected set of networks, from a user's point of view, may appear simply as a larger network. However, if each of the constituent networks retains its identity, and special mechanisms are needed for communicating across multiple networks, then the entire configuration is often referred to as an **internet,** and each of the constituent networks as a **subnetwork.**

Each constituent subnetwork in an internet supports communication among the devices attached to that subnetwork; these devices are referred to as **end systems** (ESs). In addition, subnetworks are connected by devices referred to in the ISO documents as **intermediate systems** (ISs).[1] ISs provide a communications path and perform the necessary relaying and routing functions so that data can be exchanged between devices attached to different subnetworks in the internet.

---

[1]The term *gateway* is sometimes used to refer to an IS or to a particular kind of IS. Because of the lack of consistency in the use of this term, we will avoid it.

TABLE 10.1   Internetworking Terms

Communication Network

A facility that provides a data transfer service among stations attached to the network.

Internet

A collection of communication networks interconnected by bridges and/or routers.

Subnetwork

Refers to a constituent network of an internet. This avoids ambiguity since the entire internet, from a user's point of view, is a single network.

End System (ES)

A device attached to one of the subnetworks of an internet that is used to support end-user applications or services.

Intermediate System (IS)

A device used to connect two subnetworks and permit communication between end systems attached to different subnetworks.

Bridge

An IS used to connect two LANs that use similar LAN protocols. The bridge acts as an address filter, picking up packets from one LAN that are intended for a destination on another LAN and passing those packets on. The bridge does not modify the contents of the packets and does not add anything to the packet. The bridge operates at layer 2 of the OSI model.

Router

A device used to connect two subnetworks that may or may not be similar. The router employs an internet protocol present in each router and each end system of the network. The router operates at layer 3 of the OSI model.

Two types of ISs of particular interest are bridges and routers. The differences between them have to do with the types of protocols used for the internetworking logic. In essence, a **bridge** operates at layer 2 of the open systems interconnection (OSI) seven-layer architecture and acts as a relay of frames between like networks. A **router** operates at layer 3 of the OSI architecture and routes packets between potential networks. Both the bridge and the router assume that the same upper-layer protocols are in use. In this chapter, we examine these two types of IS in turn.

10.1

BRIDGES

Functions of a Bridge

The simplest of the internetworking devices is the bridge. This device is designed for use between local area networks (LANs) that use identical

protocols for the physical and medium access layers (e.g., all conforming to IEEE 802.3 or all conforming to FDDI). Because the devices all use
the same protocols, the amount of processing required at the bridge is
minimal. The concept of a bridge was introduced in Chapter 4 as a
means of linking multiple rings.

Figure 10.1 illustrates the operation of a bridge between two LANs,
A and B. The bridge performs the following functions:

- Read all frames transmitted on A, and accept those addressed to
  stations on B.
- Using the medium access control protocol for B, retransmit the
  frames onto B.
- Do the same for B-to-A traffic.

In addition to these basic functions, there are some interesting design
considerations:

1. The bridge makes no modifications to the content or format of the
   frames it receives.
2. The bridge should contain enough buffer space to meet peak demands. Over a short period of time, frames may arrive faster than
   they can be retransmitted.
3. The bridge must contain addressing and routing intelligence. At a
   minimum, the bridges must know which addresses are on each

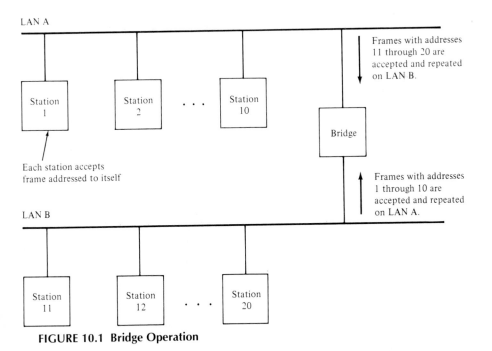

FIGURE 10.1 Bridge Operation

network in order to know which frames to forward. Further, there may be more than two networks in a sort of cascade configuration. The bridge must be able to pass along frames intended for networks further on. The subject of routing is explored later in this section.

4. A bridge may connect more than two networks. This was discussed in Chapter 4.

In summary, the bridge provides an extension to the LAN that requires no modification to the communications software in the stations attached to the LANs. It appears to all stations on the two (or more) LANs that there is a single LAN on which each station has a unique address. The station uses that unique address and need not explicitly discriminate between stations on the same LAN and stations on other LANs; the bridge takes care of that.

The bridge encompasses only layers 1 and 2 of the OSI model. In effect, the bridge operates as a layer-2 relay. Layer 3 and above must be identical in the two end systems for successful end-to-end communications.

Since the bridge is used in a situation in which all of the LANs have the same characteristics, the reader may ask why not simply have one large LAN. Depending on circumstance, there are several reasons for the use of multiple LANs connected by bridges:

- *Reliability:* The danger in connecting all data processing devices in an organization to one network is that a fault on the network may disable communication for all devices. By using bridges, the network can be partitioned into self-contained units.
- *Performance:* In general, performance on a LAN or MAN declines with an increase in the number of devices or the length of the medium. A number of smaller LANs will often give improved performance if devices can be clustered so that *intranetwork* traffic significantly exceeds *internetwork* traffic.
- *Security:* The establishment of multiple LANs may improve security of communications. It is desirable to keep different types of traffic (e.g., accounting, personnel, strategic planning) that have different security needs on physically separate media. At the same time, the different types of users with different levels of security need to communicate through controlled and monitored mechanisms.
- *Geography:* Clearly, two separate LANs are needed to support devices clustered in two geographically distant locations. Even in the case of two buildings separated by a highway, it may be far easier to use a microwave bridge link than to attempt to string coaxial cable between the two buildings. In the case of widely separated networks, two "half bridges" are needed (see Figures 10.3 and 10.4).

The description above has applied to the simplest sort of bridge. More sophisticated bridges can be used in more complex collections of LANs. These would include additional functions, such as:

- Each bridge can maintain status information on other bridges, together with the cost and number of bridge-to-bridge hops required to reach each network. This information may be updated by periodic exchanges of information among bridges. This allows the bridges to perform a dynamic routing function.
- A control mechanism can manage frame buffers in each bridge to overcome congestion. Under saturation conditions, the bridge can give precedence to enroute packets over new packets just entering the internet from an attached LAN, thus preserving the investment in line bandwidth and processing time already made in the enroute frame.

Bridge Protocol Architecture

The IEEE 802 committee has produced three specifications for bridges [IEEE90e, IEEE91a, IEEE91b]. In all cases, the devices are referred to as MAC-level relays. In addition, all of the MAC standards suggest formats for a globally administered set of MAC station addresses across multiple homogeneous LANs. In this subsection, we examine the protocol architecture of these bridges.

Within the 802 architecture, the endpoint or station address is designated at the MAC level. At the LLC level, only an SAP address is specified. Thus, it is at the MAC level that a bridge can function. Figure 10.2 shows the simplest case, which consists of two LANs connected by a single bridge. The LANs employ the same MAC and LLC protocols. The bridge operates as previously described. A MAC frame whose destination is not on the immediate LAN is captured by the bridge, buffered briefly, and then transmitted on the other LAN. As far as the LLC layer is concerned, there is a dialogue between peer LLC entities in the two endpoint stations. The bridge need not contain an LLC layer since it is merely serving to relay the MAC frames.

Figure 10.2b indicates the way in which data are encapsulated using a bridge. Data are provided by some user to LLC. The LLC entity appends a header and passes the resulting data unit to the MAC entity, which appends a header and a trailer to form a MAC frame. On the basis of the destination MAC address in the frame, it is captured by the bridge. The bridge does not strip off the MAC fields; its function is to relay the MAC frame intact to the destination LAN. Thus the frame is deposited on the destination LAN and captured by the destination station.

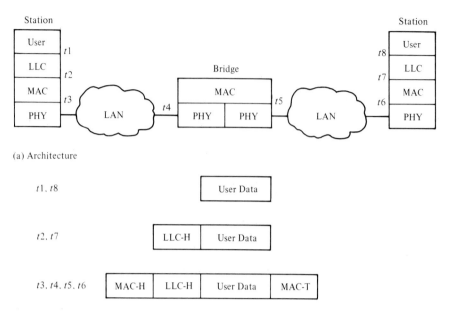

FIGURE 10.2 Connection of Two LANs by a Bridge

The concept of a MAC relay bridge is not limited to the use of a single bridge to connect two nearby LANs. If the LANs are some distance apart, then they can be connected by two bridges that are in turn connected by a communications facility. For example, Figure 10.3 shows the case of two bridges connected by a point-to-point link. In this case, when a bridge captures a MAC frame, it appends a link layer (e.g., MAN) header and trailer to transmit the MAC frame across the link to the other bridge. The target bridge strips off these link fields and transmits the original, unmodified MAC frame to the destination station.

The intervening communications facility can even be a network, such as a wide-area packet-switching network, as illustrated in Figure 10.4. In this case, the bridge is somewhat more complicated although it performs the same function of relaying MAC frames. The connection between bridges is via an X.25 virtual circuit. Again, the two LLC entities in the end systems have a direct logical relationship with no intervening LLC entities. Thus, in this situation, the X.25 packet layer is operating below an 802 LLC layer. As before, a MAC frame is passed intact between the endpoints. When the bridge on the source LAN receives the frame, it appends an X.25 packet-layer header and an X.25 link-layer header and trailer and sends the data to the DCE (packet-switching node) to which it attaches. The DCE strips off the link-layer fields and sends the X.25 packet through the network to another DCE. The target DCE appends the link-layer field and sends this to the target bridge.

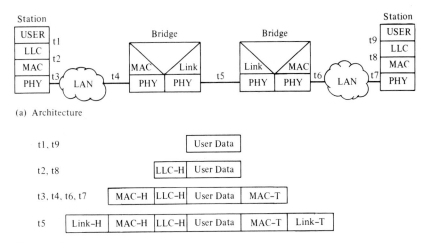

(a) Architecture

t1, t9		User Data	
t2, t8		LLC-H	User Data	
t3, t4, t6, t7	MAC-H	LLC-H	User Data	MAC-T
t5	Link-H	MAC-H	LLC-H	User Data	MAC-T	Link-T

(b) Operation

FIGURE 10.3 Bridge Over a Point-to-Point Link

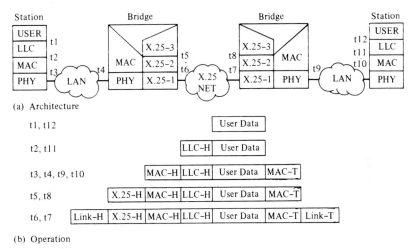

(a) Architecture

t1, t12		User Data	
t2, t11		LLC-H	User Data	
t3, t4, t9, t10	MAC-H	LLC-H	User Data	MAC-T
t5, t8	X.25-H	MAC-H	LLC-H	User Data	MAC-T
t6, t7	Link-H	X.25-H	MAC-H	LLC-H	User Data	MAC-T	Link-T

(b) Operation

FIGURE 10.4 Bridge Over an X.25 Network

The target bridge strips off all the X.25 fields and transmits the original unmodified MAC frame to the destination endpoint.

10.2

ROUTING WITH BRIDGES

In the configuration of Figure 10.1, the bridge makes the decision to relay a frame on the basis of destination MAC address. In a more complex configuration, the bridge must also make a routing decision. Consider the configuration of Figure 10.5. Suppose that station 1 transmits a frame on LAN A intended for station 5. The frame will be read by both bridge 101 and bridge 102. For each bridge, the addressed station is not on a LAN to which the bridge is attached. Therefore, each bridge must make a decision of whether or not to retransmit the frame on its other LAN, in order to move it closer to its intended destination. In this case, bridge 101 should repeat the frame on LAN B, whereas bridge 102 should refrain from retransmitting the frame. Once the frame has been transmitted on LAN B, it will be picked up by both bridges 103 and 104. Again, each must decide whether or not to forward the frame. In this case, bridge 104 should retransmit the frame on LAN E, where it will be received by the destination, station 5.

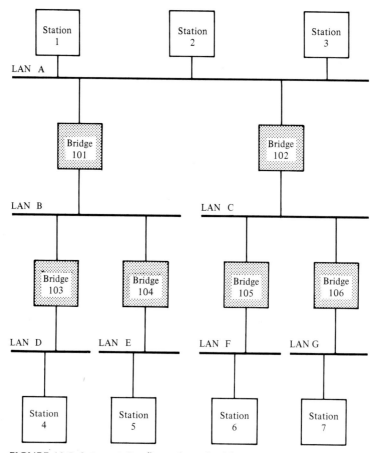

FIGURE 10.5 Internet Configuration of Bridges and LANs

Thus we see that, in the general case, the bridge must be equipped with a routing capability. When a bridge receives a frame, it must decide whether or not to forward it. If the bridge is attached to more than two networks, then it must decide whether or not to forward the frame and, if so, on which LAN the frame should be transmitted.

The routing decision may not always be a simple one. In Figure 10.6, bridge 107 is added to the previous configuration, directly linking LAN A and LAN E. Such an addition may be made to provide for higher overall internet availability. In this case, if station 1 transmits a frame on LAN A intended for station 5 on LAN E, then either bridge 101 or bridge 107 could forward the frame. It would appear preferable for bridge 107 to forward the frame, since it will involve only one "hop," whereas if the frame travels through bridge 101, it must suffer two hops. Another

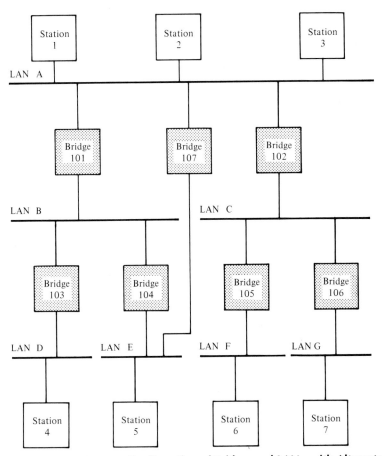

FIGURE 10.6 Internet Configuration of Bridges and LANs, with Alternate Routes

consideration is that there may be changes in the configuration. For example, bridge 107 may fail, in which case subsequent frames from station 1 to station 5 should go through bridge 101. So we can say that the routing capability must take into account the topology of the internet configuration and may need to be dynamically altered.

One final point: Figure 10.6 suggests that a bridge knows the identity of each station on each LAN. In a large configuration, such an arrangement is unwieldly. Furthermore, as stations are added to and dropped from LANs, all directories of station locations must be updated. It would facilitate the development of a routing capability if all MAC-level addresses were in the form of a network part and a station part. For example, the IEEE 802.5 standard suggests that 16-bit MAC addresses consist of a 7-bit LAN number and an 8-bit station number, and that 48-bit addresses consist of a 14-bit LAN number and a 32-bit station number.[2] In the remainder of this discussion, we assume that all MAC addresses include a LAN number and that routing is based on the use of that portion of the address only.

A variety of routing strategies have been proposed and implemented in recent years. The simplest and most common strategy is **fixed routing.** This strategy is suitable for small internets and for internets that are relatively stable. More recently, two groups within the IEEE 802 committee developed specifications for routing strategies. The IEEE 802.1 group has issued a standard for routing based on the use of a *spanning tree* algorithm. The token ring committee, IEEE 802.5, has issued its own specification, referred to as **source routing.** We examine these three strategies in turn.

Fixed Routing

For fixed routing, a route is selected for each source-destination pair of LANs in the internet. If alternate routes are available between two LANs, then typically the route with the least number of hops is selected. The routes are fixed, or at least only change, when there is a change in the topology of the internet.

Figure 10.7 suggests how fixed routing might be implemented. A central routing matrix is created, to be stored perhaps at a network control center. The matrix shows, for each source-destination pair of LANs, the identity of the first bridge on the route. So, for example, the route from LAN E to LAN F begins by going through bridge 107 to LAN A. Again consulting the matrix, the route from LAN A to LAN F goes through bridge 102 to LAN C. Finally, the route from LAN C to LAN F is directly

---

[2]The remaining bit in the 16-bit format is used to indicate whether this is a group or individual address. Of the two remaining bits in the 48-bit format, one is used to indicate whether this is a group or individual address, and the other is used to indicate whether this is a locally administered or globally administered address.

Central Routing Matrix
Destination LAN

		A	B	C	D	E	F	G
	A	–	101	102	101	107	102	102
	B	101	–	101	103	104	101	101
Source LAN	C	102	102	–	102	102	105	106
	D	103	103	103	–	103	103	103
	E	107	104	107	104	–	107	107
	F	105	105	105	105	105	–	105
	G	106	106	106	106	106	106	–

Bridge 101 Table

From LAN A		From LAN B	
Dest.	Next	Dest.	Next
B	B	A	A
C	–	C	A
D	B	D	–
E	–	E	–
F	–	F	A
G	–	G	A

Bridge 102 Table

From LAN A		From LAN C	
Dest.	Next	Dest.	Next
B	–	A	A
C	C	B	A
D	–	D	A
E	–	E	A
F	C	F	–
G	C	G	–

Bridge 103 Table

From LAN B		From LAN D	
Dest.	Next	Dest.	Next
A	–	A	B
C	–	B	B
D	D	C	B
E	–	E	B
F	–	F	B
G	–	G	B

Bridge 104 Table

From LAN B		From LAN E	
Dest.	Next	Dest.	Next
A	–	A	–
C	–	B	B
D	–	C	–
E	E	D	B
F	–	F	–
G	–	G	–

Bridge 105 Table

From LAN C		From LAN F	
Dest.	Next	Dest.	Next
A	–	A	C
B	–	B	C
D	–	C	C
E	–	D	C
F	F	E	C
G	–	G	C

Bridge 106 Table

From LAN C		From LAN G	
Dest.	Next	Dest.	Next
A	–	A	C
B	–	B	C
D	–	C	C
E	–	D	C
F	–	E	C
G	G	F	C

Bridge 107 Table

From LAN A		From LAN E	
Dest.	Next	Dest.	Next
B	–	A	A
C	–	B	–
D	–	C	A
E	E	D	–
F	–	F	A
G	–	G	A

FIGURE 10.7 Fixed Routing (Using Figure 10.6)

through bridge 105. Thus the complete route from LAN E to LAN F is bridge 107, LAN A, bridge 102, LAN C, bridge 105.

From this overall matrix, routing tables can be developed and stored at each bridge. Each bridge needs one table for each LAN to which it attaches. The information for each table is derived from a single row of the matrix. For example, bridge 105 has two tables, one for frames arriving from LAN C and one for frames arriving from LAN F. The table shows, for each possible destination MAC address, the identity of the LAN to which the bridge should forward the frame. The table labeled "from LAN C" is derived from the row labeled C in the routing matrix. Every entry in that row that contains bridge number 105 results in an entry in the corresponding table in bridge 105.

Once the directories have been established, routing is a simple matter. A bridge copies each incoming frame on each of its LANs. If the destination MAC address corresponds to an entry in its routing table, the frame is retransmitted on the appropriate LAN.

The fixed routing strategy is widely used in commercially available products. It has the advantage of simplicity and minimal processing requirements. However, in a complex internet, in which bridges may be dynamically added and in which failures must be allowed for, this strategy is too limited. We now turn to two more powerful alternatives.

IEEE 802.1 Transparent Bridge

The IEEE 802.1 committee has developed a bridge routing approach referred to as the transparent bridge [IEEE90e]. The distinguishing characteristics of this standard are:

- It is intended for use in interconnecting not just LANs with the same MAC protocol but also dissimilar LANs that satisfy any of the MAC standards (802.3, 802.4, 802.5). Hence the term *transparent*.
- The routing mechanism is a technique referred to as the spanning tree algorithm [BACK88, HART88, PERL84].

We look first at the basic operation of the transparent bridge and then in more detail at the three key aspects of bridge operation: frame forwarding, address learning, and spanning tree algorithm.

Basic Operation.   So far, we have discussed the bridge as a device that relays frames from one LAN to another. In the case of the 802.1 transparent bridge, we need to be more careful and more explicit in describing the way in which this is done. The transparent bridge must be capable of relaying a MAC frame from one type of LAN to another. However, as we know (see Figure 5.2), the MAC formats for the various 802 LANs differ. Accordingly, it is not possible to simply pick up a frame from one LAN and place it down, unaltered, on another LAN. If the two LANs use different MAC protocols, then the bridge must map the contents of the incoming frame into an outbound frame that conforms to the frame format for the outbound LAN.

Figure 10.8a, taken from the standard, indicates the bridge architecture that supports this mapping. Each bridge attachment to a LAN is referred to as a **port.** A bridge with N ports will have N MAC entities; thus the bridge has N MAC addresses, one for each port. Each MAC entity conforms to the relevant MAC standard and behaves in the normal manner with one exception: the MAC entity will capture all frames, not just those addressed to the bridge itself. Incoming MAC frames fall into three categories:

1. *Frames addressed to this bridge:* These include bridge protocol data units (BPDUs) that are part of the spanning tree algorithm described later, and management frames. All such frames are passed to higher-layer entities within the bridge using the standard MAC service for that MAC protocol.
2. *Control frames:* These are handled as part of the MAC protocol. Examples include tokens and frames involved in the maintenance of the token bus and token ring protocols. These frames are handled by the MAC entity without reference to any higher layer.
3. *User data frames:* These are frames containing LLC information. The LLC information is handed to the MAC relay entity using an internal sublayer service. If a capture frame is to be forwarded onto another LAN, the LLC information is handed down to the appropriate MAC relay entity, again using the internal sublayer service.

The internal sublayer service is defined in the usual way, namely as a set of primitives and parameters. Table 10.2 shows this service definition, and Table 10.3 defines the parameters. The operation implied by these definitions is as follows: an incoming frame is disassembled, and the LLC information field plus the values of some of the other fields are passed up to a MAC relay entity. The information is then passed down to the MAC entity for the outgoing LAN, and the MAC frame is reconstructed. Because the frame is disassembled and then reconstructed, the format can be altered to allow a bridge to function between two different types of LANs.

Several parameters in the service definition deserve additional comment. Only frames with a frame_type of user_data_frame will be relayed by a bridge between dissimilar LANs. MAC-specific frames may be relayed for a bridge between two similar LANs; this would allow certain MAC-specific management functions to be implemented. The MAC action parameter is relevant only to IEEE 802.4, which has a special feature that allows for a request/response type of exchange of MAC frames.

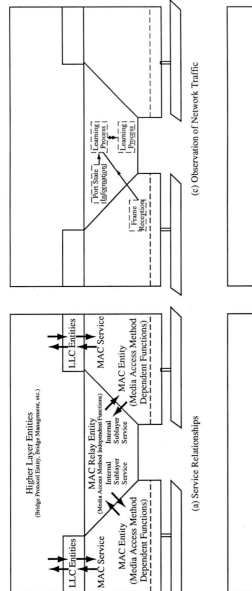

(a) Service Relationships

(b) Forwarding Mac Frames

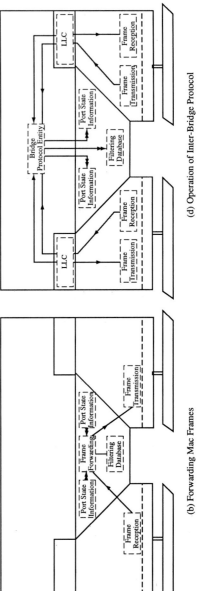

(c) Observation of Network Traffic

(d) Operation of Inter-Bridge Protocol

FIGURE 10.8 IEEE 802.1D Bridge Architecture

TABLE 10.2   IEEE 802.1D MAC Bridge Internal Sublayer Service Primitives and Parameters

M_UNITDATA.indication (frame_type, mac_action, destination_address, source_address, mac_service_data_unit, user_priority, frame_check_sequence)

M_UNITDATA.request (frame_type, mac_action, destination_address, source_address, mac_service_data_unit, user_priority, access_priority, frame_check_sequence)

TABLE 10.3   Definition of IEEE 802.1D MAC Bridge Internal Sublayer Service Parameters

Parameter	Definition
frame_type	Type of frame: value is user_data_frame, mac_specific_frame, or reserved_frame
mac_action	If the value of the frame_type parameter is user_data_frame, then the mac_action parameter is request_with_response, request_with_no_response, or response
destination_address	Address of destination MAC entity or group of MAC entities
source_address	Address of the source MAC entity that initiated transmission of the mac_service_data_unit
mac_service_data_unit	Service user data. For a user data frame, this is provided by the source LLC
user_priority	Priority requested by the originating service user
access_priority	Priority to be used by the local MAC service provider to convey the request
frame_check_sequence	Frame check sequence value of the incoming frame

The user_priority and access_priority parameters relate to the problem of how to handle priorities. In the case of IEEE 802.3, priority is not supported. IEEE 802.4 supports eight levels of priority, and IEEE 802.5 supports eight levels of priority.[3] The user_priority value provided to the MAC layer entity in an MA_UNITDATA.indication is derived from the incoming MAC frame; in the case of an incoming 802.3 frame, no

---

[3]In fact, as we have seen, 802.4 supports four classes of access: classes 6, 4, 2, and 0. However, 3 bits are reserved in the frame control field for priority. These are mapped into access classes as follows: access class 6 = priority 7 and 6; class 4 = priority class 5 and 4; class 2 = priority class 3 and 2; class 0 = priority class 1 and 0.

priority value is available and a value of *unspecified* is used. The user_
priority value issued to a MAC entity in an MA_UNITDATA.request is
to be placed in the outbound MAC frame for 802.4 and 802.5. The access
priority refers to the priority used by a bridge MAC entity to access a
LAN for frame transmission. We may not want the access priority to be
equal to the user priority for two reasons:

1. A frame that must go through a bridge has already suffered more
   delay than a frame that does not have to go through a bridge;
   therefore, we may wish to give such a frame a higher access priority than the requested user priority.
2. It is important that the bridge not become a bottleneck; therefore,
   we may wish to give all frames being transmitted by a bridge a
   relatively high priority.

In considering user priority and access priority, we can group the
alternatives into three cases:

1. *Outbound LAN = 802.3:* Priorities are not used to transmit 802.3
   MAC frames, and the frame itself has no priority field. Therefore,
   any inbound priority is ignored, and there is no access priority.
2. *Outbound LAN = 802.4 or 802.5; inbound LAN = 802.4 or 802.5:* The
   priority field in the outbound MAC frame is set equal to the priority field in the inbound MAC frame; the value is communicated
   from inbound to outbound via the user_priority parameter. The
   access priority used on the outbound LAN can be set either to the
   user_priority value or to a default access_priority value.
3. *Outbound LAN = 802.4 or 802.5; inbound LAN = 802.3:* The priority
   field in the outbound frame is set to a default user_priority value.
   The access priority used on the outbound LAN is set to a default
   access_priority value.

The frame_check_sequence value provided to the MAC layer entity
in an MA_UNITDATA.indication is derived from the incoming MAC
frame. If the outbound LAN is the same type as the inbound LAN, then
the outbound MAC frame will be the same as the inbound MAC frame,
and the FCS can be reused.

Table 10.4 summarizes these relationships, plus one other that is significant. One concern relates to the maximum frame size limitation on
the various networks. In the case of 802.3, the maximum size is 1518
octets. For 802.4, it is 8191 octets. For 802.5, the maximum frame size
may not exceed the token holding time; for the default value of 10 ms,
this results in a maximum frame size of 5000 octets at 4 Mbps and 20,000
octets at 16 Mbps. If the outbound LAN does not support a frame size
large enough to handle an inbound frame, that frame must be discarded.

TABLE 10.4   MAC-Dependent Bridge Actions

Source LAN	Destination LAN		
	IEEE 802.3	**IEEE 802.4**	**IEEE 802.5**
IEEE 802.3		Calculate frame check sequence. Set default user priority. Use default access priority.	Calculate frame check sequence. Set default user priority. Use default access priority.
IEEE 802.4	Discard frame if too long. Calculate frame check sequence. Discard user priority.	Use user priority of inbound frame. Use user priority or default access priority for access.	Discard frame if too long. Calculate frame check sequence. Use user priority of inbound frame. Use user priority or default access priority for access.
IEEE 802.5	Discard frame if too long. Calculate frame check sequence. Discard user priority.	Use user priority of inbound frame. Use user priority or default access priority for access.	Use user priority of inbound frame. Use user priority or default access priority for access.

Frame Forwarding.   In this scheme, a bridge maintains a **filtering data base** based on MAC address (Figure 10.8b). Each entry consists of a MAC individual or group address, a port number, and an aging time (described below). We can interpret this in the following fashion. A station is listed with a given port number if it is on the "same side" of the bridge as the port. For example, for bridge 102 of Figure 10.5, stations on LANs C, F, and G are on the same side of the bridge as the LAN A port, and stations on LANs A, B, D, and E are on the same side of the bridge as the LAN C port. When a frame is received on any port, the bridge must decide whether that frame is to be forwarded through the bridge and out through one of the bridge's other ports. Suppose that a bridge receives a MAC frame on port x. The following rules are applied (Figure 10.9):

1. Search the forwarding data base to determine if the MAC address is listed for any port except port x.
2. If the destination MAC address is not found, flood the frame by sending it out on all ports except the port by which it arrived.
3. If the destination address is in the forwarding data base for some port $y \neq x$, then determine whether port y is in a blocking or forwarding state. For reasons explained below, a port may sometimes be blocked, which prevents it from receiving or transmitting frames.
4. If port y is not blocked, transmit the frame through port y onto the LAN to which that port attaches.

Rule 2 is needed because of the dynamic nature of the filtering data base. When a bridge is initialized, the data base is empty. Since the bridge does not know where to send the frame, it floods the frame onto all of its LANs except the LAN on which the frame arrives. As the bridge gains information, the flooding activity subsides.

Address Learning.   The above scheme is based on the use of a filtering data base that indicates the direction, from the bridge, of each destination station. This information can be preloaded into the bridge, as in static routing. However, an effective automatic mechanism for learning the direction of each station is desirable. A simple scheme for acquiring this information is based on the use of the source address field in each MAC frame (Figures 10.8c and 10.9).

When a frame arrives on a particular port, it clearly has come from the direction of the incoming LAN. The source address field of the frame indicates the source station. Thus a bridge can update its filtering data base for that MAC address. To allow for changes in topology, each entry in the data base is equipped with an aging timer. When a new entry is added to the data base, its timer is set; the recommended default value is 300 seconds. If the timer expires, then the entry is eliminated from

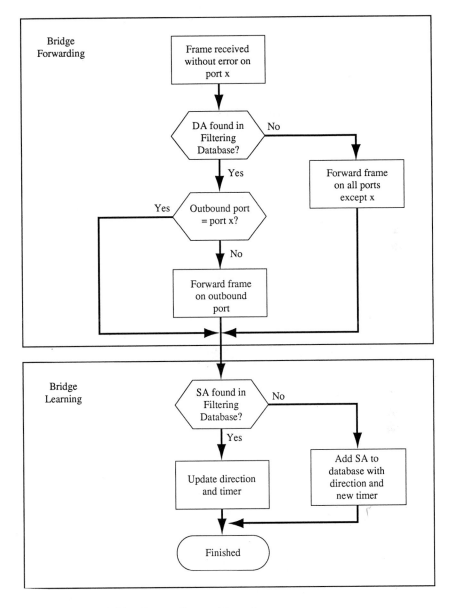

FIGURE 10.9 Bridge Forwarding and Learning

the data base, since the corresponding direction information may no longer be valid. Each time a frame is received, its source address is checked against the data base. If the entry is already in the data base, the entry is updated (the direction may have changed) and the timer is reset. If the entry is not in the data base, a new entry is created, with its own timer.

The above discussion indicates that the individual entries in the data base are station addresses. If a two-level address structure (LAN number, station number) is used, then only LAN addresses need to be entered in the data base. Both schemes work the same. The only difference is that the use of station addresses requires a much larger data base than the use of LAN addresses.

Note from Figure 10.9 that the bridge learning process is applied to all frames, not just those that are forwarded.

Spanning Tree Algorithm.   The address learning mechanism described above is effective if the topology of the internet is a tree; that is, if there are no alternate routes in the network. The existence of alternate routes means that there is a closed loop. For example in Figure 10.6, the following is a closed loop: LAN A, bridge 101, LAN B, bridge 104, LAN E, bridge 107, LAN A.

To see the problem created by a closed loop, consider Figure 10.10. At time t_0, station A transmits a frame addressed to station B. The frame is captured by both bridges. Each bridge updates its data base to indicate that station A is in the direction of LAN X, and retransmits the frame on LAN Y. Say that bridge α retransmits at time t_1 and bridge β a short time later, t_2. Thus B will receive two copies of the frame. Furthermore, each bridge will receive the other's transmission on LAN Y. Note that each transmission is a MAC frame with a source address of A and a destination address of B. Thus each bridge will update its data base to indicate that station A is in the direction of LAN Y. Neither bridge is now capable of forwarding a frame addressed to station A.

But the problem is potentially much more serious than that. Assume that the two bridges do not yet know of the existence of station B. In this case, we have the following scenario. A transmits a frame addressed to B. Each bridge captures the frame. Then, each bridge, since it does not have information about B, automatically retransmits a copy of the frame on LAN Y. The frame transmitted by bridge α is captured by station B *and* by bridge β. Since bridge β does not know where B is, it takes this frame and retransmits it on LAN X. Similarly, bridge α receives bridge β's transmission on LAN Y and retransmits the frame on LAN X. There are now two frames on LAN X that will be picked up for retransmission on LAN Y. This process repeats indefinitely.

To overcome this problem, a simple result from graph theory is used: for any connected graph, consisting of nodes and edges connecting

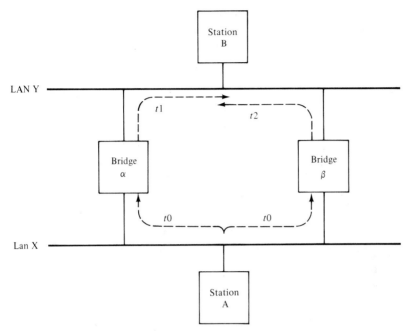

FIGURE 10.10 Loop of Bridges

pairs of nodes, there is a spanning tree of edges that maintains the connectivity of the graph but contains no closed loops. In terms of internets,
each LAN corresponds to a graph node, and each bridge corresponds
to a graph edge. Thus, in Figure 10.6, the removal of one (and only one)
of bridges 107, 101, and 104, results in a spanning tree. What is desired
is to develop a simple algorithm by which the bridges of the internet
can exchange sufficient information to automatically (without user intervention) derive a spanning tree. The algorithm must be dynamic.
That is, when a topology change occurs, the bridges must be able to
discover this fact and automatically derive a new spanning tree.

The algorithm is based on the use of the following:

1. Each bridge is assigned a unique identifier; in essence, the identifier consists of a MAC address for the bridge plus a priority level.
2. There is a special group MAC address that means "all bridges on
   this LAN." When a MAC frame is transmitted with the group address in the destination address field, all of the bridges on the
   LAN will capture that frame and interpret it as a frame address to
   itself.
3. Each port of a bridge is uniquely identified within the bridge, with
   a "port identifier."

With this information established, the bridges are able to exchange routing information in order to determine a spanning tree of the internet. We will explain the operation of the algorithm using Figures 10.11 and 10.12 as an example. The following concepts are needed in the creation of the spanning tree:

- *Root bridge:* The bridge with the lowest value of bridge identifier is chosen to be the root of the spanning tree.

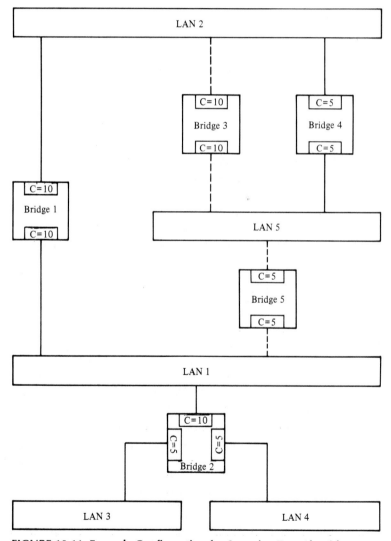

FIGURE 10.11 Example Configuration for Spanning Tree Algorithm

- *Path cost:* Associated with each port on each bridge is a path cost, which is the cost of transmitting a frame onto a LAN through that port. A path between two stations will pass through zero or more bridges. At each bridge, the cost of transmission is added to give a total cost for a particular path. In the simplest case, all path costs would be assigned a value of 1; thus the cost of a path would simply be a count of the number of bridges along the path. Alternatively, costs could be assigned in inverse proportion to the data rate of the

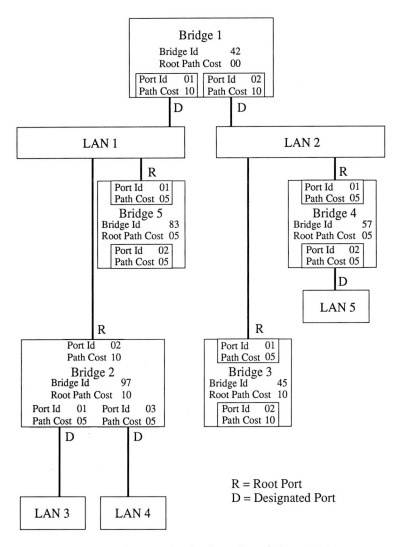

FIGURE 10.12 Spanning Tree for Configuration of Figure 10.11

corresponding LAN, or any other criterion chosen by the network manager.

- *Root port:* Each bridge discovers the first hop on the minimum-cost path to the root bridge. The port used for that hop is labeled the root port.
- *Root path cost:* For each bridge, the cost of the path to the root bridge with minimum cost (the path that starts at the root port) is the root path cost for that bridge.
- *Designated bridge, designated port:* On each LAN, one bridge is chosen to be the designated bridge. This is the bridge on that LAN that provides the minimum cost path to the root bridge. This is the only bridge allowed to forward frames to and from the LAN for which it is the designated bridge. The port of the designated bridge that attaches the bridge to the LAN is the designated port. For all LANs to which the root bridge is attached, the root bridge is the designated bridge. All internet traffic to and from the LAN passes through the designated port.

In general terms, the spanning tree is constructed in the following fashion:

1. Determine the root bridge.
2. Determine the root port on all other bridges.
3. Determine the designated port on each LAN. This will be the port with the minimum root path cost. In the case of two or more bridges with the same root path cost, the highest-priority bridge is chosen as the designated bridge. If the designated bridge has two or more ports attached to this LAN, then the port with the lowest value of port identifier is chosen.

By this process, when two LANs are directly connected by more than one bridge, all of the bridges but one are eliminated. This cuts any loops that involve two LANs. It can be demonstrated that this process also eliminates all loops involving more than two LANs and that connectivity is preserved. Thus, this process discovers a spanning tree for the given internet. In our example, the solid lines indicate the bridge ports that participate in the spanning tree.

The steps outlined above require that the bridges exchange information (Figure 10.8d). The information is exchanged in the form of bridge protocol data units (BPDUs). A BPDU transmitted by one bridge is addressed to and received by all of the other bridges on the same LAN. Each BPDU contains the following information:

- The identifier of this bridge and the port on this bridge
- The identifier of the bridge that this bridge considers to be the root
- The root path cost for this bridge

To begin, all bridges consider themselves to be the root bridge. Each bridge will broadcast a BPDU on each of its LANs that asserts this fact. On any given LAN, only one claimant will have the lowest-valued identifier and will maintain its belief. Over time, as BPDU's propagate, the identity of the lowest-valued bridge identifier throughout the internet will be known to all bridges. The root bridge will regularly broadcast the fact that it is the root bridge on all of the LANs to which it is attached. This allows the bridges on those LANs to determine their root port and the fact that they are directly connected to the root bridge. Each of these bridges in turn broadcasts a BPDU on the other LANs to which it is attached (all LANs except the one on its root port), indicating that it is one hop away from the root bridge. This activity is propagated throughout the internet. Every time that a bridge receives a BPDU, it transmits BPDUs indicating the identity of the root bridge and the number of hops to reach the root bridge. On any LAN, the bridge claiming to be the one that is closest to the root becomes the designated bridge.

We can trace some of this activity with the configuration of Figure 10.11. At startup time, bridges 1, 3, and 4 all transmit BPDUs on LAN 2 claiming to be the root bridge. When bridge 3 receives the transmission from bridge 1, it recognizes a superior claimant and defers. Bridge 3 has also received a claiming BPDU from bridge 5 via LAN 5. Bridge 3 recognizes that bridge 1 has a superior claim to be the root bridge; it therefore assigns its LAN 2 port to be its root port and sets the root path cost to 10. By similar actions, bridge 4 ends up with a root path cost of 5 via LAN 2; bridge 5 has a root path cost of 5 via LAN 1; and bridge 2 has a root path cost of 10 via LAN 1.

Now consider the assignment of designated bridges. On LAN 5, all three bridges transmit BPDUs attempting to assert a claim to be the designated bridge. Bridge 3 defers because it receives BPDUs from the other bridges that have a lower root path cost. Bridges 4 and 5 have the same root path cost, but bridge 4 has the higher priority and therefore becomes the designated bridge.

The results of all this activity are shown in Figure 10.12. Only the designated bridge on each LAN is allowed to forward frames. All of the ports on all of the other bridges are placed in a blocking state. After the spanning tree is established, bridges continue to periodically exchange BPDUs to be able to react to any change in topology, cost assignments, or priority assignment. Any time that a bridge receives a BPDU on a port it makes two assessments:

1. If the BPDU arrives on a port that is considered the designated port, does the transmitting port have a better claim to be the designated port?
2. Should this port be my root port?

The behavior of the bridges can be more precisely explained with reference to the state transition diagram of Figure 10.13. When a bridge is initialized, or when a bridge must participate in a change of configuration, all of its ports are placed in a listening state. For each port an associated timer is initialized to a value called *forward delay*. This timer is allowed to run down as long as no information is received to indicate that this port should be blocked from transmitting and receiving MAC frames. In the listening state, the spanning tree protocol information is received and transmitted, but station traffic is not forwarded to or from the bridge port, and MAC frames that arrive are not submitted to the learning process.

Once the forwarding timer expires, the bridge port transitions to the learning state, and the timer is reinitialized to the value of the forward delay parameter. Behavior in the learning state is exactly as in the listening state, with the exception that frames are submitted to the learning process. Once the forward delay timer expires a second time, the bridge port moves to the forwarding state, which means that this port is part of the spanning tree and will accept frames to be forwarded through the bridge as transmit frames out of the bridge as appropriate.

If at any time the bridge receives configuration information that indicates that this port should not be part of the spanning tree, the port is put in the blocking state. A future change in topology will move the port back to the listening state.

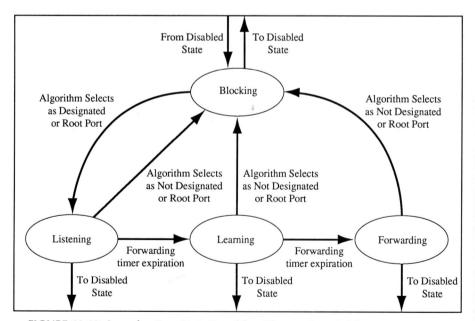

FIGURE 10.13 Spanning Tree State Transition Diagram for a Bridge Port

The motivation for this apparently complex process is to account for the propagation delays in communicating configuration information among the bridges. To move a state directly from a blocking state to a forwarding state risks having temporary data loops and the duplication and misordering of frames. Time is needed for new information to be received by all bridges and for other bridges to reply to inferior protocol information before starting to forward frames.

Bridge Protocol Data Units.   The 802.1D standard defines two bridge protocol data units: the configuration BPDU and the topology change notification BPDU. Figure 10.14 illustrates the formats.

The **configuration BPDU** consists of the following fields:

- *Protocol identifier (2 octets):* identifies the spanning tree algorithm and protocol defined by 802.1. The value is all zeros.
- *Protocol version identifier (1 octet):* identifies the version of this standard.
- *BPDU type (1 octet):* the type of BPDU. For the configuration BPDU, the value is all zeros.
- *Flags (1 octet):* consists of the Topology Change flag (bit 1 of octet 5) and the Topology Change Acknowledgment flag (bit 8 of octet 5). The use of these flags is explained below.

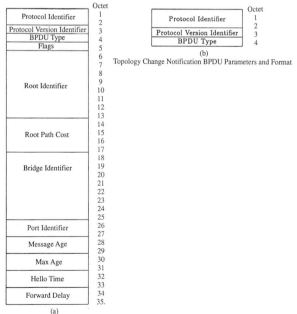

(a)
Configuration BPDU Parameters and Format

FIGURE 10.14 Bridge Protocol Data Units

- *Root identifier (8 octets):* the unique bridge identifier of the bridge assumed to be the root by the bridge transmitting this BPDU. This parameter is conveyed to enable all bridges to agree on the root.
- *Root path cost (4 octets):* the cost of the path from the transmitting bridge to the bridge identified by the root identifier above. This parameter is conveyed to enable a bridge to decide which of the bridges attached to the LAN on which this BPDU has been received offers the lowest-cost path to the root for that LAN.
- *Bridge identifier (8 octets):* the unique identifier of the bridge transmitting this BPDU. This parameter is conveyed to enable a bridge to decide, in the case of a LAN to which two or more bridges are attached and that offers equal cost paths to the root, which of the bridges should be selected as the designated bridge for that LAN.
- *Port identifier (2 octets):* the identifier of the port transmitting this BPDU. This identifier uniquely identifies a port on the transmitting bridge.
- *Message age (2 octets):* the age of the configuration message, which is the time since the generation of the configuration BPDU by the root that instigated the generation of this configuration BPDU. This parameter is conveyed to enable a bridge to discard information whose age exceeds the maximum age.
- *Maximum age (2 octets):* a time-out value to be used by all bridges in the internet. The value is set by the root. This parameter is conveyed to ensure that each bridge has a consistent value against which to test the age of stored configuration information.
- *Hello time (2 octets):* the time interval between the generation of configuration BPDUs by the root. This parameter is not directly used in the spanning tree algorithm but is conveyed to facilitate the monitoring of protocol performance by management functions.
- *Forward delay (2 octets):* a timeout value to be used by all bridges. The value is set by the root. This parameter is conveyed to ensure that each bridge uses a consistent value for the forward delay timer when transferring the state of a port to the forwarding state. This parameter is also used as the time-out value for aging filtering data base dynamic entries following changes in active topology.

The transmission of configuration BPDUs is triggered by the root (or a bridge that temporarily considers itself to be the root). The root will periodically (once every hello time) issue a configuration BPDU on all LANs to which it is attached. A bridge that receives a configuration BPDU on what it decides is its root port passes that information on to all the LANs for which it believes itself to be the designated bridge. Thus, in a stable configuration, the generation of a configuration BPDU by the root causes a cascade of configuration BPDUs throughout the spanning tree. This collection of BPDU transmissions is referred to as a **configuration message.**

A bridge may decide that it must change the topology of the spanning tree. For example, in Figure 10.12, if bridge 4 fails, it would cease to transmit configuration BPDUs as part of the periodic configuration messages. Bridge 3 would time out bridge 4 as the designated bridge on LAN 2 once the maximum-age timer expires and would enter the listening state. Eventually, the port on LAN 2 of bridge 3 would enter the forwarding state. At this point, bridge 3 must notify the root of a change in topology. This is done by transmitting a **topology change notification BPDU** on the root port of the bridge. This BPDU consists merely of a protocol identifier, protocol version identifier, and a BPDU type field with a code for this type of 10000000.

The intent is to communicate the topology change notification to the root. This is done by, in effect, relaying the change notification up the spanning tree to the root. To assure reliable delivery of the notification, the transmitting bridge will repeat the topology change notification BPDU until it receives an acknowledgment from the designated bridge for that LAN. The acknowledgment is carried in a configuration BPDU (Topology Change Acknowledgment flag). The designated bridge passes the notification to, or toward, the root using the same procedure.

When the root receives such a notification, or changes the topology itself (e.g., if a new root is declared), it will set the Topology Change flag in all configuration messages transmitted for some time. This time is such that all bridges will receive one or more configuration messages. While this flag is set, bridges use the value of forwarding delay to age out entries in the filtering data base. When the flag is reset again, the bridges revert to using a filtering timer that, typically, is much longer. It is desirable to shorten the aging time during this period of reconfiguration because, after a topology change, stations may be in a new direction with respect to the bridge. Since a bridge must endure a wait of at least two forwarding times (see Figure 10.13) to transition from listening to forwarding, this will allow enough time for currently en route frames to be delivered or eliminated by time-out.

IEEE 802.5 Source Routing Bridge

The IEEE 802.5 committee has developed a bridge routing approach referred to as source routing. With this approach, the sending station determines the route that the frame will follow and includes the routing information with the frame; bridges read the routing information to determine if they should forward the frame [DIXO88, HAMN88, PITT87b, BEDE86, PITT85, IEEE91a].

Basic Operation.   The basic operation of the algorithm can be described with reference to the configuration of Figure 10-15a. A frame from station X can reach station Y by either of the following routes:

- LAN 1, bridge B1, LAN 3, bridge B3, LAN 2
- LAN 1, bridge B2, LAN 4, bridge B4, LAN 2

Station X may choose one of these two routes and may place the information, in the form of a sequence of LAN and bridge identifiers, in the frame to be transmitted. When a bridge receives a frame, it will forward

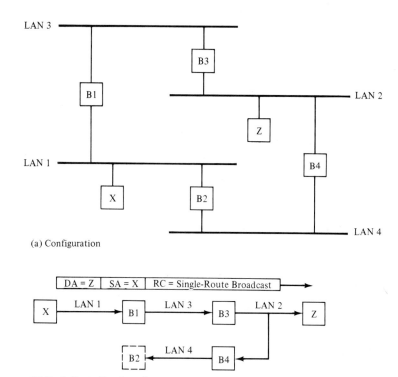

(a) Configuration

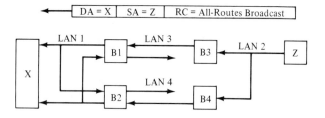

(b) Single-Route Broadcast Request

(c) All-Routes Broadcast Response

FIGURE 10.15 Route Discovery Example [DIXO88]

that frame if the bridge is on the designated route; all other frames are discarded. In this case, if the first route above is specified, bridges B1 and B3 will forward the frame; if the second route is specified, bridges B2 and B4 will forward the frame.

Note that with this scheme bridges need not maintain routing tables. The bridge makes the decision whether or not to forward a frame solely on the basis of the routing information contained in the frame. All that is required is that the bridge know its own unique identifier and the identifier of each LAN to which it is attached. The responsibility for designating the route falls to the source station.

For this scheme to work, there must be a mechanism by which a station can determine a route to any destination station. Before dealing with this issue, we need to discuss different types of routing directives.

Routing Directives and Addressing Modes. The source routing scheme developed by the IEEE 802.5 committee includes four different types of routing directives. Each frame that is transmitted includes an indicator of the type of routing desired. The four directive types are:

1. *Null:* No routing is desired. In this case, the frame can be delivered only to stations on the same LAN as the source station.
2. *Nonbroadcast:* The frame includes a route, consisting of a sequence of LAN numbers and bridge numbers that defines a unique route from the source station to the destination station. Only bridges on that route forward the frame, and only a single copy of the frame is delivered to the destination station.
3. *All-routes broadcast:* The frame will reach each LAN of the internet by all possible routes. Thus each bridge will forward each frame once to each of its ports in a direction away from the source node, and multiple copies of the frame may appear on a LAN. The destination station will receive one copy of the frame for each possible route through the network.
4. *Single-route broadcast:* Regardless of the destination address of the frame, the frame will appear once, and only once, on each LAN in the internet. For this effect to be achieved, the frame is forwarded by all bridges that are on a spanning tree (with the source node as the root) of the internet. The destination station receives a single copy of the frame.

Let us first examine the potential application of each of these four types of routing, and then examine the mechanisms that may be employed to achieve them. First, consider null routing. In this case, the bridges that share the LAN with the source station are told not to forward the frame. This will be done if the intended destination is on the same LAN as the source station. Nonbroadcast routing is used when the two stations are not on the same LAN and the source station knows a route that can be used to reach the destination station. Only the bridges on that route will forward the frame.

The remaining two types of routing can be used by the source to discover a route to the destination. For example, the source station can use all-routes broadcasting to send a request frame to the intended destination. The destination returns a response frame, using nonbroadcast routing, on each of the routes followed by the incoming request frame. The source station can pick one of these routes and send future frames on that route. Alternatively, the source station could use single-route broadcasting to send a single request frame to the destination station. The destination station could send its response frame via all-routes broadcasting. The incoming frames would reveal all of the possible routes to the destination station, and the source station could pick one of these for future transmissions. Finally, single-route broadcasting could be used for group addressings, as discussed below.

Now consider the mechanisms for implementing these various routing directives. Each frame must include an indicator of which of the four types of routing is required. For null routing, the frame is ignored by the bridge. For nonbroadcast routing, the frame includes an ordered list of LAN numbers and bridge numbers. When a bridge receives a nonbroadcast frame, it forwards the frame only if the routing information contains the sequence LAN i, Bridge x, LAN j, where

$$\text{LAN } i = \text{LAN from which the frame arrived}$$
$$\text{Bridge } x = \text{this bridge}$$
$$\text{LAN } j = \text{another LAN to which this bridge is attached}$$

For all-routes broadcasting, the source station marks the frame for this type of routing, but includes no routing information. Each bridge that forwards the frame will add its bridge number and the outgoing LAN number to the frame's routing information field. Thus, when the frame reaches its destination, it will include a sequenced list of all LANs and bridges visited. To prevent the endless repetition and looping of frames, a bridge obeys the following rule. When an all-routes broadcast frame is received, the bridge examines the routing information field. If the field contains the number of a LAN to which the bridge is attached, the bridge will refrain from forwarding the frame on that LAN. Put the other way, the bridge will forward the frame only to a LAN that the frame has not already visited.

Finally, for single-route broadcasting, a spanning tree of the internet must be developed. This can either be done automatically, as in the 802.1 specification, or manually. In either case, as with the 802.1 strategy, one bridge on each LAN is the designated bridge for that LAN, and is the only one that forwards single-route frames.

It is worth noting the relationship between addressing mode and routing directive. Recall from Chapter 5 that there are three types of MAC addresses:

1. *Individual:* The address specifies a unique destination station.
2. *Group:* The address specifies a group of destination addresses; this is also referred to as *multicast.*
3. *All-stations:* The address specifies all stations that are capable of receiving this frame; this is also referred to as *broadcast.* We will refrain from using this latter term since it is also used in the source routing terminology.

In the case of a single, isolated LAN, group and all-stations addresses refer to stations on the same LAN as the source station. In an internet, it may be desirable to transmit a frame to multiple stations on multiple LANs. Indeed, since a set of LANs interconnected by bridges should appear to the user as a single LAN, the ability to do group and all-stations addressing across the entire internet is mandatory.

Table 10.5 summarizes the relationship between routing specification and addressing mode. If no routing is specified, then all addresses refer only to the immediate LAN. If nonbroadcast routing is specified, then addresses may refer to any station on any LAN visited on the nonbroadcast route. From an addressing point of view, this combination is not generally useful for group and all-stations addressing. If either the all-routes or single-route specifications are included in a frame, then all stations on the internet can be addressed. Thus the total internet acts as a single network from the point of view of MAC addresses. Since less traffic is generated by the single-route specification, this is to be preferred for group and all-stations addressing. Note also that the single-route mechanism in source routing is equivalent to the 802.1 spanning tree approach. Thus, the latter supports both group and all-stations addressing.

Route Delivery and Selection.   With source routing, bridges are relieved of the burden of storing and using routing information. Thus the burden falls on the stations that wish to transmit frames. Clearly, some mechanism is needed by which the source stations can know the route to each destination for which frames are to be sent. Three strategies suggest themselves:

1. Manually load the information into each station. This is simple and effective but has several drawbacks. First, any time that the configuration changes, the routing information at all stations must be

TABLE 10.5 Effects of Various Combinations of Addressing and Source Routing

Addressing Mode	Routing Specification				
	No Routing	Nonbroadcast	All-Routes	Single-Route
Individual	Received by station if it is on the same LAN	Received by station if it is on one of the LANs on the route	Received by station if it is on any LAN	Received by station if it is on any LAN
Group	Received by all group members on the same LAN	Received by all group members on all LANs visited on this route	Received by all group members on all LANs	Received by all group members on all LANs
All-Stations	Received by all stations on the same LAN	Received by all stations on all LANs visited on this route	Received by all stations on all LANs	Received by all stations on all LANs

updated. Second, this approach does not provide for automatic adjustment in the face of the failure of a bridge or LAN.

2. One station on a LAN can query other stations on the same LAN for routing information about distant stations. This approach may reduce the overall amount of routing messages that must be transmitted, compared to option 3 below. However, at least one station on each LAN must have the needed routing information, so this is not a complete solution.

3. When a station needs to learn the route to a destination station, it engages in a dynamic route discovery procedure.

Option 3 is the most flexible and the one that is specified by IEEE 802.5. As was mentioned earlier, two approaches are possible. The source station can transmit an all-routes request frame to the destination. Thus, all possible routes to the destination are discovered. The destination station can send back a nonbroadcast response on each of the discovered routes, allowing the source to choose which route to follow in subsequently transmitting the frame. This approach generates quite a bit of both forward and backward traffic, and requires the destination station to receive and transmit a number of frames. An alternative is for the source station to transmit a single-route request frame. Only one copy of this frame will reach the destination. The destination responds with an all-routes response frame, which generates all possible routes back to the source. Again, the source can choose among these alternative routes.

Figure 10.15 illustrates the latter approach. Assume that the spanning tree that has been chosen for this internet consists of bridges B1, B3, and B4. In this example, station X wishes to discover a route to station Z. Station X issues a single-route request frame. Bridge B2 is not on the spanning tree and so does not forward the frame. The other bridges do forward the frame and it reaches station Z. Note that bridge B4 forwards the frame to LAN 4, although this is not necessary; it is simply an effect of the spanning-tree mechanism. When Z receives this frame, it responds with an all-routes frame. Two messages reach X: one on the path LAN 2, B3, LAN 3, B1, LAN 1, and the other on the path LAN 2, B4, LAN 4, B2, LAN 1. Note that the frame that arrived by the latter route is received by bridge B1 and forwarded onto LAN 3. However, when bridge B3 receives this frame, it sees in the routing information field that the frame has already visited LAN 2; therefore, it does not forward the frame. A similar fate occurs for the frame that follows the first route and is forwarded by bridge B2.

Once a collection of routes has been discovered, the source station needs to select one of the routes. The obvious criterion would be to select the minimum-hop route. Alternatively, a minimum-cost route could be selected, where the cost of a network is inversely proportional to its data rate. In either case, if two or more routes are equivalent by the chosen criterion, then there are two alternatives:

1. Choose the route corresponding to the response message that arrives first. One may assume that that particular route is less congested than the others since the frame on that route arrived earliest.
2. Choose randomly. This should have the effect, over time, of leveling the load among the various bridges.

Another point to consider is how often to update a route. Routes should certainly be changed in response to network failures and perhaps should be changed in response to network congestion. If connection-oriented logical link control is used (see Chapter 5), then one possibility is to rediscover the route with each new connection. Another alternative, which works with either connection-oriented or connectionless service, is to associate a timer with each selected route, and rediscover the route when its time expires.

Frame Format.   With source routing, changes must be made to the MAC frame format. Figure 10.16 shows the frame format specified by the 802.5 source routing document. Recall that the first bit of the destination address indicates whether the address is an individual or a group address. Clearly a source address must always be an individual address. To accommodate source routing, this bit becomes the routing information indicator (RII). The RII bit is set to 0 to indicate null routing and to 1 to indicate that routing information is present in the frame. In the latter case, a new field is added to the MAC frame, the routing information field, which consists of a routing control field followed by from 0 to 14 route designation fields. The routing control field consists of the following subfields:

- *Broadcast (3 bits):* indicates the type of routing directive (none, non-broadcast, all-routes, single-route).
- *Length (5 bits):* indicates the length of the routing information control field, in octets.
- *Direction (1 bit):* indicates to a bridge whether the frame is traveling from the originating station to the target or vice versa. Its use allows the list of route designation fields to appear in the same order for frames traveling in both directions along the route.
- *Largest frame (4 bits):* specifies the largest size of the MAC information field that may be transmitted on this route. This field is encoded to indicate certain common sizes. For example: 0011 indicates a maximum size of 1500 octets, which corresponds to the IEEE 802.3 CSMA/CD and Ethernet limitations; 0111 indicates 4472 octets, which corresponds to FDDI. When a bridge receives a frame, it up-

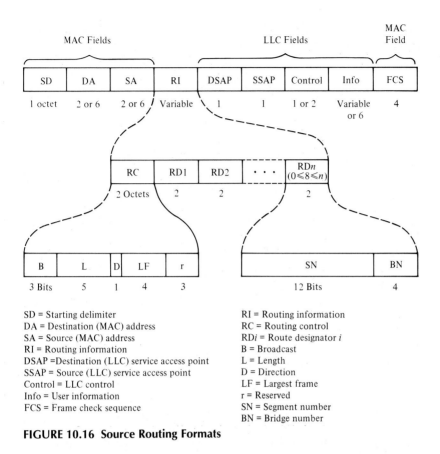

FIGURE 10.16 Source Routing Formats

dates this field if the current value exceeds what the bridge can handle or what its adjoining LANs allow. In this way, the route discovery process also discovers the maximum frame size that can be handled on a particular route.

The remainder of the routing information field consists of a sequence of route designators, each designator corresponding to one hop. The route designator consists of a 12-bit segment number (LAN number) and a 4-bit bridge number.

Spanning Tree versus Source Routing

In this subsection, a brief comparison of the two approaches to bridge routing is provided. For a further discussion, see [SOHA88], [ZHAN88], and [PITT86].

The spanning-tree approach requires no addition to the station logic and no changes to MAC frame format. Thus it preserves full transparency. That is, a collection of LANs interconnected by bridges using spanning-tree routing behaves, from the station's point of view, as a single LAN. The principal drawback of this approach is that it limits the use of redundant bridges to a standby role for availability. Only designated bridges forward frames, and other bridges are unused until a designated bridge fails. Thus redundant bridges cannot be used to share the traffic load, which would provide load leveling and perhaps improved throughput.

Source routing requires additional station logic (route discovery, route selection, insertion of the routing information field in the MAC frame) and changes to the MAC frame format. Thus this method is not fully transparent. However, source routing does permit the selection of an optimal route for each source-destination pair, and permits all bridges to participate in frame forwarding, thus leveling the load. Furthermore, this method requires additional bits to be added to each frame that traverses more than one LAN, increasing the traffic burden.

The other concern relating to source routing is the magnitude of the effect of the route discovery algorithm. We will illustrate the concern with an example from [ZHAN88], which uses the configuration of Figure 10.17. The shaded bridges in the configuration are assumed to be the designated bridges if the spanning-tree approach is used. Using the spanning-tree approach, a frame sent from H2 to H1 will traverse 2 bridges and 3 LANs; only one copy of the frame will arrive at H1. In the source routing case, the route from H1 to H2 must first be discovered. Using single-route broadcasting, a request frame is sent from H2 to H1. H1 responds with an all-routes frame. When B0, B1, and B3 receive the frame, each of them will try to forward it further to LANs it has not passed through. The original response frame will then be fabricated to multiple copies on other LANs. Specifically, 4 copies will be transmitted on LAN 2, 5 on LAN 3, and 6 on LAN 4, for a total of 16 transmissions of the frame (including the initial transmission on LAN 1). The result of this effort will be a route through B3 that is shorter than the spanning-tree route through B2 and B1.

Thus, while the source routing method may produce shorter routes and provides load leveling, the source discovery algorithm is very resource intensive. Even for this small example, 16 transmissions were required. In general, the number of frame copies transmitted for route discovery is on the order of $O(N^M)$, where N is the average number of bridges on each LAN and M is the number of LANs in the configuration [ZHAN88]. For example, a configuration consisting of 12 LANs with an average of 2 bridges per LAN, which is still a modest configuration, would generate on the order of $2^{12} = 4096$ frames for each route discovery.

In summary, source routing offers certain advantages in route selection at the cost of additional station logic, frame overhead, and consid-

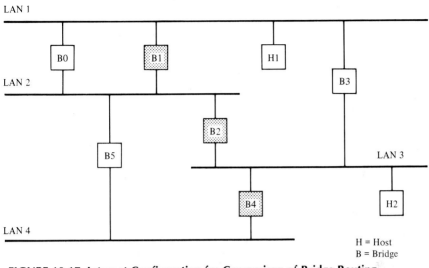

FIGURE 10.17 Internet Configuration for Comparison of Bridge Routing Approaches [ZHAN88]

erable traffic overhead. In most situations, the spanning-tree approach should prove adequate and avoids the disadvantages of the source routing approach.

Source Routing Transparent

The transparent bridge standard is available on many IEEE 802.3 and 802.4 products, and the source routing bridge standard is widely available on 802.5 products. While both types of bridges have advantages and disadvantages, a key problem with both is that they are incompatible. In order to allow the interconnection of LANs by a mixture of transparent and source routing bridges, a new standard has been developed by the 802.5 committee, referred to as the SRT (source routing transparent) technique [IEEE91b, NETR91, GREE90a].

The key to the operation of an SRT bridge is the RII bit in the MAC source address field. Recall that this bit is set to 1 by a source station to indicate that routing is desired and to 0 to indicate that no routing is to be performed (i.e., the frame should not be picked up by a source routing bridge). This bit is not used by stations that are supported by transparent bridges. As the name implies, the transparent bridge approach is transparent to the end stations. Thus the RII bit is always set to 0 by a station that is not participating in source routing.

Figure 10.18 indicates how the RII bit is used by an SRT bridge. All passing user data frames are observed by the bridge. If RII = 1, then

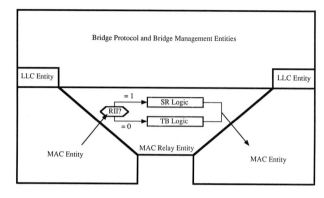

FIGURE 10.18 SRT Bridge Logic

the frame is handled by source routing logic; if RII = 0, then the frame is handled by transparent bridge logic.

So much for the basic frame forwarding logic. The difficult design problems associated with SRT bridging have to do with how routes are established. For transparent bridging, a spanning tree must be developed among all of the bridges. For source routing, a spanning tree must also be developed. The requirement for SRT operation is that the bridge must permit both transparent and source routing stations to participate within the same spanning tree. Since the SRT bridge includes transparent bridge logic, it can interoperate with pure transparent bridges to create the spanning tree. Thus, we can have a collection of LANs interconnected by a mixture of transparent bridges and SRT bridges. However, pure source routing bridges could not be incorporated into such a configuration, because they are incapable of passing transparent frames.

10.3

ROUTERS

The bridge is applicable only to a configuration involving a single type of LAN. Of course, in many cases, an organization will need access to devices on a variety of networks. For example, as Figure 1.6 illustrates, an organization may have a tiered LAN architecture, with different types of LANs used for different purposes within an organization. There may also need to be access to devices on a wide-area network. Examples of the latter are a public information source or data base for query and transaction applications and a customer or supplier computer for transferring ordering information.

A general-purpose device that can be used to connect dissimilar networks and that operates at layer 3 of the OSI model is known as a router.

We begin this section by looking at the requirements that must be satisfied by the router to support internetworking.

Requirements

Up until now, we have discussed instances in which the differences among networks were small. Now let us consider the more general problem of connecting a local network to outside resources. For now, let us limit ourselves to LANs; the principles for MANs are the same, and the protocol issues we are discussing do not apply to digital PBXs. For LAN connection, we can distinguish a number of cases:

1. *LAN-to-LAN:* A user or application process on one LAN desires access to a user or application process on another. The possibilities include:
   a. Point-to-point link, homogeneous networks. For example, a corporation might procure a LAN for each of its main offices from a single vendor.
   b. Network link, homogeneous networks. As above, but it is found more feasible to connect through a network (e.g., an X.25 long-haul packet-switched network).
   c. Point-to-point link, heterogeneous networks. An organization may have two LANs, in the same location, or separated, from different vendors.
   d. Network link, heterogeneous networks. As above, but linked by a packet-switched network.
2. *LAN-to-network:* In this case, some or all LAN subscribers need access to services available on a long-haul network (e.g., a data base or information utility available through a packet-switched network). Two possibilities are:
   a. Host-to-network link. Each host (or terminal) that requires a network link establishes one independent of the LAN.
   b. LAN-to-network link. As a service, the LAN establishes a link to the long-haul network that may be multiplexed to provide access for multiple hosts.

Of these six cases, three are of no real interest as problems in internetworking. Case 1a can be handled with a bridge. The two halves of the bridge maintain a layer 2 point-to-point link. Case 1b is also solved by a bridge, with a special adaptation to handle the long-haul network protocol. For example, consider two LANs connected via an X.25 network. The bridge on LAN A accepts frames as before. Now, it wraps that frame in a layer 3 packet and transmits it to the bridge at LAN B, which unwraps the frame and inserts it into LAN B. For this purpose, a virtual circuit may be maintained between the two bridges. Case 2a does not involve internetworking at all! Each host on the LAN is responsible for its own link to the long-haul network and for implementing the protocols of that network; the LAN is not involved.

The remaining three cases require some kind of logic or protocol beyond that needed for intranetwork routing and delivery. This logic can be considered to reside in a router. Figure 10.19 depicts these three cases. It can be seen (or will be seen) that these three cases are fundamentally the same. The internetworking requirements are the same for all these cases. In essence, we wish to permit process-to-process communication across more than one network.

Before turning to the architectural approaches to providing the service of Figure 10.19, we list some of the requirements on the internetworking facility. These include:

1. Provide a link between networks. At minimum, a physical and link control connection is needed.
2. Provide for the routing and delivery of data between processes on different networks.
3. Provide an accounting service that keeps track of the use of the various networks and gateways and maintains status information.
4. Provide the services listed above in such a way as not to require modifications to the networking architecture of any of the attached networks. This means that the internetworking facility must accommodate a number of differences among networks. These include:

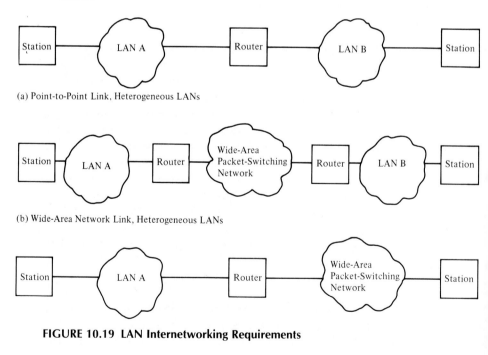

(a) Point-to-Point Link, Heterogeneous LANs

(b) Wide-Area Network Link, Heterogeneous LANs

FIGURE 10.19 LAN Internetworking Requirements

a. Different addressing schemes. The networks may use different endpoint names and addresses and directory maintenance schemes. Some form of global network addressing must be provided, as well as a directory service.

b. Different maximum packet size. Packets from one network may have to be broken up into smaller pieces for another. This process is referred to as segmentation.

c. Different network interfaces. For purposes of this discussion, we will assume that the interface is at layer 3, such as is found in an X.25 network. This assumption is a reasonable one since layers 1, 2, and 3 are specific to the communications subnetwork, while layer 4 and above relate to end-to-end host process considerations. As we discussed in Chapter 8, there are a number of protocol residency alternatives between host and NIU for LANs. In this chapter, we use the DTE, DCE terminology for the communications architecture, to avoid confusion with the host-NIU architecture.

d. Different time-outs. Generally, a connection-oriented transport service will await an acknowledgment until a time-out expires, at which time it will retransmit its segment of data. Generally, longer times are required for successful delivery across multiple networks. Internetwork timing procedures must allow successful transmission that avoids unnecessary retransmissions.

e. Error recovery. Intranetwork procedures may provide anything from no error recovery up to reliable end-to-end (within the network) service. The internetwork service should not depend on or be interfered with by the nature of the individual network's error recovery capability.

f. Status reporting. Different networks report status and performance differently. Yet it must be possible for the internetworking facility to provide such information on internetworking activity to interested and authorized processes.

g. Routing techniques. Intranetwork routing may depend on fault detection and congestion control techniques peculiar to each network. The internetworking facility must be able to coordinate these to adaptively route data between DTEs on different networks.

h. Access control. Each network will have its own user access control techniques. These must be invoked by the internetwork facility as needed. Further, a separate internetwork access control technique may be required.

i. Connection, connectionless. Individual networks may provide connection-oriented (e.g., virtual circuit) or connectionless (datagram) service. The internetwork service should not depend on the nature of the connection service for the individual networks.

Protocol Architecture

Router operation depends on a protocol at OSI layer 3 (network layer), sometimes known as an **internet protocol** (IP). Figure 10.20 depicts a typical example, in which two LANs are interconnected by a wide-area X.25 network. The figure depicts the operations involved for the transfer of data from station A on LAN 1 and station B on LAN 2. The two stations and the routers must share a common internet protocol. In addition, to communicate successfully, the two stations must share the same protocols above IP.

The data to be sent by A are passed down to A's internet protocol. IP attaches a header specifying, among other things, the global internet address of B. That address is in two parts: network identifier and station identifier. The result is called an internet protocol data unit, or simply a

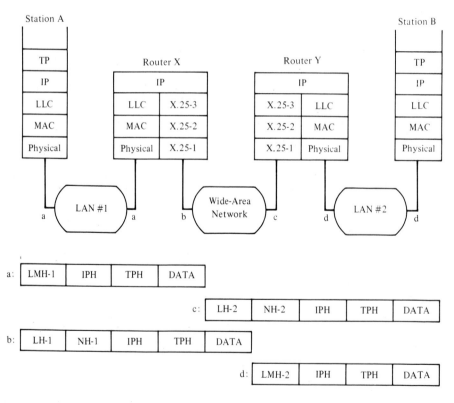

LMH-*i* : Combined LLC and MAC header for LAN i
LH-*j* : Link Header (X.25 Layer 2) for DTE = Router *j*
NH-*k* : Network Header (X.25 Layer 3) for DTE = Router *k*
IPH : Internet Protocol Header
TPH : Transport Protocol Header

FIGURE 10.20 Message Encapsulation: IP Approach

datagram. The datagram is then encapsulated with the LAN protocol and is sent to a router that strips off the LAN header. The datagram is then encapsulated with the X.25 protocol and transmitted across the network to a router. The router strips off the X.25 fields and recovers the datagram, which is then wrapped in LAN 2 headers and sent to B. If a connection-oriented service is required, A and B must share a common layer 4 protocol.

With this example in mind, we describe briefly the sequence of steps involved in sending a datagram between two stations on different networks. This is followed by a more detailed discussion of the design issues involved.

The process starts in the sending station. Station A wants to send an IP datagram to a station B on another network. The IP module in A constructs the datagram with the global internet address of B in the datagram header and recognizes that the destination is on another network. So the first step is to send the datagram to router X. To do this, the IP module passes the datagram down to the next lower layer (in this case LLC) with instructions to send it to the router. The header at this lower layer will contain the address of the router. In our example, this is the MAC-level address of router X on LAN 1.

Next, the packet travels through LAN 1 to router X. The router strips off the MAC and LLC headers and analyzes the IP header to determine whether this datagram contains control information intended for itself, or data intended for a station farther on. In our example, the data are intended for station B. The gateway must therefore make a routing decision. There are three possibilities:

1. The destination station B is connected directly to one of the subnetworks to which the router is attached.
2. To reach the destination, one or more additional routers must be traversed.
3. The router does not know the destination address.

In case 1, the router sends the datagram directly to the destination. In case 2, a routing decision must be made: To which router should the datagram be sent? In both cases, the router sends the datagram down to the next lower layer with a destination station address. Remember, we are speaking here of a lower-layer address that refers to this network (a layer 3 address for an X.25 network; a MAC address for a LAN). In case 3, the router returns an error message to the source of the datagram.

In this example, the data must be routed through router Y before reaching the destination. So router X constructs a packet by appending an X.25 header to the IP data unit containing the address of router Y. When this packet arrives at router Y, the packet header is stripped off. The router determines that this IP data unit is destined for B, which is connected directly to a network to which the router is attached. The router therefore creates a MAC frame with a destination address and sends it out onto LAN 3.

At each router, before the data can be forwarded, the router may need to segment the datagram to accommodate a smaller maximum packet size limitation on the outgoing network. The datagram is split into two or more segments, each of which becomes an independent IP datagram. Each new datagram is wrapped in a lower-layer packet and queued for transmission. The router may also limit the length of its queue for each network to which it attaches so as to avoid having a slow network penalize a faster one. Once the queue limit is reached, additional datagrams are simply dropped.

The process described above continues through as many routers as it takes for the datagram to reach its destination. As with a router, the destination host recovers the IP datagram from its network wrapping. If segmentation has occurred, the IP module in the destination host buffers the incoming data until the entire original data field can be reassembled. This block of data is then passed to a higher layer in the host.

The internet protocol does not guarantee that all data will be delivered or that the data that are delivered will arrive in the proper order. It is the responsibility of the next higher layer, the transport layer, to recover from any errors that occur. This approach provides for a great deal of flexibility.

With the internet protocol approach, each unit of data is passed from router to router in an attempt to get from source to destination. Since delivery is not guaranteed, there is no particular reliability requirement on any of the subnetworks. Thus the protocol will work with any combination of subnetwork types. Since the sequence of delivery is not guaranteed, successive data units can follow different paths through the internet. This allows the protocol to react to congestion and failure in the internet by changing routes.

Design Issues

With that brief sketch of the operation of an IP-controlled internet, we can now go back and examine some design issues in greater detail. These are:

- Addressing
- Routing
- Datagram lifetime
- Segmentation and reassembly

Addressing.   In order to transfer data from one end system to another end system, there must be some way of uniquely identifying the destination ES. Thus, with each ES, we must be able to associate a unique identifier, or address. This address will allow ESs and ISs to perform the routing function properly.

In the OSI environment, this unique address is typically equated to a **network service access point** (NSAP). An NSAP uniquely identifies an ES within the internet. An ES may have more than one NSAP, but each is unique to that particular ES. A network layer address may also refer to the network protocol entity itself. This latter is appropriate in an intermediate system, which does not support upper layers via an NSAP. In the case of an IS, the network layer address is called a **network entity title** (NET).

Both NSAPs and NETs provide an unambiguous global internet address. Frequently, this address is in the form of *(network, host)*, where the parameter *network* identifies a particular subnetwork and the parameter *host* identifies a particular ES attached to that subnetwork.

Figure 10.21 suggests that another level of addressing is needed. Each subnetwork must maintain a unique address for each ES attached to that subnetwork. This allows the subnetwork to route data units through the subnetwork and deliver them to the intended ES. Such an address is referred to as a **subnetwork point of attachment** (SNPA) address.

It would appear convenient for the *host* parameter in the global address to be identical to the SNPA for that ES. Unfortunately, this may

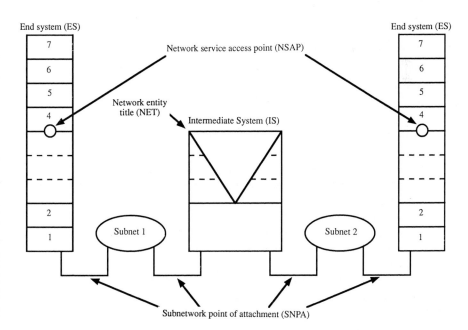

FIGURE 10.21 Network-Layer Addressing

not always be practical. Different networks use different addressing formats and different address lengths. Furthermore, an ES may enjoy more than one attachment point into the same network. Accordingly, we must assume that the *host* parameter has global significance and the SNPA has significance only within a particular subnetwork. In this case, the internetworking facility must translate from the global address to the locally significant address to route data units.

Routing.   Routing is generally accomplished by maintaining a routing table in each end system and router that gives, for each possible destination network, the next router to which the internet datagram should be sent.

Table 10.6 shows the routing table for the BBN router, which is part of the DARPA internet. If a network is directly connected, it is so indicated. Otherwise, the datagram must be routed through one or more routers (one or more hops). The table indicates the identity of the next router on the route (which must share a common subnetwork with this router or end system) and the number of hops to the destination.

The routing table may be static or dynamic. A static table, however, could contain alternate routes if a router is unavailable. A dynamic table is more flexible in responding to both error and congestion conditions. In the DARPA internet, for example, when a router goes down, all of its neighbors will send out a status report, allowing other routers and stations to update their routing tables. A similar scheme can be used to control congestion. This latter is particularly important because of the mismatch in capacity between local and wide-area networks. Section 10.4 discusses routing protocols.

Routing tables may also be used to support other internetworking services, such as security and priority. For example, individual networks might be classified to handle data up to a given security classification. The routing mechanism must assure that data of a given security level are not allowed to pass through networks not cleared to handle them.

Another routing technique is source routing. The source station specifies the route by including a sequential list of routers in the datagram. This, again, could be useful for security or priority requirements.

Finally, we mention a service related to routing: route recording. To record a route, each router appends its internet address to a list of addresses in the datagram. This feature is useful for testing and debugging purposes.

Datagram Lifetime.   If dynamic or alternate routing is used, the potential exists for a datagram to circulate indefinitely through the internet. For example, if there are sudden, significant shifts in internet traffic, the datagram might be diverted first one way and then another to avoid

TABLE 10.6   INTERNET Routing Table for the BBN Router

Network Name	Net Address	Route[a]
SATNET	4	Directly connected
ARPANET	10	Directly connected
BBN-NET	3	1 hop via RCC 10.3.0.72 (ARPANET 3/72)
PURDUE-COMPUTER SCIENCE	192.5.1	2 hops via PURDUE 10.2.0.37 (ARPANET 2/37)
INTELPOST	43	2 hops via MILLS 10.3.0.17 (ARPANET 3/17)
DECNET-TEST	38	3 hops via MILLS 10.3.0.17 (ARPANET 3/17)
WIDEBAND	28	3 hops via RCC 10.3.0.72 (ARPANET 3/72)
BBN-PACKET RADIO	1	2 hops via RCC 10.3.0.72 (ARPANET 3/72)
DCN-COMSAT	29	1 hop via MILLS 10.3.0.17 (ARPANET 3/17)
FIBERNET	24	3 hops via RCC 10.3.0.72 (ARPANET 3/72)
BRAGG-PACKET RADIO	9	1 hop via BRAGG 10.0.0.38 (ARPANET 0/38)
CLARK NET	8	2 hops via MILLS 10.3.0.17 (ARPANET 3/17)
LCSNET	18	1 hop via MIT-LCS 10.0.0.77 (ARPANET 0/77)
BBN-TERMINAL CONCENTRATOR	192.1.2	3 hops via RCC 10.3.0.72 (ARPANET 3/72)
BBN-JERICHO	192.1.3	3 hops via RCC 10.3.0.72 (ARPANET 3/72)
UCLNET	11	1 hop via UCL 4.0.0.60 (SATNET 60)
RSRE-NULL	35	1 hop via UCL 4.0.0.60 (SATNET 60)
RSRE-PPSN	25	2 hops via UCL 4.0.0.60 (SATNET 60)
SAN FRANCISCO-PACKET RADIO-2	6	1 hop via C3PO 10.1.0.51 (ARPANET 1/51)

[a]Names and acronyms identify gateways in the INTERNET system.
Source: [SHEL82].

areas of congestion. Additionally, there might be a flaw in the routing tables of the various routers that causes the datagram to stay inside the network. These problems place an undesirable burden on the internet. To avoid these problems, each datagram can be marked with a lifetime. Once the lifetime expires, the datagram is discarded.

A simple way to implement lifetime is to use a hop count. Each time that a datagram passes through a router, the count is decremented. Alternatively, the lifetime could be a true measure of time, which requires that the router must somehow know how long it has taken for the datagram to traverse the last network, so as to know by how much to decrement the lifetime field. The advantage of using a true measure of time is that it can be used in the reassembly algorithm, which is described next.

Segmentation and Reassembly.   To avoid fixing the maximum size of a packet, a constraint that is unfavorable to CSMA/CD LANs, segmentation must be done at the internet level by routers.

The ISO standard, described below, specifies an efficient technique for datagram segmentation. The technique requires the following fields in the datagram header:

- ID
- Length
- Offset
- More Flag

The ID is some means of uniquely identifying a station-originated datagram. It consists of the source and destination addresss, an identifier of the protocol layer that generated the datagram, and a sequence number supplied by that protocol layer. The Length is the length of the data field in octets, and the Offset is the position of a fragment in the original datagram in octets.

The source station IP layer creates a datagram with Length equal to the entire length of the data field, with Offset = 0, and the More Flag reset. To segment a long packet, an IP module in a router performs the following tasks:

1. Creates two new datagrams and copies the header fields of the incoming datagram into both.
2. Divides the data into two approximately equal portions along an 8-bit boundary, placing one portion in each new datagram.
3. Sets the Length field of the first datagram to the length of the inserted data, and sets the More Flag. The Offset field is unchanged.
4. Sets the Length field of the second datagram to the Length of the inserted data, and adds the length of the first data portion divided by 8 to the Offset field. The More Flag remains the same.

Table 10.7 gives an example. The procedure can be generalized to an *n*-way split.

To reassemble a datagram, there must be sufficient buffer space at the reassembly point. As segments with the same ID arrive, their data fields are inserted in the proper position in the buffer until the entire datagram is reassembled, which is achieved when a contiguous set of data exists starting with an Offset of 0 and ending with data from a segment with a reset More Flag. Typically, reassembly is done at the destination station, to avoid burdening routers with unnecessarily large buffer space and to permit segments to arrive via different routes. However, as men-

TABLE 10.7   Segmentation Example

Original Datagram	First Segment	Second Segment
Length = 472	Length = 240	Length = 232
Offset = 0	Offset = 0	Offset = 240
More = 0	More = 1	More = 0

tioned, it is an advantage in certain local networks to make the packet size as large as possible. Therefore, it might be a good design decision to dictate reassembly of datagrams entering a local network.

One eventuality that must be dealt with is that one or more of the segments may not get through: the IP service does not guarantee delivery. Some means are needed to decide to abandon a reassembly effort to free up buffer space. The ISO IP standard suggests two approaches. First, assign a reassembly lifetime to the first segment to arrive. This is a local, real-time clock assigned by the reassembly function and decremented while the segments of the original datagram are being buffered. If the time expires prior to complete reassembly, the received segments are discarded. A second approach is to make use of the datagram lifetime, which is part of the header of each incoming segment. The lifetime field continues to be decremented by the reassembly function; as with the first approach, if the lifetime expires prior to complete reassembly, the received segments are discarded.

The ISO Internetworking Standard

Now we look at the internetworking standard developed by ISO [ISO87, ISO88, PISC86]. As with any layer specification, IP can be described in two parts:

- The services provided to the next higher layer (e.g., ISO transport)
- The protocol mechanisms and formats that are used to provide the service

ISO IP Service.   The ISO internetworking service is defined by two primitives at the interface between IP and an IP user. There are:

- N-UNITDATA.request (Source Address, Destination Address, Quality of Service, NS-User-Data)
- N-UNITDATA.indication (Source Address, Destination Address, Quality of Service, NS-User-Data)

The request primitive is issued by an IP user to submit data to IP for transfer across the internet. The indication primitive is issued by IP to a higher-layer user to deliver data arriving from the internet. The *source address* and *destination address* parameters are global internet addresses that uniquely identify end stations. The *quality-of-service* parameter consists of options drawn from the list of Table 10.8. The IP entities in the source station and the routers will endeavor, within the limitations of the network services available, to provide these additional services. Finally, *NS-User-Data* is the unit of data transferred across the internet in a datagram.

ISO IP Protocol. The ISO IP protocol is best explained with reference to the IP header format (Table 10.9). The header is largely self-explanatory. Some clarifying remarks:

- *Protocol identifier:* When the source and destination stations are connected to the same network, an internal protocol is not needed. In that case, the internet layer is null and the header consists of this single field of 8 bits.

TABLE 10.8 Quality-of-Service Parameters for the ISO Connectionless-Mode Network Service

Transit Delay	The elapsed time between an N-UNITDATA.request at the source station and the corresponding N-UNITDATA.indication at the destination station
Protection from Unauthorized Access	Four options are defined: 1. no protection features 2. protection against passive monitoring 3. protection against modification, replay, addition, or deletion 4. both (1) and (2)
Cost Determinants	Permits the user to specify: 1. that the service provider (IP) should use the least expensive means available 2. maximum acceptable cost
Residual Error Probability	Probability that a particular NS-User-Data unit will be lost, duplicated, or delivered incorrectly
Priority	Specifies the relative priority of NS-User-Data units with respect to: 1. the order in which the data units have their quality of service degraded, if necessary 2. the order in which data units are to be discarded to recover resources, if necessary

TABLE 10.9   ISO IP Header Format

Name	Size (bits)	Purpose
Protocol Identifier	8	Indicates if internet service is provided
Header Length	8	Header length in octets
Version	8	Version of protocol
PDU Lifetime	8	Lifetime in units of 500 ms
Flags	3	Three 1-bit indicators
Type	5	Data or Error PDU
Segment Length	16	Header plus data length
Checksum	16	Applies to header only
Destination Address Length	8	Length of field in octets
Destination Address	Variable	Structure not specified
Source Address Length	8	Length of field in octets
Source Address	Variable	Structure not specified
Identifier	16	Unique for source, destination
Segment Offset	16	Offset in octets
Total Length	16	Length of original PDU
Options	Variable	Additional services

- *Lifetime:* Expressed as a multiple of 500 ms. It is determined and set by the source station. Each gateway that the IP datagram visits decrements this field by 1 for each 500 ms of estimated delay for that hop. When the lifetime value reaches 0, the datagram is discarded. This technique prevents endlessly circulating datagrams.
- *Flags:* The S/P flag indicates whether segmentation is permitted. The M/S flag is the More Flag described earlier. The E/P flag indicates whether an error report is desired by the source station if a datagram is discarded.
- *Checksum:* Computed at each gateway.
- *Addresses:* Variable-length addresses are provided; the structure of the addresses is not specified in the standard.
- *Options:* The optional parameters that may be specified include: Security, defined by the user; Source Routing, which allows the source station to dictate the gateway routing; Recording of Route, used to trace the route a datagram takes; Priority; and Quality of Service, which specifies reliability and delay parameters.

10.4

ROUTING WITH ROUTERS

The routers in an internet perform much the same function as packet-switching nodes in a packet-switching network. As with the nodes of a packet-switching network, the bridges or routers of an internet need to make routing decisions based on knowledge of the topology and conditions of the internet. In simple internets, a fixed routing scheme is possible. However, in more complex internets, a degree of dynamic cooperation is needed among the routers. In particular, the router must avoid portions of the network that have failed and should avoid portions of the network that are congested. In order to make such dynamic routing decisions, routers exchange routing information using a special protocol for that purpose. Information is needed about the status of the internet, in terms of which networks can be reached by which routes, and the delay characteristics of various routes.

In considering the routing function of routers, it is important to distinguish two concepts:

- *Routing information:* information about the topology and delays of the internet
- *Routing algorithm:* the algorithm used to make a routing decision for a particular datagram, based on current routing information

There is another way to partition the problem that is useful from the point of view of allocating routing functions properly and effective standardization. This is to partition the routing function into:

- Routing between end systems (ESs) and intermediate systems (ISs)
- Routing between ISs

The reason for the partition is that there are fundamental differences between what an ES must know to route a packet and what an IS must know. In the case of an ES, it must first know whether the destination ES is on the same subnet. If so, then data can be delivered directly using the subnetwork access protocol. If not, then the ES must forward the data to an IS attached to the same subnetwork. If there is more than one such IS, it is simply a matter of choosing one. The IS forwards datagrams on behalf of other systems and needs to have some idea of the overall topology of the network in order to make a global routing decision.

Accordingly, ISO has developed standards for two types of routing protocols: ES-IS protocols and IS-IS protocols. We can list three technical advantages to this approach:

1. The more difficult and complicated procedures can be placed in the ISs, which are dedicated to the internetworking function, minimizing overhead in the ESs.

2. A specialized ES-IS protocol can be made independent of the IS-IS routing procedures. This allows multiple IS-IS procedures to be used, if necessary, without burdening the ES.
3. Many subnetworks are of a broadcast nature; the ES-IS protocol can exploit this feature, where it exists, to improve efficiency.

In the remainder of this section, we provide an introduction to ES-ES and ES-IS protocols. More detail can be found in [STAL93b].

ES-IS Routing

The ES-IS protocol is designed to solve the basic routing problems associated with ESs on a subnetwork. These are:

1. When an ES is presented with data from a higher layer, in the form of a network service data unit (NSDU), with a destination NSAP, it must first decide whether the destination ES is on the same subnetwork as itself. If so, then it can deliver the user data by using the subnetwork access protocol (SNAcP) and providing that protocol with the subnetwork point of attachment (SNPA) address of the destination ES. However, direct examination of the NSAP may not provide the identity of the destination subnetwork. Therefore, the ES needs a method for discovering the existence and SNPA of other ESs on the same subnetwork.
2. If the destination ES is not on the same subnetwork, then the ES must forward the user data to an IS for routing through the internet. It does this, again, by using the SNAcP and providing that protocol with the SNPA of an IS attached to this subnetwork. Therefore, the ES needs a method for discovering the existence and SNPA of at least one IS on the same subnetwork.
3. If there is more than one IS on the subnetwork, then the ES should send datagrams to that IS which can most efficiently deliver the datagram to the destination. Therefore, the ES needs a method for deciding which IS to use for any particular destination ES.
4. For ISs, the final stage of relaying occurs when the IS is connected to the same subnetwork as the destination ES. When a datagram is forwarded to an IS, it must first decide whether the destination ES is on one of the subnetworks to which the IS is directly attached. If so, then it can deliver the datagram by using the SNAcP and providing that protocol with the SNPA address of the destination ES. However, direct examination of the NSAP may not provide the identity of the destination subnetwork. Therefore, the IS needs a method for discovering the existence and SNPA of these ESs.

To address these problems, two types of information are provided to ESs and ISs by the ES-IS protocol: configuration information and route redirection information. Configuration information deals with the existence of ESs and ISs attached to a particular subnetwork. The information includes the NSAP or NET of the system and its SNPA address. Configuration information permits ESs to discover the existence and reachability of other ESs and of ISs, and permits ISs to discover the existence and reachability of ESs. This information is provided dynamically by the protocol, eliminating the need for manual insertion of the information. Route redirection information is supplied to an ES to indicate a preferred IS to be used for a particular remote NSAP. The delivery of this information is triggered by an ES attempt to forward data through a less-preferred IS.

ISO 9542 defines an ES-IS protocol that is intended to operate with the ISO connectionless internet protocol. This protocol provides both configuration and redirection functions.

Configuration Functions.   The configuration functions of ISO 9542 include the following:

1. An ES learns the NET and SNPA of each IS on the subnet by means of an ES-IS exchange.
2. An IS learns the NSAP and SNPA of each ES on the subnet by means of an ES-IS exchange.
3. An ES learns the NSAP and SNPA of other ESs on the subnet by means of an ES-ES exchange.

These functions are accomplished by means of the ES Hello (ESH) and IS Hello (ISH) PDUs.

The ESH is broadcast to all ISs periodically by each ES on the subnetwork. It includes a list of all NSAPs (usually one, but sometimes multiple) that are valid for that ESH. On receipt of an ESH, the IS stores the associated addressing information.

The ISH is broadcast to all ESs periodically by each IS on the subnetwork. It identifies the IS by its NET address. In both the ESH and ISH, there is no SNPA address information, yet this information is needed by the recipient. However, this information is supplied by the subnetwork service. When a data unit is delivered by a subnetwork service, it is accompanied by the subnetwork source and destination SNPAs.

Route Redirection Function.   Redirection information is provided by ISs in the form of Redirect (RD) PDUs. When an IS receives a datagram for forwarding, it will attempt to forward the datagram according to the rules of the CLNP. Two cases lead to the use of the RD:

1. If the datagram is forwarded to another IS on the same subnetwork as the originating ES, then it is clear that resources could have been saved if the ES had simply forwarded the datagram

directly to the other IS. Therefore, *after* forwarding the original datagram, the IS sends an RD to the originating ES that instructs the ES to forward all future datagrams intended for that NSAP to the other IS. The NET and SNPA of the other IS are supplied to the ES.

2. If the destination system is on the same subnetwork over which the datagram arrives, then it is clear that resources could have been saved if the originating ES had simply forwarded the datagram directly to the destination ES. Therefore, *after* forwarding the original datagram, the IS sends an RD to the originating ES that informs the ES that it can directly address the destination ES. The NSAP and SNPA of the destination ES are supplied to the originating ES.

IS-IS Routing

ISO 10589 defines an IS-IS routing protocol to be used in conjunction with the ISO connectionless internet protocol.

Routing Environment.   In order to make the complexity of large internets more manageable, ISO has defined a multilevel, hierarchical routing environment. At the top level, an internet can be divided into a number of **routing domains.** A domain is a large-scale portion of an internet, generally organized along geographical or organizational lines. For example, all of the local area networks at a site, such as a military base or campus, could be linked by ISs to form a routing domain. This complex might be linked through a wide-area network to other routing domains. Domains can be further subdivided into **areas.** [MCCO91] and [TSUC89] list a number of advantages for this hierarchical approach:

- Minimizing the amount of information exchanged by ISs, thus simplifying the operation of ISs at all levels
- Allowing different routing optimizations within each level of the hierarchy
- Protecting the entire routing environment from inaccurate information generated by any intermediate system
- Construction of "firewalls" between different portions (areas, domains) that would provide access control and other mechanisms to protect and secure the environment
- Simplifying routing protocol evolution, since ISs at one level need not know the protocol or topology at other levels

Four levels of routing can be defined:

- *Level 0 routing:* routing of traffic between ESs and ISs on the same subnet

- *Level 1 routing:* routing of traffic between ISs within the same area
- *Level 2 routing:* routing of traffic between different areas within the same routing domain
- *Level 3 routing:* routing of traffic between different domains

Level 0 routing is covered by ES-IS routing protocols. Levels 1 and 2 are covered by IS-IS routing protocols. Currently, there is no standard for level 3 routing. At this level, the gross topology will generally be rather simple, and static routing based on manual configuration will usually suffice.

Figure 10.22 illustrates the routing hierarchy. Level 1 ISs know the topology in their area (by means of the level one IS-IS interchange), including all ESs and ISs in their area. However, level 1 ISs do not know the identity of ISs or ESs outside of their area. Level 1 ISs forward all traffic for ESs outside of their area to a level 2 IS in their area.

Level 2 ISs form a backbone that connects the level 1 areas within a routing domain. All the level 2 ISs in a routing domain are connected at level 2. That is, any level 2 IS can reach any other level 2 IS by going through level 2 ISs only (without visiting any level 1 ISs). Level 2 ISs know the level 2 topology and know which addresses are reachable via each level 2 IS in their routing domain. Each level 2 IS is also a level 1 IS in a particular area; this allows for final delivery of datagrams. Thus, the obligation of a level 2 IS is to forward a datagram to the destination area. The final level 2 IS on the path will also be a level 1 IS in the destination area and can forward the datagram to other level 1 ISs in the area to reach the destination subnet and ultimately the destination ES. Thus we can envisage the following set of steps. Assume that ES A receives user data from the transport layer and constructs a datagram with a destination NSAP indicating ES B. Then:

1. If ES B is on the same subnetwork as ES A, deliver the datagram directly (routing information may be preconfigured or obtained via ES-IS protocol ISO 9542).
2. Otherwise, ES A delivers the datagram to a level 1 IS on the same subnetwork for internetwork routing (routing information obtained via IS-ES protocol ISO 9542).
3. The IS examines the NSAP in the datagram to determine if ES B is in the same area as this IS. If so:
   a. The IS makes a routing decision to forward the datagram through zero or more additional level 1 ISs to reach ES B's subnetwork (routing information obtained via level 1 IS-IS protocol ISO 10589).
   b. The final IS on the path shares a subnetwork with ES B and delivers the datagram directly (routing information obtained via ES-IS protocol ISO 9542).
4. If the condition in step 3 does not prevail, then the IS forwards the

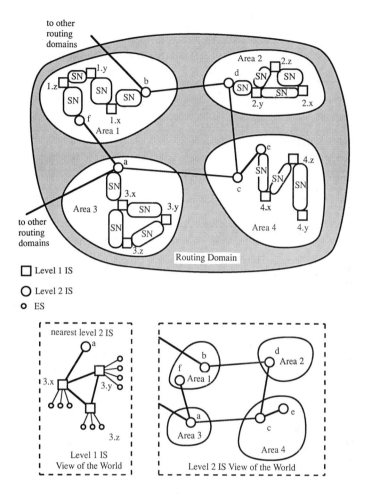

FIGURE 10.22 Routing Hierarchy [TSUC89]

datagram through zero or more additional level 1 ISs to reach a level 1 IS in this area that also acts as a level 2 IS (routing information obtained via level 1 IS-IS protocol ISO 10589).

5. The level 2 IS examines the NSAP in the datagram to determine the destination area. It then forwards the datagram through one or more level 2 ISs to a level 2 IS that is the destination area (routing information obtained via level 2 IS-IS protocol ISO 10589).

6. Once the datagram reaches a level 2 IS in the target area, that IS acts as a level 1 IS and performs step 3.

Routing Algorithm.   One of the functions of an IS is to make a routing decision in order to forward the datagram on its next hop. This routing decision is based on the IS having information about the topology of the internet and the cost associated with alternative paths through the internet. In discussing any routing algorithm, the following aspects must be considered:

- Information required
- Routing metrics
- Path calculation
- Information exchange discipline

The information required by an IS to perform the routing function is of three types:

1. *Topology information:* The information required will depend on the role of the IS (Figure 10.22). A level 1 IS needs to know only the existence of the other level 1 ISs in its area and at least one level 2 IS in its area, and the way in which these ISs are interconnected. Similarly, a level 2 IS needs to know only the identity of the other level 2 ISs in its routing domain and the way in which these are interconnected. In either case, we can abstract the topology into a graph consisting of nodes connected by edges. Each node is an IS and each edge is either a point-to-point link or a subnetwork.
2. *NSAP reachability:* In the case of a level 1 IS, it needs to know, for each ES (identified by an NSAP) in its area, the identity of the subnet that contains that ES. In the case of a level 2 IS, it needs to know, for each ES, the area that contains that ES and a level 2 IS that is in that area.
3. *Hop cost:* For either level 1 or level 2 routing, each "hop" must be assigned a cost in each direction. In the case of level 1 routing, a hop is a subnetwork or point-to-point link connecting ISs. For level 2 routing, a hop is a point-to-point link between level 2 ISs.

The cost associated with each hop, in each direction, is generally referred to as a *routing metric.* The routing metrics used in ISO 10589 are arranged in four levels and defined in such a way that a lower value indicates a more optimum (lower cost) choice. In order, the routing metrics are:

1. *Default:* assigned by routing administrators to satisfy any administrative policies. The default metric is understood by every IS in the domain. Each hop has a positive integer value assigned to it. The values may be assigned arbitrarily, but the intent is that the metric should be a function of throughput or capacity: higher values indicate lower capacity.

2. *Delay:* measure of the transit time or delay through a particular hop. This is made up of propagation delay plus queueing delay at the IS, and is measured dynamically by each IS for each hop element to which it is connected.
3. *Expense:* related to the monetary cost of moving internet traffic through a particular subnet.
4. *Error:* a measure of the probability of error over this hop.

The hop costs are used as input to the **path calculation** routine. Each IS maintains an information base containing the topology and hop costs of each link for the level of interest (level 1 area, level 2 routing domain). This information is used to perform what is referred to as a *least-cost routing algorithm,* which can be simply stated as:

> Given a network of nodes connected by bidirectional links, where each link has a cost associated with it in each direction, define the cost of a path between two nodes as the sum of the costs of the links traversed. For each pair of nodes, find the path with the least cost.

The algorithm used in ISO 10589 was originally proposed by Dijkstra [DIJK59].[4] It enables each IS to find the least-cost route to every other IS of interest.

The validity of the algorithm will, of course, depend on the validity of the information used as input. The routing information may change over time. An IS or subnetwork failure can alter the topology, and some of the costs, especially delay, are variable. Thus some sort of **information exchange discipline** is needed to govern the frequency with which ISs exchange routing information. For ISO 10589, each IS periodically transmits the current status of each hop that initiates itself to all other ISs of which it is aware.

ISO 10589 Functions. Having described the routing environment and the concept of a routing algorithm, we are now in a position to describe the key functions of ISO 10589, which are:

- Discovery
- Information exchange
- Synchronization
- Partitioning

First, let us consider **discovery.** The IS makes use of the ES-IS protocol (ISO 9542) to determine the network layer addresses (and on broadcast subnetworks, the SNPA) and identifies (ES or IS) of all adjacent neigh-

---

[4]A description can be found in [STAL91].

bors. This information is used to create link state PDUs, discussed below.

Although ISO 9542 allows an IS to identify that it has IS neighbors, by the receipt of an ISH, there is no provision in ISO 9542 to indicate whether the neighbor is a level 1 or level 2 IS. ISs convey this information through the exchange of Hello PDUs. There are three types:

1. *Level 1 LAN IS-IS Hello PDU:* used by level 1 ISs on broadcast LANs. The PDU is multicast to all ISs on the same broadcast subnetwork.
2. *Level 2 LAN IS-IS Hello PDU:* used by level 2 ISs on broadcast LANs. The PDU is multicast to all ISs on the same broadcast subnetwork.
3. *Point-to-Point IS-IS Hello PDU:* used on nonbroadcast media, such as point-to-point links and general topology subnetworks.

Link state PDUs (LSPs) are used for link state **information exchange.** The information describes the characteristics of all links (hops) to which the reporting IS is attached. Each IS floods its LSPs to all neighboring peer-level ISs, who flood it to their neighbor ISs, with the following restrictions. Level 1 LSPs are broadcast from a level 1 IS to all level 1 ISs within the same area, and level 2 LSPs are broadcast from a level 2 IS to all level 2 ISs within the same routing domain. Since every IS will receive LSPs from every other peer-level IS within the same area or routing domain, every IS can build a full topology data base.

An LSP is sent when a timer expires, or when the connectivity or status of an IS changes. Every LSP includes a sequence number incremented by the reporting IS for each LSP. Thus, the combination of NET IS address and sequence number uniquely identifies an LSP and orders all LSPs issued by a single IS.

Sequence number PDUs are used for **synchronization** of the data base information and to ensure that all ISs have a consistent view of the network topology. Synchronization serves to terminate the flooding of LSPs and to distinguish old LSPs from new ones. Four types of PDUs are used in the synchronization process:

1. *Level 1 complete sequence numbers PDU:* A designated level 1 IS will broadcast this PDU over a broadcast subnet periodically. It contains the ID of the sending system as well as the start and ending LSP sequence numbers in its data base. This PDU is viewed by all other level 1 ISs sharing the same subnetwork, to determine whether they and the sending IS have synchronized LSP data bases. If a recipient detects that the transmitter is out of date, the recipient IS multicasts the newer information in a link state PDU.
2. *Level 2 complete sequence numbers PDU:* As above, for level 2 ISs.
3. *Level 1 partial sequence numbers PDU:* If a level 1 IS, upon receipt of

a complete sequence numbers PDU, detects that the transmitter has more up-to-date information, the recipient issues a partial sequence numbers PDU containing a list of the link-state records that are not current. When the designated system receives a partial sequence numbers PDU, it supplies the missing information in a link-state PDU.

4. *Level 2 partial sequence numbers PDU:* As above, for level 2 ISs.

The failure of a level 1 IS or a subnetwork can result in the **partition** of an area. For example, if the link (subnetwork) between 1.y and 1.x in Figure 10.22 is broken, then level 1 IS 1.y could not deliver a datagram to 1.x even though a physical path exists (via level 2 ISs.) The reason is that since 1.x is part of the same area as 1.y, 1.x is precluded from using a level 2 IS for delivery. In addition, some datagrams coming from outside the area will be discarded because they enter the wrong partition. This situation is referred to as a level 1 partition.

The responsibility for repairing a level 1 partition is assigned to level 2 ISs. A level 2 IS discovers a partition when it obtains inconsistent information from (a) level 1 ISs telling which level 2 ISs are attached to an area, and (b) level 2 ISs telling which level 1 areas can be reached. The first sort of information is available since every level 2 IS must also function as a level 1 IS in its area. The partition is repaired by the establishment of a virtual level 1 link. This link is virtual in the sense that it appears to the level 1 ISs in the partitioned area that a new link between level 1 ISs has been created. This new link reestablishes connectivity between the partitions. In fact, the link makes use of the level 2 backbone to relay datagrams from one partition in an area to the other. The mechanism for establishing the link is encapsulation: any traffic between level 1 ISs is encapsulated in a CLNP PDU and routed through the level 2 network.

As an example, let us return to the case of a break in the link between 1.x and 1.y. The level 2 ISs b and f discover the partition and set up a virtual link. All traffic arriving at b destined for the other partition is wrapped in a CLNP PDU and routed through d, c, and a to f. Level 2 IS f strips off the CLNP PDU to recover the original PDU and then delivers it. For example, suppose an ES attached to a subnetwork shared with IS.2.z wishes to send a CLNP PDU to an ES that shares a subnetwork with IS 1.z. The datagram will initially be routed to level 2 IS b since it is the shortest path to that area (assuming equal link costs). Level 2 IS b will proceed to wrap the datagram in an enclosing CLNP PDU addressed to level 2 IS f. This datagram backtracks to f, which decapsulates the enclosed datagram and delivers it to IS 1.z.

Notice that no ISs other than level 2 ISs b and f are aware that a partition exists in area 1. Clearly there is considerable overhead in this approach. However, it does provide a temporary patch for a partition.

The strategy assumes that the partition can be repaired in a relatively short period of time.

A partition can also occur at level 2. For example, if the link between level 2 ISs c and d went down, traffic from area 3 could not reach area 5 even though there is a physical path available through area 1. The current version of the standard does not contain any mechanism for repairing level 2 partitions.

10.5

RECOMMENDED READING

Two special issues of the *IEEE Journal on Selected Areas in Communications* provide a number of worthwhile papers on internetworking [GREE90b, BUX87]. [GERL88] is a special issue of *IEEE Network* devoted to bridges. [PARU90] is a thoughtful discussion of the implications of high-speed networking and future trends in distributed processing for internetworking. [CERF78] remains one of the best overall discussions of the design issues related to internetworking. Considerable detail on the ISO internet protocol standard can be found in [BURG89], [ISRA87], and [WEIS87].

Good book-length treatments of the topic are [WHIT92], [MCCO88b], and [COME88]. [BERT92] and [SPRA91] examine the performance implications of transparent bridging and source routing.

10.6

PROBLEMS

10.1 Consider a token-passing local network configured as a single system with N stations or two systems with $N/2$ stations each connected by a bridge. Assume no delay at the bridge other than medium access delay. Do a breakpoint analysis of the type of Chapter 9 to show the relative delay characteristics of the two configurations as a function of the percentage of internetwork traffic.

10.2 Would the spanning tree approach be good for an internet including routers?

10.3 Describe some circumstances where it might be desirable to use source routing rather than let the routers make the routing decision.

10.4 Recall that the token ring MAC protocol specifies that the A and C bits may be set by a station on the ring to indicate address recognized and frame copied, respectively. This information is then available to the source station when the frame returns after circulating around the ring. If a bridge captures a frame and forwards it, should it set the A and C bits or not? Make a case for each policy.

10.5 Because of fragmentation, an IP datagram can arrive in pieces, not necessarily in the right order. The IP layer at the receiving host must accumulate these fragments until the original datagram is reconstituted.

    a. Consider that the IP layer creates a buffer for assembling the datagram. As assembly proceeds, the buffer will consist of data and "holes" between the data. Describe an algorithm for reassembly based on this concept.

    b. For the algorithm above, it is necessary to keep track of the holes. Describe a simple mechanism for doing this.

10.6 Consider an internet that includes both gateways and routers. Further consider a site that contains multiple LANs interconnected by bridges, with one of the LANs including a router that attaches to the remainder of the internet. How can remote stations use internet addressing to address a specific station on one of the LANs? It would appear that there is no way for the internet as a whole to know of the existence of multiple networks at this site.

10.7 What is the header overhead in the ISO IP protocol?

CHAPTER 11

Network Management

Networks and distributed processing systems are of growing importance and, indeed, have become critical in the business world. Within a given organization, the trend is toward larger, more complex networks supporting more applications and more users. As these networks grow in scale, two facts become painfully evident:

1. The network and its associated resources and distributed applications become indispensable to the organization.
2. More things can go wrong, disabling the network or a portion of the network or degrading performance to an unacceptable level.

A large network cannot be put together and managed by human effort alone. The complexity of such a system dictates the use of automated network management tools. The urgency of the need for such tools is increased and the difficulty of supplying such tools is also increased if the network includes equipment from multiple vendors.

Of course, these comments apply to the total networking facilities of an organization, including LANs, MANs, and WANs. However, LANs, and now to a growing extent MANs, are the core of any organization's networking strategy and must be the focus of any network management program.

In this chapter we attempt to provide a survey of a very big and complex subject: network management, with a special emphasis on LAN/MAN management. Specifically, we focus on the hardware and software tools and organized systems of such tools that aid the human network manager in this difficult task.

We begin by looking at the requirements for network management. This should give some idea of the scope of the task to be accomplished. To manage a network, it is fundamental that one must know something about the current status and behavior of that network.

For either LAN/MAN management alone, or for a combined LAN/MAN/WAN environment, what is needed is a network management system that includes a comprehensive set of data gathering and control tools and that is integrated with the network hardware and software. We look at the general architecture of a network management system and then examine the ISO standards for network management.

Then we look at the special requirements for LAN management and the tools that have been developed for that purpose. This is followed by an introduction to the LAN/MAN management standards developed by IEEE 802. These standards provide a set of tools and a framework for management, to be supplemented by specific logic for each type of network. As an example of the latter, we look at the management standards developed for FDDI.

11.1

NETWORK MANAGEMENT REQUIREMENTS

Table 11.1 lists key areas of network management as defined by the International Organization for Standardization (ISO). These categories provide a useful way of organizing our discussion of requirements.

Fault Management

Overview.   To maintain proper operation of a complex network, care must be taken that systems as a whole, and each essential component individually, are in proper working order. When a fault occurs, it is important, as rapidly as possible, to:

- Determine exactly where the fault is
- Isolate the rest of the network from the failure so that it can continue to function without interference
- Reconfigure or modify the network in such a way as to minimize the impact of operation without the failed component or components
- Repair or replace the failed components to restore the network to its initial state

TABLE 11.1   Elements of the ISO Network Management Architecture

Fault management	The facilities that enable the detection, isolation, and correction of abnormal operation of the OSI environment
Accounting management	The facilities that enable charges to be established for the use of managed objects and costs to be identified for the use of those managed objects
Configuration and name management	The facilities that exercise control over, identify, collect data from, and provide data to managed objects for the purpose of assisting in providing for continuous operation of interconnection services
Performance management	The facilities needed to evaluate the behavior of managed objects and the effectiveness of communication activities
Security management	Addresses those aspects of OSI security essential to operate OSI network management correctly and to protect managed objects

Central to the definition of fault management is the fundamental concept of a fault. Faults are to be distinguished from errors. A **fault** is an abnormal condition that requires management attention (or action) to repair. A fault is usually indicated by failure to operate correctly or by excessive errors. For example, if a communications line is physically cut, no signals can get through. Or a crimp in the cable may cause wild distortions so that there is a persistently high bit error rate. Certain errors (e.g., a single bit error on a communication line) may occur occasionally and are not normally considered to be faults. It is usually possible to compensate for errors using the error control mechanisms of the various protocols.

User Requirements.   Users expect fast and reliable problem resolution. Most end users will tolerate occasional outages. When these infrequent outages do occur, however, the user generally expects to receive immediate notification and expects that the problem will be corrected almost immediately. To provide this level of fault resolution requires very rapid and reliable fault detection and diagnostic management functions. The impact and duration of faults can also be minimized by the use of redundant components and alternate communication routes, to give the network a degree of fault tolerance. The fault management capability itself should be redundant to increase network reliability.

Users expect to be kept informed of the network status, including both scheduled and unscheduled disruptive maintenance. Users expect reassurance of correct network operation through mechanisms that use confidence tests or analyze dumps, logs, alerts, or statistics.

After correcting a fault and restoring a system to its full operational state, the fault management service must ensure that the problem is truly resolved and that no new problems are introduced. This requirement is called problem tracking and control. As with other areas of network management, fault management should have minimal effect on network performance.

Accounting Management

Overview.   In many corporate networks, individual divisions or cost centers, or even individual project accounts, are charged for the use of network services. These are internal accounting procedures rather than actual cash transfers, but they are important to the participating users. Furthermore, even if no such internal charging is employed, the network manager needs to be able to track the use of network resources by user or user class for a number of reasons, including:

- A user or group of users may be abusing their access privileges and burdening the network at the expense of other users.
- Users may be making inefficient use of the network, and the network manager can assist in changing procedures to improve performance.
- The network manager is in a better position to plan for network growth if user activity is known in sufficient detail.

User Requirements.   The network manager needs to be able to specify the kinds of accounting information to be recorded at various nodes, the desired interval between sending the recorded information to higher-level management nodes, and the algorithms to be used in calculating the charging. Accounting reports should be generated under network manager control.

In order to limit access to accounting information, the accounting facility must provide the capability to verify users' authorization to access and manipulate that information.

Configuration and Name Management

Overview.   Modern data communication networks are composed of individual components and logical subsystems (e.g., the device driver in an operating system) that can be configured to support many different applications. The same device, for example, can be configured to act either as a router or as an end system node or both. Once it is decided how a device is to be used, the configuration manager can choose the appropriate software and set of attributes and values (e.g., a transport layer retransmission timer) for that device.

Configuration management is concerned with initializing a network and gracefully shutting down part or all of the network. It is also concerned with maintaining, adding, and updating the relationships among components and the status of components themselves during network operation.

User Requirements. Start-up and shut-down operations on a network are the specific responsibilities of configuration management. It is often desirable for these operations on certain components to be performed unattended (e.g., starting or shutting down a network interface unit).

The network manager needs the capability to initially identify the components that comprise the network and to define the desired connectivity of these components. Those who regularly configure a network with the same or a similar set of resource attributes need ways to define and modify default attributes and to load these predefined sets of attributes into the specified network components. The network manager needs the capability to change the connectivity of network components when users' needs change. Reconfiguration of a network is often desired in response to performance evaluation or in support of network upgrade, fault recovery, or security checks.

Users often need to, or want to, be informed of the status of network resources and components. Therefore, when changes in configuration occur, users should be notified of these changes. Configuration reports can be generated either on some routine periodic basis or in response to a request for such a report. Before reconfiguration, users often want to inquire about the upcoming status of resources and their attributes.

Network managers usually want only authorized users (operators) to manage and control network operation (e.g., software distribution and updating).

Performance Management

Overview. Modern data communications networks are composed of many and varied components that must intercommunicate and share data and resources. In some cases, it is critical to the effectiveness of an application that the communication over the network be within certain performance limits.

Performance management of a computer network comprises two broad functional categories: monitoring and controlling. Monitoring is the function that tracks activities on the network. The controlling function enables performance management to make adjustments to improve network performance. Some of the performance issues of concern to the network manager are:

- What is the level of capacity utilization?
- Is there excessive traffic?
- Has throughput been reduced to unacceptable levels?
- Are there bottlenecks?
- Is response time increasing?

To deal with these concerns, the network manager must focus on some initial set of resources to be monitored in order to assess performance levels. This includes associating appropriate metrics and values with relevant network resources as indicators of different levels of performance. For example, what count of retransmissions on a transport connection is considered to be a performance problem requiring attention? Performance management, therefore, must monitor many resources to provide information in determining network operating level. By collecting this information, analyzing it, and then using the resultant analysis as feedback to the prescribed set of values, the network manager can become more and more adept at recognizing situations indicative of present or impending performance degradation.

User Requirements.   Before using a network for a particular application, a user may want to know such things as the average and worst-case response times and the reliability of network services. Thus performance must be known in sufficient detail to assess specific user queries. End users expect network services to be managed in such a way as to consistently afford their applications good response time.

Network managers need performance statistics to help them plan, manage, and maintain large networks. Performance statistics can be used to recognize potential bottlenecks before they cause problems to the end users. Appropriate corrective action can then be taken. This action can take the form of changing routing tables to balance or redistribute traffic load during times of peak use or when a bottleneck is identified by a rapidly growing load in one area. Over the long term, capacity planning based on such performance information can indicate the proper decisions to make, for example, with regard to expansion of lines in that area.

Security Management

Overview.   Security management is concerned with generating, distributing, and storing encryption keys. Passwords and other authorization or access control information must be maintained and distributed. Security management is also concerned with monitoring and controlling access to computer networks and access to all or part of the network management information obtained from the network nodes. Logs are an important security tool and therefore security management is very much involved with the collection, storage, and examination of audit records and security logs, as well as with the enabling and disabling of these logging facilities.

User Requirements. Security management provides facilities for protection of network resources and user information. Network security facilities should be available for authorized users only. Users want to know that the proper security policies are in force and effective and that the management of security facilities is itself secure.

11.2

NETWORK MANAGEMENT SYSTEMS

A network management system is a collection of tools for network monitoring and control that is integrated in the following senses:

- A single operator interface with a powerful but user-friendly set of commands for performing most or all network management tasks.
- A minimal amount of separate equipment. That is, most of the hardware and software required for network management is incorporated into the existing user equipment.

A network management system consists of incremental hardware and software additions implemented among existing network components. The software used in accomplishing the network management tasks resides in the host computers and communications processors (e.g., front-end processors, terminal cluster controllers, bridges, routers). A network management system is designed to view the entire network as a unified architecture, with addresses and labels assigned to each point and the specific attributes of each element and link known to the system. The active elements of the network provide regular feedback of status information to the network control center.

Figure 11.1 suggests the architecture of a network management system. Each network node contains a collection of software devoted to the network management task, referred to in the diagram as a network management entity (NME). Each NME performs the following tasks:

- Collects statistics on communications and network-related activities
- Stores statistics locally
- Responds to commands from the network control center, including commands to (1) transmit collected statistics to the network control center, (2) change a parameter (e.g., a timer used in a transport

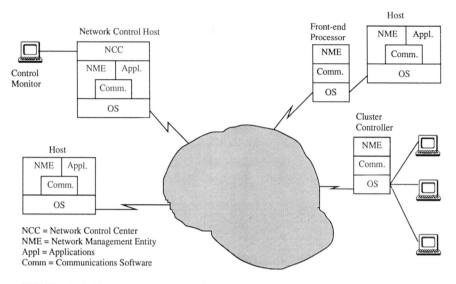

NCC = Network Control Center
NME = Network Management Entity
Appl = Applications
Comm = Communications Software

FIGURE 11.1 Elements of a Network Management System

protocol), (3) provide status information (e.g., parameter values, active links), and (4) generate artificial traffic to perform a test

At least one host in the network is designated as the network control center. In addition to the NME software, the network control host includes a collection of software called the network control center (NCC). The NCC includes an operator interface to allow an authorized user to manage the network. The NCC responds to user commands by displaying information and/or by issuing commands to NMEs throughout the network. This communication is carried out using an application-level network management protocol that employs the communications architecture in the same fashion as any other distributed application.

Several observations are in order:

1. Since the network management software relies on the host operating system and on the communications architecture, most offerings until recently have been designed for use on a single vendor's equipment. In the case of a network of personal computers, there are a number of LAN network management packages that will tie together personal computers from a number of vendors. Standards in this area are still immature, but standardized network management systems designed to manage a multiple-vendor network are becoming more common.

2. As depicted in Figure 11.1, the network control center communicates with and controls what are essentially software monitors in other systems. The architecture can be extended to include tech-

nical control hardware and specialized performance monitoring hardware as well.

3. For maintaining high availability of the network management function, two or more network control centers are used. In normal operation, one of the centers is idle or simply collecting statistics, while the other is used for control. If the primary network control center fails, the backup system can be used.

11.3

OSI NETWORK MANAGEMENT

The International Organization for Standardization (ISO) has issued a set of standards for network management, referred to by ISO as systems management. The first standard related to network management issued by ISO was ISO 7498-4, which specifies the management framework for the OSI model. This document dictates that OSI management support user requirements for:

- Activities that enable managers to plan, organize, supervise, control, and account for the use of interconnection services
- The ability to respond to changing requirements
- Facilities to ensure predictable communications behavior
- Facilities that provide for information protection and for the authentication of sources of and destinations for transmitted data

Since then, ISO has issued a voluminous set of standards and draft standards for network management. The Consultative Committee on International Telegraphy and Telephony (CCITT) is the joint sponsor of this effort and has set aside the X.700 series of numbers for their recommendations. The standards fall into five general categories:

1. *OSI management framework and overview:* includes ISO 7498-4, which provides a general introduction to management concepts, and ISO 10040, which is an overview of the remainder of the documents
2. *CMIS/CMIP:* define the common management information service (CMIS), which provides OSI management services to management applications, and the common management information protocol (CMIP), which provides the information exchange capability to support CMIS
3. *Systems management functions:* define the specific functions that are performed by OSI systems management
4. *Structure of management information:* defines the management information base (MIB), which contains a representation of all objects within the OSI environment subject to management

5. *Layer management:* define management information, services, and functions related to specific OSI layers

OSI Management Framework

An architectural model of an OSI system participating in network management is shown in Figure 11.2. Key elements of this architecture include:

1. *System management application process:* This is the local software within a system that is responsible for executing the network management functions on a single system (host, front-end processor, router, etc.). It has access to an overall view of system parameters and capabilities and can, therefore, manage all aspects of the system and can coordinate with SMAPs on other systems.

2. *System management application entity:* This application-level entity is responsible for communication with other nodes, especially with the system that exercises a network control center function. A standardized application-level protocol, common management in-

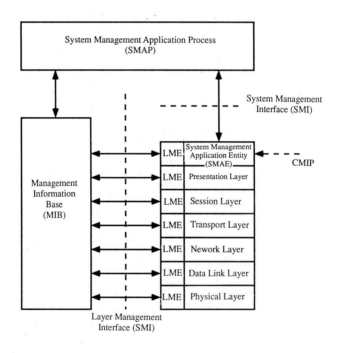

LME = Layer Management Entity
CMIP = Common Management Information Protocol

FIGURE 11.2 Architectural Model of OSI Management

formation protocol (CMIP), is used for this purpose. The SMAE provides services to the SMAP by means of a common management information service (CMIS).

3. *Layer management entity (LME):* Logic is embedded into each layer of the OSI architecture to provide network management functions specific to that layer.

4. *Management information base (MIB):* The collection of information at each node pertaining to network management.

Of course, all of the elements illustrated in Figure 11.2 must be implemented in a distributed fashion across all of the systems that are subject to network management. The interactions that take place among systems are depicted, in abstract fashion, in Figure 11.3. The management activities are effected through the manipulation of managed objects. Each system contains a number of such objects. Each object is a data structure that corresponds to an actual entity to be managed. The SMAP in a system is allowed to take on one of two possible roles, either an agent role or a manager role.

The manager role for an SMAP occurs in a system that acts as a network manager or network control center. The manager issues requests

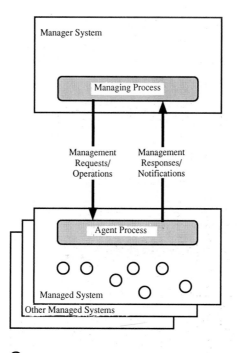

O = Managed Object (may contain other objects)

FIGURE 11.3 Systems Management Interactions

for information and operations commands for execution to the managed systems in the network. In each managed system, the agent interacts with the manager and is responsible for managing the objects within its system.

Systems Management Functions

A set of standards has been issued under the general category *systems management functions* (SMF). Each SMF standard defines the functionality to support system management functional area (SMFA) requirements; the SMFAs are described in Section 11.1 of this chapter. A given SMF may support requirements in one or more of the five SMFAs; for example, the event report management function may be applicable to all SMFAs. Of course, each of the SMFAs requires several of the SMFs.

Each of the SMF standards defines the functionality for the SMF and provides a mapping between the services provided by the SMF and the common management information service (CMIS). This relationship is depicted in Figure 11.4.

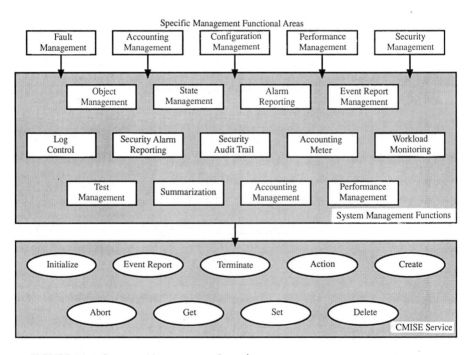

FIGURE 11.4 Systems Management Overview

Structure of Management Information

The foundation of the systems management activity is the management information base (MIB), which contains a representation of all of the resources under systems management. The structure of management information (SMI) defines the general framework within which a MIB can be defined and constructed. The SMI identifies the data types that can be used in the MIB, and how resources within the MIB are represented and named.

OSI systems management relies heavily on the concepts of object-oriented design. Each resource that is monitored and controlled by OSI systems management is represented by a managed object. A managed object can be defined for any resource that an organization wishes to monitor and/or control. Examples of hardware resources are switches, work stations, PBXs, LAN port cards, and multiplexers. Examples of software resources are queuing programs, routing algorithms, and buffer management routines. Managed objects that refer to resources specific to an individual layer are called (N)-layer managed objects. Managed objects that refer to resources that encompass more than one layer are called system managed objects.

A managed object is defined in terms of attributes it possesses, operations that may be performed on it, notifications that it may issue, and its relationships with other managed objects. In order to structure the definition of a MIB, each managed object is an instance of a managed object class. A managed object class is a model or template for managed object instances that share the same attributes, notifications, and management operations. The definition of a managed object class, as specified by the template, consists of:

- Attributes visible at the managed object boundary
- System management operations that can be applied to the managed object
- Behavior exhibited by the managed object in response to management operations
- Notifications that can be emitted by the managed object

Table 11.2 lists the object classes that have so far been defined as part of the SMI.

Attributes. The actual data elements contained in a managed object are called attributes. Each attribute represents a property of the resource that the object represents, such as the operational characteristics, current state, or conditions of operation. The data type of an attribute may be integer, real, boolean, character string, or some composite type constructed from the basic types. An attribute may have a single value or a

TABLE 11.2   Object Classes (X.721/DIS 10165-2)

Object Class	Description
Alarm record	Used to define the information stored in the log as a result of receiving alarm reports. Object classes are communicationAlarm, qualityofServiceAlarm, processingErrorAlarm, equipmentAlarm, and environmentalAlarm
Attribute value change record	Used to define the information stored in the log as a result of receiving attribute value change notification.
Discriminator	Used to define the criteria for controlling management services.
Event forwarding discriminator	Used to define the conditions that shall be satisfied by potential event reports before the event report is forwarded to a particular destination.
Event log record	Used to define the information stored in the log as a result of receiving events. This is superclass from which records for specific event types are derived.
Log	Used to define the criteria for controlling the logging of the information received in management protocol data units.
Log record	Used to define the records in a log-managed object.
Object creation record	Used to define the information stored in the log as a result of receiving object creation notification.
Object deletion record	Used to define the information stored in the log as a result of receiving object deletion notification.
Object name change record	Used to define the information stored in the log as a result of receiving object name change notification.
Relationship change record	Used to define the information stored in the log as a result of receiving relationship change reports.
State change record	Used to define the information stored in the log as a result of receiving state change reports.
Security alarm report	Used to define the information stored in the log as a result of receiving security alarm reports.
System	Used to represent a set of hardware and software that forms an autonomous whole capable of performing information processing and/or information transfer.
Top	That class of which every object class is a subclass.

set value. A set-valued attribute is one whose value is a set of members of a given data type.

In addition to a data type, each attribute has access rules (read, write, read/write), and the rules by which it can be located as the result of a filtered search (matching rules).

Operations.   Systems management operations apply to the attributes of an object or to the managed object as a whole (Table 11.3). An operation performed on a managed object can succeed only if the invoking managing system has the access rights necessary to perform the operation, and consistency constraints are not violated.

Behavior.   A managed object exhibits certain behavioral characteristics, including how the object reacts to operations performed on it and the constraints placed on its behavior. The behavior of a managed object occurs in response to either external or internal stimuli. External stimuli are in the form of system management operations delivered in the form of CMIP messages. Internal stimuli are events internal to the managed object and its associated resource, such as timers.

Notifications.   Managed objects are said to emit notifications when some internal or external occurrence affecting the object is detected. Notifications may be transmitted externally in a protocol, or logged. Managing systems may request that some or all of the notifications emitted by a managed object are to be sent to it. Notifications that are sent to a manager are contained in an event report.

Common Management Information Service

The Common Management Information Service (CMIS) defines the services provided for OSI systems management (ISO 9595). These services are invokable by management processes in order to communicate remotely.

Table 11.4 lists the CMIS services in terms of service primitives. CMIS services are of two types: confirmed services require a remote management process to send a response to indicate receipt and success or failure of the operation requested; nonconfirmed services do not use responses.

Three categories of service are relevant to CMIS:

1. *Association services:* CMIS users need to establish an application association to communicate. The CMIS user relies on the association control service element (ACSE), which is a separate OSI application entity, for the control of application associations.

TABLE 11.3 Systems Management Operations (X.720/DIS 10165-1)

(a) Attibute oriented operations

Operation	Scope	Semantics	Behavior
Get attribute value	All attributes types, unless they are defined as not readable.	Read all attribute values or list of attribute values; return values that can be read and indicate an error for values that cannot be read.	Return error indications for those attributes that could not be read.
Replace attribute value	Does not apply to group attributes or attributes that are not writable.	Replace the values of specified attributes with supplied values.	Return error indications for those attributes whose values could not be replaced, because the attributes were non-writable.
Replace-with-default value	All attribute types, unless they are defined as not writable.	Replace the value of some attributes with the defaults defined as part of the object class specification.	Return error indication for those attributes whose values could not be replaced, due to attribute not writable, no default defined, or general failure of the replace-with-default request.
Add member	Attributes whose values are sets and whose values are writable.	Add supplied attribute members to the set that currently comprises the attribute's value.	Return error indication for attribute where members could not be added, because attribute is not writable.
Remove member	Attributes whose values are sets and whose values are writable.	Remove from the set that currently comprises the attribute's value those members supplied by the operation.	Return error indication for attribute whose members could not be removed, because attribute is not writable.

(b) Operations that apply to managed objects as a whole

Create	All objects that are creatable as defined by the object class definition.	Create and initialize a managed object. The operation has analogous effects on the resource, as defined by the managed object class definer.	The create request may specify explicit values for individual attributes and may specify a reference object from which values may be obtained. The managed object class definition may specify initial attribute values. An error indication is provided if the managed object cannot be created.
Delete	All managed objects that can be deleted remotely.	Delete the managed object. The operation has analogous effects on the resource, as defined by the managed object class definer.	The execution of the delete operation may depend on the whether other managed objects are contained in this object and on relationships with other managed objects.
Action	All managed object classes.	The managed object performs the specified action and indicates the result.	Action results and/or error indications are returned.

TABLE 11.4   CMIS Services

(a) Management notification service

Service	Type	Definition
M-EVENT-REPORT	confirmed/non-confirmed	Report an event about a managed object to a peer CMIS-service user.

(b) Management operation services

M-GET	confirmed	Request the retrieval of management information from a peer CMIS-service user.
M-SET	confirmed/non-confirmed	Request the modification of management information by a peer CMIS-service user.
M-ACTION	confirmed/non-confirmed	Request a peer CMIS-service user to perform an action
M-CREATE	confirmed	Request a peer CMIS-service user to create an instance of a managed object.
M-DELETE	confirmed	Request a peer CMIS-service user to delete an instance of a managed object.
M-CANCEL-GET	confirmed	Request a peer CMIS-service user to cancel a previously requested and currently outstanding invocation of the M-GET service.

2. *Management notification service:* This service is used to convey management information applicable to a notification. The definition of the notification and the consequent behavior of the communicating entities is dependent on the specification of the managed object that generated the notification and is outside the scope of CMIS.

3. *Management operation service:* These six services are used to convey management information applicable to systems management operations. The definition of the operation and the consequent behavior of the communicating entities is dependent on the specification of the managed object at which the operation is directed and is outside the scope of CMIS.

The CMIS provides two structuring facilities:

1. Multiple responses to a confirmed operation can be linked to the operation by the use of a linked identification parameter.
2. Operations can be performed on multiple managed objects, selected to satisfy some criteria and subject to a synchronizing condition.

The M-GET, M-SET, M-ACTION, and M-DELETE service primitives include a parameter to select the managed object or objects to be used in the given operation. Managed object selection involves three concepts: scoping, filtering, and synchronization. These three facilities are provided as parameters.

Scoping.   Scoping refers to the identification of an object or objects to which a filter is to be applied. Scoping is defined with reference to a specific managed object instance referred to as the **base managed object.** The base managed object is the starting point for the selection of one or more objects to which a filter is to be applied. Using the base object as the root, a subtree of the overall object tree is obtained. With this in mind, four specifications of scoping level are possible:

- The base object alone
- The nth level subordinates of the base object
- The base object and all its subordinates down to and including the nth level
- The base object and all of its subordinates, that is, the entire subtree

Filtering.   A filter is a boolean expression, consisting of one or more assertions about the presence or values of attributes in a scoped managed object. Each assertion may be a test for equality, ordering, presence, or set comparison. The filter test is applied to all of the managed objects selected by the scoping parameter, and only those managed objects that match the filter are selected for the performance of the operation.

Synchronization.   The scoping parameter may result in the selection of more than one managed object to be subject to filtering. In turn, if more than one object is scoped, the filtering parameter may result in the selection of more than one object for which the operation is to be performed. The question then arises as to the order in which objects will be processed. Since the order in which object instances are selected by the filter is not specified, but is left as a local implementation matter, this order cannot be used. Instead, the CSIME service user may request one of two types of synchronization:

1. *Atomic:* All managed objects selected for the operation are checked to ascertain if they are able to successfully perform the operation. If one or more managed objects is not able to do so, then none perform it.
2. *Best effort:* All managed objects selected for the operation are requested to perform it.

Common Management Information Protocol

The Common Management Information Protocol (CMIP) supports the services provided for OSI systems management by means of a set of protocol data units that implement the CMIS (ISO 9596). These PDUs are transmitted in response to CMIS service primitives issued by CMIS service users.

Table 11.5 lists the 11 PDUs that make up the CMIP. There are up to three types of information carried in each data unit. The Argument entry defines the arguments, or parameters, carried in the data unit that are derived from the triggering CMISE service primitive. The Results and Errors entries contain information from the performing entity about the result of the systems management operation. These values are derived from the CMISE response primitive.

Most of the PDUs can easily be seen to be derived from the service that they support. The one exception is the m-linked-Reply PDU, which is used to support the linkage facility. The M-GET, M-SET, M-ACTION, and M-DELETE service primitives, which are the primitives that can specify operation on multiple objects, also include a linkage parameter to provide for multiple replies to be sent for the operation. The parameter is the Linked Identifier parameter that appears in each of the response and confirm primitives. The value of the parameter is the same as the Invoke Identifier that appears in the request and indication primitives. The Invoke Identifier is a unique identifier assigned to each operation.

11.4

LAN-SPECIFIC NETWORK MANAGEMENT

A LAN by itself seems to be a much more manageable network than one involving wide-area components. For one thing, the transmission technologies used are reduced in number. Also, everything is at hand; it is much easier to localize faults and to monitor everything, since it is all clustered together in a small area. Nevertheless, for a local network supporting a substantial amount of equipment, network management is required. In many cases, the LAN vendors provide many of the tools needed for network management in a package of hardware and software that can be optionally acquired with the network. In this section, we give an overview of the types of capabilities typically found in such products.

The Special Importance of Local Area Network (LAN) Management

Most LANs start out as a homogeneous set of equipment from a single networking vendor. At that time, they usually have one main application, such as multiuser accounting, desktop publishing, electronic mail, or host communications. But rapid growth breeds complexity. And, as users come to depend on the LAN, the network's applications expand.

Thus, LANs evolve from being a nice extra to being a critical part of an organization's day-to-day operations. Downtime can cost a corporation dearly as work backs up. Slowdowns, due to increased server and network loads, can lead to wasted time as users wait for transactions to finish or customer accounts to be called up. Unfortunately, most users do not recognize the difficulties of managing LANs until serious problems are encountered. Networks are easy to install and deliver substantial benefits when their size and scope are limited. Network popularity, however, often outpaces users' understanding of network management and methods for spotting and identifying network problems.

The combination of larger size, more internetworking, and multivendor configurations can rapidly change a simple network into a maze that can leave all but the most sophisticated users confused and stymied. Isolating problems and improving performance in complex and feature-laden networks is one of the major challenges in today's LAN environments.

LANs that were once small and easy to use become very easy to misuse when they grow to meet users' ever-expanding needs. For example, one naive user could utilize the wrong boot disk, containing last year's version of network drivers. This could have a catastrophic effect on hundreds of users in a large network installation. Another user innocently utilizing a workstation for a particular data base application might discover that by simply exceeding some internal limit, the application unexpectedly starts to use all of the resources of the file server.

In yet another problem scenario, a network manager installs a file server, which should routinely send out a single packet regarding the health of the file server every 15 minutes. If a mistake is made in setting parameters, the server may send out a flood of packets, which can cause

TABLE 11.5 CMIP Data Units

CMIP Data Unit	Argument	Result	Errors
m-EventReport	EventReportArgument	—	—
m-EventReport-Confirmed	EventReportArgument	EventReportResult	InvalidArgumentValue, noSuchArgument, noSuchEventType, noSuchObjectClass, noSuchObjectInstance, processingFailure
m-Get	GetArgument	GetResult	accessDenied, classInstanceConflict, complexityLimitation, getListError, invalidFilter, invalidScope, noSuchObjectClass, noSuchObjectInstance, operationCancelled, processingFailure, syncNotSupported
m-linked-Reply	LinkedReplyArgument	—	accessDenied, classInstanceConflict, complexityLimitation, invalidFilter, invalidScope, noSuchObjectClass, noSuchObjectInstance, processingFailure, setListError, syncNotSupported
m-Set	SetArgument	—	—
m-Set-Confirmed	SetArgument	SetResult	—
m-Action	ActionArgument	—	—

m-Action-Confirmed	ActionArgument	ActionResult	accessDenied, classInstanceConflict, complexityLimitation, invalidScope, InvalidArgumentValue, invalidFilter, noSuchAction, noSuchArgument, noSuchObjectClass, noSuchObjectInstance, processingFailure, syncNotSupported
m-Create	CreateArgument	CreateResult	accessDenied, classInstanceConflict, duplicateManagedObjectInstance, invalidAttributeValue, invalidObjectInstance, missingAttributeValue, noSuchAttribute, noSuchObjectClass, noSuchObjectInstance, noSuchReferenceObject, processingFailure
m-Delete	DeleteArgument	DeleteResult	accessDenied, classInstanceConflict, complexityLimitation, invalidFilter, invalidScope, noSuchObjectClass, noSuchObjectInstance, processingFailure, syncNotSupported
m-Cancel-Get-Confirmed	getInvokedId, InvokeIdType	—	mistypedOperation, noSuchInvokeId, processingFailure

a service "brownout" due to retransmissions and broadcasts through the network. To the unsophisticated network manager, such a brownout has the same symptoms as a saturated network.

These problems are quite common and in many instances the network manager does not know the cause. A sophisticated and easy-to-use network control center can make the job of LAN management much easier.

LAN Network Control Center

With many local area network (LAN) products, a network control center (NCC) is provided. Typically, this is a separate dedicated microcomputer attached to the network through a network interface unit (NIU). All of the functions of a LAN network control center involve observation, active control, or a combination of the two. They fall into three categories:

- Configuration functions
- Monitoring functions
- Fault isolation

Configuration Functions. One of the principal functions of an NCC is to maintain a directory of names and addresses of resources available on the network. This allows users to set up connections by name. A resource may be any device or service—terminals, hosts, peripherals, application programs, or utility programs. For example, a user at a terminal who wishes to use the accounts payable package could request it with LOGON ACCOUNTS PAYABLE. Because the directory linking names with addresses can be altered, the manager, via the NCC, has the ability to move applications around (for load balancing or because a host is down). The directory is maintained at the NCC, but portions or all of it can also be downloaded to NIUs to reduce the network traffic required for directory look-up.

The NCC can also control the operation of the NIUs. The NCC could have the ability to shut down and start up NIUs and to set NIU parameters. For example, an NIU may be restricted to a certain set of NIUs or destination names with which it can communicate. This is a simple means of setting up a type of security scheme. Another example is to assign different priorities to different NIUs or different users.

Monitoring Functions. In a typical LAN control center, monitoring functions fall into three categories: performance monitoring, network status, and accounting.

Table 11.6 lists the types of measurements reported in a typical LAN facility [AMER82, AMER83]. These measurements can be used to an-

TABLE 11.6 Performance Measurement Reports

Name	Variables	Description
Host communication matrix	Source × destination	(Number, %) of (packets, data packets, data bytes)
Group communication matrix	Source × destination	As above, consolidated into address groups
Packet-type histogram	Packet type	(Number, %) of (packets, original packets) by type
Data packet–size histogram	Packet size	(Number, %) of data packets by data byte length
Throughput-utilization distribution	Source	(Total bytes, data bytes) transmitted
Packet interarrival time histogram	Interarrival time	Time between consecutive carrier (network busy) signals
Channel acquisition delay histogram	NIU acquisition delay	(Number, %) of packets delayed at NIU by given amount
Communication delay histogram	Packet delay	Time from original packet ready at source to receipt
Collision count histogram	Number of collisions	Number of packets by number of collisions
Transmission count histogram	Number of transmissions	Number of packets by transmission attempts

swer a number of questions. Questions concerning possible errors or inefficiencies include:

- Is traffic evenly distributed among the network users or are there source-destination pairs with unusually heavy traffic?
- What is the percentage of each type of packet? Are some packet types of unusually high frequency, indicating an error or an inefficient protocol?
- What is the distribution of data packet sizes?
- What are the channel acquisition and communication delay distributions? Are these times excessive?
- Are collisions a factor in getting packets transmitted, indicating possible faulty hardware or protocols?
- What is the channel utilization and throughput?

These areas are of interest to the network manager. Other questions of concern have to do with response time and throughput by user class and determining how much growth the network can absorb before certain performance thresholds are crossed.

Because of the broadcast nature of LANs, many of the measurements can be collected passively at the NCC without perturbing the network. The NCC can be programmed to accept all packets, regardless of destination address. For a heavily loaded network, this may not be possible, and a sampling scheme must be used. In a LAN containing bridges, one collection point per segment is required.

However, not all information can be centrally collected by observing the traffic on the LAN. To get end-to-end measures, such as response time, would require knowing the time that a packet is generated by a host or terminal and having the ability to identify the responding packet. This sort of measure requires some collection capability at the individual NIUs. From time to time, the NIUs can send the collected data to the NCC. Unfortunately, this technique increases the complexity of the NIU logic and imposes a communication overhead.

Another major area of NCC monitoring is that of network status. The NCC keeps track of which NIUs are currently activated and the connections that exist. This information is displayed to the network manager upon request.

Finally, the NCC can support some accounting and billing functions. This can be done on either a device or user basis. The NCC could record the amount of traffic generated by a particular device or user and the resources to which a device or user connected and for how long.

Fault-isolation Functions.   The NCC can continuously monitor the network to detect faults and, to the extent possible, narrow the fault down to a single component or small group of components. As an example, the NCC can periodically poll each NIU, requesting that it return a status packet. When an NIU fails to respond, the NCC reports the failure and also attempts to disable the NIU so that it does not interfere with the rest of the LAN.

11.5

IEEE 802 LAN/MAN MANAGEMENT

The IEEE 802.1 committee has issued draft standards for LAN/MAN management [IEEE91c]. The standards are intended to be complementary to the OSI systems management standards.

Figure 11.5 depicts the key elements of the LAN/MAN management communications architecture. These elements are:

- *LAN/MAN management user (LMMU):* a user of management func-

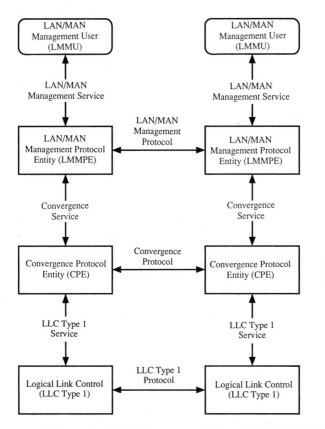

FIGURE 11.5 LAN/MAN Management Communications Architecture

tionality (typically a process) specific to the management of IEEE 802 LANs and MANs.

- *LAN/MAN service (LMMS):* defines the service available to the LMMU for the exchange of management information with another LMMU. The LMMS makes use of service primitives defined in CMIS.

- *LAN/MAN management protocol (LMMP):* protocol between LMMP entities that supports the LMMS. The LMMP makes use of the procedures and protocol data units defined in CMIP. In OSI terms, LMMP is a layer management protocol.

- *Convergence service:* provides enhancements to LLC type 1 service in order to provide for the specific requirements of the LMMP entity.

- *Convergence protocol:* protocol that supports the convergence service.

- *LLC type 1 service and protocol:* connectionless service and protocol that is the underlying service for LAN/MAN management.

LAN/MAN Management Service and Protocol

The use of the LAN/MAN management service and protocol does not preclude the use of OSI systems management functionality. The LMMS and LMMP make use of elements of CMIS and CMIP. Table 11.4, which lists the CMIS primitives, also applies to LMMS, and Table 11.5, which lists the CMIP data units, also applies to LMMP. The concepts of managed objects and management information used in 802.1B are based on the OSI systems management concepts.

Figure 11.6 indicates the use of the LAN/MAN management service and protocol to perform management functions. Two basic types of information exchange are possible: operations and notifications.

A process acting as a manager requests an **operation** to be performed by a remote LMMU, the agent. One or more operations are performed on managed objects as a result of the request, and the results of those operations are reported back to the manager LMMU by means of a service confirm primitive.

A managed object may emit a **notification** that contains information related to events that have occurred within the managed object. The agent, on the basis of event forwarding information held locally, determines whether notification-related information should be forwarded to one or more managers, to be delivered in a service indication primitive.

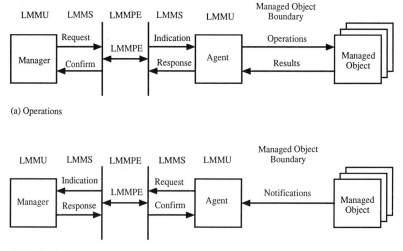

(a) Operations

(b) Notifications

FIGURE 11.6 LAN/MAN Management Information Exchanges

Convergence Service and Protocol

The necessary services and protocol for managing objects within a LAN or MAN configuration can be provided by means of CMIS and CMIP operating as part of a seven-layer OSI architecture. However, there are two reasons listed in the 802.1B document why this may not always be desirable or practical:

1. Management of the communication capability of a station is often required when part of the communication capability is unavailable, inoperable, or approaching inoperability. This may require the management protocol to be carried directly by simple, lower-layer services. Examples of such requirements are initializing and loading of a station's system software during bootstrapping of the system.
2. Many of the devices that make up a communications network are constrained by memory or other resource limitations in ways that prohibit support of a full seven-layer connection-oriented OSI protocol stack for management purposes (e.g., modems, MAC layer bridges, repeaters, hubs) and more economical methods of operation are a practical necessity.

To meet the requirement for a streamlined management architecture, 802.1B defines a convergence service and protocol that support the LAN/MAN functionality and that require only the services of the lower two layers, specifically the simple connectionless services available through LLC.

Figure 11.7 compares the use of the convergence service and protocol to the use of the full OSI suite. The purpose of the convergence service is to provide a means of exchanging managing information between LAN/MAN management users by mapping the LMMS service into the LLC type 1 service.

Affiliate.   The convergence service and protocol make use of the concept of *affiliate*. An affiliate is a remote convergence protocol entity (CPE) whose address is known to the local CPE. An affiliation exists if both remote and local CPEs know each other's addresses.

Each CPE maintains an identifier known as the CPE instance number, which is set when the CPE is initialized (e.g., at system boot time). The combination of LLC address and CPE instance number form a CPE instance identifier that is unique within the LAN/MAN environment.

The purpose of the use of affiliates is to provide a logical association between management requests and responses, both in the case of a sin-

CMIP   LMMP

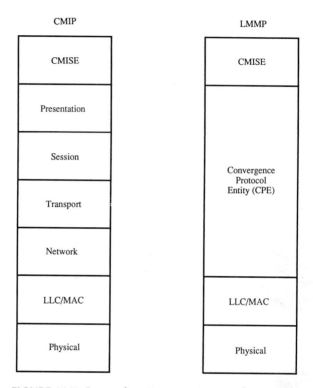

FIGURE 11.7 Comparison Between CMIP and LMMP Protocol Stacks

gle request/response and in the case of multiple responses linked to a single request. There are three types of affiliates:

1. *New affiliate:* a remote CPE instance identifier for which the CPE address was previously unknown to the local CPE.
2. *Old affiliate:* a remote CPE instance identifier already known to the local CPE. Once a CPE communicates with a remote CPE, it retains the instance identifier of the remote CPE for future use.
3. *Changed affiliate:* a remote CPE instance identifier for which the CPE address was previously unknown to the local CPE, but where the remote CPE instance number is different from the one known to the local CPE. This change occurs when a CPE has been reinitialized (e.g., a system initialization after a crash) at a remote CPE address since the last communication with that address.

Convergence Service.   The convergence service is a PDU delivery service for the LAN/MAN management protocol entity (LMMPE). The convergence service accepts PDUs from an LMMPE for delivery to a particular destination, and delivers them to the peer convergence protocol entity (CPE) at that destination. The receiving CPE then passes the received PDU to its service user. In addition to this delivery service, the convergence service includes an abort indication service that alerts the convergence service user to service provider aborts.

Table 11.7 lists the primitives and parameters of the convergence service. The CPE__send service is used for passing an LMMP data unit from a source to a destination LMMPE. The requesting user can request a quality of service consisting of the following parameters:

- *Priority:* This is passed down to LLC.
- *Reliability:* The convergence service user may request basic or enhanced reliability. The basic option makes direct use of the underlying connectionless service. The enhanced option causes the CPE to provide enhancements that improve the reliability of the underlying LLC.

The status parameter indicates the status of the CPE from which the CPE user information was received. The permitted values are new affiliate, old affiliate, or changed affiliate.

If the CPE is unable to deliver information as requested in a CPE__Send.request, it issues a CPE__Abort.indication to the requesting user, giving the reason. The reason parameter may take on the values timeout, resource limitation, and failure of underlying service.

The CPE__Status.indication primitive is used to report to a convergence service user a change in information about an old affiliate.

Convergence Protocol. The convergence protocol defines:

- Procedures for exchanging convergence protocol data units (CPDUs), including a simple retry mechanism to permit the provision of the reliable quality-of-service option
- Instance and sequence numbering information to support the requirements of the convergence service

There is only a single type of convergence protocol data unit, simply called CPDU. A CPDU contains header information relating to the convergence protocol, as explained below. It may also contain user data

TABLE 11.7   Convergence Service Primitives and Parameters

CPE__Send.request (Destination Address, Quality of Service, CPE User Information)

CPE__Send.indication (Source Address, Quality of Service, Status, CPE User Information)

CPE__Abort.indication (Reason, CPE User Information)

CPE__Status.indication (CPE identifier, Status)

consisting of a LAN/MAN management PDU being transferred from one CPE user to another.

The convergence protocol is based on the concept of a **request.** A request occurs when a CPE transmits a CPDU containing user information to an affiliate. Requests are of two types:

- *Confirmed:* A confirmed request is said to be outstanding until such time as a confirmation is received or a time-out occurs. This type of request supports the reliability of the quality-of-service option.
- *Unconfirmed:* No confirmation is required.

The convergence protocol provides a mechanism by which the CPE can manage incoming and outgoing requests and support the reliability option. Requests are organized as follows. At any time, between a given pair of affiliates, there may be a single request group in existence in each direction referred to as a **request group instance** and assigned a unique sequence number. A request group comprises requests destined for a particular affiliate, some or all of which may be outstanding at any time. Each request in a request group also has a sequence number assigned to it.

With the above concepts in mind, we can now describe the CPDU. The contents of the CPDU depend on the purpose for which it is transmitted. There are three cases:

1. When a CPDU is issued to carry a request for the first time. Such a CPDU may also be used to carry an acknowledgment of an outstanding request received from the same affiliate.
2. When a CPDU is issued to repeat a request after a time-out has occurred. Such a CPDU may also be used to carry an acknowledgment of an outstanding request received from the same affiliate.
3. When a CPDU is issued only to acknowledge a request received from an affiliate.

Table 11.8 lists the fields that are contained in the CPDU for each of the three cases. For case 1, if the request requires acknowledgment, the CPDU is saved as a request record until acknowledgment is received. If the acknowledgment is not received within a given time limit, the request record is retransmitted.

The CPDU is transmitted and received by means of the LLC type 1 service and protocol. When a CPDU is received, the following actions occur:

- If the incoming CPDU contains an acknowledgment of an outstanding outgoing CPDU (incoming RRG and RRI match the LRG and LRI of an outstanding request), the request record for the outstanding CPDU may be deleted.
- If the incoming CPDU contains user information, and if the received

TABLE 11.8 Convergence Protocol Data Unit Fields

	Case 1	Case 2	Case 3
Remote CPE instance number	Most recent CPE instance number received from remote CPE address. Zero if not known.	Most recent CPE instance number received from remote CPE address. Zero if not known.	Most recent CPE instance number received from remote CPE address. Zero if not known.
Local CPE instance number	Instance number of the sending CPE	Instance number of the sending CPE	Instance number of the sending CPE
Local request group instance (LRG)	Sequence number that identifies the request group of this request	Sequence number that identifies the request group of this request	0
Local request instance (LRI)	Sequence number that identifies this request	Sequence number that identifies this request	0
Remote request group instance (RRG)	Most recent request group instance received from remote CPE address. Zero if not known.	Most recent request group instance received from remote CPE address. Zero if not known.	Most recent request group instance received from remote CPE address. Zero if not known.
Remote request instance (RRI)	Most recent request instance received from remote CPE address for current RRG. Zero if RRG is zero.	Most recent request instance received from remote CPE address for current RRG. Zero if RRG is zero.	Most recent request instance received from remote CPE address for current RRG. Zero if RRG is zero.
Reliable QOS flag	TRUE if the request requires acknowledgment	TRUE if the request requires acknowledgment	FALSE
User information	User information passed to the CPE in a CPE_Send.request	Information held in a request record	Null

request is next in sequence, then the user information is passed up to the CPE user; otherwise the incoming request is ignored.

The definition of in-sequence is as follows:

((Received LRG = RRG stored for this affiliate) AND (LRI is next in sequence))
OR (Received LRG is next in sequence) AND (LRI = 0))

11.6

FDDI MANAGEMENT

The FDDI station management (STM) specification consists of three major components:

- Connection management (CMT)
- Ring management (RMT)
- SMT frame services

Connection Management

Connection management is concerned with the insertion of stations onto the ring and removal of stations from the ring. This involves establishing or terminating a physical link between adjacent ports and the connection of ports to MAC entities. Connection management is comprised of three subcomponents:

- Entity coordination management
- Physical connection management
- Configuration management

Entity Coordination Management.   Entity coordination management (ECM) is responsible for the media interface to the FDDI ring, including the coordination of the activity of all the ports and the optional optical bypass switch associated with that station. For example, ECM coordinates the trace function, which is part of ring management. ECM signals physical connection management when the medium is available and ready for initialization of the port.

Physical Connection Management.   Physical connection management provides for managing the point-to-point physical links between adjacent PHY/PMD pairs. This includes initializing the link and testing the quality of the link (referred to as link confidence).

Initialization is accomplished by signaling between the adjacent ports. One port transmits a continuous stream of symbols until the neighbor responds with another stream of symbols. PCM sequences through a number of these request-response exchanges to communicate the following information:

- Port type (A, B, M, S)
- Willingness to establish a link
- Duration of the link confidence test performed
- Availability of the MAC entity for a link confidence test
- Outcome of the link confidence test
- Availability of the MAC for a local loop test
- Intent to place a MAC in the connection if established

Once the connection has been verified, configuration management is invoked.

Configuration Management. Configuration management provides for configuring PHY and MAC entities within a node. Essentially, configuration management is concerned with the internal organization of the station entities, and may be thought of as controlling a configuration switch that implements the desired interconnections.

Ring Management

Ring management receives status information from media access control (MAC) and from connection management. Services provided by ring management include:

- Stuck beacon detection
- Resolution of problems through the trace process
- Detection of duplicate addresses

Stuck Beacon Detection. A beacon is a MAC control frame used to isolate a serious ring failure such as a break in the ring. A station that suspects a ring failure will transmit a continuous stream of beacons. Eventually, it should receive either a beacon from an upstream station or its own beacon. If neither event occurs, the station will continue to transmit its own beacon indefinitely, a condition known as a stuck beacon. A stuck beacon indicates that a station is locked into sending continuous beacon frames.

A stuck-beacon timer under the control of ring management measures the duration of beacon transmission. If a time limit is exceeded, ring management initiates a stuck-beacon recovery procedure. The procedure begins with the transmission of a *directed beacon,* which is addressed to its nearest upstream neighbor and informs the ring of the stuck condition. The directed beacons are sent for a sufficiently long time to assure that they are seen by all the MACs. After the directed beacons are sent and the stuck-beacon condition is still unresolved, a trace function is initiated.

Trace Function.   The trace function uses PHY signaling of symbol streams to recover from a stuck-beacon condition. The result of the directed beacon is to localize the fault to the beaconing MAC and its nearest upstream neighbor.

Duplicate Address Detection.   If two or more MAC entities have the same address, then the ring cannot function properly. Duplicate address detection is performed during ring initialization and consists of monitoring the ring for conditions indicating that duplicate addresses are present.

If two or more MACs have the same address, at least one of the MACs will experience one of the following conditions:

- Receive own beacon while issuing claim frames for longer than the maximum delay of the FDDI ring (DMax). This indicates that the other duplicate is sending beacon frames while this duplicate is sending claim frames.
- Receive own claim frames while issuing beacon frames for longer than DMax. This indicates that the other duplicate is sending claim frames while this duplicate is sending beacon frames.
- Receive own claim frames for a period of time greater than DMax after having "won" the claim-token contest. This indicates that the other duplicate is sending claim frames while this duplicate has stopped claiming and issued a token.
- Receive own claim frame with different value of TTRT. This indicates that duplicates with different requested TTRT values are both claiming.

When a station detects the duplicate address condition, it can respond by changing its MAC address, configuring the MAC to lose the claim process and disabling its LLC services, or removing the MAC from the ring.

SMT Frame Services

The frame services portion of SMT deals with the management of the station after the ring has achieved an operational state. These services are implemented by a set of SMT frames. Table 11.9 lists the frames and Figure 11.8 illustrates the frame format. The frames are:

- *Neighborhood information frame:* used to transmit own address and basic station descriptor to downstream neighbors. Each station periodically issues the frame using next station addressing (NSA).

TABLE 11.9   FDDI SMT Frames

Frame Class	Abbreviation	Frame Types in Class
Neighbor Information	NIF	Announcement, Request, Response
Station Information	SIF	
Configuration		Request*, Response
Operation		Request*, Response
Echo	ECF	Request*, Response
Resource Allocation	RAF	Announcement, Request, Response
Request Denied	RDF	Response
Status Report	SRF	Announcement*
Parameter Management	PMF	
Get PMF		Request*, Response*
Change PMF		Request*, Response*
Add PMF		Request*, Response*
Remove PMF		Request*, Response*
Extended Service	ESF	Announcement*, Request*, Response*

* = optional

NSA is a special addressing mode that permits a station to send a frame to the next station in the token path without knowing the address of that station.

- *Station information frame:* used to request and supply a station's configuration and operating information.
- *Echo frame:* used for SMT-to-SMT loopback testing.
- *Resource allocation frame:* intended to support a variety of network

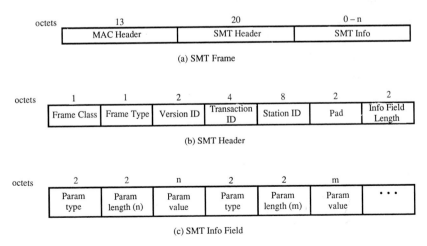

(a) SMT Frame

(b) SMT Header

(c) SMT Info Field

FIGURE 11.8 SMT Frame Format

policies for the allocation of resources. A typical use is the allocation of synchronous bandwidth to the stations within a ring.

- *Request denied frame:* issued in response to an unsupported optional frame class or type request or unsupported version ID.
- *Status report frame:* used by stations to periodically announce station status, which might be of interest to the manager of an FDDI ring.
- *Parameter management frame:* provides the means for remote management of station attributes via the parameter management protocol.
- *Extended service frame:* user-defined frames that extend or exercise new SMT services.

11.7

RECOMMENDED READING

One of the few textbooks on the subject of network management technology is [TERP91]. [STAL93c] is an in-depth examination of both the OSI and SNMP sets of standards. [STAL93d] contains reprints of key recent papers on network management.

11.8

PROBLEMS

11.1 List useful protocol-specific performance measures for the following protocols. Indicate whether collection can be centralized or must be distributed.
  a. Token bus
  b. Token ring
  c. Slotted ring
  d. Register insertion
  e. DQDB
11.2 For centrally collected measurement data, there is a timing bias due to the propagation delay of the medium. Give examples of performance measures that are (are not) affected by this bias.
11.3 For the LAN/MAN management architecture, is it possible to support LMMP directly on type 3 LLC (acknowledged connectionless) or type 2 LLC (connection-oriented) rather than use a convergence protocol. If not, why not? If so, is anything lost?

Glossary

ALOHA. A medium access control technique for multiple access transmission media. A station transmits whenever it has data to send. Unacknowledged transmissions are repeated.

AMPLIFIER. An analog device designed to compensate for the loss in a section of transmission medium. It increases the signal strength of an analog signal over a range of frequencies.

ANS X3T9.5. A committee sponsored by the American National Standards Institute (ANSI) that is responsible for a variety of system interconnection standards. The committee has produced draft standards for high-speed coaxial cable bus and fiber optic ring local networks.

BANDWIDTH. Refers to a relative range of frequencies, that is, the difference between the highest and lowest frequencies transmitted. For example, the bandwidth of a TV channel is 6 MHz.

BASEBAND. Transmission of signals without modulation. In a baseband local network, digital signals (1's and 0's) are inserted directly onto the cable as voltage pulses. The entire spectrum of the cable is consumed by the signal. This scheme does not allow frequency-division multiplexing.

BRIDGE. A device used to link two or more homogeneous LANs or MANs. It accepts frames from attached networks addressed to devices on other networks, buffers them, and retransmits them in the direction of the other network. A bridge does not alter the frame content but acts merely as a relay. It operates at the MAC layer.

BROADBAND. The use of coaxial cable for providing data transfer by means of analog or radio-frequency signals. Digital signals are passed through a modem and transmitted over one of the frequency bands of the cable.

BUS.   A topology in which stations are attached to a shared transmission medium. The transmission medium is a linear cable; transmissions propagate the length of the medium and are received by all stations.

CARRIERBAND.   Same as single-channel broadband.

CATV.   Community antenna television. CATV cable is used for broadband local networks.

CENTRALIZED BUS ARCHITECTURE.   A bus topology in which the bus is very short and the links to attached devices are relatively much longer.

CENTREX.   A voice and data-switching service that performs switching functions in the telephone company's central office as opposed to a digital PBX, which performs switching on the customer's premises.

CHEAPERNET.   A baseband local area network that uses a thinner cable and less expensive components than Ethernet or the original IEEE 802.3 standard. Although the data rate is the same (10 Mbps), the network span and number of stations is less for Cheapernet.

CIRCUIT SWITCHING.   A method of communicating in which a dedicated communications path is established between two devices through one or more intermediate switching nodes. Unlike packet switching, digital data are sent as a continuous stream of bits. Bandwidth is guaranteed, and delay is essentially limited to propagation time. The telephone system uses circuit switching.

COAXIAL CABLE.   An electromagnetic transmission medium consisting of a center conductor and an outer, concentric conductor.

CODEC.   Coder–decoder. Transforms analog voice into a digital bit stream (coder), and digital signals into analog voice (decoder), usually using pulse code modulation (PCM).

COLLISION.   A condition in which two packets are being transmitted over a medium at the same time. Their interference makes both unintelligible.

CONTENTION.   The condition when two or more stations attempt to use the same channel at the same time.

CRC.   Cyclic redundancy check. A numeric value derived from the bits in a message. The transmitting station calculates a number that is attached to the message. The receiving station performs the same calculation. If the results differ, then one or more bits are in error.

CSMA.   Carrier sense multiple access. A medium access control technique for multiple-access transmission media. A station wishing to transmit first senses the medium and transmits only if the medium is idle.

CSMA/CD.   Carrier sense multiple access with collision detection. A refinement of CSMA in which a station ceases transmission if it detects a collision.

DATAGRAM.   A packet-switching service in which packets (datagrams) are independently routed and may arrive out of order. The datagram is self-contained and carries a complete address. Delivery confirmation is provided by higher-level protocols.

DCE.   Data circuit-terminating equipment. A generic name for network-owned devices that provide a network attachment point for user devices.

DIFFERENTIAL ENCODING.   A means of encoding digital data on a digital signal such that the binary value is determined by a signal change rather than a signal level.

DIFFERENTIAL MANCHESTER ENCODING. A digital signaling technique in which there is a transition in the middle of each bit time to provide clocking. The encoding of a 0(1) is represented by the presence (absence) of a transition at the beginning of the bit period.

DIGITAL DATA SWITCH. A star topology local network using circuit switching. Usually refers to a system that handles only data but not voice.

DIGITAL PRIVATE BRANCH EXCHANGE. A local network based on the private branch exchange architecture. Provides an integrated voice/data switching service. See PBX.

DTE. Data terminal equipment. A generic name for user-owned devices or stations that attach to a network.

DUAL CABLE. A type of broadband cable system in which two separate cables are used: one for transmission and one for reception.

ETHERNET. A 10-Mbps baseband local area network specification developed jointly by Xerox, Intel, and Digital Equipment. It is the forerunner of the IEEE 802.3 CSMA/CD standard.

FRAME. A group of bits that includes data plus one or more addresses. Generally refers to a link layer (layer 2) protocol.

FREQUENCY-AGILE MODEM. A modem used on some broadband systems that can shift frequencies in order to communicate with stations in different dedicated bands.

FREQUENCY-DIVISION MULTIPLEXING (FDM). A technique for combining multiple signals on one circuit by separating them in frequency.

FREQUENCY TRANSLATOR. In a split broadband cable system, an analog device at the headend that converts a block of inbound frequencies to a block of outbound frequencies.

FSK. Frequency-shift keying. A digital-to-analog modulation technique in which two different frequencies are used to represent 1's and 0's.

GATEWAY. A device that connects two systems, especially if the two systems use different protocols. Recently, the term *gateway* has been reserved for the interconnection of networks at layer 7 of the OSI model.

GRADE OF SERVICE. For a circuit-switched system, the probability that, during a specified period of peak traffic, an offered call will fail to find an available circuit.

HEADEND. The endpoint of a broadband bus or tree network. Transmission from a station is toward the headend. Reception by a station is from the headend.

HIGH-SPEED LOCAL NETWORK (HSLN). A local network designed to provide high throughput between expensive, high-speed devices, such as mainframes and mass storage devices.

HIGHSPLIT. A type of broadband cable system in which the available frequencies are split into two groups: one for transmission (5 to 174 MHz) and one for reception (232 to 400 MHz). Requires a frequency translator.

HOST. The collection of hardware and software that attaches to a network and uses that network to provide interprocess communication and user services.

HYBRID LOCAL NETWORK. An integrated local network consisting of more than one type of local network (LAN, HSLN, digital PBX).

IEEE 802. A committee of IEEE organized to produce a LAN standard.

INBOUND PATH. On a broadband LAN, the transmission path used by stations to transmit packets toward the headend.

INFRARED. Electromagnetic waves whose frequency range is above that of microwave and below the visible spectrum: 3×10^{11} to 4×10^{14} Hz.

INJECTION LASER DIODE (ILD). A solid-state device that works on the laser principle to produce a light source for optical fiber.

INTERNET. A collection of packet-switched networks connected via gateways.

INTERNETWORKING. Communication among devices across multiple networks.

LASER. Electromagnetic source capable of producing infrared and visible light.

LIGHT-EMITTING DIODE (LED). A solid-state device that emits light when a current is applied. Used as a light source for optical fiber.

LISTEN BEFORE TALK (LBT). Same as carrier sense multiple access (CSMA).

LISTEN WHILE TALK (LWT). Same as carrier sense multiple access with collision detection (CSMA/CD).

LOCAL AREA NETWORK (LAN). A general-purpose local network that can serve a variety of devices. Typically used for terminals, microcomputers, and minicomputers.

LOCAL NETWORK. A communications network that provides interconnection of a variety of data communicating devices within a small area.

MANCHESTER ENCODING. A digital signaling technique in which there is a transition in the middle of each bit time. A 1 is encoded with a high level during the first half of the bit time; a 0 is encoded with a low level during the first half of the bit time.

MEDIUM ACCESS CONTROL (MAC). For bus, tree, and ring topologies, the method of determining which device has access to the transmission medium at any time. CSMA/CD and token are common access methods.

MESSAGE SWITCHING. A switching technique using a message store and forward system. No dedicated path is established. Rather, each message contains a destination address and is passed from source to destination through intermediate nodes. At each node, the entire message is received, stored briefly, and then passed on to the next node.

MICROWAVE. Electromagnetic waves in the frequency range 1 to 30 GHz.

MIDSPLIT. A type of broadband cable system in which the available frequencies are split into two groups: one for transmission (5 to 116 MHz) and one for reception (168 to 400 MHz). Requires a frequency translator.

MODEM. Modulator/demodulator. Transforms a digital bit stream into an analog signal (modulator) and vice versa (demodulator). The analog signal may be sent over telephone lines, or could be radio frequencies or lightwaves.

NETWORK CONTROL CENTER. The operator interface to software that observes and controls the activities in a network.

NETWORK INTERFACE UNIT. A communications controller that attaches to a local network. It implements the local network protocols and provides an interface for device attachment.

NETWORK MANAGEMENT. A set of human and automated tasks that support the creation, operation, and evolution of a network.

NONBLOCKING NETWORK. A circuit-switched network in which there is always at least one available path between any pair of idle endpoints regardless of the number of endpoints already connected.

OPTICAL FIBER. A thin filament of glass or other transparent material through which a signal-encoded light beam may be transmitted by means of total internal reflection.

OUTBOUND PATH. On a broadband LAN, the transmission path used by stations to receive packets coming from the headend.

PACKET. A group of bits that includes data plus source and destination addresses. Generally refers to a network layer (layer 3) protocol.

PACKET SWITCHING. A method of transmitting messages through a communications network, in which long messages are subdivided into short packets. The packets are then transmitted as in message switching. Usually, packet switching is more efficient and rapid than message switching.

PASSIVE HEADEND. A device that connects the two broadband cables of a dual-cable system. It does not provide frequency translation.

PASSIVE STAR. A star-topology local network configuration in which the central switch or node is a passive device. Each station is connected to the central node by two links, one for transmit and one for receive. A signal input on one of the transmit links passes through the central node where it is split equally among and output to all of the receive links.

PBX. Private branch exchange. A telephone exchange on the user's premises. Provides a switching facility for telephones on extension lines within the building and access to the public telephone network. May be manual (PMBX) or automatic (PABX).

PCM. Pulse code modulation. A common method for digitizing voice. The data rate typically used for a single digitized voice channel is 64 kbps.

PROPAGATION DELAY. The delay between the time a signal enters a channel and the time it is received.

PROTOCOL. A set of rules governing the exchange of data between two entities.

REGISTER INSERTION RING. A medium access control technique for rings. Each station contains a register that can temporarily hold a circulating packet. A station may transmit whenever there is a gap on the ring and, if necessary, may hold an oncoming packet until it has completed transmission.

REMODULATOR. In a split broadband cable system, a digital device at the headend that recovers the digital data from the inbound analog signal and then retransmits the data on the outbound frequency.

REPEATER. A device that receives data on one communication link and transmits it, bit by bit, on another link as fast as it is received, without buffering. An integral part of the ring topology. Used to connect linear segments in a baseband bus local network.

RING. A topology in which stations are attached to repeaters connected in a closed loop. Data are transmitted in one direction around the ring, and can be read by all attached stations.

RING WIRING CONCENTRATOR. A site through which pass the links between repeaters, for all or a portion of a ring.

ROUTER. A device used to link two or more networks. The router makes use of an internet protocol, which is a connectionless protocol operating at layer 3 of the OSI model.

SINGLE-CHANNEL BROADBAND. A local network scheme in which the entire spectrum of the cable is devoted to a single transmission path; frequency-division multiplexing is not used. Also known as carrierband.

SLOTTED ALOHA. A medium access control technique for multiple-access transmission media. The technique is the same as ALOHA, except that packets must be transmitted in well-defined time slots.

SLOTTED RING. A medium access control technique for rings. The ring is divided into slots designated empty or full. A station may transmit when an empty slot goes by, by marking it full and inserting a packet into the slot.

SPACE-DIVISION SWITCHING. A circuit-switching technique in which each connection through the switch takes a physically separate and dedicated path.

SPECTRUM. Refers to an absolute range of frequencies. For example, the spectrum of CATV cable is now about 5 Hz to 400 MHz.

SPLITTER. Analog device for dividing one input into two outputs and combining two outputs into one input. Used to achieve tree topology on broadband CATV networks.

STAR. A topology in which all stations are connected to a central switch. Two stations communicate via circuit switching.

STAR WIRING. A method of laying out the transmission medium that is installed for a local network. All cables are concentrated in a wiring closet, with a dedicated cable run from the closet to each device on the network.

STATISTICAL TIME-DIVISION MULTIPLEXING. A method of TDM in which time slots on a shared transmission line are allocated to I/O channels on demand.

SUBSPLIT. A type of broadband cable system in which the available frequencies are split into two groups: one for transmission (5 to 30 MHz) and one for reception (54 to 400 MHz). Requires a frequency translator.

SYNCHRONOUS TIME-DIVISION MULTIPLEXING. A method of TDM in which time slots on a shared transmission line are assigned to I/O channels on a fixed, predetermined basis.

TAP. An analog device that permits signals to be inserted or removed from a twisted pair of coax cable.

TDM BUS SWITCHING. A form of time-division switching in which time slots are used to transfer data over a shared bus between transmitter and receiver.

TERMINAL. A collection of hardware and possibly software that provides a direct user interface to a network.

TERMINATOR. An electrical resistance at the end of a cable that serves to absorb the signal on the line.

TIME-DIVISION MULTIPLEXING (TDM). A technique for combining multiple signals on one circuit by separating them in time.

TIME-DIVISION SWITCHING. A circuit-switching technique in which time slots in a time-multiplexed stream of data are manipulated to pass data from an input to an output.

TIME-MULTIPLEXED SWITCHING (TMS). A form of space-division switching in which each input line is a TDM stream. The switching configuration may change for each time slot.

TIME-SLOT INTERCHANGE (TSI). The interchange of time slots within a time-division multiplexed stream.

TIMING JITTER. Deviation of clock recovery that can occur when a receiver attempts to recover clocking as well as data from the received signal. The clock recovery will deviate in a random fashion from the transitions of the received signal.

TOKEN BUS. A medium access control technique for bus/tree. Stations form a logical ring, around which a token is passed. A station receiving the token may transmit data, and then must pass the token on to the next station in the ring.

TOKEN RING. A medium access control technique for rings. A token circulates around the ring. A station may transmit by seizing the token, inserting a packet onto the ring, and then retransmitting the token.

TOPOLOGY. The structure, consisting of paths and switches, that provides the communications interconnection among nodes of a network.

TRANSCEIVER. A device that both transmits and receives.

TRANSCEIVER CABLE. A twin-pair cable that connects the transceiver in a baseband coax LAN to the controller.

TRANSMISSION MEDIUM. The physical path between transmitters and receivers in a communications network.

TREE. A topology in which stations are attached to a shared transmission medium. The transmission medium is a branching cable emanating from a head-end, with no closed circuits. Transmissions propagate throughout all branches of the tree and are received by all stations.

TWISTED PAIR. An electromagnetic transmission medium consisting of two insulated wires arranged in a regular spiral pattern.

VIRTUAL CIRCUIT. A packet-switching service in which a connection (virtual circuit) is established between two stations at the start of transmission. All packets follow the same route, need not carry a complete address, and arrive in sequence.

WIRING CLOSET. A specially designed closet used for wiring data and voice communication networks. The closet serves as a concentration point for the cabling that interconnects devices, and as a patching facility for adding and deleting devices from the network.

References

ABBO84 Abbot, G. "Digital Space Division: A Technique for Switching High-Speed Data Signals." *IEEE Communications Magazine*, April, 1984.

ABEY91 Abeysundara, B., and Kamal, A. "High-Speed Local Area Networks and Their Performance: A Survey." *ACM Computing Surveys*, June, 1991.

ABRA70 Abramson, N. "The ALOHA System—Another Alternative for Computer Communications." *Proceedings, Fall Joint Computer Conference*, 1970.

AIME79 Aimes, G.T., and Lazowska, E.D. "The Behavior of Ethernet-like Computer Communications Networks." *Proceedings, Seventh Symposium on Operating Systems Principles*, 1979.

AMER82 Amer, P.D. "A Measurement Center for the NBS Local Area Computer Network," *IEEE Transactions on Computers*, August, 1982.

AMER83 Amer, P.D.; Rosenthal, R.; and Toense, R. "Measuring a Local Network's Performance." *Data Communications*, April, 1983.

BACK88 Backes, F. "Transparent Bridges for Interconnection of IEEE 802 LANs." *IEEE Network*, January 1988.

BAL85 Bal, S. "Core Modules Speed System Design." *Systems & Software*, November, 1985.

BARC81 Barcomb, D. *Office Automation: A Survey of Tools and Technology.* Bedford, MA: Digital Press, 1981.

BART85 Bartee, T. *Data Communications, Networks, and Systems.* Indianapolis, IN: Howard W. Sams and Co., 1985.

BASC87 Basch, E. *Optical-Fiber Transmission.* Indianapolis, IN: Howard W. Sams, 1987.

BEDE86 Bederman, S. "Source Routing." *Data Communications*, February, 1986.

BELL90 Bellcore (Bell Communications Research). *Telecommunications Transmission Engineering, Third Edition.* Three volumes. 1990.

BELL91 Bellamy, J. *Digital Telephony,* New York: Wiley, 1991.

BERT92 Bertsekas, D., and Gallager, R. *Data Networks.* Englewood Cliffs, NJ: Prentice-Hall, 1992.

BEUE88 Beuerman, S., and Coyle, E. "The Delay Characteristics of CSMA/CD Networks." *IEEE Transactions on Communications,* May, 1988.

BEVA86 Bevan, M. "Image Processing May Cause Future Problems with Network Loading." *Data Communications,* March, 1986.

BHUS85 Bhushan, B., and Opderbeck, H. "The Evolution of Data Switching for PBX's." *IEEE Journal on Selected Areas in Communications,* July, 1985.

BIND75 Binder, R. "A Dynamic Packet Switching System for Satellite Broadcast Channels." *Proceedings of the ICC, 1975.*

BRAY85 Bray, J. "The Resurgence of Centrex." *Telecommunications,* September, 1985.

BURG84 Burg, F.; Chen, C.; and Folts, H. "Of Local Networks, Protocols, and the OSI Reference Model." *Data Communications,* November, 1984.

BURG89 Burg, F., and Iorio, N. "Networking of Networks: Interworking According to OSI." *IEEE Journal on Selected Areas in Communications.* September, 1989.

BURK79 Burke, R. G. "Eliminating Conflicts on a Contention Channel." *Proceedings, Fourth Local Computer Network Conference,* 1979.

BUX81 Bux, W. "Local-Area Subnetworks: A Performance Comparison." *IEEE Transactions on Communications,* October, 1981.

BUX83a Bux, W.; Closs, F.; Kummerle, K.; Keller, H.; and Mueller, H. "Architecture and Design of a Reliable Token-Ring Network." *IEEE Journal on Selected Areas in Communications,* November, 1983.

BUX83b Bux, W., and Schlatter, M. "An Approximate Method for the Performance Analysis of Buffer Insertion Rings." *IEEE Transaction on Communications,* January, 1983.

BUX84 Bux, W. "Performance Issues in Local-Area Networks." *IBM Systems Journal,* no. 4, 1984.

BUX87 Bux, W.; Grillo, D.; and Maxemchuk, N. editors. *Interconnection of Local Area Networks. Special issue of IEEE Journal on Selected Areas in Communications,* December, 1987.

BYTE85 Bytex Corporation. *Autoswitch Technical Manual,* 1985.

CELA82 Celano, J. "Crossing Public Property: Infrared Link and Alternative Approaches for Connecting a High Speed Local Area Network." *Proceedings, Computer Networking Symposium,* 1982.

CERF78 Cerf, V.G., and Kristein, P.T. "Issues in Packet-Network Interconnection." *Proceedings of the IEEE,* November, 1978.

CERR87 Cerruti, M., and Voce, M. "Zap Data Where It Really Counts—Direct-to-Host Connections." *Data Communications,* July, 1987.

CHEN82 Cheng, W. *Performance Evaluation of Token Networks.* Ph.D. thesis, University of Illinois at Urbana-Champaign, 1982.

CHER83 Cheriton, D. "Local Networking and Internetworking in the V-System." *Proceedings, Eighth Data Communications Symposium,* 1983.

CHU82 Chu, W.W.; Haller, W.; and Leung, K.K. "A Contention Based Channel Reservation Protocol for High Speed Local Networks." *Proceedings, Seventh Conference on Local Computer Networks,* 1982.

CLAI88 Clair, M., and Orlov, M. "Is It Wise for Users to Run Ethernet Over Existing Nonshielded Twisted Pair?" *Network World,* January 11, 1988.

CLAN82 Clancy, G.J. et al. "The IEEE 802 Committee States Its Case Concerning Its Local Network Standards Efforts." *Data Communications,* April, 1982.

COME88 Comer, D. *Internetworking with TCP/IP: Principles, Protocols, and Architecture.* Englewood Cliffs, NJ: Prentice-Hall, 1988.

COOP84 Cooper, E. *Broadband Network Technology.* Mountain View, CA: Sytek Press, 1984.

COOV85 Coover, E. "Notes from Mid-revolution: Searching for the Perfect PBX." *Data Communications,* August, 1985.

COOV86 Coover, E. "Voice-Data Integration in the Office: A PBX Approach." *IEEE Communications Magazine,* July, 1986.

COOV89 Coover, E. *Digital Private Branch Exchanges.* Washington, DC: IEEE Computer Society Press, 1989.

COTT81 Cotton, J.; Giesken, K.; Lawrence, A.; and Upp, D. "ITT 1240 Digital Exchange: Digital Switching Network." *Electrical Communication,* No. 2/3, 1981.

COUC90 Couch, L. *Digital and Analog Communication Systems, Third Edition.* New York: Macmillan, 1990.

COUC87 Couch, D. Measuring the Performance of a Mixed-Vendor Ethernet." *Data Communications,* August, 1987.

CROC83 Crochiere, R.E., and Flanagan, J.L. "Current Perspectives in Digital Speech." *IEEE Communications Magazine,* January, 1983.

CROW73 Crowther, W.; Rettberg, R.; Walden, D.; Orenstein, S.; and Heart, F. "A System for Broadcast Communication: Reservation ALOHA." *Proceedings, Sixth Hawaii International System Science Conference,* 1973.

CUNN80 Cunningham, J.E. *Cable Television.* Indianapolis: Howard W. Sams, 1980.

CZOT87 Czotter, T. "Network Interface Design Guide." *Proceedings, 12th Conference on Local Computer Networks,* October, 1987.

DAHO83 Dahod, A.M. "Local Network Standards: No Utopia." *Data Communications,* March, 1983.

DAVI73 Davies, D.W., and Barber, D.L. *Communication Networks for Computers.* New York: Wiley, 1973.

DAVI77 Davidson, J.; Hathaway, W.; Postel, J.; Mimno, N.; Thomas, R.; and Walden, D. "The ARPANET Telnet Protocol: Its Purpose, Principles, Implementation, and Impact on Host Operating System Design." *Proceedings, Fifth Data Communications Symposium,* 1977.

DAVI83 Davidson, J. "OSI Model Layering of a Military Local Network." *Proceedings of the IEEE,* December, 1983.

DAVI90 Davidson, R., and Muller, N. *LANs to WANs: Network Management in the 1990s.* Norwood, MA: Artech House, 1990.

DAY80 Day, J. "Terminal Protocols." *IEEE Transactions on Communications,* April, 1980.

DAY81 Day, J. "Terminal, File Transfer, and Remote Job Protocols for Heterogeneous Computer Networks." In *Protocols and Techniques for Data Communication Networks*, edited by F.F. Kuo. Englewood Cliffs, NJ: Prentice-Hall, 1981.

DCA85 Defense Communications Agency. *DDN Protocol Handbook.* Menlo Park, CA: DDN Information Center, December, 1985.

DIAM90 Diament, P. *Wave Transmission and Fiber Optics.* New York: Macmillan, 1990.

DIGI80 Digital Equipment Corp.; Intel. Corp.; and Xerox Corp. *The Ethernet: A Local Area Network Data Link Layer and Physical Layer Specifications.* September 30, 1980.

DIJK59 Dijkstra, E. "A Note on Two Problems in Connection with Graphs." *Numerical Mathematics*, October, 1959.

DINE80 Dineson, M.A., and Picazo, J.J. "Broadband Technology Magnifies Local Network Capability." *Data Communications*, February, 1980.

DINE81 Dineson, M.A. "Broadband Local Networks Enhance Communication Design." *EDN*, March 4, 1981.

DIXO83 Dixon, R.; Strole, N.; and Markov, J. "A Token-ring Network for Local Data Communications." *IBM Systems Journal.* Nos. 1/2, 1983.

DIXO88 Dixon, R., and Pitt, D. "Addressing, Bridging, and Source Routing." *IEEE Network,* January, 1988.

DONN79 Donnelly, J.E., and Yeh, J.W. "Interaction Between Protocol Levels in a Prioritized CSMA Broadcast Network." *Computer Networks*, March, 1979.

DRAV91 Dravida, S.; Rodrigues, M.; and Saksena, V. "Performance Comparison of High-Speed Multiple-Access Networks." *Proceedings of the International Teletraffic Congress*, June, 1991.

ENOM85 Enomoto, O.; Kohashi, T.; Aomori, T.; Kadota, S.; Oka, S.; and Fujita, K. "Distributed Microprocessors Control Architecture for Versatile Business Communications," *IEEE Journal on Selected Areas in Communications*, July, 1985.

ESTR86 Estrin, J., and Cheney, K. "Managing Local Area Networks Effectively." *Data Communications*, January, 1986.

FARM69 Farmer, W.D., and Newhall, E.E. "An Experimental Distributed Switching System to Handle Bursty Computer Traffic." *Proceedings, ACM Symposium on Problems in the Optimization of Data Communications*, 1969.

FLEM79 Fleming, P. *Principles of Switching.* Geneva, IL: Lee's abc of the Telephone, 1979.

FRAN80 Franta, W.R., and Bilodeau, M.B. "Analysis of a Prioritized CSMA Protocol Based on Staggered Delays." *Acta Informatica*, June, 1980.

FREE89 Freeman, R.L. *Telecommunication System Engineering.* New York: Wiley, 1989.

FREE91 Freeman, R.L. *Telecommunication Transmission Handbook.* New York: Wiley, 1991.

FREE85 Freeman, R. *Reference Manual for Telecommunications Engineering.* New York: Wiley, 1985.

GERL88 Gerla, M.; Green, L.; and Rutledge, R. Special Issue on Bridges and Routers. *IEEE Network*, January, 1988.

GOEL83 Goeller, L.F., and Goldston, J.A. "The ABCs of the PBX." *Datamation*, April, 1983.

GONS88 Gonsales, T., and Tobagi, F. "On the Performance Effects of Station

Locations and Access Protocol Parameters in Ethernet Networks." *IEEE Transactions on Communications*, April, 1988.

GOOD88   Goodman, J.; Greenberg, A.; Madras, N.; and March, P. "Stability of Binary Exponential Backoff." *Journal of the ACM*, July, 1988.

GRAN83   Grant, A.; Hutchinson, D.; and Shepherd, W. "A Gateway for Linking Local Area Networks and X.25 Networks." *Proceedings, SIGCOMM 83 Symposium*, 1983.

GRAU84   Graube, M., and Molder, M. "Local Area Networks," *IEEE Computer*, October, 1984.

GREE90a   Greenfield, D. "An End to a Bridging Feud?" *Data Communications*, May, 1990.

GREE90b   Green, P.; Naemura, K.; and Williamson, R. editors. *Heterogeneous Computer Networks Interconnection. Special issue of IEEE Journal on Selected Areas in Communications*, January, 1990.

GRNA80   Grnarov, A.; Kleinrock, L.; and Gerla, M. "A Highly Reliable Distributed Loop Network Architecture." *Proceedings, International Symposium on Fault-Tolerant Computing*, 1980.

HAFN74   Hafner, E.R.; Nenadal, Z.; and Tschanz, M. "A Digital Loop Communications System." *IEEE Transactions on Communications*, June, 1974.

HAHN90   Hahne, E.; Choudhury, A.; and Maxemchuk, N. "Improving the Fairness of Distributed-Queue-Dual-Bus Networks." *Proceedings, INFOCOM '90*, June, 1990.

HALL85   "Factory Networks." *Micro Communications*, February, 1985.

HAMM86   Hammond, J., and O'Reilly, P. *Performance Analysis of Local Computer Networks*. Reading, MA: Addison-Wesley, 1986.

HAMN88   Hamner, M., and Samsen, G. "Source Routing Bridge Implementation." *IEEE Network*, January, 1988.

HANS81   Hanson, K.; Chou, W.; and Nilsson, A. "Integration of Voice, Data, and Image Traffic in a Wideband Local Network." *Proceedings, Computer Networking Symposium*, 1981.

HART88   Hart, J. "Extending the IEEE 802.1 MAC Bridge Standard to Remote Bridges." *IEEE Network*, January, 1988.

HAYE81   Hayes, J.F. "Local Distribution in Computer Communications." *IEEE Communications Magazine*, March, 1981.

HELD87   Held, G. "A Dozen Ways to Beef Up Your Network with a Port Selector." *Data Communications*, June, 1987.

HENR89   Henry, P. "High-Capacity Lightwave Local Area Networks." *IEEE Communications Magazine*, October, 1989.

HERR79   Herr, D.E., and Nute, C.T. "Modeling the Effects of Packet Truncation on the Throughput of CSMA Networks." *Proceedings, Computer Networking Symposium*, 1979.

HEYM82   Heyman, D.P. "An Analysis of the Carrier-Sense Multiple-Access Protocol." *Bell System Technical Journal*, October, 1982.

HEYW81   Heywood, P. "The Cambridge Ring Is Still Making the Rounds." *Data Communications*, July, 1981.

HOHN80   Hohn, W.C. "The Control Data Loosely Coupled Network Lower Level Protocols." *Proceedings, National Computer Conference*, 1980.

HONG86   Hong, J. "Timing Jitter." *Data Communications*, February, 1986.

HOPK77 Hopkins, G.T. *A Bus Communications System.* MITRE Technical Report MTR-3515, 1977.

HOPK79 Hopkins, G.T. "Multimode Communications on the MITRENET." *Proceedings, Local Area Communications Network Symposium,* 1979.

HOPK80 Hopkins, G.T., and Wagner, P.E. *Multiple Access Digital Communications System.* U.S. Patent 4,210,780, July 1, 1980.

HOPP83 Hopper, A., and Williamson, R. "Design and Use of an Integrated Cambridge Ring." *IEEE Journal on Selected Areas in Communications,* November, 1983.

HUBE83 Huber, D.; Steinlin, W.; and Wild, P. "SILK: An Implementation of a Buffer Insertion Ring." *IEEE Journal on Selected Areas in Communications,* November, 1983.

IBM82 IBM Corp. *IBM Series/Local Communications Controller Feature Description.* GA34-0142-2, 1982.

IBM84 IBM Corp. *A Building Planning Guide for Communication Wiring.* G320-8059, March, 1984.

IEEE89a Institute of Electrical and Electronics Engineers. *Logical Link Control.* IEEE Std 802.2, 1989.

IEEE89b Institute of Electrical and Electronics Engineers. *Token Ring Access Method.* ANSI/IEEE Std 802.4, 1989.

IEEE90a Institute of Electrical and Electronics Engineers. *IEEE Standard 802: Overview and Architecture.* IEEE Std 802-1990, December, 1990.

IEEE90b Institute of Electrical and Electronics Engineers. *Carrier Sense Multiple Access with Collision Detection (CSMA/CD) Access Method and Physical Layer Specifications.* ANSI/IEEE Std 802.3, 1990.

IEEE90c Institute of Electrical and Electronics Engineers. *Token Passing Bus Access Method and Physical Layer Specifications.* ANSI/IEEE Std 802.4, 1990.

IEEE90d Institute of Electrical and Electronics Engineers. *Distributed Queue Dual Bus (DQDB) Subnetwork of a Metropolitan Area Network (MAN).* ANSI/IEEE Std 802.6, 1990.

IEEE90e Institute of Electrical and Electronics Engineers. *Media Access Control (MAC) Bridges.* ANSI/IEEE Std 802.1D, 1990.

IEEE91a Institute of Electrical and Electronics Engineers. *Source Routing Annex to MAC Bridges.* IEEE Draft Standard P802.5M/D4, 1991.

IEEE91b Institute of Electrical and Electronics Engineers. *SRT Route Determination Entity.* IEEE Draft Standard P802.5M,E1, 1991.

IEEE91c Institute of Electrical and Electronics Engineers. *LAN/MAN Management.* IEEE Draft Standard 802.1B, 1991.

IRSH92 Irshid, M., and Kavehrad, M. "Star Couplers with Gain Using Fiber Amplifiers." *IEEE Photonics Technology Letters,* January, 1992.

ISO87 International Organization for Standardization. *Network Service Definition, Addendum 1: Connectionless-mode Transmission,* ISO 8348/Add. 1, 1987.

ISO88 International Organization for Standardization. *Protocol for Providing the Connectionless-mode Network Service (Internetwork Protocol),* ISO 8473, 1988.

ISRA87 Israel, J., and Weissberger, A. "Communicating Between Heterogeneous Networks." *Data Communications,* March, 1987.

JACK63 Jackson, J.R. "Job Shop-like Queueing Systems." *Management Sciences,* 1963.

JACO78 Jacobs, I.; Binder, R.; and Hoversten, E. "General Purpose Packet Satellite Networks." *Proceedings of the IEEE,* November, 1978.

JACO87 Jacobson, D., et al. "A Master/Slave Monitor Measurement Technique for an Operating Ethernet Network." *IEEE Networks,* July, 1987.

JAIN91 Jain, R. "Performance Analysis of FDDI Token Ring Networks: Effect of Parameters and Guidelines for Setting TTRR." *IEEE LTS,* May, 1991.

JAJS83 Jajszczyk, A. "On Nonblocking Switching Networks Composed of Digital Symmetrical Matrices." *IEEE Transactions on Communications,* January, 1983.

JAYA84 Jayant, N., and Noll, P. *Digital Coding of Waveforms.* Englewood Cliffs, NJ: Prentice-Hall, 1984.

JAYA87 Jayasumana, A. "Performance Analysis of Token Bus Priority Schemes: *Proceedings, INFOCOM '87,* 1987.

JEWE85 Jewett, R. "The Fourth-Generation PBX: Beyond the Integration of Voice and Data." *Telecommunications,* February, 1985.

JOEL77 Joel, A.E. "What Is Telecommunications Circuit Switching?" *Proceedings of the IEEE,* September, 1977.

JOEL79a Joel, A.E. "Circuit Switching: Unique Architecture and Applications." *Computer,* June, 1979.

JOEL79b Joel, A.E. "Digital Switching—How It Has Developed." *IEEE Transactions on Communications,* July, 1979.

JOEL85 Joel, A., ed. *Special Issue on Serving the Business Customer Using Advances in Switching Technologies. IEEE Journal on Selected Areas in Communications,* July, 1985.

JOHN87 Johnson, M. "Proof That Timing Requirements of the FDDI Token Ring Protocol Are Satisfied." *IEEE Transactions on Communications,* June, 1987.

JONE85 Jones, K. "Cheapernet Makes Local Area Networking More Affordable." *Mini-Micro Systems,* January, 1985.

JORD85 Jordan, E., ed. *Reference Data for Engineers: Radio, Electronics, Computer, and Communications.* Indianapolis, IN: Howard Sams & Co., 1985.

KAJI83 Kajiwara, M. "Trends in Digital Switching System Architectures." *IEEE Communications Magazine,* May, 1983.

KANA88 Kanakia, H., and Cheriton, D. "Universal Network Device Interface Protocol (UNDIP)." *Proceedings, 13th Conference on Local Computer Networks,* October, 1988.

KANE80 Kane, D.A. "Data Communications Network Switching Methods," *Computer Design,* April, 1980.

KARO90 Karol, M., and Gitlin, R. "High-Performance Optical Local and Metropolitan Area Networks: Enhancements of FDDI and IEEE 802.6 DQDB." *IEEE Journal on Selected Areas in Communications,* October, 1990.

KARP82 Karp, P.M., and Socher, I.D. "Designing Local-Area Networks." *Mini-Micro Systems,* April, 1982.

KASS79 Kasson, J.M. "Survey of Digital PBX Design." *IEEE Transactions on Communications,* July, 1979.

KATK81a Katkin, R.D., and Sprung, J.G. "Simulating a Cable Bus Network in a Multicomputer and Large-Scale Application Environment." *Proceedings, Sixth Conference on Local Computer Networks,* 1981.

KATK81b Katkin, R.D., and Sprung, J.G. *Application of Local Bus Network Tech-

nology to the Evolution of Large Multi-computer Systems. MITRE Technical Report MTR-81W290, November, 1981.

KAUF86 Kaufman, H. "PBX Versus LAN." *Telecommunications,* May, 1986.

KEIS85 Keiser, B., and Strange, E. *Digital Telephony and Network Integration.* New York: Van Nostrand Reinhold, 1985.

KELL83 Keller, H.; Meyr, H.; and Mueller, H. "Transmission Design Criteria for a Synchronous Token Ring." *IEEE Journal on Selected Areas in Communications,* November, 1983.

KESS92 Kessler, G., and Train, D. *Metropolitan Area Networks: Concepts, Standards, and Services.* New York: McGraw-Hill, 1992.

KILL82 Killen, M. "The Microcomputer Connection to Local Networks." *Data Communications,* December, 1982.

KIM88 Kim, G. *Broadband LAN Technology.* Norwood, MA: Artech House, 1988.

KLEI75 Kleinrock, L., and Tobagi, F.A. "Packet Switching in Radio Channels: Part I: Carrier Sense Multiple-Access Modes and Their Throughput-Delay Characteristics." *IEEE Transactions on Communications,* December, 1975.

KLEI76 Kleinrock, L. *Queueing Systems, Vol. II: Computer Applications.* New York: Wiley, 1976.

KLEI86 Kleinrock, L."Channel Efficiency for LANs." In [PICK86].

KLIN86 Klinck, C. "Just When You Thought It Made Sense to Get Rid of Centrex." *Data Communications,* March, 1986.

KOBA78 Kobayashi, K. *Modeling and Analysis: An Introduction to System Performance and Evaluation Methodology.* Reading, MA: Addison-Wesley, 1978.

KURO84 Kurose, J.; Schwartz, M.; and Yemini, Y. "Multiple-Access Protocols and Time-Constrained Communication." *ACM Computing Surveys,* March, 1984.

LE88 Le, K., and Raghavendra, C. "Fault-Tolerant Routing in a Class of Double Loop Networks." *Proceedings, IEEE INFOCOM '88,* March, 1988.

LEBA86 LeBarre, L., and Brusil, P. "Metrics and Measurements for Evaluating LAN Terminal Communications." *Proceedings, Fifth Annual International Phoenix Conference on Computers and Communications,* March, 1986.

LI87 Li, V., editor. Performance Evaluation of Multiple-Access Networks. *IEEE Journal on Selected Areas in Communications,* July, 1987.

LI88 Li, T., and Linke, R. "Multigigabit-Per-Second Lightwave Systems Research for Long-Haul Applications." *IEEE Communications Magazine,* April, 1988.

LIBO85 Liboff, R., and Dalman, G. *Transmission Lines, Waveguides, and Smith Charts.* New York: Macmillan, 1985.

LISS81 Lissack, T.; Maglaris, B.; and Chin, H. "Impact of Microprocessor Architecture on Local Network Interface Adapters." *Proceedings, Conference on Local Networks and Office Automation Systems,* 1981.

LIU78 Liu, M.T. "Distributed Loop Computer Networks." In *Advances in Computers, Vol. 17.* New York: Academic Press, 1978.

LIU82 Liu, M.T.; Hilal, W.; and Groomes, B.H. "Performance Evaluation of Channel Access Protocols for Local Computer Networks." *Proceedings, COMPCON 82 Fall,* 1982.

LOWE83 Lowe, H. "OSI Virtual Terminal Service." *Proceedings of the IEEE,* December, 1983.

MAGL80 Maglaris, B., and Lissack, T. "An Integrated Broadband Local Network Architecture." *Proceedings, Fifth Conference on Local Computer Networks,* 1980.

MAGL81 Maglaris, B.; Lissack, T.; and Austin, M. "End-to-End Delay Analysis on Local Area Networks: An Office Building Scenario." *Proceedings, National Telecommunications Conference,* 1981.

MAGL82 Maglaris, B., and Lissack, T. "Performance Evaluation of Interface Units for Broadcast Local Area Networks." *Proceedings, COMPCON Fall,* 1982.

MAGN79 Magnee, F.; Endrizzi, A.; and Day, J. "A Survey of Terminal Protocols." *Computer Networks,* November, 1979.

MANF91 Manfield, D., and Beshai, M. "Traffic Analysis of Large TST Networks." *IEEE Transactions on Communications,* March, 1991.

MARA82 Marthe, M., and Hawe, B. "Predicted Capacity of Ethernet in a University Environment." *Proceedings, SOUTHCON 82,* 1982.

MARK78 Mark, J.W. "Global Scheduling Approach to Conflict-Free Multiaccess via a Data Bus." *IEEE Transactions on Communications,* September, 1978.

MART72 Martin, J. *Systems Analysis for Data Transmission.* Englewood Cliffs, NJ: Prentice-Hall, 1972.

MART88 Martin, J., and Leban, J. *Data Communication Technology.* Englewood Cliffs, NJ: Prentice-Hall, 1988.

MART89 Martin, J., and Chapman, K. *Local Area Networks: Architectures and Implementations.* Englewood Cliffs, NJ: Prentice-Hall, 1989.

MART90 Martin, J. *Telecommunications and the Computer.* Englewood Cliffs, NJ: Prentice-Hall, 1990.

MATS82 Matsukane, E. "Network Administration and Control System for a Broadband Local Area Communications Network." *Proceedings, COMPCON Fall,* 1982.

MAXE88 Maxemchuk, N. "Twelve Random Access Strategies for Fiber Optic Networks." *IEEE Transactions on Communications,* August, 1988.

MCCO88a McCool, J. "FDDI: Getting to know the Inside of the Ring." *Data Communications,* March, 1988.

MCCO88b McConnell, J. *Internetworking Computer Systems: Interconnecting Networks and Systems.* Englewood Cliffs, NJ: Prentice-Hall, 1988.

MCCO91 McConnell, J. "OSI Internetwork Routing." *Open Systems Data Transfer,* Omnicom, Inc., February, 1991.

MCDO83 McDonald, J., ed. *Fundamentals of Digital Switching.* New York: Plenum, 1983.

MCGA85 McGarry, S. "Networking Has a Job to Do in the Factory." *Data Communications,* February, 1985.

MCNA88 McNamara, J.E. *Technical Aspects of Data Communication.* Bedford, MA: Digital Press, 1988.

MEHT87 Mehta, S. "Who Needs a LAN?" *LAN Magazine,* June, 1987.

MEHT88 Mehta, S. "The Big Switch." *LAN Magazine,* June, 1988.

METC76 Metcalfe, M., and Boggs, D.R. "Ethernet: Distributed Packet Switching for Local Computer Networks." *Communications of the ACM,* July, 1976.

METC77 Metcalfe, M.; Boggs, D.R.; Thacker, C.P.; and Lampson, B.W. "Multipoint Data Communication System with Collision Detection." *U.S. Patent* 4,063,220, 1977.

METC83   Metcalfe, R. "Controller/Transceiver Board Drives Ethernet into PC Domain." *Mini-Micro Systems,* January, 1983.

MITC81   Mitchell, L.C. "A Methodology for Predicting End-to-End Responsiveness in a Local Area Network." *Proceedings, Computer Networking Symposium,* 1981.

MITC86   Mitchell, L., and Lide, D. "End-to-End Performance Modeling of Local Area Networks." *IEEE Journal on Selected Areas in Communications,* September, 1986.

MOLL87   Molle, M.; Sohraby, K.; and Venetsanopoulos, A. "Space-Time Models of Asynchronous CSMA Protocols for Local Area Networks." *IEEE Journal on Selected Areas in Communications,* July, 1987.

MUKH91   Mukherjee, B. "Integrated Voice-Data Communication over High-Speed Fiber Optic Networks." *Computer,* February, 1991.

MULL87   Muller, N. "Enhanced Data Switches May Outshine LAN, PBX Alternatives." *Data Communications,* May, 1987.

MULQ88a   Mulqueen, J. "Flashing Images Across Networks—A Technology Whose Time Is Coming." *Data Communications,* May, 1988.

MULQ88b   Mulqueen, J. "Phone Wire Loses Its Wimp Image in High-Speed Ethernet LANs." *Data Communications,* December, 1988.

MURA88   Murata, M., and Takagi, H. "Two-Layer Modeling for Local Area Networks," *IEEE Transactions on Communications,* September, 1988.

MYER82   Myers, W. "Toward a Local Network Standard." *IEEE Micro,* August, 1982.

NAKA90   Nakagawa, K., and Shimada, S. "Optical Amplifiers in Future Optical Communication Systems." *IEEE LCS,* November, 1990.

NAUG91   Naugle, M. *Local Area Networking.* New York: McGraw-Hill, 1991.

NETR91   Netronix, Inc. *Source Routing Transparent: Facts and Myths.* Petaluma, CA: Netronix, Inc., 1991.

NEWM88   Newman, R.; Budrikis, Z., and Hullett, J. "The QPSX MAN." *IEEE Communications Magazine,* April, 1988.

OCHE90   Ocheltree, K. "Using Redundancy in FDDI Networks." *Proceedings, 15th Conference on Local Computer Networks,* October, 1990.

OHSH86   Ohshima, S.; Ito, T.; Donuma, K.; Sugiyama, H.; and Fujii, Y. "Small Loss-Deviation Tapered-Fiber Star Coupler for LANs." *Journal of Lightwave Technology,* June, 1986.

OLSE83   Olsen, R.; Seifert, W.; and Taylor, J. "Tutorial: RS-232-C Data Switching on Local Networks." *Data Communications,* September, 1983.

OREI82   O'Reilly, P.J.; Hammond, J.L., Schalg, J.H.; and Murray, D.N. "Design of an Emulation Facility for Performance Studies of CSMA-Type Local Networks." *Proceedings, Seventh Conference on Local Computer Networks,* 1982.

ORLO88   Orlov, M. "Another Twist: Twisted-Pair Ethernet May Not Be All It's Cracked Up to Be." *LAN Magazine,* August, 1988.

PARK92   Park, Y., et al. "2.488 Gb/s-318 km Repeaterless Transmission Using Erbium-Doped Fiber Amplifiers in a Direct-Detection System." *IEEE Photonics Technology Letters,* February, 1992.

PARL85   Parlatore, P. "Hooking Into AT&T Networks." *Systems & Software,* September, 1985.

PARU90   Parulkar, G. "The Next Generation of Internetworking." *Computer Communications Review,* January, 1990.

PATE87 Paterakis, M.; Georgiadis, L.; and Papantoni-Kazakos, P. "On the Relation Between the Finite and Infinite Population Models for a Class of Random Access Algorithms." *IEEE Transactions on Communications,* November, 1987.

PERL84 Perlman, R. "An Algorithm for Distributed Computation of a Spanning Tree." *Proceedings, Ninth Data Communications Symposium,* 1984.

PFIS82 Pfister, G.M., and O'Brien, B.V. "Comparing the CBX to the Local Network—and the Winner Is?" *Data Communications,* July, 1982.

PICK86 Pickholz, R. *Local Area and Multiple Access Networks.* Rockville, MD: Computer Science Press, 1986.

PIER72 Pierce, J.R. "Network for Block Switches of Data." *Bell System Technical Journal,* July/August, 1972.

PITT85 Pitt, D.; Sy, K.; and Donnan, R. "Source Routing for Bridged Local Area Networks." *Proceedings, Globecom '85,* December 1985.

PITT86 Pitt, D., and Sy, K. "Address-Based and Non-Address-Based Routing Schemes for Interconnected Local Area Networks." In [PICK86].

PITT87 Pitt, D., and Winkler, J. "Table-Free Bridging." *IEEE Journal on Selected Areas in Communications,* December 1987.

PRES88 Press, L. "Benchmarks for LAN Performance Evaluation." *Communications of the ACM,* August, 1988.

PROT82 Protunotarios, E.N.; Sykas, E.P.; and Apostolopoulos, T.K. "Hybrid Protocols for Contention Resolution in Local Area Networks." *Proceedings, Seventh Conference on Local Computer Networks,* 1982.

PRYC91 Prycker, M. *Asynchronous Transfer Mode: Solution for Broadband ISDN.* Chichester, England: Ellis Horwood Ltd., 1991.

RAGH81 Raghavendra, C.S., and Gerla, M. "Optimal Loop Topologies for Distributed Systems." *Proceedings, Seventh Data Communications Symposium,* 1981.

RAUC83 Rauch-Hindin, W.B. "Upper-Level Network Protocols." *Electronic Design,* March 3, 1983.

RAWS78 Rawson, E.G., and Metcalfe, R.M. "Fibernet: Multimode Optical Fibers for Local Computer Networks." *IEEE Transactions on Communications,* July, 1978.

REAM75 Reames, C.C., and Liu, M.T. "A Loop Network for Simultaneous Transmission of Variable-Length Messages." *Proceedings, Second Annual Symposium on Computer Architecture,* 1975.

RICH80 Richer, J.; Steiner, M.; and Sengoku, M. "Office Communications and the Digital PBX." *Computer Networks,* December, 1980.

RICH90 Richer, M. "Who Needs Universal Network Interface Standards?" *Data Communications,* September 21, 1990.

ROBE73 Roberts, L.G. "Dynamic Allocation of Satellite Capacity Through Packet Reservation." *Proceedings, National Computer Conference,* 1973.

ROBE75 Roberts, L.G. "ALOHA Packet System With and Without Slots and Capture." *Computer Communications Review,* April, 1975.

RODR90 Rodrigues, M. "Evaluating Performance of High-Speed Multiaccess Networks." *IEEE Network Magazine,* May, 1990.

RONA86 Ronayne, J. *Introduction to Digital Communications Switching.* Carmel, IN: Sams, 1986.

ROSE88 Rosenberg, R. "The Shots Seen Round the World," *Data Communications,* December, 1988.

ROSS86   Ross, F. "FDDI: A Tutorial." *IEEE Communications Magazine*, May, 1986.

ROSS87   Ross, F. "Rings Are 'Round for Good!" *IEEE Network*, January, 1987.

ROUN83   Rounds, F. "Use Modeling Techniques to Estimate Local-net Success." *EDN*, April 14, 1983.

RUBI90   Rubin, I., and Baker, J. "Media Access Control for High-Speed Local Area and Metropolitan Area Communications." *Proceedings of the IEEE*, January, 1990.

RUSH82   Rush, J.R. "Microwave Links Add Flexibility to Local Networks." *Electronics*, January 13, 1982.

SACH88   Sachs, S. "Alternative Local Area Network Access Protocols." *IEEE Communications Magazine*, March, 1988.

SALT83   Saltzer, J.; Progran, K.; and Clark, D. "Why a Ring?" *Computer Networks*, March, 1983.

SALW83   Salwen, H. "In Praise of Ring Architecture for Local Area Networks." *Computer Design*, March, 1983.

SAND82   Sanders, L. "Manchester Code Gaining on NRZ" *Electronic Design*, August 5, 1982.

SAUE81   Sauer, C.H., and Chandy, K.M. *Computer Systems Performance Modeling*, Englewood Cliffs, NJ: Prentice-Hall, 1981.

SCHM83   Schmidt, R.; Rawson, E.; Norton, R.; Jackson, S.; and Bailey, M. "Fibernet II: A Fiber Optic Ethernet." *IEEE Journal on Selected Areas in Communication*, November, 1983.

SCHM88   Schmidt, R. "Developing Ethernet Capability on Unshielded Twisted Pair." *Telecommunications*, January, 1988.

SCHO84   Schoeffler, J. "Distributed Computer Systems for Industrial Process Control." *Computer*, February, 1984.

SCHO88   Scholl, F., and Coden, M. "Passive Optical Star Systems for Fiber Optic Local Area Networks." *IEEE Journal on Selected Areas in Communications*, July, 1988.

SCHW77   Schwartz, M. *Computer-Communication Network Design and Analysis.* Englewood Cliffs, N.J.: Prentice-Hall, 1977.

SEAM82   Seaman, J. "Local Networks: Making the Right Connection." *Computer Decisions*, June, 1982.

SEE86   See, M. "Specifying Fiber." *Data Communications*, March, 1986.

SEVC87   Sevcik, K., and Johnson, M. "Cycle Time Properties of the FDDI Token Ring Protocol." *IEEE Transactions on Software Engineering*, March, 1987.

SHOC80   Shoch, J.F., and Hupp, J.A. "Measured Performance of an Ethernet Local Network." *Communications of the ACM*, December, 1980.

SHOC82   Shoch, J.F.; Dala, Y.K.; and Redell, D.D. "Evolution of the Ethernet Local Computer Network." *Computer*, August, 1982.

SOHA87   Soha, M. "A Distributed Approach to LAN Monitoring Using Intelligent High Performance Monitors." *IEEE Network*, July, 1987.

SOHA88   Soha, M., and Perlman, R. "Comparison of Two LAN Bridge Approaches." *IEEE Network*, January, 1988.

SKAP79   Skaperda, N.J. "Some Architectural Alternatives in the Design of a Digital Switch." *IEEE Transactions on Communications*, July, 1979.

SLON91   Slone, J., and Drinan, A., editors. *Handbook of Local Area Networks.* New York: Auerbach, 1991.

SMIT91 Smith, W., and Kain, R. "On the Validity of Assumptions Used to Model Local Area Networks." *Proceedings, Tenth Annual Phoenix Conference on Computers and Communications,* March, 1991.

SPAN86 Spanier, S. "FEPs Ease Migration to New LAN Protocols." *Mini-Micro Systems,* September, 1986.

SPEC82 Spector, A. "Performing Remote Operations Efficiently on a Local Computer Network." *Communications of the ACM,* April, 1982.

SPRA91 Apragins, J.; Hammond, J.; and Pawlikowski, K. *Telecommunications Protocols and Design.* Reading, MA: Addison-Wesley, 1991.

STAC80 Stack, T.R., and Dillencourt, K.A. "Protocols for Local Area Networks." *Proceedings, NBS Symposium on Computer Network Protocols,* 1980.

STAH82 Stahlman, M. "Inside Wang's Local Net Architecture." *Data Communications,* January, 1982.

STAL90a Stallings, W. *Handbook of Computer-Communications Standards: Volume II: Local Area Network Standards.* New York: Macmillan, 1990.

STAL90b Stallings, W. *Business Data Communications.* New York: Macmillan, 1990.

STAL90c Stallings, W. *The Business Guide to Local Area Networks.* Carmel, IN: Prentice-Hall Computer Publishing, 1990.

STAL90d *Handbook of Computer-Communications Standards,* Second Edition. *Volume III, The TCP/IP Protocol Suite.* Indianapolis, IN: Howard W Sams & Co., 1990.

STAL91 Stallings, W. *Data and Computer Communications, Third Edition.* New York: Macmillan, 1991.

STAL92 Stallings, W. *Computer Communications: Architectures, Protocols, and Standards, Third Edition.* Los Alamitos, CA: IEEE Computer Society Press, 1992.

STAL93a Stallings, W. *Advances in Local and Metropolitan Area Network Technology.* Los Alamitos, CA: IEEE Computer Society Press, 1993.

STAL93b Stallings, W. *Networking Standards.* Reading, MA: Addison-Wesley, 1993.

STAL93c Stallings, W. *SNMP, SNMPv2, and CMIP: The Practical Guide to Network Management Standards.* Reading, MA: Addison-Wesley, 1993.

STAL93d Stallings, W. *Network Management.* Los Alamitos, CA: IEEE Computer Society Press, 1993.

STIE85 Stieglitz, M. "X.25 Standard Simplifies Linking of Different LANs." *Computer Design,* February, 1985.

STRA87 Straus, J., and Kawasake, B. "Passive Optical Components." in [BASC87].

STRO86 Strole, N. "How IBM Addresses LAN Requirements with the Token Ring." *Data Communications,* February, 1986.

STUC85 Stuck, B., and Arthurs, E. *A Computer Communications Network Performance Analysis Primer.* Englewood Cliffs, NJ: Prentice-Hall, 1985.

SUDA83 Suda, T.; Miyahara, H.; and Hasegawa, T. "Performance Evaluation of an Integrated Access Scheme in a Satellite Communications Channel." *IEEE Journal on Selected Areas in Communications,* January, 1983.

SUNS77 Sunshine, C. "Interconnection of Computer Networks." *Computer Networks,* February, 1977.

TAKA85 Takagi, H., and Kleinrock, L. "Output Processes in Contention

Packet Broadcasting Systems." *IEEE Transactions on Communications*, November, 1985.

TAKA88 Takagi, H. "Queuing Analysis of Polling Models." *ACM Computing Surveys*, March, 1988.

TANE88 Tanenbaum, A.S. *Computer Networks*. Englewood Cliffs, NJ: Prentice-Hall, 1988.

TASA86 Tasaka, S. *Performance Analysis of Multiple Access Protocols*. Cambridge, MA: MIT Press, 1986.

TASS85 Tassey, G. *Technology and Economic Assessment of Optoelectronics*. National Bureau of Standards, Planning Report 23, October, 1985.

TERP91 Terplan, K. *Communication Networks Management*. Englewood Cliffs, NJ: Prentice-Hall, 1991.

TOBA80a Tobagi, F.A., and Hunt, V.B. "Performance Analysis of Carrier Sense Multiple Access with Collision Detection." *Computer Networks*, October/November, 1980.

TOBA80b Tobagi, F.A. "Multiaccess Protocols in Packet Communications Systems." *IEEE Transactions on Communications*, April, 1980.

TOBA82 Tobagi, F.A. "Distributions of Packet Delay and Interdeparture Time in Slotted ALOHA and Carrier Sense Multiple Access." *Journal of the ACM*, October, 1982.

TOBA83 Tobagi, F.; Borgonova, F.; and Fratta, L. "Expressnet: A High-Performance Integrated Services Local Area Network." *IEEE Journal on Selected Areas in Communications*, November, 1983.

TSUC89 Hagens, R. "Components of OSI: IS-IS Intra-Domain Routing." *Connexions*, Interop, Inc., August, 1989.

VALE92 Valenzano, A.; DeMartini, C.; and Ciminiera, L. *MAP and TOP Communications: Standards and Applications*. Reading, MA: Addison-Wesley, 1992.

VERE91 Vereen, L. "High Speed Twist." *LAN Magazine*, September, 1991.

VONA80 Vonarx, M. "Controlling the Mushrooming Communications Net." *Data Communications*, June, 1980.

WARN80 Warner, C. "Connecting Local Networks to Long-Haul Networks: Issues in Protocol Design." *Proceedings, Fifth Conference on Local Computer Networks*, 1980.

WATS80 Watson, W.B. "Simulation Study of the Configuration Dependent Performance of a Prioritized, CSMA Broadcast Network." *Proceedings, Fifth Conference on Local Computer Networks*, 1980.

WEBB84 Webb, M. "Build a VLSI-Based Workstation for the Ethernet Environment." *EDN*, February 23, 1984.

WEIS87 Weissberger, A., and Israel, J. "What the New Internetworking Standards Provide." *Data Communications*, February, 1987.

WHIT92 White, G. *Internetworking and Addressing*. New York: McGraw-Hill, 1992.

WILK79 Wilkes, M., and Wheeler, D. "The Cambridge Digital Communication Ring." *Proceedings, Local Area Communications Network Symposium*, 1979.

WILL73 Willard, D. "MITRIX: A Sophisticated Digital Cable Communications System." *Proceedings, National Telecommunications Conference*, 1973.

WOLT90 Wolter, M. "Fiber Distributed Data Interface (FDDI)—A Tutorial." *Connexions*, Interop, Inc., October, 1990.

WONG84 Wong, J. and Bux, W. "Analytic Modeling of an Adapter to Local Area Networks." *IEEE Transactions on Communications*, October, 1984.

YEN83 Yen, C., and Crawford, R. "Distribution and Equalization of Signal on Coaxial Cables Used in 10-Mbits Baseband Local Area Networks." *IEEE Transactions on Communications*, October, 1983.

ZANG91 Zanger, H., and Zanger, C. *Fiber Optics: Communication and Other Applications*. New York: Macmillan, 1991.

ZHAN88 Zhang, L. "Comparison of Two Bridge Routing Approaches." *IEEE Network*, January, 1988.

Index

College Division
Macmillan Publishing Company
Front & Brown Streets
Riverside, NJ 08075

ORDER FORM

Ship To: **Bill to:**
(Please print or type)   (If different from shipping address)

Name _____   Name _____

Co. _____   Co. _____

Address _____   Address _____

_____   _____

City _____ St ____ Zip _____   City _____ St ____ Zip _____

Mail your order to the above address or call 800-548-9939 (in New Jersey call
609-461-6500) or Fax 609-461-9265

Shipping Method **(select one)**
_____ UPS ground
_____ 2nd Day Air
_____ Book Rate

Payment Method **(select one)**	
_____ Check	_____ Visa
_____ Bill Me	_____ MasterCard
Authorized Signature	
Card Number Exp Date	

(*continued*)

TEAR OUT THIS PAGE TO ORDER OTHER TITLES BY WILLIAM STALLINGS:

SEQ.	QTY.	ISBN NO.	TITLE	SINGLE COPY PRICE	TOTAL
1	_____	002-415495-4	Computer Organization & Architecture 3/e	69.00	_____
2	_____	002-415454-7	Data and Computer Communications 3/e	69.00	_____
3	_____	002-415465-2	Local and Metropolitan Area Networks 4/e	60.00	_____
4	_____	002-415431-8	Business Data Communications	49.00	_____
5	_____	002-415475-X	ISDN and Broadband ISDN 2/e	55.00	_____
6	_____	002-415481-4	Operating Systems	56.00	_____

Handbooks of Computer Communications Standards

SEQ.	QTY.	ISBN NO.	TITLE	SINGLE COPY PRICE	TOTAL
7	_____	002-415521-7	Volume 1, The Open Systems Interconnection (OSI) Model and OSI-Related Standards, 2/e	47.00	_____
8	_____	002-415522-5	Volume 2, Local Area Network Standards, 2/e	47.00	_____
9	_____	002-415523-3	Volume 3, The TCP/IP Protocol Suite, 2/e	47.00	_____

GRAND TOTAL _____

A small shipping charge will be added. Prices subject to change without prior notification.

PSR-PSL 350-3500   FC# 1355

ACRONYMS

ANS	American National Standard
ANSI	American National Standards Institute
ASK	Amplitude-Shift Keying
CATV	Community Antenna Television
CBX	Computerized Branch Exchange
CCITT	Consultative Committee on International Telegraphy and Telephony
CRC	Cyclic Redundancy Check
CSMA	Carrier-Sense Multiple Access
CSMA/CD	Carrier-Sense Multiple Access with Collision Detection
DCE	Data Circuit-Terminating Equipment
DES	Data Encryption Standard
DOD	Department of Defense
DQDB	Distributed Queue, Dual Bus
DTE	Data Terminal Equipment
FCS	Frame Check Sequence
FDDI	Fiber Distributed Data Interface
FDM	Frequency-Division Multiplexing
FNP	Front-End Network Processor
FSK	Frequency-Shift Keying
HAM	Hybrid Access Method
HDLC	High-Level Data Link Control
IEEE	Institute of Electrical and Electronics Engineers
IP	Internet Protocol
ISO	International Standards Organization